Introduction to Political Psychology

Introduction to Political Psychology, fourth edition, explores the many psychological patterns that influence political behavior. The authors introduce readers to a broad range of theories, concepts, and case studies of political activity, arguing that individuals are driven or motivated to act in accordance with personality characteristics, values, beliefs, and attachments to groups. The book explains many aspects of political behavior—whether seemingly pathological actions or normal decision-making practices, which sometimes work optimally, and sometimes fail.

Thoroughly updated throughout, the book examines patterns of political behavior in areas including leadership, group behavior, voting, race, nationalism, terrorism, and war. This edition features coverage of the 2016 election and profiles former U.S. President Donald Trump, while also including updated data on race relations and extremist groups in the United States. Global issues are also considered, with case studies focused on Myanmar and Syria, alongside coverage of social issues including Black Lives Matter and the #MeToo movement.

Accessibly written and comprehensive in scope, it is an essential companion for all graduate and upper-level undergraduate students of psychology, political science, and political psychology. It will also be of interest to those in the policy-making community, especially those looking to learn more about the extent to which perceptions, personality, and group dynamics affect the policy-making arena. It is accompanied by a set of online instructor resources.

Martha L. Cottam is Professor Emeritus of Political Science in the School of Politics, Philosophy, and Public Affairs at Washington State University, USA. She specializes in political psychology, international politics, and intercommunal conflict. She has published books and articles on U.S. foreign policy, decision making, nationalism, and Latin American politics. She received her Ph.D. from UCLA.

Elena Mastors is a lecturer at Johns Hopkins University, USA. She was an academic administrator for over a decade and also served as an associate professor in the National Decision Making Department of the Naval War College. She has held various senior intelligence and policy positions the Department of Defense. She specializes in the political psychology violence.

Thomas Preston is Professor of Political Science in the School of Politics, Philosophy, and Public Affairs at Washington State University, USA. He specializes in political psychology, leadership analysis, and international politics. He has written numerous books and articles on presidential leadership, weapons of mass destruction, and American foreign policy. He received his Ph.D. from The Ohio State University.

Beth Dietz is Professor of Psychology at Miami University, USA, where she teaches a variety of courses in psychological science. Her research interests include social identity theory, computer-mediated communication, and the scholarship of teaching and learning. She also has interests in online teaching and using technology to enhance student learning.

Introduction to Political Psychology

Fourth Edition

Martha L. Cottam
Elena Mastors
Thomas Preston
Beth Dietz

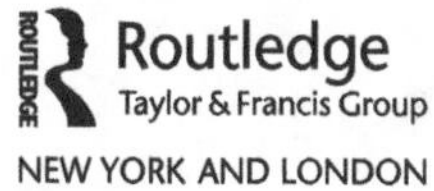

New York and London

Cover image: © Olmo Couto (Getty Images)

Fourth edition published 2022
by Routledge
605 Third Avenue, New York, NY 10158

and by Routledge
4 Park Square, Milton Park, Abingdon, Oxon, OX14 4RN

Routledge is an imprint of the Taylor & Francis Group, an informa business

First edition published by Psychology Press 2004
Third edition published by Routledge 2016

Library of Congress Cataloging-in-Publication Data
A catalog record has been requested for this book

ISBN: 978-0-367-20000-8 (hbk)
ISBN: 978-0-367-20001-5 (pbk)
ISBN: 978-0-429-24464-3 (ebk)

DOI: 10.4324/9780429244643

Typeset in Warnock Pro
by Newgen Publishing UK

Access the Support Material: www.routledge.com/9780367200015

Contents

Preface

When colleagues from other disciplines ask us what we specialize in, they are often puzzled when we say "political psychology". "What's that?" or "I didn't know there was such a thing" are frequently heard comments. That is primarily a result of the fact that political psychology is not a traditional field in the social sciences. First, it is interdisciplinary, using psychology to explain political behavior. The field is so interdisciplinary that calling it "political psychology" is misleading because it includes scholars from political science and psychology, but also from sociology, public administration, criminal justice, anthropology, and many other areas. Second, unlike many fields in the social sciences, political psychology uses multiple methodologies, from experiments to surveys to qualitative case studies and beyond. And if our colleagues from other disciplines have not heard of political psychology, they will soon, because it is exploding. It is a burgeoning field because it is inherently interesting and because it is enormously important. Understanding the psychological causes of political behavior is crucial if we are to affect patterns of behavior that are harmful to humanity and to promote patterns of behavior that are beneficial to humanity. Political psychology is an important domain of academic research: students find it fascinating and often troubling as they are exposed to some of the most shocking examples of political violence, while policy-makers would undoubtedly benefit greatly from a better understanding of political psychology.

As the field of political psychology has grown, so has the need for a comprehensive textbook that pulls together many strands of research in political psychology. This book is a result of the authors' frustration produced by teaching courses in political psychology without a foundational text. Rather than having students purchase a textbook on psychology (of which they will read only a portion) and a number of books describing political behavior (without a psychological explanation of that behavior), we decided to produce a book that presents the psychology used in *political* psychology, and explains types of political behavior with political psychological concepts in a single book. We introduce readers to a broad range of theories of political psychology and sketch many cases of political activity to illustrate the behaviors. Readers do not need a background in psychology or political science to understand the material. However, knowing that an introduction will stimulate a desire for more, we also include suggested reading in the details of the cases. Such readings are rich, nuanced studies of each of the political behaviors we introduce in this book.

Once we embarked upon this project, we quickly discovered that the field of political psychology is much broader than those of us who teach and do research in the area may realize. It ranges from voting behavior to nuclear deterrence, from the politics of race to the politics of genocide. In the following pages, many of the patterns of behavior researched by political psychologists are presented, including leadership, group behavior, voting, media effects, race, ethnicity, nationalism, political extremism, social movements, genocide, and war and deterrence. Because political psychology is so broad, many of those who teach the courses tend to stick to the familiar portion of political psychology. Consequently, another goal of this book is to educate educators by making it easier to acquire a background in unfamiliar areas of political psychology. Specialists in voting behavior, for example, may not know much about genocide, but both topics are covered here, and using this book as a primer will enable those who teach political psychology to expand the content of their courses. Students, in turn, will learn the interconnectedness of many patterns of behavior that at first glance seem quite distinct. They will learn, for example, that people who exercise their political rights in a democracy could, under the right circumstances, support an authoritarian dictatorship that forbids political competition and tortures its opponents. Relatedly, we include examples of political behavior from around the world, so students will see that these patterns of behavior are universal, not restricted to people who live in one particular culture or in one type of political system.

In this book, many of the major topics of political psychology are covered. We begin with an introductory chapter that discusses what political psychology is, and presents some of its history as well as methodological issues. The introduction also presents a representation of the "Political Being," a drawing of the generic political person, depicting the minds and hearts of people in a political environment. It places components of our thinking and feeling—personality, social identity, values, attitudes, emotion, and cognitive processes—in layers of the mind, with personality at its core, social identity and values in the next layers, and attitudes, cognitive processes, and emotions closest to the surface. The Political Being is also depicted in his or her political environment, with in-groups and out-groups representing the importance of group psychology as well as perceptions of political opponents.

Chapters 2, 3, and 4 introduce the reader to the central psychological theories used in political psychology and some of the most prominent frameworks used in the field. In this fourth edition of the book, findings from evolutionary psychology and neuroscience are included in the first four chapters. Many of these theories and frameworks reappear in the following chapters' discussion of patterns of behavior in various contexts. In addition, other frameworks not presented in the preliminary theory chapters are introduced where appropriate. Chapter 2 discusses personality-based theories and frameworks. Chapter 3 involves cognitive processes, attitudes, identities, and emotions, and Chapter 4 presents group psychology in politics. After Chapter 4, the book turns to patterns of behavior in politics.

Chapter 5 looks at leadership—specifically, presidential leadership in domestic and international politics, and includes detailed case studies of George W. Bush and Donald Trump. Chapter 6 looks at political psychology and the political behavior of the average citizen in the United States, with some comparison with Great Britain provided. The chapter examines arguments concerning the structure and function of attitudes, how people process information, and how they decide who to vote for. The 2008, 2012 and 2016 elections are used to illustrate the complexities of voting in the United States. The effect of the media on voters' attitudes toward politics and politicians, as well as the media's roles in campaigns, is the topic of Chapter 7.

Chapters 8–12 draw upon psychological findings in studies of social identity, cognitive processes, group dynamics, and emotions in explorations of race, ethnic conflict, nationalism, social movements, and terrorism. Chapter 8 looks at race in the United States, Europe, Brazil, and South Africa. Careful consideration is given to arguments concerning the rise of racism in the United States in the past decade. Chapter 9 examines ethnic relations and conflict in several cases across the globe, including Nigeria, Bosnia, Guatemala, Iraq, Syria, and Myanmar, and concludes with a discussion of genocide and the cases of the Holocaust, Rwanda, and Darfur. Chapter 10 presents an examination of the effects of nationalism on the behavior of citizens and leaders in both domestic and international politics. The cases used to illustrate the effect of nationalism on domestic politics include the conflicts in Northern Ireland, Yugoslavia, Kosovo, Cyprus, Chechnya, the issue of the Kurds in Turkey, and German unification. The effects of nationalism on foreign policy behavior are illustrated in this chapter with the cases of World War II, the American war on drugs, and the dispute between Ukraine and Russia. Chapter 11 explores the political psychology of social movements, and includes the cases of the American Civil Rights Movement, the Tea Party, Occupy Wall Street, the Arab Spring, Black Lives Matter and the #MeToo movement. Terrorism is the topic of Chapter 12, which concentrates on the political psychological causes of terrorism, recruitment and motivational patterns among terrorists, and state-sponsored repression and torture. Finally, Chapter 13 examines the political psychology of nuclear deterrence and conventional warfare, while Chapter 14 concludes with a look at possible approaches to conflict prevention and/or resolution.

Throughout the book, a number of learning tools are provided. These include a number of key terms, defined in the Glossary; concluding chapter lists of theories, concepts, and cases introduced in the chapter; text boxes with interesting related topics for class discussion; and tables and illustrative figures that summarize text discussion.

Like previous editions, the fourth edition of *Introduction to Political Psychology* is designed for upper division undergraduate and graduate courses on political psychology, but it also has other uses. We introduce readers to many different methods of research; hence, it is useful to scholars outside of the classroom. The book also contains material that should be of interest to those in the policy-making community. It presents academic findings in a user-friendly way, and policy-makers may be quite surprised to discover the extent to which perceptions, personality, and group dynamics affect the policy-making arena. In a challenge to the commonly held assumptions that self-interest drives behavior, this book shows over and over again, in one context after another, how psychological factors affect our behavior and that of others in ways we rarely recognize at the time the behaviors take place.

In many respects, this is a disturbing book, for it describes some of the saddest events in human history and some of the most horrific things people do to each other for political purposes. But the book also presents many discoveries about how to prevent, resolve, and recover from conflict. We hope that after reading this book the reader will understand the enormous complexity of human behavior and realize the importance of understanding and using political psychology to improve the human condition.

Acknowledgments

We have benefited from the comments, insights, and ideas of a number of colleagues and students. We are grateful to Travis Ridout, Bruno Baltodano, Isabel Beck, Bob Hanes, Martin Garcia, Peg Hermann, Rick Herrmann, Joe Huseby, Bob Jackson, Faith Lutze, Otto Marenin, Craig Parks, Claudia Reye-Quilodran, Ann Rumble, Hayden Smith, Craig Whiteside, and Michael Young for their input of previous editions. We also are grateful to our editors for their help and patience.

Chapter 1

Political Psychology

Introduction and Overview

WHY STUDY POLITICAL PSYCHOLOGY?

Why do people behave the way they do in politics? What causes conflicts such as those in Bosnia, Rwanda, or Northern Ireland? Is racism inevitable? Why do presidents make the decisions they do? Why did 9/11 happen? These and many other questions about politics are of great concern to all of us, whether we are directly affected or are only eyewitnesses through the news. So much of political behavior seems to defy explanation and seems incomprehensible when looked at with hindsight: people start wars that are, in the end, regarded as pointless and futile, such as World War I or the Vietnam War; civil wars erupt among people who have lived together harmoniously for years, but then commit hideous acts of barbaric violence against one another, as in the former Yugoslavia, Liberia, or Sierra Leone; groups commit acts of terrorism that kill numerous innocent civilians each year; and a scandal-plagued president cannot resist tempting fate by engaging in an extra-marital affair when he knows full well the extent of the scrutiny of those looking for more scandals. Unless one understands the thoughts and feelings of the people who make the decisions to commit those acts, one cannot fully understand why those things occurred. But an exploration of the psychology—the personalities, thought processes, emotions, and motivations—of people involved in political activity provides a unique and necessary basis for understanding that activity.

This is a book about the psychology of political behavior. In the chapters that follow, we will explore many psychological patterns that influence how individuals act in politics. At the outset, we challenge the traditional notion that people act in politics in a rational pursuit of self-interest. This argument concerning rationality is based on a set of assumptions that are common in political science, but ignore the many studies done by psychologists. Many people assume psychology is common sense because they believe behavior is rational and predictable. But decades of research by psychologists have revealed that behavior is anything *but* common sense. Although psychologists recognize much of human behavior is not always rational, human beings, as social perceivers, often operate on the belief that

DOI: 10.4324/9780429244643-1

behavior (their own and that of others) is quite rational. The motivation to expect behavior to be rational is based on two fundamental needs. First, people have a need to make sense of—to *understand*—their world. Second, people have a need to *predict* the likely consequences of their own and others' behavior. To the extent that behavior is perceived as rational, these two needs become easier to fulfill.

A more accurate picture of human beings as political actors is one that acknowledges that people are driven or motivated to act in accordance with personality characteristics, values, beliefs, and attachments to groups. People are imperfect information processors, struggling mightily to understand the complex world in which they live. People employ logical, but often faulty, perceptions of others when deciding how to act, and they often are unaware of the causes of their own behavior. People often do things that are seemingly contrary to their own interests, values, and beliefs. Nevertheless, by understanding the complexities of political psychology, we can explain behavior that often seems irrational. A few illustrations help us to bring this point home. These are examples of common behavior.

A common argument is that people vote in accordance with self-interest; therefore, people in higher income brackets will vote for the Republican Party and those in lower income brackets will vote for the Democratic Party. However, the authors of this book vote for the same candidates and party, despite the fact their incomes and personal circumstances are quite different. Is one rational and the others not, or do we share certain values and beliefs that we put above economic self-interest? Another assumption is people are fully aware of their beliefs and attitudes and they act in accordance with them, behaving in such a way as to maximize values. As the following example illustrates, we often act in ways that violate our beliefs and values:

> A friend of ours was sitting on a bench in a crowded shopping mall when he heard running footsteps behind him. Turning, he saw two black men being pursued by a white security guard. The first runner was past him in a flash, but he leapt up in time to tackle the second runner, overpowering him. From the ground, the panting black man angrily announced that he was the store owner. Meanwhile, the thief escaped. Our friend, who is white and devotes his life to helping the oppressed, was mortified.
>
> (Fiske & Taylor, 1991, p. 245)

Here the power of social stereotypes lay unknowingly deep inside the mind of the friend, despite his outward, and no doubt deeply held, values opposed to such stereotyping. This is an example of the power of what psychologists call social categorization, a process wherein we nonconsciously categorize others into groups. On the surface, the act of categorizing people into groups appears logical and rational. The danger, however, lies in the consequences of categorizing people into groups on the basis of characteristics they might not possess. (The process of social categorization is one to which we will devote a great deal of attention in this book.) In the example above, little harm was done, but the same process can occur at society-wide levels, and can produce acts of terrific violence. Racial discrimination, ethnic cleansing in Bosnia, and genocide in Rwanda are all, in part, outcomes of stereotyping. They are political actions that cannot be understood through conventional political science explanations, yet they constitute some of the most important and damaging forms of behavior in human societies.

Consider the following account:

> The army was determined to stamp out the grass roots support for the guerillas. A company of one hundred soldiers from Santa Cruz del Quiché moved into Nebaj the next day and installed a detachment of military police. Within days, leading citizens of the towns began to disappear. Later their bodies were found mutilated and strung up on posts in the town square.
>
> (Perera, 1993, p. 71)

Now consider this example:

> Juliette's family, who were well-off Tutsis, stayed inside their house that first night. The next night, Thursday, when the militia came searching for them, they ran and hid in a banana plantation. On Friday they ran to the school where her uncle ... was an administrator. Two days later the family decided to go to the place where the Belgian United Nations soldiers were and seek protection from them. But 11 Belgian soldiers had been lined up against a wall and shot the day before, so all the other Belgian soldiers had left. Juliette's family then went to a sports stadium where a lot of other people were sheltering. But here the Interahamwe [militia men] caught up with them and ordered them to another place, an open field where thousands of others had also been rounded up. The Interahamwe told all the people who were Hutus to go; then they told all the others to sit down and they threw grenades at them. When Juliette became conscious the next morning, she found her mother and brothers dead. Her father was also dead and his body had been hacked to pieces.
>
> (Bone, 1999, p. 1)

These two stories depict real-life examples of two politically motivated atrocities committed during war that cannot be explained unless the psychology of the perpetrators is understood. What objective self-interest is served by using a machete to chop up a human being? Why not just quickly kill and be done with it if his or her death serves one's interests? These are true stories: the first is from Guatemala during the 1980s; the second is from Rwanda roughly 10 years later. These are two very different places, and these acts occurred at different times, yet these two countries encountered similar experiences in terms of brutal acts of violence waged by one group against another. And people in many other countries have similar stories to tell. Political psychology helps explain political behavior along the continuum from everyday political behavior, such as voting, to the most extraordinary kinds of behavior, such as mass terror and violence.

WHAT IS POLITICAL PSYCHOLOGY?

Understanding the psychological underpinnings of these behaviors gives us a different, and arguably a much more complex, understanding of political behavior. Traditional explanations of political behavior often fail to adequately explain some of the most important political decisions and actions people take. Political psychology emerged as an important field in both political science and psychology that enables us to explain many aspects of political behavior—whether it is seemingly pathological actions, such as those described above, or normal decision-making practices, which sometimes work optimally and other times fail. Both psychologists and political scientists became interested in expanding their knowledge of issues and problems of common interest, such as foreign and domestic policy decision-making by elites, terrorism, conflicts ranging from ethnic violence to wars and genocide, the minds of people who are racists, and more peaceful behaviors such as voting, among many other problems and issues that are traditionally of concern in political science. For example, if we understand the limitations of the abilities of policy-makers to recognize the significance of specific pieces of information, then we can institute organizational changes that will help improve our abilities to process information adequately. Likewise, if we can understand the deeper personality elements of the most important of our political leaders, we can comprehend which situations they will handle well, and which situations will require more assistance and advice from others. If we understand what motivates terrorists to act, we can find ways in which to try to address those motivations and counter terrorism.

One goal of political psychology is to establish general laws of behavior that can help to explain and predict events that occur in a number of different situations. The approach used by political psychologists to understand and predict behavior is the **scientific method**. This approach relies on four cyclical steps that a researcher repeatedly executes as he or she tries to understand and predict behavior. The first step involves *making observations*, both systematic and unsystematic, of behavior and events. From these observations, a researcher begins to form hunches about the likely factors, or **variables** (see box) that affect the behavior under observation. The second step involves *formulating tentative explanations*, or a *hypothesis*. During this stage, a researcher makes predictions about the nature of the relationship between variables. The third step involves making *further observations and experimenting* (see box). During this stage of the scientific method, observations are made to test the validity of the hypothesis. In the fourth step, *refining and retesting explanations*, researchers reformulate their hypothesis on the basis of the observations made in Step 3. This might involve exploring the limits of the phenomenon, exploring causes of relationships, or expanding on the relationships discovered. Clearly, the scientific method requires a great deal of time spent making careful observations.

At the same time, it is important to mention the replication crisis currently being experienced in psychology. Replication is what gives science credibility. It is the key to important scientific results and is at the heart of generalizability. The "crisis" that results do not replicate is a recent concern in the social sciences, and especially psychology. The replication issues were brought to the attention of social scientists almost 20 years ago, with the publication of two seminal papers. First, Simmons, Nelson, and Simonsohn (2011) argued "questionable research practices" lead to many "false positive" results. Briefly, "questionable research practices" include such things as "p-hacking" (using ostensibly permitted or unpermitted data strategies to turn null findings into significant ones), selective reporting of dependent variables, and failure to disclose all experimental conditions, to name a few. Second, John, Lowenstein, and Prelec (2012) sampled a large number of studies by social scientists and reported a "surprisingly" high rate of questionable research practices. There are, of course, many reasons why a study might fail to replicate. It may be that the replication studies were poorly designed, leading to "false negatives." Or, it may be that the original studies were poorly designed. The replication crisis might be a result of a publication bias, which is the tendency of journals to only publish statistically significant results.

Regardless of the reasons for the replication crisis, psychologists are responsive to the crisis and have taken significant steps to solve the issues. Some of the practices currently in place include changes in the ways statistical analyses are reported, and moving toward a more open science, where replicability and transparency are promoted (Open Science Collaboration, 2015). For example, it is now common practice to either pre-register a study before data collection begins or to share the data and materials freely. Other solutions to the crisis include changes to journals and publishing, including the addition of replication and null-effects journals, and open source publishing.

Variables

A **variable** is what we call something that is thought to influence, or be influenced by, something else. One seeks to identify variables in the first stage of the scientific method. Variables can vary in degree or differentiation. One question of interest in social sciences is the question of how variance in one variable explains change in something else. When variables are measured, the researcher ideally wants a measurement instrument that is *reliable*—that is, one that will produce the same results when used by another researcher. In addition, the measurement should have *validity*—that is, it should provide an accurate measurement of what it claims to measure.

Essentially, political psychology represents the merging of two disciplines, psychology and political science, although other disciplines contributed to the literature and growth of the field. Political psychology can be described as a marriage of sorts that fosters a very fruitful dialogue. Political psychology involves explaining what people do by adapting psychological concepts so they are useful and relevant to politics, then applying them to the analysis of a political problem or issue. For example, psychologists have been helpful to political scientists who study negative political advertising. Psychologists have done studies whose outcomes provide evidence to suggest negative political advertisements are often ineffective because the sponsor of the negative ad is evaluated negatively by same-party voters. Psychologists brought fresh perspectives to political science regarding how to make sense of politics, thus expanding our knowledge of the political world. Political scientists bring to the field their knowledge and understanding of politics. For example, psychologists often study the decision-making process employed by groups. Some of the ideas psychologists use to guide their theories about how groups make decisions come from real-life group decisions made by political groups (e.g., Bay of Pigs, the decision to enter the Vietnam War). Each must be well versed in the other field, and together they are able to expand the scope of study in both political science and psychology. As a result, political psychology makes a very important contribution to our understanding of politics and expands the breadth of that understanding.

Experiments

The three characteristics that define experimental research are the *manipulation* of an independent variable, *control* over extraneous variables, and random assignment of participants to conditions. The values of an *independent variable* are set and chosen by the experimenter. If an experimenter wanted to examine the effects of room temperature on mood, then room temperature would be the independent variable. The experimenter can randomly assign participants to a room that is 70°F or a room that is 90°F and then observe their moods. Manipulation of the independent variable involves exposing participants to various levels of it, and observing its effects on another variable, the *dependent variable.* In an experiment, the values of the dependent variable are predicted to change as a function of the independent variable. For example, mood is predicted to change as a function of varying temperatures in a room, with a temperature of 90°F predicted to cause a more negative mood than a temperature of 70°F. Another characteristic of an experiment is control over extraneous variables. *Extraneous variables* are variables that may affect the behavior a researcher is studying, but that he or she has no interest in at the moment. If some of the participants learned they had won the lottery just before showing up for the study, then their mood in response to room temperature may be different than if they didn't. The variable "winning the lottery" is an extraneous variable. Because of the manner in which experiments are designed, they allow a researcher to have a great deal of control over extraneous variables.

Merging the two fields is not an easy enterprise. For example, one cannot use many of the experimental techniques utilized in psychology to study politics, yet experiments are vital to psychological research and confidence in their findings. Because experiments in psychology are conducted under carefully controlled conditions, they allow psychologists to make inferences about relationships that they suspect exist. Such insights are not possible with other research methodologies, especially those used by political scientists. The patterns of behavior observed in the laboratory, are therefore not likely to be observed in such pristine quality in the real world, where many extraneous factors cannot be filtered out as influences on behavior. If, for example, when psychologists want to study group behavior, they can design an experiment in which all other factors (such as competing group loyalties, personality characteristics, gender, or ethnicity) can be made irrelevant to the study. In the real world of politics, these things cannot be extracted from behavior. The simple point is that we cannot expect to see an exact parallel between what the psychologist sees and explains, and what we will see and explain in political behavior. Instead, we must take psychological concepts or explanations of behavior and ask ourselves how these things are likely to manifest in the real world of politics. This is one of the most difficult aspects of the development of the field of political psychology.

Some simple examples may clarify this problem. If psychologists tell us that personality traits influence behavior, political psychologists must figure out which personality traits are important in politics. Are there certain political personality traits? If so, what are they and why are they politically important? Political psychologists argue that certain political personality traits are indeed important in influencing political behavior, such as how a person deals with conflict, how complex the person's thought processes are (that is, their **cognitive complexity**), and so on. If psychologists tell us that certain conditions and attitudes affect behavior, and we wish to know how this applies to deciding how to vote, then the political question becomes: Which attitudes about politics, under what circumstances, affect how we vote? In the United States, attitudes about candidates, issues, parties, and groups affect how people vote. Those attitudes vary in importance in determining how someone votes under differing circumstances. These are examples of the steps that must be taken in applying psychology to the explanation of political behavior. The consequence is that psychology benefits political science because political scientists use psychological theories to understand political behavior. But political science also benefits psychology because tests of psychological theories in political settings can help psychologists to refine their theories.

Despite these difficulties, political psychology is a rapidly growing field. Psychology has been used to explain political behavior for many years, but there has been an explosion in its application to politics since the early 1970s. The field began in the 1920s with studies of personality and politics, and in particular with psychoanalytic studies of political leaders. As time and psychology's understanding of personality progressed, political psychologists began looking at personal characteristics, such as motivation and traits in their analyses of political leaders. While the psychoanalytic studies tended to use psychobiographies—that is, life stories of a person for data, later studies relied upon new social scientific techniques such as questionnaires, interviews, experiments, and simulations for their research. This research is examined in Chapters 2 and 5.

A second wave in the development of political psychology came in the 1940s and 1950s, with increased interest in the systematic study of public opinion and voting behavior in the United States. Beginning in 1952, researchers at the University of Michigan began collecting survey data on public opinion and voting preferences. With the publication of *The*

American Voter, by Campbell, Converse, Miller, and Stokes (1960), the tradition of using political psychology to study public attitudes toward politics took off. This book presented a number of centrally important findings about the nature of political attitudes in the United States. It sparked debate and fueled important, and often differing, models of attitudes and behavior. In the years that followed, political psychology was used in analyses of political socialization, the role of the media in affecting political attitudes, racial politics in the United States, and a number of other aspects of American political behavior. Analyses of public attitudes and political behavior are done in many other countries in addition to the United States. Chapters 3, 6, and 7 explore research in these areas.

The application of political psychology, and the development of political psychological frameworks for the analysis of behavior in international affairs was the third wave, and it came a bit later, beginning in the 1960s with studies of Soviet–American perceptions of each other and studies of the conflict in Vietnam (Kelman, 1965; White, 1968). By the 1970s and continuing until today, concepts of political psychology were applied to our understanding of nuclear deterrence, past wars, such as World Wars I and II, decision-making in crises, nationalism, ethnic conflict, terrorism, and a wide variety of additional topics in international politics. This book explores many of these topics in Chapters 5 and 7–12.

A fourth arena in which political psychology was used to explain behavior is what Sears (1993) refers to as "death and horror." This is another growing body of literature, which covers the study of terrorism, ethnic cleansing, genocide, and other patterns of behavior that involve extraordinary levels of politically motivated violence. We review this literature in Chapters 9 and 12.

More recently, both **evolutionary psychology** and neuroscience have been used to explain such political psychological concepts as voting behavior, in-group bias, and party affiliation. Briefly, evolutionary psychology suggests that we cannot fully understand human behavior without understanding its biological origins. More specifically, understanding how particular traits, behaviors, and abilities evolved over time allows for a richer and more comprehensive understanding of human behavior today (Barkow, Cosmides, & Tooby, 1992; Bridgeman, 2003). You are likely familiar with the roots of the evolutionary approach—Darwin's ideas about natural selection, for example. We will explore the evolutionary approach in Chapters 3, 4, and 9.

You have also likely heard a lot about **cognitive neuroscience**. This term refers to a field of study that focuses on how the function and structure of the brain and nervous system explain thoughts, feelings, and actions (e.g., Gazzaniga, 2014). Neuroscience is likely one of the hottest areas of inquiry within psychology. In part, this emphasis is attributed to the advanced techniques (such as functional MRIs and EEGs) available to study the brain. The more we unlock techniques for studying the brain, the more we can use that knowledge to understand humans. Political behavior is no exception. In Chapters 2, 3, and 6, we explore neuroscience perspectives on personality, social identity, and voting behavior.

Thus, there are many realms of political behavior amenable to a psychological analysis, and we will explore quite a few of them. There are so many ways of exploring political behavior that the number of concepts can become confusing. In part, this is because different concepts emerged in psychology over time as that field grew. The growth of a field, be it political science, psychology, or political psychology, is always haphazard. Concepts often appear under a new name that may seem strikingly similar to old concepts. Discoveries are made in one area that were made long before in another area. The lack of cross-fertilization has meant scholars looking at one aspect of behavior have often been unaware of what those looking at another aspect of behavior are doing, and therefore they reinvent the wheel over and over again. One of the tasks of this book is to draw connections between ideas in different realms of the study of political behavior to lessen the confusion that arises from so many similar ideas, concepts, and arguments.

Another outcome of the haphazard development of political psychology is that related, but slightly different, concepts became popular as explanatory tools for different kinds of political behavior. Attitudes, beliefs, schemas, images, and many other concepts appear in the literature, but are rarely discussed in terms of how they overlap and still differ. We will undertake some clarification in this regard, but for the moment let us present our own general picture of how and why people think and act politically, based on the work generated by political psychologists over the years. To put it simply, people are driven to act by internal factors such as personality, attitudes, and self-identity. They evaluate their environment and others through cognitive processes that produce images of others, and they decide how to act when these factors are combined. In politics, people often act as part of a group, and their behavior in this context can be very different from their individual behavior. Therefore, the political psychology of groups is an essential part of political psychology as a field. As the book proceeds, each of these factors is developed. By the end, the picture in Figure 1.1 will be described and explained in detail; this is the generic political being in his or her political universe.

THE POLITICAL BEING

At the core of our Political Being is **personality**. Personality is a central psychological factor influencing political behavior. As we shall see in Chapter 2, personality is unique to the individual, although certain personality traits appear in many people. Many people have traits in common, such as a particular degree of complexity in their thinking processes and desires for power and achievement, but the combination of those traits differs, so each individual is unique. Consequently, we place personality in the center of the Political Being's brain. It affects other aspects of the thought process and is itself affected by life experiences. However, personalities tend to be very stable in terms of amenability to change, and they influence our behavior and behavioral predispositions on an ongoing, constant basis. Moreover, personality affects behavior nonconsciously in that people rarely sit down and consider the impact of their personalities on their political preferences. It drives behavioral predispositions without our having to give conscious consideration to the source of those preferences. Personality is, in that sense, a core component of the engine of political thinking and feeling. Much of the discussion of personality in political psychology concerns the personality traits of political leaders and the impact of particular combinations of those traits on their leadership styles. Consequently, much of our discussion of personality in Chapter 2 is focused on the leadership dimension, and we have devoted Chapter 5 to leadership.

Next we have **values** and **identity**. These concepts involve deeply held beliefs about what is right and wrong (values) and a deeply held sense of who a person is (identity). Values often include a strong emotional component. We often feel very strongly about some of our beliefs and goals for ourselves and those we care about, and political principles. For example, a person may have a strongly held value that violence is wrong, which translates into a political predisposition to oppose war, refuse military service, and go to prison if necessary to defend that value. That person's identity involves personal self-descriptions that are usually tied to, and emerge from, close and enduring personal relationships. For our person with a strong value opposing violence, identity may include a strong attachment to a religion and religious affiliation. Being religious would be an important part of his or her identity and the person would strongly value the religious group that is part of this identity. Values, emotions, and identities are also deeply held and fairly permanent aspects of one's psychology, and hence we place them deep in the mind of our Political Being. They are discussed further in Chapter 3. Political values, emotions, and identity are also important concepts in our case studies of voting, race and ethnic conflicts, and nationalism—Chapters 6, 8, 9, and 10, respectively.

Next, our Political Being has **attitudes**. As we will see in Chapter 3, scholars define *attitudes* in different ways. Generally, they can be thought of as units of thought composed of some cognitive component (that is, knowledge) and an emotional response to it (like, dislike, etc.). For example, a person with an attitude on funding for public education may think it is a good thing, know how much his or her state spends on public education, and strongly feel this particular level of spending is too low. Many important political attitudes are acquired through socialization, as we shall see in Chapter 6. In the diagram of the Political Being, they are placed toward the top of the mind because they are accessible to thinkers (who can be asked what they think and feel about an issue and can articulate an answer), and because they are subject to change based on new information, changes in feeling, or persuasion. Attitudes are the focus of attention in political psychology when it comes to voting decisions, political socialization, the impact of the media on how and what people think, and important political notions such as tolerance, all of which we will explore in Chapter 6. Studies of voting behavior are central to political psychology in general, and Chapter 6 introduces the topic with a look at public opinion and voting in the United States, Great Britain, and other countries. Voting is, of course, a central component of democratic politics, so it is a logical focus of political psychology.

We left **emotions** floating in the mind of the Political Being in Figure 1.1. Politics can be an extremely emotion-evoking arena of life. Emotions affect all aspects, and are affected by all aspects of the Political Being's mind. Values, identities, and attitudes are emotional and have emotional components, and emotions interact with the next portion of the Political Being's mind: cognition. Emotions permeate politics and the mind of the

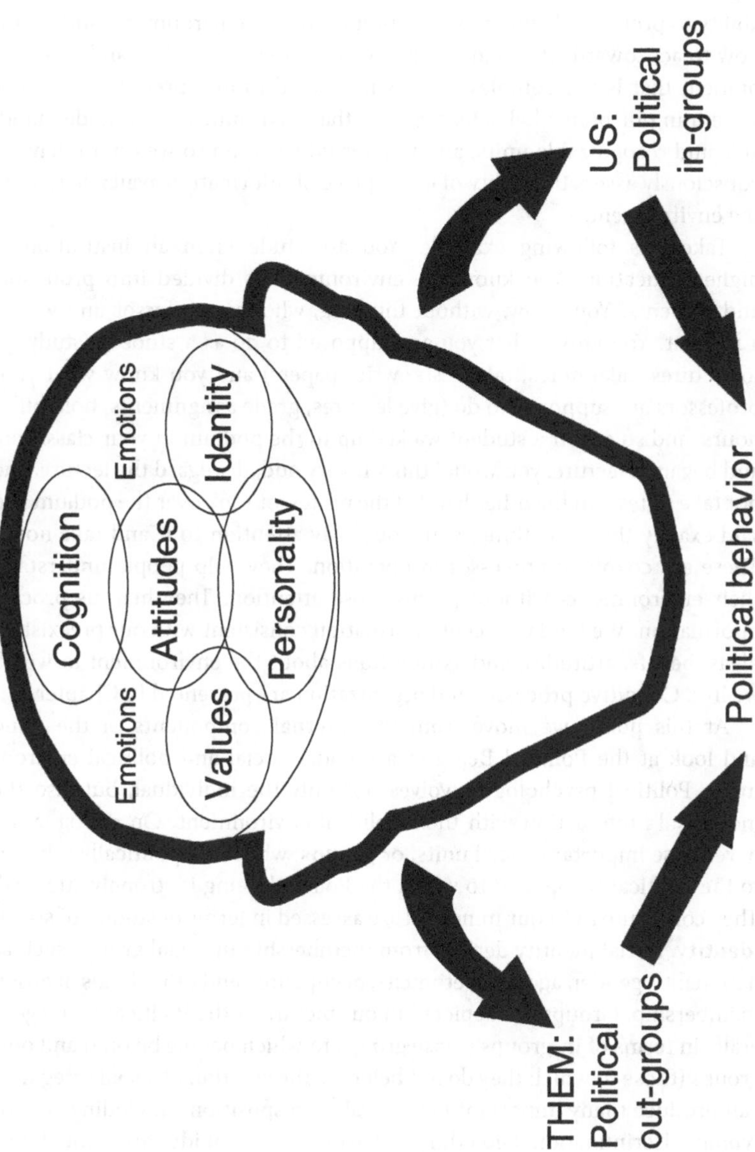

Figure 1.1 The Political Being

Political Being; hence, they are left to freely move about in our picture of the mind of the Political Being. We discuss emotion in every topical chapter in this book.

The final component of the Political Being is **cognitive processes**, which are the channels through which the mind and the environment first interact. They involve receiving and interpreting information from the outside. They are the mind's computer in that they facilitate the individual's ability to process information, interpret his or her environment, and decide how to act towards it. Cognitive processes help us to understand an environment that is too complex for any individual to interpret. The cognitive system in our brains helps us organize that environment into understandable and recognizable units, and to filter information so we do not have to consciously assess the utility of every piece of information available to us in the environment.

Take this following example. You are students in an institution of higher education. You know the environment is divided into professors and students. You know, without thinking, who is a professor and who is a student. You know what you are supposed to do as a student (study, go to lectures, take notes, take tests, write papers) and you know what your professors are supposed to do (give lectures, grade assignments, hold office hours, and so on). If a student walked up to the podium in your classroom and began to lecture, you would think it very odd, disregard the lecture, and not take notes. On the other hand, if the professor took over the podium and said exactly the same thing, you would pay attention to it and take notes. These are cognitive processes in operation. They help people understand their environments without paying close attention. They help us process information. We tend to accept information consistent with our preexisting ideas, beliefs, attitudes, and assumptions about the environment in which we live. Cognitive processes and organization are presented in Chapter 3.

At this point, we move from the internal components of the mind and look at the Political Being in a broader social and political environment. Political psychology involves not only the individual, but also the individual's interaction with their political environment. On one side, we have those important social units, or **groups**, which are politically relevant to the Political Being, and to which the Political Being is strongly attached. They constitute *us* in our mind and are assessed in terms of studies of **social identity**. Social identity derives from membership in social groups such as nationality, gender, age, race, ethnicity, occupation, and other kinds of group membership. Groups are depicted in our picture of the Political Being generally in terms of in-groups (those groups to which people belong) and out-groups (those to which they do not belong). The creation of social categories can produce many important behavioral predispositions, including stereotyping, discrimination, and ethnocentrism. Our social identities, much like our values and attitudes, can strongly motivate behavior. We discuss social identity and groups in Chapters 3 and 4, then provide several illustrations of their impact on behavior in the chapters that follow.

People belong to many different groups, and we are interested in the role played by attachment to politically relevant groups. Groups themselves have particular dynamics that influence people's behavior. This is the subject of Chapter 4, where group psychology is introduced, both in and of itself and in the context of distinctly political groups. Groups demand loyalty, compliance, and obedience, and those psychological factors can override even strongly held values. Take, for example, perpetrators of genocide during the Holocaust who explained their behavior in terms of obedience to the norms of the group (e.g., "I did it because I was ordered to"). But social identity goes beyond group dynamics. People are influenced by groups, but they are also personally driven to support groups to which they are strongly attached. They make sacrifices that are sometimes extraordinary for the sake of the group. Illustrations of that behavior, as well as social identity factors, are found in Chapter 8 (race), Chapter 9 (ethnic conflict and genocide), Chapter 10 (nationalism), Chapter 11 (social movements), and Chapter 12 (terrorism). As we shall see, group dynamics can make people do things they would never consider doing on their own.

These topics were chosen for in-depth analyses for several reasons. Racial discrimination and conflict are a central aspect of American history and current politics, but they also mark the political systems of other countries. Ethnic conflict has many similarities with racial conflict. Its prevalence in the post-Cold War world, as well as our failure to prevent it from causing hundreds of thousands of deaths, makes it an important issue for political psychology to consider. The same can be said for nationalism, which cost millions of deaths in World War II and reappeared with ferocity after the Cold War. Terrorism is also of central importance in domestic and international politics, and not just because of the 9/11 attacks. It is a global concern and, sadly, mass killings for political reasons continue.

The Political Being also interacts in the environment with *them*—those groups to which the Political Being does not belong but with which it must interact in politics. People organize the political environment just as they do the social environment, and we will look at how people do so. There are a variety of perspectives on this, one of which is Image Theory, which argues people look at the world around them, and organize it in terms of important political actors, such as enemies and allies (and many other categories, as we will see in Chapter 3). Some of those actors threaten deeply held values and/or groups with which the Political Being strongly identifies. The enemy is such an actor. Others, such as allies, provide opportunities to achieve desired goals, things important to the individual Political Being and to the groups he or she identifies with. In Chapter 13, we examine the ultimate conflict with the other; war and efforts to deter it, a matter of importance to everyone in the nuclear era.

All of these psychological elements interact, and all of the patterns of behavior we illustrate are important. Of course, not all of them are functioning all the time. One's attitudes toward political candidates do not affect political preferences every day, but they do during elections. Nationalism is not important in affecting behavior until the nation is either threatened or an opportunity for its advancement appears. Moreover, at any point in time one of these factors may be more important than others. Personality can become overwhelmingly important when Presidents are dealing with a major crisis. Perceptions that another country is an enemy may be important during that crisis as well. A President's social identity with an ethnic group may not play a role during a crisis but may be important when pressing for a particular piece of legislation.

Our conceptualization of political psychology sees the political mind as composed of layers or levels. Different layers take on a more or less important role in different kinds of behavior or at different points in the political action process. Consequently, the following chapters focus on central psychological causes of different types of political behavior. When it comes to small group behavior and intricate decisions made by the members of that group, we look specifically at the personality of leaders and small group dynamics. When it comes to nationalism-based conflicts, we look at social identity, perceptions or images of other groups, and cognitive processes.

The organization of this book blends concepts and patterns in political psychology and political behavior with detailed illustrations of those concepts and patterns. Chapters 2, 3, and 4 introduce central concepts in political psychology with examples from psychology and politics for illustration. Then Chapters 5 through 13 examine some forms of political behavior, using the concepts introduced in Chapters 2 through 4, where appropriate, to explain those behaviors. Chapter 14 explores various conflict resolution and reconciliation strategies applicable to the cases in the previous chapters. We encourage you to try to amplify upon our explanations as you read the descriptions of the types of political behavior in each chapter. Chapter 5 focuses on political personality traits and leaders. Chapter 6 addresses the political psychology of the average citizen in the voting booth, and in his or her efforts to learn about and respond to political information. Chapter 7 takes a more detailed look at the role of the media in politics, and its influence on information processing by citizens generally and by voters during campaigns in particular. Chapter 8 moves us from the individual level to individuals and groups in an examination of racial politics, and Chapter 9 explores similar patterns in ethnic conflicts and cases of genocide. Chapter 10 looks at individual and group political psychology and behavior in the context of nationalism, and its impact on domestic politics and foreign policy behavior. Chapter 11 is an overview of the political psychology of social movements, with numerous case studies. Chapter 12 also focuses on individuals and groups in a look at terrorists and state terror. Chapter 13 explores individual and group decision-making in international politics, specifically international security, and efforts to prevent war. Finally, in Chapter 14 we conclude with a look at possible approaches to conflict prevention and/or resolution. Each chapter includes important terms, which are defined in the Glossary at the end of the book, and suggestions for further reading.

CONCLUSION

We began this introductory chapter with examples of political behavior that are both disturbing and difficult to explain. Let us conclude the chapter on a more personal note. The psychological causes of political behavior are interesting to study. However, for the individuals who live the realities the following chapters describe, political behavior is not an academic exercise, but a life-shaping and altering experience. At the heart of political psychology is the question of whether by understanding why people behave as they do in politics, we can prevent the worst of human behavior and promote the best. In the following pages, we present the work of many political psychologists who believe this is an achievable goal, and a reasonable one to pursue. Without an understanding of political psychology, it is an impossible one.

Key Terms

attitudes
cognitive complexity
cognitive neuroscience
cognitive processes
evolutionary psychology
identity
personality
scientific method
social identity
values

Suggestions for Further Reading

Huddy, L., Sears, D. O., and Levy, J. S. (2013). Introduction: Theoretical foundations of political psychology. In. L. Huddy, D. O. Sears, & J. S. Levy (Eds.), *The Oxford handbook of political psychology* (2nd ed., pp. 1–21): Oxford: Oxford University Press.

Kressel, N. (Ed.). (1993). *Political psychology: Classic and contemporary readings*. New York: Paragon House.

Monroe, K. R. (Ed.). (2002). *Political psychology*. Mahwah, NJ: Lawrence Erlbaum.

Chapter 2

Personality and Politics

As we mentioned in the previous chapter, personality is a central concept in psychology. For this reason, personality is placed at the bottom of the Political Being's brain, representing its roots, and therefore the most fundamental element. Personality does not just affect how people think and behave in the political arena; it is also affected by their life experiences. In this chapter, we consider some central questions about personality addressed in political psychology, including questions such as: How does personality affect political behavior? How deep must we go in understanding the development of a person's personality to understand his or her political inclinations (to the unconscious or more surface, conscious traits, and motivations)? What personality characteristics are most politically relevant? Are people completely unique, or do they share personality traits in various combinations, making individuals more or less similar in their political behavior? How should we study personality when we cannot very well put political figures on the couch and ask them questions?

The study of personality and politics is the oldest tradition in political psychology (Adorno et al., 1950; Lasswell, 1948a, 1960; Leites, 1951). Personality as a concept is used to evaluate a wide variety of political behaviors, from the psychology of political leaders to psychopathologies of people who have committed politically motivated atrocities (such as Hitler, with the Holocaust), to the average citizen and the role personality factors play in attitudes toward race and ethnicity, interest in politics, and willingness to obey authority. However, most studies employing personality-based frameworks focus on the impact of the characteristics of leaders on major decisions and policy-making issues such as leader–adviser relations. In fact, the studies of political personality and political leadership developed conjointly in political psychology. As a result, separating political personality from political leadership research in any textbook on political psychology is problematic.

In this chapter, we discuss some of the broader theoretical arguments about personality and its effect on political behavior. We begin with some of the central questions about the role of personality in political behavior before turning to the study of personality in psychology and looking at some of the major scholars and approaches from the psychological perspective.

DOI: 10.4324/9780429244643-2

Next we present an overview of some of the ways in which personality in politics, and particularly personality factors relevant to political leadership, are studied. The portion of the Political Being emphasized in this chapter is, of course, the personality circle. There are also links between personality and cognition, and the impact of personality on interactions with people in the political environment—shown as *US* and *THEM* in the Political Being diagram in Figure 1.1.

Despite the central role personality plays in psychology, political science, and political psychology, coming to an acceptable definition of *personality* is problematic, with research in psychology and political science tending to focus (and define) the concept quite differently. As Robert Ewen (1998, p. 3) points out, within the discipline of psychology, "there is no one universally accepted definition of 'personality,' nor is there any one recognized "theory of personality." Greenstein (1969, pp. 3–4) observed that the psychologist's usage of the term "personality" is comprehensive, subsumes all important psychic regularities, and refers to an inferred entity rather than to a directly observable phenomenon. In other words, personality refers to a construct that is introduced to account for the regularities in an individual's behavior as he or she responds to diverse stimuli (Hermann, Preston, & Young, 1996). Or, as Ewen notes, personality in the psychological literature refers to "*important* and *relatively stable* aspects of a person's behavior that account for consistent patterns of behavior," which "may be observable or unobservable, and conscious or unconscious" (1998, pp. 3–4). Gordon DiRenzo offers a related definition: personality is "one's acquired, relatively enduring, yet dynamic, unique, system of predispositions to psychological and social behavior" (1974, p. 16). At the same time, there is tremendous disagreement within the field between social psychologists and personality theorists regarding exactly what should be incorporated into such a comprehensive definition. Personality theorists include cognition, affect, motivation, identification, and processes of ego-defense in their conceptions of personality, while social psychologists usually seek to limit personality to a residual category, absent of emotion, cognition, or motivation (see George & George, 1998; Greenstein, 1969). There are many different theories of personality in psychology. Schultz (1981), for example, reviewed 20 personality theories organized into nine categories: psychoanalytic, neopsychoanalytic, interpersonal, trait, developmental, humanistic, cognitive, behavioristic, and limited domain.

In the political psychology literature, in contrast, analysts typically do not worry about arriving at a specific, comprehensive definition of personality. Instead, the focus is on how particular aspects of personality translate into political behavior. Indeed, the study of personality in political psychology is best characterized as the study of individual differences. Rather than seek the whole, researchers selectively focus on any number of individual aspects of a person's makeup (i.e., cognition, motivation, affect, ego, attitudes) to explain behavior. Obviously, this is a much narrower and more restrictive view of personality than that taken by most psychologists (especially the personality theorists). As a result, in our view it is unproductive to attempt to provide a commonly agreed-upon definition of personality for this textbook—there isn't one (Ewen, 1998; Maddi, 1996; Magnavita, 2002).

Further, we clearly cannot explore all theories of personality in this chapter. Instead, since our focus is on political psychology rather than psychology, we limit our discussion to those theories most used in political psychology: psychoanalytic, trait, and motivation. Furthermore, we address research in this field that centers upon various kinds of individual differences to explain leadership, leadership style, and political behavior.

WHEN DO PERSONALITIES MATTER IN POLITICS?

Of course, just because personalities may sometimes matter with regard to policy outcomes, it would be a mistake to argue that they *always* matter. In fact, during the 1930s and 1940s, Kurt Lewin argued that to understand behavior, it is necessary to understand both a person's personality and the context in which the behavior is observed. Lewin (1935) emphasized that the interaction between the person and the situation was most important to understanding behavior. Similarly, Mischel (1973) focused attention on the degree to which situational factors govern behavior. In the early 1970s, Mischel (1973) reviewed research on the importance of personality in predicting behavior across a variety of situations. He found that people behave far less consistently across situations than previously thought. Instead, it appears that the situation exerts powerful effects on behavior. Indeed, scholars who work in the fields of personality or leadership generally accept that *context* (or situation) matters more (George, 1980; Greenstein, 1969; Hermann, 1987, 2000; Preston, 2001; Preston & 't Hart, 1999). The situational context is the stage upon which the person will interact with his or her environment, providing both opportunities for action and constraints upon it. For example, in his classic book *Personality and Politics*, Fred Greenstein (1969) observed while personality is often unimportant in terms of either political behavior or policy outcomes, the likelihood of personal impact: (1) increases to the degree that the environment requires restructuring; (2) varies with the political actor's location in the environment; and (3) varies with the personal strengths and weaknesses of the actor (1969, p. 42). In other words, when individuals have the personal power resources due to their position in the political system (i.e., as president, prime minister, general, mayor, etc.) and the situation allows them to exert this power to influence the policy process, what these people are like (i.e., strengths/weaknesses, personality, experience) will have an impact on policy. For Abraham Lincoln, this situation allowed him to educate his cabinet on the importance of the individual leader when, after a particularly contentious vote, he observed, "Gentlemen, the vote is 11 to 1 and the 1 has it." For Saddam Hussein, it meant Iraq invaded Kuwait. On the other hand, in contrast to foreign policy, where there is more freedom of action, American presidents are well acquainted with their far weaker influence upon domestic policy, with Congress, the courts, interest groups, and many other actors playing substantial roles in determining policy outcomes (see Burke, 1992; Cronin, 1980; Light, 1982; Neustadt, 1990).

THEORIES AND APPROACHES TO STUDYING PERSONALITY

There are many different approaches or theories to personality, but only some of them were used in the study of personalities of political actors. Among the most important are psychoanalytic theories, trait-based theories, and motive-based theories. More recently, the genetic approach to personality, as it applies to political psychology, gained enough traction to warrant mention. We will explain that approach as well. As mentioned above, many of the frameworks in political psychology go beyond a single theoretical orientation. Below, we review some personality theories from psychology, then explore their use in political psychology. With each theoretical approach, we discuss some of the research methods typically used to study political actors.

Psychoanalytic Approaches

Among the oldest traditions in personality in psychology are **psychoanalytic or psychodynamic theories**. Psychoanalytic theories highlight the role of the **unconscious** in human behavior, and the motives and drives that underlie behavior. The father of psychoanalytic theory is Sigmund Freud (1932, 1950, 1962). Freud introduced the idea that the mind is like an iceberg. Only a small part of the iceberg is visible floating above the water. Around 90% is under water and unobservable. Similarly, people are conscious of only a small part of the mind. The majority of the mind's operation is like the portion of the iceberg underwater. It is unconscious. Freud viewed the personality as an energy system driven by aggressive and sexual drives. People are motivated to satisfy those drives, a force Freud called the **pleasure principle**. Behavior is a product of these drives and the unconscious efforts by individuals to suppress and channel the desire to act out in search of satisfaction. Living in society, from Freud's perspective, requires people to deny the pleasure principle. The consequence, in Freud's view, is pathologies such as anxiety, obsessions, and defense mechanisms.

Freud argued that the structure of personality is based upon three elements: the id, the ego, and the superego. The **id**, which is inherited, includes instincts and responses to bodily functions (e.g., hunger). The id follows the pleasure principle. The **ego** is the part of the personality that moderates between the id and its desire for pleasure and the realities of the social world. The ego therefore follows the **reality principle**. According to the reality principle, the demands of the id will be blocked or channeled in accordance with reality, but also in accordance with the final element of the personality, the **superego**. This is the moral arm or conscience of the personality (Hall & Lindzey, 1970). Thus, if you interact with an individual who you do not like at all, the id may inspire you to lash out angrily at that person, but the ego keeps you from doing it because it is socially inappropriate, and the superego tells you to be kind to all people and forgive them for their obnoxious behavior. When the ego is threatened, people feel anxiety. The anxiety can be realistic, or it may be neurotic. **Neurotic anxiety** is a person's fear of being punished for doing something the id wants to do. Another type of anxiety is moral anxiety, which occurs when there is a conflict between the id and the superego. **Defense mechanisms** are also used to defend the ego. Defense mechanisms are unconscious techniques used to distort reality and prevent people from feeling anxiety. They include **repression**, wherein someone involuntarily eliminates an unpleasant memory. **Projection** is another defense mechanism, and it involves attributing one's own objectionable impulses to another person, projecting them onto another. **Rationalization** is a third defense mechanism. When people rationalize, they reinterpret their own objectionable behavior to make it seem less objectionable. A fourth defense mechanism is **denial**, wherein people may deny reality (e.g., denying that the country is going to war despite the mobilization of troops), or they may deny an impulse (e.g., proclaiming that they are not angry when they really are).

Freud's ideas were evident in the theories of many psychologists who succeeded him. Eric Fromm (1941, 1955, 1964), for example, explored the interactions between people and society. He argued that change in human society produced freedom from certain restraints such as serfdom and slavery, but in the process, people experienced an increase in alienation and insecurity. To ameliorate this, they could pursue the positive freedom of a humanistic society in which people treat one another with respect and love, or they could renounce freedom and accept totalitarian and authoritarian political and social systems. Eric Erikson (1950, 1958, 1969) was also a depth psychologist trained as a Freudian who made many contributions to psychoanalysis. He too maintained an interest in politics and political leaders. Erikson is best known for his work on individual stages of personality development and identity. He maintained that the ego continues to grow after childhood and that society has an impact on personality. Among his important works are studies of Mahatma Gandhi (Erickson, 1969) and Martin Luther (Erickson, 1958).

Psychoanalysts employed several techniques that served the roles of data collection, broadly defined, and therapy. Freud and other psychoanalysts believed much of the unconscious was repressed to avoid painful recollections, and one important component of therapy was to try to bring those repressed ideas and memories to the conscious level. One Freudian approach to therapy is known as free association. This involves having the patient lay on a couch, thinking of things in the past (free association), and saying everything that comes to mind. A second therapeutic technique is dream analysis. Freud believed dreams were symbolic representations of thoughts—desires, fears, things that happened. Freud's research was based upon notes taken after therapeutic sessions with patients took place.

Clearly the couch and dream analysis are not options in political psychological research that uses psychoanalytical theories. Access problems, particularly to political leaders, prevent direct person-to-person psychoanalysis. Therefore, many scholars who adopt a psychoanalytic approach to the analysis of political figures use the psychobiographical method. **Psychobiographies** involve an examination of the life history of an individual. It is important to note that not all psychobiographies are psychoanalytic.[1] Some focus upon Freudian analysis or notions of ego-defense (e.g., Glad, 1980; Hargrove, 1988; Link & Glad, 1994; Renshon, 1996), whereas others concentrate upon specific kinds of personality disorders, ranging from narcissism to paranoid personality disorders (e.g., Birt, 1993; Post, 1991; Volkan, 1980; Volkan et al., 1999). Usually, psychobiographies take the form of quite detailed, in-depth case studies of individual leaders, tracing their personal, social, and political development from early childhood onwards through young adulthood. Since it is assumed that leaders' personalities or political styles are shaped by their early childhood socialization experiences, psychobiographies generally seek to identify consistent patterns of behavior across time that can be explained using psychoanalytic analysis (see Renshon, 2012; Schultz, 2005).[2]

One of the most important examples of high-quality psychobiography is the study of Woodrow Wilson by Alexander and Juliette George (1964). In their classic book *Woodrow Wilson and Colonel House*, they use a psychoanalytic approach to explain Wilson's highly moralistic, rigid and uncompromising political style while in the White House. They argue that it was a result of a strict Calvinist childhood, where morality and distinctions between good and evil were emphasized above all else and where Wilson's minister father constantly belittled and severely punished him for any perceived transgressions. As a result, Wilson developed a rigid, driven political personality in which he sought to accomplish great moral deeds to compensate for his own feelings of low self-esteem. Given his difficult relationship with his stern, disciplinarian father, Wilson bridled at authority figures and internalized their criticism as personally directed at him. As well as seeing the world in absolute terms, Wilson felt that compromise on moral issues was immoral. The Georges argue that these very patterns, developed throughout his childhood and young adult life, followed him into the White House. Indeed, Wilson's efforts to create the League of Nations took on the form of a great moral crusade. His conflict with Senate Majority Leader Henry Cabot Lodge (who ultimately defeated Wilson's efforts to bring the United States into the organization) took the form of a renewed conflict with another rigid, authoritarian figure—his father. The Georges saw Wilson's political personality and his inability to compromise (not only on what he saw as a moral issue, but also in his conflict with Lodge) as the ultimate reasons for his political defeat over the League of Nations.

As mentioned, another focus of psychoanalytic studies of personality and politics is on psychopathology, or psychological disorders. The examination of political leaders' behavior as a possible product of psychopathologies began with Harold Lasswell's *Psychopathology and Politics* (1960), in which he maintained that the behavior of some people in political roles is affected by their psychopathologies. Lasswell attributed modern understanding of psychopathology to Freud's innovative ideas. Many political figures were analyzed based upon the identification of psychopathologies. For example, McCrae and Costa (1997) examined **neuroticism**, a personality disorder they argue is characterized in individuals by anxiety, self-consciousness, vulnerability, hostility, depression, and impulsiveness. In his study of **narcissism**, Volkan (1980) argued that narcissistic people seek leadership roles in a relentless search for power, and use others in their climb to power. Further, such individuals often seem charismatic and rise to power in times of crisis when followers are searching for strong leaders who will improve things. Birt's (1993) analysis of Joseph Stalin found descriptions of his personality fit the pattern associated with **paranoia**. Paranoid personalities are quite complex. Birt argued that they function along two continua: aggression and narcissism. Aggression can be manifested at one extreme as a victim and at the other as an aggressor. Narcissism ranges from feelings of inferiority to superiority. Paranoid people swing from one end of each continuum to the other. Birt argued Stalin's paranoia not only affected the international policies of the Soviet Union, but also his career: Stalin "is the classical example of a paranoid individual whose paranoia helped him rise to the top of a highly centralized political structure and, once there, turn the bureaucratic institutions of the Soviet Union into extensions of his inner personality disorders" (Birt, 1993, p. 611). Birt's analysis of a particular time period in Soviet foreign policy, the blitzkrieg attack by Germany during World War II, demonstrated that before the attack, Stalin was in an aggressor/superior phase and did not believe Hitler would attack. After the attack, Stalin "assumed the position of victim/superior. He deserved better from Hitler. He was slighted. Insecurity set in. To Stalin, he, not the Soviet Union, was under attack" (1993, p. 619). As time progressed, he moved into the aggressor/inferior and then the victim/inferior modes; he then climbed out of his depression back to the aggressor/superior mode, where he was ready for action. The rest of the war was fought with Stalin in that mode.

Political psychologists examining personality disorders in leaders will usually employ the widely accepted American Psychiatric Association's diagnostic criteria to guide and structure their analysis of leader personality and behavior.

Freud and psychoanalysis in general received numerous criticisms. Indeed, the criticisms of Freud were so extensive that "no other psychological theory has been subjected to such searching and often bitter criticism than has psychoanalysis. Freud and his theory have been attacked, reviled, ridiculed, and slandered" (Hall & Lindzey, 1970, p. 68). Among the more legitimate criticisms are the empirical problems that arose because Freud's research was not controlled, and he relied upon his recollections of therapy sessions with patients, which he recorded after the fact. He presented his findings as personal conclusions, without the original data, and those conclusions may have been subject to biases because he relied on his own recollection of discussions. His method for reaching conclusions was not revealed, and there was "no systematic presentation, either quantitative or qualitative, of his empirical findings" (Hall & Lindzey, 1970, p. 69).

A second criticism often made of Freud's theory and psychoanalysis in general is that it is not amenable to empirical testing. This is partly because much of Freud's theory about personality is based upon unobservable abstract ideas, and partly because there are so many theoretically possible behaviors that are manifestations of psychoanalytic issues. For example, recall the study of Stalin's paranoia. If diametrically opposite patterns of behavior can result from the same psychoanalytic condition, it is difficult to develop testable and therefore falsifiable hypotheses. Because of these criticisms and discussion of different perspectives on how important the unconscious is, a number of additional personality theories emerged in psychology, to which we now turn.

TRAITS, MOTIVES, AND INDIVIDUAL DIFFERENCES

A wealth of personality theories and research exist that look at individual characteristics (or traits), motivations, and cognitive style variables, and how these shape styles of decision-making, interpersonal interaction, information processing, and management in office.

Trait Theories

If you were asked to describe your mother, you might say she is smart, funny, loving, tidy, and humble. These are personality traits, which we all use to characterize other people and ourselves. **Traits** are personality characteristics that are stable over time and in different situations (Pervin & John, 1997). Traits produce predispositions to think, feel, or act in a particular pattern toward people, events, and situations. Trait theorists also regard traits to be hierarchically organized. Trait theories in psychology began with the work of Gordon Allport (1937, 1961, 1968). Allport disagreed with Freud's contention that personality dynamics were governed by the unconscious. He also believed childhood experiences were less important in the adult's personality than Freud maintained. Allport regarded personality traits as central in determining how people respond to their environments. He distinguished among cardinal traits, central traits, and secondary traits. *Cardinal traits* are critically important and dominate a person's life. An example would be authoritarianism, which is discussed below. Allport believed these were rare and most people had few cardinal traits, or none at all. A second type of trait is the *central trait*, which affects people regularly, but not in every situation. An example would be honesty. Finally, there are *secondary traits*, which are least important and most irregular in affecting behavior. Allport also emphasized the importance of understanding motivation as a driving force in human behavior. For Allport, motivation was not hidden in the unconscious or derived from childhood experience, but consciously considered through cognitive processes.

Another trait theorist whose work influenced political psychology is Hans Eysenck (1975, 1979). He identified three personality trait dimensions: introversion–extroversion, neuroticism, and psychoticism. The *introvert-extrovert trait* refers to how outgoing a person is, the *neuroticism trait* to how emotionally stable a person is, and the *psychoticism trait* to how isolated and insensitive to others a person is. Eysenk used questionnaires to gather data on personality traits and employed a statistical technique called *factor analysis* to identify which traits cluster together. Other important early trait theorists include Raymond Cattell (1964, 1965; Cattell & Child, 1975) and David McClelland (1975), both of whom wrote extensively about motivation, a trait factor we consider below.

In recent years, psychologists sought to develop a taxonomy of personality traits that constitute the basic units of personality. Using several different research techniques, including factor analyses of trait terms commonly used in everyday language and the analysis of trait questionnaires, they developed five central personality traits. The **Big Five** personality dimensions or traits have received considerable attention over the last two decades (Costa & McCrae, 1992; Dietrich et al., 2012; Hofstede & McCrae, 2004; Rubenzer & Faschingbauer, 2004). These traits are neuroticism, extraversion, agreeableness, openness to experience, and conscientiousness.

Each trait is arranged on a continuum. For example, those high in neuroticism are characterized as people who worry and are nervous and insecure, whereas those low in neuroticism are calm, secure, and unemotional. People who are high in **extraversion** are sociable, optimistic, fun loving, and affectionate, while those low in extraversion are quiet, reserved, and aloof. A person high in **openness** is curious, creative, and has many interests, while someone low in openness is conventional and has narrow interests. People high in **agreeableness** are trusting, good natured, helpful, and soft-hearted, while a person low in agreeableness tends to be cynical, rude, irritable, and uncooperative. Finally, a person high in **conscientiousness** is organized, hard-working and reliable, while a person low in conscientiousness is aimless, unreliable, negligent, and hedonistic (Pervin & John, 1997).

The Big Five traits are viewed as superordinate and universal (Marsella et al., 2000), though some Big Five researchers have found some gender and cultural differences in these traits in studies across several countries (Costa et al., 2001). Indeed, Eagly and Carli (2007) found that women scored higher than men on the warmth and positive emotion aspects of extraversion, but lower on the assertiveness aspect of extraversion. Other studies looked at a variety of behavioral patterns associated with the Big Five personality traits. Olson and Evans (1999) examined the relationship between the "Big Five" personality dimensions or traits and social comparisons. The authors used a new technique (the Rochester Social Comparison Record, or RSCR), wherein experimental subjects keep a diary recording their social comparisons, measuring who they compare themselves with. The researchers also examined how people feel about those comparisons. They found people high in neuroticism felt more positive when they compared themselves "downward"—that is, with others of less stature or status. People high in extraversion compared downward more than people low in extraversion, in part because they had stable positive moods. In addition, the authors argued that, "along with their greater tendency to experience positive affect, extraverts also might compare downward because of their tendency to be dominant, masterful, and assertive, attributes that are reflected in studies showing them to have a high degree of leadership ability" (1999, p. 1506). We shall see this illustrated later in this chapter, and in Chapter 5, where we consider leadership in detail. People low in agreeableness tend to see themselves as superior to others, and therefore compare downward more than those high in agreeableness. Finally, people high in openness compare themselves to superior groups more than those low in openness, and tend not to experience a diminution of positive affect in the process. Still, Judge, Bono, Ilies, and Gerhard (2002) found leadership effectiveness and emergence was significantly related to the traits of extraversion, conscientiousness, and openness to experience, with agreeableness related to leader effectiveness. For U.S. presidents, Gallagher and Allen (2014) found those high in excitement-seeking were more likely to use force to carry out their foreign policy objectives, while openness to action led to greater variation in their decision-making. This builds upon previous work that found leader risk propensities in decision-making correlated with four Big Five measures: excitement-seeking, openness to action, deliberation, and altruism (Kowert & Hermann, 1997; Nicholson, Soane, Fenton-O'Creevy, & William, 2005; Rubenzer & Faschingbauer, 2004). There is also a body of literature on personality trait affect that explores the question of whether traits have particular associated affects. Schimmack, Oishi, Diener, and Suh (2000) argue that extroversion includes pleasant affects, and neuroticism has unpleasant affects.

The traits used in political psychology are related to traits described in the psychological literature, but they are presented in their political manifestation. Openness to experience, for example, appears as cognitive complexity, interest in politics, integrative complexity, and other traits named and described in political form. Traits commonly used in political psychology and their measurement are discussed later in our section on profiling leader characteristics. But again, recent personality research in psychology emphasizes that some people vary in their trait expression over time, situations, or contexts more than others (Fleeson, 2004; Kernis, 2003; Roberts & Donahue, 1994), so it remains important to view traits as not simply static or driven purely by situational factors (Mischel, 1968), but rather as more nuanced and dynamic (Hermann, 1999a; La Guardia & Ryan, 2007; Marcus, 2013).

Somewhat similar to the Big Five is the application of the Myers-Briggs Type Indicator (MBTI) personality assessment measure to the study of political personality. The MBTI assumes individual personality is revealed in the form of specific preferences for certain kinds of environments, tasks, and cognitive patterns (Lyons, 1997, p. 793). Compared with the Big Five personality traits, the MBTI scales mirror similar factors, with the exception of neuroticism, which is not included. As illustrated in Figure 2.1, the MBTI comprises four scales of preferences allowing for a total of 16 potential MBTI personality types (Lyons, 1997, p. 794).

For example, applying these measures to former President Bill Clinton's life prior to his arrival in the White House, Michael Lyons (1997, p. 801) argued that Clinton fell squarely into the Extroversion, Intuitiveness, Feeling, and Perceiving categories (an ENFP type). Given the predictions of the MBTI for the ENFP personality type, Lyons suggested Clinton would be expected to seek close attachments to other people; be very adept at establishing such attachments; seek out "people-to-people work" professionally; be optimistic, warmly enthusiastic, high spirited, and charismatic; be brilliantly perceptive about other people; draw followers, and be an excellent politician; appear insincere sometimes because of a tendency to adapt to other people in the way he presents his objective; be innovative, yet undisciplined, disorganized, and indecisive; hate rules and find it difficult to work within the constraints of institutions; thrive on constant change and begin more projects than he can reasonably complete; find difficulty relaxing and commonly work himself into exhaustion; have his energies divided between competing interests and personal relationships; be ingenious and adaptable in a way that allows him to often improvise success; and exhibit a highly empathetic world view, yet focus on data that confirm his biases, leading to a propensity to make poor choices and make serious errors of judgment (Lyons, 1997, p. 802).

Introversion	vs.	Extroversion
(Introspective, Reserved, Seeking Solitude)	(Expressiveness and Gregariousness)	
Sensing	**vs.**	**Intuition**
(Favoring Literal, Empirical Perception)	(Favoring Abstract, Figurative Perception)	
Thinking	**vs.**	**Feeling**
(Favoring Objective, Detached, Logical Decision Making)	(Favoring Subjective, Value- or Emotion-based Decision Making	
Judging	**vs.**	**Perceiving**
(Seeking Resolution and Order)	(Curious, Spontaneous, Tolerant of Disorder)	

Figure 2.1 MBTI Personality Types

Source: From Lyons (1997, p. 794).

Though the Myers-Brigg typology and test were widely popular for decades as a means of assessing job candidates in business and advising people on careers, they are not without their problems—especially from a scientific point of view (Grant, 2013; McCrae & Costa, 2006; Paul, 2004; Pittenger, 1993). Numerous studies suggest that little empirical support exists for the view that the MBTI actually measures truly dichotomous preferences or qualitatively distinct types, although four of the MBTI indices were shown to measure aspects of four of the five major Big Five dimensions (McCrae & Costa, 2006). In fact, Gardner and Martinko (1996) found few consistent relationships between MBTI type and managerial effectiveness; others found a 50% chance of test takers being in an entirely different category when retaking the exam five weeks later (Krznaric, 2013). So, while the use of the MBTI remains highly popular because of familiarity and marketing, many scholars argue that it merely picks up on Big Five factors, lacks empirical support for some of its dimensions (the thinking–feeling dichotomy in particular), and does not merit the continued reliance of business upon it for assessment purposes (Grant, 2013; Paul, 2004).

Motive Theories

Some researchers look at the motives of individuals. There are many motive theories in psychology and many definitions of the term. In a study done over 40 years ago, Madsen (1961) considered the works of 20 different motive theorists. Interest in motivation has come and gone and come around again in personality theory in psychology. **Motives** are those aspects of personality concerned with goals and goal-directed actions. Motives "energize, direct, and select behavior" (Emmons, 1997, p. 486). The motives receiving the most attention are regarded as the Big Three in both psychology and political psychology. These are the **need for power** (i.e., concern for impact and prestige), **need for affiliation-intimacy** (i.e., concern for close relations with others), and **need for achievement** (i.e., concern with excellence and task accomplishment) (McClelland, 1975; McClelland & Boyatzis, 1982; Winter, 1973, 1987; Winter, Hermann, Weintraub, & Walker, 1991; Winter & Carlson, 1988; Winter & Stewart, 1977). For example, Winter and Stewart (1977) argue that those high in power and low in affiliation make better presidents. Those high in power also require a far greater degree of personal control over the policy process and the actions of subordinates than low power personalities. In terms of interpersonal relationships, people high in the need for power exhibit more controlling, domineering behavior towards subordinates than low power people (McClelland, 1985; Winter, 1973, 1987). Motivation and leadership receives attention in Winter's (1987) study of the appeal of U.S. presidents. He argues that a leader's popular appeal (measured by electoral success) is a function of the fit between his or her motives and those of society.

In psychology, a method for assessing motives used by clinical psychologists is the Thematic Apperception Test, or TAT. This method involves giving participants a picture, having them write imaginative stories about it, then doing a content analysis of the stories. The stories reveal underlying personality characteristics. This method was criticized as unreliable; regardless of its reliability, it is not available for the assessment of political leaders, so techniques for measuring motives from a distance were developed using **content analysis** of texts, in particular the inaugural speeches of U.S. presidents.[3]

What is Content Analysis?

Content analysis is a research method used frequently by political psychologists taking a wide variety of analytical approaches, including those discussed in this chapter and Chapter 3. Because in political psychology we often lack direct access to policy-makers, we look at their statements and infer from those statements some aspects of their political psychological make-up. This is content analysis. To conduct a systematic content analysis, a researcher must: (1) decide what materials he or she will use in the study—for example, only statements written by the official you are examining, public statements written by others, interviews, and so on; and (2) establish how the material will be analyzed (or coded)—that is, how inferences will be drawn and recorded.

Genetic Theories

When thinking about genetic influences on personality, there are two related areas we can explore. The first area is evolutionary psychology, which we mentioned in the first chapter. As applied to personality, evolutionary psychologists take the position that certain traits or patterns of behavior have persisted and strengthened because they possess high survival value. In other words, certain patterns of behavior help a species to survive because they are adaptive. Evolutionary psychologists studied such behavioral patterns as aggression (e.g., Lorenz, 1966), altruism (e.g.,

Dawkins, 1976), and self-esteem (e.g., Leary, 1999). For example, altruism is said to have survival value because we are more likely to help out members of our own species, thereby ensuring its survival.

Related to evolutionary psychology is **behavioral genetics**, which explains how individual traits and patterns of behavior get passed down from parents to children, and how those traits are shared between siblings. Basically, it asks whether there is a family resemblance with regard to personality. In this section of the chapter, we focus more on behavioral genetics because there is research to suggest a genetic component to personality.

First, to understand the research on behavioral genetics in political psychology, it might be helpful to review the basic aim of behavioral genetic research. You may recall from a biology or genetics class that a phenotype refers to the observable traits a person possesses, while a genotype refers to the underlying genetic structure. Of course, the picture is quite a bit more complicated than that, as evidenced by the Human Genome Project, which mapped about 25,000 genes. For our purposes, it is important to understand behavioral genetics is concerned with the degree of variation in a phenotype attributable to the genotype. One way to answer that question is to engage in research on twins. Here again, it is wise to recall some information from your biology classes: monozygotic twins come from one egg, while dizygotic twins come from two eggs. Therefore, monozygotic twins are genetically identical.

Why is it relevant that monozygotic twins are identical? As you can imagine, there are many factors that can influence our personality. Some of these, such as motives and the unconscious, were already discussed. But there may be other influences on our personality, such as social situations or the environment. Behavioral geneticists do not discount or ignore those influences, but instead try to measure how much of our personality is attributable to genes and how much is attributable to environmental factors. This is where studies of twins are highly valuable. If a trait or a behavioral pattern is influenced by genes, then the trait or behavioral scores of monozygotic twins should be more highly correlated than they are for dizygotic twins or siblings. And, of course, close relatives should have more highly correlated scores on traits or behavioral patterns than more distant relatives. So how highly correlated are the traits of monozygotic twins? It turns out to be about .60 for monozygotic and .40 for dizygotic (Borkenau et al., 2001), suggesting that genes matter. Also, it appears that growing up in the same household does not lead to similar personalities. Adoptive siblings raised in the same household have a correlation of about .05 on personality traits (Funder, 2010).

There is increasing evidence for a genetic component to political behavior (Funk, 2013). More of this will be explored in later chapters, but for now we will focus on the role of genetics in personality as it relates to political behavior. Specifically, there is evidence that many of our political beliefs have a strong genetic component. In a large-scale study of about 8000 twins, Funk et al., (2013) studied a number of political traits and measured the variability in those traits that was likely due to genetics, and to the environment. With regard to political attitudes, they found attitudes of political ideology and egalitarianism had strong genetic components, with about 58% of the variability in political ideology, and 50% of the variability in egalitarianism attributable to genes.

Recall the prior section on the Big Five personality traits. There is strong evidence to suggest many of those traits are heritable. Funk et al. (2013) found one of the reasons we are the way we are is because of genetics. For example, consider the trait of extroversion. Funk et al. found about 70% of the variability of that trait is due to genetic factors. The other four traits in the Big Five were also shown to have high heritability scores, with agreeableness at 38%, conscientiousness at 42%, neuroticism at 42%, and openness at 43%. One important trait for political psychology studied by the authors was authoritarianism. The twins in the study were asked for responses to statements such as "Our country needs a powerful leader, in order to destroy the radical and immoral currents prevailing in society today" and "Our country needs free thinkers, who will have the courage to stand up against traditional ways, even if this upsets many people." Their results showed that about 48% of the variability in responses to these questions was attributable to genes.

Another approach to the examination of biological differences among liberals and conservatives uses fMRI studies to examine brain activity. FMRI stands for functional magnetic resonance imaging. Subjects are placed in a MRI machine and their brains are scanned looking for changes in electrical activity. In studies by John Hibbing (2019) and others, the psychological and physiological differences between liberals and conservatives were examined as they were exposed to images of positive and negative events, including threatening, negative, positive, or disgusting images. Hibbing found that, in general, conservatives were more sensitive to threat than liberals. They spotted threat more readily, categorized it more easily, and remembered it better than liberals. Hibbing's studies also examined the adamant supporters of Donald Trump, and those findings are discussed in Chapter 6.

SOME FRAMEWORKS FROM POLITICAL PSYCHOLOGY

In the following sections, we introduce readers to political psychological frameworks that employ various combinations of personality psychology discussed above. As mentioned at the outset of this chapter, the use of personality theories by political psychology is eclectic. The frameworks presented below draw liberally from a variety of psychological theories. Most importantly, they tried to adapt those theories and concepts to political contexts. For example, personality traits and motivations discussed in psychology may be used directly in political analyses, or they may be presented in a political manifestation. The need for power is directly applicable to politics. **Ethnocentrism** has been determined to be an important *politically relevant trait,* but is not considered to be a central personality trait in the personality literature.

The Authoritarian Personality

Although research into the **authoritarian personality** has a long history, interest in exploring authoritarian personality characteristics increased as a result of World War II and the Nazi regime in Germany. The rabid anti-Semitism of that regime, along with its extreme right-wing fascist political principles, led researchers to explore the question of whether this political authoritarianism could be traced to a personality syndrome. The post-World War II study of an authoritarian personality type began with *The Authoritarian Personality* (Adorno, Frenkel-Brunswick, Levinson, & Sanford, 1950), which was based on psychoanalytic arguments. The authors argued that authoritarian personalities were the product of authoritarian patterns of childhood upbringing and a resultant weak ego. The parents of authoritarians were insensitive to the difficulties experienced by children as they try to learn how to control id-derived impulses relating to sexual desires, bodily functions, and aggression. Instead of helping their children develop, these parents were demanding, controlling, and used severe disciplinary techniques. The parents were also described as being determined to raise their children to be highly conventional. As a result, the children did not develop effective ways of controlling their sexual and aggressive impulses, yet feared those impulses. They developed iron-tight defensive techniques that would prevent them from confronting those impulses. They regarded their parents, and subsequent authority figures in their lives, with a mixture of resentment and dependence.

Adorno et al. (1950) saw the authoritarian personality as composed of several central personality traits, including conventionalism (rigid adherence to conventional values), submission to authority figures, authoritarian aggression (aggressive impulses towards those who are not conventional), anti-intraception (rejection of tenderness, imagination, subjectivity), superstition and stereotype (fatalistic belief in mystical determinants of the future and rigid thinking), high value placed on power and toughness, destructiveness and cynicism, projectivity (the projection outward of unacceptable impulses), and an excessive concern with the sexual activity of others. Given the era in which the study was conducted, there was a natural interest in the extent to which authoritarian personalities would be susceptible to fascism of the Nazi Germany variety—anti-democratic and right wing in political ideology, anti-Semitic, ethnocentric, and hostile toward racial and other minorities.

The Authoritarian Personality study used a wide variety of research tools including questionnaires (with factual questions, opinion-attitude scales, and open-answer questions) and clinical measures (interviews and TAT). The authors developed scales to measure several elements of authoritarian political attitudes. Scales combined several items from a questionnaire on the same topic, enabling the researcher to get a broader range of scores for a single person. This increased the reliability of the score. The Fascism scale, or F scale, was developed to test for a person's propensity toward fascism. The other scales were the Anti-Semitism (A-S) scale, the Ethnocentrism (E) scale, which included Negro (N), Minority (M), and Patriotism (P) subscales, and the Politico-Economic Conservatism (PEC) scale. Each scale was designed to assess different elements of political authoritarianism. Adorno et al. (1950) argued that their empirical evidence demonstrated this syndrome was closely associated with anti-Semitism, ethnocentrism, and in turn with political conservatism. But criticisms quickly emerged on conceptual and methodological grounds. One of the more important criticisms was presented by Edward Shils (1954), who noted that communists who also held authoritarian political values scored low on the Adorno et al. measurement scale, the F scale. Therefore, he argued, they apparently tested only for right-wing authoritarianism and not left-wing authoritarianism. Therefore, their F scale was not a true measure of authoritarianism. Other criticisms noted that Adorno and his colleagues did not control for education and income, and the F scale question wording *provoked* a tendency to agree (acquiesce), thereby producing false positives (Bass, 1955; Gage, Leavitt, & Stone, 1957; Jackson & Messick, 1957). In short, much of the criticism was methodological and related to the question of whether the F scale actually tapped true authoritarianism, and whether it actually established a relationship between those nine authoritarian personality traits and fascistic political principles.

Additional criticisms were made of the work of Adorno and his colleagues. For example, John Levi Martin (2001) argued that there was a fundamental flaw in the theoretical construct because it assumed that those who were high in authoritarianism had certain syndromes, and those who were low did not. Instead, he suggested the whole issue should be approached as a question, and the difference between low and high should be studied on a continuum. What, for example, were those in the middle like? Second, Martin noted that the Adorno group was willing to distort or dismiss data showing non-authoritarian tendencies among the highs and authoritarian tendencies among the lows. This reached its acme in a differential interpretation strategy by which anything good said by a high (but not a low) was evidence of the suppression of its opposite, and anything bad said by a low (but not by a high) was taken as evidence of a healthy acceptance of one's shortcomings (Martin, 2001, p. 10).

The authoritarian personality debate, and renewed interest in the personality syndrome, was revitalized by the work of Robert Altemeyer (1981, 1988, 1996). Altemeyer's approach is trait based rather than psychoanalytic. He used three of the nine personality traits identified by Adorno et al. (1950): authoritarian submission, authoritarian aggression, and conventionalism. He regarded these as central attitudinal clusters—orientations to respond in the same general way toward certain classes of stimuli (Altemeyer, 1996, p. 6) in right-wing authoritarianism. Altemeyer did not include the more psychoanalytical traits because he was not convinced by the original psychoanalytic argument, noting there was little inter-item consistency among the F scale questions that attempted to trace those traits. Instead, he conceptualized right-wing authoritarianism psychologically rather than politically (that is, one ideology versus another). Psychologically, **right-wing authoritarianism** is submission to perceived authorities, particularly those in the establishment or established system of governance (1996, p. 10). That system could be a repressive right-wing system, as in Apartheid South Africa, a communist system as in the People's Republic of China (PRC), or a democratic system as in the United States. Hence, right-wing authoritarianism can occur in any political system. Altemeyer developed a Right-Wing Authoritarianism (RWA) scale. The scale includes statements with which the respondent must agree or disagree, such as "life imprisonment is justified for certain crimes" and "women should have to promise to obey their husbands when they get married" (1996, p. 13).

In Altemeyer's view, right-wing authoritarianism is a product of social learning, a combination of personality predispositions and life events. Altemeyer argued that those high in right-wing authoritarianism have greater difficulty than low scorers in engaging in critical thinking. They are more likely to agree with a statement of a fact without examining it critically (1996, p. 95). This is a consequence of having truths dictated to them by those in authority and being prohibited from challenging that authority. Therefore, when a scapegoat is selected upon whom a country's problems are placed, people high in right-wing authoritarianism are more likely to uncritically believe that the scapegoat is responsible. It follows that a second pattern of thinking among those high in right-wing authoritarianism is the acceptance of contradictory ideas and an ability to compartmentalize them, thereby ignoring the contradictions. Any idea that comes from an authority figure is accepted as correct, even if it is in direct contradiction to another idea. Third, Altemeyer argues that those high in right-wing authoritarianism see the world as a very dangerous place. Their parents taught them this, and the resulting fear drives a lot of their aggression; this makes them vulnerable to precisely the kind of overstated, emotional, and dangerous assertions a demagogue would make (1996, pp. 100–101). Fourth, high authoritarians are much more careful in looking for evidence to disprove ideas they are predisposed to reject than to disprove ideas they are predisposed to accept. Finally, he suggests that high authoritarians are particularly susceptible to the *fundamental attribution error*, wherein people attribute the behavior of others to internal dispositions and their own behavior to external forces (discussed further in Chapter 3).

Further research into the authoritarian personality is ongoing. In Chapter 8, we also discuss some research regarding race-related attitudes and right-wing authoritarianism. Lambert, Burroughs, and Nguyen (1999) used Altemeyer's RWA scale to examine the relationship between authoritarianism, belief in a just world, and perceptions of risk. They found that high authoritarians perceived risk to be lower if people believed in a just world (i.e., good things come to good people). Low authoritarians did not have the same perception. Tam, Leung, and Chiu (2008) found that when people high in authoritarianism are more "mindful" or attentive to information, they become more punitive in their reactions to criminal behavior, contrary to the general assumption that individuals become less punitive when more attentive to information. The opposite was the case for authoritarians.

While Altemeyer (1996) argues that several political attitudes, such as anti-Semitism and hostility toward foreigners, correlated with his three central authoritarian attitude clusters, others such as Raden (1999) suggest that the clustering of such attitudes is influenced by political and social change. Raden found anti-Semitism was decreasingly likely to correlate with authoritarian personality characteristics as the twentieth century progressed. Martin (2001) weighed in on Altemeyer's work, arguing that although he avoided the methodological problems of Adorno's F scale, he still failed to see authoritarianism as a continuum, and did not compare the behavior of lows and highs, sticking to the examination of the behavior of highs. Furthermore, Altemeyer did not adequately explain why conventionalism is a manifestation of authoritarianism, and he used evidence of differences in degree (that is, some lows agreeing with highs and some highs agreeing with lows in some question items) as evidence of a clear-cut, mutually distinct typological difference.

As mentioned at the beginning of this chapter, studies of personality and leadership in political psychology are rather eclectic in that they draw not only from psychological personality concepts, but other areas too. As a result, scholars built some frameworks used to analyze political leaders (although many could also be used to examine the average citizen). Below we provide an overview of some of those frameworks with some examples of their applications to political leaders. Political leaders are discussed in much greater depth in Chapter 5.

In their analysis of authoritarianism in the United States and the Trump administration, Dean and Altemeyer (2020) pulled together many advances that have occurred in the study of authoritarianism since the 1990s. They distinguished between authoritarian followers, social dominators, and "double highs," who are high in both authoritarianism and social dominance. The description of authoritarian followers is consistent with the discussion above but adds some interesting examples and additional ideas. One example used of the authoritarian followers' submission to authority concerns COVID-19:

> Nothing demonstrates right-wing authoritarians' submission to their leaders as clearly as Trump's supporters' acceptance of his pronouncements and guidance regarding COVID-19. Polls show they believed Trump's dismissal of the threat during January and February and up to March 11, 2020. Accordingly, they would have been more likely to ignore the advice coming from medical experts to socially distance themselves from others. Considerable numbers of them likely became infected and proceeded to infect others, including their loved ones.
>
> Dean & Altmeyer (2020, p. 125)

The dominant characteristics Dean and Altemeyer identified in those high in RWA involve highly compartmentalized thinking, enabling them to hold contradictory ideas; double standards (for example, advocating extreme punishment for those they dislike and little or no punishment for those they like – for example, Hillary Clinton vs. Donald Trump); conflicting and contradictory ideas; difficulty judging evidence; high ethnocentrism; high levels of prejudice; and dogmatism (resulting from memorizing instead of thinking about and understanding why they believe what they believe).

Earlier studies of authoritarians note that they can be submissive to authority and aggressive toward those who do not conform. As work progressed, greater scrutiny was devoted to those who aggressed against others. A new scale was developed (discussed at greater length in Chapter 7) called the Social Dominance Scale (SDO). This measured the extent to which people believe in social hierarchies and established inequalities between groups, and will act to maintain that social order. This scale enables scholars to distinguish better between submissive authoritarians and those who will act more aggressively against outsiders and norm violators. As Dean and Altemeyer explain, social dominators become submissive:

> Mostly because they got beat. A persona driven to control others will eventually lose to someone in his [they are usually male] world, unless he is fierce enough, endowed enough, and lucky enough to become Number One. When social dominators meet their match, they can quit the game. But it is much more rewarding to claim a place in the hierarchy.
>
> Dean & Altmeyer (2020, p. 111)

Finally, Dean and Altemeyer discuss "double highs," people who score high in both right-wing authoritarianism and SDO. They note that previous studies found few double highs, but state that they do exist, and tend to have the worst characteristics of both the RWA and SDO highs:

> Take dogmatism, which RWAs have by the bucketful, which High SDOs can carry theirs in a cup because they do not care about creeds and philosophies enough to be dogmatic about them. But Double Highs need a bucket. High RWAs, in turn, are not power-mad or amoral deceitful manipulators, but high SDOs are and so are Double Highs. High SDOs do not effervesce with religious fundamentalism and religious ethnocentrism, but Double Highs tend to, like High RWAs. So, like an unfortunate child who has his father's alligator skin and bowlegs plus his mother's bad hearing and poor digestion, Double Highs generally carry with them the worst features of high SDOs and high RWAs. You can say about high RWAs, for example, they may be dogmatic, but at least they are not power-mad. But Double Highs tend to be both. And this spells real trouble.
>
> Dean & Altmeyer (2020, p. 196)

Leader Analysis Frameworks

There is an extensive literature in political psychology on the leadership or management styles of political leaders using many different frameworks. Below we introduce several frameworks used to study political leaders: the presidential character framework developed by James David Barber, several trait assessment approaches, and the Operational Code. There also is no common, agreed-upon empirical approach to the study of political leaders in political psychology. Instead, there is a broad, methodologically diverse, interdisciplinary body of literature on the topic tolerant of hybrid research approaches that borrow individual concepts or variables from a variety of sources. As a result, variables that psychologists would be quick to describe as personality based (whether Freudian concepts, authoritarian measures, personal traits like need for power, self-confidence, distrust of others, and so on) are routinely combined with non-personality-based variables, such as an individual's first political success, their socialization experiences, their prior policy experience, or operational code belief systems, in the same analysis. Since the literature in political psychology addressing the impact of personal variables upon political leader behavior developed over a long process of selective borrowing by political scientists from a broad range of psychological literatures (on personality, cognition, groups, and so on), it is practically impossible to draw crisp, clear delineations between personality and political leadership in political psychology. Like the problem often facing surgeons in separating infants born conjoined, these two research traditions in political psychology share too many common elements to easily separate them into two distinct bodies. This reality will become more apparent as many of the approaches to the study of personality and politics, as well as political leadership, are viewed in this chapter. Some personality-based studies are applied to both leaders and the average person, such as authoritarian personality studies. Below we will provide an overview of several theories and frameworks that focus on individual characteristics, and their impact on political behavior.

Trait-Based Studies

Presidential Character

James David Barber's well-known book *The Presidential Character* (1972), employs psychobiography to explain the personalities, styles, and character of modern presidents. Avoiding the psychoanalytic focus on Freudian concepts (the id, ego, and superego), Barber's psychobiographies seek patterns in the early lives or political careers of leaders that create, through a process of socialization, the subsequent patterns of personality, style, and leadership one sees in office. Moreover, Barber argues that personality should not be studied as a set of idiosyncratic traits unique to individual presidents, where some presidents have a trait that others do not. Instead, he argues that personality is a "matter of tendencies," in which traits such as aggressiveness, detachment, or compliancy are possessed by all presidents, but in differing amounts and combinations (1972, p. 7). As a result, the components of presidential personality (*character*, *world view*, and *style*) are patterned, fitting together in a "dynamic package understandable in psychological terms" (p. 6). *Style* reflects the habitual way a president performs the three political roles (rhetoric, personal relations, and homework), whereas *world view* consists of the leader's primary politically relevant beliefs regarding such things as social causality, human nature, and the central moral conflicts of the time (pp. 7–8). Lastly, *character* is seen as the way in which a president orients himself or herself towards life and his or her own merits – that is, a sense of self-esteem and the criteria by which the president judges who he or she is, such as by achievement or affection (p. 8). To put these pieces together, Barber employs a psychobiographical approach to trace the sociological development within presidents of the three patterns comprising personality (character, world view, and style) from their early lives on through to their critically important *first independent political successes*. It is that first political success that sets the pattern that follows, giving the leader a template for successful action and positive feedback that they emulate and seek to copy throughout their subsequent careers.

Perhaps one of the most famous typologies in political science, Barber's seeks to capture how *presidential character*, or "the basic stance a man [sic.] takes toward his Presidential experience," finds itself reflected in two basic dimensions: (1) the energy and effort he puts into the job (*active or passive*);

Table 2.1 Barber Typology of Presidential Character

	Personal satisfaction with presidential duties	
Energy put into the job	*Positive*	*Negative*
Active	Derives great personal satisfaction and is highly engaged (examples: Jefferson, Roosevelt, Truman, Kennedy, Ford, Carter, Bush, Clinton)	Derives little personal satisfaction yet is highly engaged (examples: Adams, Wilson, Hoover, Johnson, Nixon)
Passive	Enjoys great personal satisfaction from the job, but puts little energy into it (examples: Madison, Taft, Harding, Reagan, George W. Bush)	Derives little personal satisfaction and puts little energy into it (examples: Washington, Coolidge, Eisenhower)

and (2) the personal satisfaction he derives from his presidential duties (*positive or negative*) (Barber, 1972, p. 6). The resulting typology is presented in Table 2.1, along with Barber's examples of U.S. presidents who fit within each of the cells.

Applied to both Bill Clinton and George W. Bush, Barber's (1972) typology leads to a very generalized prediction of behavior and style in office. In Clinton's case, he fits into the *active-positive* category of Barber's typology. Indeed, few presidents in American history were so actively engaged personally in the details of policy-making on a day-to-day basis, or enjoyed their presidential duties and responsibilities as much as Bill Clinton did in office (Preston, 2001). Barber's predictions for this type of personality are that such individuals want to achieve results and direct much of their energy towards achievement, tend to be self-respecting and happy, open to new ideas, flexible and able to learn from mistakes, and tend to show great capacity for growth in office. While one might quibble with some of the problematic predictions in light of Clinton's White House behaviors regarding interns and the ability to learn from mistakes, the general predictions regarding his emphasis on results and achievement, his generally happy demeanor, and his widely reported openness to new ideas and policy flexibility are strongly supported by his record in office. Similarly, Barack Obama would also be seen as *active-positive*, and despite obstructionism by Congressional Republicans throughout his two terms in office, he remained engaged, open to new ideas, flexible regarding policy, and focused on results and achievement, while enjoying being president.

In contrast, George W. Bush would likely be classified as a *passive-positive* according to Barber's typology. The early evidence of Bush's style in office supports this designation. He is an individual who tends to be less personally engaged or involved in the formulation and making of policy, preferring instead to delegate these tasks to subordinates, but who nevertheless greatly enjoyed being president (Dowd, 2001; Khan, 2000; Milbank, 2001). In terms of predicted behaviors arising from this style type, Barber describes passive-positives as primarily being after affirmation, support, or love from followers, while showing a tendency for policy drift—especially during times of crisis, where confusion, delay, and impulsiveness are expected. There certainly were numerous examples of confusion, delay, and impulsiveness with regard to Bush's policies in the Middle East (especially the Israeli–Palestinian conflict and Iraq), in his reaction toward U.S. participation in many international treaties (ABM and Kyoto being only the most notable), and in his enunciation of an "axis of evil." Moreover, the Iraq War and U.S. actions in Afghanistan were, throughout Bush's presidency, characterized by considerable policy drift and inconsistencies (Preston, 2011).

Obviously, the typology is exceedingly general in nature, examines only two possible dimensions relating to presidential style, and is intensely subjective. Clearly, one could take issue with either the accuracy or usefulness of the Barber model, especially given that it basically places Franklin Roosevelt, Harry Truman, John Kennedy, Gerald Ford, Jimmy Carter, George Bush Sr., Clinton, and Obama all in the active-positive category, while Ronald Reagan, Warren Harding, and William Taft join George W. Bush as passive-positives. Given such minimal differentiation among such varied presidents, many leadership analysts argued for a more nuanced approach (Hermann & Preston, 1994, 1998; Preston, 2001; Winter et al., 1991). Indeed, while Barber's later book achieved the most notoriety, many see his book *The Lawmakers* (1965), which explored the motivations for Connecticut legislators running for office in the first place (i.e., making laws, doing their public service, etc.), and how these shaped their legislative behaviors and styles once in office, as being a superior approach to looking at leaders than his later typology. In fact, similar relationships between motivation for leadership and political behavior were found in a study of Middle Eastern revolutionaries (Winter, 2011).

Looking at other traits, in a study of twentieth-century U.S. presidents and foreign policy advisers, Etheredge (1978) notes the importance of traits such as dominance, interpersonal trust, self-esteem, and introversion–extroversion in shaping policy-maker views and policy preferences. American leaders scoring high on measures of dominance tended to favor using force to settle disputes with the Soviet Union over the use of arbitration or disarmament. Moreover, leaders scoring high on introversion tended to oppose cooperation, while extroverted ones generally supported cooperation and negotiation with the Soviets. These results built upon earlier studies reported by Etheredge of over 200 male U.S. foreign service officers, military officers, and domestic affairs specialists, where those who scored high on traits of dominance and competitiveness were more likely to advocate the use of force and to see the Soviet Union as threatening, while those high on interpersonal trust and self-esteem tended to hold a more benign view of the Soviets and to oppose the use of force (Winter, 2003). Other significant work applying traits to political leaders was done by Weintraub (1981, 1986, 1989) in his studies of U.S. presidential press conference responses, and by Hermann (1984, 1987, 1988) in studies of the foreign policy orientations of world leaders.

Leaders' Characteristics: Motives and Traits

A wealth of research also exists on the impact various individual characteristics of leaders have on their styles of decision-making, interpersonal interactions, information processing, or management behaviors in office (cf., Hermann, 1980a, 1980b, 1983, 1984, 1987; Hermann & Preston, 1994, 1998; Mitchell, 2005; Preston, 2001, 2011; Preston & 't Hart, 1999; Stogdill & Bass, 1981; Vertzberger, 1990; Winter et al., 1991). Ample illustrations of leader characteristics and decision-making patterns are presented in Chapter 5. Table 2.2 provides basic descriptions of several of the most important leader characteristics, along with the measurement techniques discussed.[4]

A few brief illustrations of several of these individual characteristics (power, complexity, expertise) provide the reader with a clearer understanding of how these measures tend to be thought of in the literature.

The need for power (or dominance) is a personality characteristic extensively studied and linked to specific types of behavior and interactional styles with others (Browning & Jacob, 1964; Hermann, 1987; House, 1990; McClelland, 1975; Winter, 1973, 1987; Winter & Stewart, 1977). Specifically, leaders with progressively higher psychological needs for power are

Table 2.2 Descriptions of Selected Individual Characteristics

Need for power	Concern with establishing, maintaining, or restoring one's power (i.e., one's impact, control, or influence over others).
Locus of control	View of the world in which an individual does or does not perceive some degree of control over situations he/she is involved in and whether government can influence what happens in or to the nation.
Ethnocentrism	View of the world in which one's own nation holds center stage; strong emotional ties to one's own nation; emphasis on national honor and identity.
Need for affiliation	Concern with establishing, maintaining, or restoring warm and friendly relationships with other persons or groups.
Cognitive complexity	Ability to differentiate the environment: Degree of differentiation person shows in describing or discussing other people, places, policies, ideas, or things.
Distrust of others	General feeling of doubt, uneasiness, and misgiving about others; inclination to suspect and doubt others' motives and actions.
Self-confidence	Person's sense of self-importance or image of his/her ability to cope with the environment.
Task-interpersonal emphasis	Relative emphasis in interactions with others on getting the task done versus focusing on feelings and needs of others.

increasingly dominant and assertive in their leadership styles in office, and assert greater control over subordinates and policy decisions. For example, Fodor and Smith (1982, pp. 178–185) found that leaders high in need for power are more associated with the suppression of open decision-making and discussion within groups than low power leaders. Similarly, a number of studies found high power leaders require a far greater degree of personal control than low power leaders over the policy process and the actions of subordinates (Etheredge, 1978; Winter, 1973, 1987). In terms of interpersonal relationships, studies also found that leaders high in the need for power exhibit more controlling, domineering behavior towards subordinates than low power leaders (Browning & Jacob, 1964; Fodor & Farrow, 1979; McClelland, 1985; Winter & Stewart, 1977).

The cognitive complexity of decision-makers is another individual characteristic with a significant impact on the nature of decision-making, style of leadership, assessment of risk, and character of general information-processing within decision groups (Driver, 1977; Hermann, 1980b, 1987; Preston, 2001; Stewart, Hermann, & Hermann, 1989; Tetlock, 1985; Wallace & Suedfeld, 1988; Vertzberger, 1990). For example, Vertzberger (1990), among others, notes that as the cognitive complexity of individual decision-makers increases, they become more capable of dealing with complex decision environments and information. When making decisions, complex individuals tend to have greater cognitive need for information, are more attentive to incoming information, prefer systematic over heuristic processing, and deal with any overload of information better than their less complex counterparts (Nydegger, 1975; Schroder, Driver, & Streufert, 1967). In terms of interactions with advisers and the acceptance of critical feedback, several studies have shown that complex individuals are far more interested in receiving negative feedback from others, and are more likely to incorporate it into their own decision-making, than are those who are less complex (Nydegger, 1975; Ziller et al., 1977). Indeed, Vertzberger (1990) and Glad (1983) both note that low complexity individuals tend to show symptoms of dogmatism, view and judge issues in black-and-white terms, ignore information that threatens their existing closed belief systems, and have limited ability to adjust their beliefs to new information.

Complexity is also linked to how attentive or sensitive leaders are to information from (or to nuances from within) their surrounding political or policy environments (Hermann, 1984; Preston, 1997, 2001). In fact, Hermann (1984) notes that the more sensitive the individual is to information from the decision environment, the more receptive the leader is to information regarding views of colleagues, constituents, and outside actors, and the value of alternative viewpoints and discrepant information. In contrast, leaders with a low sensitivity to contextual information are less receptive to information from the outside environment, operate from a previously established and strongly held set of beliefs, selectively perceive and process incoming information to support or bolster this prior framework, and are unreceptive or close-minded towards alternative viewpoints and discrepant information. This is closely correlated with the degree to which individuals are *high versus low self-monitors*—that is, those focusing upon and taking cues from their external environment when interacting with others as opposed to those who ignore such cues in order to "be who they are" (Day et al., 2002; Gangestad & Snyder, 2000; Snyder, 1987). Self-monitoring is having one's antennae up to pick up on and be responsive to social situations, and is related to being high in complexity (Preston, 2001, 2011).

The **integrative complexity** literature differs slightly from the cognitive complexity literature discussed above in that it focuses on both *differentiation* (which involves evaluatively distinct dimensions of a problem taken into account by decision-makers) and *integration* (which involves the connections made by decision-makers among differentiated characteristics), whereas the general complexity literature focuses principally on differentiation alone (Tetlock, 1983). For example, according to Tetlock and Tyler (1996), integrative complexity presupposes a dialectical point–counterpoint style of thinking in which the speaker recognizes the legitimacy of contradictory points of view, then integrates those evaluatively differentiated cognitions into a higher-order synthesis. The concept of cognitive complexity, by contrast, only requires one to have many distinct ideas or thoughts on a subject, not that those cognitions be in tension with each other or that they are organized into higher-order schemata or knowledge structures. For example, one could be cognitively complex by generating lots of reasons why one is right and one's adversaries are wrong, but still be integratively simple.

In terms of impact on leaders, Suedfeld and Rank (1976) observed that successful revolutionary leaders needed the low complexity associated with single-mindedness to be successful, but those with this characteristic found it difficult to govern after their successful revolutions since governing required more "graduated, flexible, and integrated" views of the world (Suedfeld & Rank, 1976, p. 169). Indeed, it was only those revolutionary leaders who later showed a significant increase in their integrative complexity who found success in governing. Other studies looked at the complexity of U.S. presidents (Thoemmes & Conway, 2007), the U.S. Supreme Court (Gruenfeld, 1995), and communications regarding the "war on terror" (Suedfeld & Leighton, 2002).

Finally, the **prior policy experience or expertise** of leaders significantly impacts presidential style, the nature of advisory group interactions, and how forcefully leaders assert their own positions on policy issues (cf., Barber, 1972; George, 1980; Hermann, 1986; House, 1990). Past experience provides leaders with a sense of which actions will be effective or ineffective in specific policy situations, as well as which cues from the environment should be attended to and which are irrelevant (Hermann, 1986). Prior experience influences how much learning must be accomplished on the job, the inventory of behaviors (standard operating procedures) possessed, and how confident the leader will be in interactions with experts. Leaders with a high degree of prior policy experience are more likely to insist on personal involvement or control over policy-making than those low in prior policy experience, who will tend to be more dependent upon the views of expert advisers. Indeed, experienced leaders who have expertise in a policy area are far less likely to rely upon the views of advisers or utilize simplistic stereotypes or analogies to understand policy situations. Such leaders are more interested in gathering detailed information from the policy environment, and they employ a more deliberate decision-making process than their less experienced counterparts. Similarly, leaders lacking experience or expertise find themselves far more dependent upon expert advisers and more likely to utilize simplistic stereotypes and analogies when making decisions (see Khong, 1992; Levy, 1994; Preston, 2001). Knowing whether a leader is approaching foreign or domestic policy as a relative expert or novice provides insight into predicting how damaging such reliance upon analogy might be to a particular leader's information-management and information-processing styles. This individual characteristic is similar to George's (1980) *sense of efficacy*.

A major pioneer of modern leadership studies, Hermann (1983, 1984, 1986, 1999a, 2001) led the way forward with a rigorous leader assessment-at-a-distance technique, and a body of path-breaking research exploring many facets of how leaders shape and affect foreign policy. Not only has Hermann's **Leader Trait Assessment (LTA)** content-analytic technique become the most widely utilized and empirically rich of the existing approaches to leadership analysis, but Hermann's work spawned the original development of the computer-based, expert system, Profiler-Plus, developed by Social Science Automation, a company co-founded by Hermann and Michael Young. Profiler-Plus's ability to code millions of words of text systematically with ease created massive databases of world leaders. The program runs comparisons across leaders, their characteristics, and a wide range of other leadership dimensions.

The LTA approach uses the spontaneous interview responses of leaders to code for seven specific individual characteristics: need for power, conceptual complexity, **task-interpersonal emphasis**, self-confidence, locus of control, distrust of others, and ethnocentrism (Hermann, 1999b). All available materials from interviews, press conference Q&As across every issue area and across time are coded by Profiler-Plus, generating overall scores for each leader broken down by characteristic, audience, topic, and time period. This system not only has 100% intercoder reliability, and removes the subjectivity so often associated with profiling techniques coded by hand; it also allows for the comparison of leader scores against a norming population of over 250 other world leaders. These comparisons can also be made within groups of leaders within a country or across a given region.

Moreover, empirical research provides support for the behavioral correlates linked by Hermann to leader scores. For example, Preston (2001) and Dyson and Preston (2006) profiled modern U.S. presidents and British prime ministers respectively, then compared the theoretical expectations for given LTA scores (given the psychological literatures) with the leaders' actual behavior across foreign policy cases using archival materials (i.e., their need for personal involvement/control, need for information, structuring/use of advisory systems). Similarly, in a study of sub-Saharan African leaders, Hermann (1987) found that—unlike the styles of Western political leaders, who generally tended to emphasize task completion in office—African leaders emphasized constituent morale over task accomplishment. At the same time, Hermann's study also found substantial variability across the individual characteristics scores of these African leaders, meaning there was no single style type for sub-Saharan African leaders, illustrating the need to study each in depth and in context to predict foreign policy behavior. Interestingly, across this broad leadership literature, Hermann and Preston (1994, p. 81) note five main types of leadership variables routinely identified as impacting the style of leaders, and their subsequent structuring and use of advisory systems: (1) leader involvement in the policy-making process; (2) leader willingness to tolerate conflict; (3) leader's motivation or reason for leading; (4) leader's preferred strategies for managing information; and (5) leader's preferred strategies for resolving conflict.

Other studies applying the LTA approach looked at UN Secretaries General (Kille, 2006), Iranian leaders (Taysi & Preston, 2001), European prime ministers (Kaarbo & Hermann, 1998); President Assad of Syria (Hermann, 1988); Soviet leaders (Winter et al., 1991); Irish nationalist leaders (Mastors, 2000); Indian prime ministers (Mitchell, 2007); Saddam Hussein and Bill Clinton (Hermann, 2006); the impact of leader characteristics upon bureaucratic and group dynamics (Preston & 't Hart, 1999; Stewart et al., 1989); leader selection and socialization dynamics (Hermann, 1979); democratic peace theory (Hermann & Kegley, 1995); use of analogy in decision-making (Dyson & Preston, 2006); and leader management of crisis contexts (Boin et al., 2010; Preston, 2008). Across all these studies, the differences in leader characteristics and styles had substantial foreign policy impacts.

Operational Code

A final approach to studying characteristics of political leaders to be presented in this chapter is studies of **operational codes**, a concept originally introduced by Leites (1951, 1953) in his study of the ideology and belief structures of the Soviet Bolsheviks. His work was later modified and stripped of its psychoanalytic elements by Alexander George (1969), who reconceptualized the operational code (as illustrated in Table 2.3) to represent the answers to ten questions about a leader's *philosophical beliefs* (what the nature of the political universe is) and *instrumental beliefs* (what are believed to be the best strategies and tactics for achieving goals).

Table 2.3 Operational Code: Philosophical and Instrumental Beliefs of Leaders

Philosophical beliefs	*Instrumental beliefs*
The fundamental nature of politics and political conflict, and the image of the opponent	The best approach for selecting goals for political action
The general prospects for achieving one's fundamental political values	How such goals and objectives can be pursued most effectively
The extent to which political outcomes are predictable	The best approach to calculation, control, and acceptance of the risks of political action
The extent to which political leaders can influence historical developments and control outcomes	The matter of "timing" of action
The role of chance	The utility and role of different means for advancing one's interests

Source: George (1979, p. 100).

Operational codes are constructs representing the overall belief systems of leaders about the world—that is, how it works, what it is like, what kinds of actions are most likely to be successful) (George, 1969, 1979; Holsti, 1977; Malici & Malici, 2005; Walker, 1983; Walker & Schafer, 2007; Walker, Schafer, & Young, 1998). Why is the discussion of the operational code in a chapter on personality, and not in the next chapter where beliefs are discussed? The explanation is simply that the operational code is unique to the personality of the person under examination and, more importantly, because the operational code links **motivation** (a personality factor) with beliefs. Scholars who use the framework argue that the beliefs it depicts are motivating forces, as well as information-processing filters.

As George (1979) observed, operational code beliefs, unlike attitudes, represent central beliefs, which "are concerned with fundamental, unchanging issues of politics and political action" (p. 99). By understanding the operational codes of leaders, scholars employing this technique argue, we gain a better understanding of their likely decision-making styles and political behavior. Operational codes are constructed either quantitatively or qualitatively through an examination of decision-makers' speeches, interviews, writings, and other verbal or written materials. This technique has a long history of use in political science and is used to examine a wide range of political leaders. Moreover, an automated coding scheme for the operational code, *Verbs in Context* (or VICS), employing the Profiler-Plus computer program, resulted in a dramatic increase in the use of operational code to assess the world. While at times lacking the qualitative richness of traditional Georgian op-code case study analysis, the VICS op-codes substitute quantitative rigor and the ability to code massive amounts of material across leaders with relative ease. Included within this operational code literature are studies of a wide range of political leaders, including John Foster Dulles (Holsti, 1970; Stuart & Starr, 1981), John F. Kennedy (Marfleet, 2000; Stuart & Starr, 1981), Henry Kissinger (Stuart & Starr, 1981; Walker, 1977), Woodrow Wilson (Walker, 1995), Jimmy Carter (Walker et al., 1998), U.S. Presidents and Secretaries of State (Walker & Falkowski, 1984), Vladimir Putin (Dyson, 2001), a large cross-section of world leaders (Shafer & Walker, 2006), Ayman al-Zawahiri (Jacquier, 2014), and leaders in a cross-cultural context (Dirlien-Gumas, 2017).

For example, in the case of President Vladimir Putin of Russia, an operational code analysis suggested that because of his *philosophical beliefs*, Putin would: (1) view political life as harmonious to the extent that it was governed and regulated by laws, rules, and norms; (2) believe that one can be optimistic about making progress towards one's goals as long as the rule of law is enforced, but that anarchy and corruption will reign in its absence; (3) believe that the political future is predictable to the extent that one can rely upon the existence of enforced rules and norms; (4) believe that it is possible to achieve very little direct control over history, but that one's own environment and circumstances can be affected by engaging in an incremental, step-by-step approach; and (5) view chance as something to be avoided as much as possible through good organization and organizational planning. In terms of his *instrumental beliefs*, Putin believes that: (1) the goals and objectives set for political action should be both achievable and measurable; (2) the best strategy for pursuing goals is to engage in an incremental, backward-mapping approach, planned step by step to stay within the norms of expected behavior; (3) political risk can be controlled by keeping a low political profile on his part while working behind the scenes; (4) the best timing of political action is one that preempts major difficulties, but does not occur so early as to cause difficulties itself; and (5) the prime tools of political interest advancement are incremental backward-mapping and flexibility on the leader's part (Dyson, 2001, pp. 339–343). Thus, Putin's operational code suggests a leader who is incremental by nature, judges the acceptability of actions by their chances of success, sees adherence to norms as essential, and views those who step outside of such norms as requiring reciprocal or violent treatment (Dyson, 2001, p. 343).

The value of such operational codes in predicting the likely pattern of leader behavior given the answers to these basic philosophical and instrumental questions is potentially quite high and of great value to policy-makers. For example, in summarizing the findings about Putin, Dyson (2001) makes a number of observations regarding the predictability of certain patterns of behavior:

> Putin's central belief in the harmony of political life when governed by rules and norms suggests a reciprocal, *quid pro quo* approach. Putin is unlikely to be impressed by unexpectedly bold or unconventional initiatives. His belief in the necessity of selecting goals which are both achievable and measurable, along with his personal propensity to "backward-map" a "step-by-step" approach towards an objective, suggests that agreements of an incremental design appeal to him … Putin's Operational Code suggests he will, chameleon-like, imitate his environment. One could not expect Putin to act in a norm-bound manner when those with which he is engaged do not. Putin is unlikely to "stick to the rules" in the face of deviation by another … instead, departure from agreed norms of behavior will in all probability entail a decisive break—an "all bets are off" attitude from Putin … [his] beliefs about political life … disposes him to prefer to retain a certain flexibility and freedom to maneuver. A recommendation would therefore be to design agreements and the like with clearly set out rules and schedules, but many "points of exit" for either side … [He] is unlikely to want to be tied to great statements of intent. Platitudes and vagaries can be expected from him, he will attempt to maintain a low profile until a clear "success" compels him to take political credit … Overall, the policymaker can feel confident that carefully constructed initiatives will not be dismissed out of hand, and that Putin is unlikely to make rash, impulsive or emotional gestures … However, the policymaker can feel warned that Putin will reciprocate "bad" as well as "good" behavior, and that a break down in co-operation will likely be quite bitter and long-lived.
>
> (Dyson, 2001, p. 344)

CONCLUSION

This chapter reviewed some of the major theoretical approaches to the study of personality in psychology, but only those used in political psychology.

There are many additional psychological theories of personality not mentioned in this chapter. In addition, the chapter presented a review of some of the frameworks in political psychology used to analyze personality and leadership in politics. In this chapter, we said little about the average person, as opposed to political leaders, because most of the personality-based studies in political psychology are of political leaders. Analyses of the political psychology of the average person are important and will be explored in Chapter 6. However, the concepts and theories used are those found in the next chapter, where we address cognition and attitudes.

Topics, Theories/Explanations, and Concepts in Chapter 2

Topics	*Theories/Explanations and Frameworks*	*Concepts*
Personality	Individual differences	Context
Greenstein's (1969) three factors determining whether personality is important or not	Psychoanalytic approaches	Id, ego, superego
	Disorders	Narcissism Neuroticism
Psychobiographies	Big Five personality traits	Neuroticism, extraversion, agreeableness, openness to experience, conscientiousness
Motivations		Power, affiliation, achievement
Behavioral genetics		
Authoritarian personality		
Leadership frameworks	Barber's (1972) typology of presidential character	Active/negative; passive/positive
	Operational code	Philosophical/ instrumental beliefs
	Hermann's Leader Trait Assessment (LTA)	
	Leader traits	Need for power, locus of control, ethnocentrism, need for affiliation, conceptual complexity, distrust, self confidence

Key Terms

agreeableness
authoritarian personality
behavioral genetics
Big Five
cognitive complexity
conscientiousness
defense mechanisms
denial
ego
ethnocentrism
extroversion
id
locus of control
motives
need for achievement
need for affiliation-intimacy
need for power
neurotic anxiety
neuroticism
openness
operational codes
paranoia
pleasure principle
projection
psychoanalytic or psychodynamic theories
rationalization
reality principle
repression
right-wing authoritarianism
superego
task-interpersonal emphasis
traits
unconscious

Suggestions for Further Reading

Altemeyer, B. (1996). *The authoritarian specter*. Cambridge, MA: Harvard University Press.

American Psychiatric Association (APA). (2000). *Diagnostic and statistical manual of mental disorders: DSM-IV-TR*. Washington, DC: APA.

Dean, J. W. & Altemeyer, R. (2020). *Authoritarian nightmare: Trump and his followers*. New York: Melville House.

Ewen, R. (1998). *An introduction to theories of personality* (5th ed.). Mahwah, NJ: Lawrence Erlbaum.

Feldman, O., & Valenty, L. (Eds.). (2001). *Profiling political leaders: Cross-cultural studies of personality and behavior*. Westport, CT: Praeger.

George, A. L., & George, J. L. (1964). *Woodrow Wilson and Colonel House: A personality study*. New York: Dover.

George, A. L., & George, J. L. (1998). *Presidential personality and performance*. Boulder, CO: Westview Press.

Greenstein, F. I. (1969). *Personality and politics: Problems of evidence, inference, and conceptualization*. Chicago, IL: Markham.

Maddi, S. R. (1996). *Personality theories: A comparative analysis* (6th ed.). Washington: Brooks/Cole.

Magnavita, J. (2002). *Theories of personality: Contemporary approaches to the science of personality*. New York: John Wiley and Sons.

Post, J. M. (Ed.). (2003). *The psychological assessment of political leaders*. Ann Arbor, MI: University of Michigan Press.

Robins, R. S., & Post, J. (1997). *Political paranoia: The psychopolitics of hatred*. New Haven, CT: Yale University Press.

Smith, C., Atkinson, J., McClelland, D., & Veroff, J. (Eds.). (1992). *Motivation and personality: Handbook of thematic content analysis*. Cambridge: Cambridge University Press.

Notes

1. For a critique of psychobiographical method and a discussion of challenges faced by researchers who employ this methodology, see George and George (1998) and Greenstein (1969).
2. Other well-known studies of political leaders relying upon psychobiography with some elements of psychoanalytic analysis include those exploring the personalities of former U.S. Secretary of Defense James Forrestal (Rogow, 1963); Vladimir Lenin, Leon Trotsky, and Mahatma Gandhi (Wolfenstein, 1971); John F. Kennedy (Mongar, 1974); former U.S. Secretary of State Henry Kissinger (Isaak, 1975); Richard Nixon (Brodie, 1981); Jimmy Carter (Glad, 1980; Hargrove, 1988); Ronald Reagan (Glad, 1989); Iraqi President Saddam Hussein (Post, 1991, 1993a); Josef Stalin (Birt, 1993); and Bill Clinton (Renshon, 1996). Some of these psychobiographies focus upon Freudian notions of ego-defense (e.g., Glad, 1980; Link & Glad, 1994; Hargrove, 1988; Renshon, 1996), whereas others concentrate upon specific kinds of personality disorders in these leaders, ranging from narcissism to paranoid personality disorders (e.g., Birt, 1993; Post, 1991, 1993b; Volkan, 1980).
3. Examples of leader studies using Winter's motive scoring technique (which looks at power, achievement and affiliation) include: Richard Nixon (Winter & Carlson, 1988), U.S. presidents (Winter, 1987); African political leaders (Winter, 1980); and Mikhail Gorbachev (Winter, Hermann, Weintraub, & Walker, 1991). For a more detailed discussion of motives and various coding techniques surrounding them, see Smith, Atkinson, McClelland, and Veroff's (1992) volume, *Motivation and Personality: Handbook of Thematic Content Analysis*, published by Cambridge University Press.
4. Among the political psychology or psychological studies that have focused upon either the traits themselves or how they relate to leaders have been ones examining personal needs for power (Etheredge, 1978; Hermann, 1984, 1987; House, 1990; McClelland, 1975; Winter, 1973, 1987); personal needs for affiliation (Browning & Jacob, 1964; McClelland & Boyatzis, 1982; Winter, 1987; Winter & Stewart, 1977); conceptual complexity (Driver, 1977; Hermann, 1984, 1987; Suedfeld & Rank, 1976; Suedfeld & Tetlock, 1977; Tetlock, 1985); locus of control (Davis & Phares, 1967; Hermann, 1984, 1987; Rotter, 1966); achievement or task/interpersonal emphasis (Bales, 1951; Byars, 1972, 1973; Hermann, 1987; Rowe & Mason, 1987; Winter & Stewart, 1977); ethnocentrism (Glad, 1983; Levine & Campbell, 1972); and self-confidence (Hermann, 1987; House, 1990; Winter et al., 1991). For a more detailed discussion of these traits, see Hermann (1999a) and Smith, Atkinson, McClelland, and Veroff (1992).

Chapter 3

Cognition, Social Identity, Emotions, and Attitudes in Political Psychology

This chapter explores how individuals make sense of others and themselves in the context of political issues, choices, and conflict. How do people understand the political world? How do they interpret information and make decisions? How organized are their thoughts? How do emotions affect thoughts and actions in politics? This chapter reflects the thinking and feeling portions of the Political Being's mind: cognition, emotion, social identity, and attitudes and beliefs. We examine a number of ideas about how people process political information, the psychological techniques and mechanisms used to understand others and the environment in which they live, the importance of the groups to which people belong, and how people regard those groups to which they do not belong. In addition, we explore the importance of emotion in politics, as well as in political attitudes. Various concepts are introduced, including cognition, cognitive categories and schemas, social identity, images, affect and emotion, and attitudes. These concepts are tied to different kinds of political behavior in this chapter and are detailed in the chapters that follow.

Once again, the depiction of the Political Being highlights the concepts covered here, and does so in a way that layers them. Attitudes and cognitive processes are at the top of consciousness. These are things we are well aware of, and they are important in information processing and everyday decision-making. Values and social identities are deeper. We have to think harder to figure out how they affect our behavior. Emotions saturate the mind and influence the entire process of deciding how to act politically. In addition, more detail is provided on the *us* and *them* portions of the Political Being's environment.

We proceed with building blocks. First, we examine the thinking part of the Political Being. We begin with the topic of information processing and the limits people have in their abilities to process information. In doing so, we introduce two theoretical areas that provide insights into the patterns

DOI: 10.4324/9780429244643-3

and causes of patterns in human information processing: attribution theory and consistency theories. Next, we turn to the question of how people make sense of the world in which they live, through a process called cognitive categorization. In examining cognitive categorization, we discuss how people organize and simplify the complex social and political world in which they live, and we introduce the related notion of a stereotype. Next, we proceed to social identity theory, which provides us with information about how people see the groups to which they belong and those to which they do not belong—in-groups and out-groups. We then introduce a model of categories of other political actors—the political equivalent of out-groups—called image theory.

From here, we turn to the emotional part of the Political Being and look at emotions in politics. This is a relatively new area of political psychological research, but it is very important because of the power of emotions in politically motivated violence and other patterns of behavior. After discussing emotions, we discuss attitudes, which combine emotion and thinking about politics. Our goal in this chapter is to introduce a wide range of central political psychological concepts regarding thinking and feeling about politics and the behavioral predispositions that result from these processes. These concepts are used throughout the rest of the book as we look at different kinds of political behavior.

Let us begin with some puzzles. First, people need to understand the world around them, and particularly the people in that world, so they can understand and know what to expect. Perceivers need to explain and predict the behavior of others. To do this, they need to process incoming information from their environments and evaluate it. People like to think that they are good at processing information. We assume that we recognize and evaluate important information and that we store it in memory quite accurately; however, this is not always correct. Consider the following example.

In the criminal justice system, eyewitness testimony is commonly accepted as both notoriously inaccurate and as having a strong impact on juries. As Loftus explains:

> Before a witness can recall a complex incident, the incident must be accurately perceived at the outset; it must be stored in memory. Before it can be stored, it must be within a witness's perceptual range, which means that it must be loud enough and close enough so that the ordinary senses pick it up. If visual details are to be perceived, the situation must be reasonably well illuminated. Before some information can be recalled, a witness must have paid attention to it. But even though an event is bright enough, loud enough, and close enough, and even though attention is being paid, we can still find significant errors in a witness's recollection of the event, and it is common for two witnesses to the same event to recall it very differently.
>
> (Loftus, 1979, p. 22)

Second, people tend to see what they expect to see. They fit incoming information into the ideas or beliefs they already hold to be true, and typically they do not recognize they are doing this. Discrepant information is often not noticed or rejected as incorrect. This is known as the *misinformation effect*, which occurs when someone incorporates misinformation into their memory of the event after receiving misleading information about it (Loftus, 1979, 2001). Consider some examples from the battlefields of World War II:

> Common also are cases of outright refusal to believe reports that contradict a firm belief ... When Hermann Göring was informed that an Allied fighter has been shot down over Aachen, thus proving that the Allies had produced a long-range fighter that could protect bombers over Germany, he told the pilot who had commanded the German planes in the engagement: "I'm an experienced fighter pilot myself. I know what is possible. But I know what isn't too ... I officially assert that American fighter planes did not reach Aachen ... I herewith give you an official order that they weren't there." Similarly, when the secretary of the navy was told of the Japanese attack on Pearl Harbor, he said, "My God, this can't be true. This [message] must mean the Philippines." It is not without significance that the common reaction is not that the report is incorrect, but that it must be incorrect.
>
> (Jervis, 1976, pp. 144–145)

These examples illustrate several important topics with which we begin this chapter. The eyewitness testimony example shows important instances in which people do not process or remember information very well. People are sometimes imperfect information processors, and of course this will affect their processing, evaluation, and retention of political information – just like any other kind of information. Second, people do not process information on a tabula rasa. They have certain psychological mechanisms that facilitate the processing of information.

In psychology, the concept of **cognition** is central to understanding how people process information and understand the world around them. Cognition is "a collective term for the psychological processes involved in the acquisition, organization, and the use of knowledge" (Bullock & Stallybrass, 1977, p. 109). The knowledge is organized in our minds in a cognitive system. For example, our knowledge of birds might be organized as follows: birds have wings, feathers, and beaks; they use their wings to fly; they eat insects or seeds and are eaten by people. The terms *beliefs* or *attitudes* are often used to describe these components of the cognitive system. **Beliefs** are associations people create between an object and its attributes (Eagly & Chaiken, 1998). We believe that birds have wings and that Democrats are liberal. **Cognitive processes** refer to what happens in the mind while people move from observation of a stimulus to a response to that stimulus. Cognitive processes include everything from perception, memory, attention, and problem-solving to information processing, language, thinking, and imagery. Let us turn first to cognitive processes involved with the acquisition of information from the environment and its evaluation.

INFORMATION PROCESSING

People are bombarded with vast amounts of information all the time. They cannot attend to all of it, and the mind has developed techniques for deciding what information is important and relevant, and what information can be ignored. Several theories in psychology address patterns of information processing and provide explanations for different propensities in attending to and interpreting information. One theoretical perspective in psychology that focuses on how people judge and evaluate others is **attribution theory**. One of the earliest attribution theorists was Heider (1958), along with Jones and Davis (1965), Kelley (1967), and Weiner (1986). Attribution theorists also have a number of insights into information processing. They argue that people process information as though they are "naïve scientists"—that is, they search for causes in the behavior of others, just as scientists search for the cause of a disease. However, people often do not properly employ the scientific method, and tend to make errors in this quest for the cause of others' behavior. Attribution theorists argue that individuals use **heuristics**, which are mental shortcuts, in processing information about others. Among the most important heuristics is the **availability heuristic**, wherein people predict the likelihood of something based on the ease with which they can think of instances or examples of it (Tversky & Kahneman, 1982)—for example, estimating the distribution of A's in a political science class based on how many people you can think of who got A's in the class last year.

Imaginability is another aspect of the availability heuristic. It is the tendency to retrieve plausible information without any regard for actual probabilities. As a result, individuals construct a series of possible behaviors based on their ability to imagine their occurrence. More specifically:

> Imaginability plays an important role in the evaluation of probabilities in real life situations. The risk involved in an adventurous expedition, for example, is evaluated by imagining contingencies with which the expedition is not equipped to cope. If many such difficulties are vividly portrayed, the expedition can be made to appear exceedingly dangerous, although the ease with which disasters are imagined need not reflect their likelihood. Conversely, the risk involved in an undertaking may be grossly underestimated if some possible dangers are either difficult to conceive of, or simply do not come to mind.
>
> (Tversky & Kahneman, 1982, pp. 12–13)

Biases can also occur due to the availability of instances. Thus, "when the size of a class is judged by the availability of its instances, a class whose instances are easily retrieved will appear more numerous than a class of equal frequency whose instances are less retrievable" (Tversky & Kahneman, 1982, p. 11):

> This bias is demonstrated by an experiment that used lists of male and female personalities. Individuals were asked whether a list of well-known personalities contained more men than women and they responded positively if the men were better known than the women were (and vice versa).
>
> (Tversky & Kahneman, 1982, p. 11)

This happened even though there were equal numbers of men and women. Increased familiarity made the male names more available, resulting in the bias. Salience is also influential. If you have just finished watching a news program about a local house fire, you will believe your chances of your own house catching fire to be greater.

The **representativeness heuristic** is another common example. This is a probability judgment. A person may, for example, evaluate the characteristics of another person and estimate the likelihood that person belongs to a particular occupation (Fiske & Taylor, 1991). For example, medical professionals are commonly seen with stethoscopes. If you see someone with a stethoscope, you will assume it is probable that the person is a medical professional.

Another consequence of the representative heuristic is misrepresentations of chance. A manifestation of this is the gambler's fallacy. This is illustrated by the game of roulette where, after a long run of one color—say, black—red is believed to now be due. Thus, "chance is commonly viewed as a self-correcting process in which a deviation in one direction induces a deviation in the opposite direction to restore the equilibrium" (Tversky & Kahneman, 1982, p. 7). If you have ever gambled, even if you only play the slots, you have probably experienced the gambler's fallacy: You don't leave the machine while losing because losing has to be followed by winning. Finally, another outcome of the representative heuristic is the "law of small numbers", wherein individuals believe small samples randomly drawn from a population are representative of the populations from which they are drawn (Tversky & Kahneman, 1982). For example, you meet an international student from a particular country and view him or her as representative of a larger population. The danger of holding on to such perceptions is that they can skew our perceptions, beliefs, and attitudes.

Anchoring and adjustment involve how individuals make estimates. Specifically, they refer to when individuals make estimates by starting from an initial value that is adjusted to yield the final answer:

> The initial value, or starting point, may be suggested by the formulation of the problem, or it may be the result of partial computation. In either case, adjustments are typically insufficient. Different starting points yield different estimates, which are biased toward the initial values.
>
> (Tversky & Kahneman, 1982, p. 14)

In interpreting and evaluating information regarding the cause of behavior of other people, one of the most important aspects of perceptions of causality is whether it is attributed to internal states (personality) or to external forces (situation). People are more likely to attribute others' behavior to their general dispositions (personality traits or attitudes) than to the situation they are in. This is known as the **fundamental attribution error** (Ross, 1977). A study by Jones and Harris (1967) provided a clear illustration of the fundamental attribution error. Participants in the study were asked to read essays about a controversial topic—Cuba under the rule of Fidel Castro. Participants were either told the essay writer had freely chosen to take a pro-Castro or anti-Castro position, or that the essay writer was assigned a particular essay position. Even when the essay writer was assigned the position, participants overestimated the role of internal dispositions (the writer's true position on Castro) and underestimated the role of the situation (lack of choice about which position to take) when asked to explain the position taken in the essay.

The fundamental attribution error is the most recognized, but there are others. For example, the **positivity effect** is the tendency to attribute positive behaviors to dispositional factors and negative behaviors to situational factors with individuals we like (Plous, 1993). When dealing with individuals we dislike, we tend to do the opposite—that is, attribute behavior to dispositional rather than situational factors (Plous, 1993). This is the **negativity effect**. There are numerous other biases identified in the literature. For example, the **self-serving bias** is when individuals are more likely to take responsibility for successes than failures (Plous, 1993). The **egocentric bias** is the tendency of individuals to accept more responsibility for joint outcomes than others attribute to them (Plous, 1993). The **confirmation bias** is seen when individuals tend to favor information that confirms already-existing beliefs. The **hindsight bias** is commonly described as "I knew it all along." Another bias is referred to as **childish games**. This occurs when individuals communicate something to another person that is familiar and meaningful to them, but not to the person communicated with (Pronin, Puccio, & Ross, 2002).

Another set of theories that contributes to our understanding of information processing comes under the general category of consistency theories. One of the earliest consistency theories was Heider's (1946, 1958) balance theory, which posits that people try to keep the components of the cognitive system in balance. He described **balance** as "a harmonious state, one in which the entities comprising the situation and the feelings about them fit together without stress" (Heider, 1958, p. 180). In other words, people want to see their environment, the people in it, and their feelings about it as a coherent, consistent picture. For example, if you consider yourself a responsible and serious student, you would not neglect your studies and go out partying with your friends the night before an exam. If you did, the cognitive system representing your knowledge about yourself would be out of balance, and you would try to change it. Partying, rather than studying the night before an exam, is not consistent with your self-perception that you are a serious student. A friend of one of the authors presents another example. She is a lifelong liberal Democrat from an eastern city, who advised a politician on his state's education policy. That politician was a Republican. She liked him, found him charming, and was proud that his policies improved education in his state. She would like to vote for him, and she is appalled at herself. How can she, a lifelong liberal Democrat, consider voting for a conservative Republican? That behavior would not be balanced, because it is inconsistent with her political beliefs. To achieve balance, she would either have to vote Democratic, change her ideology and join the Republican Party, or consider this single Republican vote an anomaly.

A related type of consistency pattern is described in dissonance theory, which addresses the inconsistencies between people's attitudes and behaviors (Festinger, 1957). **Dissonance** refers to an aversive state that results when our behavior is inconsistent with our attitudes. Dissonance creates psychological tension, which people feel motivated to avoid through selective attention to information. Once dissonance is experienced, people are motivated to relieve it. For example, suppose you ate a big piece of chocolate cake while you were on a diet. There are at least three ways that people can reduce dissonance: they can change their behavior (in this case that is not possible, because you already ate the cake); they can engage in cognitive strategies, such as trivialization (e.g., "It's not really that bad if I ate a big piece of chocolate cake") or distortions of information (e.g., "Chocolate cake has lots of nutritional value"); or they can change their attitude (e.g., "I really don't need to be dieting anyway"). Typically, people reduce dissonance by changing their attitude.

People can live with inconsistency and imbalance, but they would prefer not to. When inconsistency is extreme, it can be psychologically painful—for example, when your significant other and best friend cannot abide one another. Individuals can avoid inconsistency through information processing, and they can reestablish consistency in their cognitive system by changing whatever is easiest to change. If our friend's attachment to the Democratic Party is weaker than her liking for the Republican politician, she will change parties. If not, she will either vote Democrat or consider the situation an anomaly (incidentally, she voted for the Democrat, which is an illustration of the power of political socialization, which we discuss in Chapter 6).

Vertzberger notes that the drive for consistency occurs on three levels; within attitudes between affect and cognition (thinking and feeling the same way); across attitudes; and throughout what he calls the "cognitive entirety" (1990, p. 137)—attitudes, beliefs, and values. The drive for consistency affects information processing in a number of ways. First, it produces selective perception, which includes "selective exposure (seeking consistent information not already present), selective attention (looking at consistent information once it is there), and selective interpretation (translating ambiguous information to be consistent)" (Fiske & Taylor, 1991, p. 469). Inconsistent information can be ignored, or distorted so it appears consistent with attitudes or cognitive categories. Inconsistent behaviors can be compartmentalized so people refuse to recognize their own actions as serious. The process of balancing and avoiding inconsistency can also lead to **bolstering**, which involves selective exposure to information, as people search for information supporting their decisions and avoid information critical of them. Bolstering also occurs when people denigrate the alternative not chosen and amplify the attractive aspects of the decisions they did make. Bolstering occurred in the Kennedy administration, before the Bay of Pigs invasion, when decision-makers convinced themselves that American involvement would remain secret by avoiding arguments to the contrary. This incident is discussed (in Chapter 4) in the context of *groupthink*, a group decision-making error involving faulty information processing. President Johnson's decision in 1965 to use air power in Vietnam shows evidence of bolstering as well, in his belief the air campaign would not have to last long and that the war would end quickly (George, 1980).

The drive for consistency in information processing has a number of important political consequences. Accepting only information that conforms with expectations can lead people to miss important information—for example, about a candidate's stand on a political issue if that position is inconsistent with their party's or with the candidate's other issue positions. Interpreting information so it conforms to expectations, rather than to some other possibility, can lead to spiraling conflicts between countries or political groups. Distorting information in a search for consistency can produce a failure to recognize the need for value trade-offs in politics. The **avoidance of value trade-offs** occurs when people mistakenly believe that a policy that "contributes to one value ... also contributes to several other values, even though there is no reason why the world should be constructed in such a neat and helpful manner" (Jervis, 1976, p. 128). An example comes from the Vietnam War:

> Officials who favored bombing North Vietnam felt that this would: (1) decrease American casualties, (2) drastically increase the cost of the war to the North; (3) increase the chance of the North's entering negotiations, without increasing the danger of Soviet or Chinese intervention. Those who opposed bombing disagreed on all points.
>
> (Jervis, 1976, p. 134)

These patterns are tendencies, not absolutes. They occur often, but not always. People may be aware of, but ignore, inconsistent information if it is unimportant to them. They may be forced by situational conditions to attend and respond to inconsistent information.

CATEGORIZATION

So far, we have noted that people organize and simplify their environment; they process information about that environment, based on the way they understand it, and they search for causes in the behavior of others. People retain the most useful knowledge about an environment, then use it to filter subsequent information. We expect the environment to be consistent and that what we know about it will be repeated. We accept as true information that conforms to our preexisting knowledge, and reject as untrue, or irrelevant, information that does not conform. Consequently, the cognitive system helps us filter incoming information. If, for example, your cognitive system of politicians includes the belief that all politicians are dishonest, if you have evidence both confirming and disconfirming that politician Smith took a bribe, then you will believe the confirming evidence. But cognitive systems are more than a set of bits of knowledge. They are organized to enable people to move through their worlds without thinking too much and yet manage their environments effectively. Cognitive systems help people understand their world. Knowledge about the environment in which people live is organized, simplified, and used to make sense of complex social and physical realities. If we did not organize and simplify the environment, then we would not be able to process all the information available to us and could never make decisions. The world is too complex for our brains to handle. As Allport wrote in 1954:

> The human mind must think with the aid of categories ... Once formed, categories are the basis for normal prejudgment. We cannot possibly avoid this process. Orderly living depends upon it ... What this means

> is that our experience in life tends to form itself into clusters ... and while we may call on the right cluster at the wrong time, or the wrong cluster at the right time, still the process in question dominates our entire mental life. A million events befall us every day. We cannot handle so many events. If we think of them at all, we type them ... Bertrand Russell ... has summed up the matter in a phrase, "a mind perpetually open will be a mind perpetually vacant."
>
> (Allport, 1954, pp. 19–20)

People form and use cognitive categories that aid them in their need to process information efficiently. There is no set recipe by which categories are formed. Categories, the attributes or characteristics associated with them, and the beliefs about them are formed through experience. Rosch and Lloyd (1978) argue that two principles are involved in category formation. First, categories must provide the perceiver with a large amount of information with as little mental effort as possible. People need categories that enable them to discern and understand the world around them, but that also allow them to reduce small and irrelevant differences among people and objects. Second, people need categories suited to their own social and physical realities. If you live in a high-crime, heavily populated urban area, you will need different social categories to understand and deal with people than if you live in a rural area with almost no crime and few people.

One way of looking at this is to think of the way people organize and simplify their environment as creating a mental model of the environment that emphasizes only the most important points. People form categories of the most important elements of the environment. For example, in the natural world we think of categories such as dogs, cats, horses, and birds. As we said before, the category of birds is filled with important information about what a bird is and how it behaves. The same is true of the categories of dog, cat, and so on. Of course, some birds are not good fits with the common characteristics associated with birds. Penguins do not fly, but they swim and have scrawny wings that they use like flippers. They do not fit the bird category very well in our minds. The same is true of the human world. We categorize people into groups, such as racial groups (Caucasian, Black, Asian), ethnic groups (Latino or Hispanic, Italian-American), nationality groups (American, German, Chinese), and religious groups (Christian, Muslim, Jewish). In other words, we organize the social world in terms of social categories. We all make assumptions about other people, ourselves, and the situations we are in. Sometimes we are very wrong, but often our expectations are functional. The first step in perceiving another person is to classify the person or situation as fitting a familiar category. Once you recognize someone as filling a particular role (e.g., a police officer or a professor) on the basis of particular attributes (uniform, gun, billy club; glasses, briefcase, lecture notes), then you can apply your knowledge about the role to guide the subsequent interaction with that person.

Once a person or situation is classified into a category, people apply organized generic knowledge, in the form of a category or **schema**, to process information about the person or situation and to make decisions about it or them. The terms *cognitive category* and *schema* are often used interchangeably. Psychologists define schema as "a cognitive structure that represents knowledge about a concept or type of stimulus, including its attributes and the relations among those attributes" (Fiske & Taylor, 1991, p. 8).

Stereotypes are a particular type of social cognitive category. The psychological roots of stereotypes, the reasons for their occurrence, and the impact they have on the behavior of those using them and those viewed through them, are widely studied in psychology and political science (see Fiske, 1998 for a review). Stereotypes are beliefs about the attributes of people in particular groups or social categories, and should be a very familiar concept. Everyone has stereotypes or at least knows about the stereotypes of others. Consider, for example, the well-known stereotype of Jewish people, called the anti-Semitic stereotype, which assumes a particular group is an over-achieving minority, superior in wealth and talent. It is also assumed that they are able to construct complex conspiracies to increase their material wealth and influence. Finally, they are seen as standoffish, cliquish, and considering themselves superior to everyone else (Hunter, 1991). Other people who are seen through the same stereotype are the Indians and Pakistanis in East Africa, the overseas Chinese in Southeast Asia, the Armenians in the Middle East, and the Ibos in Nigeria. Other stereotypes familiar to most readers denigrate people who are considered inferior. Most Americans are familiar with American racism, which is a result of holding negative stereotypes of Black people, for example. Stereotypes are not limited to personality trait descriptions (e.g., "Germans are conscientious and hardworking"), but can include any personal attribute—physical, affective, visual, or behavioral—seen as characteristic of that group (e.g., "Germans are fair, tall, and rigid"). Stereotyping, like all social categorization, is a mental short-cut that enables people to know quite a bit about a person or group of persons, whether that knowledge is accurate or not. It occurs quickly and without conscious thought (Fiske, 1998). We discuss social stereotypes in more detail in Chapters 8, 9, and 10.

Discrimination is not an inevitable consequence of stereotyping. Research (e.g., Devine & Elliot, 1995) suggests that even though people possess knowledge of stereotypes, they are not necessarily prejudiced. Only those high in prejudice tend to accept stereotypes about a group of people. A person can have knowledge of stereotypes and not discriminate. For the moment, we will define stereotypes as social categories, and accept that when people are evaluated through a stereotype, they often suffer from discrimination. They are assumed to have the characteristics of a stereotype whether they do or not. Those who hold the stereotype and behave toward that group in a discriminatory fashion are said to be prejudiced.

Once information about a person is noticed, it is classified nominally in terms of what it is about, or which category or attitude it is relevant to. If you notice a person who is tall, blond, blue-eyed, and speaks with an accent, you may classify that person in the category "German." The availability heuristic is important in this stage, because information is more likely to be classified in readily accessible categories. Hence you may be more likely to use the German social category if you are in a town with a high percentage of German immigrants. Once this judgment is made, the information is evaluated in terms of its fit into the category. If, for example, you walk into a classroom and the professor looks like he is 15 years old, and is wearing shorts, a ripped t-shirt, and no shoes, that information about him is not typical of what you expect to see when interacting with a professor. It affects how you regard this particular person in his role as professor: you may think he is not very qualified because he looks young and dresses like a teenager.

Moreover, when this kind of social judgment is made, it is also influenced by **assimilation** and **contrast effects**. The prototypical example of a social category serves as an anchor or central reference point for incoming information. Information is compared with that anchor and, when it is different from expectations, the contrast effect makes it seem more so. For example, most people would expect a priest to be honest. Learning that a priest did something objectively moderately dishonest will be interpreted as extremely dishonest because complete honesty is expected. The assimilation effect produces the opposite perception. Information similar to what is expected can be perceived as even more similar than it objectively is (Eiser & Stroebe, 1972; Herr, 1986; Manis, Nelson, & Shedler, 1988). The category in which a person, group, or country is placed has yet another effect on information and information processing. Missing information can be supplied by the category or image itself. If you do not know whether a person has a particular characteristic because you do not have the information, then you can guess based on the social category in which the person is placed (Taylor & Crocker, 1981).

We also categorize the political world. Some scholars argue that we organize the international environment in terms of types of states, such as the enemy or the ally. These cognitive categories are called images, and images function very much like stereotypes. **Image theory** is a political psychological approach that draws connections between policy-makers' images of other countries and their resulting behavior (Blanton, 1996; Cottam, 1977, 1986, 1994; Herrmann, 1985a, 1985b, 1988, 1991; Herrmann, Voss, Schooler, & Ciarrochi, 1997; Holsti, 1962; Schafer, 1997; Shimko, 1991). **Images** contain information about a country's capabilities, culture, intentions, kinds of decision-making groups (lots of people involved in decision-making or only a few), and perceptions of threat or opportunity. Capabilities include economic characteristics, military strength, domestic political stability, and effective policy-making and implementation. Cultural attributes consist of judgments of cultural sophistication. When assessing a country, decision-makers judge whether its capabilities and culture are equal, inferior, or superior to those of their own country. Another appraisal is whether the country or group has threatening or defensive (good) intentions, or presents an opportunity to achieve an important goal. Lessons of history that policy-makers associate with a particular type of state are also included in each image. In other words, leaders use historical incidents to explain a conflict and to make predictions about the outcome of a conflict.

Policy-makers also draw upon a variety of policy options, which are measures they see as appropriate in dealing with a country. Some policy options include military threat, economic sanctions or incentives, and diplomatic protests. The model also proposes certain tactics that are deemed relevant to each image. For example, when decision-makers hold the so-called colonial or client image of another country, they consider that country and its people to be inferior in terms of culture and capabilities. They also assume the people are incompetent and childlike, and ruled by a small elite, who are generally not a threat and are often corrupt. This image produces coercive and uncompromising behavioral tendencies (you do not negotiate with children—you tell them what to do). When an enemy image is held, that country is seen as equal in capability and culture, and threatening in intentions. The enemy is ruled by a small elite, but one that can cleverly strategize policies that will attempt to hurt the perceiver's country. The tactics used in responding to such a state are global in focus, competitive, and uncompromising, because you cannot trust such a country to keep its word.

The ally is perceived as equal in terms of its capability and culture, but also as very similar to your own group in values. The intentions of an ally are believed to be good. Barbarians are superior in capability and inferior in culture. They are also aggressive in intentions, which makes them very frightening. An imperialist country is perceived to be superior in culture and capability, but its intentions can be either harmful or benevolent. Either way, imperialists are a dominating people, and resisting them would be very difficult. The rogue is inferior in capability and culture, but is also very harmful in intentions. This is the bad seed, the irresponsible child, who can and should be punished until they reform their ways. Lastly, there is the degenerate image. A degenerate may be powerful and culturally advanced, but also undisciplined and lacking the will to follow through on expressed goals and plans of action.

The ways policy-makers distinguish among these types of images are a matter of their perceptions of the country's capabilities, culture, threat, response alternatives, and event scripts. The images are summarized in Table 3.1.

Although this particular example demonstrates images of other countries used by policy-makers in foreign affairs, images are used to organize and guide responses to people's action in any political domain. In fact, Jackson (2001) gathered impressive data concerning the images used by police officers of the communities in their districts and the patterns of response to crime associated with those images. We return to the discussion of images later, after introducing some additional psychological concepts. Chapters 8, 9, and 10 also contain many examples of how images affect political behavior.

SOCIAL IDENTITY

We classify ourselves and others into groups. The groups to which we belong are called in-groups, and those to which we do not belong are out-groups. Conflict among political groups is, of course, a central issue in political psychology. Group conflict and behavior are examined in detail in Chapter 4. Here we consider groups as social categories and as part of the general cognitive organization of the social and political world. Much of the work on the social psychology of intergroup relations has focused on intergroup conflict and discrimination. The seminal research using this approach is found in Tajfel's (1970) work on intergroup conflict, in which the author speculated that something about group membership alone might stimulate conflict with other relevant groups. He postulated that individuals are likely to act in a discriminatory manner whenever they are in a situation in which intergroup categorization is made salient and relevant.

Table 3.1 Images of Cultures

Images	*Capability*	*Culture*	*Intentions*	*Decision-makers*	*Threat or opportunity*
Enemy	Equal	Equal	Harmful	Small elite	Threat
Barbarian	Superior	Inferior	Harmful	Small elite	Threat
Imperialist	Superior	Superior	Exploitive	A few groups	Threat
Colonial	Inferior	Inferior	Benign	Small elite	Opportunity
Degenerate	Superior or equal	Weak-willed	Harmful	Confused, differentiated	Opportunity
Rogue	Inferior	Inferior	Harmful	Small elite	Threat
Ally	Equal	Equal	Good	Many groups	Threat/opportunity

In other words, whenever individuals find themselves in a situation where clear evidence exists of an "us" and a "them," they are likely to discriminate against the out-group (them) and in favor of the in-group (us). To test this idea, Tajfel (1970) designed a series of experiments based on the minimal group paradigm, in which individuals were arbitrarily assigned to one of two groups. In one typical experiment, assignment to a group was based on whether individuals tended to overestimate or underestimate a series of dots presented on a screen. Individuals participating in the experiment were then assigned to either the overestimator or underestimator group, presumably on the basis of their estimating tendencies. In reality, this assignment was purely arbitrary; the tendency to over- or underestimate was in no way related to accuracy. This arbitrary assignment procedure proved to be important and necessary for several reasons. First, it ensured there was no personal reason for one group to discriminate against the other group. An individual presumably had nothing to gain personally by discriminating against the other group. Second, the procedure ensured there was no existing hostility between the groups. Prior to categorization, individuals never thought of themselves as being a member of a group that tended to underestimate, or that other individuals were members of a group that tended to overestimate, for example. Further, there was no chance for the groups to interact with one another, thus eliminating any possibility that group members would come to like the in-group or dislike the out-group. Third, such a procedure ensured individuals had no conflicts of interest. There was nothing inherently valuable about being a member of a group that underestimated or overestimated.

Following this categorization procedure, individuals were asked to assign rewards and penalties by allocating small amounts of money to two anonymous group members (Brewer, 1979; Insko & Schopler, 1987; Turner, 1978, for a review of allocation matrices). To eliminate self-interest as a possible influence, individuals were told that they should not allocate any money to themselves. The results of this experiment showed that, even in this minimal group, the allocation decisions concerning both an in-group and out-group member led to in-group favoritism and out-group discrimination. Individuals gave more money to members of their own group than to members of the other group. Thus, even though these individuals were assigned to a group on the basis of unimportant and seemingly meaningless criteria, they still acted in a discriminatory or competitive manner. Providing an explanation for this effect is what led to Tajfel and Turner's (1979, 1986) social identity theory.

According to Tajfel (1978), social identity is "that part of an individual's self-concept which derives from his [her] knowledge of his [her] membership in a social group (groups) together with the value and emotional significance attached to that membership" (p. 63). Tajfel and Turner (1979) summarized this theory with three theoretical principles. First, group members strive to achieve or maintain a sense of positive social identity. Second, group members base this social identity on favorable comparisons that can be made between in-group and relevant out-group members. The social categories or groups to which individuals belong provide individuals with a social identity by enabling them to compare their in-group with relevant out-groups. These comparisons are said to contribute to individuals' self-esteem because they allow individuals to define the members of their group as being better than other groups. In other words, in an attempt to gain a positive sense of self, individuals compare their group with other groups to create a favorable distinction between the groups. Third, group members will attempt to leave their group or join a more positively distinct group when their social identity is not satisfactory to them.

Tajfel and Turner (1979) imply that intergroup discrimination is a result of a motivation to evaluate one's own group more positively than a relevant out-group. By comparing one's in-group to a relevant out-group, individuals attempt to differentiate their group from other groups so their social identity will be enhanced. In addition to the necessary precondition of social categorization into in-group and out-group, Tajfel and Turner (1979) maintain that at least three additional variables exist that should influence intergroup differentiation. First, members of a group must have internalized their group membership as an aspect of their self-concept. In other words, if asked a question such as "Who are you?," they must clearly perceive themselves as a member of the in-group and be likely to describe themselves as a group member. Second, the social situation must allow for intergroup comparisons. Group members must be able to make evaluative group comparisons to perceive their in-group as positively distinct from the out-group. Third, the out-group must be perceived as a relevant comparison group. Members of an in-group do not compare their group to any available out-group. Instead, factors such as similarity, proximity, and situational salience determine whether an out-group is considered a valid and reliable comparison group (see Campbell, 1958).

Tajfel (1978) and Tajfel and Turner (1979) also discuss three ways individuals might react to threatened or actual negative social identity. Social mobility is the enhancement of positive social identity by advancement to a group of higher status. If an individual's social identity is threatened or is perceived as being negative, the individual will attempt to dissociate himself or herself from the in-group by joining a group that is higher in status. A second reaction to threatened or negative social identity is social creativity, which includes three strategies: (1) comparing the in-group to the out-group on a different dimension; (2) reevaluating the comparison dimension, so that previously negative dimensions are perceived as positive; and (3) comparing one's in-group to a different or lower status out-group. Finally, social competition is another reaction to a threatened or negative social identity. In-group members might directly compete with the out-group to attain positive distinctiveness or positive social identity, or at least with the intention of attaining a positive social identity.

In a review of research examining strategies of identity enhancement, van Knippenberg and Ellemers (1990) concluded that the permeability of group boundaries appears to play a key role in determining which strategy is used to enhance social identity. For example, when it is relatively easy for a group member to move to a higher status group, that member is more likely to move to the new group than when it is more difficult to change group membership.

Much of the research on social identity tested the original in-group bias effect—that is, whether individuals tend to favor their own group over a relevant out-group—and has shown this to be true (see Brewer, 1979). The arbitrary assignment of individuals to groups was repeatedly demonstrated to result in preferential reward allocations to in-group members (e.g., Billig & Tajfel, 1973; Tajfel & Billig, 1974), heightened in-group attractiveness (e.g., Rabbie & Wilkins, 1971), perceptions of in-group similarity and homogeneity (e.g., Allen & Wilder, 1979; Linville & Jones, 1980), and assignment of positive traits to in-group members (e.g., Howard & Rothbart, 1980). Thus, when individuals are categorized into two distinct groups, there is a tendency for individuals to favor their own group over another relevant group, presumably to enhance their social identity. However, some research has sought to identify ways in which in-groups and out-groups may cooperate with one another or extinguish the tendency to compete.

To add to the body of knowledge on social identity, in particular categorization (Hogg & McGarty, 1990), other research by Turner and colleagues (Turner, 1985, Turner et al., 1987) focused on the role of the social self-concept—"the concept of self based on comparison with other people and relevant to social interaction" (Turner, 1985; Turner et al., 1987, p. 42). *Self-categorization theory* explains these processes and argues when the self and others are categorized into in-groups and out-groups, the self and other become prototypical group members. The process whereby the self cognitively integrates into the group is known as *depersonalization.* As Hogg elaborates:

> The core idea is that we categorize ourselves just as we categorize others, and thus we depersonalize ourselves ... Prototype-based depersonalization of the self is the process that makes group behavior possible. It transforms self-conception so that we conceive of ourselves prototypically (prototypes define and evaluate the attributes of group membership), and our behavior assimilates or conforms to the relevant ingroup prototype in terms of attitudes, feelings, and actions. Self-conception in terms of an ingroup prototype is a representation and evaluation of the self in collective terms—a representation of self in terms of qualities shared with others.
>
> (Hogg, 2004, p. 208)

As Hogg (2000) further explains, a collective self represents the social identities obtained through belonging to groups. Self-categorization results in uncertainty reduction, whereby the prototype defines things such as beliefs, attitudes, and so forth.

Collective or group action is also evident in a fairly recent extension of social identity theory. More specifically, the **Social Identity Model of Collective Action (SIMCA)** explores the motivations of individuals who engage in collective action (van Zomeren, Postmes, & Spears, 2012). Briefly, collective action refers to actions taken by group members in pursuit of social change. The original SIMCA model posits that group identification, group efficacy beliefs (individual group members' belief that actions on the part of the group to achieve its goal will be successful), and a perceived sense of injustice about a group's disadvantage will motivate group members to engage in collective action. The more strongly an individual identifies with a (typically disadvantaged) group, the more likely they are to believe that a group can achieve its goals through collective action. A recent extension of

SIMCA (van Zomeren, Kutlaca, & Turner-Zwinkels, 2018) added a morality motivation to the model, arguing that group identity is typically linked with a motivation to fight for what the group stands for, "integrating who 'we' are with what 'we' (will not) stand for" (p. 124).

More recent research has focused on the role of evolution in in-group bias. You may recall from previous chapters that evolutionary psychologists contend behavior persistent over time is the sort of behavior that allows us to survive as a species. If one group in a population thrives, then the genes of those in that group survive. What does this have to do with how groups interact with one another? There is evidence suggesting our tendency to favor our own groups over others may be motivated by a desire to insure the continuation of our group, which offers, among other things, survival and reproductive benefits (e.g., McDonald, Navarrete, & Van Vugt, 2012). In other words, it is adaptive for humans, and other species as well, to display in-group favoritism.

Evolutionary psychologists looked more closely at ethnocentrism, which is the belief that our own ethnic group is superior to all others. The preference for our own ethnic group is so widespread that all ethnic groups and cultures exhibit this preference (e.g., Mullen, Brown, & Smith, 1992). But, exactly what evolutionary factors can explain why this is, and how ethnocentrism is displayed, are still uncertain (Sidanius & Kurzba, 2013). For example, we know group norms dictate that members of a group will behave in roughly the same manner (Boyd & Richerson, 1985), which is basically conformity. And the greater the extent to which all members of the group conform to the group norms, the more likely those behaviors, and the group, will be to survive. But of course, some groups have stronger norms than others, and some members of a group are more likely than others to adhere to the norms. Environmental factors might also play a role. According to Sidanius and Kurzba (2013), the strength of ethnocentrism might be related to such factors as the economic uncertainty, population density, and the tendencies of political elites.

There are instances in which people accept a group's inferior situation if they believe their position is just and legitimate. These kinds of patterns were evident historically in the submission to and eventual rejection of colonial domination. People in territories conquered by colonial powers such as Britain, France, Germany, and others often accepted that domination. They perceived the colonial powers through the imperialist image and saw them as superior in culture and capability. Resisting domination would bring severe punishment, and they often accepted domination as just and legitimate. Over time, though, independence movements grew, and political activists in the colonies argued their subservience to the colonial power was unfair, unjust, and illegitimate. Once that change in perception occurred, they began to compare their situations with that of the colonial power and decided that the colonial country was rich and they were poor—an unacceptable difference, particularly because the colonial power took the resources of the colonies and used them for self-enrichment. Subjugated colonized people were willing to risk everything—even their lives—for independence. They did so when they believed independence was a real possibility. In other words, they compared themselves with the other group (the colonial power), found the comparison to be unacceptably negative, sought and found an alternative, and engaged in social competition (rebellion) to achieve it.

AFFECT AND EMOTION

Our discussion so far has centered on cognition and politics. But the discussion of social identity leads easily to another important element in political psychology: emotion. People respond emotionally to political issues, actors, and events, and to political principles and ideals they value. When social categories and stereotypes are discussed, there is a tendency for the emphasis to be placed on cognitive processes and properties, such as beliefs, assumptions, and knowledge about different kinds of people, groups, or countries. But clearly cognitive phenomena, such as stereotypes, information processing, and making political decisions—such as who to vote for—involve affect and emotion too. Analysts tend to focus on cognition versus affect, depending upon what they are studying and the relative importance of each in affecting how people think. Affect and emotions are difficult to study because of considerable disagreement about what they are and how to measure them. Political scientists often argue that rational decision-making is unemotional. Nevertheless, political psychology must make advances in understanding the impact of affect and emotions on behavior. Not only is emotion, in the form of prejudice, more closely associated with behavior than the cognitive component (Fiske, 1998), but we cannot understand mass violence, including genocide, without understanding the role of emotions. Moreover, emotion can play a positive role in decision-making (e.g., Baumeister, Vohs, & Tice, 2006). One study found, for example, that suppressing emotions impairs memory (Richards & Gross, 1999). Thus, not only is emotion important, but trying to be unemotional can actually impede important elements in decision-making.

Various scholars have defined affect and emotion differently. Fiske and Taylor (1991) define affect as "a generic term for a whole range of preferences, evaluations, moods, and emotions" (p. 410). Neuman, Marcus, Crigler, and MacKuen (2007) define affect as "the evolved cognitive and physiological response to the detection of personal significance" (p. 9). Affect can be positive or negative—that is, evaluations or preferences are either pleasant or unpleasant. Ottati and Wyer (1993), on the other hand, have a more narrow definition and consider affect to be a physiological state experienced as either pleasant or unpleasant, positive or negative. Fiske and Taylor (1991) regard emotion as a "complex assortment of affects, beyond merely good feelings or bad to include delight, serenity, anger, sadness, fear and more" (p. 411), but Ottati and Wyer (1993) define emotions as affective states more precisely labeled as anger, hatred, fear, love, and respect.

How affect and cognition are interrelated is an issue of debate. As we have already noted, cognition is "a collective term for both the psychological processes involved in the acquisition, organization, and the use of knowledge" (Bullock & Stallybrass, 1977, p. 109). Some argue that affect follows cognition. In other words, when a person makes a cognitive appraisal, then affect is evoked. The alternative picture is that people feel first, and then evoke cognition (Marcus, Neuman, & MacKuen, 2000; Zajonc, 1980a).

Marcus, Neuman, and MacKuen (2000) also emphasize the role of emotion in information processing. They argue that emotion plays a dual role, in which emotion both forms a dispositional system that affects our responses to normal, familiar situations, and performs a surveillance role, alerting us to novel and possibly threatening situations. Information processing in the former is below the conscious level, while in the latter it is in the forefront of consciousness. Stephan and Stephan (1993) present a network model of affect and cognition, in which they maintain cognition and affect are a set of interconnected parallel systems. In other words, people have a cognitive system (a system of thoughts, ideas, knowledge), and an affective system (a system of feelings and various emotions). They are separate systems in the mind, linked by various cognitive and affective nodes. The links can vary in strength.

Is having a better understanding of the relationship between affect and cognition important? We suggest it is. As we will see in Chapter 6, the relationship between affect and cognition with regard to influencing political tolerance in the United States is an important area of research. Another important area of inquiry is the role of cognition and emotion in politically motivated violence, and we examine many cases of such violence in Chapters 8–13. When does emotion take over in the process of committing acts of violence? Are some conflicts dominated by cognitive factors and others dominated by affect? An interesting study by a clinical psychologist, Beck (1999), compared domestic violence with group-to-group violence and to international violence. Beck emphasized the cognitive side of violent actions, in the sense of exploring what people were thinking before they attacked someone—their spouse or children—and he noted that getting people to recognize what they were thinking before they lashed out violently was difficult; they really do not think they are thinking anything in particular but, when really pressed, they recognize the self-demeaning thoughts and hurt feelings that precede the violence. On the flip side, there is the question of what happens to the thought process when emotions are essentially turned off—if they are—when people commit atrocities over a long period of time. We see cases of this in Chapter 9, when we look at people who have committed torture and genocide.

Affect and emotions clearly influence information processing, decision-making, and some predispositions for behavior. In a review of studies of positive affect, Isen (1993) noted that positive affect and emotions promote improvements in problem-solving, negotiating, and decision-making. Positive affect seems to expand people's abilities to see interrelationships and connections among cognitive items. On the other hand, when compared with neutral affect, positive and negative affect—but particularly positive affect—reduces people's ability to perceive variability in other groups (Park & Banaji, 2000; Stroessner & Mackie, 1993). Cassino and Lodge (2007) argue that positive affect is associated with a greater use of heuristics in information processing, while negative affect results in deeper information-processing strategies.

Predispositions for behavior resulting from particular emotions were also studied. Anger, for example, was found to be associated with moving against, or lashing out at, the perceived source of the anger (Izard, 1977). Contempt, on the other hand, was described by Izard (1977) as cold and distant, leading to depersonalization and dehumanization of others: "It is because of these characteristics that contempt can motivate murder and mass destruction of people" (p. 340). Anxiety leads to intensified attention to the environment and heightened perceptions of threat (Cassino & Lodge, 2007).

Emotions and the behaviors they influence are intricately related to the goals at stake in a situation. Political goals naturally vary over time, given particular political contexts and values. Even so, people generally assume that out-groups hinder in-group goals, and therefore the out-group is automatically associated with negative emotions. Out-groups, by definition, are assumed to be different and thus have different goals.

Emotions also vary in intensity, which can increase in response to certain psychological properties, as well as to the nature and impact of events. One of those event characteristics is simply how real the event seems to the person experiencing the emotion (Ortony, Clore, & Collins, 1988). Second, the closer the emotion-producing situation is in time—that is, its proximity—the greater the intensity of the emotion. Third, unexpected events or actions increase intensity. Fourth, physical arousal and the flow of adrenaline increase the emotional intensity. Fifth, in terms of psychological properties, leaving aside individual differences, the salience of social identity groups will increase emotional intensity. The stronger the sense of belonging to a group, the more important belonging is to members' self-esteem, the more salient group membership becomes, and the more intense are the emotions generated by that membership. Emotional reactions to events affecting the group may not be observed often, even when one identifies strongly with that group. As long as things are normal, there may be little emotion; however, intense relationships produce the potential for strong emotions, when that relationship, as well as normal forms of behavior in the context of that relationship, is interrupted (Berscheid, 1987). Thus, one can expect politically motivated emotions to be intense when important political identity groups face threats or unusual opportunities. The intensity of the emotion may come as a great surprise to outside observers if it was not witnessed before.

The intensity of affect and emotion is also determined by perceptions of the other group. Out-groups are reacted to more negatively and with greater intensity than in-groups. Moreover, extreme stereotyping corresponds with more extreme affect. Groups perceived to be threatening (e.g., out-groups) are seen as more homogeneous and extreme as threat perceptions increase (Corneille, Yzerbyt, Rogier, & Buidin, 2001). Conversely, more complex cognitive processes are associated with more moderate reactions (Linville, 1982). Thus, because a group member perceives their group in a more complex way than the out-group, evaluations of the in-group are typically less extreme than evaluations of the out-group. However, research (Marques, Abrams, Paez, & Hogg, 2001) shows that when an in-group member engages in positive behavior or is described in positive terms, they are evaluated more favorably than an out-group member who engages in the same behavior, or who is described in the same positive terms. But when an in-group member engages in negative behavior, or is described in unfavorable terms, that person is evaluated more unfavorably than an out-group member who engages in similar behavior, or who is described in unfavorable terms. This was termed the *black sheep effect* (Marques, Yeerbyt, &

Leyens, 1988). Group members might derogate a "bad" in-group member so they can distance themselves from that member, thus restoring their sense of positive social identity. The purpose of that study was to test the hypothesis that the strength of group identification is related to the strength of derogation of an errant in-group member.

Generally, we would expect positive emotions to be associated with in-groups and negative emotions to be associated with out-groups. This is an important principle to keep in mind when looking at emotion and political behavior. Social psychologists examined the emotions associated with social groups lower or higher in power and status, under varying circumstances, which helped with another important pattern regarding emotion and politics (Smith, 1993; Duckitt, 1994). Intergroup Emotions Theory (IET), the roots of which are in social identity theory, predict which emotions group members feel in certain situations (Mackie & Smith, 2015, 2018). In certain social situations, a person's group identity will be more salient to them, such as when they perceive a threat to their group. When this happens, the individual engages in group-level appraisals of the situation—much like we do as individuals. But in group-level appraisals, a group member first assesses whether the situation is harmful to the group, thus generating either negative out-group-directed emotions or positive in-group-directed emotions. Once such appraisals are made, the corresponding behavior follows. For example, anger tends to lead to aggression or confrontation (e.g., Leonard, Mackie, & Smith, 2011; Leonard, Moon, Mackie, & Smith, 2011; Mackie & Smith, 2015). Disgust often leads to attempts to attack the out-group or efforts to avoid them (e.g., Esses & Dovidio, 2002; Mackie, Smith, & Ray, 2008). Shame and humiliation may lead to feelings of powerlessness and efforts to withdraw from threats (e.g., Leidner, Sheikh, & Ginges, 2012).

These studies are complex because emotions can be bundled together. Prejudice, the affective partner of a cognitive stereotype, is a good example of this. "Hot prejudices" are composed of disgust, resentment, hostility, and anger. Let us turn to a number of politically relevant emotions first, and then consider how they may cluster with different political groups.

The list of negative emotions is long, and one in particular—anger—is often found in political behavior. Anger is a negative emotion whereby blame for undesirable behavior, and resulting undesirable events, is directed at another person or group. It occurs when goals are thwarted and attention is focused on the source of the obstacle to the goal (Stein, Trabasso, & Liwag, 1993). Anger produces a desire to regain control, remove the obstruction and, if necessary, attack the source of injury (Frijda, 1986; Izard, 1977; Lazarus, 1991). Whether a person acts on anger depends on the situation, norms and values, and the characteristics of the offending party. Anger can also be triggered by a particular schema. When a person has experienced intense emotions such as anger in a previous situation, the schema of that situation can trigger anger when a similar situation is identified. If, for example, a person witnessed an act of cruelty and was angered by it, the same emotion can be triggered by similar situations, or even by thinking about acts of cruelty in general.

Other emotions are closely related to anger, and are also politically important, including frustration, resentment, contempt, and disgust. Disgust involves being repulsed by the actions or characteristics of others.

It can be quite severe and lead people to fear the social order is being contaminated. The behavior that can be produced by disgust includes the possibility of wanting to destroy the offending group. On the other hand, because the level of interest and degree of distress when one is disgusted is lower than when one is angry, disgust does not produce as much aggression as anger. Contempt, on the other hand, involves feeling superior to another group and can lead to domination and dehumanization of others (Frijda, 1986). Dehumanization, in turn, leads to extremely violent behavior—even genocide (Izard, 1977; Kressel, 1996). The less human another person or group appears to be, the easier it is to kill them en masse.

Guilt, shame, sympathy, pity, envy, and jealousy can also affect political behavior. Guilt occurs when people do something they consider morally unacceptable, and want to atone or make amends to those they hurt (Lazarus, 1991; Swim & Miller, 1999). Shame, on the other hand, occurs when a person does something that violates how they see themselves. When feeling shame, people tend to avoid others who have observed what they did to produce the shame. Humiliation is another strong emotion; it produces a desire for revenge (Gilligan, 1997; Lindner, 2006; Weingarten, 2004).

Fear and anxiety—two other emotions important in politics—both occur when danger is perceived, but they differ in that fear is associated with a clear and certain threat, and anxiety is associated with uncertainty about the threat. Typically, when people experience fear they want to avoid or escape the threat. When they experience anxiety, however, they do not really know what to do or how to respond, and they tend to worry about what to do and how to do it (Lazarus, 1991; Marcus, Neuman, & MacKuen, 2000; MacKuen, Marcus, Neuman, & Keele, 2007).

Some positive emotions are important in politics, such as pride in the achievements of one's group or country, or happiness when an opportunity to achieve an important goal occurs. As mentioned earlier, positive emotions tend to make people more flexible and more creative in problem-solving. They are able to see more nuances and have more complex evaluations of other people when feeling positive emotions. Clearly, these emotions—such as pride in your country, or joy and happiness when the country does well in things such as economic development and growth or in international athletic competitions—are associated with politics.

As alluded to earlier, there are a few psychological studies of emotions associated with groups of varying degrees of power, in different contexts. Duckitt (1994), for example, looked at emotion and behavior patterns associated with groups considered malicious, superior, oppressive, inferior, threatening, and powerful. He found punitiveness, intropunitive abasement, extrapunitive hostility, hostility, derogation, and superficial tolerance associated with each, respectively. Smith (1993) also examined perceptions of different groups (strong or weak, compared with the perceiver's group and the emotions associated with it), in a study of emotions and stereotyping. Smith found that minorities with low power felt fear regarding high-power or majority groups; members of high-status groups felt disgust in regard to low-status groups; contempt was felt by any group toward any outgroup; anger was felt by members of high-power or majority groups when low-power or minorities made demands or threats; and jealousy emerged among low-status groups toward high-status groups.

Image of other political actor		Threat/ opportunity		Strategic preference
Enemy image	→	Threat high	→	Containment
Barbarian image	→	Threat high	→	Search for allies, augment power
Imperial image	→	Threat high	→	Submit/revolt when possible
Rogue image	→	Threat moderate/low	→	Crush
Degenerate image	→	Opportunity high/ moderate	→	Challenge, take risks
Colonial image	→	Opportunity high	→	Control, exploit
Ally image	→	Threat/opportunity (will help in either context)	→	Negotiate agreements, common strategy

Figure 3.1 Political Images and Strategic Preferences

Mackie, Devos, and Smith (2000) also examined an important issue regarding the experience of negative emotions resulting from interactions with an out-group. They argue that either fight (e.g., anger) or flight (e.g., fear) emotions are possible, depending upon appraisals of the out-group by and in relation to the in-group. In an interesting study drawing on neuroscience and other fields, Marcus et al. (2000) looked at emotion in the American electoral context. They argued there are "two systems associated with the brain's limbic region, the disposition and the surveillance systems" (p. 9). From the dispositional system come the emotions of satisfaction and enthusiasm, or frustration and depression. The surveillance system determines feelings of relaxation and calm, or anxiety and unease, depending upon political conditions. Both cause people to be more or less attentive to the political arena and their evaluation of candidates and participation in politics. In looking at emotions and images of other states, Cottam and Cottam (2001) argue that certain emotions are closely associated with particular images. Some of these images can be translated to domestic contexts as well. Following is a review of the images and emotions associated with them. These patterns received some empirical verification from experimental studies (Alexander, Brewer, & Herrmann, 1999). The images and strategic patterns discussed next are summarized in Figure 3.1.

The Diabolical Enemy

The image of an enemy is associated with intensely perceived threat and very intense affect and emotions. The enemy is perceived as relatively equal in capability and culture. In its most extreme form, the diabolical enemy is seen as irrevocably aggressive in motivation, monolithic in decisional structure, and highly rational in decision-making (to the point of being able to generate and orchestrate multiple complex conspiracies). Citizens who do not share this image, or who merely have a more complex view of the enemy, are often accused of being, at best, dupes of the enemy, and possibly even traitors. This is unfortunate, particularly because the ability to view the threatener in more complex terms makes it possible to identify a broader range of policy options, some of which might stave off a crisis or at least allow for a more complex strategic response.

Some of the emotions associated with the enemy include anger, frustration, envy, jealousy, fear, distrust, and possibly grudging respect. An enemy's successes are considered unfair, and when bad things happen and goals are not met, the enemy is blamed. People tend to be both antagonistic and reactant in responding to an enemy. People compete with the enemy and try to prevent the enemy from gaining anything. The approach to conflict makes sense in light of the cognitive properties of the image. The enemy is as powerful and capable as one's own country, so there is an even chance of losing if the approach to the conflict is entirely zero sum. Thus the enemy image makes a strong, aggressive defense the logical choice. If such a defense should eliminate the threatener altogether, so much the better. However, a strategy of containment may be the only recognized alternative in most political contexts, simply because the odds of defeating an enemy are 50–50 at best. Containing your enemy, preventing them from becoming more powerful or achieving their desired goals, may be all you can do.

The consequences of stereotypical enemy image can be tragic when the motivations of the country considered to be an enemy are really misunderstood—that is, when the people and leaders are essentially acting toward that country based upon a stereotype of an enemy. It can produce a self-fulfilling prophecy. The people and leaders of enemy countries will see themselves as having been aggressed against and will develop an enemy image (or mirror image) because each sees the other as an enemy and will adopt the same tough strategy. The result could be an unnecessary and disastrous security dilemma that would be extremely difficult to overcome. **Security dilemmas** are situations in which the efforts made by one state to defend itself are simultaneously seen as threatening to its opponents, even if those actions were not intended to be threatening. They easily lead to **spiral conflicts**, in which each side matches and one-ups the actions taken by the other side. This can produce arms races and other types of aggression that result from misunderstanding each other's motives. The enemy stereotype is virtually non-falsifiable. It can explain any response, including appeasement, on the part of the enemy. In Chapters 9 and 10, a number of cases are presented in which this image is evident. Spiral conflicts and the security dilemma are discussed in more depth in Chapter 13.

The Barbarian

The barbarian image appears when an intense threat is perceived as emanating from a political entity viewed as superior in terms of capability, but as inferior culturally. Historical examples of this image are found in the ancient Greek depiction of the Germanic tribes to the north. The image of the barbarian is of an aggressive people who are monolithic in decisional structure, cunning, and willing to resort to unspeakable brutality, including genocide, and who are determined to take full advantage of their superiority. Emotions commonly associated with this image are disgust rather than contempt (because the barbarian is considered greater in capability, even though culturally inferior), anger, and fear. The latter is a product of the superior capability of the barbarian. People who do not share this image will be accused of cowardice and treason.

Because of both cognitive and emotional properties, this image does not lead to an aggressive defense posture. Fear produced by capability asymmetries will mean people prefer to avoid direct conflict. A more reasonable primary course of action for dealing with a barbarian is a search for allies who can be persuaded that a failure to deal with this threat will seriously and adversely affect their own national interests. In social identity theoretical terms, perceivers would probably engage in direct competition with this hated and disgusting opponent in the most violent form of eliminating the threat altogether, but they cannot because they are too weak. Instead, they must build coalitions to overcome their weakness and improve their ability to at least contain the barbarian.

There are some examples of this image in recent international and domestic political conflicts. International cases include Israeli perceptions of the Arab world. Although the Arab states are not superior to Israel in military capability, their large populations and resource advantages lead to an Israeli expectation they have the potential to become superior. Despite perceived cultural inferiority, the probability is seen as high that superiority in conventional arms is not only attainable but unavoidable. A second example occurred in the disintegration of Yugoslavia (explored in detail in Chapter 9), in which the Croatians believed themselves to be culturally superior to the Serbs, but much weaker in capability (Cottam & Cottam, 2001). In both cases, allies were sought: Israel looked to the United States and Europe, and the Croatians looked to Slovenia and other European states for support in their efforts to achieve independence from Yugoslavia.

The Imperial Image

This image occurs when the people of a polity perceive a threat from another polity viewed as superior in terms of both capability and culture—a fairly commonplace situation during the height of colonialism in the nineteenth century. The imperial stereotype is now viewed primarily in a neocolonial variation, reflecting the disappearance of formal colonialism. People view the imperial power as motivated by the desire to exploit the resources of the colonized people. The decisional structure of the imperial power is viewed as less monolithic than in the enemy and barbarian images because an anti-imperialism element is frequently perceived to be present in the imperial power. People assume decisions are made in a subtle and discreet manner in the imperial power, in the form of an elaborate web of institutions and individuals. People also believe that even though their own country has its own institutions and leader, the imperial power is pulling the strings, often at a very detailed level. The imperial power is viewed as having the capacity to orchestrate developments of extraordinary complexity and to do so with great subtlety. The style is often described as operating through a hidden hand, which is what gives the imperial power superiority in capability. People who collaborate with the imperial power are viewed by those resisting it as profiting hugely from the relationship and are judged as having betrayed their nation. But the reality is that, historically, many people in colonial and neocolonial countries did collaborate with the imperial powers. From a social identity standpoint, this makes sense if collaborators made comparisons not between themselves and the imperial power, but between themselves and other groups in the colony dominated by the imperial power. They may have seen imperial control as just and legitimate, and thereby accepted their own inferior status, if they saw their own circumstances improved in comparison with other groups because of the imperial power's presence. Therefore, the image is sometimes associated with strong perceptions of injustice and illegitimacy, but not by everyone.

The complex of emotions associated with this image is affected by perceptions of whether or not the relationship is a just or legitimate one. When the colonial–imperial relationship is seen as legitimate or just, emotions associated with the image include fear of the imperial power. The behavioral tendencies that result involve self-protection and avoiding conflict with the fear-inducing agent (Duckitt, 1994). In addition, when the relationship is considered just and legitimate, respect is likely by the subordinate people for the imperial group, as is benevolent paternalistic affection by the imperial group for the subordinate group (Duckitt, 1994). The behavioral preferences would simply be to maintain the relationship as it is currently conducted, with the imperial group making major decisions and allowing symbolic concessions to the colonial subject group.

Emotions and action preferences are different on both sides when the relationship and interaction is considered unjust by the weaker, subordinate group. The extremity of mutual stereotyping increases in such situations, and the people in the subordinate position start to make demands for greater equality. They may feel jealousy, anger, and shame that they are in the inferior position (Smith, 1993). These perceptions and emotions can push people toward antagonistic and hostile actions against the superior group, including rebellion, even though they are well aware of the potential consequences. However, actions as risky as outright rebellion tend to occur only when social mobility and creativity options are not available and when real alternatives are perceived to exist. For example, after World War II, the European colonial powers were so weak that the prospect of actually achieving independence looked good enough to leaders of independence movements to push hard for the end of colonialism. This image is also important in a case study presented in Chapter 10 of relations between the United States and Mexico in relation to the war on drugs.

The Rogue Image

The rogue image is relatively new. During the Cold War, leaders of the West held an image of a dependent of the enemy, in which a country was viewed as inferior in capability and culture but controlled and supported by the enemy. That image disappeared with the end of the Cold War and the demise of the Soviet Union. Nevertheless, the West saw former allies of the Soviet Union, along with some other countries (such as North Korea, Cuba, Iraq, Libya, Serbia, and Iran) as both inferior and threatening. American policy-makers often referred to these as rogue states. For example, while he was national security adviser, Anthony Lake wrote:

> Our policy must face the reality of recalcitrant and outlaw states that not only choose to remain outside the family [of nations] but also assault its basic values. There are few "backlash" states: Cuba, North Korea, Iran, Iraq and Libya. For now they lack the resources of a superpower, which would enable them to seriously threaten the democratic order being created around them. Nevertheless, their behavior is often aggressive and defiant ... These backlash states have some common characteristics. Ruled by cliques that control power through coercion ... these nations exhibit a chronic inability to engage constructively with the outside world, and they do not function effectively in alliances ... Finally, they share a siege mentality. Accordingly, they are embarked on ambitious and costly military programs.
>
> Lake (1994, pp. 45–46)

Look at the words Lake used. There are references to a family (bad children), the weakness of these states, the incompatibility of their values with those of the rest of the family of nations, their aggressive behavior, decisions made by a small elite, and the impossibility of dealing with them rationally and constructively. Responses to this type of state are driven by a sense of superiority. They are bad children who must be taught a lesson with force. One does not negotiate with bad children; one punishes them. There are many examples. Americans reacted to Saddam Hussein's resistance to weapons inspection with a full-force attack. President Bush repeatedly stated that there would be no negotiations with Saddam Hussein and if he didn't do as he was told, he would be punished. When Slobodan Milošević resisted points in the Rambouillet accords that would give North Atlantic Treaty Organization (NATO) forces the right to wander unimpeded throughout Yugoslavia, negotiations ceased, and Yugoslavia was bombed. When Manuel Noriega thumbed his nose at U.S. efforts to promote free elections, Panama was bombed. Often, one individual is assumed to be responsible for the behavior of the rogue state (e.g., eliminate Noriega, Saddam, or Milošević and the problem will be solved overnight).

The Degenerate Image

The degenerate image is associated with the perception of an opportunity to achieve a goal at the expense of a country seen as relatively equal or even greater in capability and culture. Even though a degenerate country may be more powerful than the perceiver's country, it is also seen as uncertain and confused in motivation and characterized by a highly differentiated leadership lacking a clear sense of direction and incapable of constructing an effective strategy. They are believed to be unable to muster the will and determination to make effective use of their power instruments or to mobilize effective public support. Fellow citizens who do not share this image are seen as wimps. As in the case of the enemy stereotype, disconfirming evidence is likely to be interpreted as confirming, and the image is extremely difficult to falsify.

The emotions associated with the image are disgust, contempt, scorn, and anger, all of which may ultimately turn to hatred. This combination leads to a desire to eliminate the offensive group and can lead to a dangerous underestimation of an adversary's abilities (Izard, 1977). Contempt and disgust combine with anger and scorn, and this can lead to dehumanization and to genocidal violence. Because the motivations of a country seen as a degenerate are assumed to be harmful, the drive to eliminate the problem is likely to be strong. The leaders of Germany and Japan before World War II made statements about, and committed acts toward, Great Britain, the United States, and France, indicating their degenerate image of those countries. A more recent example of this stereotypical view was Saddam Hussein of Iraq in his confrontation with the United States and its allies in 1990. Saddam Hussein apparently believed to the end that the United States and its allies would not have the will to engage him on the issue of the invasion of Kuwait. More typical was the operating worldview of Hitler, Mussolini, and the Japanese military. They at least did possess formidable war capabilities, and all saw a reality that made plausible the achievement of their aggressive ends.

The Colonial Image

A second stereotypical image associated with perception of opportunity is the **colonial image**, which is the flip side of the imperial image. It occurs when an opportunity is identified to gain control over another polity or group perceived as significantly inferior in capability and culture. The people are perceived as childlike and inferior, and the political elite are typically perceived to fall into one of two groups: one group is seen as behaving moderately and responsibly, as is indicated by its willingness to collaborate with the imperial power; the other group, in contrast, is seen as behaving in an agitating and irresponsible manner, opposing the imperial purpose, sometimes to the point of allying with and serving the interests of enemies of the imperial power. The moderate, responsible section is motivated to support what is perceived as the civilizing mission of the imperial power. The agitating group is seen as monolithic in decisional structure and cunningly destructive as it tries to mobilize the most alert elements in a mostly apolitical and passive populace. The imperial power capability advantage rests on the perceived immaturity of the colonial population, as manifested in an inability to effectively recruit, organize, and lead a military force, and to make effective use of advanced weaponry. Those citizens of the imperial power who do not share this essentially contemptuous view will be regarded as having "gone native" and lost perspective.

Members of the imperial power polity tend to regard the colonial populace with disgust and contempt, but also pity. Behaviors associated with the image and its emotional baggage include wanting to avoid contamination from contact with the inferior, or moving forcefully against them to punish bad behavior. This was the Cold War pattern in U.S. foreign policy. Countries in this image, who moved in political directions that U.S. policy-makers did not approve of, were punished, sometimes through the overthrow of their governments. Examples include the overthrow of the governments in Iran (1953), Guatemala (1954), and Chile (1973). The fear was that they would become infected with socialism, and it would spread to other countries. They were not going to allow this to happen. In less-dangerous contexts, such as disagreements regarding economic matters, there is little a colonial country can do to seriously threaten the imperial power, and policy preferences are for nonviolent repression in the form of economic sanctions, isolation, refusal to give trade preferences, and so on. The actions and demands of the colonial country are still considered illegitimate and inconsistent with the goals of the perceiver, and responsibility for the conflict is attributed to the colonial country.

We describe this image in terms of international politics, but the dynamic repeats itself in any domestic political context in which one group considers itself vastly superior to, and therefore rightfully in control of, another group. White resistance to the Civil Rights Movement in the South of the United States in the 1960s is an example. Black political leaders were also divided into "moderate" and "irresponsible" classifications. This image is also evident in the case study of United States–Mexico interaction in Chapter 10.

ATTITUDES

The discussion of images and their emotional components tells us something about the interaction of cognition and emotion. There is a great deal of research on the cognitive and emotional elements in the individual attitudes that make up a cognitive system. The concept is defined and thought of in different ways by different psychologists. A standard definition of attitudes is that they are an enduring system of positive or negative beliefs (the cognitive component), **affective** feelings and emotions, and action tendencies regarding **attitude objects**—that is, the entity being evaluated. Stone and Schaffner (1988), for example, regard attitudes as "an organized set of beliefs, persisting over time, which is useful in explaining the individual response to tendencies" (p. 63). Eagly and Chaiken (1998) define attitudes as "a psychological tendency that is expressed by evaluating a particular entity with some degree of favor or disfavor" (p. 269). Duckitt (1994) reviews two different ways in which attitudes are conceptualized in psychology. In one, they are seen to be composed of cognitive, affective, and behavioral components. However, there were many criticisms of this conceptualization of attitudes because there was little in the way of specifics as to how these three components interacted, and whether they were always consistent with each other. We saw earlier, in our discussion of balance and consistency, that affect and cognition are not always consistent, and most people know from personal experience that attitudes and behavior are often inconsistent.

One of the most important controversies in attitude research concerned the behavioral component in the original conceptualization of attitudes. Originally, it was assumed that a person's attitudes determine behavior. A person who favors a certain politician is likely to vote for that candidate.

A person who smokes marijuana is likely to support legislation legalizing marijuana. A person who is racially prejudiced is unlikely to send their child to a school where Blacks and Hispanic Americans, or whoever the person does not like, are in the majority. In 1934, however, a major study was done that found interesting results and challenged the notion that there is a direct connection between attitudes and behavior. This study was conducted by La Pierre, a White professor. He toured the United States with a Chinese couple during a period when there was a great deal of prejudice against Asian people in the country. They stopped at 66 hotels and 184 restaurants. Only once were they turned away by a hotel, and never by a restaurant. Later, a letter was sent to the same hotels and restaurants asking whether they would accept Chinese customers. Ninety-two percent of those who responded (128) said they would not. The study showed people do not always behave in accordance with their attitudes. Later studies raised similar concerns (Deutscher, 1973; Katz & Stotland, 1959; Kuntner, Wilkins, & Yarrow, 1952; Minard, 1952). This, of course, led to the question of when and under what circumstances attitudes and behavior are likely to coincide.

Attitudes that are strong, clear, and consistent over time, and directly and specifically relevant to the behavior under examination, are more likely to be associated with attitude–behavior consistency (Fazio & Williams, 1986; Fishbein & Ajzen, 1980; Krosnick, 1989). Inconsistencies can come from weak or ambivalent affect. In addition, the affective and cognitive components of an attitude may be in some conflict, which also reduces the changes of attitude–behavior consistency. For example, some men and women may think intellectually gender-based discrimination is wrong, but they are emotionally upset when men and women do not conform to gender-related roles. Also, if one is going to study the relationship between attitudes and behaviors, one needs to look at behaviors directly related to attitudes to get an accurate picture of the relationship. For example, several studies examined the relationship between religious attitudes and religious behavior by asking subjects whether they believe in God or consider themselves religious, then noting whether they attended church. Usually, there was only a weak relationship between the two. The problem is that going to church is not directly related to belief in God or even to being religious. Many people who believe in God do not go to church. Other people go to church for social reasons more than because they believe in God. In addition, looking at a series of actions over time to get an accurate picture of the relationship between attitudes and behavior is important (Epstein, 1979; Fiske & Taylor, 1991). This eliminates interference from situational conditions that affect the attitude–behavior relationship.

This brings us to situational pressures, which can also affect the relationship between attitudes and behavior. Whenever a person engages in overt behavior, they can be influenced both by their attitudes and by the situation. When situational pressures are very strong, attitudes are not likely to be as strong a determinant of behavior as when situational pressures are relatively weak. Situational pressure can include social norms (a person may be a bigot, but know that others will think poorly of him or her for acting that way) or contextual effects, which heighten the salience of or perspective on, a certain attitude (Bentler & Speckart, 1981; Fishbein & Ajzen, 1975; La Pierre, 1934). Individual differences are also important in explaining inconsistencies between what people think and how they behave. Some people are high self-monitors, meaning they are very attentive to social norms and the impression they make in social situations. They are less likely to act consistently on the basis of their attitudes and instead act as they think the situation demands (Perloff, 1993; Snyder, 1987).

Given these issues, others offered perspectives on attitudes. Fishbein and Ajzen (1980) offered a unidimensional approach to attitudes, wherein they regarded attitudes solely as affect. They separated the cognitive and behavioral components and argued these should be observed and measured separately. As Duckitt (1994, p. 13) explains:

> This approach does not expect a strong relationship between an attitude to an object and specific behaviors to that object. To predict a specific act, both the attitude to that act and act-specific social norms need to be considered as well. On the other hand, a generalized attitude toward an object should predict the overall tendency to behave in a generally favorable or unfavorable way toward that object, as aggregating over a variety of different situations and acts should largely average out normative and situational influences.

Judd and Krosnick (1989) take a similar approach and define an attitude as "an evaluation of an attitude object that is stored in memory" (p. 100). Others have limited attitudes to affect and beliefs alone (Levin & Levin, 1982).

No agreement exists on a universally accepted understanding of what an attitude is and how its component parts relate to each other, but as we show in Chapter 6, the attitude concept is widely used in studies of voting behavior, persuasion, and media effects on political behavior. Unlike the image and stereotype concepts, the attitude concept can more easily separate cognition and affect, and for that reason it can be very useful in studying voting behavior, particularly in a country such as the United States, where people have political attitudes that are often based on little, and often inaccurate, cognition. An attitude can be driven mostly by affect. But, as our discussion of images and stereotypes showed, there is considerable knowledge—although often inaccurate—embodied in them. Alternatively, an attitude may be primarily cognitive in content, based solely on beliefs without affect (Eagly & Chaiken, 1998).

Attitude studies were conducted on many issues, one of which, as mentioned, is the relationship between cognition and affect—particularly when they are not consistent (i.e., what you think about an object and how you feel about it are different). Marcus et al. (2000) examined the role played by affect in the behavior of American citizens in elections and regarding important issues. They argue that emotions help people to monitor and take surveillance of politics. Their study included survey results demonstrating the importance of enthusiasm and anxiety in electoral preferences for the presidency in the 1980s. For example, enthusiasm for Reagan and lack of anxiety about the country's circumstances contributed strongly to Reagan's reelection in 1984. They also explained the lack of everyday interest in politics in America by noting the average citizen uses emotions to act as an alarm; when the citizen starts to feel anxiety, they then turn to the news to find out more. The emotional system is a watchdog that operates unconsciously. We discuss this research in more detail in Chapter 6.

Another broad issue concerns the consistency among, and structure of, attitudes—for example, whether Republicans are consistently conservative and Democrats are consistently liberal on all political issues, and how those attitudes are linked together. Attitudes can be bipolar, wherein people recognize and understand both sides of an issue, or they can be unipolar, in which case people see only their preferred position. Eagly and Chaiken (1998) cite a number of studies suggesting attitudes on controversial issues are likely to be bipolar (e.g., Pratkanis, 1989; Sherif, Sherif, & Nebergall, 1965). In addition, there is a large body of literature on the complexity of beliefs, which we introduced in Chapter 2 and will explore in more detail in Chapter 5, where political leaders are discussed. Many studies concerning how political attitudes are formed, and how they change, are examined in Chapter 6.

CONCLUSION

This chapter has introduced readers to many different concepts in cognitive and social psychology, and their application to political psychology. We began with basic patterns in information processing, and then turned to an overview of the cognitive system. To this, we added the importance of the groups to which people belong (**in-groups**), and their reactions to groups to which they do not belong (**out-groups**). We presented a model of out-groups (image theory), which depicts out-groups in international politics, but can also be used in domestic political arenas. In subsequent chapters, where we examine race, ethnicity, nationalism, and political extremists, we explore some of the groups in politics to which people have powerful attachments, as well as patterns of behavior toward out-groups. We looked at emotion in politics. Readers may find that although emotions were not systematically examined in the patterns of political behavior, they are deeply important, as discussed in subsequent chapters. Indeed, readers may find themselves having powerful emotional reactions to some of the cases presented in the following chapters. Finally, we presented the concept of attitudes, to which we return when we look at public opinion and voting in Chapter 6. Thus far, in Chapters 2 and 3, we explored the content of the Political Being's mind. In the next chapter, we turn to the Political Being and the outside world, with a look at groups and group behavior.

Topics, Theories/Explanations, and Concepts in Chapter 3		
Topics	*Theories*	*Concepts*
Information processing	Attribution theory	Heuristics: availability, representativeness, fundamental attribution error
	Balance theory	Need for consistency
	Dissonance theory	Selective exposure, attention, interpretation; avoidance of value trade-offs; bolstering
Cognition and cognitive systems	Categorization; social identity	Cognitive categories; schemas; stereotypes; in-groups and out-groups
	Image theory	Enemy, barbarian, imperial, rogue, degenerate, colonial
Emotions		
Attitudes		

Key Terms

affect
ally image
anchoring and adjustment
assimilation effect
attitudes
attribution theory
availability heuristic
avoidance of value trade-offs
balance
barbarian image
beliefs
bolstering
childish games
cognition
cognitive processes
colonial image
compliance
confirmation bias
contrast effect
degenerate image
dissonance
emotion
enemy image
fundamental attribution error
heuristic
hindsight bias
image theory
imperialist image
in-group
out-group
representativeness heuristic
rogue image
schema
security
social identity
Social Identity Model of Collective Action (SIMCA)
spiral conflicts
stereotypes

Suggestions for Further Reading

Alexander, M. G., Brewer, M. B., & Herrmann, R. K. (1999). Images and affect: A functional analysis of out-group stereotypes. *Journal of Personality and Social Psychology, 77*, 78–93.

Cottam, M. (1994). *Images and intervention*. Pittsburgh, PA: University of Pittsburgh Press.

Cottam, M., & Cottam, R. (2001). *Nationalism and politics: The political behavior of nation states*. Boulder, CO: Lynne Rienner.

Eagly, A. H., & Chaiken, S. (1998). Attitude structure and function. In D. T. Gilbert, S. T. Fiske, & G. Lindzey (Eds.), *The handbook of social psychology* (4th ed., pp. 269–322). New York: McGraw-Hill.

Fiske, S., & Taylor, S. E. (1991). *Social cognition*. New York: McGraw-Hill.

Frijda, N. (1986). *The emotions*. Cambridge: Cambridge University Press.

Mackie, D., & Hamilton, D. (Eds.). (1993). *Affect, cognition and stereotyping: Interactive processes in group perception*. New York: Academic Press.

Marcus, G., Neuman, W. R., & MacKuen, M. (2000). *Affective intelligence and political judgment*. Chicago, IL: University of Chicago Press.

Neuman, R. Marcus, G., Crigler, A., & MacKuen, M. (Eds.). (2007). *The affect effect*. Chicago, IL: Chicago University Press.

Tajfel, H. (1982). *Human groups and social categories*. Cambridge: Cambridge University Press.

Westen, D. (2007). *The political brain: The role of emotion in deciding the fate of the nation*. New York: Public Affairs.

Chapter 4

The Political Psychology of Groups

This chapter looks at Political Beings in their environment—that is, in the presence of, and as a member of, groups. Groups have a prominent role in politics. Small groups are often given the responsibility for making important political decisions, creating political policies, and generally conducting political business. Larger groups, such as the Senate, also hold a special place in politics, and are responsible for larger-scale decisions and tasks, such as passing legislation. Finally, large groups, such as states and countries, carry with them their own dynamics, especially regarding how they view each other and how they get along. Because so much political behavior is performed by groups, it behooves us to learn more about the basic processes that govern groups. Although groups are composed of individuals, group behavior cannot be understood by studying individual behavior. Obviously, understanding groups involves an understanding of the individuals who compose a group, but there are dynamics of groups that cannot be observed from examining individuals alone. Many observers (e.g., Durkheim, 1966; LeBon, 1960) have noted that individuals often behave quite differently when they are together compared with when they are alone. Consequently, although the workings of the Political Being's mind are still operative, in this chapter we are interested in the impact of the sociopolitical environment on behavior.

The study of groups in social psychology has a short history, with some of the first studies being conducted just before World War II (e.g., Lewin, Lippitt, & White, 1939; Newcomb, 1943; Sherif, 1936; Whyte, 1943). Nonetheless, a vast amount of information is available about group behavior, and most of it can be applied to the study of groups in political settings. In this chapter, we review a variety of information about groups. The first half of the chapter focuses on the structural characteristics of groups, such as composition, formation, and development. The second half of the chapter focuses on the unique behaviors that take place in groups or because of groups, including influence, performance, decision-making, and intergroup conflict.

DOI: 10.4324/9780429244643-4

THE NATURE OF GROUPS

Definition of a Group

Imagine all the different types of collectives that exist in political settings. People work together to solve problems, set political policies and agendas, serve constituents, make legal decisions, run political campaigns, and make decisions about world problems. Do all of these collectives constitute groups? Group researchers were unable to answer that question. There is little consensus in the field about what characteristics of a collective make a group. Although most social psychologists would agree that a group is a collection of people who are perceived as belonging together and dependent on one another, there are other ways to conceptualize groups. For example, Moreland (1987) discussed "groupiness" or social integration as a quality possessed by every collection of individuals to some degree. As the level of social integration increases, people start to think and act more like a group than a collection of individuals. Other social psychologists (Dasgupta, Banji, & Abelson, 1999; Lickel et al., 2000) have pointed to **entiativity**, which refers to the extent to which a collection of people is perceived as a coherent entity. Some groups, such as people in line at a bank, are perceived as being low in entiativity. Other groups, such as members of a family or members of a professional sports team, are perceived as being high in entiativity.

Types of Groups

When thinking about groups, it is sometimes useful to consider the various types. Several groups researchers provided typologies of groups. For example, Prentice, Miller, and Lightdale (1994) investigated **common-bond** and **common-identity groups.** Common-bond groups, such as social groups, are based mostly on the attachments between group members. In common-bond groups, the attachments to the group are based on such things as member similarity, likability of fellow group members, and familiarity with group members. Common-identity groups, on the other hand, are based primarily on attachments to the group identity. Examples of common-identity groups include music groups, sports teams, and performing groups. Individuals in common-identity groups are far more attached to the group identity than they are to individual members of the group.

Deaux, Reid, Mizrahi, and Ethier (1995) provide another perspective on types of groups. In research focusing on the dimensions of social identity, they identified five types of social identities: personal relationships (e.g., friend, husband); vocations/avocations (e.g., student, gardener); political affiliation (e.g., Democrat, Republican); stigmatized groups (e.g., alcoholic, unemployed person); and ethnic/religious groups (e.g., Catholic, Hispanic).

Lickel et al. (2000) provided a more recent typology of groups. In their study, participants were asked to rate a variety of groups on such dimensions as perceived entiativity, interaction, common goals, similarity, permeability, duration, size, and importance. The results of their investigation showed groups could be divided into three types. One type, intimacy groups, consisted of small groups with frequent interactions, high similarity, and importance to their members. Examples of intimacy groups include families, friends, and fraternities. A second type, task groups, consists of groups that are fairly small in size, but with high interaction, similarity, and importance. Task groups are groups such as members of a jury, labor unions, and student study groups. The third type of group, social categories, consists of large groups that are usually low in interaction, importance, and similarity of group members. These groups include women, Blacks, and Jews, for example.

Why is it important to consider types of groups? One reason may be the different functions groups serve or the types of needs they fulfill. For example, Johnson et al. (2005) show that intimacy groups tend to fulfill needs for affiliation, task groups tend to fulfill the need for achievement, and social category groups are associated with the need for identity. Understanding the relationship between group types and individual needs can be useful for knowing what types of groups to look for to satisfy various social needs. In addition, knowing what types of groups fulfill which needs might help to explain dissatisfaction with a group. For example, if a person has a strong need for affiliation but is not getting that need satisfied in their study group, then it is likely because study groups usually do not help to fulfill a need for affiliation.

Group Composition

Groups come in all shapes and sizes, and political groups are no exception. Groups can differ in size, composition, and type. Research suggests naturally occurring groups are typically small, containing just two or three persons (Desportes & Lemaine, 1988). People may prefer smaller groups because they are confused by large groups (James, 1951) or because they cannot easily control what happens to them in larger groups (Lawler, 1992). Research examined some interesting effects of group size. For example, as the size of the group increases, group members participate less (Patterson & Schaeffer, 1977), display less commitment to the group (Widmeyer, Brawley, & Carron, 1990), and show higher levels of tardiness, absenteeism, and turnover (Durand, 1985; Spink & Carron, 1992). Other group dynamics are also affected by group size. In larger groups, there tends to be more conflict (O'Dell, 1968), less cooperation (Brewer & Kramer, 1986), and less conformity to group norms (Olson & Caddell, 1994). Finally, group performance can also be affected by the size of a group. In large groups, coordination is more difficult (Diehl & Stroebe, 1987; Latane, Williams, & Harkins, 1979), leading to decrements in performance, and it is easier to social loaf and free ride, which can have harmful effects on the performance of a group (Karau & Williams, 1993). In the following chapters, we examine large groups, such as ethnic, national, and racial groups, as well as small groups involved in political decision-making and political violence.

Groups can also differ in terms of their composition. The characteristics of individual group members, such as sex, race, ethnicity, and physical attractiveness, can be very important to the functioning of the group. However, attention has also been focused on diversity within a group (Levine & Moreland, 1998). Research examining the effects of diversity on communication suggests diversity can be harmful. As the degree of diversity increases, group members tend to communicate with each other less and in more formal ways (Zenger & Lawrence, 1989). When group members communicate less often, interpersonal conflicts become more likely (Maznevski, 1994). Diversity, however, can also be beneficial to group performance (McLeod & Lobel, 1992) because it allows a group to be more flexible, foster innovation, and improve the quantity and quality of relationships outside of the group.

Groups can also be distinguished by their type. In a study, Lickel et al. (2000) asked participants to categorize a large number of groups. Their sorting resulted in four categories of groups: first, some groups, such as families and romantic relationships, were categorized as *intimacy groups*; second, *task-oriented groups* consisted of groups such as committees and work groups; third, groups such as women and Americans were categorized as *social categories*; and, finally, *weak social relationships or associations* included such groups as those who enjoy a certain type of music or those who live in the same neighborhood. Political groups certainly fall into the task-oriented type, whether they are government working groups, juries, political interest groups such as Greenpeace or Human Rights Watch, or committees and subcommittees in Congress. Political groups can also be social categories, such as ethnic groups, racial groups, or women, all with particular political issues of concern.

Group Structure

Another important characteristic of a group is its structure. Every group has a structure, and it tends to develop quickly and change slowly (Levine & Moreland, 1998). Apparently group members need to know what the structure of a group is, and are reluctant to alter it once it is set. For example, understanding the structure of a group, and how aspects of a group's structure can influence conflict and performance, is important. Aspects of group structure include status, roles, norms, and cohesion.

Status in a group refers to how power is distributed among its members. Indicators of high status include nonverbal behavior, such as standing more erect, maintaining eye contact, and being more physically intrusive (Leffler, Gillespie, & Conaty, 1982), as well as verbal behavior, such as speaking more, interrupting more, and being more likely to be spoken to (Skovertz, 1988). The manner in which people acquire or are assigned status is explained by two theories: expectation states theory (Berger, Rosenholtz, & Zelditch, 1980), suggested the expectations of a person, based on their personal characteristics, contribute to group members' sense of the sorts of accomplishments a person can achieve, and ethological theories (Mazur, 1985), which maintain that a group member acquires status when other group members assess the person's strength by evaluating their demeanor and appearance. However status is acquired, it is generally slow to change. Because high status is associated with rewards, those high in status are reluctant to give it up. And, because those high in status are usually evaluated more favorably than those low in status, other group members are reluctant to remove status (Messe, Kerr, & Sattler, 1992).

The various **roles** group members hold constitute another important component of group structure. Roles are expectations about how a person ought to behave. Little is known about how roles in groups develop (Levine & Moreland, 1998), except that task roles emerge before socioemotional ones. Regardless of how roles develop, well-played roles can be beneficial to a group (Barley & Bechky, 1994; Bastien & Hostager, 1998). Much of the research on roles in groups focuses on the conflicts they create. Some role conflicts occur as a result of *role assignment*, which refers to the decisions made about who plays what role. Other conflicts center on *role ambiguity* (uncertainty about how to behave in a role) or *role strain* (lacking knowledge or ability to fulfill the role).

The **norms** of a group can be an important aspect of group structure. Norms refer to expectations about how all group members should behave. Like roles, the formation of norms in a group can be difficult to identify. Some argue that a group's initial behavior can be transformed into norms (Feldman, 1984). Others argue that norms can arise from the expectations for behavior people bring with them when they join a group (Bettenhausen & Murnighan, 1991). Regardless of how norms are formed, there is strong pressure to maintain them. Group members can impose strong sanctions on members who violate the standards of behavior, and with good reason. Research suggests adherence to norms improves the performance of a group (Seashore, 1954). For example, in groups that have norms of productivity or success, group members become more motivated to engage in behaviors or tasks that ensure the success of the group. On the other hand, adherence to norms can sometimes impede the performance of a group. If a norm of laziness develops, for example, then group members might work less hard to achieve their goals.

Cohesion refers to the factors that cause a group member to remain in the group (Festinger, 1950). The importance of cohesion to a group's well-being cannot be underestimated. It exerts powerful effects on a group's longevity. As such, understanding how cohesion in a group develops is important. There are several factors that affect the development of group cohesion. First, the more time group members spend together, the more cohesive they become (Griffith & Greenlees, 1993). Second, the more group members like each other, the more cohesive the group is (Lott & Lott, 1965). Third, groups that are more rewarding to their members are more cohesive (Ruder & Gill, 1982). Fourth, external threats to a group can increase the group's cohesiveness (Dion, 1979). Fifth, groups are more cohesive when leaders encourage feelings of warmth among group members. Most studies of the effects of cohesion on wellbeing and performance find a positive relationship. For example, members of cohesive groups are more likely to participate in group activities and to remain in the group (Brawley, Carron, & Widmeyer, 1988) and, in a meta-analysis of the effects of cohesion on performance, Mullen and Copper (1994) found cohesive groups tend to perform better.

There are many studies of political decision-making groups, particularly U.S. presidents and their close advisers, that show differences among those groups in status, roles, norms, and cohesion. These studies are reviewed extensively in Chapter 5. Here we provide a few examples. President John

F. Kennedy preferred a collegial advisory group. Although he was at the top in terms of status, he saw the various advisers as colleagues. The group formed at the outset of the administration, and members had their own domain of expertise, which provided him with a particular role. In terms of norms, conflicting viewpoints were encouraged, and all sides were taken into account in searching for solutions to problems. President Nixon was very different. His advisory group structure was hierarchical, with him on top. Again, each adviser had a role to play, but conflict and brainstorming were not encouraged. The emphasis in problem-solving was on technical rather than political considerations. In the Clinton administration, role assignments were ambiguous, which led to many delays and much turmoil in policy-making.

Group Formation

If you think about all the groups of which you are a member, do you know how or why each of those groups formed? What were the circumstances surrounding the formation of each of your groups? Some of the answers may be easier than others. For example, the animal shelter at which you volunteer formed because there was a need to care for stray dogs and cats, and the group of people with whom you spend free time formed because the members liked one another. But how did the church you attend get started? Why did the Tuesday night intramural softball team you play on come to be? Groups researchers have yet to develop a comprehensive theory to explain how and why groups form, but there are two perspectives that offer promise. The *functional perspective* suggests groups form because they serve a useful function or fulfill a need for their individual members (Mackie & Goethals, 1987). For example, your animal shelter formed to fulfill the need created by so many homeless dogs and cats. The *interpersonal attraction perspective* suggests groups form because members like one another and seek to spend time together. Thus, the group of friends with whom you spend time formed because you all liked one another and wanted to spend time together.

Functional Perspective

According to the functional perspective, groups satisfy many needs, including survival, psychological, informational, interpersonal, and collective. Groups can be functional, in that they can fulfill many of our *survival* needs, including feeding, defense, nurturance, and reproduction (Bertram, 1978; Harvey & Greene, 1981; Scott, 1981). Many of these needs were stronger during earlier periods in history, but we still rely on groups to fulfill many of these functions today. For example, we rely heavily on our military forces to defend our country. We depend on farmers to provide some of our food. And, to the extent we have a need to defend our country, we might decide to join the armed forces. From an evolutionary psychology perspective, membership in groups can help groups to fulfill their evolutionary goals of survival, for most of the reasons expressed above.

Political Action Groups and the Internet

The internet seems to affect everything, even group-formation patterns. Consider, for example, a political action group called MoveOn. Two Silicon Valley entrepreneurs, Joan Blades and Wes Boyd, organized MoveOn in 1998 when they reached a level of frustration with the effort to impeach President Clinton. Then, after 9/11, Eli Pariser started an online petition for peace. They joined forces and formed the MoveOn.org political action committee, creating an international association of over two million online activists.

This is an example of a cyber group that formed to achieve functional goals of affecting politics through interest group activity. Will the opportunity to form and join cybergroups affect group psychology? Will it affect group influence in politics? (To learn about MoveOn, naturally, you should visit their website, www.moveon.org.)

Groups can also satisfy a host of psychological needs, some of which we introduced in Chapter 2. For example, joining a group can satisfy the need for affiliation. Those with a high need for affiliation join groups more often, communicate with others frequently, and seek social approval (McClelland, 1985). Groups also satisfy the need for power. People with a high need for power want to control others (Winter, 1973). Schutz's **Fundamental Interpersonal Relations Orientation (FIRO)** also explains how joining a group fulfills psychological needs (Schutz, 1958). According to this perspective, joining a group satisfies three basic needs: *inclusion* (the desire to be part of a group), *control* (the need to organize an aspect of the group), and *affection* (the desire to establish positive relations with others). Joining a group offers individuals a way to fulfill these needs.

Another category of needs is informational needs. Festinger (1950, 1954) argued that people join groups to provide standards with which to compare their own beliefs, opinions, and attitudes. People often need to determine whether their own viewpoints are correct or accurate. One way to make such determinations is to seek similar people with whom to compare our views. This perspective suggests people join groups to better understand social reality.

Groups also meet people's interpersonal needs. Many groups provide social support, giving emotional sustenance, advice, and valuable feedback. Social support can be a valuable function of groups. Groups protect us from the harmful effects of stress (Barrera, 1986). The social support of groups also protects us from loneliness. Research indicates that people who were members of many groups reported less loneliness (Rubenstein & Shaver, 1980). College students who eat dinner with others and spend time with their friends also report being less lonely (Russell, Peplau, & Cutrona, 1980).

Finally, groups fulfill important collective needs. Sometimes, groups are more productive and efficient than individuals working alone. Groups often form because individuals believe pooling the efforts of multiple people will lead to better outcomes. Some of the collective goals sought by groups include engaging in the performing arts, enriching the leisure time of their members, changing the opinions of persons outside the group, and making routine individual tasks more tolerable (Zander, 1985).

Interpersonal Attraction Perspective

Sometimes, groups form because individuals discover they like each other and want to spend more time together. There are many factors that influence our liking of another. First, we tend to be attracted to those who are most similar to us in attitudes, beliefs, socioeconomic status, physical appearance, and so on (Newcomb, 1960). This suggests we prefer to form or join groups with people who are most similar to us. Second, we tend to form relationships with those who are physically closer to us (Festinger, Schachter, & Back, 1950). Thus, we tend to make friends with those who live next door, those we sit next to in class, and those with whom we work closely. We are likely, then, to form or join groups with people who are physically close. Third, we like people who like us (Newcomb, 1979). We are thus more likely to form or join groups with people who are fond of us. Fourth, we are attracted to people who are physically attractive. With the exception of those who are extremely attractive, physically attractive people are more accepted than those less physically attractive.

In summary, people join groups for a variety of reasons. One reason people join and form groups is to satisfy a number of important needs, including survival, psychological, informational, interpersonal, and collective needs. We are more likely to join groups that can effectively satisfy our needs. Another reason people join groups is to spend more time with the people they like. Such situations, especially when reciprocal, can be very rewarding.

Group Development

Think again about the groups to which you belong. Have they remained the same over time or have they changed somehow? Most likely, groups of which you are a member have changed somewhat over time, but how? **Group development** refers to the stages of growth and change that occur in a group, from its formation to its dissolution (Forsyth, 1990). Of course, there is disagreement among researchers about the number and types of stages, but most models include the following basic stages: forming, storming, norming, performing, and adjourning (Tuckman, 1965; Tuckman & Jensen, 1977).

The first stage refers to the point during which the collection of individuals is **forming**. This stage is also referred to as the orientation stage because prospective members are orienting themselves to the group. During this stage, individuals are getting to know one another. The stage is often characterized as one with a fair amount of tension—prospective group members are on guard, reluctant to share much information or discuss their personal views. Also, as you can imagine, group norms have not yet formed, making this a difficult period of development. In fact, the tension can be so high that those who believe they lack the skills necessary to effectively handle such a situation try to avoid group membership (Cook, 1977; Leary, 1983). Over time, tensions lessen and group members begin to exchange more information. Also, feelings of interdependence—one of the defining features of a group—increase during this stage. In Chapters 10 and 12, we look at a number of groups of political extremists, such as the Nazi SS and terrorists. In such cases, careful attention is given to this stage to ensure only people with particular characteristics are included.

The second stage of group development, **storming**, is characterized as one of conflict. Many types of conflict exist. Some conflicts occur when a person's position or action is misinterpreted (Deutsch, 1973). Other conflicts arise when a group member's behavior is deemed to be distracting, such as when a group member consistently arrives 15 minutes late for meetings. Other types of conflicts can escalate, such as when minor disagreements turn into major points of contention. Although conflicts, especially those that escalate, can disrupt the group, they can serve as important catalysts for group development. Conflicts can serve to promote group unity, interdependence and stability, and cohesion (Bennis & Shepard, 1956; Coser, 1956; Deutsch, 1969).

Norming, the third stage of group development, is a phase in which conflict is replaced with cohesion and feelings of unity. When groups become more cohesive, they have a heightened sense of unity. The relationships among members become stronger, as do individual members' sense of belonging. The degree of group members' identification is heightened during this period. Another characteristic of groups in this stage of development is stability. There is a low turnover of members, a low absentee rate, and a high rate of involvement.

Urban Street Gangs as Groups

Urban street gangs in the United States, and elsewhere, provide illustrations of the power of group demands for loyalty, conformity, and obedience. In the book *Monster: The Autobiography of an L.A. Gang Member* (Shakur, 1993), Sanyika Shakur, a.k.a. Monster Kody, describes those group dynamics.

(1) Belonging to the group enhances self-esteem, and cohesive groups demand strong loyalty:

> Actually, I wasn't fully aware of the gang's strong gravitational pull. I knew, for instance, that the total lawlessness was alluring, and that the sense of importance, self-worth, and raw power was exciting, stimulating, and intoxicating beyond any other high on this planet. But still I could not explain what had happened to pull me in so far that *nothing* outside of my set mattered (p. 70).

(2) Loyalty and solidarity are described in passages such as this:

> I went to trial [for murder] three months later. The gang turnout was surprising. Along with my family, at least fifteen of my homeboys came. All were in full gear (gear as in gang clothes, colors and hats—actually uniforms) (p. 23).

(3) He describes the norms of his gang as "You are your brother's keeper"; when war is declared, all members are expected to fight; reject family and other agents, like the schools and teachers and police, to associate

(*Continued*)

(*Continued*)

with the gang; respect and honor others according to their status; protect the gang turf; and retaliate against all perceived offenses.

(4) Shakur also outlines what the gang values, including trouble (fighting, drinking, drugs, and sex), toughness, smartness (respect for streetwise savvy), and fatalism (they did not believe they would grow old).

During this stage of development, group members also report a high degree of satisfaction with the group. They enjoy the group more, note increases in self-esteem and security, and experience lower levels of anxiety. Finally, the internal dynamics of the group begin to intensify. There is greater acceptance of the group's goals by group members, a low tolerance for disagreement, and increased pressures to conform.

The fourth stage of group development is characterized by **performing**. Performance usually only occurs when groups mature and have successfully gone through the previous stages of development (Forsyth, 1990). In a study of neighborhood action groups (Zurcher, 1969), only one of 12 groups reached the performing stage. All others were stuck in the conflict or cohesion stages.

A group's decision to dissolve (**adjourning**) can either be planned or spontaneous. A planned dissolution occurs when the group accomplishes its intended goals or exhausts its time and resources. Examples of groups with planned dissolutions include a jury that has reached a verdict, a softball team playing its last game of the season, or a class that dissolves because the semester has ended. Spontaneous dissolutions occur when unanticipated problems arise that prevent the group from continuing. Examples of groups with unplanned dissolutions include those that repeatedly failed, or those that fail to satisfy their members' needs.

INFLUENCE IN GROUPS

Groups can exert a great deal of influence over their members. When people are in a group, there is a strong tendency to adhere to the group's norms. When group members act in accord with group norms, they are conforming. **Conformity** refers to the tendency to change one's beliefs or behaviors so they are consistent with the standards set by the group. Americans tend to be ambivalent about the notion of conformity. On the one hand, to conform is to be "spineless" and "wishy-washy"; because Americans tend to value individualism, being labeled a conformist can be a negative label. On the other hand, conformity is valued because it leads to harmony and peace. Imagine a world in which no one conformed. In this section, we examine some of the early studies on norm formation and conformity. We also explore the reasons why people conform, as well as when people conform.

One of the earliest studies of conformity was conducted by Sherif (1936), who was interested in how group norms form. To understand norm formation, he made use of the **autokinetic effect**, which refers to a perceptual illusion that occurs when a single point of light in a darkened room appears to be moving. In Sherif's experiments, he asked participants to stare at the point of light and estimate how far it moved. In reality, the light did not move at all, so there was no correct answer on this task. In his first experiment, Sherif asked individual participants to estimate, over a series of trials, how far the light moved. The pattern of responses was nearly identical for all participants; initially, their estimates were quite variable, but over time they settled on a single estimate, such as 3 inches. In the next experiment, Sherif asked pairs of participants to estimate, over a series of trials, how far the light moved. Again, the pattern of responses for each pair was nearly the same—variability in their initial estimates, then convergence on how far the light moved. These experiments were important in showing how norms form. Eventually, individual or pairs of participants formed a standard for how far the light moved. In Sherif's third experiment, he sought to determine whether people could be persuaded to conform to the judgment of another person. Participants in this experiment made judgments in groups of two. In reality, only one of those in each pair was a real participant; the other was a confederate of the researcher. The confederate was asked to make estimates either lower or higher than the real participant. Over time, the participant began to make estimates closer to the estimates of the confederate, suggesting participants were conforming to the standards set by the confederate. These experiments were important in demonstrating that, in ambiguous situations where there is no correct answer, people tend to conform to a norm. Another researcher, Asch (1955), wondered whether participants would be as likely to conform when the situation was not so ambiguous—that is, when there was a correct answer on a judgment task. To answer this query, Asch asked five participants to take part in a perceptual judgment task. The participants were shown a series of three lines, varying in length. Their task was to determine which of the three lines matched a target line. The task was designed to be unambiguous: there was clearly a correct answer. Each participant, in turn, was asked to indicate, aloud, his answer to the experimenter. In reality, the first four participants were confederates of the experimenter. The person sitting in the fifth position was the real participant. On half of the trials, they instructed the four confederates to give the (clearly) wrong answer. The question was whether the fifth (real) participant would also give the wrong answer. The results showed 75% of the participants went along with the group and gave the wrong answer at least once. Apparently, the pressure to conform was so strong that, even on this unambiguous task with a clearly correct answer, participants were willing to give an answer they knew was wrong.

Both these experiments are important in showing that people conform. But why do they? Research suggests people conform for two reasons: to be liked, and to be correct (Cialdini & Trost, 1998). In Sherif's (1936) study, people conformed because they wanted to be correct. One way to be correct is to gather as much information as possible before acting or making a decision. For example, one of the authors was recently in London and had to take a train to the airport. Not knowing where or how to buy a train ticket or where to board the train, she spent time observing what other people were doing. In doing so, she gathered enough information so that she was able to successfully purchase a train ticket and board the correct train. Whenever we use other people's actions or opinions to define reality, we conform because of **informational social influence**.

Conformity on the basis of informational social influence occurs whenever we are uncertain about the correct or appropriate action. In the Sherif (1936) studies, for example, the task was novel and ambiguous. Under these circumstances, the best course of action is to gather information from other participants, in order to arrive at the best answer. If we have a great deal of confidence in our knowledge or ability to make the right decision, then there is little reason to rely on others for information. Research suggests that when our motivation to be correct is high, we tend to conform more when we are uncertain about the correct answer than when we are certain (Baron, Vandello, & Brunsman, 1996).

In Asch's study (1955), people may have conformed not because they wanted to be correct, but because they wanted to be liked; this is called **normative social influence**. Sometimes, as in the Asch study, people clearly gave a wrong answer in order to be liked and accepted by the group. In these situations, the group has a powerful, if unspoken, influence over group members' behavior. In an interesting twist on normative social influence, two social psychologists investigated "jeer pressure," or the tendency to conform in order to avoid rejection from peers (Janes & Olson, 2000). When we observe another person being rejected by the group, there is a tendency to conform even more strongly to the standards set by the group, presumably to avoid similar rejection from group members.

Situational Conformity

If you think about your own behavior, there probably were times when you conformed or felt the pressure to conform more than others. Some aspects of a situation lead to more pressure to conform than others. These factors include the size of the group, group unanimity, commitment to the group, and individuation and deindividuation.

Intuitively, one would predict that the pressure to conform is greater as the size of the group increases. Early research (Asch, 1956) suggested that as group size increased, so did conformity – but only to a point. Once the size of the group reached about three members, conformity seemed to level off. But later research (Bond & Smith, 1996) suggests conformity increases up to a group size of eight members. So, it seems the larger the group, the greater our tendency to conform. Group unanimity is also important. Imagine being in the Asch line study—in which all the group members give the (clearly) wrong answer. Now, it is your turn to give your answer. What do you do? Asch's results suggest you would give the wrong answer at least once. But now imagine just one other member of the group gives the correct answer, one that disagrees with the other group members. Now, what answer would you give? Research (Asch, 1955; Morris & Miller, 1975) suggests conformity drops if there is even one dissenter in the group.

Groups with highly committed members are more likely to conform than members with less commitment (Forsyth, 1990). Obviously, highly committed group members want to be liked and accepted by other group members. One way to ensure being liked and accepted is to go along with the group.

One individual difference variable that predicts the tendency to conform or not is **individuation**. Individuation refers to the desire to be distinguishable from others in some aspect (Maslach, Stapp, & Santee, 1985; Whitney, Sagrestano, & Maslach, 1994). Some people have a greater desire than others to differentiate themselves. Those high in the desire for individuation are less likely to conform than those low in individuation. Conversely, **deindividuation** can increase conformity. When this occurs, people attribute their behavior to being part of the group's behavior and there is a diffusion of responsibility. People feel less responsible for their actions when those actions take place in a group context than they would if they committed those acts alone.

The Tulsa Race Riot, May 31–June 1, 1921

Mobs and riots are one of the most frightening and destructive instances of group behavior, resulting, in part, from situational conformity factors. One example of mob behavior with racist motivations occurred in Tulsa, Oklahoma, in 1921. At that time, Tulsa was home to the most prosperous Black community in the United States, called Greenwood. About 10,000 people lived in this 34-block neighborhood. It was separated from the White community by railroad tracks. Tensions between the Black and White communities increased in May 1921, when a Black man was accused of assaulting a White woman. Fighting ensued, and on May 31 a White mob pushed the Blacks across the railroad track and proceeded to burn down Greenwood. It soon became evident the Whites would settle for nothing less than the complete destruction of the Black community and every vestige of Black prosperity. They spread gasoline inside homes and businesses and set them on fire. Blacks fled; some were shot down while they ran, and some burned to death in the buildings. The Whites arrested any Blacks they caught but didn't kill. Before they burned, they looted and stole personal property. It still is not known whether the mob acted spontaneously, or was organized by the Klu Klux Klan (KKK), the police, or another entity. For the full story, read Tim Madigan's book, *The Burning* (2001).

Power

Implicit in our discussion of influence in groups is power. *Power* is the capacity to influence other people (French & Raven, 1959). In groups, power can be advantageous. Powerful group members can resolve group conflicts more efficiently than those with less power (Levine & Moreland, 1998), and powerful members are better liked and are deferred to more than less powerful group members (Shaw, 1981). Of course, having power can also serve as a disadvantage; those with power are granted the responsibility to be effective leaders (Hollander, 1985), exercising power can be stressful (Fodor, 1985), and it can lead to faulty perceptions of oneself and others (Kipnis, 1984). In this section, we examine the bases of power, as well as the reactions of group members to the exercise of power.

One of the most influential typologies of power is French and Raven's (1959; Raven, 1965) **critical bases of power**. The typology assumes that a group member's ability to exert power over another member or the entire group can be derived from one or more of the following kinds of power: reward, coercive, legitimate, referent, and expert. **Reward power** is defined as the ability to control the distribution of positive and negative reinforcers. In groups, there are many rewards: praise for good performance, money for work completed, and trophies for winning championships. Group members who control the distribution of those rewards are granted the most power. For example, teachers exert power over students to study hard because they control the distribution of good grades. Of course, the group member who controls the distribution of rewards is only powerful if the rewards are valued by the group member, the group member depends on the power-holder for the reward, and the power-holder's promises are sincere (Forsyth, 1990). When a power-holder is the only one in the group who can distribute rewards, their position as a power-holder becomes more secure. **Coercive power** refers to the capacity to punish those who do not comply with requests or demands. For example, if one country threatens another with attacks or boycotts, then the country is using coercive power. Teachers can use coercive power to get students to work harder by assigning extra work. Research suggests that given the choice of using reward or coercive power, most will choose reward (Molm, 1987, 1988). Those with **legitimate power** have a right, by virtue of their position, to require compliance. For example, when a military officer orders troops into battle, that officer is exerting legitimate power. With legitimate power, the power-holder has the right to exercise power, and the target has a duty to obey the power-holder. An interesting characteristic of legitimate power is the power-holder is typically chosen to occupy the position of power, granting them the support of the majority.

When we identify with someone because they are similar to us or because we want to be like that person, the person then possesses **referent power**. When a child imitates an older sister because the child wants to be like her, this is an example of referent power. Of course, advertisers make use of referent power when, for example, they encourage young people to purchase cigarettes by implying they will make them look like the attractive models in the advertisements. Special knowledge, skill, or ability one possesses can serve as a basis for **expert power**. Physicians, for example, are often afforded a great deal of power because of their knowledge and ability. Of course, expert power can only be exerted if the target of power is aware of the power-holder's special knowledge or talent (Foschi, Warriner, & Hart, 1985).

Reactions to the Use of Power

One of the goals of power exertion is to affect change. When one country threatens to attack another country if that country does not comply with certain demands, there is an expectation that the target country will change. Of course, other changes may occur in the target country as a result of the use of power tactics, including compliance, attraction, conflict, rebellion, motivation, and self-blame (Forsyth, 1990). **Compliance** occurs when a powerful member of the group asks a less powerful member of the group to do something, and the member does what is asked. This response is consistent with the *complementarity hypothesis* (Carson, 1969; Gifford & O'Connor, 1987; Kiesler, 1983), which suggests that when one person acts in a powerful manner, the other person will become submissive. Such a response also ensures the power-holder will retain their power. Of course, the complying group member need not change his or her attitudes or behaviors permanently. In fact, although a group member agrees to the demands or requests of the power-holder, this does not necessarily correspond to a permanent change in behavior or attitude (Kelman, 1958, 1961). It is only when the target of power internalizes the power-holder's views that a permanent change in behavior or belief occurs. Note that compliance is different from conformity, although both types of social influence can result in a change in behavior. Compliance involves behavior motivated by a particular request, and conformity involves behavior motivated by a need to be liked or correct.

Attraction is also affected by having power. A potential consequence of having power is not being liked by targets of power. In general, we tend not to like those who use power in direct and irrational ways (Forsyth, 1990). This is not to suggest we dislike all powerful people. Research indicates targets of power tend to like those who influence them via discussion, persuasion, or expertise more than those who influence them via manipulation, evasion, or threat (Falbo, 1977). Regarding the bases of power discussed earlier, research shows managers who use referent power are liked the most, and those who use coercive power are liked the least (Shaw & Condelli, 1986).

Another consequence of the use of power in a group is conflict and tension (Forsyth, 1990). Some types of power engender more conflict than others. For example, group members often respond to coercive power with anger and hostility (Johnson & Ewens, 1971), except in situations when the group is successful (Michener & Lawler, 1975), they have a trusted leader (Friedland, 1976), or the use of coercive power is normative for the group (Michener & Burt, 1975). One problem with responses that involve anger and conflict is that the functioning of the group may be compromised (Forsyth, 1990). One group member's anger can be fueled by another group member's anger, which can result in an escalation of anger and hostility. Research suggests if a group member abuses power, a typical response is **rebellion** on the part of other group members (Lawler & Thompson, 1978). Abuses of power can also lead to *reactance*, a feeling one's freedom was limited or taken away (Brehm, 1976). When group members believe their freedom (of choice, for example) has been removed, they respond by becoming defiant and refusing to go along with the leader (Worchel & Brehm, 1971).

Motivation can also be influenced when power is exercised in a group. Often, group members are motivated intrinsically—that is, they enjoy being productive and doing good work because they derive personal satisfaction from it. But if a leader uses reward or coercive power, which often involves the use of extrinsic rewards (e.g., money, promises), group members may become less motivated to work hard and do a good job.

In some circumstances, a leader might be so abusive that they cause group members to suffer tremendously. If group members believe the world is just, then they are likely to think they got what they deserve (Lerner & Miller, 1978). They might come to believe they deserve to suffer and engage in self-blame. A belief such as this allows suffering group members to make sense of their plight.

Group leaders exercise power in a number of ways. There are several bases of power, some of which are more conducive to certain situations than others. If group leaders can choose which bases of power to use, it behooves them to carefully consider the consequences. As we have seen, the use of power can engender many reactions, some of which can be good for the functioning and wellbeing of the group, but others detrimental.

Minority Influence

A final topic of interest for the study of social influence in groups is minority influence. Sometimes there are lone dissenters or a small faction of the group that will refuse to go along with the others. Of interest to social psychologists is the success of minorities in exerting influence. Research suggests minorities successfully influence majorities under specific circumstances (Kaarbo, 1998; Kaarbo & Beasley, 1998; Moscovici, 1985). First, for minorities to be successful in exerting influence on majorities, they must be consistent in their opposition (Wood, Lundgren, Ouellette, Busceme, & Blackstone, 1994). Members of a consistent minority are perceived as being more honest and competent (Bassili & Provencal, 1988). If they are inconsistent or appear divided in any way, then their influence is greatly diminished. Second, minorities are more successful if they are able to refute the majority's arguments successfully (Clark, 1990). Third, minorities are more successful if the issue is not of great personal relevance to members of the majority (Trost, Maass, & Kendrick, 1992). Finally, minorities are likely to be successful when they are similar to the majority groups in most respects, except for the disagreement at hand (Volpato, Maass, Mucchi-Faina, & Vitti, 1990). For example, if a member of the Republican Party were trying to convince other Republicans to change their views on homeland security, that member would be more successful than if the would-be persuader were a Democrat. In this case, the Republican dissenter is more similar (in terms of party membership) to the majority than is the Democrat.

Successful minorities may be able to change the position of the majority, which in the political realm may amount to a policy change. Short of affecting policy as a whole, they may be able to indirectly affect it through pressuring the majority to move in a particular direction, or affecting the information received by the majority. Finally, studies show minorities can improve the quality of a group's decision-making (Nemeth, 1986). Given the inter-agency nature of many government decision-making units, which makes the presence of minorities a frequent occurrence, understanding the role of minorities helps us to understand both change in policy and shifts in policy. Kaarbo and Gruenfeld (1998) point to a number of examples: change in Japan's foreign aid policy from one that emphasized Japan's self-interest to one reflecting humanitarian interest occurred because of a small minority in the foreign ministry, which was pitted against the large and powerful ministries of finance and international trade. Soviet policy toward Czechoslovakia in 1968 changed because of the pro-interventionist minority who, through manipulation of information and the decision-making process, moved themselves from the minority to the majority.

GROUP PERFORMANCE

One of the primary functions of a group is to perform a task, and one of the unique characteristics of a group is that its tasks typically are performed in the presence of others. For some groups, tasks are performed in the presence of other people, such as in a factory. For other groups, tasks require group members to depend on one another to successfully complete them, such as in an assembly line. In this section, we examine research suggesting that sometimes the presence of other people enhances performance (social facilitation) and at other times it hinders performance (inhibition).

Groups are often assumed to accomplish more than individuals and to perform better than individuals. Yet research suggests groups do not always perform better than individuals. We examine the various productivity losses in groups, including coordination and motivation losses. Finally, we explore some of the techniques used to help groups function more effectively.

Social Facilitation and Inhibition

Have you ever noticed that when you run a five kilometer race your time is always better than when you time yourself during training? Why is it the speech you gave in your communications class was better than when you practiced it at home by yourself? In some situations, we appear to perform better in the presence of other people than when alone, which is an effect known as *social facilitation*. One of the first experiments ever conducted in social psychology was designed to examine the effects of the presence of others on an individual's performance. Norman Triplett (1898) tested the hypothesis that people perform better in the presence of others than when alone. In his study, he had children play a game alone or with one other person. His results confirmed his hypothesis: when paired with another person, individual performance is better than when performing alone. This and subsequent research suggested that, if given a choice between working alone or in the presence of other people, we would be better off performing a task in the presence of others.

Now imagine another situation. You are playing on a basketball team. Your coach spends hours helping you learn to shoot a left-handed layup, which is not an easy shot for a right-handed person. When by yourself, you can shoot 20 left-handed layups easily. But what happens when you are playing a game in front of a cheering audience? Evidence suggests you would miss the layup. This effect, known as *social inhibition*, occurs when the presence of others inhibits performance. According to research in this area, we would be better off working alone than in the presence of others.

These two effects—facilitation and inhibition—seem contradictory. One suggests working in groups can enhance performance; the other suggests the opposite. Zajonc (1965) reconciled these two seemingly contradictory findings by arguing that the presence of others enhances performance on well-learned or simple tasks, but inhibits performance on difficult or novel tasks. The presence of other people enhances the tendency to display the *dominant* (well-learned) response and inhibits the tendency to suppress the *nondominant* response. Because running is a fairly simple task, the presence of others during a race should enhance performance. But shooting a left-handed layup when you are right-handed is a difficult task, so the presence of a cheering crowd or other teammates should hurt performance because our tendency is to shoot the ball with our right hand. A comprehensive review of research in this area basically confirmed Zajonc's perspective (Bond & Titus, 1983). The presence of others improves the quantity of performance on simple tasks and decreases the quality and quantity of performance on difficult tasks.

Zajonc's (1965) perspective explains when facilitation and inhibition occur, but why do these effects occur? What is it about the social situation that causes improvement in performance on simple tasks, but decreases performance on difficult tasks? Researchers in the area developed three explanations; arousal, evaluation apprehension, and distraction. Zajonc (1965, 1980b) argues that the mere presence of others increases the arousal level of the performer. When individuals are in a heightened state of arousal, the tendency to display a dominant response is increased. If the dominant response (shooting the ball with your right hand) is the correct one, then social facilitation occurs. If the dominant response is not the correct one, then social inhibition occurs. Cottrell (1972) agrees that the presence of others causes arousal, but he argues that the source of arousal is evaluation apprehension, or the anxiety created by the fear one is being evaluated. In a study to test this idea (Cottrell, Wack, Sekerak, & Rittle, 1968), participants were asked to work on a task alone, in the presence of others who were also working on the task, or in the presence of others who were blindfolded (and thus could not see what participants were doing). The results showed social facilitation occurred only when the others present could see the participant perform the task. When the possibility of evaluation was removed (in the blindfolded participants' condition), social facilitation did not occur. Finally, according to the distraction explanation, the presence of others is potentially distracting. When one is distracted, paying attention to the task at hand can be difficult. Such distractions create conflict as to whether to pay attention to the audience or to the task. When one is distracted, more effort is required to focus attention on the task, thereby improving performance on simple or well-learned tasks. When tasks are difficult, even the increase in effort is not enough to improve performance and usually leads to impaired performance (Baron, 1989; Groff, Baron, & Moore, 1983).

Productivity Losses

As mentioned previously, there is a belief that groups are more productive than individuals. More than likely, you were in a group that seems not to have lived up to its fullest potential. Clearly, groups are not always as productive as they should be. According to Steiner (1972), there are two reasons for process losses in groups. One is that the responses of individual group members are not combined in a way that enhances group productivity. Decrements in performance caused by poor coordination are known as *coordination losses*. In an operating room, for example, coordination losses occur if the surgeon is not handed the correct surgical instruments. Another reason for productivity losses is known as *motivation losses*. These occur when individual group members fail to exert their maximum effort on a task. The operating room team will not perform at its maximum level if one of the team members does not complete his or her assignment effectively. Although both coordination and motivation losses in groups are interesting, most attention has been paid to motivation losses. One such motivation loss that has received a great deal of attention is social loafing.

Social loafing refers to the tendency of group members to work less hard when in a group than when working alone. One of the earliest studies of social loafing was conducted by Ringelmann (1913), who found people exert less effort when pulling a rope or pushing a cart if they work in a group than if they work alone. In another interesting study (Latane et al., 1979), groups of six participants were asked to wear a blindfold, sit in a semicircle and listen (via headphones) to the noise of people shouting. Participants were asked to shout as loudly as they could while listening to the noise through their headphones. On some trials, participants believed they were shouting alone or with one other person. On other trials, they believed everyone was shouting. When participants thought they were shouting with one other person, they shouted 82% as intensely as when they thought they were alone. When they thought everyone was shouting, they shouted 75% as intensely.

Because social loafing can lead to severe performance decrements in groups, efforts are made to reduce or eliminate it. First, social loafing can be reduced if each group member's contributions are clearly identifiable (Hardy & Latane, 1986; Kerr & Bruun, 1981). When the possibility of being evaluated is evident, group members appear to give maximum effort (Harkins, 1987). Second, if group members find the work to be interesting and involving, they are less likely to loaf (Brickner, Harkins, & Ostrom, 1986; Harkins & Petty, 1982; Zaccaro, 1984). Third, if group members take personal responsibility for the group's outcome, then they are less likely to loaf (Kerr & Bruun, 1983). Group members need to believe their individual efforts will have an impact on the group's outcome.

Improving Productivity

In addition to efforts to reduce social loafing in groups, researchers developed techniques to help groups function more effectively and avoid production losses of any kind. One such technique is *team development*, which includes a variety of techniques, such as sensitivity training, problem identification, and role analysis (Dyer, 1987). Techniques such as these are designed to improve both the task and interpersonal skills of group members. A similar technique involves the use of *quality circles* (Marks, Mirvis, Hackett, & Grady, 1986). If group members engage in regular meetings to discuss problems with productivity and ways to solve the problems, then productivity losses can often be reduced. Another technique involves the use of *autonomous work groups* (Pearson, 1992). This technique involves the use of self-managed work teams who can control how tasks are performed.

Many of these techniques require groups to change how they function. There are also techniques that focus on individual group members. For example, in *participative goal-setting*, individual group members are responsible for setting the group's productivity goals (Pearson, 1987; Pritchard, Jones, Roth, Stuebing, & Ekeberg, 1988). Another technique, *task design*, involves changing the attributes of the task to make it more attractive to group members (Hackman & Lawler, 1971). Both these techniques involve changing group members' perceptions of the task, rather than the task itself.

GROUP DECISION-MAKING

The discussion of group productivity attests to the fact that groups are frequently called upon to perform a variety of activities. An important activity that groups—especially political groups—are often asked to do is to make decisions. Political groups are often responsible for making decisions with large-scale consequences, such as whether to send troops to a region in conflict or to escalate an existing conflict. As in productivity tasks, groups are often assumed to make better decisions than individuals. Groups can pool all the best resources that individual group members can offer. In this section, we examine the group decision-making process, including how decisions are made, the stages of group decision-making, and how individual resources are pooled; then we examine research on the effectiveness of individual versus group decisions. We also look at research suggesting that groups often make bad decisions, and finally, we explore some tactics to improve the decisions made by groups.

The Decision-Making Process

Imagine that a group of people, such as a jury, were assembled to make an important decision. A jury spends time listening to testimony and the presentation of evidence. When all the evidence is presented, the jury meets to discuss its verdict. At the end of their deliberations, which can last from a couple of minutes to weeks and months, the jurors reach a final, typically unanimous decision. From the perspective of an observer, the jury appears to leave the courtroom and magically return with a verdict. But what happened between the time the jury left the courtroom to deliberate and when they returned with a verdict? How did this group of people reach a decision about what should happen to the defendant? The group decision-making process has been studied extensively, and several models help us understand how groups arrive at a decision.

Three-Stage Model of Group Decision-Making

According to Bales and Strodtbeck (1951), groups proceed through a **three-stage model of group decision-making** before eventually arriving at a decision. In the *orientation* stage, group members spend time defining the problem and planning their strategy for solving the problem. Research (Hackman & Morris, 1975) suggests most groups spend little time in this phase, assuming planning is a waste of their time, but groups that spend a fair amount of time in the orientation phase are more successful (Hackman, Brousseau, & Weiss, 1976; Hirokawa, 1980). In the *discussion* stage, group members spend their time gathering information, identifying and evaluating alternatives. The amount of time groups spend in this stage is also related to the quality of the group's decisions (Harper & Askling, 1980; Laughlin, 1988). However, groups do not often make full use of this stage (Janis & Mann, 1977; Stasser & Titus, 1987). In addition, the use of information by groups at this stage is problematic, in that new information brought forth by one member of the group, but unknown to other members, is not fully considered in discussion. In fact, groups tend to "omit unshared information from discussions while focusing on information that all members already know" (Wittenbaum & Stasser, 1996, p. 5). In the *decision-making* stage, groups choose a solution. How groups combine the individual preferences to reach a group decision can be explained by understanding the group's social-decision scheme.

Social-Decision Schemes

Social-decision schemes refer to the process by which groups combine the preferences of all the members of the group to arrive at a single group decision (Stasser, Kerr, & Davis, 1989). If groups use the *majority-wins rule*, then they combine individual preferences by opting for whatever position is supported by the greatest number of group members. For example, if 10 of 12 jury members believe they should deliver a "guilty" verdict, then the group's final decision will be "guilty." In the *truth-wins rule*, group members tend to be persuaded by the truth of a particular position. This rule tends to be adopted when group members are discussing facts rather than opinions. Another decision scheme that groups use is the *first-shift rule*, by which groups tend to adopt the decision that is consistent with the first shift in group members' opinions.

Describing social-decision schemes from a research perspective may leave you with a sense that the process occurs without pressures or emotions, but pressures, such as conformity pressures, occur during this process—and they can be extreme. A book describing jury deliberations in a murder case, written by the foreman of the jury, describes the pressure put upon the only person reluctant to vote "Not guilty":

> Without pausing, I took the cards out of my pocket and passed them around ... There was silence as the cards started to come back, each folded in half. I counted them. Nine. We waited, and two more came in. Eleven. We waited. Still eleven. At this point there was no confusion about who still held a card. Adelle [the holdout] sat at the corner of the table to my left ... She was looking fixedly away, up, behind her, out the window. No one spoke ... One sensed everyone in the room concentrating on the blank card in rapt meditation. Adelle breathed audibly, wrote something rapidly on the card, closed it on itself, and pushed it into the middle of the table. I placed it, consciously and more or less conspicuously, at the bottom of the pile. I wanted the full dismay of the room to land on her if she had voted for a conviction.

> Then I began to open the cards and read them: not guilty, not guilty …
> And the last one: Not guilty.
>
> (Burnett, 2001, p. 166)

Emotions and Decisions

As you can imagine, people and groups make decisions for a variety of reasons ranging from the mundane (e.g., choosing the background on a print advertisement) to the serious (e.g., deciding whether or not to engage in a terrorist activity). As such, some decisions are made with weak emotion; others with quite strong emotions. One question that is useful to ponder is what effect emotions have on decision-making. The answer to this question is more complicated than it may appear on the surface. Research (Leith & Baumeister, 1996) on the effects of emotion on risky decisions shows when people are angry, embarrassed, or upset, they tend to make risky decisions, presumably in an attempt to gain a positive outcome, thereby offsetting or neutralizing the negative emotion. Why do people experiencing negative emotions make riskier decisions? The answer is that when people are angry, embarrassed or upset, their ability to cognitively process rational information is diminished. They appear to be less able to think things through and consider all possible outcomes (Leith & Baumeister, 1996).

Emotions also impact how people search for information when making decisions. Often, the quality of a decision is impacted by the amount of information a decision-maker uses. In addition, decision-makers typically strive for information-search efficiency, which refers to the amount of information gathered relative to the total amount of information available. As it turns out, a decision-maker's mood can impact how risky they are in their search for information. Blay, Kadous, and Sawers (2012) found that when decision-makers are in a negative mood, their information search efficiency improved when the risk is high. When the risk is low, however, being in a good mood impairs efficiency because decision-makers are less focused in their search.

So does this mean that people should not make decisions when they are feeling emotional? Not necessarily. Baumeister, Vohs, and Tice (2006) suggest that sometimes being emotional can lead to good decisions and sometimes bad decisions. What matters is the type and nature of the emotion. Some emotions are anticipatory in nature—that is, they are emotions people expect to feel once they made a decision. Consider a decision such as deciding whether to break up with your significant other. How you expect to feel once the break-up happened influences your decision about whether to initiate the break-up or not. Baumeister, Vohs, and Tice (2006) found anticipated emotion can have beneficial effects on decision-making because people are likely to base their decision on trying to achieve the best emotional outcome, such as feeling better or feeling good. On the other hand, one's current (as opposed to anticipated) emotional state can lead to poor decisions because people want to make a decision that will improve their mood or affect, thus causing them to engage in risky decisions. Current emotional states, if they are negative, motivate people to make decisions that will make them feel better right now. Such a strategy often causes people to make irrational and bad decisions.

Groups and Political Decision-Making Units

Political decisions are made in response to a perceived problem, and they tend to occur sequentially—that is, frequently a set of decisions is made, one after another, without pausing to evaluate the effect of each decision along the way. Decisions are also made by different actors, agencies, and coalitions. The type of group making authoritative decisions can impact policies. Hermann (2001) proposed a model of foreign policy decision-making by groups, which can also be used in domestic political contexts. She argued there are three types of decision-making groups, or units. The **predominant leader** group has "a single individual who has the ability to stifle all opposition and dissent as well as the power to make a decision alone, if necessary" (p. 56). The **single group** is a decision unit that includes "a set of individuals, all of whom are members of a single body, who collectively select a course of action in consultation with each other" (p. 57). This can be an ad hoc group set up to respond to a crisis, such as the Office of Homeland Security established by President Bush after the attacks of September 11, 2001, a standing bureaucracy (which Homeland Security eventually became), or an interagency committee. Finally, a **coalition of autonomous actors** is a decision unit composed of multiple groups that can act independently. U.S. trade policy, for example, is affected by a wide variety of domestic and international interest groups, multilateral organizations, government bureaucracies, and so forth. Each can act independently, and each has some impact at different times on decisions and policies.

Hermann (2001) maintains that each kind of decision-making unit has different decision processes and different behavioral patterns. The first two kinds of decision units can be analyzed with political psychological concepts. In the *predominant leader unit,* the most important factors affecting how the group behaves and makes decisions are the personality characteristics of the leader, which are discussed in Chapter 2. The *single group pattern* is determined by group psychology, particularly the techniques used by the group to handle disagreements and conflict in the group. There are three alternatives: groupthink (discussed in more detail later), wherein groups attempt to minimize disagreement by promoting conformity; bureaucratic politics, wherein group members acknowledge that disagreements will occur and attempt "to resolve the conflict through debate and compromise" (Hermann, 2001, p. 65); and, finally, the implementation of a social-decision scheme, discussed earlier.

Individual vs. Group Decision-Making

Evidence indicates that groups are not necessarily better decision-makers than individuals (Hill, 1982). According to Hastie (1986), whether groups make better decisions than individuals often depends on the characteristics of the task. On numerical estimation tasks, for example, group judgments tend to be a little better than the average individual judgment. However, on problem-solving tasks, such as logic problems, group solutions tend to be much better than average individual judgments, but worse than the best individual judgment. One of the keys to determining the superiority of group or individual judgments, according to Hastie (1986), is whether the task involves a demonstrably correct solution. When there is, groups tend to perform better than individuals. Some recent research indicates groups make better decisions than individuals when they have been working together for a long time, and the task is important to group members (Michaelsen, Watson, & Black, 1989; Watson, Michaelsen, & Sharp, 1991).

Individual solutions were also compared with group solutions in *brainstorming* tasks, which require participants to generate as many different suggestions as they can. Intuition suggests groups would perform better than individuals on brainstorming tasks (more people should produce more ideas), but research suggests individuals often produce more and better ideas when working alone than when working in brainstorming groups (Mullen, Johnson, & Salas, 1991; Taylor, Berry, & Block, 1958). Several explanations were offered for the failure of groups to perform as well as individuals on brainstorming tasks. First, when one group member is speaking, another is prevented from speaking at the same time, which often causes other group members to forget what they were going to say (Brown & Paulus, 1996). This situation might lead to a loss of ideas. Second, group members may have evaluation anxiety and fear their ideas will be ridiculed by other group members (Camacho & Paulus, 1995). As a consequence, they might be reluctant to share new ideas.

Consistent with the idea that groups often perform worse than individuals on problem-solving or brainstorming tasks is the notion that groups often make worse decisions than individuals. In fact, many group decisions in political history (e.g., the Bay of Pigs, the Vietnam War) suggest groups often make bad decisions with serious consequences. Researchers identified several faulty decision-making processes to describe some of the bad decisions made by groups, including groupthink, new group syndrome, bureaucratic politics, group polarization, and the **escalation of commitment**.

Groupthink

Groupthink refers to an irrational style of thinking that causes group members to make poor decisions (Janis, 1972). Janis argues that many major political decisions, such as the Bay of Pigs invasion, the United States' failure to defend against the attack on Pearl Harbor, the Vietnam War, and Watergate, provide evidence for groupthink. According to Janis (1982), there are a number of observable features of these groups proving the existence of groupthink. First, in all these decision-making groups, group members felt a strong pressure to *conform* to the group. There were strong sanctions for disagreeing with other group members or criticizing their opinions. Second, *self-censorship* was present in most of the groups. Although many group members may have disagreed with the decisions, they felt pressured to not express these disagreements openly. Third, *mindguards* in the group prevented group members from learning of new information that might disrupt the flow of the group's proceedings. Fourth, there was an *apparent unanimity* of opinion. All the group members seemed to agree with one another. Fifth, *illusions of invulnerability* allowed group members to feel confident in their decisions. Most group members believed their judgments could not be wrong. Sixth, *illusions of morality* prevented group members from ever questioning the morality of their decisions. Because this was an elite decision-making group, they believed all their decisions were moral and justified. Seventh, group members had a *biased perception of the other group*. In the Bay of Pigs decision, a decision by the Kennedy administration to sponsor a group seeking to overthrow Fidel Castro in Cuba in 1961, members of the President's advisory committee believed Castro was a weak and evil leader. Derogatory comments about Castro were frequently voiced during meetings. Finally, many of the decisions made by these groups represented *defective decision-making strategies*. Decisions made in groupthink situations are often described as fiascos, blunders, and debacles.

In addition to specifying the characteristics of the group and the group decision-making process, Janis (1972) specified the causes of groupthink. One cause is *cohesiveness*. When groups are very cohesive, as was the case in the Bay of Pigs advisory committee, disagreements are typically held to a minimum, creating the perfect conditions for faulty decision-making. Another cause of groupthink is *isolation*. When groups, such as the president's advisory committee, discussed top-secret issues, they did so in isolation, which prevented outsiders from entering the group to review deliberations. Another cause of groupthink is the presence of a *directive leader*, who controls the discussion and can prevent disagreements from being voiced. Finally, *stress* can also create symptoms of groupthink.

't Hart (1990, 1994) expanded Janis's concept and found that, in addition to groupthink being a product of high in-group cohesion under stress, it may also emerge because of anticipatory compliance by group members seeking to reach decisions they believe will meet the views or desires of powerful leaders or peers. Further, 't Hart notes that the situational conditions in which groupthink becomes most likely include situations of threat and stress (the context emphasized originally by Janis), and situations perceived by group members as major opportunities requiring rapid and major commitment to a pet project or policy to achieve major success (Fuller & Aldag, 1997).

Groupthink received mixed reviews (Levine & Moreland, 1998). Some studies supported parts of the model. For example, Tetlock, Peterson, McGuire, Chang, and Feld (1992) analyzed records of 12 different political decisions and found it was possible to distinguish between groups whose decisions were indicative of groupthink and those reflecting good decision-making. However, the research was not especially successful in locating evidence for all the factors thought to cause groupthink. Other work (Aldag & Fuller, 1993; Fuller & Aldag, 1997) suggested that research failed to provide convincing support for the existence of groupthink, and the model was an unnecessary constraint upon researchers seeking to adequately examine the true dynamics of group decision-making under the conditions explored by Janis. Indeed, Fuller and Aldag (1997), along with other researchers on political group dynamics (see 't Hart, Stern, & Sundelius, 1997), argue that scholars should unpack the various component parts from the model and embrace a wider range of new research and literature on group function and dynamics that better reflects the behavior of actual political decision groups.

New Group Syndrome

Another analysis of conformity problems in group decision-making is called *new group syndrome,* which is part of a collection of articles seeking to move beyond groupthink ('t Hart et al., 1997). Stern (1997; see also Stern & Sundelius, 1994) uses social psychological findings regarding the life-cycle of groups in a reexamination of the Bay of Pigs disaster, one of Janis's groupthink cases. Group cohesion, norms, status hierarchy, and strength of group identity all change as the group ages. With good performance, cohesion increases. With time, the status hierarchies and role responsibilities become clear and routine. Norms and accepted decision rules are internalized. When groups are new, Stern (1997) argues, members bring with them extragroup baggage, in the form of values, beliefs, and past experiences that affect decision-making. In addition, leaders are particularly important in the early stages of a group's life, and that is particularly the case when the leader is the president of the United States. At this stage, leaders can establish roles, norms, and group decision-making processes that lead to effective and critical policy option deliberation, rather than group conformity. Some leaders do this early on, but others do not, which leads to new group syndrome. When a leader does not establish norms and decision-making patterns, "there is a serious risk that group interaction will spontaneously evolve in a fashion leading to excessive degrees of conformity or conflict (an abrupt shift into the storming stage)" (Stern, 1997, p. 163). In this early forming stage, the group members are uncertain about how they should behave, are anxious to do a good job, and therefore are very vulnerable to conformity pressures if group leaders do not encourage the opposite by establishing roles, norms, and decision-making procedures. As an explanation of excessive group conformity, new group syndrome differs from groupthink in that it is not dependent upon situational pressures such as extreme stress. The phenomenon can occur in any group, in any context.

The Bay of Pigs fiasco showed evidence of new group syndrome. Kennedy was in office for only four months, and the plan came from the previous administration. Kennedy was under pressure to do something about Castro, and the advisory group he used was informal and interagency in nature. Kennedy campaigned against Republicans, in part on the platform that they were lackadaisical in confronting communism, and he swept away the previous administration's policy-making system. Stern describes the group culture in the decision-making group as follows:

> A number of analysts have suggested that a norm of "boldness" associated with the "New Frontier" mentality permeated the proceedings. Another important norm appears to have been "rally to the President" when his "project" came under the criticism of outsiders ... Another apparent norm that proved dysfunctional was "deference to experts." Finally, an emergent norm of deference to the leader is noticeable, a norm of which the president himself appears to have been unaware ... Kennedy, having little previous management experience, reportedly had a relatively simplistic view of small group and organizational management. He placed a premium on talent, believing that this quality was the key to achieving policy and political

> success. In other words, he believed that it was enough to assemble a number of talented people, throw them in a room together, and wait for good things to happen.
>
> (Stern, 1997, pp. 174, 177)

What he got instead was failure. The Cuban exiles, sponsored by the United States to invade Cuba and overthrow Castro, landed in a swamp, the Bay of Pigs, and were quickly captured by the Cuban military. The popular uprising against Castro, which they counted on in their plan to overthrow Castro, never happened.

Bureaucratic Politics

Another set of group-related decision-making problems plaguing political decisions consists of bureaucratic politics. Although political systems differ widely, many political decisions are affected by the interactions of groups based in governmental bureaucracies. Those groups have differing perspectives and interests; they see issues and problems differently, and compete for policy dominance and resources. At the same time, these groups interact in a variety of policy contexts and need to work together. Consequently, their interactions are often characterized as "pulling and hauling": bargaining, coalition formation, compromise, competition, and the selective use and sharing of information to enhance the position of the group or faction in question. The result is policy decision-making based upon organizational and group interests rather than on an objective assessment of the policy issue. The often-quoted phrase "Where you stand depends on where you sit" reflects this pattern.

Early studies of bureaucratic politics focused primarily on the standard operating procedures and conflicts among bureaucratic groups, both of which can negatively affect decision-making. The seminal study by Allison (1971) on the Cuban missile crisis of 1962 illustrated the impact of bureaucratic struggles in one of the most dangerous episodes of American foreign policy, which nearly led to nuclear war. Rather than maintaining a focus on the national interest, the bureaucracies fought continuously for control of the policy. In August 1962, there were increasing concerns in the Central Intelligence Agency (CIA) that the Soviet Union was placing, or would place, offensive nuclear missiles in Cuba. During the next month, these concerns spread, and the question of whether to send U-2 spy planes to take pictures of Cuba in search of missile sites was discussed. This was considered to be a risky enterprise because of the diplomatic fallout should a U-2 be shot down. Bickering between the Air Force and CIA over which agency would get to fly the U-2s over Cuba caused a 10-day delay in spotting the missiles. Those 10 days were crucial for the installation and arming of the missiles and made the conflict that followed, between the United States and Soviet Union, much more dangerous.

Other studies of bureaucratic politics focused more precisely on the group nature of decision-making in bureaucracies (Preston & 't Hart, 1999; Stern & Sundelius, 1997; Vertzberger, 1990). This enabled analyses of the whole range of decision-making patterns that can emerge from group

Optimal process				
Bureaucratic Consensus-making				**Bureaucratic confrontation**
Bureaupolitical oversimplification	←	(1) Reality testing Bureaupolitical deliberation	→	Bureaupolitical distortion
Bureaupolitical isolation	←	(2) Acceptability Bureaupolitical compromise formation	→	Bureaupolitical paralysis
Bureaupolitical haste	←	(3) Efficiency Bureaupolitical economy	→	Bureaupolitical waste

Figure 4.1 Bureaucratic Politics: The Normative Dimensions

interaction in bureaucracies—a range that spans from consensus seeking, the most extreme form of which is groupthink, to extreme intergroup conflict verging on bureaucratic warfare. Consensus and cohesion occur within groups, particularly when pressured by intense intergroup conflict. Hence, bureaucracies can be the site of a long continuum of group-produced behaviors (see Figure 4.1).

For example, Preston and 't Hart (1999) argue that the actual degree to which bureaucratic politics pervades the policy-making process is variable, and bureaucratic politics is a continuum in which such dynamics will have varying degrees of impact (both positive and negative) upon the quality of the decision-making process. They employ three criteria developed by George (1980) for evaluating the quality of decision-making on that continuum. The three criteria are *reality testing* (Does information get to the central decision-makers and are multiple options considered?), *acceptability* (Are relevant players involved in the decision-making group and are they listened to?), and *efficiency* (What are the costs of the decision-making process?). Preston and 't Hart (1999) argue that, at the consensus end of the spectrum, one sees the decision-making pathologies of bureaupolitical *oversimplification*, when reality testing is poor; *isolationism*, when acceptability is poor; and *hasty decision-making*, when efficiency is poor. On the extreme conflict end of the scale, one sees bureaupolitical *distortion*, when reality testing is poor; *paralysis*, when acceptability is poor; and *waste*, when efficiency is poor.

Manipulation

Manipulation occurs when a group member, often a leader, rigs decision-making, and may get a group to "accept a commitment which would have been rejected out of hand had the full implications and full extent of the project been revealed from the start" (Stern & Sundelius, 1997, p. 131). Manipulators use at least three strategies: they affect the group's structure so their allies dominate decision-making; they manipulate the procedures followed by the group by setting the agenda and framing issues in a particular way; and they manipulate their personal relationships with group members, both formally and informally, to put themselves in a favorable position to influence the decision's outcome (Hoyt & Garrison, 1997).

Group Polarization

Groups researchers are interested in whether groups make riskier decisions than individuals. Janis's (1972) groupthink model suggests groups take unjustified risky courses of action. Research on the *risky shift* phenomenon suggests decisions made by groups are often riskier than those made by individuals (Stoner, 1961; Wallach, Kogan, & Bem, 1962). But evidence also exists suggesting that groups sometimes make more cautious decisions than individuals (Wallach et al., 1962), and some evidence suggests that groups make both more risky *and* more cautious decisions (Doise, 1969).

Groups make both very risky and very cautious decisions compared with individuals. When in a group, there is a tendency to make extreme decisions. Whether the decision is extremely risky or extremely cautious depends on what position dominated at the outset of the discussion. **Group polarization** refers to the tendency for individuals' opinions to become more extreme after discussion than before discussion (Myers & Lamm, 1976). For example, if group member A's pre-group discussion opinion tended to be moderately cautious, then their post-group discussion opinion would probably be extremely cautious. Likewise, if group member B's pre-group discussion opinion was moderately risky, it will become even more risky after group discussion. Although there is a tendency to assume that extreme decisions, in either direction, are bad decisions, this is not the case. Extremely risky or cautious decisions can have positive or negative outcomes.

A number of explanations were offered to account for polarization effects. One explanation is based on the *persuasive arguments perspective*, which assumes people are likely to be exposed to persuasive arguments that favor their initial position (Burnstein & Vinokur, 1977). Although group discussions are likely to contain some arguments for and against an individual's initial position, there is a tendency to sample information that is consistent with our own point of view. Such biased information sampling is likely to shift a group member's opinion further in the direction of their initial position. Additionally, a group member is likely to share their initial position with the rest of the group. The mere expression and restatement of ideas may increase the shift toward a more extreme view (Brauer, Judd, & Gliner, 1995). Those members committed to a more risk-prone decision may be more committed, more vocal, and hence more influential in persuading others. However, as Vertzberger (1997) notes, when more cautious members are more committed, they can sway the group toward that pole.

Another explanation for group polarization is based on *social comparison* processes. According to this perspective, group members often compare themselves with others in order to gain approval for their views. Comparisons with other group members might lead to the realization that others have similar opinions and still others have more extreme opinions.

Motivated by a need to be viewed positively by other group members, individuals may shift their opinions to a more extreme position (Brown, 1974; Myers, 1978). Social comparison processes can be so strong that polarization is produced by merely knowing of others' positions, in the absence of exposure to supporting arguments (Isenberg, 1986).

A third explanation for group polarization is based on *social identity* processes (Hogg, Turner, & Davidson, 1990; Mackie, 1986). According to this perspective, group discussion causes individual group members to focus on the group, which can often lead to pressures toward conformity. Rather than perceiving the average opinion of the group, individual group members often perceive the group's opinion to be more extreme. Pressures to conform lead individuals to adopt a more extreme position than their initial position.

Escalation of Commitment

In making political decisions, people sometimes decide on a course of action that proves detrimental to the achievement of their goals. Both individuals and groups can become overly committed to these failing endeavors. Situations such as these have been referred to as escalation situations (Staw & Ross, 1989), or situations in which some course of action has led to losses, but in which there is a possibility of achieving better outcomes by investing further time, money, or effort (Brockner, 1992; Staw & Ross, 1987, 1989). Thus, there is still a glimmer of hope that, by investing additional resources, the project will become successful. Three characteristics define escalation situations (Staw & Ross, 1987). First, escalation situations involve some loss or cost. Second, there must be a lapse in time from the initial decision: escalation situations do not refer to one-shot decisions, but rather refer to a series of decisions made over time. Third, withdrawal from the situation is not obvious or easy. Countless examples of these escalation situations exist at both the individual and group levels (Ross & Staw, 1986). Individual-level examples include a person deciding whether to invest more money in a broken car or in a declining stock.

Decision-making during the Vietnam War illustrates the impact of commitment. In his memoir, former Secretary of Defense Robert McNamara reviews the debates within the policy advisory circles of the Johnson administration. The administration, under the influence of the *domino theory* prominent during the Cold War, believed that if South Vietnam were overtaken by the communist government of North Vietnam, regimes all over Asia would become communist as well, like dominoes falling. Yet the government of the South was corrupt and illegitimate, and the determination of the North, as well as of the Viet Cong (the guerrillas operating in the South) was clear. Important voices in the military warned that the administration's hopes in 1964—that the insurgency problem could be solved by bombing the North, thereby eliminating the need for U.S. ground troops—would not work. Bombing North Vietnam into oblivion would still not stop the Viet Cong's efforts to overthrow the government of South Vietnam. They also knew, from an intelligence report, that the chances of a stable South Vietnamese government emerging—one with popular support, which could pursue the war on its own terms—was very unlikely. As McNamara recalls:

> These two assessments should have led us to rethink our basic objective and the likelihood of ever achieving it. We did not do so, in large part because no one was willing to discuss getting out ... We ... wished to do nothing that might lead to a break in the "commitment dike" as long as there appeared to be some alternative... It is clear that disengagement was the course we should have chosen. We did not. Instead we continued to be preoccupied by the question of which military course to follow.
>
> (McNamara, 1995, pp. 154, 164)

They decided to pursue a course that led to a quagmire from which they could and would not extract themselves, a situation resulting in thousands of American and Vietnamese casualties, which would have been avoided by an earlier withdrawal of U.S. military forces.

Project, psychological, social, and organizational factors could all affect escalation behavior. Project factors are the most obvious determinants of commitment to a failing course of action. The manner in which a failing project is structured seems to influence whether an individual or group withdraws from it or persists. One such factor is whether a setback is the result of permanent or temporary causes (Leatherwood & Conlon, 1987). Commitment is more likely to escalate when the setback results from a temporary cause. In the Vietnam case, the focus on military options led the decision-making group to think a change in military strategy would work, and their inability to win the war was a temporary result of incorrect military strategy, rather than the result of permanent irremediable political realities. Similarly, when future costs required for the project's success are expected to be small, commitment is more likely to escalate (Brockner, Rubin, & Lang, 1981). Escalation of commitment can also depend on how often previous commitments succeeded (Goltz, 1992; Hantula, 1992; McCain, 1986). When previous investments are successful, people are more likely to escalate their commitment to a project, even when the project is currently failing. Commitment to a failing project is also more likely to escalate if the size of the initial investment is relatively large (Teger, 1980). Finally, escalation of commitment is stronger when the size of the payoff from continued investment is likely to be high (Rubin & Brockner, 1975).

There are also several psychological factors that can influence persistence in an escalation situation. Information-processing errors, for example, can be very important. Individuals often misinterpret or seek data in a manner that supports their beliefs (Frey, 1986), thus strengthening their commitment to a failing course of action (Bazerman, Beekun, & Schoorman, 1982; Caldwell & O'Reilly, 1982; Conlon & Parks, 1987). A related factor is the type of goal individuals set before initiating the project. If people do not set explicit goals about the maximum size of their investment (Kernan & Lord, 1989) or the extent of their commitment (Brockner, Shaw, & Rubin, 1979), then they are likely to escalate their commitment to a failing project. This pattern was also evident in Vietnam. The escalation of force was gradual and incremental, with no set limit on size or the point at which there would be an evaluation of the effort to determine whether it had failed, and no upper limit identified on how many U.S. troops would be committed.

Self-justification is another psychological factor that has been shown to influence commitment. Individuals often commit further resources to a losing course of action to justify previous behavior, such as advocating the project in the first place (Bazerman et al., 1982; Bazerman, Giuliano, & Appelman, 1984; Staw, 1976; Staw & Fox, 1977). Other research suggests conscientiousness also impacts whether individuals escalate their commitment. When individuals felt a sense of duty, they escalated less than did individuals motivated by an achievement obligation (Moon, 2001). Finally, groups whose members identify strongly with their group are more likely to escalate their commitment to a failing project than groups whose members identify weakly with a project (Dietz-Uhler, 1996).

Another set of factors that can influence the escalation of commitment is social in nature. One such factor is the need for external justification. Individuals or groups may persist in order to save face or avoid losing credibility with others (Brockner et al., 1981; Fox & Staw, 1979). Another factor that might influence persistence is external binding, which occurs when individuals or groups become strongly linked with their actions related to a project. For example, a project may become so associated with the primary decision-maker (e.g., Reaganomics) that withdrawal is difficult or impossible (Staw & Ross, 1989). Research on the "hero effect" found that, under some conditions, people who remain committed to a failing project are evaluated more favorably than people who withdraw (Staw & Ross, 1989).

Finally, structural or organizational factors can also influence commitment to a failing project. One such determinant of persistence is institutional inertia. Because change in an organization (especially a large organization) is often difficult, it may seem easier to persist in a losing course of action than to somehow mobilize the organization for change (Staw & Ross, 1989). Another organizational determinant of persistence is the operation of political forces. There may be strong political support for the continuation of a project, even though it is not economically feasible. Groups that are interdependent or politically aligned with a project may also demand support for it (Staw & Ross, 1989). Finally, cultural norms can affect the likelihood of escalating commitment (Geiger, Robertson, & Irwin, 1998; Greer & Stephens, 2001).

Escalation of commitment to a failing project is a robust phenomenon. Escalations of commitment were demonstrated in many laboratory and real-life situations, and many factors were shown to account for the phenomenon in such situations; what is so intriguing is that the decisions appear to be so irrational. From a rational point of view, it often seems the best choice in these situations is to withdraw and avoid greater losses. However, several researchers (Barton, Duchon, & Dunegan, 1989; Beeler, 1998; Beeler & Hunton, 1997; Bowen, 1987; Northcraft & Neale, 1986; Northcraft & Wolf, 1984) note that decisions to continue investment in a failing project are not necessarily irrational, at least from the perspective of the decision-maker(s). For example, Northcraft and Wolf (1984) and Whyte (1986) argue from an information-processing perspective that the manner in which decisions are framed determines whether individuals escalate their commitment to a failing project. If a decision is framed as a certain loss, then people tend to abandon the project. However, if a decision is framed as an attempt to recoup an investment, then people tend to escalate their commitment to the project. In escalation situations, decisions are often framed as an attempt to recoup an investment. Thus, to an outside observer, these decisions seem to be irrational but, to the decision-maker(s), they can seem quite rational because of the way in which they are framed.

Improving Group Decisions

Because the decisions made by groups are often disappointing, efforts have been made to develop techniques to improve groups' decisions. One suggested technique is to appoint a group member to serve as a *devil's advocate* (Hirt & Markman, 1995). The role of the devil's advocate is to disagree with and criticize whatever plan is being considered by the group. This technique can be effective because it encourages group members to think more carefully about the decisions they are contemplating. A related approach involves the use of *authentic dissent*, in which one or more members of the group will actively disagree with the group's initial plans without being assigned to this role (Nemeth, Connell, Rogers, & Brown, 2001). This technique can be effective because it encourages the group to consider alternatives and often moves the group away from its initial preferences.

A technique relevant to political decision-making is **multiple advocacy** (George, 1980; George & Stern, 2002). In this process, manipulation is avoided by having the deliberation procedures managed by a neutral person, a custodian manager, while the advocates of different positions are allowed to fully develop their proposals and advocate the advantages. Mutual criticism by the advocates of various proposals should, in theory, flesh out the strengths and weaknesses of the different policy options. This is done for the benefit of the final decision-maker, or chief executive (the president, prime minister, etc.), who listens, evaluates the options, and makes an informed decision. Many U.S. presidents tried to use this approach for improving decision-making in their administrations. In fact, the National Security Council (NSC), and particularly the national security adviser, evolved into the role of the custodian manager following its foundation in 1947. As George (1980) describes it, the NSC took on a number of tasks in its role as custodian manager:

1 balancing actor resources within the policymaking system
2 strengthening weaker advocates
3 bringing in new advisers to argue for unpopular options
4 setting up new channels of information so that the president and other advisors are not dependent upon a single channel
5 arranging for independent evaluation of decisional premises and options, when necessary
6 monitoring the workings of the policy-making process to identify possibly dangerous malfunctions and institute appropriate corrective action. (pp. 195–196)

Nevertheless, establishing and consistently using a multiple advocacy system to improve group decision-making is difficult, and many presidents fail to keep it alive. First, the custodian manager has to ensure a wide range of views and proposals are heard and the appropriate people are involved in deliberations. This is difficult to achieve, particularly given that this role is typically held by someone from the administration and therefore a person with their own political perspective and career, subject to pressure from many different agencies and individuals ('t Hart, 1997). For similar reasons, it is difficult for the chief executive to use the system. Choosing the best option is often impossible because of domestic or international political pressures and obstacles. Finally, some presidents, such as Ronald Reagan, do not want to hear debate and discussion of multiple options.

CONFLICT IN GROUPS

When people work together to achieve a goal, there will inevitably be some conflict, which occurs when group members believe their goals are not compatible (Pruitt & Rubin, 1986). Group members can conflict with one another in many ways. For example, conflict can arise if group members have to compete for scarce resources. Groups can also experience conflict when one member tries to exert influence or gain prestige in the group (Levine & Moreland, 1998). In this section, we examine the various types of conflict that can exist in a group, particularly in situations in which group members are motivated to both compete and cooperate. A discussion of the causes of conflict in groups follows; we then briefly examine the formation of coalitions in groups. Finally, we examine strategies designed to reduce conflict in groups.

Types of Conflict: Social Dilemmas

Much of the research on conflict in groups examines mixed-motive situations in which the motivation to compete is mixed with the motivation to cooperate. Perhaps the most famous mixed-motive game is the **prisoner's dilemma** (Luce & Raiffa, 1957; see Figure 4.2). Research of this type is used to determine how tendencies to cooperate and compete can lead to various outcomes for groups.

In this game, participants cannot communicate with one another, yet the outcome of the game for each person is contingent on what the other person decides. The game is set up so that: (1) if both players cooperate, they receive a moderately favorable outcome; (2) if one cooperates and the other competes, the cooperator receives an unfavorable outcome and the competitor receives a favorable outcome; and (3) if both players compete, they receive a moderately unfavorable outcome. In this situation, the dilemma is whether to compete or cooperate. The situation is rigged so both players benefit equally if they cooperate, but there is a tendency to not trust the other player, so many people compete (Pruitt & Kimmell, 1977). More recently, research on mixed-motive interactions used an N-person social dilemma, a social dilemma with more than two people (Levine & Moreland, 1998). In these dilemmas, several outcomes are possible. First, a player always benefits more from a noncooperative than a cooperative choice. Second, a noncooperative choice is harmful to others in the group.

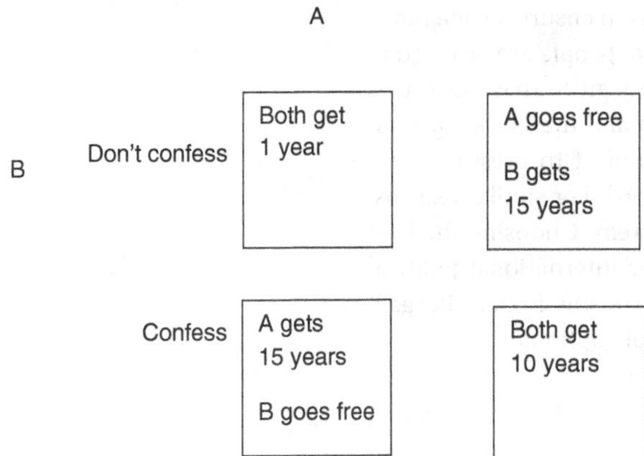

A
B
Don't confess
Both get
1 year
A goes free
B gets
15 years
Confess
A gets
15 years
B goes free
Both get
10 years

Figure 4.2 The Prisoner's Dilemma. In this classic game, two prisoners, A and B, both of whom are accused of a crime, have the options of confessing or not confessing. If they maintain their alliance and neither confesses, both get short sentences. If each of them confesses, they each get a heavy sentence. But if one confesses and the other does not, the prisoner who confesses is rewarded with freedom, while the one who does not confess gets a severely heavy sentence. The dilemma for each prisoner is that, if he or she trusts the other not to confess, the best option is to rat out his or her partner in crime.

Third, the amount of harm to others that results from a noncooperative choice is larger than the profit received as a result of any choice.

There are several types of social dilemmas (Messick & Brewer, 1983). In a **collective trap**, behaviors that reward individual group members can be harmful to the rest of the group, especially if engaged in by enough group members. For example, during a water shortage, individuals who use too much water harm everyone else by prolonging the shortage. The best strategy for the collective is if each individual takes a little. In **collective fences**, the entire group is harmed if enough people avoid costly behaviors. For example, if each person does not donate money to medical research, then everyone will be worse off. The best strategy is for everyone to give a little. In either situation, people are tempted to "free ride," or enjoy the group's resources without penalty. Research using collective traps and collective fences can tell us much about human tendencies to be selfish or prosocial, as well as how a person's value orientation (e.g., cooperative or competitive) can influence their behavior in social dilemmas.

Causes of Conflict

Conflicts such as social dilemmas typically arise when group members have competing goals or see their goals as being incompatible. There are many factors that can contribute to the origination of conflict, as well as to its escalation. In the previous chapter, the concept of **attributions** was introduced. They play a role in group conflict, as well as in individual perceptions. *Attributions* refer to the explanations generated for the causes of our own and others' behavior. Imagine playing a prisoner's dilemma game in which you realize that the best strategy is for you to cooperate, but your partner always seems to make the competitive choice. Why? You may generate many reasons why your partner makes the competitive choice: perhaps he does not understand the game; perhaps he was told by the experimenter to make consistently competitive choices; maybe he is just an evil person. Attributing the cause of another's behavior to dispositional, rather than situational, factors is the *fundamental attribution error* (Ross, 1977). If we blame another group member for conflict, it is likely to escalate rather than be resolved (Forsyth, 1990). Thus, if you blame your partner's personality for the competitive choices they make, then you are likely to also make competitive choices. People also tend to perceive their own views as correct and objective, but to perceive others' views as biased (Keltner & Robinson, 1997; Robinson, Keltner, Ward, & Ross, 1995). A consequence of this bias in perception is that we are likely to exaggerate the difference in perspective between ourselves and another group member, which is likely to serve as fuel for conflict.

Second, when in potential conflict situations, communicating effectively can be difficult. Sometimes group members criticize one another harshly. If you have ever been on the receiving end of harsh criticism, then you realize it can be unpleasant and uncomfortable. Such discomfort can often instigate revenge, which only serves to escalate the conflict (Cropanzano, 1993). If group members do not communicate reasonably and effectively, then conflict will likely occur and may even be escalated. One particularly destructive variant of faulty communication is *nay-saying*, a pattern in which group discussions are crippled and paralyzed by negativism and bickering over everything, down to the smallest details of a decision (Stern & Sundelius, 1997). Whenever conflict becomes stronger, so do anxiety and tension (Blascovich, Nash, & Ginsburg, 1978; van Egeren, 1979). According to the arousal/aggression hypothesis (Berkowitz, 1989), group members become frustrated when they are unable to attain their goals. Frustration can lead to aggression, which is often displayed by lashing out at other group members. If group members are aggressive, then conflict occurs and probably escalates.

Third, and more recent, are theories and research about the gendered nature of group conflict. Much of this thinking is based on principles of evolutionary psychology, which we discussed in earlier chapters. The primary idea of the gendered nature of group conflict is the experience and reasons for group conflict differ for males and females, and they do so because of different reproductive motivations for males and females. One of the hypotheses derived from this perspective is referred to as the "out-group male target hypothesis" (Sidanius & Kurzba, 2013). According to this hypothesis, in-group bias is more prominent for males than females. In other words, discrimination against out-group males is more pervasive and severe than discrimination against out-group females. For example, archival evidence shows Black males are six times more likely to be imprisoned than White males, while the disparity in imprisonment rates for Black and White females is about half of that rate (McDonald, Navarrete, & Sidanius, 2011). This and other evidence (see Sidanius & Kurzba, 2013 for a review) suggests that much larger gaps exist in discrimination against male than female out-groups.

Of course, this disparity in out-group discrimination against males and females begs the question "Why?" The answer lies in evolutionary psychology. Male aggression against out-group males appears to be motivated by aggressive tendencies and the desire to gather resources and status to present as ideal mates. The picture for females, however, is quite a bit different. Female motivation to discriminate against the out-group is rooted primarily in fear of sexual coercion and assault. An interesting study that led to this conclusion found females displayed more bias against out-group males when their risk of conceiving was at its highest level (Navarrete et al., 2009).

These ideas are consistent with the male warrior hypothesis that males form coalitions that allow them to plan and execute out-group aggression. McDonald et al. (2011) found males have a stronger desire than females to control and dominate out-groups, while female out-group bias is predicted primarily from their self-assessed vulnerability to sexual coercion. There seems to be ample support for the male warrior hypothesis, including findings that: (1) men discriminate against out-groups more than women; (2) men prefer group-based hierarchies more than do women; (3) males are more likely than females to defend their in-group; and (4) males are more likely than females to engage in intergroup competition and aggression (McDonald, Navarrete, & Van Vugt, 2012). Consistent with the male warrior hypothesis, the rationale for this hypothesis lies in the idea that group conflict affords males the opportunity to attract reproductive mates, property, and status, while for females, group conflict is largely avoided because it increases the opportunity and risk of being sexually assaulted by out-group males (McDonald, Navarrete, & Van Vugt, 2012).

Finally, in the review of the research on escalation of commitment, we learned that group members easily become committed to a course of action, even if it is a failing one. Group members can also become committed to their viewpoints, especially when they are under attack (Staw & Ross, 1987). There are several reasons. First, we tend to seek information to confirm, rather than refute, our beliefs (Petty & Cacioppo, 1986). Such action tends to make us even more committed to our beliefs. Second, in a public situation, there is often a desire to appear strong and have conviction in our beliefs. Third, once an individual commits to a belief, they rationalize their choice by overestimating its favorableness and increasing their dedication to it (Batson, 1975). Fourth, attacks from other group members can create reactance (Brehm, 1976), which occurs whenever we sense a loss of freedom. The consequence is that we become even more committed to our belief or position.

Coalitions

Conflicts exist between more than two group members. Sometimes, group members persuade other group members to join forces by forming a **coalition**, a small collection of group members who cooperate in order to achieve a mutually desired goal. Coalitions have a number of characteristics in common (Forsyth, 1990). First, they all typically involve group members who disagree on fundamental issues, but decide to set aside those differences and focus on the problem at hand. Second, they form for the purpose of achieving certain goals. Third, coalitions tend to be temporary, and there is often little commitment on the part of the participants, except to the current goal. Fourth, coalitions typically form in mixed motive situations, so group members who formerly competed with one another must cooperate to achieve the current goal. Fifth, coalitions are adversaries. The goal is to make sure that, in the end, they are better off and another coalition is worse off.

There are a number of theories put forth to explain when and why certain coalitions are likely to form. According to **minimum-resource theory** (Gamson, 1961, 1964), group members form coalitions on the basis of equal input–equal output; the most likely grouping of people is one that involves the fewest number of people with the fewest number of resources, yet is most likely to win. The theory makes two assumptions: (1) people in groups are primarily motivated by the need to maximize power and payoffs and believe forming coalitions will satisfy this goal; and (2) members of coalitions believe the distribution of power and rewards should be divided equally among the members.

Another theory that explains when and why coalitions form is **minimum-power theory** (Shapley, 1953). According to this theory, coalition members expect payoffs directly proportional to their ability to turn a losing coalition into a winning one. This type of power is referred to as pivotal power (Miller, 1980). In this theory, power, not resources, is the most important determinant of coalition formation. The pivotal power of any group member is determined by the number of times a member could turn a winning coalition into a losing one by withdrawing from the coalition. Thus, coalitions form on the basis of the highest chances of winning with the lowest amount of pivotal power.

According to **bargaining theory** (Komorita & Nagao, 1983), coalitions form on the basis of considering **expected payoffs**, which are based on norms of equity and equality, and group members will appeal to whichever norm provides them with the largest payoff. This theory assumes group members prefer to form coalitions with those who will not withdraw. It also assumes the amount of payoff may change over time, to compensate for extra rewards given to coalition members who are being tempted to join another coalition.

In addition to these theories of coalition formation, research identified other factors that influence the formation of coalitions, including the number and size of existing coalitions (Komorita & Miller, 1986; Kravitz, 1987), expectations of each group member in forming coalitions (Miller & Komorita, 1986), and the availability of other influence strategies that do not require the formation of coalitions (Komorita, Hamilton, & Kravitz, 1984).

CONCLUSION

This chapter has reviewed some of the central findings from psychological research on groups and their behavior. We also reviewed some of the key patterns of group behavior in politics, discussed how and why groups form, how they make decisions, and what problems arise in group decision-making. We examined intra- and intergroup conflict dynamics, and some techniques for conflict resolution. Several of the chapters that follow provide additional information and illustrations of group behavior. Chapter 5 provides examples of small-group dynamics in leadership management styles. Chapters 8, 9, and 10 provide examples of group behavior in cases of race, ethnic, and nationalist group conflicts. Chapters 9 and 12 look at the behavior of extremist groups, such as terrorist organizations, perpetrators of genocide, and others. They provide several illustrations of obedience to, and compliance with, group demands.

Topics, Theories/Explanations, and Concepts in Chapter 4

Topics	*Theories/Explanations*	*Concepts*
Definition of groups; central characteristics: size, composition, type		Entiativity
Group structure: status, roles, norms, cohesion; group formation	Expectation states theory; ethological theories; functional perspective; interpersonal attraction perspective	
Group development		Stages: forming, storming, norming, performing, adjourning
Influence in groups		Conformity
Conformity	Informational social influence; normative social influence	
Situational conformity	Group size; group unanimity; commitment to the group; individuation	
Power: reward, coercive, legitimate, referent, expert; minority influence		
Reaction to power: compliance, attraction, conflict, rebellion, motivation, self-blame	Complementarity hypothesis	
Group performance; social facilitation and inhibition	Arousal; evaluation apprehension; distraction	
Productivity losses; group decision-making	Social loafing; three stage model	
Groups and political decision-making units		Predominant leader; single group; coalitions

(*Continued*)

(Continued)

Topics, Theories/Explanations, and Concepts in Chapter 4		
Group decision-making	Groupthink; new group syndrome; bureaucratic politics; manipulation; group polarization; escalation of commitment	
Improving group decisions; conflict in groups		Social dilemmas; collective traps; collective fences
Causes of conflict	Faulty attributions; faulty communications; biased perceptions; personality; commitment; arousal and aggression	
Coalitions	Minimum resource theory; minimum power theory; bargaining theory	

Key Terms

- adjourning
- attributions
- autokinetic effect
- bargaining theory
- coalition
- coalition of autonomous actors
- coercive power
- cohesion
- collective fences
- collective trap
- common-bond groups
- common-identity groups
- compliance
- conformity
- critical bases of power
- deindividuation
- entiativity
- escalation of commitment
- expected payoffs
- expert power
- forming
- Fundamental Interpersonal Relations Orientation (FIRO)
- group
- group development
- group polarization
- groupthink
- individuation
- informational social influence
- legitimate power
- minimum-power theory
- minimum-resource theory
- motivation
- multiple advocacy
- normative social influence
- norming
- norms
- performing
- predominant leader
- prisoner's dilemma

rebellion
referent power
reward power
roles
single group
social-decision schemes
social loafing
status
storming
three-stage model of group decision-making

Suggestions for Further Reading

Brown, R. (2010s). *Prejudice: Its social psychology*. Oxford: John Wiley & Sons.

Forsyth, D. R. (1990). *Group dynamics*. Pacific Grove, CA: Brooks/Cole.

George, A., & Stern, E. (2002). Harnessing conflict in foreign policy making: From devil's advocate to multiple advocacy. *Presidential Studies Quarterly, 32*, 484–508.

Janis, I. L. (1982). *Groupthink: Psychological studies of policy decisions and fiascoes* (2nd ed.). Boston, MA: Houghton Mifflin.

LeBon, G. (1960 [1895]). *The crowd: A study of the popular mind*. New York: Viking.

Levine, J. M., & Moreland, R. L. (1998). Small groups. In D. T. Gilbert, S. T. Fiske, & G. Lindzey (Eds.), *The handbook of social psychology* (4nd ed., pp. 415–469). New York: McGraw-Hill.

Moscovici, S., & Doise, S. (1994). *Conflict and consensus: A general theory of collective decisions*. London: Sage.

Prentice, D., & Miller, D. (Eds.). (1999). *Cultural divides: Understanding and overcoming group conflict*. New York: Sage.

Preston, T., & 't Hart, P. (1999). Understanding and evaluating bureaucratic politics: The nexus between political leaders and advisory systems. *Political Psychology, 20*, 49–98.

't Hart, P. (1994 [1990]). *Groupthink in government: A study of small groups and policy failure*. Baltimore, MD: Johns Hopkins University Press.

't Hart, P., Stern, E. K., & Sundelius, B. (1997). *Beyond groupthink: Political group dynamics and foreign policy-making*. Ann Arbor, MI: University of Michigan Press.

Chapter 5

The Study of Political Leaders

The preceding chapters developed a number of important concepts, theories, and analytical frameworks in political psychology. We now examine important topics in political psychology and begin with a look at leaders. In this chapter, aspects of personality, cognition, and small group behavior, all considered in depth in the previous chapters, are brought together to explore political leaders' management and leadership styles. We begin with a consideration of types of leaders, and then explore several analytical frameworks. The case of President George W. Bush, and in less detail that of Donald J. Trump, will be used to illustrate the use of the concepts of leader analysis. The Political Being (see Figure 1.1) considered in this chapter is, of course, a leader. The elements of the Political Being of interest in this chapter are personality, cognition, emotion, and also the interaction with *us* (that is, political in-groups in the form of advisers).

We begin with an illustration of the importance of the personality of political leaders. In recalling the Cuban Missile Crisis, Robert Kennedy remarked that, "The fourteen people involved were very significant—bright, able, dedicated people, all of whom had the greatest affection for the U.S. … If six of them had been President of the U.S., I think that the world might have been blown up" (quoted in Steel, 1969, p. 22).

Robert Kennedy's chilling observation about the men within President John F. Kennedy's decision-making group (the Ex Comm, or Executive Committee of the National Security Council) during the Cuban Missile Crisis of 1962 dramatically illustrates the importance of personality and other individual leader characteristics in politics. What a leader is like in terms of personality, background, beliefs, and style of leadership can have a tremendous impact upon the policy-making process and its outcomes. In the case of Cuba, Kennedy's pragmatism, sensitivity to the needs of his adversaries, openness to advice and feedback from his staff, and his own extensive, personal foreign policy expertise led to a willingness on his part to debate the pros and cons of the airstrike option (which he initially favored), and to consider arguments in favor of the less-confrontational blockade option to remove the Soviet missiles. Within the decision group, Kennedy's collegiality enabled advisers to express their unvarnished opinions during Ex Comm sessions, and his desire for outside advice led to the inclusion within the group of several notable foreign policy experts from outside his administration. More

DOI: 10.4324/9780429244643-5

importantly, his willingness to consider the possible consequences of his policy actions, and his sensitivity to the need for his opponent (Khrushchev) to have a face-saving way out of the crisis, enabled Kennedy to successfully avoid war (Allison, 1971; Preston, 2001; Zelikow, 1999).

Would a different president have brought the same personal qualities or style of leadership to the situation? For Kennedy, the answer was clearly no. Among the Ex Comm advisers, there were many who lacked Kennedy's pragmatism, favoring instead an aggressive, immediate response to resolve the crisis. Others lacked his empathy towards Khrushchev and his awareness of his opponent's domestic political position. Some clearly had less need for information when making decisions, less desire to search out alternative viewpoints on policy matters, and far lower tolerances for dissent or disagreement over policy than Kennedy. Had any of these individuals been President instead of JFK, the outcome of the Cuban Missile Crisis might have been very different indeed.

In his classic book *Leadership*, James MacGregor Burns (1978), described two basic types of leadership: transactional and transformational. According to Burns, "leadership over human beings is exercised when persons with certain motives and purposes mobilize, in competition or conflict with others, institutional, political, psychological, and other resources so as to arouse, engage, and satisfy the motives of followers" (p. 18). This definition is significant because it distinguishes between relationships based upon "naked power" and those based upon "leadership." For Burns, true leadership involves a relationship between the leader and followers in which the leader taps the motives of followers to realize *mutually* held goals. This can take the form of either **transactional leadership**, where the leader approaches followers with an eye towards exchanging one valued thing for another (i.e., jobs for votes, subsidies for campaign contributions, etc.), or **transformational leadership**, in which leaders engage their followers in such a way that they raise each other to higher levels of motivation and morality. As Burns described it:

> Transforming leadership ultimately becomes *moral* in that it raises the level of human conduct and ethical aspiration of both leader and led, and thus it has a transforming effect on both. Perhaps the best modern example is Gandhi, who aroused and elevated the hopes and demands of millions of Indians and whose life and personality were enhanced in the process. Transcending leadership is dynamic leadership in the sense that the leaders throw themselves into a relationship with followers who will feel "elevated" by it and often become more active themselves, thereby creating new cadres of leaders.
>
> (Burns, 1978, p. 26)

On the other hand, the use of naked power is not leadership, but instead is based purely on a coercive, one-sided relationship with followers built upon a leader's own power position or resources (Burns, 1978). No exchange of valued commodities takes place and the followers' motives are irrelevant to the leader. Instead, the leader employing naked power enters into neither a transactional nor transformational relationship with followers, but merely forces them to comply with his or her own desires.

Later scholars such as Barbara Kellerman (1984) expanded upon Burns' explicitly moral, normative definition of transformational leadership by including the notion leaders can also tap into their followers' needs for authority or for the "security of a firm and coercive program" (p. 81). Thus, the transformation brought about by the leader can be elevating (as Burns argues) or debasing. In particular, charismatic leaders often embody for followers, by virtue of their unusual personal qualities, the promise or hope of salvation (or deliverance from distress) and, as a result, take on a transformational role. This relationship—in which the leader evokes such a strong emotional response that his misdeeds and mistakes are ignored or trivialized—can lead to elevation or disaster. If the charismatic leader is transforming, he or she will, according to Burns, capitalize on the strength of his followers' devotion and engagement to "raise the level of human conduct and aspiration." But another kind of charismatic leader—a Hitler, a Jim Jones—will lead his still-willing followers to destruction. Yet whether or not we who are outside the group judge the charismatic leader to be benign or malignant, the main point here is that the leader apparently emerged in response to some deeply felt group need or wish.

Are Leaders Born or Made?

A substantial debate in leadership studies has revolved around the issue of whether leaders are born or are made. The *"great man" theory of leadership* suggests people who become leaders are special—they have personal qualities or characteristics that set them apart from non-leaders. According to this line of thinking, Abraham Lincoln and Winston Churchill were special and would have become great leaders even in the absence of the crises during which they emerged (the American Civil War and World War II, respectively). On the other hand, the *situational (or zeitgeist) theory of leadership* holds that it is the context that is special, not the person, and the situation itself determines the type of leaders and leadership will occur. For example, this theory suggests that in the absence of the outbreak of World War II and Chamberlain's political humiliation by Adolf Hitler at Munich, Winston Churchill would have remained in the shadows and never risen to the rank of British Prime Minister. It was the particular nature of the times and the dire crisis facing Britain (i.e., the hardships of the blitz, Britain's isolation and lack of allies, and the danger of imminent invasion by Germany) that created the stage for the charismatic, strong, uncompromising Churchill to lead. Further, just as the war created the proper situational context for Churchill's leadership, the end of the war resulted in a dramatically altered context and his defeat in the first postwar national elections in 1945. Thus, the convergence of a unique situation with an individual whose personal qualities matched up well with the requirements of that situation led to the emergence of Churchill's leadership.

In fact, a useful distinction was proposed in the leadership literature focusing on the concept of *destructive leadership,* which is created by a "toxic triangle" of leader, followers, and environmental factors enabling it

Table 5.1 Five Features of Destructive Leadership

1	Destructive leadership is seldom absolutely or entirely destructive; there are both good and bad results in most leadership situations.
2	The process of destructive leadership involves dominance, coercion, and manipulation rather than influence, persuasion, and commitment.
3	The process of destructive leadership has a selfish orientation; it is focused more on the leader's needs than the needs of the larger social group.
4	The effects of destructive leadership are outcomes that compromise the quality of life for constituents and detract from the organization's main purposes.
5	Destructive organizational outcomes are not exclusively the result of destructive leaders, but are also products of susceptible followers and conducive environments.

Source: Padilla et al. (2007, p. 179).

(Padilla et al., 2007). This focus disagrees with Burns' notion that Hitler was not a leader by acknowledging the role played by followers and the environment in creating a form of destructive leadership, which is leadership nonetheless (see Table 5.1).

The toxic triangle leading to destructive leadership described by Padilla et al. (2007) is composed of three points: (1) *destructive leaders* (possessing charisma, personalized power, narcissism, negative life themes, and an ideology of hate; (2) *susceptible followers* (composed of either conformers or colluders); and (3) *conducive environments* (where instability, perceived threats, cultural values, and a lack of effective institutions or checks and balances provide a breeding ground for destructive leadership). Such destructive leaders may be narcissistic, dangerously charismatic, or simply have strong elements of psychopathy in their personalities, allowing them to be effective at rising to leadership positions and manipulating followers (Rosenthal & Pittinsky, 2006; Schouten & Silver, 2012). It is a form of leadership, albeit a destructive one.

Building upon and paralleling James MacGregor Burns' (1978) focus on leadership and followership are a number of studies in political science, especially in the field of presidential studies, dealing explicitly with the leadership (or management) styles of presidents and how these impact their interactions with advisers (followers). Although the primary focus of most of this work still rests squarely upon the personal qualities and characteristics of the leaders themselves, usually taking the form of discussions of types of presidential style, implicit in all of these discussions is the importance of the leader–follower relationship. This was illustrated in Chapter 2 where we discussed the presidential character studies of Barber (1972) (see also Burke & Greenstein, 1991; Campbell, 1986; Crabb & Mulcahy, 1986; George, 1980; George and George, 1998; Greenstein, 1982, 2000; Hargrove, 1988; Jones, 1988; Johnson, 1974; Porter, 1980; Pika, 1988; Haney, 1997; Preston, 1997, 2001). Beginning with Richard Neustadt's seminal *Presidential Power* (1960, 1990), which focused upon the personal rather than institutional presidency and emphasized the importance of the persuasive powers of presidents, the U.S. presidential literature began to focus much more intently upon the importance of leadership style. Indeed, this followed naturally given Neustadt's (1960, 1990) observation that, due to the inherent limitations on their institutional powers, presidents are forced to rely on their interpersonal skills and the art of persuasion to carry out their policies. Although this description of presidential power appeared at first glance to place individual presidents squarely into an institutional context that constrained most of their freedom of action, Neustadt's (1990) depiction of presidential power emphasized the fundamental importance of the *personal presidency* as well. Neustadt viewed the personal characteristics (or qualities) of presidents as critical to successful presidential leadership—and to the ability of presidents to obtain the kind of "personal influence of an effective sort on governmental action" that he defined as *presidential power* (p. ix). However, before they can persuade, presidents must formulate and develop their policies, gather and analyze immense amounts of information, adapt their strategies and policies to a rapidly changing political environment, and surround themselves with advisers and advisory systems capable of dealing with all of these difficult tasks effectively. Across all these areas, the individual characteristics of presidents play a critical role.

For Neustadt (1990), the personal qualities necessary for successful presidents were those traits found in *"experienced politicians of extraordinary temperament"*—those possessing political expertise and unpretentious self-confidence in their abilities, and who were at ease with their roles and enjoy the job (pp. 207–208). Noting that the presidency "is not a place for amateurs," Neustadt points to the importance of prior policy experience or expertise (pp. 152–153, 162). Further, Neustadt emphasizes the need for presidents to be active information-gatherers and to seek out multiple sources and differing perspectives on policy problems. This involves leaders cultivating enhanced sensitivity to the policy environment through both "sensitivity to processes" (who does what and how in the political environment) and "sensitivity to substance" (the details and specifics of policy) (pp. 128–130). The clear message from Neustadt's work is that the personal qualities of leaders play a significant role in successful (or unsuccessful) presidential leadership, and presidents who fail to effectively utilize their advisory systems, or lack appropriate *sensitivity to the policy context,* are unlikely to develop the foundations of power necessary to persuade anyone.

Indeed, reflecting upon the centrality of this leader–follower relationship, Greenstein (1988, p. 352) observes that, "Leadership in the modern presidency is not carried out by the president alone, but rather by presidents with their associates. It depends therefore on both the president's strengths and weaknesses and on the quality of the aides' support." Yet, across this broad literature, Hermann and Preston (1994, p. 81) argue there are five main types of leadership variables that appear to be routinely identified as having an impact upon the style of leaders and their subsequent structuring and use of advisory systems: (1) leader involvement in the policy-making process; (2) leader willingness to tolerate conflict; (3) leader's motivation or reason for leading; (4) leader's preferred strategies for managing information; and (5) leader's preferred strategies for resolving conflict.

The focus on types of leadership style, personality, or character in the political science literature can be traced back to Harold Lasswell (1930,

1960), who first argued in his classic *Psychopathology and Politics* that it was possible to classify leaders as particular types because, although leaders are different in fine details, important similarities are seen across leaders that allow us to argue two or more leaders are of the same type. For example, after Barber's (1972) active-passive/positive-negative typology of presidential character, perhaps the best known typology of presidential management style is Johnson's (1974) classification scheme. Johnson argued among modern-day presidents there were three management styles: **formalistic**, **collegial**, and **competitive** (see Table 5.2).

These management styles essentially established group norms, an important part of the group behavior presented in Chapter 4. The formalistic style (Harry S. Truman, Dwight Eisenhower, Richard Nixon) is designed to reduce the effects of human error through a well-designed hierarchical management system, which is non-confrontational, focused on issues rather than personalities, and oriented toward generating options and making the best decision. The focus of this style is on preserving the president's time for the big decisions. In contrast, the collegial and competitive styles emphasize less hierarchical organization. The collegial style (John F. Kennedy, Jimmy Carter, Bill Clinton) focuses on working as a team, sharing responsibility, and consensus-building, with an interest in generating options, openness to information, and reaching a doable as well as best decision. Leaders organizing their advisers around the collegial style want to be involved in policymaking, and are uncomfortable when they are not in the middle of things. On the other hand, the competitive style (Franklin Roosevelt) centers around confrontation, with the leader setting up an organization with overlapping areas of authority to maximize the availability of information and differing perspectives. The emphasis in competitive systems is upon debate and advocacy, with the leader playing the role of final arbiter.

Alexander George (1980) built on Johnson's work, abstracting out three stylistic variables that seemed to shape what presidential advisers do. The first, **cognitive style**, refers to the way the president gathers and processes information from the environment. Does the president come with a well-formulated vision or agenda that helps to shape how he or she perceives, interprets, and acts on information or is he or she interested in sounding out the situation and political context before defining a problem and seeking options? The way this question is answered suggests the types of advisers the president will have around him or her and the kinds of information the president will require to make a decision. In the first instance, the president seeks advisers and information supportive of his predispositions; in the second instance, he is interested in experts or representatives of his various constituencies who will provide him with insights into the political context and problem at any point in time. At issue in this second instance is what fits with the context: what is doable at this particular moment.

The second stylistic variable centers on a **sense of efficacy** or competence. Sense of efficacy for George relates to how the president's agenda is formed. The problems presidents feel most comfortable tackling and the areas they are most interested in are likely to dominate the agenda. If, like George Bush, the president feels more at ease with foreign than domestic policy, his presidency will probably favor foreign over domestic policy. If, like Ronald Reagan, he has an arena of problems that are of particular

Table 5.2 General Characteristics of Johnson's (1974, pp. 3–7) Typology of Formalistic, Competitive, and Collegial Management Styles

Management style	*Advisory system characteristics*
Formalistic (examples: Truman, Eisenhower, Nixon administrations)	Emphasis upon strictly hierarchical, orderly decision structures. Formalized staff system funnels information to top where leader weighs options on their merit. Emphasis upon technical over political considerations (underplays politics). Analytical and dispassionate advisers selected. Stress upon finding best solution to problems instead of working out compromises among conflicting views. Discourages staff conflict; emphasis on order and analysis.
Competitive (example: Franklin Roosevelt administration)	Relatively unstructured information network with leader placed in arbiter position among competing advisers with overlapping areas of authority. Leader thrives on conflict and uses it to stay informed and exploits existing political environment. Seeks aggressive advisers with divergent opinions. Encourages staff conflict as means of generating creative ideas and opposing viewpoints. Emphasizes bargaining over analysis with tendency to settle upon short-term solutions.
Collegial (examples: Kennedy, Carter and G. H. W. Bush administrations)	Emphasizes teamwork, shared responsibility, and problem solving within group. Advisers seen as colleagues who work as cooperative group to fuse strongest elements of divergent views. Leader has strong interpersonal skills and will work collegially with advisers rather than dominate group by pushing one position. Discourages staff conflict, encourages conflicting viewpoints, takes into account all sides of issues to forge solutions that are substantive and politically acceptable.

importance, such as building the military strength of the United States *vis-à-vis* the Soviet Union, these issues may dominate much of the time of his administration.

The third stylistic variable George calls **orientation toward political conflict**. How open is the president to face-to-face disagreements and confrontations among presidential advisers? The more open the president is to such debate and crossfire, the easier it is for the president to forge an advisory system exhibiting the characteristics of Johnson's competitive model; the more uncomfortable such a milieu makes the president, the more likely he or she will be to want an advisory system that either emphasizes teamwork (all of us work together) or formal rules (here are the gatekeepers who manage what gets to the president). George argues that this orientation tends to shape the president's dealings with the cabinet and the executive bureaucracy as well as the White House staff. It colors the way the president wants his or her advisory system to run. Moreover, it helps to define the type of control the president will want over the policy-making process and how much loyalty will be demanded from those around him or her. If conflict is to be minimized, the president needs to expend resources to keep it under control; one way to achieve such control is to choose advisers who are loyal to the president and serve for some time. If conflict can be tolerated and perhaps even used, the president may see high turnover among staff as egos are bruised or tempers flare. But advisers are more likely to be policy advocates and know what they want the president to do. Examples of presidents with low tolerances for political conflict include Richard Nixon and Lyndon Johnson. Indeed, Johnson's intolerance of dissent from advisers and desire for loyalty among advisers on policy lines adopted by the administration were defining characteristics of his Vietnam War policy style (Preston, 2001, 2012; Preston & 't Hart, 1999). On the other hand, Franklin Roosevelt's skillful use of a competitive management style provides the prototypical example of the leader high in tolerance of political conflict (George, 1980; Johnson, 1974).

Other scholars particularly interested in the presidency (Campbell, 1986; Crabb & Mulcahy, 1986; Smith, 1988) have contributed to what Johnson and George describe. These writers are interested in relational leadership style variables; they focus on what the president does *vis-à-vis* advisers and the bureaucracy. One such variable is the degree to which the president does business personally or through institutionalized routines. Is the president a hands-on person like Lyndon Johnson, who wanted to talk to commanders in Vietnam or the ambassador in the Dominican Republic about what was really going on, or more likely to want what comes up through the bureaucracy to be culled and organized before it gets to the presidential level for reflection? Anyone can become an adviser to the first type of president: the gatekeepers at the end become the advisers for the second type of president.

Another relational variable concerns how proactive versus reactive the president's policy-making is. Is the president interested in shaping policy and enlisting the aid of others in selling the policy, or is the president more responsive to what comes from others rather than searching out activities? The proactive president is more likely to want a loyal staff with similar predispositions who are sold on the president's program and ready to enlist support for it. Consider the staff that supported Reagan in seeking the release of American hostages in Lebanon by selling arms to Iran. The reactive president becomes more dependent on how others define and represent problems and the pressure they place on the president to act. The issues that the more reactive president focuses on are a function of who is on the presidential staff.

A third relational variable centers on distrust of the bureaucracy. How much does the president trust the executive branch bureaucracy to carry out the president's decisions and program? Those presidents like Nixon with an inherent distrust of what the bureaucracy will do to their policies often centralize authority so it rests with those they can trust, or they bypass the bureaucracy altogether by bringing policy-making into the White House and under their own control. With more trust of the bureaucracy comes more interest in recommendations from those further down in the hierarchy and more interest in interagency commissions and task forces. Two scholars writing about political leadership in general (Hermann, 1987; Kotter & Lawrence, 1974) have stressed several further leadership styles that can influence how advisers are chosen. The first focuses on the leader's preferred strategies for resolving conflict. Which of the following strategies does the leader generally use to resolve conflict among advisers: leader preferences, unanimity/consensus, or majority rule? Each strategy suggests a difference in the advisory system. If the strategy focuses on ensuring that the leader's preferences prevail, the leader is going to play a more forceful role in the proceedings than if the strategy involves building a consensus or engaging a coalition to make a majority. Consensus-building demands more of a facilitative role from the leader, while engaging in coalition formation suggests an emphasis on negotiation and bargaining with trade-offs and side payments. Moreover, the advisers the leader selects may differ with these strategies. If the leader generally wants his or her preferences to prevail, then he or she will probably seek out advisers who have a similar philosophy, are loyal, and predisposed to please. If consensus is the name of the game, the leader will seek out advisers who are also interested in facilitating the process of bringing different views together and more conciliative than confrontational. Advisers to leaders whose preferred strategy is coalition-building probably need skills at ascertaining where constituents stand and persuading others to join with them (Preston, 2001, 2011).

Another leadership style variable focuses on *social identity* and, given that true leadership involves getting followers to actually follow, scholars such as Haslam et al. (2011, p. xxii) suggest the need for an *identity leadership* approach in which leaders are: (1) seen as "one of us," or part of the in-group prototype; (2) seen as "doing it for us," or advancing in-group interests; (3) seen as actively "crafting a sense of us," by involvement as a skilled entrepreneur of identity in shaping a shared understanding of who the in-group is; and finally, (4) seen to be "making the group matter," taking in-group values and priorities and making them become reality. It is a view of leadership not necessarily the interaction between leaders and followers as individuals, but as group members (Haslam, 2001; Haslam & Platow, 2001; Haslam et al., 2011).

Also impacting leadership is the role played by individual beliefs and generational effects. Abelson (1986) warned that beliefs are like the cherished possessions leaders hold onto dearly before relinquishing them, which has significant implications for the types of political questions/environments likely to be salient to leaders and the goals and strategies subsequently adopted. These can take the form of operational code beliefs, various worldview beliefs about other countries (Rosati, 1987, 1990), or the relevance of historical lessons and analogies in framing current events or policy options (Dyson & Preston, 2006; Hagan, 2001; Khong, 1992; Neustadt & May, 1986). Common generational experiences among leaders, who share having lived through certain historical events/periods, the cultural norms and values of earlier times, and so on, often lead to disconnects or radical differences between older and younger leadership cohorts in countries (Jennings 2004; Strategic Assessment Group, 2003). For example, generations of leaders who came of age in Eastern Europe during the Cold War will have very different perceptions of their relationship to the United States and Russia than will a younger generation of leaders in the coming years who did not live through that conflict. Similarly, those in the older generation of Iranian leadership and clergy who took part in the revolution against the Shah in 1979 have a fundamentally different world-view from that of the majority of the current Iranian population that is 16 years old and younger, who were not even alive during that period—which would eventually be expected to impact policy (whether in terms of a new Green Revolution or a softening of the hard line of the original revolutionaries in Iran's foreign policy).

Indeed, prior experiences can significantly affect leaders' behavior, how they perceive their environments, and how they process information. For example, David Kay, the former UNSCOM weapons inspector who President Bush sent to Iraq in 2004 to lead the hunt for WMDs, was chosen primarily because of his preexisting beliefs (which fit the narrative being pushed by the administration at the time). But, while Kay's previous experiences in Iraq after the First Gulf War led him to believe strongly, prior to going, that WMDs were being hidden, once he was on the ground, his expertise as a weapons inspector quickly led him to the conclusion that none existed. Here, the individual difference of prior expertise on the part of Kay allowed him to modify his pre-existing views in the face of new evidence. In contrast, Vice President Cheney, with his own ideological beliefs and experiences from the First Gulf War (when WMDs were found), refused to accept the truth of this reporting, and CIA Director George Tenet literally told Kay he didn't care what he said, and he was always going to believe that there were WMDs in Iraq (Preston, 2011). This illustrates the difficulty of new information breaking through these strong beliefs, which in the case of Cheney and Tenet were truly cherished possessions, and the importance of expertise over ideology in allowing new, disconfirming information to be considered. Interestingly, during conversations with former Iraqi Foreign Minister Tariq Aziz, Kay was told Saddam Hussein was so convinced, given his own past experiences of the United States bombing for a while and then going away (and of not being willing to occupy Iraq in 1991), that the initial invasion of March 2003 was not really perceived for what it really was, with the Iraqi leader even ordering his front-line troops to not engage the Coalition forces because it was all a bluff (Preston, 2011).

Another interesting variable impacting leadership involves the physical and mental health of leaders, and how illness can influence their decision-making, policies, and styles of interacting with others (Post & Robins, 1993; McDermott, 2008). For example, the Shah of Iran's efforts to modernize Iran (the White Revolution) in the 1970s was intended to be a slow process, but his diagnosis of terminal cancer led to him to push for change more rapidly—resulting in instability and ultimately the Iranian Revolution and his overthrow (Post & Robins, 1993). Advancing age in leaders can sometimes result in lower capacities to deal with chronic stress, the need for medications can impact cognition, or hardening of the arteries, for example, impairs intellect, judgment, and emotional stability (McDermott, 2008). Examples of the impacts of health cited among scholars exploring this field of leadership include Hitler's and Stalin's extreme paranoia (a mental health issue perhaps brought on by physical ailments) late in their rule, Franklin Roosevelt's hardening of the arteries during the last years of his life (impacting his World War II decision-making), John Kennedy's Addison's disease and need for powerful painkillers to deal with his chronic back pain (impacting cognition), British Prime Minister Anthony Eden's bizarre behavior during the Suez Crisis in 1956 (possibly linked to amphetamine withdrawal), Ronald Reagan's Alzheimer's disease during his second term (impacting his cognition, engagement, and memory), and Woodrow Wilson's strokes (and earlier hypertension), possibly influencing his ability to achieve ratification of U.S. entry into The League of Nations in the U.S. Senate, and later his ability to govern at all (George & George, 1998; Link, 1996; McDermott, 2008; Park, 1993; Post & Robins, 1993; Weinstein, 1981). Clearly, the potential for leaders' personalities and styles to be impacted by underlying physical or mental health issues, drugs, or simple aging is a significant factor to be taken into account when assessing leaders at a distance (for scholars or practitioners), since these often have significant real-world consequences.

The last leadership style variable centers on the *general operating goal* of the leader—what is driving the leader to accept a leadership position. Why is a person interested in running for president? The type of goal indicates whom the leader is likely to seek for advisers. Leaders interested in a particular cause seek advocates around them; those interested in support seek a cohesive group around them; those interested in power and influence seek implementers around them; those who want to accomplish some task or change some policy seek experts around them. Advisers are sought that complement the leader's needs and facilitate the leader doing what he or she perceives needs to be done.

Thinking more broadly regarding the leader–follower relationship, Hermann, Preston, and Young (1996) propose a typology of foreign policy leadership style types for world leaders based upon three dimensions: (1) their responsiveness to (or awareness of) constraints; (2) their openness to information; and (3) their motivational focus (i.e., task/problem accomplishment versus interpersonal/relationship emphasis). As Table 5.3 illustrates, the dimensions result in eight specific foreign policy styles; expansionistic, evangelistic, actively independent, directive, incremental, influential, opportunistic, and collegial.

Finally, another typology of leadership style focused on two main dimensions: (1) the leader's need for control and involvement in the policy process; and (2) the leader's need for information and general sensitivity

Table 5.3 Leadership Style as a Function of Responsiveness to Constraints, Openness to Information, and Motivation

		Motivation	
Responsiveness to constraints	*Openness to information*	*Problem focus*	*Relationship focus*
Challenges constraints	**Closed to information**	*Expansionistic* Focus of attention is on expanding leader's, government's, and state's span of control.	*Evangelistic* Focus of attention is on persuading others to join in one's mission; in mobilizing others around one's message.
Challenges constraints	**Open to information**	*Actively independent* Focus of attention is on maintaining one's own and the government's maneuverability and independence in a world that is perceived to continually try to limit both.	*Directive* Focus of attention is on maintaining one's own and the government's status and acceptance by others by engaging in actions on the world stage that enhance the state's reputation.
Respects constraints	**Closed to information**	*Incremental* Focus of attention is on improving state's economy and/or security in incremental steps while avoiding the obstacles that will inevitably arise along the way.	*Influential* Focus of attention is on building cooperative relationships with other governments and states in order to play a leadership role; by working with others, one can gain more than is possible on one's own.
Respects constraints	**Open to information**	*Opportunistic* Focus of attention is on assessing what is possible in the current situation and context given what one wants to achieve and considering what important constituencies will allow.	*Collegial* Focus of attention is on reconciling differences and building consensus—on gaining prestige and status through empowering others and sharing accountability.

Source: Hermann, Preston, & Young (1996).

to context (Preston, 2001). Measuring the individual characteristics of past American presidents using the LTA technique, discussed in Chapter 2, Preston (2001) suggests that a leader's need for power and prior experience/ policy expertise in a given policy domain will shape how much control or involvement a president will insist upon having in the policy-making process. Indeed, as the psychological literature on the need for power suggests, individuals differ greatly in their desire for control over their environments, with some insisting on a more active role than others (see Table 5.4).

Table 5.4 Presidential Need for Control and Involvement in Policy Process

	Prior policy experience or expertise in policy area (general interest level of desire for involvement in policy)	
	High	*Low*
	Director	*Magistrate*
Need for power high	Decision-making centralized in inner circle; Preference for direct control and involvement throughout policy process; Advocate own policy views, frame issues, and set specific policy guidelines; Leader relies upon own policy judgments more than those of expert advisers.	Decision-making centralized in inner circle; Preference for direct control over decisions but limited need for involvement throughout policy process; Sets general policy guidelines, but delegates policy formulation and implementation; Leader relies more upon views of expert advisers than own.
	Administrator	*Delegator*
Need for power low	Decision-making less centralized and more collegial. Leader requires less direct control over policy process and subordinates; Enhanced roles of subordinates; Actively advocates own views, frames issues, and sets specific policy guidelines; Leader relies more upon own judgments than those of expert advisers.	Decision-making less centralized and more collegial. Leader requires little/no direct control/ involvement in policy process; Enhanced roles of subordinates; Delegates policy formulation and implementation to subordinates; Tendency to rely upon (and adopt) views of expert advisers in final policy decision.

In terms of the second dimension, Preston (2001) uses cognitive complexity and prior experience/policy expertise in the policy domain as indicators of a president's *general sensitivity to context* (i.e., general cognitive need for information, attentiveness and sensitivity to the characteristics of the surrounding policy environment and the views of others). As the literature on complexity and experience illustrates, individuals differ greatly in terms of their general awareness of, or sensitivity towards, their surrounding environments. Indeed, individuals vary radically even in their general cognitive need for information when making decisions; some prefer a broad information search before reaching conclusions, while others prefer to rely more upon their own existing views and other simplifying heuristics. As shown in Table 5.5, the leaders'

Table 5.5 Sensitivity to Context (Including Policy Environment, Institutional Constraints, Views of Subordinates)

	Prior policy experience or expertise in policy area	
	High	*Low*
Cognitive complexity high	**Navigator** High general need for information & interest in foreign policy (FP). Active collector of information from policy environment. Greater sensitivity to constraints and enhanced search for information and advice from outside actors.	**Observer** High general need for information, but limited personal interest in FP. Interested in information on policy specifics, but heavily dependent on expert advice. Reduced sensitivity to constraints on policy & less awareness of (search for) information and advice from outside actors.
Cognitive complexity low	**Sentinel** High personal interest in FP, but low need for information. Greater sensitivity to constraints and advice from outside actors. Seeks to guide policy along path consistent with own personal principles, views, or past experience. Avoids broad search for policy information beyond that deemed relevant given past experience or existing personal views.	**Maverick** Low need for information and limited personal interest in FP. Avoids broad collection of general information—decisions driven by own idiosyncratic policy views and principles. Reduced sensitivity to constraints on policy and less awareness of (search for) information and advice from outside actors.

cognitive complexity interacts with their prior substantive policy experience or expertise to produce an overall style regarding the need for information and sensitivity to external context.

Developed through empirical testing of its hypothesized relationships between leader characteristics and their foreign policy decision-making, and uses of advisory systems against the archival record in the presidential libraries, Preston's (2001) model produced a nuanced, composite style typology sensitive to differences in leaders across these two dimensions and differing policy domains (see Table 5.6). In other words, this allows presidents to vary from one another in more than just the one simple dimension of their need for control and involvement in the policy process—as in the typologies of Barber (1972), discussed in Chapter 2, and Johnson (1974)—but also in terms of their general sensitivity to policy information and context. In addition to providing greater variation in style types, the resulting typology provides greater analytical capability to study the impact of leadership styles across different policy domains by incorporating a more contingent notion of leadership style into the analysis of presidents. For example, a serious weakness of previous typologies was their firm roots in either foreign or domestic policy, with presidential styles generally appearing to be incompatible between the two domains. Although personality traits (i.e., need for power and complexity) are stable over time, and should impact presidential behavior regardless of policy domain (foreign or domestic), this is not the case for non-personality-based characteristics such as prior policy experience or expertise (McCrae, 1993; Winter, 1973). In the typology presented above, leadership styles for presidents vary across the foreign and domestic policy domains based upon the leaders' degree of prior policy experience in the particular area. Table 5.6 compares the composite leadership style designations for a number of modern U.S. presidents across both foreign and domestic policy.

Table 5.6 Composite Leadership Style Types

	Foreign policy	*Domestic policy*
Truman	Magistrate-Maverick	Director-Sentinel
Eisenhower	Director-Navigator	Magistrate-Observer
Kennedy	Director-Navigator	Magistrate-Observer
Johnson	Magistrate-Maverick	Director-Sentinel
Reagan	Director-Maverick	Sentinel-Maverick
G. H. W. Bush	Administrator-Navigator	Delegator-Observer
Clinton	Delegator-Observer	Administrator-Navigator
G. W. Bush	Delegator-Maverick	Delegator-Maverick
Obama	Administrator-Observer	Administrator-Navigator

(Preston, 2001)

AN ILLUSTRATION OF APPLICATION OF POLITICAL PSYCHOLOGY APPROACHES TO LEADERS

In the final section of this chapter, an illustration is provided to demonstrate how a number of the political psychological approaches discussed so far can be applied to a political leader, George W. Bush. Obviously, examples of all of the techniques discussed would be impractical given space constraints in a textbook. While some illustrations were provided in Chapter 2, a lengthy examination of Bush's characteristics using two additional approaches demonstrates the utility of leadership analysis for understanding the behavior of this president. This will be followed by an examination of the case of a more recent president, Donald J. Trump.

The Example of George W. Bush

Political psychological approaches to the study of political leaders range from those that make fairly general, simple predictions of overall styles of behavior to those providing much more involved, detailed analysis. An example of the former would be Barber's (1972) typology focusing upon the two dimensions of active/passive (i.e., how much energy presidents put into the job) and positive/negative (i.e., the personal satisfaction they derive from presidential duties), which we discussed in Chapter 2 with reference to Presidents Clinton, Bush, and Obama. Examples of more complex approaches would include more involved leader profiles using the LTA approach of Hermann (1999a), discussed in Chapter 2, or the style typology developed by Preston (2001).

Again using the example of Clinton, Hermann's (1999b) LTA technique, employing content analysis of leader interviews to produce profile scores along seven characteristics (i.e., need for power, locus of control, ethnocentrism, task-interpersonal focus, complexity, self-confidence, and distrust of others), suggests quite different style consequences for the two presidents. For example, in terms of Hermann, Preston, and Young's (1996; see also Keller, 2005) typology focusing on whether leaders challenge or respect constraints and whether they are open or closed to information, Bill Clinton (based upon his measured, moderate profile scores on need for power and locus of control) is seen as generally accepting (or respectful) of constraints, but under certain circumstances willing to challenge what appear to be inappropriate or unfounded limitations on his role (Hermann, 1999b, p. 3). As Hermann (1999b) notes, leaders with moderate scores such as Clinton's will work within the parameters they perceive to structure their political environment, and because of the limitations within which they perceive they have to work, building consensus and achieving compromise are important skills for a politician to have and exercise. Clinton's high scores on complexity and self-confidence suggested he is open to information, will be more highly attuned to feedback from the political environment, and will be much more active in monitoring his surroundings and gathering advice when making decisions. At the same time, such intensive monitoring of the environment for feedback and information before taking actions can lead outside observers to see a leader's behavior as erratic and opportunistic (Hermann, 1999b). In terms of the degree to which he is motivated by the problem or the relationship, Clinton's moderate score on task-interpersonal emphasis suggests he can direct his attention to the problem when that is appropriate to the situation at hand, or to building relationships when that seems more relevant; essentially shifting between these as called for by the context (Hermann, 1999b). As Hermann explains:

> Clinton's pattern of scores on the seven traits help us determine the kind of leadership style he will exhibit. By ascertaining that he is likely to (1) generally respect constraints in his political environment, (2) be open to, and search out, information in the situation, (3) be motivated by both solving the problem and keeping morale high, and (4) view politics as the art of the possible and mutually beneficial, we know from extensive research that Clinton will exhibit a collegial leadership style. His focus of attention is on reconciling differences and building consensus, on retaining power and authority through building relationships and taking advantage of opportunities to work with others toward specific ends. Clinton's leadership style predisposes him toward the team-building approach to politics. Like the captain of a football or basketball team, the leader is dependent on others to work with him to make things happen. Such leaders see themselves at the center of the information-gathering process. With regard to the advisory process, working as a team means that advisers are empowered to participate in all aspects of policymaking but also to share in the accountability for what occurs. Members of the team are expected to be sensitive to and supportive of the beliefs and values of the leader.
>
> (Hermann, 1999b, pp. 4–5)

Another approach to Clinton and Bush is Preston's (2001) typology of leadership style, which also makes use of the LTA technique to obtain scores for a president's need for power and complexity, but adds a measure for prior policy experience or expertise. In the foreign policy arena, Clinton, who scored low in need for power and prior policy experience but high in complexity, was classified as a Delegator-Observer. As a result, the typology would predict that while interested in policy matters, Clinton would require less direct personal control over the policy process, actively delegate policy formulation and implementation tasks to subordinates, and rely heavily upon the expertise or policy judgments of his senior specialist advisers when making decisions. On the other hand, his high complexity suggested he has a high need for information when making decisions. This would lead him to seek out multiple policy perspectives from advisers, engage in extensive research in the policy environment for information and feedback, and exhibit a more tentative, less decisive decision style that avoids rigid, black-and-white reasoning while focusing upon the shades of gray in issues. Clinton would be expected to demonstrate a pragmatic approach to policy issues and not rigidly adhere to a given ideological or political position if feedback from the policy environment suggested a different context.

Advisers would be drawn not only from those who share his views, but also from those who express varied and competing viewpoints.

In contrast, George W. Bush, who scores low in power, complexity, and prior policy experience, would fit the Delegator-Maverick style (the same style as Ronald Reagan). LTA profile scores for George W. Bush showed him to be low in cognitive complexity, but high in self-confidence and in-group bias (nationalism). Further, in terms of his prior foreign policy experience and degree of expertise in that domain, Bush scored low on both counts. As a result, Bush's foreign policy style was found in previous research to be one characterized by low sensitivity to the surrounding context, heavy dependence upon expert advisers (to whom most policy formulation/implementation tasks were delegated), a closed advisory system emphasizing limited search for information or divergent viewpoints, and the assembly of like-minded advisers into the White House inner circle (Preston 2008; Preston & Hermann 2004. Moreover, Bush's low complexity scores suggested his own personal information processing style would be characterized by black-and-white, absolute categorizations of the surrounding policy environment, heavy use of stereotypes and analogies, a strongly ideological approach to policy and the framing of problems, and more uncritical adoption of preexisting images of other countries (Preston, 2001; Preston & Hermann, 2004; Dyson & Preston, 2006; Cottam & Preston, 2007). Further, such use of images by Bush would be expected to not only be uncritical of their fit to the existing policy environment (to which he is generally insensitive), but also be highly resistant to modification or reconsideration once adopted. Bush's high score on *in-group bias* (or nationalism) would be expected to further exacerbate this dynamic.

One consequence of Bush's extremely delegative nature is to enhance the potential for bureaucratic conflict over policy among subordinates (see, Preston & 't Hart, 1999; Preston, 2011). Bureaucratic in-fighting and conflicts over the shape of Bush's foreign policy were quite visible, pitting administration hard-liners like Defense Secretary Donald Rumsfeld and Vice President Cheney against the more moderate Secretary of State Colin Powell (Sipress, 2002; Zakaria, 2002). For example, Powell's efforts to pursue mediation to break the deadlock between the Israelis and the Palestinians were repeatedly undercut and blocked by Bush's more influential hardline advisers (Preston, 2011; Sipress, 2002). As a result of this in-fighting, Bush's foreign policy in the Middle East and elsewhere was inconsistent and at times incoherent (Duffy, 2002; Preston, 2011; Sanger, 2002). Similar conflicts occurred between Powell, Rumsfeld, and Cheney over policy towards Iraq, North Korea, the United Nations, and over continued U.S. commitments to international agreements. Further, Bush's own personal dislike of conflict and controversy, along with his lack of substantive policy knowledge, made it difficult for him to end these adviser conflicts (Preston, 2011). Instead, Bush sought the comfort zone provided by those advisers (principally Rumsfeld and Cheney) who shared his own ideological beliefs and was usually more influenced by their advice. This often resulted in a rather closed information-gathering advice system, where the more hard-line inner circle excluded the participation of Powell or external actors who differed with them over policy.

Bush also tended to see the world in stark, undifferentiated terms, a pattern complicated by his often-reported lack of attention to the details of policy (Bruni, 2002; Mitchell, 2000). For example, Bush's categorization of Iraq, Iran, and North Korea as an axis of evil served to simplify three quite distinct regions and policy situations into a more easily understood, black-and-white frame for policy-making. After the events of 9/11, Bush's simple moral clarity about the world seemed to resonate with a changed political climate in America, in which good and evil seemed easily delineated. Making statements like "either you are with us or you are with the terrorists," Osama bin Laden would be brought back "dead or alive," the new struggle was between good versus evil, civilization versus anarchy, and a "crusade" on which America had now embarked, resonated with the American public, if not always with foreign publics (Buzbee, 2001; Duffy, 2002). As the administration's manipulation of evidence and extremely selective ("cherry picking") search for information to justify the invasion of Iraq in 2003 (and its subsequent conduct of the war since then) illustrated, Bush's advisory system strongly fit what his LTA scores predicted. Namely, it is best characterized as closed to information contradicting favored (often ideologically derived) policy conclusions, preferring simplistic analogies and images of opponents, and rigidly adhering to failing policies despite overwhelming, contradictory evidence from the surrounding domestic and international policy environments—to which he was largely insensitive (Alfonsi, 2006; Baker & Hamilton, 2006; Bamford, 2005; Fallows, 2006; Isikoff & Corn, 2006; Preston, 2011; Woodward, 2004).

Moving beyond the above discussion, which lays out how some of the many different types of political psychological approaches might explain or predict a political leader's behavior, we now take Preston's (2001) typology and discuss in a more detailed fashion the empirical evidence supporting its predictions to illustrate the application of such approaches to the study of the personality and styles of leaders. At the same time, it should be emphasized there are many available elaborations of the approaches discussed in this chapter in published research on political leaders that are worth examining in more depth. For example, several approaches were applied to Bill Clinton: the psychoanalytic approach (Renshon, 1996), operational code (Schafer & Crichlow, 2000), and Myers-Briggs (Lyons, 1997). All provide useful cues on the different dimensions of his personality or individual characteristics. Together, they provide a more nuanced, well-rounded portrait of a complex individual. None of the approaches alone provides all of the answers. Rather, the scholarship on personality and leadership across the literature provides multiple methods and approaches to the study of individuals across many differing dimensions. Such approaches can be applied to political leaders across cultural and national boundaries, as well as applied to non-leaders and individual citizens (see Hermann, 1984, 1987; Kaarbo & Hermann, 1998; Taysi & Preston, 2001; Winter et al., 1991).

George W. Bush as a *Delegator-Maverick*: A Case Study

Based upon his LTA profile scores, George W. Bush would be expected to exhibit the *Delegator*'s preferences for control and involvement in the policy process and the *Maverick*'s needs for information and sensitivity

Table 5.7 Expectations for the Composite Delegator-Maverick Leadership Style

Composite style (The Delegator-Maverick)	*Expectations: Leader style and use of advisers*
Dimensions of leader control and involvement in policy process	Relegative presidential style in which leader requires limited direct personal control over the policy process; Preference for informal, less hierarchical advisory structures designed to enhance participation by subordinates; Leader actively delegates policy formulation and implementation tasks to subordinates and adopts (relies upon) the expertise and policy judgments of specialist advisers when making decisions; Inner circle decision rule: Advisory group outputs and leader policy preferences reflect the dominant views expressed by either expert advisers or the majority of group members.
Dimension of leader need for information and general sensitivity to context	Leader has low need for information & advice, limited search for broad-ranging information, selective processing favoring information & advice consistent with existing beliefs, extreme dependence on subordinate advice. Leader is largely insensitive to external constraints on policy-making (due to lack of information gathering and reliance on simplifying frames (such as ideology) to gap-fill. (*Challenger*) Advisers selected based on loyalty & ideological fit with leader and his/her beliefs over expertise/competence. Decisions driven by leader's own idiosyncratic policy views, ideology, and principles. Heavy use of simplifying heuristics like analogies, ideologies, & stereotypes to frame the decision environment, assess its feedback, and consider policy options.

to the contextual environment in his foreign policy decision-making. Table 5.7 provides a summary of the composite *Delegator-Maverick* leadership style predicted for Bush in foreign affairs. In the following section, the predictions of the typology will be compared to the secondary literature on Bush, as well as interviews conducted with White House advisers from his administration.

In looking at the personal characteristics of George W. Bush, it is useful to note that, like Ronald Reagan and Lyndon Johnson, Bush saw the world in absolute, black-and-white terms and had hardly any prior experience or exposure to foreign affairs before entering the White House. In this, Bush exhibits a *Maverick* style as far as his *sensitivity to context.* On the other hand, in terms of his *need for personal control and involvement in the policy process,* Bush was far more interpersonally oriented (placing far more emphasis upon maintaining personal relationships) and was much lower in his personal need for involvement and control over policy-making. As a result, Bush falls into the *Delegator* style category, thereby heightening the importance of key, influential advisers around him in policy-making.

This becomes critically important as we consider the amalgam of Bush's quite hierarchical, centralized advisory structures that existed alongside his highly delegative style—a setup that at first glance would seem out of place. However, for leaders who require less personal, active engagement in policy and who lack their own personal policy experience, it is the *nature* of the delegation to subordinates that plays a major role in the shaping of the subsequent inner circle structures. For Bush, the trusted adviser to whom he delegated much of the transition-related organization and staffing of the White House was Dick Cheney, his eventual Vice President. Unlike Bush, Cheney's own personal style was very control-oriented and he developed probably the most powerful vice presidential staff organization in history to assert his control over policy. Indeed, Cheney falls into the *Director-Sentinel* style of leadership—one that emphasizes high control and engagement along with a moderate to low degree of sensitivity to context.

For the *Delegator-Maverick* Bush, the selection of a more hands-on, directive vice president was quite complementary to his style, allowing him to focus more upon the personal side of the presidency he enjoyed (while Cheney focused more on the task side). As a result, Cheney and other subordinates like Defense Secretary Donald Rumsfeld were allowed to play a quite powerful policy-making role in the administration, and given their loyalty and ideological fit with Bush, served to provide policy substance (or flesh) to the President's own, preexisting ideological views on policy. They would serve to frame (or explain) the policy environment for him, and largely formulate the types of policy choices the President would choose among during the decision process. And during the Iraq War policy-making process (both pre- and post-March 2003), this would have the consequence of limiting dissenting policy views and isolating the White House within a closed advisory system housing an insular inner circle at the top (Preston, 2011). It would encourage subordinates, who had been delegated substantial freedom of action, to compete with one another for influence with the President and over policy (e.g., Cheney's office or Rumsfeld's Pentagon competing with Powell's State Department over Iraq policy). Given Bush's style and the inner circle advisers he selected, the policy-making dynamics that would be seen within his administration over Iraq (and in many other areas) were largely to be expected, and were quite consistent with what was predicted (Preston, 2008; Preston & Hermann, 2004). Let us now explore these style effects on the President's inner circle in more detail.

The Importance of Loyalty in the Bush Inner Circle

One quality that certainly played a major role in defining George W. Bush's interpersonal style in the White House (and how he would structure his inner circle) was the heavy emphasis placed on loyalty—both in the expectation that staff would be unfailingly loyal to him, and his own belief that he should reward that loyalty with loyalty in return. It was a tendency the younger Bush shared with his father; it was a Bush family standard (Dowd & Friedman, 1990; Draper, 2007; Moens, 2004). It represented a kind of social contract for Bush, a two-way street of responsibilities between those he worked closely with and himself. And, as even the most ardent supporters of the administration acknowledge, within the President's inner circle loyalty and absolute fidelity to White House policy were unquestioned components (Burke, 2004; Moens, 2004).

Yet, while laudable on a personal level, the down-side of such an emphasis upon loyalty is that leaders tend (as a result) to surround themselves with political or policy doppelgängers who never provide healthy criticism or challenges to policy (or to the leader). The higher the degree to which loyalty is emphasized by leaders, the more likely they are to become insulated inside a phalanx of supporters and detached from a more healthy process, whereby negative (and potentially useful) feedback might reach the inner circle. In fact, many of the inner circle advisers surrounding Bush, even if they did influence the specifics of policy, did not markedly differ from the President's own predispositions (in terms of ideology, world view, etc.) (Preston, 2011). They generally tended to add flesh to the skeleton, not create the skeleton itself—with Rove, for example, being described by Heclo (2003) as providing experience and merely complementing Bush's own political mind. And among leaders who seek the warm cocoon of loyalty within their inner circles, one often also sees a lower comfort zone for dissent. As Gellman observes:

> Bush generally hated it when advisers disagreed, demanding that they get their acts together. At decision time, according to Cheney aide Ron Christie, Bush wanted to hear that "your senior advisers believe X" ... Bush valued not only consensus but finality. "Once he's made up his mind, controversy ceases, so getting to him at just the right time is extremely important."
>
> (Gellman, 2008, p. 79)

Moreover, an emphasis on loyalty also results in leaders often selecting subordinates for roles in their administrations based more upon that dimension than upon their competence, expertise, or prior experience dealing with a given issue or policy area. Unfortunately, this is often coupled with a slow response to making personnel changes, and an ineffective blame-avoidance response, when loyal, yet unqualified subordinates become political liabilities due to their ineffective or incompetent handling of policy problems. For Bush, this resulted in his hanging on to Secretary of Defense Donald Rumsfeld long after his mishandling of the Iraq War had become a major political liability in 2006, provoking even former senior military leaders to publicly criticize him. It also led Bush to stand firmly behind former FEMA Director Michael Brown during the Hurricane Katrina response and, much to his detriment, express publicly the belief that "Brownie" had done "a heck of a job"—despite obvious evidence to the contrary (Preston, 2008). Indeed, as one exasperated senior administration official observed, "the president thinks cutting and running on his friends shows weakness," even though politically it would have been the smart move (Baker, 2007).

Unfortunately, equating "conformity with existing policy" with loyalty on the part of advisers has the effect of allowing advice that disagrees with the existing policy line, even if only in terms of means to be dismissed by the broader group. In an echo of the Vietnam inner circle dynamics that occurred during the Johnson administration, different bureaucratic actors or advisers who disagreed with President Bush and his core inner circle's policy views on Iraq were not only dismissed, but viewed with hostility as opponents. As Assistant Secretary of State Richard Armitage noted:

> Tenet, the CIA, and the State Department were the hated enemies of the White House. They hated us! Because sometimes the intelligence didn't comport with whatever the bullshit the White House wanted to come up with. Or we would raise issues. So we were both seen, for different reasons, as not being on the team.
>
> (Preston, 2011, p. 28)

When it was observed that a lot of people would use the term "cherry-picking of information" to describe that kind of dynamic, Armitage replied:

> That's fair. Yeah. That's fair. See, I'm, by the way, I'm thrilled that they dropped us out of meetings! It speaks very well of us. For instance, on detainees and abuse, water-boarding. We were not even told there were meetings. Why? Because we raised objections.
>
> (Preston, 2011, p. 28)

The Need for Control and Involvement in the Policy Process

George W. Bush reveled in seeing himself as "The Decider" who made all the tough, final policy decisions, almost channeling his own inner Harry Truman to model his leadership image upon (Woodward, 2002). And it is certainly true that Bush often (though not always) made the final call on policy matters within his inner circle, much as Truman made the final decisions after staff brought him questions to be decided (Preston 1997, 2001). But such deciding does not necessarily require active presidential engagement in the policy-making process preceding the decision point (where policy formulation and the fashioning of options take place), nor does it preclude a heavy reliance on the leader's part upon expert advisers to frame the policy environment and provide options to decide among. Indeed, in the case of Truman these earlier elements were delegated to subordinates (like Secretary of State Dean Acheson), who would fashion policy and lay out the option(s) for the President to decide upon—while still preserving his final yea or nay (Preston, 1997, 2001). This was similarly the case with Bush, who retained the final decision authority, but delegated much of the policy formulation tasks to his tight inner circle of advisers. And as former White House press secretary Scott McClellan (2008, p. 154) observed, the President "liked to compartmentalize information within the White House.

There were regular meetings between the President and the Vice President, or Andy Card or Karl Rove that were strictly private." Indeed, in terms of the tightness of Bush's inner circle, Thomas and Wolffe (2005, p. 33) remark that he "may be the most isolated president in modern history, at least since the late-stage Richard Nixon." But unlike Nixon, who insisted on retaining a great deal of personal control over policy, Bush tended to delegate. And this would have a significant effect on policy-making, as Colin Powell's former chief of staff, Lawrence Wilkerson, later observed during an interview:

> Now, here's the point where I think he really failed, in a major sense! Not only was he a President who *believed* in being aloof from the details, being the "great decision maker" as he himself has said. The guy who makes the big ones. And then leaves them alone for execution. Not only was that his nature ... he was also lazy in my view. Intellectually, and what I would call execution-wise. And he'd say, "My decision's made! It's sacrosanct!" A certain amount of hubris and arrogance associated with this too. "No one would *dare* not carry out my decision the way I have conceived that decision!" But he may not have even articulated the way he conceived of that decision. He just made the decision. You know? And then the bureaucracy went out and did what it damned well pleased, usually with its own pre-dispositions and its own biases, and so forth. And the President had no *attentiveness* to that execution.
>
> (Preston, 2011, p. 29)

And just as would sometimes happen during the Truman administration, where bureau-political competition between lower level subordinates would determine how policy decisions were implemented (see Preston, 1997), this would also happen with the delegative style of Bush. As Wilkerson observed:

> A great case in point was when the brouhaha occurred over who made the decision to disband the Iraqi Army down to the lowest private. Well, the President had made the decision just a week or two earlier that the Iraqi Army would not be disbanded any further than battalion—about six to nine hundred men—those units would be kept intact. The brigade commanders, the division commanders, and their staffs maybe will go away, but the battalions and their people would stay, and they would form a new Iraqi Army. That's the decision the President made! Well, a couple of weeks later, without telling anybody, Jerry Bremer issues an order disbanding the Iraqi Army down to the lowest private. No one *knew* who made that decision! And the President *himself*, as far as I know, has made the same statement! I listened to him one day in an interview, and I think what I heard him say was, "I don't know who changed that decision."
>
> (Preston, 2011, pp. 29–30)

Off-the-record descriptions of the President by many former White House officials and other colleagues who knew him well tend to provide more support for an explanation based on his general lack of interest in details and delegation to subordinates. Indeed, Armitage recalls a presidential style that was highly delegative and not focused on the details of policy:

> I'll give you a couple of examples ... the President wanted to get out of the ABM Treaty. We wanted the Treaty of Moscow. Powell said, "I can get ya this. I can do this! Just keep the animals off my back basically." And the President, "okay." But there, he wasn't interested in the details, he was interested in the result, and we got it. We get to war planning and what-not, the President would always say to the generals, whoever they were, "You get what you need? You have what you need?" And they'd say, "yes" or "I need this." Generally, they'd say, "yes sir!," because Mr. Rumsfeld had brow-beat them so much. But he wasn't interested in the, what's it gonna be used for, etc. Part of it, I think, was what he's read about Vietnam. That Vietnam was run from the President's desk and all that, and you let the generals fight the war. It's gotta be both. The President commits young men and women to battle and then he wants to be sure that he's fighting in the best possible way. And Mr. Bush, in my view, took a very, too much hands-off view.... he wasn't steeped in details.
>
> (Preston, 2011, pp. 30–31)

The resulting combination of a President who saw loyalty as the first-and-foremost quality in advisers and wanted to be a decisive decider while tending to delegate substantially to subordinates is what characterized Bush's need for control or involvement in the policy *process*. While questioning whether Bush's national security adviser, Condaleezza Rice, really did an adequate job of calibrating for the President's "headstrong style of leadership" or "appreciate the need to keep his beliefs in proper check," McClellan (2008, p. 128) observes:

> Overall, Bush's foreign policy advisers played right into his thinking, doing little to question it or to cause him to pause long enough to fully consider the consequences before moving forward. And once Bush set a course of action, it was rarely questioned. That is what Bush expected and made known to his top advisers. The strategy for carrying out a policy was open for debate, but there would be no hand-wringing, no second-guessing of the policy once it was decided and set in motion.

But how do we reconcile the view of Bush as "The Decider" versus the image of him as a leader heavily influenced (or dominated) by the views of his inner circle advisers—two competing images around which much of the literature on his presidency revolves? Essentially, it could be argued that these debates between the two poles miss the fundamental point. Bush could be in charge of the final decisions and have similar world views to his inner circle advisers, yet still be dependent upon their judgment and expertise in formulating policy approaches and deciding upon courses of action. This is the difference between the caricature of a puppet (which no doubt was incorrect regarding Bush) and the more accurate depiction of a leader lacking experience in substantive policy areas who delegates to expert advisers and is dependent upon their guidance during the policy-making process. In this, Bush was hardly dissimilar from Bill Clinton, Lyndon Johnson, or Harry Truman in the foreign policy realm—as a president who leaned heavily upon his inner circle foreign policy experts (Preston, 2001, 2011).

Indeed, George W. Bush entered the White House as arguably the least experienced or knowledgeable about foreign affairs of any modern American president! Not only had he not traveled abroad to any significant degree (lacking even a passport until only a few years prior to his presidential run), but he possessed no real prior experience or knowledge of foreign policy matters. This lack of knowledge required a crash course under the tutelage of Condoleezza Rice during the campaign to try to avoid his obvious weakness in this area during the debates and in speaking with reporters on the trail. Soon, the campaign focused upon emphasizing the degree to which Bush would be surrounding himself with experienced policy experts if he were elected, such as his Vice President Dick Cheney, who had served in many capacities in Washington. Experienced advisers with names such as Rice, Colin Powell, Donald Rumsfeld, and others were described as individuals likely to play key roles in the new administration—roles that would compensate for the public's concerns about Bush's own relative inexperience. As Lawrence Wilkerson, Powell's chief of staff, observed, this emphasis being placed upon surrounding Bush with experienced advisers was critical because "it allowed everybody to believe that this Sarah Palin-like president—because, let's face it, that's what he was—was going to be protected by this national-security elite, tested in the cauldrons of fire" (Preston, 2011, p. 32).

And, as would be expected for an inexperienced leader, Bush tended to delegate substantial authority to subordinates and defer to his loyal, inner circle policy experts. During foreign policy meetings, Bush "often deferred to Cheney" on issues (Draper, 2007, p. 114), a pattern that he often repeated even in domestic affairs (where he also had limited substantive experience)—with former Treasury Secretary Paul O'Neill recalling that Bush "seemed to be limited in his knowledge of most domestic issues" (Suskind, 2004, p. 88). Indeed, for O'Neill, the problem was that:

> This President's lack of inquisitiveness or pertinent experience—Jack Kennedy, at least, had spent a decade in Congress—meant he didn't know or really care about the position of the U.S. government. It wasn't just a matter of doing the opposite of whatever Clinton had done, which was a prevalent theme throughout the administration. This President was starting from scratch on most issues and relying on ideologues like Larry Lindsey, Karl Rove, and, he now feared, his old friend Dick. Not an honest broker in sight.
>
> (Suskind, 2004, p. 126)

For O'Neill, it was clear that Bush often ceded significant authority over policy to others inside his administration and was clearly signing on to strong ideological positions that had not been fully thought through. But, of course, "that's the nature of ideology. Thinking it through is the last thing an ideologue wants to do" (Suskind, 2004, p. 127). As McClellan (2008, p. 85) would observe, because the President lacked "a deep background in foreign policy, Bush counted on a team of foreign policy heavyweights with diverse expertise to help him formulate policy based on his guiding principles, such as freedom, a strong military, and free trade." Unfortunately for a President who is less sensitive to context, having a team of heavyweights with diverse expertise only helps to compensate for a closed advisory-information gathering system if they also possess diverse viewpoints and perspectives. And this, the Bush inner circle lacked, with the exception of Colin Powell, who generally was ignored and whose influence was minimal when compared with the central core advisers such as Cheney, Rumsfeld, and Rice (Preston, 2011).

Bush's Sensitivity to Context/Use of Information

The *Maverick* style of Bush, with his low sensitivity to context and limited, highly selective information search, is one that is pretty well documented and reinforced by interviews with many former advisers, staffers, and individuals who briefed him (see Preston, 2011).[1] As would be expected for such a leadership style, the Bush inner circle was one in which diversity of views and wide information-search were severely constrained. Advisers within the inner circle tended to share very similar views (both politically and ideologically) and, as is typical within closed advisory systems, those with policy views or perspectives that challenged the prevailing ones within the core group were either ignored or never granted access. Where information search occurred, it often was highly selective, and sought out only material that supported existing policy or assisted in implementing or selling it politically. The *Maverick* style is also quite idiosyncratic, and certainly Iraq policy was driven from a basic foundation, an absolute view of the world, based within George W. Bush's own personal ideological beliefs. While it is true that Bush was extremely dependent upon his inner circle advisers to provide the details and substance of the formulation of policy, it is equally true that the basic directions which Iraq policy took were not divergent from the President's own personal views or beliefs. In this way, again, it is inaccurate to characterize him as a puppet of the neocons. Though they influenced his thinking and suggested paths to follow, these roads were not ones that Bush was disinclined to take. Moreover, typical of belief systems that are of the simple, black-and-white variety, leaders possessing them tend to be more decisive and confident in their own idiosyncratic policy choices, and see no need to search for lots of additional information or alternative viewpoints. After all, if you already see the world in terms of "you are either with us or against us," and you know what is right or wrong or true or false, the decisions are much more straightforward in your mind. And you don't need to gather information that challenges those absolutes. For the *Maverick* Bush, these elements played a central role in how the Iraq policy was developed and later implemented—and governed much of the inner circle dynamics governing the policy debate (Preston, 2011).

One of the characteristics normally associated with less sensitive leaders is their tendency to rely more upon their own idiosyncratic beliefs (whether these be ideological or religious) in judging situations, as opposed to gathering lots of varied information from multiple sources. Certainly, George W. Bush's general pattern fits perfectly into that description. As his former White House Press Secretary Scott McClellan (2008, p. 127) observed:

> Bush has always been an instinctive leader more than an intellectual leader. He is not one to delve deeply into all the possible policy options—including sitting around engaging in extended debate about them—before making a choice. Rather, he chooses based on his gut and his most deeply held convictions. Such was the case with Iraq."

Indeed, as Woodward (2002, p. 342) remarked, during interviews,

> the president spoke a dozen times about his "instincts" or his "instinctive" reactions, including his statement, "I'm not a textbook player, I'm a gut player." It's pretty clear that Bush's role as politician, President, and commander in chief is driven by a secular faith in his instincts—his natural and spontaneous conclusions and judgments. His instincts are almost his second religion.

This style of gathering information and making decisions has the tendency to often short-circuit policy debate and reduce circumspection on the part of leaders. And, as Baker (2007) notes, this certainly appeared to be the case with the way Bush interacted with his environment:

> To an extent, Bush walls himself off from criticism. He does read newspapers, contrary to public impression, but watches little television news and does not linger in the media echo chamber. "He does a very good job of keeping out the extreme things in his life ... He doesn't watch Leno and Letterman. He doesn't spend a lot of time exposing himself to that sort of stuff. He has a terrific knack of not looking through the rearview mirror." Rep. Jack Kingston (R-Ga.), who attended a legislative meeting with Bush last month, said his impervious nature works both ways. "The things that make him unpopular also help him deal with all the pressure ... He's stubborn. He's loyal to his philosophy."

This insensitivity to context, and more black-and-white manner of viewing the world, also contributed to a tendency that many former Bush administration officials noted during interviews, of a president who was relatively incurious (intellectually) about the details of policy beyond big picture or broad brush-stroke treatments of subjects. For example, former Treasury Secretary Paul O'Neill remarked that whether it was in large or small meetings, Bush tended to be relatively unresponsive and behave differently than had previous presidents he had served under, and related this experience briefing Bush on a detailed memo he had written on the economy:

> There were a dozen questions that O'Neill had expected Bush to ask. He was ready with the answers ... Bush didn't ask anything. He looked at O'Neill, not changing his expression, not letting on that he had any

> reactions—either positive or negative… . The President said nothing. No change in expression. Next subject. Certainly, each president's style is different. But O'Neill had a basis for comparison. Nixon, Ford, Bush 41, and Clinton, with whom he had visited four or five times during the nineties for long sessions on policy matters. In each case, he'd arrived prepared to mix it up, ready for engagement. You'd hash it out. That was what he was known for. It was the reason you got called to the office. You met with the President to answer questions. "I wondered, from the first, if the President didn't know the questions to ask," O'Neill recalled, "or did he know and just not want to know the answers? Or did his strategy somehow involve never showing what he thought? But you can ask questions, gather information, and not necessarily show your hand. It was strange."
>
> (Suskind, 2004, pp. 57–58)

But for those inner circle advisers who briefed Bush frequently, it was apparent that while the President would often engage more than O'Neill experienced, it still took the more limited form typical of leaders who don't look for the minutiae. Richard Clarke (2004, p. 243) recalls that "Bush was informed by talking with a small set of senior advisers" rather than casting his net more widely for advice, and that "early on we were told that 'the President is not a big reader' and goes to bed at 10." As a result, the type of advice Bush sought from his inner circle, or those who briefed him, did not lend itself to broad information-gathering or a focus on the details of policy. For example, McClellan (2008, p. 128) recalled that Bush believed "it's important for his advisers to think about specific actions in terms of larger, strategic objectives—how they fit into the bigger picture of what the administration seeks to accomplish." As Clarke (2004, p. 243) would later note regarding Bush:

> It was clear that the critique of him as a dumb, lazy rich kid were somewhat off the mark. When he focused, he asked the kind of questions that revealed a results-oriented mind, but he looked for the simple solution, the bumper sticker description of the problem. Once he had that, he could put energy behind a drive to achieve his goal. The problem was that many of the important issues, like terrorism, like Iraq, were laced with important subtlety and nuance. These issues needed analysis and Bush and his inner circle had no real interest in complicated analyses; on the issues that they cared about, they already knew the answers, it was received wisdom.

However, as one former White House official who worked for Bush for more than two years observed, "With argument comes refinement, and there was none of that … It's fine to say he's a big-picture leader and doesn't get bogged down in the details. But that's another way of saying he's lazy—not physically lazy, but intellectually lazy."[2] Indeed, Draper (2007, p. 416) noted that "most of all, Bush evinced an almost petulant heedlessness to the outside world." This detachment from the context and strategy of avoiding information would certainly not be one advocated by most business schools advising future CEOs. It is far more common for books on leadership in business to emphasize flexibility and the gathering of a variety of different kinds of information in order to make optimal decisions. Instead, according to several former White House officials, Bush generally preferred "short conversations—long on conclusion, short on reasoning," which often served to short-circuit the kinds of inner circle policy debates that fleshed out problems:

> In subtle ways, Bush does not encourage truth-telling or at least a full exploration of all that could go wrong. A former senior member of the Coalition Provisional Authority in Baghdad occasionally observed Bush on videoconferences with his top advisers. "The president would ask the generals, 'Do you have what you need to complete the mission?' as opposed to saying, 'Tell me, General, what do you need to win?'—which would have opened up a whole new set of conversations," says this official, who did not want to be identified discussing high-level meetings. The official says that the way Bush phrased his questions, as well as his obvious lack of interest in long, detailed discussions, had a chilling effect. "It just prevented the discussion from heading in a direction that would open up a possibility that we need more troops."
>
> (Thomas & Wolffe, 2005, p. 37)

Interestingly, a similar observation was made during an interview with Dr. David Kay, the former Chief UNSCOM inspector in Iraq, who briefed Bush several times on the search for Iraqi WMD:

> I briefed him directly twice on what was going on in Iraq (I met other times) ... And usually when you give a briefing you know where all the holes are in your own briefing. There's no briefing that doesn't have holes when you're dealing with something as complex as Iraq. And so you're prepared for the tough questions. Or you at least know that they're coming. In his case, he just expressed confidence... and all he said afterwards was essentially, "What else can we do for you?" ... Everyone whose dealing with a complex issue, and particularly if you go to the White House, everyone has their own agenda. Their own sets of issues. Things are *never* as good as you'd like the people to believe they are. And so, you expect ... I expected greater curiosity and skepticism from the President. And I got a lot less than I'd gotten when I was doing my own graduate work, or certainly than I gave my own graduate students when they would come in with it. And it was just not at that level, it was just a lack of intellectual curiosity as much as anything else. The questions, even later on, tended to be questions that went to, sort of personality issues, not to the deep factors that might be involved.
>
> (Preston, 2011, pp. 35–36)

Comparing Bush to Clinton, under whom he also served, Clarke (2004, pp. 243–244) observed that not only were there "innumerable differences between Clinton and Bush ... the most telling ... was how the two sought and processed information," with Bush wanting "to get to the bottom line and move on" while "Clinton sought to hold every issue before him like a Rubik's Cube, examining it from every angle to the point of total distraction for his staff." And in this comparison, one sees the difference between how the complex, highly sensitive to context Clinton sought out information (see Preston, 2001) and the pattern typical of less sensitive leaders like Bush. As McClellan would later observe:

> (Bush's) leadership style is based more on instinct than deep intellectual debate. His intellectual curiosity tends to be centered on knowing what he needs in order to effectively articulate, advocate, and defend his policies. Bush keenly recognizes the role of marketing and selling policy in today's governance, so such an approach is understandable to some degree. But his advisers needed to recognize how potentially harmful his instinctual leadership and limited intellectual curiosity can be when it comes to crucial decisions, and in the light of today's situation, it has become reasonable to question his judgment.
>
> (McClellan, 2008, pp. 145–146)

It should be emphasized again that this notion of *sensitivity to context* is completely unrelated to intelligence or IQ in leaders, and refers merely to how much they tend to differentiate in their environments and attend to information. Indeed, Harry Truman's less sensitive to context style was augmented by tremendous basic common sense and intelligence. Lyndon Johnson could be accused of being many things, but unintelligent would certainly not be among them. But like these former presidents, Bush shared with them a less sensitive, big-picture focus that was driven by a commitment to his own idiosyncratic policy beliefs (see Preston, 2001). As David Kay would later observe, during an interview recounting his experience briefing Bush on the ongoing problems impacting the search for WMDs in Iraq, his general style of information-gathering was definitely not detail-oriented:

> Certainly in my case, and what I observed, it was *very* broad-brush. It was like, ten thousand feet above the details. Now like I say, at one stage, I certainly appreciated this because I was trying to pick apart something that was very complex and I didn't know exactly what the shape of this elephant was either… I remember coming back, I guess it was in October, and talking to him. And … things were *not* going well in Iraq on the security problem. And that was affecting how we carried out our activities of discovering. And he was concerned about *safety*, but he wasn't concerned about *what does that mean*? What are the broader implications? Why is it like that now issues? And I remember describing to him that one of the hurdles we had in trying to find weapons of mass destruction was the vast amount of looting that took place immediately after the war. And he didn't show any curiosity at all in the extent of the looting, why it might have taken place, all of that. I mean, issues that, just for me, were of great concern

> and understanding, and I didn't find, I didn't have someone across the table that seemed to be that interested in it.
>
> (Preston, 2011, p. 37)

Indeed, as Armitage recalled about Bush, "he doesn't look around corners, in my view" (Preston, 2011, p. 37) And to some extent, as one senior official who played key roles in the 9/11 and WMD Commissions observed, this lack of interest in information (and divergent views) may be related to the lesson that George W. Bush took away from the electoral defeat of his father, the belief that this had occurred primarily because "he wasn't *enough* of a decider! He was *too* inclusive. He sought too many conflicting views" (Preston, 2011, p. 37). In fact, when Senator John McCain was asked by Brent Scowcroft whether Bush had ever asked his opinion on policy, McCain admitted, "No, no, he hasn't ... As a matter of fact he's not intellectually curious. But one of the things he did say one time is he said, 'I don't want to be like my father. I want to be like Ronald Reagan'" (Woodward, 2006, pp. 407–408). And while Henry Kissinger liked Bush personally, he told colleagues that it was not clear to him that the President really knew how to run the government. One of the big problems, he felt, was that "Bush did not have the people or a system of national security policy decision making that ensured careful examination of the downsides of major decisions" (Woodward, 2006, pp. 407–408).

Given Bush's absolute views of the world, there was almost a belief on the President's part that the policy clarity provided by his beliefs alone would allow his Iraq policies to succeed (and reduced his tolerance of information questioning that view). As a result, Bush had "little patience for briefings," often telling briefers to "speed it up, this isn't my first rodeo!" (Woodward, 2008, p. 408). Indeed, as Woodward (2008) reported from an interview with David Satterfield, who served as Senior Adviser on Iraq to Secretary of State Condaleezza Rice:

> If Bush believed something was right, he believed it would succeed. Its very rightness ensured ultimate success. Democracy and freedom were right. Therefore, they would win out. Bush ... tolerated no doubt. His words and actions constantly reminded those around him that he was in charge. He was the decider.
>
> (Woodward, 2008, p. 407)

In fact, Satterfield recalled that "it was difficult to brief him because he would interject his own narrative, questions or off-putting jokes," which meant "presentations and discussions rarely unfolded in a logical, comprehensive fashion" (Woodward 2008, p. 408). Moreover, Woodward (2008, p. 431) notes that for Bush, "his instincts are almost his second religion," and as a result, he "didn't want an open, full debate that aired possible concerns and considered alternatives. He was the 'gut player,' the 'calcium-in-the-backbone' leader who operated on the principle of 'no doubt.'" And this had implications for the types of advisers that Bush wanted around him, with the President noting to Woodward (2008, p. 431) that "I don't need people around me who are not steady ... And if there's kind of a hand-wringing going on when times are tough, I don't like it." In fact, one former aide remarked that no matter how many people Bush consulted, he heeded only two or three (Baker, 2007). A similar concern was expressed by former national security adviser Brent Scowcroft, who worried that "the White House was taking the wrong advice and listening to a severely limited circle" of like-minded advisers on Iraq (Goldberg, 2005, p. 57). For Scowcroft, the influence of Vice President Dick Cheney on Bush was seen as particularly powerful:

> The real anomaly in the Administration is Cheney ... I consider Cheney a good friend—I've known him for thirty years. But Dick Cheney, I don't know anymore ... I don't think Dick Cheney is a neo-con, but allied to the core of neo-cons is that bunch who thought we made a mistake in the first Gulf War, that we should have finished the job.
>
> (Goldberg, 2005, p. 57)

Indeed, the influence on Bush's thinking by his inner circle advisers was far more complex than just the standard neocon influence. Undoubtedly it was important, but not all the key players within the inner circle were actually neoconservatives. Agreeing with Scowcroft's interpretation, Powell's former chief of staff Lawrence Wilkerson noted during a recent interview that he didn't even think Bush was a neocon:

> I think there was an unholy alliance there between hyper-nationalists like Cheney and Rumsfeld, neo-cons like Feith, Bolton, Wolfowitz ... although Paul's in a category all by himself. And Bush's tendency to be evangelical and to be a hyper-nationalist himself if rubbed the right way. I think that all came together in this unholy conglomeration of decision making that haunts us still. Although Condi has attenuated it a lot.
>
> (Preston, 2011, p. 38)

But the less complex lens through which Bush tended to view his environment combined the President's own, quite personal, idiosyncratic beliefs (including his evangelical views) with those of hyper-nationalists like Cheney and neoconservatives like Wolfowitz to greatly shape Iraq policy. During a White House meeting on the Middle East with scholars and theologians, participants saw these characteristics in play in shaping how Bush viewed the world. One noted that "Bush seemed smarter than he expected," but that the discussion about the Middle East took on a predictable, low-complexity flavor, with "much of the discussion focused on the nature of good and evil, a perennial theme for Bush, who casts the struggle against Islamic extremists in black-and-white terms" (Baker, 2007). Similarly, Michael Novak, a theologian who participated, later remarked that "it was clear that Bush weathers his difficulties because he sees himself as doing the Lord's work" (Baker, 2007). In observing that Bush tended to lack intellectual curiosity and view things in absolute terms, Wilkerson noted that "I don't think you can get at Bush and his decision-making style, and some of the decisions he's made, without thinking about the evangelical aspect, without thinking about the spiritual aspect, in the sense that he gets advice from a 'higher authority'" (Preston, 2011, p. 39). But again, even those who worked for Bush quickly acknowledge that the President's views (and the influences upon them) were more complicated than simply his religious beliefs. As Wilkerson observed:

> The President did listen to a lot of voices. He had *pre-dispositions*, if you will, and those pre-dispositions if they were not fed by some of the voices—reinforced, confirmed by some of the voices—then the tendency was to quicker rather than later turn those voices away, or off, or not listen ... if the advice being rendered didn't fit, more often than not, with pre-conceived notions, then that began to taper off in its importance and ... his listening began to taper off too. Plus, the pre-conceived ideas were very hard to penetrate. Some have said, the most revealing remark about him was when he said he listened to a "higher father". And that had a lot to do with those pre-conceived notions. Someone, somewhere, in prayer at night on bended knee, had told the President, or indicated to the President, or the President felt he perceived that this was the right way to go. And come Hell or high water, he was gonna go the right way. It's my firm view ... strong view ... buttressed by some experience up-close-and-personal, but more, my 35 years in the government and understanding how these things work bureaucratically. That oftentimes, the pre-disposition was influenced not by God, but by Dick Cheney. And the fact that Dick Cheney is the most unprecedentedly powerful Vice President we've ever had. Steeped in defense, and military-industrial complex, congressional issues. The President isn't. He's the gray eminence, if you will, the President isn't. He's the guy whose done foreign policy before, national security policy, the President hasn't. He's the guy that goes into the Oval Office after everyone else has left and gets the last bite at the apple. So, I think a lot of the President's pre-disposition was not necessarily, exclusively the Vice-President's influence, but if there was a single influence that *hardened*, and that might be a better word, rather than created that pre-disposition, it was the Vice President. The Secretary of State put it this way to me one time. "Bush has a lot of shoot-from-the-hip, cowboy hat, buck-skin inclinations. The Vice President knows how to bring those out." So, maybe the pre-disposition was there. For whatever reason. In a nascent form. The Vice President astutely recognized that and then used that "shoot-from-the-hip", that "you're with us or against us" type pre-disposition to reinforce a much wider perspective on an issue or a foreign policy. So it wasn't like the President didn't have any complicity in this. He was pre-disposed, perhaps, to listen to the piper.
>
> (Preston, 2011, p. 39)

Even as the Iraq situation was spinning out of control in mid-2007, and Bush was forced to remain heavily focused on Iraq policy, he still refused to second-guess himself. As Irwin Stelzer, a senior fellow at the Hudson Institute who met privately with Bush in the White House during this time, noted, "You don't get any feeling of somebody crouching down in the bunker ... this is either extraordinary self-confidence or out of touch with reality. I can't tell you which" (Baker, 2007). Similarly, Henry Kissinger noted that he found Bush "serene" and of the view that "he feels he's doing what he needs to do and he seems to me at peace with himself" (Baker, 2007). Yet this certainty shown by Bush also led to some strong criticisms of his decision-making style:

> A president must be able to get a clear-eyed, unbiased assessment of the war. The president must lead. For years, time and again, President Bush has displayed impatience, bravado and unsettling personal certainty about his decisions. The result has too often been impulsiveness and carelessness and, perhaps most troubling, a delayed reaction to realities and advice that run counter to his gut.
>
> (Woodward, 2008, p. 433)

As one senior administration official later observed, Bush clearly "is a very self-confident man, which in the view of many, including myself is both his greatest strength and his greatest weakness" when it comes to policymaking (Preston, 2011, p. 40)! Not only did Bush like "to appear to be the Decider," the official noted, but his sense was that the President "*believes* himself to be the Decider" and that this was used "as a reference point" for him (Preston, 2011, p. 40).

Bush's Interpersonal Style

One of Bush's foremost strengths as a leader is his engaging, charming interpersonal style. It is a basic likability acknowledged by both his friends and political opponents. Those who know Bush remark that he "finds being around people invigorating and uplifting" (McClellan, 2008, p. 40). Even during his days as a student at Harvard, Draper (2007, p. 29) observed that the "young Bush's particular genius—the facility for wiping out in milliseconds the distance separating himself from total strangers"—was one that drew other boys to him through the use of his uncanny ability to generate instant familiarity through "remembering their names (or, if one's surname twisted the tongue, assigning a nickname), flinging arms around shoulders, acute eye contact, a gruff yet seductive whisper." Indeed, Draper (2007, p. 29) notes that "formality never suited him—he wasn't really a prince, just a senator's grandkid—so George W. swept it aside." Even in his critical memoir about his time as White House Communications Director, Scott McClellan (2008, p. xi) notes that Bush possesses a "disarming personality" and observes "that much of what the general public knows about Bush is true. He is a man of personal charm, wit, and enormous political skill." Yet as McClellan (2008) also suggests, this great skill could be a double-edged sword for the President:

> Bush likes familiarity and does not like change, especially in regard to key staff members he has come to trust and rely on. This had led to a close bond between Bush and a number of us senior staffers, particularly fellow Texans and people like Andy. His personal charm and approachable demeanor also make for an enjoyable working environment where people *want* to stick round—maybe longer than they

should. It's a great personal strength of George W. Bush that he is able to inspire such loyalty. But for President Bush it is also a potential source of weakness. Bush's discomfort with change makes it difficult for him to step back from the bonds he develops and make clear-eyed decisions about what is best.

(McClellan (2008, p. 242)

Similarly, Wilkerson also emphasized the *very* high emphasis placed by Bush upon personal relationships, characterized by his quickly "giving you a nickname," followed by the "hail Fellow, well met!" and "all that good Texas stuff" (Preston, 2011, p. 41). Agreeing with this characterization, Armitage recalled Bush "was a big nicknamer, and everybody's got a nickname—I was Tiny, for instance. And he likes that. I mean we used to joke, call it locker-room talk, but he's kind of that way. The dynamic of talking with the President, he wasn't intimidating in his manner or anything of that nature" (Preston, 2011, p. 41). And since advisers within Bush's inner circle were selected based upon their perceived loyalty and ideological fit, there tended not to be a lot of direct conflict among advisers during meetings with the President (although there was often a tremendous amount of bureaucratic conflict between various department heads outside of Bush's sight competing for policy influence). Avoiding head-on collisions was also accomplished by excluding outside players who might disagree with policy positions from having access to the inner circle, where their views might upset the group's harmony. For example, while former NSC adviser Brent Scowcroft was appointed chairman of the President's Foreign Intelligence Advisory Board in the first term, he was not consulted on plans for Iraq and (after he publicly criticized the policy) was not reappointed to the position at the end of 2004 (Goldberg, 2005, p. 58). Observing that the White House "ignores ideas that conflict with its aims," a colleague of Scowcroft noted that he was "not the only person to be frozen out," a clear reference to James Baker and other officials who had also expressed reservations about Iraq policy (Goldberg, 2005, p. 58).

Another consequence of avoiding head-on collisions and open conflict within inner circles (especially ones where loyalty is emphasized—and loyalty is usually seen as a two-way street)—is a reluctance to fire close subordinates. For Armitage, this element within the Bush style is in no place seen more clearly than in the handling of Defense Secretary Donald Rumsfeld and the degree to which the White House stuck with him long after he had become a political liability. According to Armitage:

I think a leader, to be a great leader, you need three primary attributes. You gotta have a vision, which people can believe in. He had that. Whether you agree with it or not is different, he had the vision. So that part of leadership he got right. But a leader demands, in various ways, and each leader's different, is execution of that vision. And then, right alongside of execution he demands accountability. So, vision, execution, accountability. Mr. Bush had, first, vision. He didn't have any demand for execution, he didn't hold anyone accountable. I once described in a speech here, I was asked, not so long ago, what I thought of the firing of Mr. Rumsfeld. And I described it as a national tragedy! It came five and a half years too late! *(laughs)* So, you know, he didn't man the execution, didn't man the accountability.

(Preston, 2011, p. 42)

The Case of Hurricane Katrina (2005)

From the standpoint of presidential crisis management, Hurricane Katrina, which hit in August 2005, posed stark challenges to an administration already losing credibility with the public over its handling of the war in Iraq, a leak inquiry, and its truthfulness regarding its use of intelligence surrounding WMDs. This *preexisting political context* meant the administration could ill afford to appear unprepared, ineffectual, or purposefully misleading over Katrina—primarily because this would serve to immediately activate preexisting political frames in the public's mind that could all too readily link this event with other perceived policy failings. During the initial response to Katrina, the overly optimistic responses by Bush and White House spokespeople about the federal response and the situation on the ground in New Orleans were immediately refuted by media coverage of the situation and rescue workers on the scene (Stevenson, 2005; Thomas, 2005). This caused immense political damage to the President, who was seen by detractors as being either out of touch with events (at best) or downright duplicitous (at worst)—neither of which helped the administration to deflect blame. Past political decisions also increased Bush's vulnerability to blame. In the case of Katrina, Bush's own style of substantial delegation to subordinates, limited active involvement, and emphasis on loyalty over expertise in appointments served to preset the roles of many of the policy actors prior to Katrina—actors whose performances would later be criticized as lacking (such as FEMA director Brown and Homeland Security Secretary Chertoff). Media investigations of the backgrounds of Bush political appointees afterwards further opened the administration up to charges of cronyism and placing officials (such as Brown) into positions for which they weren't qualified (Tumulty, Thompson, & Allen, 2005)—an especially damaging charge given the obvious importance (and failure) of the federal emergency managers during Katrina.

In the case of Katrina and its aftermath, those who long worried about and modeled the impact of a major hurricane on New Orleans (and lobbied for the matter to be given higher priority) viewed the crisis as a long-standing vulnerability that existed for many years. For the Bush administration, Katrina was generally argued to be an event difficult to fully anticipate ahead of time. Obviously, crises with long run-ups (providing ample warning or time to react had policy-makers been more vigilant and competent) are much easier to assign blame to than crises that could legitimately arrive as a *bolt-from-the-blue* (Parker & Stern, 2005). For example, Bush's statement on 1 September that "no one could have foreseen the levees being breached" can be seen as an attempt to define the crisis one way, while a competing definition would note that Bush was told 56 hours before landfall by the National Weather Service and the National Hurricane Center there was an "extremely high probability" New Orleans would be flooded (Hsu, 2006).

Leaders must also calculate the contestability of existing perceptual frames held by the public, the media, and the political system regarding their allotment of responsibility (or blame) for an event. As long as policy-makers believe the final image (or perceptual frame) of the crisis and its aftermath remain contestable—or malleable enough to be shaped by either denial of responsibility, deflection of blame to others, or positive spin (showing themselves or their management of events in a positive light)—leaders continue to adopt various tactics of blame avoidance to protect themselves (Boin et al., 2010). Obviously, less sensitive leaders like Bush, who employ closed advisory systems gathering limited information from the surrounding political environment, are far more likely to miscalculate such contestability than more sensitive leaders, who closely monitor that environment. Further, given their general rigidity towards changing adopted policy positions, insensitive leaders tend to contest the public frame for as long as possible—often long past the point where political damage is avoidable. Indeed, the Bush administration, which made a hallmark of never admitting to policy mistakes or reverses publicly, followed this general pattern on Iraq, WMDs, and Katrina—contesting frames long after public opinion on the topics shifted away from the image the White House continued to try to present.

Consistent with his delegative, less engaged style, Bush took lengthy vacations on his Crawford, Texas, ranch during the summers, leaving most policy tasks to trusted subordinates in Washington. Such delegation, especially given his closed advisory system and tight inner circle, makes it critical for trusted advisers to be on hand to adequately monitor the policy environment. Unfortunately, as Katrina formed, not only was Bush on vacation, but other senior members of the administration were as well, with Vice President Cheney in Wyoming, Condoleezza Rice in Manhattan, White House chief of staff Andy Card in Maine, and both White House communications director Nicolle Devenish and senior media adviser Mark McKinnon in Greece (Cooper 2005, p. 51). This served to impede the flow of advice and information to the President, magnifying the seeming disconnect between Bush's actions/statements and developing events. It was fully 24 hours after Katrina hit (August 30) before senior aides finally decided Bush should cut his five-week vacation short to return to Washington, where he could meet top advisers the next day (Thomas, 2005, pp. 30–31).

That Bush remained on vacation, and didn't immediately return to Washington, during such a catastrophe was broadly criticized by the media, and the lack of strong presidential statements regarding the situation aggravated this public perception of detachment. While often boasting that he didn't read newspapers or watch the media, in the case of Katrina Bush did seem surprisingly uninformed throughout the crisis about events that were being covered live by most U.S. news networks. For example, observers noted that four days after Katrina, during a briefing for his father and Bill Clinton, Bush's own rosy perception of the progress being made in New Orleans "bore no resemblance to what was actually happening" (Allen, 2005, p. 44). Indeed, White House staffers who had been watching the increasingly dire reports coming out of New Orleans made up a DVD of the newscasts so Bush could watch them (and presumably catch up with events) as he flew over the Gulf Coast on the morning of 31 August (Thomas, 2005, p. 32). Although photos taken of Bush aboard Air Force One, peering intently out of his window at the devastation below, were intended by the White House to show the President's engagement and concern, their impact on public opinion and how they were covered by the media (especially when coupled with the lack of significant federal assistance to the region and his perceived slowness to end his vacation) conveyed the entirely unintended image of detachment. Later that day, in a Rose Garden speech, Bush sought to demonstrate that he was engaged, reciting statistics on the number of ready-to-eat meals delivered, and of people rescued or in shelters (Sanger, 2005). But significant political damage had already occurred, as the photos aboard Air Force Once became the first visual image of the President's response to Katrina.

As days passed and the situation in New Orleans continued to deteriorate in the absence of effective relief efforts, the administration faced a growing need to reverse the political damage being inflicted upon it due to the growing public perception that it was out of touch or incompetent. Competing with the President during this period, where he sought to show his engagement and an effective federal response, was the constant, largely negative, media coverage coming out of New Orleans. This coverage was uncomfortably juxtaposed against Bush's September 1 Oval Office statement expressing sympathy for the victims, his belief that the federal government had "an important role to play," and his expressed desire "to make sure I fully understand the relief efforts" (Stevenson, 2005, p. A8). This response again fell short of what the public expected and was roundly criticized in the media. Bush argued in an ABC interview that same day that no one had expected the levees in New Orleans to be breached. However, the intensity and salience of the media images continued to overwhelm the White House explanations. On September 2, Bush acknowledged on the South Lawn of the White House (as he left for his first, highly visible tour of the Gulf Coast and New Orleans) that the results of the federal relief efforts were not acceptable thus far—with the symbolism of his trip intended to convey a more engaged, active leadership role on his part for the efforts (Stevenson, 2005, p. A8).

Although his visits to Alabama, Mississippi, and Louisiana were timed to coincide with the arrival of relief supplies and National Guard troops in some of the areas, a series of well-publicized statements by Bush weakened these efforts. For example, during his visit to Mobile, Alabama, Bush touched only briefly on the hundreds of thousands of displaced people in the region, and instead focused upon wealthy Senator Trent Lott's intentions to rebuild his upscale home and his own desire to sit on Lott's porch when it was done (Stevenson, 2005, p. A8). This public identification with his wealthy friend's plight, which hardly compared to the situation facing poorer evacuees or those still stranded in New Orleans, was immensely damaging politically and widely criticized. Even more damaging politically was Bush's infamous public congratulations on camera to FEMA director Michael Brown ("You're doing a heck of a job, Brownie!") during a meeting with government officials in Mississippi (Stevenson, 2005, p. A8)—while tens of thousands still remained stranded and without aid days after the storm. When *Time* magazine published its own investigation of cronyism in the administration (Tumulty et al., 2005), it found numerous examples similar to that of Brown (where appointees had no relevant professional experience to qualify for their posts, beyond being Bush loyalists). Such charges and continued publicity about Brown's (and Chertoff's) qualifications served to undercut White House efforts to avoid blame.

As this brief example of Katrina illustrates, leaders and their management styles play a critical role in shaping not only how they approach the task of crisis management, but also how vulnerable to blame they will be in the face of policy reversals. The personalities of leaders don't just shape their strategies for dealing with blame, but also create (through the development of various types of advisory systems) decision-making and management processes that either strengthen or greatly reduce their ability to cope with (and deflect blame arising from) crises. During Katrina, as expected for a less-controlling, insensitive leader, Bush's lack of personal engagement and substantial delegation to subordinates, coupled with his lack of attention to the surrounding policy environment, greatly slowed his personal response to the crisis. Moreover, given the insular, closed nature of the White House advisory system, where information tended to flow in primarily from loyal insiders, it is hardly surprising that Bush's political response to the crises was often out of step with the views (and perceptions) of those outside of his inner circle. This led to the clear disconnect observed during the Katrina response between those events being widely covered by the media (and viewed by the public) and White House pronouncements on the subject. Given the normal policy rigidity associated with such styles, it was to be expected that Bush would be slow to either adapt his policy approach once it had been adopted or accept blame. This rigidity was particularly damaging given the immense emotive power of the imagery coming out of New Orleans, which easily overpowered the White House's attempts at positive spin. Bush's own leadership style was ill-suited to the nature of the crisis, serving to greatly exacerbate his administration's vulnerabilities to blame through appointment of loyalists rather than experts to critical positions and lack of focus on the details of policy problems or environment.

The Case of Donald J. Trump

Political psychology has several tools useful for examining the personality of former president Donald J. Trump. Below we provide a number of different frameworks for analysis of Trump, and there is clearly a great deal of agreement about Trump's personality, whether using psychoanalysis, the Big Five, the Operational Code, LTA, or image analysis.

The behavior of Trump so worried psychiatrists, psychologists, and other mental health professionals that in 2017 they published the book *The Dangerous Case of Donald Trump*, and their findings were portrayed in the documentary *Unfit*. It is not practice to evaluate sitting leaders without their full evaluation and consent because of the Goldwater Rule (Trent, 2020), but Trump so alarmed them, and others, that they publicly released their psychological assessments. Indeed, many argued that, of any president, Trump had unprecedented personality disorder traits, and these were dangerous to the democratic process.

These professionals, and others making independent assessments such as psychiatrist and former CIA analyst Jerrold Post, who labeled Trump dangerous (Trent, 2020), agreed that Trump exhibited narcissistic personality disorder, "which entails entitlement, exploitation, and empathy impairment, along with the typical characteristics of narcissism" (Narvaez, 2020). The characteristics of narcissism include:

- believing you are superior to others
- fantasizing about success
- exaggerating talents and achievements
- expecting constant admiration and praise
- believing you are special and acting that way
- failing to recognize others' feelings
- expecting others to do what you want
- taking advantage of others
- expressing disdain for the "inferior"
- jealousy of others
- being easily hurt and rejected
- having fragile self-esteem
- appearing tough and unemotional
- setting unrealistic goals
- being unable to maintain healthy relationships

(Narvaez, 2020).

One of the contributors, forensic psychiatrist Bandy Lee, explained that Trump was "hungry for adulation to compensate for an inner lack of self-worth" and "projects grandiose omnipotence" (Lewis, 2021). His "autocratic disposition," coupled with narcissism, makes him predisposed to delusions and psychotic episodes (Lewis, 2021). Others pointed to antisocial personality disorder exhibited by failure to conform to laws and social norms, deceitfulness, impulsivity, irritability and aggressiveness, reckless disregard for safety of others and of self, pattern of irresponsibility, lack of remorse, and conduct disorder (impulsivity, aggressiveness, callousness, and deceitfulness starting before age 15) (Narvaez, 2020).

Using the Millon Inventory of Diagnostic Criteria (MIDC) (expressive behavior, interpersonal conduct, cognitive style, mood/temperament, self-image, regulatory mechanisms, object representations, and morphologic organization), Immelman and Griebie (2020) found Trump to primarily be ambitious/self-serving (bordering on exploitative), dominant/controlling (bordering on aggressive), and outgoing/gregarious (bordering on impulsive). Furthermore, he exhibited dauntless/dissenting, distrusting/suspicious, and erratic/unstable tendencies. The authors connected these traits to expected behavior; however, of note is their assessment of his leadership orientation:

> Given his supreme self-confidence and high dominance, Trump will likely be more goal directed than relationship oriented. As a task-oriented leader, Trump will not permit the maintenance of good relations to stand in the way of goal achievement. This orientation will be offset to some extent by Trump's outgoing tendencies which,

> in addition, will also prime him to place a high premium on loyalty among his advisers and members of his administration.
>
> (Immelman & Griebie, 2020, p. 27)

Using the Big Five personality trait approach (extroversion, neuroticism, conscientiousness, agreeableness, and openness to experience) McAdam (2016) similarly found Trump to be extremely extroverted, a trait that can produce an inclination toward reward-seeking in fame, wealth, recognition, and so forth. Other U.S. presidents—for example, Bill Clinton and George W. Bush, discussed above—have this trait. Unlike those presidents, Trump—along with Richard Nixon—is extremely low in agreeableness. This means Trump was also predisposed to be rude, callous, lacking empathy, and a convention breaker while still desiring accolades about his superiority. McAdam argued that when the traits of extroversion and disagreeableness are combined, one sees a tendency to take risks as a result of high extroversion, and "hard-nosed realpolitik" caused by a lack of agreeableness.

Other researchers used trait analysis to explain Trump's behavior, bringing additional insights. Using operational code analysis, Walker and Schafer (2018) found Trump believed others were hostile, and that he was high in distrust, had a strong belief in his ability to control events, making him challenge constraints, and was prone to conflict. In their assessment of Trump, Siniver and Featherstone (2020) argued that low cognitive complexity shaped his foreign policy orientation:

> We suggest that a constant and simplified plutocratic worldview underpins Trump's low-conceptual complexity. It can be summed up as a transactional, money-first prism through which Trump understands his environment and deals with people and policy issues: those who pay their "fair share" are allies; the ones who do not are adversaries. Similarly, complex political and diplomatic questions are often treated as business opportunities or economic endeavors which supersede broader geopolitical considerations.
>
> (Siniver & Featherstone, 2020, p. 1)

Specifically, the authors examined his cognitive complexity in relation to NATO, and why limited information and low sensitivity to his environment explained his "confrontational courses of action and violation of international norms" (Siniver & Featherstone, 2020, p. 9).

The Leader Trait Analysis of Donald Trump adds another layer to this picture of his personality. Preston (2017) found Trump to be low in prior policy experience, low in cognitive complexity, extremely high in distrust of others, low in self-confidence, high in need for affiliation, with a pronounced internal locus of control (meaning a strong belief he can control events), and medium to high in need for power (Preston, 2017). Taken together, "these traits predict a pattern of behavioral predispositions to be heavily reliant on like-minded and loyal advisors irrespective of expertise, uninterested in information, particularly when he has strong beliefs about an issue, a black and white view of the world, and a desire to be the principal decision maker." Trump's "nationalism" and identification with both the Republican Party and his base is questionable. "He does not have strong in-group attachments ...

Rather than being a nationalist, he knows how to use nationalism to attract followers" (Cottam, 2020, p. 131).

Looking at Trump's image-based world view, there is ample reason to expect that his low cognitive complexity will lead him to have simple, highly stereotyped images of others. For example, Trump's rogue image of North Korea and Iran is evident in the denigrating and demanding language he used. He referred to North Korea's Kim Jong Un as "rocket man" and "little rocket man," and threatened to pour "fire and fury" on North Korea if it threatened the United States with its nuclear program (Woodward, 2018, p. 280). He also threatened Iran in the following tweet:

> "To Iranian President Rouhani: NEVER, EVER THREATEN THE UNITED STATES AGAIN OR YOU WILL SUFFER CONSEQUENCES THE LIKES OF WHICH FEW THROUGHOUT HISTORY HAVE EVER SUFFERED BEFORE," Trump tweeted after returning to the White House from a weekend at his golf resort in Bedminster, New Jersey. "WE ARE NO LONGER A COUNTRY THAT WILL STAND FOR YOUR DEMENTED WORDS OF VIOLENCE & DEATH BE CAUTIOUS!"
>
> (CNN, 2018)

Trump also displayed the classic colonial image of a variety of poorer less developed countries such as Haiti and the African "shit hole" countries. He also accused Mexico of being composed of criminals and rapists, although he did acknowledge there may be some good people in Mexico (Time, 2015). On the other hand, Trump's lack of strong in-group attachments meant he did not have the typical attachment to ally image relationships. He threatened NATO and was disrespectful of European leaders at NATO and other meetings.

CONCLUSION

This chapter serves as only a starting point for students interested in political psychological approaches to personality or leadership. However, this overview of a number of the more widely known psychological approaches used in research on political questions, as well as the case study application examples above, should give the reader a sense of how these approaches tend to be employed. The leader personality and style variables discussed in this chapter also significantly impact the political behavior of the masses, which is discussed in Chapter 6.

Topics, Theories/Frameworks, and Cases Covered in Chapter 5		
Topics	*Theories/frameworks*	*Cases*
Burn's transactional and transformational types of leadership		
Leader management style	Johnson's (1974) formalistic, competitive, and collegial management styles George's (1980) cognitive style, sense of efficacy, tolerance of political conflict Hermann et al.'s (1996) three leadership style dimensions: responsiveness to constraints, openness to information, and motivational focus Preston's (2001) typology and three style dimensions: leader need for control, prior policy experience/expertise, and sensitivity to context	Bush Trump

Key Terms

cognitive style
collegial management style
competitive management style
formalistic management style
orientation toward political conflict
sense of efficacy
transactional leadership
transformational leadership

Suggestions for Further Reading

George, A. L. (1980). *Presidential decisionmaking in foreign policy: The effective use of information and advice.* Boulder, CO: Westview Press.

George, A. L., & George, J. L. (1998). *Presidential personality and performance.* Boulder, CO: Westview Press.

Greenstein, F. I. (1988). *Leadership in the modern presidency.* Cambridge, MA: Harvard University Press.

Hermann, M. G., Preston, T., Korany, B., & Shaw, T. M. (2001). Who leads matters: The effects of powerful individuals. *International Studies Review, 3(2),* 83–131.

Hill, D. (2019). *Two cheers for democracy: How emotions drive leadership style.* Minneapolis, MN: Sensory Logic Books.

Preston, T. (2001). *The president and his inner circle: Leadership style and the advisory process in foreign policy making.* New York: Columbia University Press.

Preston, T. & Hermann, M. G. (2004). Presidential leadership style and the foreign policy advisory process. In E. Wittkopf & J. McCormick (Eds.), *The domestic sources of American foreign policy: Insights and evidence* (4th ed., pp. 33–61). Lanham, MD: Rowman & Littlefield.
Preston, T. & 't Hart, P. (1999). Understanding and evaluating bureaucratic politics: The nexus between political leaders and advisory systems. *Political Psychology, 20*, 49–98.

Notes

1. Interviews with multiple senior Bush administration policy-makers and staff who requested anonymity, as well as briefers from various government departments and agencies.
2. Allen, M., & Broder, D. S. (2004, August 30). Bush's leadership style: Decisive or simplistic? *Washington Post*, p. A1.

Chapter 6

The Political Psychology of Mass Politics

How Do People Decide Who to Vote For?

How do Americans think and feel about politics? The political thoughts and feelings of the American public have been the subject of intense and prolific research since the 1950s. Political psychology asks questions such as: How sophisticated is the public about politics and democratic ideals? How much attention do Americans pay to political information? How do people process and use information (particularly during electoral campaigns)? How do Americans make decisions when deciding for whom to vote?

Another important question raised by political psychologists about American political beliefs concerns the issue of how tolerant Americans are of views that are contrary to their own. Needless to say, in a democracy this is an extremely important matter because democratic ideals hinge upon the notion that even very unpopular views may be expressed without fear of reprisal or repression. This chapter looks at some of the findings and controversies in political psychology regarding the political attitudes of ordinary American citizens. The Political Being in this chapter is an average citizen. We focus primarily upon the attitudes and cognition component of the citizen's mind and the "us" part of the political environment. While we look at the Political Being in the context of politics in the United States, we also discuss studies conducted about voting behavior in the United Kingdom and other countries. In addition, we touch upon the "political brain," and explore how genetics and biology play a role in political thinking and behavior.

We begin with some concepts and then turn to the classic study by the Michigan School of thought on the nature of American political attitudes and sophistication. We then consider some critics of the Michigan School's perspective. From that topic, we turn to studies of how people process information during campaigns and how their feelings affect who they decide to vote for, and political tolerance in America. After that, we compare American political attitudes with those in the United Kingdom, and discuss voting behavior in other countries. To begin, let us review some of the central concepts used by analysts to study public opinion.

DOI: 10.4324/9780429244643-6

BELIEFS, VALUES, IDEOLOGY, ATTITUDES, AND SCHEMAS

In Chapter 3, the term *beliefs* was defined as associations people create between an object and its attributes (Eagly & Chaiken, 1998). Another useful definition of beliefs is "cognitive components that make up our understanding of the way things are" (Glynn, Herbst, O'Keefe, & Shapiro, 1999, p. 104). When beliefs are clustered together, we call it a **belief system**. Most Americans, for example, have a belief system about democracy that includes such beliefs as "Free speech is a necessity," "The people have a right to decide who holds political power," and "All citizens should have the right to vote."

Values are closely related, but have an ideal component. Beliefs reflect what we think is true; values reflect what we wish to see come about, even if it is not currently true. Rokeach (1973) argues that there are two types of values: *terminal values,* which are goals; and *instrumental values,* which endorse the means to achieve those goals. For example, Americans want a safe society and want the police to maintain law and order. This is a terminal value—a concern for the wellbeing of the people. At the same time, Americans value civil liberties, defined in the constitution, and endorse only those behaviors by the police that enforce public safety and order through means that do not violate civil liberties. This is an example of instrumental values.

Values and beliefs are closely related, and when we refer to political values and belief systems, we call it an **ideology**, which is "a particularly elaborate, close-woven, and far-ranging structure" of attitudes and beliefs (Campbell, Converse, Miller, & Stokes, 1960, 1964, p. 111). American political values and ideology are rooted in Lockean liberalism, that is, the philosophical ideas of John Locke, and, although attitudes about many issues changed over time, these values remain much the same, even after more than 200 years (McClosky & Zaller, 1984).

A central concept in the study of political psychology used in this chapter is *attitudes,* which we presented in Chapter 3 as an enduring system of positive or negative beliefs, affective feelings and emotions, and subsequent action tendencies regarding an attitude object, that is, the entity being evaluated. Some of the controversies regarding this type of definition were discussed in Chapter 3. In terms of research on the political psychology of Americans and their subsequent political behavior, some central questions regarding attitudes were: (1) Are attitudes consistent with one another? In other words, do people have consistently liberal or consistently conservative attitudes? (2) Are political attitudes consistently related to political behavior? For example, do people who consider themselves Republicans, and hold Republican views on political issues, also vote for Republican Party candidates? (3) How do people use attitudes to process political information? (4) How do people acquire their political attitudes? (5) How sophisticated are political attitudes in a given population? Are they cognitively complex? (6) If people do have inconsistent attitudes, how do they balance the inconsistencies?

The attitude concept has a long tradition in the study of public opinion, but subsequently the schema concept was introduced. As we saw in

Chapter 3, a *schema* is defined as a "cognitive structure that represents knowledge about a concept or type of stimulus, including its attributes and the relations among those attributes" (Fiske & Taylor, 1991, p. 8). There is some debate as to whether schemas and attitudes are the same thing. Kuklinski, Luskin, and Bolland (1991) maintain they are the same concept; Conover and Feldman (1991) maintain they are not. They argue that, "The central meaning of the attitude concept—the meaning common to all competing definitions—is fundamentally *affective* in nature." At its core, an attitude is a "person's evaluation of an object of thought" (Pratkanis & Greenwald, 1989, p. 247). The central meaning of the schema concept stands in sharp contrast. Although it, too, was defined in a variety of ways, at its core a schema is fundamentally a *cognitive* structure ... Traditionally, attitudes are linked to consistency theories while schemata are tied to information-processing theories. Others claim attitude theories always looked at attitudes as information-processing filters, hence they are cognitive in nature and the same as schemas (e.g., Eagly & Chaiken, 1998). Each argument has some validity but, in our view, the debate is overblown. Neither concept needs to replace the other, and the different concepts were used mostly to examine different questions. Early research on public opinion found that American political attitudes were sorely lacking in cognitive content (i.e., Americans know little about politics), and hence the concept of attitude did emphasize affect (as in art, people may not know much about politics, but they know what they like and dislike). Later researchers were curious about how people process political information. Newly developed theories about information processing, emphasizing cognitive properties, were used to explore information processing, using the concepts of schema and heuristics.

POLITICAL SOPHISTICATION AND VOTING IN AMERICA

Beginning in the late 1940s, researchers armed with surveys set out to investigate the nature of American political attitudes. They were interested in the question of how sophisticated Americans were, as well as in the internal consistency of their attitudes. The deeper question underlying this research concerned the quality of democracy in America. Presumably, a functioning democracy requires citizens to make informed decisions when they vote. This requires some degree of political sophistication—that is, knowledge about the political system in which they live and the issues that are important. However, despite the importance attributed to political sophistication, there is considerable disagreement about whether it should be considered knowledge about politics or, more broadly, knowledge, attention, interest, and involvement in politics (McGraw, 2000).

The Michigan School

The groundbreaking study of American political sophistication, *The American Voter* (Campbell et al., 1964), was discouraging for those who believed democracy must be founded on a citizenry interested in, and informed and thoughtful about, democratic principles and political issues of the day. Because *The American Voter* was based upon survey results from the Survey Research Center at the University of Michigan, its model of the American voter became known as the Michigan School, or **Michigan model**. Specifically, the researchers were interested in finding out whether people had consistently liberal or conservative values, whether those values were related to their party identification and loyalty, and to their policy preferences, and how they determined who they would vote for.

The authors began with the assumption that Americans should have an integrated mental map of the political system:

> The individual voter sees the several elements of national politics as more than a collection of discrete, unrelated objects. After all, they are parts of one political system and are connected in the real world by a variety of relations that are visible in some degree to the electorate. A *candidate* is the nominee of his *party*; party and candidate are oriented to the same *issues* or *groups*, and so forth. Moreover, we may assume that the individual strives to give order and coherence to his image of these objects.
>
> (Campbell et al., 1964, p. 27)

In other words, these are the cognitive categories utilized by Americans to simplify and organize American politics.

Campbell and colleagues then anticipated American attitudes about candidates, issues, party, and group interests would be structured—that is, that they would be functionally related to each other and to an ideology. Ideally, people should know what liberal and conservative values are, what positions on important political issues are liberal and conservative stances, which party represents liberal and which party represents conservative principles, and which issues candidates stand for. For example, a person who opposes big government (a conservative ideological attitude) should also feel an attachment to the Republican Party (the conservative party in the United States), vote for candidates espousing similar views, and belong to groups benefiting from minimal government. In addition, that person should favor other conservative positions on other issues, such as taxes, labor rights, federal versus state power, and so on. This type of person could justifiably be called an **ideologue.** A liberal ideologue would be equally consistent, with liberal attitudes regarding party (Democratic Party), issues, and candidate preferences. An ideologue is considered a political sophisticate in the sense that such a person would presumably be politically aware, could understand and process political information consistently, and would make political choices suitable for their personal, group, and value-based interests.

What the authors of *The American Voter* (Campbell et al., 1964) reported, however, was that very few Americans fit the profile of an ideologue—that is, of a person who understood the differences between liberal and conservative principles, and who could locate each party and the issues along liberal and conservative dimensions. They conducted surveys in which they asked people what they liked and disliked about the parties and candidates, and coded the surveys in terms of the nature of the response. If the respondent expressed likes and dislikes in terms of ideological principles, that person was considered an ideologue. They classified people into one of several possible **levels of conceptualization** on the basis of the primary attitudes used to express likes and dislikes about the parties and candidates. The levels of conceptualization are arranged in terms of degrees of sophistication. In fact, they found that only about 2.5% of their respondents fell into the ideologue level of conceptualization. The second level of conceptualization of respondents was called the "near-ideologues." These people claimed to know the differences between liberal and conservative principles, but were less confident about, and less able to articulate, those principles. About 9.5% of the sample fell into the near-ideologue level of conceptualization.

The next level of conceptualization, the "group benefits" level, was populated by people who saw political issues in terms of concrete benefits for their group, compared with those for other groups in society. At this level, "there is little comprehension of 'long-range plans for social betterment,' or of basic philosophies rooted in postures toward change or abstract conceptions of social and economic structure or causation" (Campbell et al., 1964, p. 135). Forty-two percent of the respondents fell into this category. Level four was populated by "nature of the times" folks, who had no conception of ideology, no recognition of group interests, and who, when they did think of politics, thought simply in terms of whether times were good or bad for themselves and their families. Good times meant that the party of the president was good; bad times meant that the party of the president should be punished. The category also included people who identified a single isolated issue with a party (e.g., Social Security benefits and the Democratic Party). Twenty-four percent of the respondents fell into this category.

The final level was "absence of issue content"—the booby prize level. These people, 22.5%, knew nothing about political issues and approached politics solely in terms of party membership (absent any understanding of the party's position on issues) or candidate appeals (looks, religion, or sincerity, rather than issue positions), when they had anything resembling a political opinion. Few of the people at this level of conceptualization bothered to vote.

This study demonstrates that Americans are not political philosophers, and that a deep understanding of politics and democracy is not the foundation of their decisions on how to vote. Subsequent studies using similar survey tools (but with important changes in question wording, which positively affected respondents' ability to express knowledge of politics) found an improvement in knowledge after the 1950s. In particular, *The Changing American Voter* (Nie, Verba, & Petrocik (1976), covered elections from 1952 through 1976, and found that, as politics became more exciting in the 1960s, levels of conceptualization improved in terms of the numbers in the highest levels (they identified 31% ideologues), as did levels of issue consistency (i.e., people tended to take consistently liberal or conservative positions on a number of issues). However, a significant number of people remained fairly ignorant about politics. Later works, such as *The Unchanging American Voter* (Smith, 1989), although critical of important components of *The American Voter* (particularly the levels of conceptualization idea, which Smith argues is not a valid measurement of how people actually think about politics), provided further data supporting the argument that American political

Table 6.1 Levels of Conceptualization Over Time

Levels of conceptualization	*1956*	*1960*	*1964*	*1968*	*1972*	*1976*	*1980*	*1984*	*1988*
Ideologues	12%	19%	27%	26%	22%	21%	21%	19%	18%
Group benefit	42	31	27	24	27	26	31	26	36
Nature of the times	24	26	20	29	34	30	30	35	25
No issue content	22	23	26	21	17	24	19	19	21
N	1,740	1,741	1,431	1,319	1,372	2,870	1,612	2,257	2,040

Source: Niemi & Weisberg (1993, p. 89).

attitudes do not revolve around sophisticated political ideologies and ideological thinking. The political attitudes of Americans do not have a cognitive component that is sophisticated enough to understand abstractions such as liberalism and conservatism. Table 6.1 shows trends in levels of conceptualization over time. From this table, the reader can easily see there was an upsurge in ideologues during the "hot politics" years of the 1960s and early 1970s; however, by and large, the American public remains non-ideological.

Just how little Americans know about politics is revealed in the findings of survey researchers. For example, for many years, pollsters asked people after a national election which party had won the most seats in the House of Representatives, and which party had the most members in the House. In 1980, only 14% knew both (Smith, 1989). In 1986, 24% of Americans were either unable to recognize Vice President George Bush's name or could not identify his office, even though he had been in the office of Vice President for six years (Zaller, 1992). In a 1966 national election study, only 1.9% of the public could name even half of the members of the Supreme Court, and not one of the 1500 people surveyed could name all nine members of the Supreme Court (Zaller, 1992). In March 2000, after months of intense and often bitter competition, both Al Gore and George W. Bush secured enough delegates to get the nomination for the presidential candidacy from the Democratic and Republican Parties, respectively. But only 66% of Americans could correctly name both candidates, and 20% could name neither (Gallup Poll, 2000). A Gallup poll taken in July 2001 found that only 11% of Americans claimed to follow the national missile defense issue closely, despite heavy news coverage of that controversial proposal by the Bush administration. Fifty-eight percent thought the United States already had a missile defense system, and only 28% knew the United States did not have a missile defense system. On a more humorous note, a 1998 study by the National Constitution Center found that only 41% of American teenagers can name the three branches of government, but 59% know the names of the Three Stooges; although only 2% know the name of the chief justice of the Supreme Court, we can all be comforted by the fact that 95% know the name of the actor who played the Fresh Prince of Bel Air on television (Will Smith) ("Teens Sharper," 1998).

Knowledge is at least improving about the Constitution and separation of powers, according to a 2019 survey by the Annenberg Policy Center. For example, the survey found 39% of Americans could name the three branches of government, which was the highest proportion in five years. The Center attributed this and other knowledge changes about the government and constitution to high school civics classes (Annenberg Public Policy Center, 2019).

The political attitudes many Americans do have are not constrained or consistent, nor are they stable—that is, the same over time (Converse, 1964). In terms of constraint, this means people do not have consistently liberal or conservative attitudes; they may be conservative on one issue and liberal on another. Without an underlying ideological guideline, such a lack of constraint is not surprising, but the implication in terms of American political sophistication is controversial. In terms of stability, Converse (1964) notes that responses to attitude questions from some people remained very stable, but for others the responses changed in an apparently random pattern. He calls this the **black and white model** of attitude change. We return to the issue of how Americans organize and process political information later, but let us turn now to the question of which attitudes affect how Americans vote, and how they changed.

The authors of *The American Voter*, and others included in the Michigan School, presented a model of political attitudes, and their relationship to each other, that depicted the causes of the vote. The model is called the **funnel of causality** (see Figure 6.1), and it distinguishes between long-term factors or attitudes that affect how Americans vote (which are attachment to a party, or **party identification**, and group interests) and short-term factors (currently important **issues** and candidates' personal characteristics). Party identification is an attitude by which a person considers him- or herself to be a Democrat or a Republican. Party identification is acquired through socialization and other life experiences and, the authors argue, tends to remain fairly stable—that is, it does not change over one's lifetime. Partisanship does vary in intensity, and the Michigan School scholars argued that those who were more strongly attached to a political party were more likely to be interested and involved in politics. They were more likely to know more about politics and vote. In the United States, the strength of attachment to the political parties has diminished over the generations, since the height of party loyalty and attachment in the Great Depression, at which time the Democratic Party became the majority party. Bartels (2000), however, presents data indicating that attachment to the parties reached its low point in 1996, and has since increased, but only for those who actually vote. Additionally, since the Depression, new generations entered the electorate, and the Democratic Party's majority status changed. The Depression generation was strongly attracted to the Democratic Party because of its perception Franklin Roosevelt and his New Deal policies, designed to end the Depression, were beneficial to the workers, the young, and immigrants who had recently acquired citizenship. As that generation passed on, and new generations come of voting age without the same strong pull, the Democratic and Republican parties became about equal in voter identification, and over one-third of voters (about 35% in the 1990s) considered themselves to be

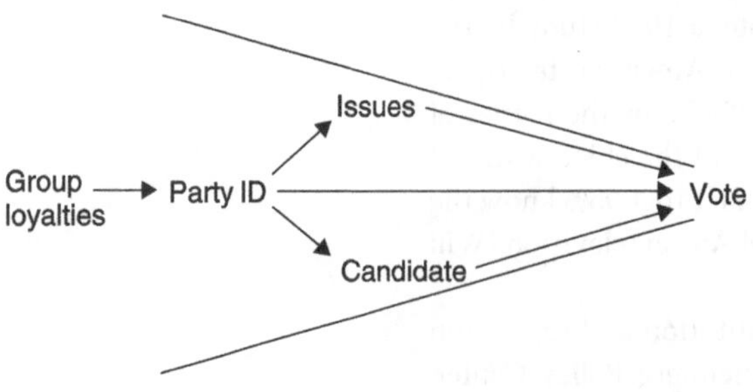

Figure 6.1 The Funnel of Causality

Independent (although two-thirds of the self-identified Independents in fact lean toward one of the two parties). In 2008, the Pew Research Center found a decline from 2004 in those identifying with the Republican Party. They found 36% identifying as Democrats, 27% as Republican (down from 33% in 2004), and 37% as Independent. However, among those Independents, 15% leaned Democratic, 10% leaned Republican, and 12% indicated no leaning at all (Pew Research Center, 2008a). Fluctuations have occurred since then, and surveys from 2018/19 indicated 34% of registered voters identified as Independent, 22% as Democrats, and 29% as Republicans. Among Independents, 49% identified or leaned toward the Democratic Party, while 44% identified or leaned Republican (Pew Research Center, 2020).

Party identification strongly affects how people vote—particularly those who identify intensely with their party. When you consider how little Americans know about politics, the importance of party identification seems obvious. If people know little about the current issues, those who identify always have their party attachment to guide them in the voting booth. Party identification also affects how people view short-term forces, such as issues and candidates. It is used to screen information, and it colors the voter's interpretation of issues and candidates. But people do not always vote for candidates of their own party, nor do they always agree with their party's stance on particular issues. When people defect and vote for the other party's candidates, it is the result of short-term forces. For example, a moderate conservative who is a member of the Republican Party, but who favors reproductive choice, might decide not to vote for George W. Bush, because he is opposed to abortion rights. Or recall our friend from Chapter 3, a lifelong Democrat and a strong party loyalist, who briefly considered voting for George W. Bush but ended up voting for Al Gore. Education policy was one of several important short-term forces for her (the others favoring Gore), and partisanship kept its strong pull.

The Michigan School developed a formula for analyzing the impact of partisanship, issues, and candidate characteristics in each election. Because partisanship is a long-term factor affecting the vote, they reasoned that an election in which people voted according to their party identification, and in which Independents are split evenly between the two parties, could be considered a baseline, or an ideal typical election. They labeled such an election a **normal vote** (Converse, 1966). They could then look at different elections and determine the relative importance of partisanship, issues, and candidate characteristics. In the 1950s, 1960s, and 1970s, when the Democratic Party was the majority party, a normal vote was 54% Democratic and 46% Republican. Thus, the 1952 and 1956 elections deviated from the normal vote because Dwight Eisenhower, the Republican candidate for the presidency, won. His election was mostly the result of candidate appeal and short-term forces (he was immensely popular), pro-Republican foreign policy attitudes, and a negative popular reaction to Democratic skills in managing government. The distribution of party identification changed in the last part of the twentieth century, so that Republican and Democratic identifiers were each roughly 33% and Independents were the other 33%. As noted above, Republican identifiers were an even smaller percentage as of 2008, but 10 years later, these figures were Democrats 22%, Republicans 29%, and Independents 34%.

The arguments that partisanship lasts a lifetime, even when one defects repeatedly and votes for the other party, and that it outweighs short-term factors when people decide how to vote, came under attack. Rational choice analysts, who are not political psychologists, argue that people vote on issues in terms of self-interest calculations and partisanship is a collage of short- and long-term forces (e.g., Brody & Rothenberg, 1988; Fiorina, 1981; Franklin, 1992; Franklin & Jackson, 1983; Markus & Converse, 1979; Page & Jones, 1979). Political psychologists, on the other hand, studied candidate evaluations from a cognitive information-processing perspective, findings to which we turn a little later. Miller and Shanks (1996) defended the Michigan model's emphasis on partisanship in *The New American Voter*.

More recently, evidence suggests the brain plays a role in partisanship and the strength of political affiliation. For example, recent studies examined the heritability of party affiliation. It was largely accepted that party affiliation is primarily environmental, with family members generally affiliating with the same political party. And it turns out that the environment is still influential in determining party affiliation, but genetics are equally important. Funk, Smith, Alford, and Hibbing (2010) found that although environment played a strong role in predicting party identification, so did genetics. Dawes and Fowler (2009) found a genetic correlate (the DRD2 dopamine receptor) of party identification, suggesting that the tendency to affiliate with a particular political party is inherited. This dopamine receptor, by the way, plays a role in cognitive functioning and in social attachments (such as to a political party). Of course, this also explains why party affiliation seems to be environmental—we often identify with the same party as our parents, and that affiliation may have environmental as well as genetic origins.

There also seems to be a genetic role in the strength of political affiliation. Settle, Dawes, and Fowler (2009) found that although the environment explains why people are strongly attached to a political party, so do genetic factors. Similarly, Hatemi, Funk, Medland, Maes, Silberg, Martin and Eaves (2009) found very strong political ties were explained by a combination of genetic and environmental factors. All this recent work on genetics and heritability is important as it suggests that the environment alone cannot account for party affiliation or the strength of our partisan ties. The more we can explain the variability in party affiliation and the strength of those ties, the better we are able to make predictions about political behavior.

The Maximalists

The Michigan model is not the final word on the sophistication of the American voter. Lane (1962; see also Lane & Sears, 1964) and others had a more optimistic evaluation of the quality and quantity of political knowledge. Some argued that even if Americans do not have consistently liberal or conservative political attitudes, they may still organize their attitudes, but in a way different from that expected by the Michigan School. Perhaps the biggest political psychological challenge to the Michigan model is the Maximalist school. **Maximalists** maintain that the Michigan model is a minimalist picture of the American political worldview. Looked at differently, Americans are much more politically sophisticated than the Michigan model maintains.

Sniderman, Brody, and Tetlock (1991) traced the challenge to the minimalist picture of the American political thinker to the alternative picture painted in *The Changing American Voter* (Nie, Verba, & Petrocik, 1976), and to an article by Stimson (1975). We have already mentioned the former—they provided data indicating that when politics gets more exciting, the public becomes more informed and sophisticated. Stimson, and later Neuman (1986), argued that the problem with the Michigan model was that it attempted to treat the public as one group, but in reality great variation exists across the public. Neuman (1986) maintains that there are three publics: (1) the political sophisticates (about 5%), who know a great deal about politics and who are very active; (2) the majority (about 75% of the public), who have advanced education and, in effect, have cognitive abilities, but are not often strongly motivated to use them in the realm of politics; and (3) those who are truly apolitical (about 20% of the population), who will never be interested or involved, and who lack the cognitive capabilities to be involved, even if they wanted to.

The Maximalists challenged the Michigan model's basic premises about how people think about politics (the cognitive component), and they added the importance of affect into the process of thinking about politics (Sniderman et al., 1991). Thus, the Michigan School's assumption that people organize their political thoughts in a linear (liberal to conservative) manner diverts attention from how people actually think about politics. In their own words:

> Belief systems, we reasoned, acquired structure through reasoning about choices. To see the structure they possessed, it was necessary to identify how people managed choices—that is, the considerations that they took into account and the relative weights they placed on them. The standard approach in effect asked: To what extent is one idea element connected to another *on the assumption the connections are approximately the same for everyone.*
>
> From our perspective, idea elements could, and likely were, connected in a variety of ways depending upon both the characteristics of the problem that a person was trying to work through and the characteristics of the person trying to work it through. Political choices pose problems, and the object of political psychology accordingly is to give an account, not simply of how people recollect their preferred solution to a problem, but of how they figured it out in the first place.
>
> (Sniderman et al., 1991, pp. 3–4)

The authors posed a question: the minimalist model assumes liberals and conservatives should have consistent positions on two issues—for example, government spending and pornography—but how does one get from one of those issues to the other (Sniderman et al., 1991)? Because they are not obviously related, one can connect them using only a higher order construct—that is, liberal or conservative ideology. Using ideology as a guide, a person is expected to take either a liberal or conservative position on both issues, to be considered politically sophisticated by the minimalists. But why should we assume that this is the reasoning path people follow, and why grant this path the honor of being the hallmark of political sophistication? Why assume that such a deductive inference (i.e., using the higher order construct to connect the issues) is more likely to occur than a paired association—in this case, there is none, so why should one expect a related position on both issues? According to Sniderman et al. (1991, p. 7), the minimalist school

> asks us to suppose that the positions we take on issues, so far as we arrive at them through reasoning, are the product of logical entailment. This is an excessively cerebral account of political thinking, minimizing the role of affect, or feelings in political reasoning.

The Maximalists maintain that, although people are not experts in political philosophies of liberalism and conservatism, they can process political information and decide where they stand on political issues, which we consider later. Sniderman and Tetlock (1986) argue the minimalist view of belief system structure assumes it is, and should be, organized in a straight line along a liberal–conservative continuum. They offer a different perspective that beliefs can also be seen as organized in a weblike structure, with pockets of beliefs consistently related to other pockets. They note studies of Americans during the Cold War, demonstrating that people have internally coherent outlooks on topics such as the rights of communists to speak freely, write, and work in mass media, universities, and even in defense plants. A person who granted communists one of those rights tended to grant them the others too. Moreover, this pocket of beliefs would often be linked to other pockets. People who granted civil rights to one group of people did so not only because of their beliefs about civil liberties, but also because of their feelings toward other groups—beliefs about tolerance and so forth. The authors further argued that, depending on how cognitively complex a person is, there can be many such pockets or only a few. Cognitive complexity, in turn, depends on how adept the person is at abstract reasoning. From this perspective, they determined that at least one-third of the mass public is cognitively complex, and another third is well organized, at least in terms of the basic American values regarding democracy and capitalism.

Having reviewed some of the debate on the level of political sophistication in America, at least in terms of how much people know about politics, we turn to the question of whether it matters. Do people take issue positions and vote in accordance with their interests, despite variations in levels of information and knowledge? Delli Carpini and Keeter (1996) argue that they do not, noting that those who were poorly informed did not connect their votes to their views on issues. Bartels (1996) agrees that there is an important difference in the voting patterns of informed and uninformed voters, and believes many uninformed voters would vote differently if they had full information. On the other hand, Lau and Redlawsk (1997, 2006) conducted experiments on voting and information. They defined "correct" voting as voting in accordance with the voters' own values. Subjects in the experiments were given limited information before voting and full information after voting, with the chance to change their vote. Only 30% chose to change their votes when given additional information.

Knowledge Structures

A related approach to reconceptualizing attitude complexity looks at **knowledge structures**. In a recent review of this literature, McGraw (2000) divided it into three categories: The first focuses on how people mentally organize information about political actors; a second body of research explores how those knowledge structures (e.g., stereotypes of the political parties) affect learning and decisions about political candidates; and a third body of literature examines how attitudes about issues are represented in the mind. Lavine (2002) divided the literature somewhat differently. He argued one body of literature maintains attitudes are affected by people's memory—what they recall about a candidate when they decide who to vote for and what they think about issues. Another body of literature examines online information processing, wherein people keep a running tally of information as they form attitudes on political issues.

The architecture of knowledge (or online) structures is a subject of debate. As mentioned earlier, Sniderman et al. (1991) believe the architecture varies in complexity from individual to individual, but that it exists in weblike pockets of attitudes related to one another. Similarly, Judd and Krosnick (1989), along with McGraw and Steenbergen (1995), argue that people have **associative networks**—that is, knowledge structures embedded in long-term memory, which consist of nodes linked to one another, forming a network of associations. When nodes are linked together, thinking about one draws thoughts about the other(s). This is illustrated with a network of knowledge regarding a candidate, which becomes more complex as more is learned about the candidate. An associative network of a candidate would look like Figure 6.2.

As Judd and Krosnick (1989) explain, the linked nodes may be within a single category of political objects, or between different categories altogether:

> Thus, for instance, the policy of affirmative action may be linked to the policy of school integration. At the same time, the policy of affirmative action is also likely to be linked to more abstract value nodes, such as freedom or equality, as well as to object nodes representing political reference groups (e.g., Blacks) and candidates.
>
> (Judd & Krosnick, 1989, p. 109)

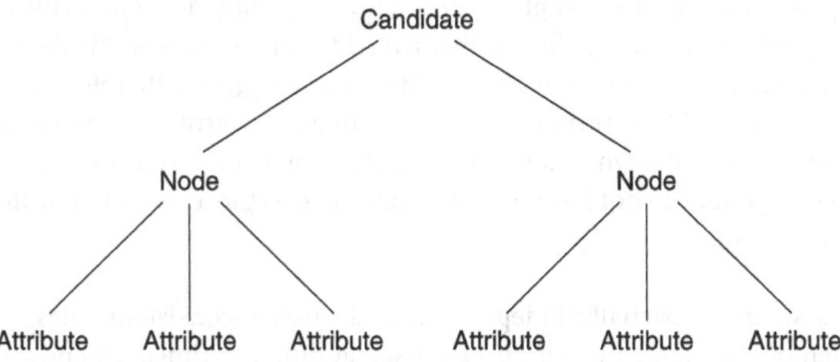

Figure 6.2 Associative Networks

Linked nodes imply a positive or negative relationship between them (e.g., affirmative action is positively associated with equality and negatively associated with freedom). Nodes, and subsequently their links, also vary in strength, which affects the probability that the activation of one node will activate another, as well as the likelihood that the associated evaluations will be consistent (Judd & Krosnick, 1989). The stronger a node, the more likely it is to be linked to other relevant nodes in a consistent manner. The more nodes, and the more links among them, the more consistent and complex a person's attitudes toward politics will be. One interesting aspect of this model is that it is entirely conceivable that a person may be quite sophisticated about politics in one domain, such as domestic politics, but not at all in another domain, such as foreign affairs. Indeed, in Chapter 5, we saw that this occurs among people very sophisticated about politics, such as President Bill Clinton. In addition, when people are more complex in their thinking, they look for and process more information when an attitude is important to them (Berent & Krosnick, 1995).

There is, however, considerable debate about whether Americans hold such precomputed opinions about issues (Lavine, 2002). Part of the reason for this debate about the political sophistication of Americans is that this research relies very heavily upon surveys. As Zaller explains, surveys are likely to pick up what is on the top of the respondent's head:

> Most people really aren't sure what their opinions are on most political matters, including even such completely personal matters as their level of interest in politics. They're not sure because there are few occasions, outside of a standard interview situation, in which they are called upon to formulate and express political opinions. So, when confronted by rapid-fire questions in a public opinion survey, they make up attitude reports as best they can as they go along. But because they are hurrying, they are heavily influenced by whatever ideas happen to be at the top of their minds.
>
> (Zaller, 1992, p. 76)

Zaller took this point beyond surveys, however, maintaining that people are ambivalent on many political issues much of the time. Putting the public in the context of politics, in the midst of debate about an issue, enables one to see the complexity of the multiple attitudes involved. A person may, for example, support a woman's right to reproductive choice generally, but may be very ambivalent about late-term partial birth abortions. When politicians discuss complex issues, they frequently do so in terms of summary judgments, a conclusion that overrides underlying ambivalence. Survey questions ask respondents to do the same thing, and therefore pick up seeming instability in responses, because ambivalent attitudes can swing in different directions when a summary judgment is required. In Zaller's (1992) view, people do not have true attitudes, such as those expected by the Michigan school,

> but a series of partially independent and often inconsistent ones. Which of a person's attitudes is expressed at different times depends on which has been made most immediately salient by change and

> the details of questionnaire construction, especially the ordering and framing of questions.
>
> (Zaller, 1992, p. 93)

The debate now turns to the question of how people actually process political information in America.

INFORMATION PROCESSING AND VOTING

A central question addressed by the knowledge structure inquiries concerns how those structures are used to process information and make political choices, such as how to evaluate a candidate and who to vote for. Those who know a lot about politics, and are interested in it, process information differently from those who know little and are not interested in politics (Lodge & Hamill, 1986; Sniderman, Glaser, & Griffin, 1990). But even people who have a great deal of interest in, and knowledge about, politics will take information shortcuts. They rely upon *attitudes, schemas,* and *heuristics* to help process information and make decisions. Pratkanis reminds us that a schema (or category) consists of

> both *content* (information in the schema and its organization) and *procedure* (the usage of this information in knowing). The dual role of a schema ... is similar to that of the heuristic as cue (an evaluation stored in memory) and strategy (the use of this cue in problem solving). A schema differs from a heuristic in its complexity. A heuristic is one simple rule, whereas a schema is an organization of many rules and pieces of data within a domain.
>
> (Pratkanis, 1989, p. 89)

Associative network models argue that nodes and links with greater strength are more easily summoned for thinking and information processing than those with weak links (Judd & Krosnick, 1989; McGraw & Steenbergen, 1995). Associative network studies drew upon schema research to develop ideas about information processing. The accessibility of political schemas influences how people think and what they are alert to. Those that are more frequently and most recently used are readily available for use again (Popkin, 1994; Ottati & Wyer, 1993). Schemas are used to filter information, providing people with a means for deciding which information is correct, irrelevant, or incorrect. Schemas or category-based knowledge—that is, pre-existing beliefs already present in a person's political mind—are also used as a source for substitute information when current information about a political issue or candidate is missing.

How do people process political information? The steps through which people presumably proceed upon receiving information are as follows: information is received and the appropriate node or schema is primed; the information is matched to the knowledge structure and appropriate nodes; the information is assessed and stored in memory; finally, that evaluation is retrieved from memory when the individual is called upon to make a decision about a political action (how to vote, what to think about a policy, etc.)

(Anderson, 1983; Brewer, 1988; Fiske & Pavelchak, 1986; Graber, 1984; Lodge & Stroh, 1995; Ottati & Wyer, 1990). In the process, feelings about candidates also emerge and are stored in memory (Rahn, Aldrich, Borgida, & Sullivan, 1990). Rather than placing feeling along a continuum from very negative to very positive, Lavine (2002) argued that people have stores or stockpiles of negative and positive feelings toward candidates, issues, and groups.

Of course, attention to information can be very selective (Iyengar, 1990; Ottati & Wyer, 1990). Some people are interested in particular issues. For example, the so-called soccer moms were intensely interested in education, childcare, and health insurance issues during the 1992 and 1996 elections. People can easily be more interested in one issue than another, and hence attentive to information about the issues that interest them, but not to information about the issues that do not. Delli Carpini and Keeter (1993, 1996) found political elites have a remarkably large amount of information about politics and the political system. They pay very close attention to politics. For these people—political elites and issue publics—schemas related to political issues will be quite accessible. The more accessible a schema or node is, the more information related to it will be noticed by the perceiver. Accessibility varies, depending on how important an attitude is to the perceiver (Berent & Krosnick, 1995; Holtz & Miller, 1985; Huckfeldt, Levine, Morgan, & Sprague, 1999; Krosnick, 1988, 1989). Moreover, Lau (1995) maintains that people use those schemas or nodes that are primed—that is, those that are most readily accessible. In addition, as is discussed in more detail later, issue nodes can be made more accessible when the media focus on a particular issue in depth (Iyengar, 1990).

People are selective in their attention to information, and studies also questioned how well they actually remember information as campaigns progress. Lodge and Stroh (1995; see also Lodge, 1995; Lodge, McGraw, & Stroh, 1989) argue that, as information is acquired, it is used to enhance or update beliefs about a candidate or party, and the specific details of the information are forgotten. Likes and dislikes are influenced by the information, and are remembered, but a person may well be hard-pressed to explain what the liking or disliking is based upon. This **impression-based model of information processing**, memory, and evaluation of political candidates stands in contrast to more traditional models, which argue that people store in memory the evidence supporting their evaluations (see Dreben, Fiske, & Hastie, 1979; Hastie & Park, 1986; McGraw, Lodge, & Stroh, 1990; Srull & Ottati, 1995; Srull & Wyer, 1989). In another study looking at voters' use of information, Lodge, Steenbergen, and Brau (1995) also addressed the question of how much information voters remember from the campaign when they vote. They argue that voters do forget lots of information, but that does not mean the information did not have an impact on their knowledge level when it was received. Voters keep a running tally, or an online tally, from which information is used in forming an impression of the candidates. The specifics of the information may be forgotten, but the overall impression remains, and is important in determining the vote.

A number of different heuristics, knowledge structures, and schema are important in processing political information (Lau, 1986; Ottati & Wyer, 1990; Rahn, Borgida, & Sullivan, 1990). There are many different heuristics serving as shortcuts in political information processing and judgments. Fiorina (1981) presented evidence of a retrospective voting heuristic, wherein voters make decisions about current candidates for office based upon those candidates' performance in the past. The representativeness heuristic, presented in Chapter 3, also plays an important role in political judgments. Recall that the representativeness heuristic is a rule of thumb for deciding what kind of person someone is based on how closely that person fits a stereotype.

In deciding who to vote for, according to Popkin (1994), "the most critical use of this heuristic involves projecting from a personal assessment of a candidate to an assessment of what kind of leader he[sic] was in previous offices or to what kind of president he[sic] will be in the future" (p. 74). People decide how well a candidate will perform in office based upon the goodness of fit between the candidate and the perceiver's stereotype of a good president or mayor, or whatever office the person is running. Popkin went on to argue that this results in the generation of narratives about people, wherein specific traits serve as the foundation of a fuller picture of the individual under observation. This, in turn, results in **Gresham's law of political information,** which says that

> personal information can drive more relevant political information out of consideration. Thus there can be a perverse relationship between the amount of information voters are given about a candidate and the amount of information they actually use: a small amount of personal information can dominate a large amount of historical information about a past record.
>
> (Popkin, 1994, p. 79)

Another informational shortcut is the **drunkard's search,** named after the drunkard who loses his keys in the street and looks for them under the lamp-post because the light is better there—not because that is where he lost the keys. This is analogous to when people reduce complicated issues and choices among candidates to simple comparisons because it is easier. This occurs in comparisons of candidates for office, when people use one-dimensional searches, focusing on obvious single issues or candidate characteristics, rather than searching for the complexities of both candidates and issues (Jervis, 1995; Popkin, 1994).

Heuristics are one form of mental shortcuts, and schemas are another. Among the most important schemas for Americans are partisanship, issues, and candidate schemas. The roles of each type of schema are difficult to separate, because they interact with one another. Ottati and Wyer illustrate this with the following possibilities:

> A voter may infer that a candidate endorses a given set of issue positions (e.g., favors bombing Libya or favors military intervention in Nicaragua) because he or she believes the candidate has certain personal traits (e.g., assertive) that combine to form the candidate's "image." Conversely, a voter may infer the candidate's personal traits from his or her stands on various issues. Analogously, a voter's perception of a candidate's personal characteristics or issue orientation

> may elicit emotional responses to the candidate. On the other hand, a voter's assessment of his or her own reactions to the candidate may lead the voter to infer that the candidate has certain personal characteristics or holds issue positions that are evaluatively consistent with these reactions.
>
> (Ottati and Wyer, 1990, p. 205)

The earliest studies of voting behavior demonstrated the importance of partisanship as a schema. *The American Voter* (Campbell et al., 1964) describes *partisanship* as an attitude used early on in information acquisition and states that a candidate's party is the first consideration, with issue positions and a candidate's personal characteristics second. Party also affects people's impressions of candidates, so, from this perspective it is the most important schema (Markus & Converse, 1979). For example, the schema or category "Democrat" has multiple pieces of information embodied in it. If a person is a Democrat, has the appropriate schema, and knows that candidate Smith is a Democrat, but has not bothered to get any information about where candidate Smith stands on issues, the association with the Democratic Party will lead to assumptions that Smith agrees with the perceiver on important issues. A study by Lodge and Hamill (1986) showed some of the effects of partisan schema on information processing. When presented with statements by a fictitious congressional leader, people with party schemas were more able to correctly categorize statements as being Republican or Democrat than people without party schemas. Those with schemas were better able to recall statements that were consistent with the party than those that were inconsistent. Schematics also "systematically distort the congressman's stance on the issue by imposing more schematic order on his policy positions than was actually present in the campaign message" (Lodge & Hamill, 1986, p. 518) indicating a bias in political information processing.

Candidate schemas or knowledge structures were studied extensively, and are believed to be closely associated with how a particular candidate appeals to voters on particular issues (Funk, 1999; Graber, 1984; Jacobs & Shapiro, 1994; Kaid & Chanslor, 1995; Kinder, 1986; Markus, 1982; Miller & Shanks, 1996; Rahn et al., 1990). Miller, Wattenberg, and Malanchuk (1986) examined whether there exists a presidential schema, or a prototype of the president. In other words, do individuals have a pre-existing schema about the current President that they use to evaluate a candidate? In their examination of elections from 1952 to 1985, the authors found individuals do in fact hold a presidential schema, central to which is the notion of competence (past political experience, ability as statesman, comprehension of political issues, and intelligence), which they regard as a performance-related criterion. Other dimensions, such as integrity (i.e., trustworthiness, honesty, sincerity, just another politician) and reliability (i.e., dependable, strong, hardworking, decisive, aggressive) became more relevant after 1964. Miller et al. (1986) notes that these expectations about the performance of presidents "appear to reflect in part the actions of past presidents and in part the agenda set by the media or by current candidates" (p. 535).

The importance of candidate schemas in information processing is further emphasized by Rahn et al. (1990), who maintain that although different people rely differentially on schemas of parties, issues, candidates, or groups, almost all the massive amount of information available to voters during an election can be used in evaluating candidates. Hence, candidate appraisals are particularly important. Moreover, they argue that in election after election, five characteristics of candidates are important in determining how much voters like or dislike a candidate: competence, integrity, reliability, charisma, and personal characteristics (Rahn et al., 1990). Funk (1999) found that candidates and campaigns vary in the underlying trait dimensions that emerge as important in evaluations of candidates. The substantive content of traits makes a difference. In her study, Funk found leadership characteristics significantly affected overall evaluations of George Bush and Michael Dukakis in 1988. In 1992, Bush was evaluated in terms of leadership and empathy characteristics. Ronald Reagan, in 1984, was evaluated in terms of empathy and integrity; Walter Mondale, his opponent, was evaluated in terms of leadership during that election. In 1992 and 1996, Bill Clinton was evaluated in terms of all three characteristics: leadership, empathy, and integrity.

Schemas and attitudes about issues compose a third important element in the American view of politics. An **issue** is a dispute about public policy. Popkin (1994) argues that issues are effective in waging a campaign for office only when voters see connections "(1) between the issue and the office; (2) between the issue and the candidate; and (3) between the issue and the benefits they care about" (p. 100). People are more likely to attend to issues about which information is easily acquired—that is, issues that are immediate in their lives and are easy to understand. This presents a formidable task for candidates for office. If candidates wish to campaign on issues, they must make the potential voters aware of where they stand on issues, that their position will benefit the voter, and that once in office they will actually have the power to effect the promised change.

Consequently, how issues are **framed** by candidates for office makes a big difference regarding whether or not, and how, the public will consider the issues (Gamson, 1992; Nelson & Oxley, 1999; Popkin, 1994; Zaller, 1992). **Issue frames** are "alternative definitions, constructions, or depictions of a policy problem" (Nelson & Oxley, 1999, p. 1041). How issues are framed influences the way voters look at the issues, and also affects how accessible the issue attitude is in the perceivers' minds. Studies showed framing to be important in presidential politics, as well as in race-related politics in the United States, which is a topic covered in Chapter 8 (Kinder & Sanders, 1996; Mendelberg, 2001; Popkin, 1994). The studies done at Columbia University in 1948, for example, showed that the campaign changed the relative importance of international issues versus domestic issues in voters' minds. Thinking about the positions of the candidates on domestic issues, instead of on international issues affected voter preference in that election, because they framed the candidates differently. Popkin (1994) summarized the findings regarding presidential politics and framing as follows:

> There is enough differentiation in people's images of presidents for formulation effects to matter; changing people's ideas about problems facing the president changes the way people think about presidents;

> and changing the ways people think about presidents affects their assessments of presidents as well as their votes.
>
> (Popkin, 1994, p. 84)

Candidates who engage in *frame alignment* (pointing out how their position on issues is consistent with voters' position) are likely to gain more support than candidates who do not.

Many of these information processing patterns are pulled together in Lau and Redlawsk's *How Voters Decide* (2006). They note four models of decision-making commonly found in the political science literature: the Rational Choice Model, wherein it is assumed that people carefully evaluate all information and make a voter choice based on self-interest; an early socialization and cognitive consistency model, the Confirmatory Decision Making Model, which is essentially that of the *American Voter*, where people start with the identification of a candidate's party and then passively acquire short-term information; a Fast and Frugal Decision Making Model, in which people look for specific bits of information about matters of importance to them and ignore everything else; and a bounded rationality model, the Semiautomatic Intuitive Decision Making Model, in which people only get as much information as they need to make a voting decision and no more. Lau and Redlawsk then examined a variety of cognitive processes, which were discussed in Chapter 3, in order to devise propositions about the decision strategies and information processing patterns associated with each model.

Beginning with the notion that processing all information is simply beyond what people are capable of, Lau and Redlawsk (2006) argue that there are five heuristics voters are likely to use. In the **affect referral heuristic**, people vote for a candidate with whom they are both familiar and regard highly. The **endorsement heuristic** refers to a shortcut wherein people select a candidate who has been endorsed by people the voter has confidence in. The **familiarity heuristic** comes into play when people are familiar with one candidate, but not the others, and they are at least neutral toward that candidate. The **habit heuristic** is simply voting the same way as last time. Finally, the **viability heuristic** is a selection of a candidate based on the likelihood he or she will win (Lau and Redlawsk, 2006, p. 28).

The models presented are considered broad decision strategies. Lau and Redlawsk (2006, p. 30) classify decision strategies by "the extent to which they confront or avoid conflict". When a voter experiences conflict between his or her preferences on one issue, and a preference on another issue, they can use one of two decision strategies. The first is a **compensatory strategy,** which involves the careful assignment of positive or negative values to each position. The voter then engages in an assessment of the trade-offs involved and resolves the conflict with a choice. The second strategy is a **noncompensatory strategy,** which essentially avoids the conflict by not getting complete information.

The authors also argued that new techniques are needed to observe how people acquire information. It is only by understanding how people acquire information that we can understand the decision rules and heuristics they use to make a decision. The *content* of the information sought is the well-known items reviewed above: party affiliation, issues and the positions candidates take, candidate traits, group interests and so on. The *process*, Lau and Redlawsk argue, is also central. It involves the depth of the search for information, the comparability of the search across alternatives, and the sequence of the search (2006, pp. 33–34). They add additional variables, which were introduced above as well, such as political sophistication, campaign dynamics, memory, and candidate evaluation, to develop their theory of voter decision-making. Lau and Redlawsk (2006) conclude with the following assessments of decision strategies for each model:

- *Rational Choice Model:* "the most cognitively difficult decision strategy, albeit one that promises a value maximizing outcome ... more likely to be chosen when there are only two alternatives in the choice set, by experts in any particular domain, and when decision makers are primarily motivated to make good decisions" (p. 45). The consequences of these decision strategies are "more moderate, less polarized candidate evaluations, higher quality decisions when decision tasks are relatively easy, or when the strategy is employed by a relative expert" (p. 46).
- *Confirmatory Decision Making Model*: "most likely to be chosen by strong political partisans ... [D]ecision makers should be motivated to learn candidates' party affiliations as soon as possible. And particularly when they are exposed to information that might lead them to question their standing decision, they should be motivated to seek disproportionate information about their in-party candidate" (p. 45). The consequences of these decision strategies include "Polarized candidate evaluations; lower quality decisions" (p. 46).
- *Fast and Frugal Decision Making Model:* "most likely when a decision is particularly difficult or when decision makers are working under severe time pressure" (p. 45). The consequences of these decision strategies include "[m]ore moderate, less polarized candidate evaluations; better quality decisions when decisions are—or are perceived to be—extremely difficult" (p. 46).
- *Semiautomatic Intuitive Decision Making Model:* "Any factor that leads decision makers to be primarily motivated by desires to make an easy decision, particularly increasing task difficulty" (p. 45) leads to the use of this model. The consequences include "Polarized candidate evaluations, better quality decisions when decisions are (perceived to be) relatively difficult" (p. 46).

The authors also introduce a method of assessing information processing that does not rely on surveys, as so much of the research in the study of public opinion does. Instead, Lau and Redlawsk use a dynamic processing methodology in which they create information boards that provide subjects with changing information about candidates during a hypothetical election. The information ebbs and flows, moving from information about the candidates to their issue positions, support base, and so on. The subjects react to the information as it comes in, which allows the researchers to gather data on their information processing as it occurs and changes.

We cannot discuss information processing and voting without mentioning the role of the brain in voting and voter turnout. In *The*

Political Brain, Westen (2007) highlights the role of the brain, based on brain scanning studies, in voting behavior. The origins of this research are the multitude of studies on brain activity and political ideology, with results showing that different areas of the brain are activated for those with liberal versus conservative beliefs. Clearly, the brain plays an important role in determining voting behavior.

With regard to actual voter turnout, Fowler, Baker and Dawes (2008), using a twin-study methodology, found a genetic component to habitual voter turnout. More specifically, they found more than half (53%) of the variance in voter turnout can be attributed to genetic factors. Similarly, Fowler and Dawes (2008) examined the relationship between MAOA (an enzyme that is sometimes called the "warrior gene") and the 5HTT gene (sometimes referred to as a depression gene) on self-reported voter turnout. Their results found a small effect of MAOA on self-reported voter turnout. There was an effect of 5HTT on voter turnout, but only through an association with religious involvement. In fact, this result makes some sense, as political activity and religious involvement both represent an interest in affiliating with a social group.

Later, French, Smith, Alford, Guck, Birnie and Hibbing (2014) examined voter participation rates in the United States, which historically have been low (40–60% voter turnout). They measured cortisol levels to determine whether they could predict voting behavior. Cortisol is a hormone often referred to as the "stress hormone" or the "fight or flight" hormone because it plays an important role in our body's reaction to stress. Our body produces more cortisol when it is stressed or in fearful situations. Their results showed that lower cortisol levels (when measured in the late afternoon) were associated with increased voting activity in major elections. Interestingly, cortisol levels were not associated in any meaningful way with non-voting political behavior.

Other research examined particular parts of the brain to determine their role in voting behavior. One brain structure implicated in this research is the amygdala, a structure in the brain responsible for several cognitive processes, but also emotional responses such as anxiety. Rule, Freeman, Moran, Gabrieli, Adams and Ambady (2010) examined the role of the amygdala in voting behavior across cultures. The basis for their study involved the observation that American and Japanese voters agreed in their judgments of candidates' faces, but they chose to elect different candidates. Japanese voters selected candidates they judged to be warm; American voters selected candidates they judged to be powerful. Rule et al. (2010) were interested in brain activity while making these voting choices. Making use of functional Magnetic Resonance Imaging (fMRI), their study emphasizes two important findings. First, activity in the amygdala was able to predict the preferred candidate of the potential voter. Moreover, this held true regardless of the potential voter's culture, or the culture of the candidate. Second, activity in the amygdala was more pronounced for out-group candidates than for in-group candidates. This latter result, of course, has implications for a host of group behaviors, but most specifically, for out-group bias discussed previously in this text. As we will see below, emotions do indeed play a role in voting.

EMOTION AND VOTING

The importance of emotion in political behavior was discussed in Chapter 3, and the work of Marcus, Neuman and MacKuen (2000) was introduced. In 1993, Marcus and MacKuen published a study pointing to the importance of anxiety and enthusiasm in political learning and involvement. They argued that people do not simply respond to candidates positively or negatively (i.e., valence), but rather with specific emotions. Traditional notions of the effect of emotions on voting showed that positive or negative feelings toward candidates directly influence how people vote. Marcus and MacKuen (1993), however, offered a more precise picture of how emotions affect political behavior during election time. Two emotions central to responses to political events and candidates are fear (or anxiety) and enthusiasm. Enthusiasm affects the decision about who to vote for, while anxiety increases the search for information about candidates. When people do not experience anxiety, they tend to rely upon habit in determining how they will vote (e.g., party identification). Thus, anxiety has an important role in information processing, and it stimulates learning.

This argument is presented as a theory of affective intelligence in *Affective Intelligence and Political Judgment* (Marcus et al., 2000). Those authors examined interviews with people during the 1980, 1984, 1988, 1992, and 1996 presidential election campaigns, looking for trends in emotional responses to the candidates and voting decisions. They made assessments of voters' preferences, using the "standing choice" factors for these elections—that is, partisanship, issues, and the candidates' personal qualities. Then they added in an analysis of voters' enthusiasm and anxiety. For example, in the 1980 election, President Jimmy Carter began the campaign with public support and sympathy in the midst of the Iran hostage crisis and the Soviet invasion of Afghanistan. By October, however, the hostage rescue scheme had failed, the economy was in the doldrums, and public enthusiasm for Carter had waned. In addition, public anxiety regarding the competence of the administration grew, albeit modestly. Enthusiasm for Ronald Reagan, Carter's 1980 opponent, was modest; however, the study showed an increase in anxiety regarding Reagan after the Democrats launched a scare campaign in an effort to persuade voters that Reagan would be dangerous in foreign policy. In the 1984 campaign, enthusiasm for Reagan—by then a popular president—was high, and anxiety was not. The challenger, Walter Mondale, evoked neither enthusiasm nor anxiety. In 1988, when Vice President George Bush ran against Massachusetts Governor Michael Dukakis, the public's anxiety about Dukakis was increased by the famous Willie Horton ads (discussed in more detail in Chapter 8) that portrayed Dukakis as weak on crime. Overall, in their analyses of all five races from 1980 to 1996, Marcus et al. (2000) found that anxious voters were much less likely to rely upon partisanship in making a voting decision and much more likely to look for and attend to information about the candidates' personal qualities and issue positions. A caveat is that this anxiety must involve the voter's own candidate, the one for whom they would ordinarily vote, based upon partisanship. To be anxious about the other candidate is normal—one is always anxious about the candidate from the other party; there is nothing unusual about that—but doubts about the person one would ordinarily vote for produce anxiety.

Redlawsk, Civettini, and Lau (2007) tested some of the hypotheses generated by the Affective Intelligence theory using their dynamic processing method discussed above. They considered several hypotheses:

1. When voters agree with a candidate on an issue they will be enthusiastic about the candidate. When they disagree, they will be angry. When there is some distance, but not enough to make them angry, voters will experience anxiety.
2. New information that produces enthusiasm will not be processed more rapidly than neutral information. However, new information that prompts the surveillance system into action (discussed in Chapter 3) will produce anxiety (or anger) and will take longer to process.

3a. When the surveillance system is activated and anxiety is produced, voters will search for more information about the candidate who is associated with anxiety. Anger, on the other hand, produces aversion to more information.

3b. Anxiety about a candidate will result in greater accuracy in knowing where the candidate stands on issues. Anger and enthusiasm produce the opposite, less accuracy in assessing the candidate's issue positions.

These hypotheses were tested with respect to a preferred candidate and a rejected candidate. Their findings supported hypothesis 1. Hypothesis 2 was supported in terms of the effect of enthusiasm. However, they found that both anxiety and anger did increase processing time, but only for candidates the subjects preferred. Regarding hypotheses 3a and 3b, they found that "in a high-threat environment, anger and anxiety both show learning effects, and subjects are much better able to place their preferred candidate. In the low-threat environment, however, both affective responses lead to *less accurate* placement" (Redlawsk, Civettini, & Lau, 2007, p. 176). They concluded:

> The weight of the evidence supports aspects of the affective intelligence thesis, albeit with important caveats. Anxiety, which is presumed to cause heightened attention and processing, only operates for preferred candidates and in an environment where there is substantial information that defies expectations. In a high-threat environment anxiety leads to more careful processing, more effort to learn about the candidate who generates the anxiety, and better assessment of that candidate's position on the issue ... But in a low threat environment, anxiety appears to do very little to increase either processing efforts or learning. Furthermore, regardless of threat environment, anxiety does not have any effects on processing information about rejected candidates ... Anger, which ought to generate aversion, exhibits the expected effect, at least in low-threat environments. In such environments greater attention is paid to information that invokes anger, but then that anger is aimed at an initially liked candidate, aversion occurs as voters turn toward other candidates. The result is to incorrectly recall where such as candidate stands with regard to issues.
>
> (Redlawsk, Civettini, & Lau, 2007, p. 177)

The Presidential Election of 2008

The election of 2008 in the United States, which resulted in the election of the first African American to the American presidency, provided an opportunity to look at both cognitive and emotional elements in voting. Democrat Barack Obama won by 52% to Republican John McCain's 46%. Thousands of people raced through Grant Park in Chicago to get a view of Obama during his victory speech, and the tears of joy on so many faces showed the powerful emotions felt by Obama supporters. Many Americans—his supporters and opponents alike—felt great pride when America crossed that highest racial threshold and elected an African American to the country's highest office. Clearly, short-term factors were extremely important in determining Barack Obama's success. The economy was in crisis by October 2008, and the wars in Afghanistan and Iraq—the latter of which Obama opposed—were increasingly unpopular. The standing president, George W. Bush, was the least popular president ever, and despite John McCain's efforts, the McCain campaign was unable to break the public association of McCain with the Bush administration. At the time of the election, 71% disapproved of President Bush and 48% thought McCain would continue along the same policy lines (Pew Research Center, 2008b). The two candidates had strengths and weaknesses in terms of candidate characteristics. Obama had less experience, and he was African American, and McCain was seen as too old and somewhat volatile. Turnout was very high, at over 60%. As it turned out, Obama did well among many different demographic groups. Sixty-one percent of Obama's votes were cast by Whites compared with 90% of McCain's, 23% of Obama's votes came from African American voters compared with 1% of McCain's, 11% of Obama's votes were from Hispanics compared with 6% of McCain's, and 30% of Obama's votes came from people under the age of 30, compared with 13% of McCain's (Curry, 2008). Forty-six percent of White women voted for Obama, more than the percentage of White women who voted for either Al Gore in 2000 (42%) or John Kerry in 2004 (41%) (Barnes & Shear, 2008). The Republican Party was less able to attract Independent voters in this election than in the previous two. Clearly, neither partisanship nor candidate characteristics won the election for Barack Obama, but issues did.

The race issue was very interesting during the campaign and the election itself. The Obama campaign was determined he would not be seen as a Black candidate. They wanted his campaign to transcend race. There were times when race became a direct issue, such as the controversy that erupted after Obama's former minister, Reverend Jeremiah Wright, was shown on video denouncing the United States. Nevertheless, race did not play a large role in the voters' choice. There were significant concerns all along that race would be important and cast a negative impact on the Obama candidacy. A 2008 study of Democrats and Independents by researchers at Stanford University found survey results indicated racial prejudice could have an important role in the 2008 election. They found that over a third of White Democrats and Independents agreed with at least one negative characterization of Blacks, and their negative feelings could prevent them from voting for Obama (AOL News, September 20, 2008). This, among other developments, raised concerns about a repeat of the so-called **Bradley effect**. Los Angeles Mayor

Tom Bradley ran for the governor's office in California in 1982. Despite his lead in the polls, he lost the election, and analysts believed this was a result of White voters lying about their willingness to vote for a Black candidate. This did not occur in the 2008 election. Polls showed Obama ahead of McCain by 51 to 43% (NBC News-Wall Street Journal), 53 to 42% (Gallup) and 51 to 42% (CBS News) (Curry, 2008). Those figures were pretty close to the actual vote. Years later, academic studies addressed the role of race in the election. For example, Schaffner (2011) examined the extent to which racial salience had a moderating influence on Whites' (and, in particular, racial conservatives') support for Obama. He found when race was salient for White voters, they were less likely to vote for Obama, and maintained that the president-elect focused too much on Blacks. Tesler and Sears (2010) and Kinder and Dale-Riddle (2012) also provided strong evidence that racial animosity affected both the vote for Obama, who would have won by a much larger margin in 2008 had he not been Black.

Issues and Emotions

The economy was the issue of greatest concern to Americans in the 2008 election. Sixty-three percent of the voters cited the economy as their greatest concern, and Obama was favored on that issue. Fifty-nine percent of those who said the economy was their greatest concern voted for Obama (Pew Research Center, 2008b). One-third of the voters expressed concern about access to affordable healthcare, and among those voters 65% voted for Obama (Pew Research Center, 2008b). Those who said the war in Iraq was their top issue also voted for Obama over McCain by 59% to 39%. The one issue area in which McCain dominated was terrorism, and he got 86% of the votes from people who cited terrorism as their top issue (Pew Research Center, 2008b). However, only 9% of the electorate saw terrorism as the most important issue.

Early analyses showed how important the issues and emotion both were in this election. Obama's supporters were more likely to express excitement and optimism at the prospect of his election than McCain's supporters by a ratio of 56% to 28%. When asked whether an Obama or McCain presidency "scared" them, 24% said Obama scared them and 28% said McCain scared them (Pew Research Center, 2008b).

The 2012 Election

In the 2012 election, exit polls indicated "more than 90% of self-identified Democrats voted for Obama, with 45% of Independents doing so as well" (Norpoth & Bednarczuk, 2013). Further, according to the Pew Research Center, Romney did not poll favorably throughout the campaign:

> Just 47% of exit-poll respondents viewed him favorably, compared with 53% for Mr. Obama. Throughout the campaign, Mr. Romney's favorable ratings were among the lowest recorded for a presidential candidate in the modern era. A persistent problem was doubt about his empathy with the average voter. By 53% to 43%, exit-poll respondents

said that Mr. Obama was more in touch than Mr. Romney with people like themselves.

(Kohut, 2012, p. 1)

Election and survey results reported by the Roper Center (2012) revealed insights from the election. Fifty-nine percent of Whites voted for Romney and 93% of Blacks, 71% of Hispanics, and 73% of Asians voted for Obama. Sixty percent (down from 66% in 1988) of those aged 18–28 years, and 45% of men and 53% of women voted for Obama. Fifty-four percent of voters making over $100,000 voted for Romney, while 60% of those making under $50,000 voted for Obama. The most important issue for Obama voters was healthcare, while Romney voters cited defense and then the economy. In their analysis of the election, Norpoth and Bednarczuk (2013) argued that Obama had the incumbency advantage and was given the benefit of the doubt. This was demonstrated in exit polls where Obama was punished less than George Bush for the economy. While Romney was a strong Republican nominee, he could not "trump" the incumbent advantage.

THE 2016 ELECTION OF DONALD TRUMP

On January 20, 2017, Donald Trump was inaugurated as President of the United States. Republican candidate Trump defeated Democratic candidate Hillary Clinton in the electoral college 306 to 232. Clinton won the popular vote by 2.86 million votes. Trump won narrow margins in the so-called "rust belt" states: Michigan, Wisconsin, Iowa, Ohio, and Pennsylvania. The election was a surprise since Clinton was in the lead in the national polls. It was the electoral college vote that revealed where Trump's strengths and Clinton's weaknesses lay.

What happened in this election? As Jacobson (2017) argues, Trump's candidacy in and of itself was very improbable. First, he was opposed by the Republican Party establishment; second, he personally, his lack of knowledge, and his style of insulting and lying were not well received by the public. He did not run a standard campaign, and even after his nomination many in the party leadership did not embrace him (Jacobson, 2017). Explaining this election is complicated. To do so, we must look at candidate characteristics, issues, and the people who voted for each candidate.

Candidates

Hillary Clinton was not a popular figure. As Jacobson wrote: "were it not for Trump, she would have been the most unpopular major-party candidate on record" (2017, p. 16). There are many reasons for her lack of popularity. She had been in politics for decades and had a track record. She was a former first lady and "stuck by her man" Bill Clinton after his affair with Monica Lewinsky was revealed. Her actions as first lady were controversial, including her efforts to promote healthcare. She was also Secretary of State during the Obama administration and came under criticism and investigation for her use of a private email server during that time. There was suspicion about the Clinton Foundation's activities, and she was suspected of having close relationships with Wall Street executives. All of this fed into impressions of her as dishonest and secretive, an impression that was fueled by Bernie Sanders and the more progressive wing of the Democratic Party. Clinton's association with the Obama administration was a positive for Democrats, but Republicans generally disliked him immensely, believing he was not born in the United States (28 per cent not born in the US, 17 per cent not sure), and he was a Muslim (43%), and they transferred that animosity to Clinton (Jacobson, 2017, p. 18).

Donald Trump had even more negatives in terms of personal popularity. He began his candidacy with a speech at Trump Tower that was filled with racist and anti-immigrant rhetoric:

> Our country is in serious trouble. We don't have victories anymore. We used to have victories, but we don't have them. When was the last time anybody saw us beating, let's say, China in a trade deal? They kill us. I beat China all the time. All the time.
>
> When did we beat Japan at anything? They send their cars over by the millions, and what do we do? When was the last time you saw a Chevrolet in Tokyo? It doesn't exist, folks. They beat us all the time.
>
> When do we beat Mexico at the border? They're laughing at us, at our stupidity. And now they are beating us economically. They are not our friend, believe me. But they're killing us economically.
>
> The U.S. has become a dumping ground for everybody else's problems.
>
> Thank you. It's true, and these are the best and the finest. When Mexico sends its people, they're not sending their best. They're not sending you. They're not sending you. They're sending people that have lots of problems, and they're bringing those problems with us [sic]. They're bringing drugs. They're bringing crime. They're rapists. And some, I assume, are good people.
>
> (*Time,* June 16, 2015)

Statements such as this were perceived to be reflections of Trump's racial attitudes. His comments to *Access Hollywood* reporter Billy Bush bragging about his ability to assault women with impunity because he was a celebrity, and his alleged extra-marital affairs with porn star Stormy Daniels and other women were perceived as evidence of his contempt for women. He was also clearly a bully, insulting his opponents, and a man who had difficulty with the truth. These characteristics contributed to an initial lack of enthusiasm for Trump among his supporters. According to a Pew Research Center study, "about a third of Trump's November 2016 voters (35%) had cold or neutral feelings toward him earlier that year" (Pew Research Centre, 2016b, p. 6). Basically, a significant proportion of Republican partisans were uncertain about Trump, but not enough to shift their votes to Clinton. Another Pew Research Center study (2016a) showed that voters were not satisfied with their choices, as 41% in their study said neither Trump nor Clinton would make a good president (2016a, p. 1).

A number of issues were in play in the 2016 election, as discussed below.

The Economy

In 2008 the United States and the rest of the world entered into the Great Recession. It included a stock market crash, a global credit crisis, a housing mortgage crisis, the collapse of the automobile industry, and other dire economic conditions. The Obama administration pulled the United States out of the recession and left office with a strong stock market and low unemployment rates. Nevertheless, the recovery benefited some more than others. The recession, along with long-term trends in globalization, shifted the American economy forever from a manufacturing economy to a service economy. This meant many people who worked in mining and manufacturing, as well as smaller retail and service jobs, did not benefit from the recovery as much as big corporations and banks (Francis, 2017). Trump promised to "make America great again" by restoring jobs lost from the recession and/or globalization. Thus, many of his supporters came from the sector of the population suffering from this reality. Eighty-four percent of respondents in the Pew Research Center study said the economy was their top issue, with 90% of Trump voters and 80% of Clinton voters seeing the economy as the most important issue in the election (Pew Research Center, 2016a, p. 4).

Terrorism

Terrorism was also an important issue in the 2016 election, with 80% overall and 74% of Clinton voters and 89% of Trump voters ranking the issue as very important (Pew Research Center, 2016a, p. 4). While both candidates advocated for the defeat of Islamic State, Trump's rhetoric was much more violent, saying he would eradicate Islamic fundamentalism, return to using torture, and even going so far as killing the families of terrorists (Francis, 2017). Forty-eight percent of voters favored Trump on dealing with terrorism, while 43% favored Clinton (Pew Research Center, 2016a, p. 4).

Immigration

Sixty-five percent of Clinton supporters and 79% of Trump supporters saw immigration as an important issue in 2016 (Pew Research Center, 2016a, p. 4). The campaigns could not have been more different on the issue. Trump made stopping illegal immigration, prohibition on immigration from certain Muslim countries, and the deportation of those who were in the United States illegally—even if they were brought to the country as children by their parents—a key platform. He promised to build a "big beautiful wall" along the U.S.–Mexico border and make Mexico pay for it. As Francis (2017, p. 123) notes:

> Keeping migrants out of the country became his signature issue. It hit all his bases: fears about jobs, terror, and crime; hatred of globalization; uneasiness about cultural change; anger at unfairness; aspirations to keep Americans first; helping the disrespected feel heard and heeded.

Clinton, in contrast, favored legislation that would develop a path to citizenship for illegal immigrants, preferred enhanced technology and border patrol along the entire border, and supported the continuation of President Obama's Dreamer program, protecting children of immigrants brought to the United States illegally from deportation (NPR, 2016). Over all, Clinton was favored on this issue with 51% thinking Clinton would do a better job and 42% thinking Trump would do a better job on the issue (Pew Research Center, 2016a, p. 4).

Trump's "Drain the Swamp" Theme

Trump's campaign depicted him as the anti-government populist out to defend those affected by the economic downturn, the fixing of which had not benefited them enough. He described the political establishment of both Democrats and Republicans as "the swamp," which he promised to "drain." In addition to the political establishment, Trump's swamp included the mainstream media and institutions, particularly the intelligence community and the FBI. He threw Hillary Clinton into the swamp as well, saying that "Hillary Clinton's corruption is on a scale we've never seen before" (quoted in Nazaryan, 2017, p. 1). Fifty percent of voters thought Trump would be better able to deal with the lobbyists and the access that special interests had to the political establishment than Clinton would (30%) (Pew Research Center, 2016a, p. 4).

Foreign Policy

There were dramatic differences between Trump and Clinton in the area of foreign policy. Clinton, the former Secretary of State, backed the foreign policy approach of the Obama administration: negotiate agreements in multilateral and bilateral forums, respect international norms, and participate in international institutions. She advanced the policy of defeating the Islamic State terrorist organization, and continuing to pursue American national interests. Her policy was essentially the status quo.

Trump, on the other hand, offered a very different picture of America's future role in international politics. "America first" was not a call for isolationism, but a rejection of international norms and institutions. Trump called for the withdrawal of American forces from Afghanistan and Syria, the withdrawal of the country from international treaties and agreements such as the Paris Accord on environmental policies, and the Iran nuclear accord. He deemed NATO "obsolete" and demanded that NATO members pay more for the organization (Cottam, 2020). Trump was equally critical of America's trade deals, believing previous administrations had given away too much and let the United States be taken advantage of. He threatened to withdraw from trade deals being negotiated like the Trans Pacific Partnership (TPP), impose high tariffs, particularly on goods from China, and to withdraw from the North American Free Trade Association (NAFTA) and the World Trade Organization (WTO) (Cottam, 2020). Once again, polls before the election indicated voters thought Clinton would do better in making foreign policy decisions (54% to 36%) and in negotiating trade deals (48% to 46%) (Pew Research Center, 2016a, p. 4).

WHO VOTED FOR TRUMP AND WHY

Given these issue differences and the general preference for Clinton, and given the equal lack of candidate attractiveness, it was surprising that Clinton lost, despite winning the popular vote by 2.86 million votes. She only lost the electoral college and therefore the votes from six crucial states by small margins, but it cost her the presidency.

First, the commonly held idea that Trump's supporters were poor, unemployed, working-class people is a myth. Trump's voters were actually better off than the average American. Their median income during the 2015 primaries was about $72,000 while the national median income was $56,000 (Silver, 2016). That figure is also higher than the $61,000 median income of both Clinton's and Bernie Sanders' supporters (Silver, 2016).

One thing that clearly differentiated Clinton vs. Trump voters was education. College graduates supported Clinton over Trump by 52% to 43%. Voters without a college education favored Trump by 52% to 44% (Pew Research Center, 2016b). However, Trump won *White* non-college *and* college educated voters, the latter by four points over Clinton. This brings us back to the question of whether those without a college degree had fewer economic opportunities. This argument is refuted by Jacobson (2017) and by Schafner, MacWilliams and Nteta (2018). Jacobson argues of Trump supporters:

> Against expectations ... they were individually no worse off economically than other Americans in similar occupations and were actually less likely to work in industries threatened by foreign competition. But they were more likely to live in areas that are homogeneously white, less cosmopolitan, and further from the Mexican border and that have lower intergenerational mobility, higher mortality rates among middle-aged whites, and a larger proportion of working-age adults receiving disability payments.
>
> (Jacobson, 2017, p. 22)

Clearly, there was something more than economic inequality going on. Some analysts (e.g., Pettigrew, 2017; Rothwell & Diego-Rosell, 2016) argue that although Trump supporters are not generally poorer than non-supporters, they may suffer from relative deprivation, or a sense they were not doing as well as other Americans. They have little social mobility and do not believe their children's futures will be better than their own.

Returning to the demographics of the 2016 vote, men supported Trump over Clinton by 53% to 41% and women supported Clinton by almost the exact opposite, 54% to 42% (Pew Research Center, 2016b, p. 1). Looking at racial alignments, as a group White people voted for Trump by 57% and for Clinton by 37%. African Americans voted overwhelmingly for Clinton (87% to 8% for Trump). Hispanics voted in favor of Clinton by 66%; and Asians voted for her by 65% (Roper Center 2016).

These figures lead us to the question of what role gender and race played in the election. White people overwhelmingly voted for Trump, and there was a male voter preference for the male candidate. Trump and his campaign made no effort to hide their misogyny. Pins worn by participants at the

Republican National Convention, for example, had slogans such as "Don't be a pussy. Vote for Trump," "Trump that bitch," and "Life's a bitch: Don't vote for one" (Frances, 2017: 129–30). More generally Bos, Schneider and Utz (2017) argue that role incongruity theory may explain why women in general, and by extension Hillary Clinton, have difficulty getting elected to the highest office in the United States. Women are expected to be well behaved and polite, but politicians are expected to be aggressive and assertive. When women behave like politicians, their behavior is incongruous and disliked. Schaffner, MacWilliams, and Nteta (2018) argue that "when Trump referred to Clinton as a 'nasty woman' during a debate, the reaction from voters may have been conditioned by their underlying views about how women should behave" (p. 14). Using two surveys of American adults, they found that those without college education scored higher on hostile sexism scales (p. 20).

Racism is another factor to consider in the 2016 election. Despite Donald Trump's repeated declaration that he is the least racist person ever, his lifelong record of racist behavior speaks for itself. In 1973, the Justice Department sued Trump, his father, and his real estate company for discriminating against African Americans who wished to rent an apartment. (The case was settled with no admission of guilt.) In 1989, Trump called for the death penalty for several young minority men accused (falsely) of raping a jogger in Central Park. After Barack Obama was elected to the presidency, Trump pushed forward his argument that Obama was not born in the United States, thereby making him ineligible to be the first African American president. While in the presidency, he repeatedly refused to condemn radical right racist groups who committed acts of violence and repeated prejudiced ideas about Muslims and Mexicans. Despite the diminution of racism in America generally, it was evident among Trump supporters, who scored higher than non-supporters on denial of racism scales (that is, that racism is no longer a problem), and a standard scale of modern racism (Pettigrew, 2017; Schaffner, MacWilliams, and Nteta, 2016).

The role of race in the 2016 election is complicated, and we will address it from several perspectives here, and in Chapters 8 and 11. Although Trump had a lifelong record of racist attitudes in his business dealings, he used race in this election to position himself as the champion of White identity and racism that already existed both systemically and as a backlash from the first Black American president. As Fording and Schram (2020) note, blatant racism was profoundly disliked by American voters by the time we reached the twenty-first century, and Trump's racist rhetoric should have ended his candidacy under normal circumstances. His campaign included more negative comments about Blacks and Latino/Latinx[1] Americans than any other candidate, as well as somewhat more negative rhetoric against Muslims (Fording & Schram, 2020, p. 113), so he certainly did not hide his views on race. Instead, Trump took advantage of the growth of White identity-based hostility to outgroups such as liberals, Blacks, Latino, and Muslims. He "provided much-needed leadership for the entire range of racially inspired movements in the post-Obama era" (Fording & Schram, 2020, p. 99). Despite the growth in White identity, which we discuss more thoroughly in Chapter 8, Fording and Schram (2020) argue that responses to questions about White identity in the 2012 and 2016 American National Election Studies indicate that outgroup hostility was more important than

White identity in producing the pro-Trump vote in 2016 (p. 161). Trump may have mainstreamed racism and racist rhetoric, and outgroup hostility, but that is not the same as White identity producing 2016 electoral support. Jardina (2019), on the other hand, provided evidence that White identity and consciousness did produce strong positive affective evaluations of Trump. We flesh out the White identity arguments in Chapter 8.

A number of additional studies found Trump supporters to be high in authoritarianism and social dominance orientation (Choma & Hanoch, 2017; Dean & Altemeyer, 2020; Francis, 2017; MacWilliams, 2020; Pettigrew 2017). For example, MacWilliams used four national panel surveys from 2016 through 2020 to study the extent to which Americans are authoritarians and found 18% were high authoritarians, with another 23% somewhat less authoritarian. Accordingly:

> This roughly 40 percent of Americans tend to favor authority, obedience and uniformity over freedom, independence, and diversity. This group isn't a monolith, and these findings don't mean that 4 in 10 Americans prefer dictatorship to democracy. Authoritarianism is best understood not as a policy preference, the way we talk about lower taxes or strong defense, but rather as a worldview that can be "activated" in the right historical moment by anyone with a big enough megaphone who is willing to play on voters' fears and insecurities.
>
> When activated by fear, authoritarian-leaning Americans are predisposed to trade civil liberties from strongman solutions to secure law and order; and they are ready to strip civil liberties from those defined as the "other"—a far cry from the image of America as a country built on a shared commitment to liberty and democratic governance.
>
> (MacWilliams, 2020, p. 4)

Social isolation is another characteristic of Trump supporters that appears to be important for their political stance on issues such as immigration and race. They have less contact with minorities, and intergroup contact is shown to decrease prejudice (Pettigrew, 2017). As Pettigrew notes, there is a "delicate balance between threat and contact" (2017, p. 112). While contact diminishes prejudice, a sudden influx of outsiders (immigrants, people of color, etc.) can be very threatening and can cause an adverse reaction to the newcomers. This helps us to understand why such strong opposition to immigration (particularly from Mexico) resonated in the Midwest, far from the border.

POLITICAL POLARIZATION

Polarization in American politics has been growing since the 1970s. There are many structural reasons for this trend. Although we are most interested in the psychological causes and consequences, some of the structural reasons are important to mention. Earlier in this chapter we discussed the changes in partisan alignment during the 1960s, which produced a realignment in the South, with White southerners becoming more Republican in their identification. As time went on, the issues and socio-economic status of Republican and Democratic identifiers continued to evolve, or "sort" (Carsey & Layman, 2018; Mason, 2018; McCarty, 2018). The two parties became increasingly distinct, with the Republican Party's movement to the right accounting for more of the partisan divergence (McCarty, 2018). Conservative voters more strongly identify with the Republican Party, and liberals more strongly identify with the Democratic Party. The Democratic Party's movement to the left is more of a result of the disappearance of Southern White identifiers along with an increase in Black and Latino identifiers (McCarty, 2018). Finally, Carsey and Layman (2018) note that while American political parties were always polarized on political issues, the focus typically was on one issue at a time, such as slavery. Today, however, through a process they term "conflict extension," Democrats and Republicans are polarized on three different issue areas simultaneously: social welfare (e.g., wealth distribution and healthcare); racial equality; and culture and morality (e.g., abortion).

America experienced increased polarization before Donald Trump came into office, but it grew stronger during his administration. Moghaddam's (2018) model, which we also discuss in Chapter 12, argues that this fits the pattern of mutual radicalization, which occurs through three stages. The first is group mobilization, wherein two groups begin to perceive members of the other group through stereotypes with deindividuation of group members. This, in turn, causes an exaggeration of the differences between the groups; an increase in group salience; a sense of injustice and relative deprivation; identity mobilization; and denigration of the out-group (pp. 31–32). In the second stage, "processes leading to intense pressure to conform and obey within each group [begin], with more aggressive styles of behavior becoming normative for both leaders and followers" (p. 33). The groups rally around an ideology, which is taken as "truth." In the third stage, intergroup hostilities increase further, issue positions become more extreme, perceptions of the out-group become more demonized, and identities become hardened. Trigger events during this stage can produce more violence and hostility (pp. 34–5).

These patterns were certainly evident in the United States by 2020. For example, a 2019 study by the Pew Research Center found:

> The share of Republicans who give Democrats a "cold" rating on a 0–100 thermometer has risen 14 percentage points since 2016—with virtually all of the increase coming in "very cold" ratings (0–24). Democrats' views of Republicans have followed a similar trajectory; 57% give Republicans a very cold r, up from 41% three years ago ... [B]oth Republicans and Democrats express negative about several traits and characteristics of those in the opposing party, and in some cases these opinions have grown more negative since 2016. For example, 55% of Republicans say Democrats are "more immoral" when compared with other Americans; 47% of Democrats say the same about Republicans.
>
> (Pew Research Center, 2019, pp. 1–2)

The report went on to note that 63% of Republicans see Democrats as more unpatriotic than other Americans, while 23% of Democrats see Republicans that way. Sixty-four percent of Republicans see Democrats as more closed minded than other Americans, while 75% of Democrats see Republicans that way (Pew Research Center, 2019, p. 2). Republicans and Democrats both see partisan divisions increasing (85% to 78%); there are major differences between the parties (74% to 59% respectively); they disagree on what is factual (77% to 72% respectively); and the other party does not share their basic values (61% to 54% respectively) (Pew Research Center, 2019, pp. 2–5). One quite interesting aspect of these findings is the perceptions of differences is greater than the actual differences on policy issues such as immigration and taxation, and perceptions of ideological polarization are twice as great than it actually is (Enders & Armaly, 2019; Moore-Berg, et al., 2020). However, the perceptions have a large effect despite not being grounded in substantial evidence. They can produce strong prejudices against the out-group, including less trust for and discrimination of the out-group party (Moore-Berg et al., 2020). These patterns match those described generally by Moghaddam.

A related outcome of polarization is dehumanization of the other party members. A number of studies note a pattern of dehumanizing among both Republicans and Democrats (Cassese, 2019; Matherus, et al., 2019; Moore-Berg et al., 2020). Cassese (2019) argues that dehumanization can be subtle or extreme (for example, Eric Trump proclaiming about people who supported the Mueller investigation that "to me they're not even human"). It leads to a desire for social distance and even violence. Dehumanization does occur among partisans of both parties. As Moore-Berg et al. (2020, p. 201) explain:

> While conservatism correlates among Republicans with their dehumanization of Democrats, Democrats' dehumanization of Republicans is just as strongly correlated with strength of adherence to liberal ideology. Therefore, liberals dehumanize just as readily and just as strongly as conservatives in this context, and dehumanization of the political outgroup is just as strongly associated with liberalism among Democrats as it is with conservatism among Republicans. Therefore, although liberal ideology is associated with the rejection of the idea that some groups are better than others (i.e., lower in Social Dominance Orientation) and liberals are less likely to dehumanize marginalized groups, adherence to liberal political ideology and rejection of social dominance does not immunize liberals from making dehumanizing evaluations ...

Perceptions that the other party is homogeneous in values—unlike one's own group—and the tendency to dehumanize produce a desire for social distance. Therefore, it is decreasingly likely that partisans from both parties will interact socially with partisans from the other. By socializing with like-minded people, the perceptions of the other party are rarely, if ever, challenged. Mason (2018) argues that because of these patterns, partisanship is part of Americans' social identity. Partisanship is no longer simply the default for where Americans stand on issues, and as a central part of social identity it can potentially produce existential threats to the very existence of a group's core to individual identities. Thus, "social polarization is an increasingly intense conflict between our two partisan groups. It is based on the same impulses that drive racial and religious prejudice" (Mason, 2018, p.16). This type of social polarization produces prejudice toward the other group, a willingness to fight to defend one's group, anger and humiliation when the group loses, and joy when it wins.

Clearly, there is an increase in intergroup differentiation going on in the United States. How deep is it? Mason (2018) argues that the increase in liberal identification among Democrats, and conservative identification among Republicans reflects more than ideological issue position consistency. It also reflects changes in social identity: there is stronger increase in partisan identity differences than policy differences. This partisan social pattern is accompanied by a racial one. Identification with one or the other of the parties is increasingly predicted by race, not issue positions on race-related policies. Non-Whites identify strongly with the Democratic Party but, more importantly, White racial identity coincides with identification with the Republican Party (Abramowitz, 2018; Mason, 2018). At the same time, the religious right, beginning in the 1990s, became politicized and moved toward the Republican Party.

The growing racial and ethnic diversity in the United States, which is reflected in party alignments, is unlikely to change. What has changed is that the White alignment with the Republican Party is now part of a shift in White identity. For most of the history of the United States, Whites didn't have a strong racial identity. Whiteness was the default, and everyone who was not White was a "different" race. As Jardina explains:

> The scholarly consensus has been that whites do not, by and large, think about their whiteness—at least not in a way that is politically meaningful. They are not, according to conventional wisdom, influenced by an inward attachment to their racial group, or by a sense of group identity. Whiteness, according to this line of reasoning, is invisible. Thus, for whites, our perspective on their attitudes and behavior when it comes to race has been almost exclusively outward focused; it attends to the nature and consequences of racial prejudice, resentment, and animus among whites, particularly that which is directed toward blacks.
>
> (Jardina, 2019, pp. 6–7)

White identity as a group is now seen as threatened by many Whites, and this is reflected in their support for the policy positions of the Republican Party. It is also reflected in the growing urban–rural divide, which is also a Democrat–Republican divide. We will address this issue in much greater depth in Chapter 8. For now, the main point is that this is a change in American politics, and it is not going away any time soon.

DONALD TRUMP AND POPULISM IN AMERICA

Donald Trump's campaign for the 2016 election threw a populist cover over the changes we described above to add additional transformations to

American politics and discourse. Populism is not new in American politics, and before Trump was most recently evidenced in the 1992 campaign for the Republican nomination by Patrick Buchanan, as well as the Tea Party and the vice presidential campaign by Sarah Palin. Norris and Inglehart (2019) define populism as "a style of rhetoric reflecting first-order principles about who should rule, claiming that legitimate power rests with 'the people' not political elites" (p. 5). Populists typically denigrate the "establishment" of traditional politicians, but they add into that "swamp" the media, the judiciary, and other components of a political system. Their message is that the system is depriving natural citizens of their power and ability to influence public policy.

In Trump's case, the swamp included the media ("enemies of the people"), government bureaucrats, interest groups, the electoral system (which is "rigged"), immigrants, scientists, intellectuals, "politically correct" speaking, and other countries—except those whose leaders he admires, such as Vladimir Putin. Trump knowingly or intuitively took advantage of the social and psychological trends we noted above and spoke to the existential fears of those who feel America is leaving them behind, notably less educated White people, particularly men and rural residents. What was different about Trump was his willingness to reject the norms of discourse acceptable to both political parties. Neither party accepted blatantly racist, sexist, anti-immigrant, or anti-Islamic extremism. Trump, on the other hand, did just that in the name of rejecting political correctness. As Norris and Inglehart argue:

> The President has been further deepening divisions between the major parties, and within the Congressional GOP, on the classic wedge issues of race/ethnicity, immigration, and gender. Trump's defeat of his rivals to become the Republican nominee, his belligerent campaign against Hillary Clinton, and the shock of his unexpected victory in the 2016 Electoral College, posed a major challenge to the liberal consensus, and energized the cultural backlash in the American electorate. Trump galvanized support through authoritarian-populist appeals, especially by articulating a dog-whistle version of racist and xenophobic rhetoric, and by appeals to strongman executive rule, disregarding conventional constitutional checks and balances.
>
> (Norris & Inglehart, 2019, p. 338)

This approach appealed to potential Trump supporters, who are different from liberals and non-Trump supporting conservatives in terms of their greatest political concerns. Hibbing's (2019) study found the major issues of concern of Trump "venerators" are immigration, national defense, guns rights, and law and order, while Liberals' main issue concerns are racial justice, healthcare, women's rights, and income inequality. Clearly Trump's message was aimed at a receptive political group amenable to such populist appeals.

POLITICAL SOCIALIZATION

How do people acquire their political attitudes in America? Research on political socialization began in the 1950s, and looked at the ways in which "people acquire relatively enduring orientations toward politics in general and toward their own particular political systems" (Merelman, 1986, p. 279). The research reached its peak in the 1970s, and suffered a decline, then a renewed interest in the 1990s (for earlier reviews, see Merelman, 1986; Niemi, 1973; Sears, 1975). Why did the field suffer a decline? As Niemi and Hepburn (1995) put it, "The field atrophied because it was based on exaggerated premises and because of misinterpreted and misunderstood research findings (and lack of findings)" (p. 7). Thus, there were several efforts to revitalize the field and offer new directions for research (see Merelman, 1986; Niemi & Hepburn 1995; Sigel, 1995). We begin with a brief look at the development of this body of literature, as seen through the eyes of the scholars themselves, then discuss the ways they suggest bringing it back to life.

The earliest socialization studies focused on children. Studies were conducted on their views of political authority figures (e.g., Easton & Dennis, 1973) and on their acquisition of political attitudes. The first authority figures recognized by children, as they became aware of politics, were the president and policeman (Easton & Dennis, 1973). As children mature, their cognitive abilities increase, and they can advance from thinking of government in personal, concrete terms (e.g., George Washington and the flag) to more abstract notions, such as institutions and law-making. Moreover, these studies found children liked the government. Easton and Dennis (1973) suggested children proceed through stages in political socialization: politicization (learning there is authority beyond family and school); personalization (becoming aware of authorities, through individuals such as police and the president); idealization (the belief that political authority is trustworthy and benevolent); and institutionalization (association with depersonalized objects, such as government) (Niemi, 1973). Concerning the acquisition of political attitudes, family was considered to be the most important agent of transmission (Jennings & Niemi, 1974; Maccoby, Matthews, & Morton, 1954), followed by schools (Hess & Torney, 1967), then peers, media, and events (Jennings & Niemi, 1974). Jennings and Niemi (1974), for example, found parents transmit partisanship to their children, although the attachment tends to be weaker in the children.

The aforementioned studies shed considerable light on how children are socialized, but whether or not they continued to have those same attitudes into adulthood was also an important question. The early socialization studies examined children precisely because they thought socialization was completed by age 18 years or so, and that the attitudes were retained through the life-cycle. But, as Niemi and Hepburn explain:

> These studies were fascinating and often had amusing twists. The problem, however, was in trying to determine their long-term significance. Here, socialization research fell victim to two assumptions that are, at best, highly questionable. First, it was assumed that what was learned prior to adulthood remained unchanged later in life. This "primacy" principle was most explicit in political science with respect to partisanship ... Party identification was very nearly immutable both between generations and across lifetimes. Yet even as socialization work was getting up a full head of steam, the first cracks in this

> assumption were appearing, as the number of independents underwent a significant increase in the late 1960s.
>
> (Niemi & Hepburn, 1995, p. 8)

The primacy principle, advanced by the claims in *The American Voter* (Campbell et al., 1964), was subsequently challenged by many studies indicating that partisanship is not necessarily constant. Other elements, such as political trust, also change over time. Niemi and Hepburn's (1995) conclusion is that attitudes and behavior do change over time, and what is learned early on may not be relevant later in life. Instead of the focus being on children, it should turn to individuals between the ages of 14 and 25 years. Why? "First, there is little dispute that youth is a time of extraordinary psychological and social change. Second, these are the years during which our society traditionally attempts to educate youth for citizen participation" (Niemi & Hepburn, 1995, p. 9). Those authors also offer several ways to "reestablish socialization as a viable and vibrant field of study" (pp. 13–14). The first is to eliminate what, for many purposes, is the artificial distinction between those aged under 18 and those 18 and over. Second, undertake a major new socialization study devoted specifically to the study of intergenerational and youthful change and development. Third, conduct more major youth studies and be more involved in new studies at the design stage. Fourth, pay more attention to high school and college courses, and their probable effects on young people. Fifth, think more theoretically and write about all aspects of socialization. Sixth, conduct more comparative socialization work, especially if it is to contribute to our understanding of the significance of learning in early childhood.

In another assessment, Sigel (1995) points out there are four problems with socialization research: a lack of conceptual clarity; poor choice of subjects; insufficient attention to historical and cultural factors; and inappropriate methodology. Sigel explains the first problem:

> What really do we understand by the term *political socialization*? As currently used in the literature, the term is applied to many different phenomena. Scholars not only disagree among themselves in their definitions of it, but at times operate with a variety of definitions or conceptualizations even in their own work, applying one definition at one time and another—not necessarily a compatible one—at another, and often doing so in the same research enterprise.
>
> (Sigel, 1995, p. 17)

Reviewing the literature, Sigel found numerous definitions of political socialization, including learning (political knowledge and comprehension), the developmental sequence through which knowledge and comprehension are acquired, continuity over time of knowledge and attitudes, acquisition and internalization of society's norms and behaviors, and synonyms for civic or political education.

The second problem is the focus of the studies on young children. Like Niemi and Hepburn, Sigel (1995) asked whether these views carry over into later years. In addition, "virtually no literature exists that has actually studied and observed the manner by which 'agents' [those who do imprinting] do or do not make influence attempts" (p. 18). Finally, she questioned the idea that young people are passive and gullible to outside influences. The author suggested taking a lifespan approach to understanding why orientations are maintained, modified, or abandoned. In addition, more attention should be paid to the historical and cultural context in which the observations of attitudes are made. Finally, political scientists need to pay more attention to methodology. The reliance upon close-ended survey questionnaires was criticized as inappropriate for studying the process of attitude change along the lifespan. Sigel (1995) also suggests other methods, such as field observations, collection of life histories, simulations, or direct observations.

Socialization studies are certainly interesting and important. They can help us understand the foundations of support for a political system. There is, as mentioned, a renewed interest in studying political socialization. In September 1999, for example, a collection of articles on political socialization appeared in *Political Psychology*. The studies are cross-national, including studies in Germany, the Netherlands, Sweden, the United States, and on the Arab–Israeli conflict. As special editor Richard Niemi points out, although these authors concentrated on different aspects of socialization research, they demonstrate the resurgence of the subject, and a new approach that is cognizant of the problems with previous research.

In addition to those studies, there is another, broader, approach to the study of political socialization, which is particularly evident in the works of Milburn and his colleagues (Milburn & Conrad, 1996; Milburn, Conrad, Sala, & Carberry, 1995). Drawing upon earlier works by Lasswell (1960) and Merelman (1969), these scholars argue that much of the traditional political socialization literature focuses too narrowly upon the transmission of political attitudes from parents to children. Instead, Milburn et al. (1995) take an approach to political socialization employing cognitive and emotional elements in the development of political ideas, or the lack thereof. A central thesis is that "childhood experiences can affect the way we view the world and the political perceptions and understanding we develop" (Milburn & Conrad, 1996, p. 3), but that understanding includes not only what we think and feel, but what we refuse to think about—that is, the political realities that people cannot face because they are too painful and threatening. They also argue that anger from childhood treatment by parents contributes to long-term political attitudes. That anger is displaced onto political issues, and people with particularly punitive upbringings tend to be attracted to conservative ideologies.

POLITICAL TOLERANCE

If asked, most Americans are likely to say that the United States is a country with a great deal of tolerance for minority viewpoints on political issues. After all, the Constitution provides assurances that majority rule will not result in the repression of the rights of minorities. Since 1937, researchers have asked how much tolerance Americans have for politically deviant groups. At that time, the questions mainly revolved around tolerance for civil liberties for communists and their rights to free speech, to hold public office, to have public meetings, and so forth. The early studies found that most Americans favored restrictions on communists' rights in these areas. A major study conducted by Stouffer (1955) found high levels of intolerance. For example, only 59% thought a person who favored government ownership of all the railroads and big industries (an indicator of socialist ideas) should be allowed to speak in their community. Only 37% would allow a person to speak against religion. Only 27% would allow an admitted communist to speak. Community leaders were more tolerant than the average citizen, however: 84% would allow a socialist to speak, 64% an atheist, and 51% an admitted communist. Higher levels of education also correlated with greater tolerance. Stouffer argues that education teaches people not to stereotype, or to rigidly categorize people into groups, and to respect differing points of view.

Studies showed an increase in tolerance between 1954 and 1973, when another major study (Nunn, Crockett, & Williams, 1978), in an effort to replicate Stouffer's (1955) study, was conducted. Now 52% would permit an admitted communist to speak publicly, and 65% would let an atheist speak. However, Sullivan et al. (1979, 1982) suggested that, although tolerance toward communists, atheists, and socialists had increased, it may only be a product of diminished perceptions of threat from these groups. People may have become less worried about these groups, and thus felt less motivation to deny them freedoms, but that does not necessarily mean tolerance in general increased. They argued that tolerance should only be said to exist when one is willing to tolerate those groups one dislikes. It is irrelevant in responses to groups one likes.

Sullivan et al. (1982) are essentially making the argument that tolerance, or the lack thereof, is a political position driven primarily by emotion rather than by cognition. One can only test levels of tolerance by looking at attitudes toward groups a person dislikes. Therefore, a person on the left end of the political spectrum who expresses a willingness to grant civil liberties to a communist is probably not expressing tolerance because that person does not dislike communists in the first place. Ask that same person how they feel about granting civil liberties to a Nazi and you will see how tolerant they really are. Sullivan et al. (1982) were fairly pessimistic about levels of tolerance in the United States, because it was studied mostly in the context of attitudes toward leftist political groups—which, as noted above, are less threatening now, and therefore are less likely to evoke negative emotions. Therefore, increased willingness to grant those groups their civil liberties is meaningless as a reflection of growth in tolerance. Empirical studies supported this argument. In their 1982 study (Sullivan et al.,1982), the researchers let their respondents decide which groups they disliked rather than presenting them with a group the researchers assumed they disliked—a technique they called a "content-controlled" measurement of tolerance. When looked at in this way, they found that levels of tolerance had not increased since the 1950s. Another implication of this approach to the study of tolerance is that American ideals regarding basic civil liberties are much less important in producing tolerance than emotional responses to groups people dislike.

Sniderman et al. (1991) disagree. They examined tolerance toward a different variety of groups, including

> people who are against all churches and religion; people who believe that blacks are genetically inferior; people who admit they are communists; people who advocate doing away with elections and letting the military run the country; and people who admit they are homosexual.
>
> (Sniderman et al., 1991, p. 123)

This assortment of groups was guaranteed to evoke dislike for at least one group by the various respondents. They found consistent responses toward the groups, meaning that if people were tolerant toward one group, they were tolerant toward the others. Therefore, the implication is that, if people hold tolerance as a value, their attitudes toward all groups reflect that attitude, even if they personally dislike the group in question. Given that every respondent would dislike at least one group, the researchers maintained people were responding on the basis of their principles regarding tolerance, rather than on the basis of which group they disliked or liked.

The difference between these two assessments of tolerance is a reflection of different emphases: affect versus cognition. The relative role of thinking and feeling when it comes to political tolerance in the United States is an interesting and important topic. A study by Kuklinski, Riggle, Ottati, Schwartz, and Wyer (1991), for example, found that although people initially endorse tolerance—that is, they respond in support of the value, the more they think about the group in question, the more intolerant they become because negative affect toward the group takes precedence over principle. The role of affect and cognition will continue to be debated and studied as time goes on. In the meantime, one clear trend is that the increase in tolerance evident from the 1950s to the 1970s has slowed down, although public opinion polls in some areas, such as civil liberties for homosexuals, continue to show increases in tolerance. In 1977, for example, 56% of respondents to a Gallup poll supported equal rights in terms of job opportunities for homosexuals, whereas in 1999, 83% supported equal rights (Gallup, 1999). Later survey data from Schwadel and Garneau (2017) indicated social class was no longer as important to political socialization when it came to millennials because, overall, they were a tolerant generation.

VOTING BEHAVIOR IN BRITAIN

Needless to say, the United States is not the only country where the public's political behavior was studied. However, the approaches used to study voting behavior in other countries are generally American in origin, with a heavy reliance on survey data. Like the United States, party identification in Britain was studied extensively. During the 1950s and 1960s, people tended to align strongly with either the Conservative Party or the Labour Party. Two widely accepted factors determined a person's party identification: parents' affiliation and class. People tended to identify with their parents' party; working-class folks belonged to the Labour Party and middle- and upper-class people overwhelmingly identified with the Conservative Party. The association between class and partisanship in Britain was very strong. The central difference between Britain and the United States, in terms of party alignment, was the greater importance of class in partisan alignment in Britain than in the United States. Other factors, such as age, sex, religion, and region, had some influence in British party alignments, but much less than class and family (Butler & Stokes, 1974; Denver, 1994). As in the United States, British voters were affected by short-term factors, which caused them to defect and vote for the other party. Indeed, during the 1950s and 1960s, the Conservative Party would never have won an election were it not for short-term factors that led the majority Labour Party identifiers to defect and vote Tory.

What is Social Class?

Although an important concept in social science, the term "social class" does not have a universally accepted definition. We generally think about class in terms of occupation, income, and lifestyle. Often, classes are divided into upper, middle, and working class. For purposes of measuring public opinion, classes are categorized as (A) high-level professional, managerial and administrative; (B) middle management, professional or administrative; (C1) supervisor, clerical, nonmanual; (C2) skilled manual labor; (D) semi-or unskilled manual; and (E) occasionally employed or reliant upon government benefits (Denver, 1998). These are then grouped together as manual workers (C2, D, E) and nonmanual workers (A, B, C1). This is known as the Alford Index. In recent years, there has been considerable debate as to whether or not a manual worker–nonmanual worker basis for distinguishing class is useful for postindustrial societies in which heavy industry is no longer dominant in the economy.

Beginning in 1970, Britain began to experience both partisan and class dealignment, which means fewer people identified with the traditionally dominant Labour and Conservative Parties, and those who did identify with a party did so with less strength of attachment. By 1997, less than 20% of the electorate in Britain identified strongly with either the Labour Party or Conservative Party, down from 38% in 1964 (Jones & Kavanagh, 1998). In part, partisan dealignment was a result of the pull from other parties, including the Liberal Party and the nationalist parties in Scotland and Wales: the Scottish Nationalist party and Plaid Cymru, respectively. Other factors leading to dealignment were increases in levels of education, enabling more independent judgments by voters, rather than reliance upon the parties for issue positions; a decline in support for more social welfare; the pro-union principles of the Labour Party; changes in campaigns, allowing for more direct and challenging reporting on candidates and issues; and general dissatisfaction with the performance of the two dominant parties when in office (Denver, 1994). Class dealignment also took place after 1970, meaning people were less and less likely to vote for the party associated with their class. As Britain moved from a predominantly blue-collar to white-collar society and economy, class interests became more diverse. For example, the pre-World War II working class had divided into different subclasses, with vestiges of the old working class—those who worked in factories, lived in council houses (i.e., government-funded housing), and so on—and a newer, more affluent working class with more skills, who worked in light manufacturing and owned their homes. As Norris (1997) puts it, "The nature of class inequalities has become more complex in postindustrial society" (p. 90). Other social identities, including region, ethnicity, and religion, increased in importance and influence on the vote in Britain, as class identity fragmented (Bartle, 1998; Norris, 1997).

During the alignment era, British voters—like Americans—tended to be fairly ignorant about political issues. Butler and Stokes (1974) found that when British voters did express attitudes on issues, their attitudes changed frequently, indicating that they were not true attitudes, but randomly changing opinions. In a series of four interviews with the same respondents, only 43% were consistent in their positions on nationalization of industries, which was an important issue in Britain at the time. In addition, respondents' attitudes were not consistently related to other attitudes. For example, in principle, a person who is pro-private enterprise should oppose a growth in trade union power, but this was not often the case in Britain in the era of alignment. Most people used partisanship to make a voting decision, rather than attitudes toward issues.

After dealignment, however, British voters began to engage in issue voting. Studies of voting in Britain use the same standards of analysis as studies of American voting. A voting decision is considered to be based on an issue (issue voting), if the voter is aware of the issue, has a position on the issue, understands where the parties stand and how they differ from each other on the issue, and finally, votes for the party perceived to be closest to their own position on the issue (Butler & Stokes, 1974). A number of studies showed the majority of British voters were casting issue votes in the dealignment era (summarized in Denver, 1994). Issues such as taxes and government spending, unemployment, privatization of publicly owned industries, the European Union, racial conflict, and the status of Scotland and Northern Ireland, among others, influenced the vote in Britain.

The transformation of the Labour Party in Britain, and its spectacular success in the 1997 election, is plausibly a reflection of the changes in the British voter. Starting in 1974, the Conservative Party regularly beat the Labour Party. In 1979, Margaret Thatcher became prime minister and stayed in office for 12 years. She was succeeded by another Conservative, John Major, and, even in the context of a struggling economy, Labour lost in 1992. This sparked a reform effort and the emergence of new leadership. According to the Labour Party's former director of communications, David Hill, the party came to be regarded as "too old fashioned, too tied to the past, too linked to minorities rather than majorities, and too associated with old images of the trades unions" (quoted in Seyd, 1998, p. 51). The public became mistrustful of Labour's stance on taxation, support for income redistribution, support for trade unions, and other traditional positions. Tony Blair, a relatively young man of 41, became the party's new leader in 1994. He set about devising some fundamental reforms of the party, referring to it as New Labour. Among those reforms was a revision of clause 4 in the party's charter, which changed the party's emphasis from primarily supporting trade unions to making trade unions only one among many important sectors, along with a thriving private sector, for which the party promised to work. This move was strongly supported by the party's members, and was a reflection of change in class, society, and the economy in Britain. The Labour Party was set to target the middle class and to address increases in issue voting. The Conservative Party, on the other hand, had made a series of blunders since 1992, including economic failures, which destroyed its reputation for financial competence, and association with a number of scandals (Denver, 1998; King, 1998). The Labour Party continued its electoral gains, but Tony Blair resigned in 2007, having lost favor due to a variety of issues, such as the war in Iraq, the weapons of mass destruction (WMD) fiasco, support for Israel, and the terrorist attack in London.

More recent studies, such as Webb (2013), identified two types of British voters: the dissatisfied democrat, and the stealth democrat. While both types exhibited low trust in political elites, dissatisfied democrats were more politically interested and wanted to participate. In another study, Benoit and Benoit-Bryan (2013) analyzed the first-ever three live prime minister debates before the 2010 elections between Gordon Brown (Labour incumbent), David Cameron (Conservative) and Nick Clegg (Liberal Democrat). The authors looked at the use of claims, attacks and defenses, the topics of policy and character, and the target of attack. They found that candidates used claims most commonly, and Brown used them the most. Further, the discussion of issues trumped character. Brown and Cameron, the forerunners in the election, were the targets of most attacks, with Brown attacking less.

National identity is an issue in discussions of Great Britain and the United Kingdom. The drive for Scottish independence was carefully watched as it had implications for Wales, England, and even Northern Ireland. There exists a perception that Westminster Parliament and executive governance is an English-dominated enterprise. Scotland, Wales, and Northern Ireland have devolved governments responsible for local governance. The future members and configuration of Great Britain and the United Kingdom will greatly depend on perceptions of identity (Mycock & Hayton, 2014). Are they English, Scottish, Welsh, British, or some combination of both? In Northern Ireland, for example, the majority of Protestants identify as British and are committed to the union with the United Kingdom. They are prepared to defend their identity and stake in the United Kingdom.

Identity issues emerged again in the campaign to leave the European Union, commonly referred to as Brexit. The European Union began in 1957 as the European Economic Community (EEC) with the goal of facilitating economic cooperation among European countries after World War II. Britain applied to join in 1963 and was rejected. The United Kingdom finally entered the organization in 1973. By the 1990s, the (now) European Union had ambitions far beyond the original goals. It now sought a unified market and political institutions, the EU Parliament, a shared approach to international politics, common rights for citizens, a common currency, the euro, and free flow of citizens across the EU border. The last of these meant that anyone, once admitted to a member country, could freely, and without inspection, cross EU borders.

Before getting into political psychological explanations of Brexit, we should look at changes in the British electorate over time. As in the

United States, political realignments took place in Britain after the 1960s. Traditionally, Britain had a large working-class population and small proportion of the population with university education. After the 1960s, this began to change. By the 2000s, only about 20% of the electorate was working-class, and over a third had university degrees (Goodwin, 2017). This meant the Labour Party could no longer rely on a large working-class support base. The Conservative Party, traditionally the party of the elite, needed to expand its electoral base to win office in the past. By the 1990s, the Labour Party had shifted to attract the growing middle class and university graduates whose values were similar to those of the liberal wing of the U.S. political spectrum, concern with social justice, gender, race, LGBTQ rights and so on (Goodwin, 2017). Meanwhile, the Conservative Party was taking aim at "socially conservative, working-class white voters with few educational qualifications" (p. 60) who no longer automatically supported Labour. As Goodwin explains:

> A ... long running social change overlapped with these demographic shifts and magnified their importance—growing value divides over national identity, diversity and multiculturalism, and liberalism more generally. The newly ascendant groups in Britain, including ethnic minorities, graduates, and middle-class professionals, held values that were very different from the more conservative and even authoritarian outlook that was held by many older, white, middle-class voters, as well as those who had left the educational system early in life. As the UK's two main parties reoriented themselves to focus on the rising liberal groups, a new "liberal consensus" emerged. This was a more socially liberal outlook on the world, which saw rising ethnic diversity as a core strength ... The increased prominence of this outlook was not just a matter of electoral expediency. It reflects the typical worldview of the university-educated professionals whose weight in the electorate is rapidly increasing, and who also came to dominate politics and the media. But such values contrasted sharply with the more nationalistic and communitarian outlook of those white, working class and economically marginalized voters ... Among these voters, national identity is linked to ancestry and birthplace, not just institutions and civic attachments, and a greater value is placed on order, stability and tradition.
>
> (Goodwin, 2017, p. 60)

As will be seen below, these trends had an important impact on Brexit. Looking at the British association with the EU in general, it is evident the British people and government had a number of issues with the EU, and membership was often uneasy or problematic. Although the Conservatives were early advocates of EU membership, complaints about membership in the EU began in the late 1980s during Margaret Thatcher's term as prime minister. The Conservative Party was increasingly associated with "Euroscepticism," which was coupled with a sense of British exceptionalism and fundamental difference from Europe. This accelerated after the 1992 Maastricht Treaty, which resulted in a common currency for the EU, the euro. The United Kingdom never adopted the euro as its currency, keeping the British pound.

The campaign against the EU picked up steam again when the Conservatives returned to power in 2010 amid the international financial crash. There was also growing concern that immigrants from EU countries, particularly the newer members from Eastern Europe, would take advantage of Britain's welfare system. On the political right, Nigel Farage formed a Brexit party, the UK Independence Party (UKIP), which picked up some support in the 2000s, and the campaign to get Britain out of the EU gained speed in the 2010s. The Conservative Party leader, David Cameron, promised to hold a referendum on membership in the EU if he became prime minister (even though he opposed such a move), and it passed by 51.9% to 48.1%, much to the world's amazement, in 2016. The vote was uneven, as Scotland and Northern Ireland voted strongly to remain in the EU, while Wales and England voted to leave. There were innumerable complications and much deal-making in an effort to plan an exit strategy, and the final moment of exit did not occur until 2020. David Cameron resigned and Theresa May became the first post-Brexit vote prime minister to try to negotiate the exit, followed by Boris Johnson.

A debate ensued about why Britain had narrowly, and surprisingly, voted to leave the EU. The initial explanation, similar to the initial explanation of Trump's votes in 2016, was that this was a vote of the economically dispossessed, the people whose jobs evaporated as globalization increased (Rodrik, 2018; Roubini, 2016). Individual-level analyses looking at surveys argue differently that the Brexit leave vote was a product of more complicated political psychological factors. As discussed above, class-based political alignments eroded in Britain over the years. Using data from the British Election Study, Norris and Inglehart (2019) found that left–right economic attitudes did not explain popular behavior as well as the libertarian/authoritarian cleavage. People higher in authoritarianism were more likely to vote to leave the EU. The increasing importance of these attitudes opened the door to other issues and grievances related to identity and resentment toward the "political establishment," as was seen in the United States in the 2016 election. As Norris and Inglehart explain,

> the Leave vote [was] being driven by a populist protest directed "upwards" against the establishment such as party leaders, journalists, economists, scientists, Eurocrats, bankers, and world leaders telling "us" what to think, and by authoritarian antipathy toward perceived threats from "Them" (whether Polish shopkeepers, Syrian refugees, or second-generation Bangladeshi)
>
> (Norris & Inglehart, 2019, p. 378)

One of the major themes of the Leave camp was immigration, which is consistently a strong predictor of authoritarian populism in Europe (Norris & Inglehart, 2019). In Britain, attitudes toward immigration were very important in determining the vote to leave the EU. Immigration was changing the face of the United Kingdom, particularly in urban areas. The Leave camp's argument was that the only way to curb the influx of immigrants from the EU to the United Kingdom was to leave the EU, its open borders policy, and the threat posed by immigrants to British culture, economy, and security (Clarke et al., 2017). The anti-immigration position of UKIP was its main appeal, and it went on to become the first British party other than Labour and the Conservatives to win at the national level since 1906. It won nearly 13% of the national vote in 2015 (Goodwin, 2017, p. 61). This support was absorbed by the Conservative Party as it increasingly took up the Leave mantle. The Remain supporters focused on the potential economic impact of leaving the EU, but that appeal was not as strong as hostility to cultural change and immigration. More generally, authoritarian and populist attitudes were central to the Leave vote, with UKIP voters the most populist (Norris & Inglehart, 2019, p. 392).

Voting Behavior in Other Countries

The study of voting behavior is heavily focused on the United States, Great Britain, and Europe, and in particular in democratic societies, but there is some research focused on other countries throughout the world. We will review some of these diverse studies here for particular insights into their electorates.

Latin American countries have complex histories with cycles of authoritarianism. Additionally, due to literacy requirements, segments of the population have been disenfranchised (Kellam, 2013). Given this history, what can we say about Latin American voting behavior? Kellam (2013) looked at 12 countries and data from 1945–2000, and discovered that after suffrage restrictions were lifted, increases in electoral participation led to disruptions in voting behavior patterns in the short term, but no long-term effect on the party system, as these new voters adjusted to their partisan attachments. In a study of Turkish voting behavior, Toros (2014) found political and personal values, along with social factors were influential, but their particular impact differed across political parties. Tambe (2016) looked at eight East Asian countries by drawing on data from the Asian Barometer survey. The study indicated that older people were more likely than younger people, those who were part of civic society organizations were more likely to participate, and political cultural attitudes did not impact behavior, with the partial exception of Japan. However, most importantly, political institutional context mattered; namely proportional representation, parliamentarism, and closeness of elections. Shi (1999) examined voting behavior in China, where voters are limited in their choices. Even so, Shi found those with greater political resources did not abstain from voting as a form of protest. Similar findings on protest were demonstrated by Daghagheleh (2018) in a study on Iran, although this dynamic was inconsistent across time and elections.

CONCLUSION

This chapter has examined public opinion and voting behavior in the United States and Britain, as well as other countries. We began the chapter with a review of some of the concepts first presented in Chapter 3, such as attitudes, beliefs, and schemas, in addition to new concepts such as values and ideology, all of which are commonly used in the analysis of public opinion and voting behavior. The analysis of American voting behavior was more thorough, looking at the Michigan School versus Maximalist views on a variety of topics: attitudes and political sophistication in the United States; ideology, information processing and voting behavior; emotions and voting; the elections of 2008 and 2016; and political tolerance. In the case of Great Britain, the British were noted to be traditionally much more reliant upon class as a basis for partisanship than Americans. We also looked at issue trends in British elections and the reemergence of the Labour Party under the auspices of New Labour, as well as Brexit. Finally, we examined voting behavior in other countries.

One of the central issues underlying the study of voting behavior is the question of how those who participate in politics—the average voters—affect the quality of a democracy. Ideally, a democracy should run on the basis of decisions made by informed and thoughtful citizens. We believe that a careful study of the political psychology of voting behavior, particularly the roles of ideology and information-processing patterns, provides students with a better basis for reaching their own conclusions about the quality of democracy in America and elsewhere.

Topics, Theories/Explanations, and Cases Covered in Chapter 6

Topics	*Theories/Explanations*	*Cases*
Public opinion	Beliefs, belief systems Values Attitudes Schema Ideology	Political sophistication in the United States
Voting in the United States	Michigan school Levels of conceptualization Funnel of causality Genetics and biology	Normal vote Long-term and short-term forces
	Maximalists	Knowledge structures
Information processing and voting	Cognitive patterns Role of emotion	Elections
Political socialization	Primacy principle	New studies
Political tolerance		
Voting in Great Britain	Class	

Key Terms

- affect referral heuristic
- associative networks
- belief system
- black and white model
- Bradley effect
- compensatory strategy
- drunkard's search
- endorsement heuristic
- familiarity heuristic
- funnel of causality

Gresham's law of political information
habit heuristic
ideologue
ideology
impression-based model of information processing
issue
issue frames
knowledge structures
levels of conceptualization
Maximalists
Michigan model
noncompensatory strategy
normal vote
party identification
viability heuristic

Suggestions for Further Reading

Ansolabehere, S., Behr, R., & Iyengar, S. (1993). *The media game*. New York: Macmillan.
Campbell, A., Converse, P., Miller, W., & Stokes, D. (1964 [1960]). *The American voter*. New York: Wiley.
Denver, D. (1994). *Elections and voting behaviour in Britain*. London: Harvester Wheatsheaf.
Fording, R.C., & Schram, S.F. (2020). *Hard white: The mainstreaming of racism in American politics*. Oxford: Oxford University Press.
Glynn, C., Herbst, S., O'Keefe, G., & Shapiro, R. (1999). *Public opinion*. Boulder, CO: Westview Press.
Hopkins, D.J., & Sides, J. (2018). *Political polarization in American politics*. New York: Bloomsbury.
Iyengar, S. (1991). *Is anyone responsible? How television frames political issues*. Chicago, IL: University of Chicago Press.
Iyengar, S., & McGuire, W. (Eds.). (1995). *Explorations in political psychology*. Durham, NC: Duke University Press.
Jardina, A. (2019). *White identity politics*. Cambridge: Cambridge University Press.
Marcus, G., Neuman, W. R., & MacKuen, M. (2000). *Affective intelligence and political judgment*. Chicago, IL: University of Chicago Press.
Miller, W., & Shanks, M. (1996). *The new American voter*. Cambridge, MA: Harvard University Press.
Norris, P.& Inglehart R. (2019). *Cultural backlash: Trump, Brexit, and authoritarian populism*. Cambridge: Cambridge University Press.
Patterson, T. (1993). *Out of order*. New York: Knopf.
Popkin, S. (1994). *The reasoning voter: Communication and persuasion in presidential campaigns*. Chicago, IL: University of Chicago Press.
Ridout, T.N., & Franz, M.M. (2011). *The persuasive power of campaign advertising*. Philadelphia: Temple University Press.
Smith, E. (1989). *The unchanging American voter*. Berkeley: University of California Press.

Note

1. We recognize the term "Latinx" emerged as a gender-neutral term to describe Latinos in the United States. This term is not widely used to date, and for continuity we use the census term "Latino" in this and other chapters.

Chapter 7

THE POLITICAL PSYCHOLOGY OF THE MEDIA IN POLITICS

Communication is central to human society, and therefore to politics. It involves the production and dissemination of political information, which occurs through the media as well as personal interactions. In this chapter, we will examine the role of the media in influencing political opinions in general, and the effects of the media on influencing the vote during campaigns in particular. First, we review several important points about communication between people in societies. Harold Lasswell (1948b) called attention to three central aspects of communication in a society: it provides surveillance of events that may affect a society, correlates knowledge of those events among members of society, and enables the transmission of norms and values among members of the society.

The range of communications media important in political communication is now very broad, and includes print, advertising, broadcast, electronic, and social media, among others. It has become centrally important in political communication as technological advances have made it cheap and easily disseminated. It was only in the mid-1800s that technological advances made newspapers available to the average person (Glynn, Herbst, O'Keefe, & Shapiro, 1999). Radios and movies were important sources of information during the 1930s and 1940s, and by the 1950s televisions had become an important source of political information (Glynn et al., 1999). Satellite technology in the 1980s expanded television news to real-time global news coverage. Then, of course, the internet and social media—now familiar tools of communication—further expanded communication capabilities.

Despite these developments, people are still people, and their information-processing limitations, discussed in Chapter 3, remain. The use of heuristics, the fundamental attribution error, the positivity and negativity effects, the drive for balance, the desire to avoid cognitive dissonance, and the avoidance of value tradeoffs all affect the processing of information coming from the media. In addition, attitudes held by people for a long period have a strong affective component, which automatically comes to mind. For example, a strong partisan Democrat is likely to react to information about Republicans with a preset negative emotion. People are also cognitively lazy. They want to be accurate and have reasonable ideas, but they also often lack the motivation to assess whether new information warrants a reconsideration of their attitudes. This pattern is reinforced because people

DOI: 10.4324/9780429244643-7

tend to associate with other people who share their views, so exposure to contrary information or opinions is not part of everyday life (Valentino & Nardis, 2013). People are also often stubbornly unwilling to admit that they are factually wrong with regard to information they believe supports their attitudes.

This brings us to the controversial issue of selective exposure. Do people maintain their political attitudes by selectively exposing themselves to information that supports their pre-existing attitudes? The evidence on this issue is mixed and complex. Looking at several studies showing contradictory patterns of selective exposure, Stroud and Muddiman (2013) argue that studies show several important aspects of selective exposure:

> First, they tell us that selective exposure doesn't always occur. Different contexts can affect the extent to which selective exposure occurs. Interview situations may motivate different information selection patterns in comparison to political brochures. Strong arguments may motivate different selection patterns in comparison to weak arguments. Second ... it appears that politics may inspire a greater degree of selective exposure in comparison to other topics ... Why might politics inspire the selection of like-minded information? Politics can spark strong emotions and feelings of self-identity—just the sort of circumstances that may lead people to prefer information matching their beliefs.
>
> (Stroud & Muddiman, 2013, pp. 7–8)

Therefore, it should not be surprising that Republicans tend to watch Fox News and Democrats watch CNN (Stroud & Muddiman, 2013). Given the information-processing patterns discussed above and in Chapter 3, the desire to avoid dissonance, the use of heuristics, and cognitive laziness would all contribute to selective exposure. People do not want to experience the dissonance to which contrary information would expose them, and they are not strongly motivated to seek out massive amounts of information since they already limit their conscious use of information by using heuristics and other cognitive shortcuts. Selective exposure is not necessarily a bad thing: some studies found exposure to views and information contrary to their own views can have a boomerang effect, making people even firmer in their original beliefs (Stroud & Muddiman, 2013, p. 17).

Finally, information is not neutrally observed and evaluated. The influence informational items have is affected by the source, as the discussion of selective exposure would imply. Democrats are more likely to believe news from NPR; Republicans are more likely to believe Fox News. The credibility and likability of the communicators themselves also influences the acceptability of one source over another (Valentino & Nardis, 2013). Given all these information-processing factors, there are many questions and mysteries in the general issue area of how political information affects political opinions and behaviors of the average citizen.

What is the role of the media in influencing public opinion? There are different schools of thought. Thus, the study of the media is approached from different perspectives, often couched in terms of **agenda-setting**, priming, framing, or attitude change and persuasion. We also focus on the research on social media and discuss the limited attention devoted to this important new area of research. In this chapter, we introduce the different perspectives and look at the research and empirical studies associated with each. As will be apparent, studies agree that the media are important, but they are often focused on different areas and variables. As a result, the literature is far from conclusive, and some of it overlaps from one category to another. Further, research is conducted in multiple disciplines, such as political science, psychology, and communications, and uses different methodologies. While many studies use the same terminology, the definitions can differ.

Before beginning our discussion of the media, we first address the prevailing assumption of media bias. The Media Research Center reports on survey research in the area of ideological research. Clearly, the public maintains the view there is a **media bias**. A commonly held argument, particularly among conservatives, is that the media are biased in a liberal direction. In fact, in a poll reported by the Pew Research Center (2012), "67% of Americans see 'a great deal' or 'fair amount' of 'political bias' in the news media." Men (41%) were more likely than women (33%) to assert bias. Further, those who watch Fox News or listen to Fox Radio as their predominant source of campaign news are more likely to assert liberal bias in the news. But do academic studies bear this out? In a study of the 1992 election, Beck, Dalton, Greene, and Huckfeldt (2002) found no clear pattern of bias in volume of coverage. In fact, they argue that "where there was partisan favoritism in news reports and editorials, it was demonstrably small in most cases. A majority of those exposed to television received messages close to evenly balanced; similarly, biases in newspaper coverage were often slight" (p. 62). They also found people who were highly partisan perceived a bias against their preferred candidate, even when none existed. While studies do not bear out partisan favoritism, media outlets exist that are known for their partisanship in agenda and editorial content. MSNBC blogs and *Huffington Post* are known for their liberal slant, while the Drudge Report and Fox News are known for their conservative slant. In another study, media bias was also examined in a foreign context. Specifically, Goltz (2012) looked at Western reporting of the Armenian–Azerbaijani conflict in western Azerbaijan called Karabakh between 1991 and 1994. The preponderance of media reports supported the Armenian side of the story. The author found that this was due to the Armenian propaganda machine's ability to spin stories and thus frame the conflict.

There are additional structural types of media bias that are different from the partisan/ideological bias accusations. The media can engage in **gatekeeping**, wherein the editors or program managers decide which stories will be told. This means some stories are not reported. This can lead to a bias in favor of the status quo as new perspectives and issues are left unreported. Another type of bias is **coverage bias**, which refers to how much time or space is devoted to a particular story. Fewer lines in a newspaper article, and placement on page 12, will result in less attention given to the story. Then there is **statement bias**, wherein a member of the media inserts his or her own views in the reporting of a story (D'Alessio & Allen, 2000; Denton & Kuypers, 2008). In addition, the news media are often accused of negative reporting, particularly by presidents and presidential candidates. However,

Groeling and Kernell (1998) found that while negative coverage is a pattern in presidential elections, negative reporting coincides with increases in negative polls about the candidates.

AGENDA-SETTING

Many analysts agree with Cohen (1963), who wrote, "The press may not be successful much of the time in telling people what to think, but it is stunningly successful in telling its readers what to think about" (p. 13). People are limited in how much time and attention they can or wish to devote to politics. They rely upon the media to tell them which issues need attention and in what form. This is referred to as *agenda-setting.* Studies examined the amount of reporting issues received and found strong correlations between quantity of coverage and the importance attributed to issues by the public (McCombs & Shaw, 1972). Other studies looked at the order in which issues were covered by the press and regarded as important by the public, and found press reporting comes first, followed by public perceptions of an issue's importance (Glynn et al., 1999; Miller, 2007); however, they argue that content is paid attention to if it invokes negative emotions. Kim and McCombs (2007) maintain that attributes in the news, whether positive or negative, affect views of gubernatorial and U.S. Senate candidates. Those attributes receiving the most attention in the media had more impact on those who were heavy readers of newspapers.

PRIMING

Priming is another psychological concept. As Hobert and Tchernev (2013) note, "Intricately connected to the process of salience transfer (from the media to the public) detailed in agenda setting theory is the subsequent process of political media priming effects." According to Dragojlovic (2011) "priming effects occur when the mention of a specific consideration in one context (the prime) increases the *accessibility* of that consideration, leading to an increase in the use of that trait later in later evaluations of a social target" (p. 991). Because political issues are many in number and extraordinarily complex, people need help in deciding which issues are important and which aspects of those issues need to be attended to. The news media deliver guidance by priming—that is, pointing out to the public which elements of which issues are important, providing a context for understanding (Glynn et al., 1999; Iyengar & Kinder, 1987; Iyengar, Peters & Kinder, 1982). For example, when primed by the media on an issue such as rising gas prices, individuals judged President Obama on how well they thought he kept rising prices at bay. How does this work? As Miller and Krosnick (1996) explain, when making day-to-day decisions, people tend to **satisfice**—that is, they make an adequate decision rather than an optimal one based on full consideration of all relevant information. They also do this when making political judgments. Using the example of how people rated presidential performance, those authors elaborated:

> To decide how well the president is doing his job, a person could evaluate how well he has been handling all issues on which he has been working. This would be a very tough task, however, because presidents typically address a great many issues in very short periods of time. In his first year in office, for example, President Clinton worked on a number of issues, including reform of the U.S. health care system, staffing of the U.S. military, abortion laws, reducing the deficit, appointments to his Cabinet, U.S. involvement in Somalia, the North American Free Trade Agreement, Supreme Court appointments, and more. A careful evaluator could have graded his handling of each of these issues and then averaged those grades together into an overall assessment. Most Americans, however, probably had neither the information nor the motivation to do such labor-intensive thinking. Instead, they probably satisficed his handling of just a few issues.
> (Miller & Krosnick, 1996, p. 260)

Again, the media play an important role in the priming process because they determine which issues come to the forefront. Therefore, to use another of Miller and Krosnick's (1996) examples, if the media pay attention to the economy, and people think about this issue, then the economy will probably become a consideration when evaluating presidential performance. What is the specific impact of any media story—in other words, does one story about an issue prime another issue? Those authors believe in related issues, so this may occur. In their view, if policies are viewed as related, coverage of one will prime the other. For example, affirmative action and school busing (the former priming the latter) are viewed as related because both could be seen as related to improving the lives of minorities. However, news coverage of affirmative action probably would not prime inflation.

The existence of priming is supported by several experimental studies (see Druckman, 2004; Iyengar, 1991; Iyengar & Kinder, 1987; Iyengar, Peters, & Kinder, 1982; Iyengar, Peters, Kinder, & Krosnick, 1984). Krosnick and Kinder (1990), for example, found the decline in the popularity of President Reagan was a result of two elements: (1) the media's newfound fascination with covert aid to the Contras; and (2) the public's opposition to intervention in Central America. In their look at priming and presidential evaluations through several case studies (President Bush and the Gulf War and the 1992 election, Ronald Reagan and Iran–Contra), Miller and Krosnick (1996) argue that what the media decide to cover does impact the standards by which people evaluate the president. Moreover, media coverage can affect the cognitive complexity of the public's evaluation of issues. Milburn and McGrail (1992) found the effect of vivid images in news coverage was a reduction of recall of information among viewers, as well as a reduction in cognitive complexity in their discussions of the issues involved.

Having noted the importance of the media in priming people to attend to particular issues, some caveats must necessarily be added. First, the impact of the media is, not surprisingly, strongest on those who have little independent interest in politics, who are weakly attached to a party, and who are less educated (Iyengar & Kinder, 1987). In addition, personal involvement with an issue affects its salience, so people for whom an issue is personally salient will attend to that issue, regardless of the amount of media coverage. Iyengar and Kinder (1987), for example, found in their experiments that subjects who were unemployed attended to media stories about employment more than those who were employed during a period of low unemployment, but that even people who were employed attended to unemployment stories during periods of higher unemployment. They concluded that employment was of concern only to the unemployed during periods of low unemployment, but everyone felt a stronger personal stake in employment issues during periods of higher unemployment.

Another way of examining priming is through nonexperimental studies. For example, using content analysis of media campaign coverage and exit polling of the U.S. Senate race in Minnesota in 2000, Druckman (2004) found the campaign primed those voters who were exposed and focused so they based their decisions of the candidate on the issues and images prevalent in the campaign. In a more recent study, Dragojlovic (2011) examined priming, the Obama effect, and evaluations by Canadians of the United States. The "Obama effect" refers to President Barack Obama's popularity with foreign audiences. In particular, the study asked whether this effect was the result of his effective management of high-level diplomacy or foreign policy changes that in turn influenced foreign perceptions of the United States. After the 2008 election, there was an increase in the salience of his image in the Canadian media and in coverage of the United States beginning in 2007 regarding the election. Because of the increase in coverage, there was a high degree of awareness of U.S. policy and frequent exposure to coverage mentioning Obama. Priming resulted in a more positive opinion of the United States. Pardos-Prado, Lancee, and Sagarzazu (2014) found apprehension over immigration fostered stronger identification with a center-right party owning the issue, particularly when primed by the media. Focusing on a foreign context, Bilali and Vollhardt (2013) investigated the role of priming in the aftermath of genocide in Rwanda as it related to Radio La Benevolencija's fictional radio drama *Musekeweya*. The drama aims to thwart violence and instead promote reconciliation. The Rwandan participants in the study listened to an audio-delivered questionnaire that was either recorded in the voice of a main character from Musekeweya or from an unknown person. Those who were primed by the main character were less distrustful of the out-group and exemplified more historical perspective-taking and less competitive victimhood.

The literature also distinguishes between explicit and implicit psychological processes. Explicit processes are those that are accessible and able to be self-reported, while those that are implicit are "expressed in behavior, but are generally unavailable to consciousness, and so are not readily measured by surveys or questionnaires" (Weinberger & Westen, 2008, p. 632). Studies focused on implicit processes often address subliminal stimulation (e.g., Dijksterhuis et al., 2005; Westen, 1998). For instance, in two experiments, Weinberger and Westen (2008) examined subliminal messages via the Web and the influence on evaluations of politicians. The second experiment examined whether subliminal presentations of one known political figure (President Clinton) could affect evaluations of another candidate (Governor Gray Davis). Negative evaluations as opposed to positive evaluations were easier to influence and, regardless of subliminal messaging, positive evaluations of Clinton resulted in positive evaluations of Davis. The same held true of low evaluations. Yet the meaning of the findings was not conclusive. In the second study, they focused on this ambiguity. Those holding strong attitudes with regard to party and ideology were less influenced by being shown a photograph of Clinton and with regard to views of Davis, as opposed to swing voters, who were highly influenced.

FRAMING

Another area of research is **framing**, which refers to when the media not only provide the content but also "how to understand and think about it" (Slothuus, 2008). Put another way, framing influences the understanding of the issue and also the evaluation of it. Another important aspect regarding issue framing, and what the media focus on, concerns the presentation of an issue, or what is often referred to as *spin*. How an issue is reported on can make a difference. Most political issues have multiple elements, but the media may focus on only one or two.

There are different schools of thought on framing (Slothuus, 2008). Some, such as Kinder and Nelson (2005), suggest framing depends on the individual and attention to the issue. In other words, the pre-existing views are made more accessible. This is referred to as the *accessibility model* (Slothuus, 2008). In another, the *importance change model*, proposed frames make some considerations more important than others (Slothuus, 2008). For example, Nelson, Clawson and Oxley (1997) presented an example in a study of local television news outlets and a rally by the Ku Klux Klan (KKK) in Ohio. Among their findings, media framing influenced the opinions of individuals toward the KKK. Specifically, if the media presented the story as having implications for free speech, individuals were more tolerant of the KKK. However, they had less tolerance for the KKK if the media framed the rally as one that may bring about a clash between two angry groups. Those elements then receive attention, and the resulting debate regarding moral and/or policy implications revolved around those elements, rather than others. Finally, those such as Zaller (1992) maintain new issues are brought to the forefront, and can therefore influence thinking. This is referred to as the content change model (Slothuus, 2008).

In a related argument, Patterson (1993) notes journalists operate with different schemas than those used by voters, which in turn produces a particular pattern in framing issues and candidates during campaigns. In particular, he argues, journalists' dominant schema "is structured around the notion that politics is a strategic game" (p. 57), rather than competing ideas about issues, appropriate policies, and matters of principle. The public, on the other hand, functions with a schema that views politics as an arena in which policies are discussed and in which leaders are selected who will attempt to implement particular policies. These game and governance schemas interact, and voters and journalists are cognizant of each other's perspective; however, Patterson (1993) contends that because of the press game schema, the focus of the news buries and distorts the substance of the information conveyed to the public during a campaign.

Most of the literature on framing cites some or multiple perspectives in the literature, either building on the schools of thought or presenting it as background in a literature review. The literature on framing is robust and replete with different issues and approaches. Some studies are highlighted below.

Entman (1993) examined framing with an example from the Cold War. During that time, civil wars in other societies were discussed in the U.S. media in terms of the implications for alliances with either the United States or the Soviet Union, rather than in terms of the domestic issues in those societies that led up to civil war. Bayulgen and Arbatli (2013) assessed U.S. newspaper reporting related to the 2008 Russia–Georgia war. The authors concluded U.S. newspaper framing was anti-Russian. Further, with an increase in exposure to media reports finding fault with Russia, there was an increased likelihood of blame being focused on Russia. In another study, Woods (2011) applied framing to perceptions of threat regarding terrorism. The author exposed participants to articles and found the term "terrorism" did not invoke a threat response; however, the threat was more pronounced when it specifically came from radical Islamist groups as opposed to homegrown terrorists and when nuclear versus other technology was mentioned. Another article by Gulati (2011) focused on coverage of human trafficking by the *New York Times* and *Washington Post* between 1980 and 2006. Interestingly, it found media coverage consisted mostly of official sources, so the framing paralleled the same view. In turn, policy-makers legitimized their views and alternative views were marginalized. The exception was investigative journalists who reported alternative views. In a study of the nightly news and framing of the Iraq War, Coe (2013) maintained the presentation of rationales regarding the war only had some impact on attitudes regarding U.S. military action. In another approach, Heim (2013) examined the 2008 Democratic presidential nomination race prior to the Iowa caucus. The author analyzed blogs, major news sources, and candidate press releases. In the case of Hillary Clinton, the author found journalists and her campaign had a "second-level intermedia agenda setting effect" (p. 511). Additionally, bloggers followed the lead from journalists and "were unable to seize control of the campaign narrative from other actors" (p. 511).

In his study, Slothuus (2008) investigated the role of frame mediation. Specifically, he looked at which individual-level factors moderated issue framing effects and which mediated issue framing effects. He found "framing effects on opinion are mediated not only through a process of changing cognitive importance of a receiver's issue-relevant considerations," as indicated in the literature, "but also through a process of altering the content of issue-relevant considerations" (p. 2). This, he argued, was a "two-process model." In another study focused on the identity of the messenger, Schatz and Levine (2010) examined framing with regard to U.S. public diplomacy and Central Asia. They found that the identity of the messenger had an impact. Specifically, they discovered that a quote attributed to President George Bush invoked lower opinions of the United States, rather than the same quote attributed to an unnamed U.S. Ambassador, an ordinary American, or no one.

In other work on elite framing, Druckman and Holmes (2004) examined elite framing, specifically, President George W. Bush's 2002 State of the Union address. Prior to the address, Bush was encountering a flailing economy but high approval ratings on his handling of security (86%). They found in their analysis that he framed the address in terms of terrorism/homeland security (49%) and only 10% on the economy. In another study, Druckman, Jacobs, and Ostermeier (2004) found President Nixon would focus framing domestic issues based on public support.

Recent work on framing looks at competitive frames. Typically, people are exposed to more than one frame regarding candidates or issues. When there are **competitive frames**, which is likely to win? Initially, it was argued that the frames would cancel each other out, and people would rely on their values when deciding what to think. Sniderman and Theriault (2004) found that when people were exposed to free speech frames and public safety frames in the context of a hate group demonstration, they chose the position consistent with their values. They argued that "competing frames make alternative positions equally accessible, which increases the likelihood that people will be able to identify and choose the side that is consistent with their ideological values" (Klar, Robison, & Druckman 2013, p. 180). However, Druckman and Chong (2007) postulated that frames may differ in strength and stronger frames will dominate when there are competitive frames. Strength is determined by the availability of the frame (the perceiver's ability to see a connection between the frame and the issue), the accessibility of the frame ("the frame must actually come to mind as a consideration when thinking about the topic"), and the applicability of the frame (the "individual must view the consideration as compelling or persuasive for it to be considered strong") (Klar et al., 2013, p. 180).

Other authors extended research to foreign media, although this seems to be an area with a need for further scholarship. One such study by Rane and Ewart (2012) studied Australian television news and the tenth anniversary of September 11, 2001. They found the news media shifted from conflating terrorism with Muslims and Islam. Instead, the news focused on U.S.–Australian relations and reconciliation, and the tenth anniversary coverage was presented with the frames of reconciliation. As the authors elaborated:

> The dominant frame across the five free-to-air Australian television news broadcasts was commemoration through the memorials and ceremonies taking place both in the USA and Australia for which the central focus was the remembrance of the victims. Notably absent from the coverage was any reference to Islam or Muslims in terms of responsibility for the 9/11 attacks.
>
> (Rane & Ewart, 2012, p. 320)

What about the role of emotions in framing? Gross (2008) argued that investigating the role of emotion had received limited attention in the literature and has since examined emotions in a specific context or issue (e.g., Gross & D'Ambrosio, 2004; Kinder & Sanders, 1990). Gross looked at the general rhetorical devices of episodic and thematic framing applicable to a range of issues where there are "ways of telling a story to make it more understandable, accessible and compelling to the audience" (p. 170). There are differences between the type of frames: episodic provides an example, case study, or event-oriented report on an issue and thematically takes an issue and puts it into a greater context. Building on the work of Iyengar (1991), Gross (2008) examined "how the use of episodic and thematic framing in a persuasive message affects emotional response and how these emotions might help us understand the link between these frames and policy views" in the case of mandatory minimum sentencing (p. 170). The author concluded there were both cognitive and affective routes, and episodic framing influences the emotional response. The influence of the frame depends on the ability to bring about sympathy and pity, and individuals use these emotions to form opinions. Frames can actually minimize attitudinal change in the case of individuals as opposed to societal matters, yet they can also increase persuasion in the case of an individual if the story is persuasive enough to elicit "intense emotional reactions" (p. 184).

ATTITUDE CHANGE AND PERSUASION

If the media influences what people think about, does it also influence how they think—that is, their attitudes toward an issue or a political candidate? Many of the aforementioned studies take on the study of attitudes; however, this subject warrants further attention here due to the focus and attention this question receives and the multiple perspectives on attitude change.

A related body of research has examined the role of **persuasion** and attitude change of the media. Fishbein and Ajzen (1972) note the lack of coherence in the early literature. Petty and Cacioppo (1986) also argue that while multiple studies were conducted on the role of persuasion, "there was surprisingly little agreement concerning if, when, and how the traditional source, message, recipient and channel variables ... affected attitude change" (p. 125). Research thus focused on organizing and framing the literature. In doing so, Petty and Cacioppo (1986) proposed the **Elaboration Likelihood Model (ELM)**, which integrated the disparate approaches. The ELM focuses on cognition and rests upon the concept of the elaboration likelihood continuum, which is "defined by how motivated and able people are to assess the merits of a person, issue or a position (i.e., the attitude object). The more motivated and able people are to assess the central merits of the attitude object, the more likely they are to effortfully scrutinize all available object-relevant information" (Petty & Wegener, 1998, pp. 327–328). The ELM purports that there are two routes to attitude change through persuasion: a central route and a peripheral route. The central route is when an individual has "careful and thoughtful consideration of the true merits of the information presented in support of an advocacy" (p. 125). Via this route, the elaboration likelihood is high. People arrive at a decision through a reasoned and informed thought process. The peripheral route is different in that it results from an attractive cue without scrutiny. The higher a person goes along the elaboration continuum, the more central route processes are important. Conversely, the farther down one goes along the continuum, the less important central route processes become. The ELM shows that attitude change varies depending on the mental effort put into considering the attitude object. The attitudes that result through the peripheral route tend to be weaker than those formed through the central route (Petty & Wegener, 1998). Related research focused on mood and messaging. Taking these into account, Wegener and Petty (1994) offered the **Hedonic Contingency Model**, which distinguished between happy and sad moods. If an individual is in a sad mood, they pay little attention to information. The reverse is true for those in a happy mood. Wegener, Petty, and Smith (1995) tested this proposition and found that when individuals had an expectation of happiness from a message, those in a happy mood paid more careful attention. Handley, Lassiter, Nicket and Herchenroeder (2004) maintain that mood is automatic; they found support for their hypothesis by studying individuals who were brought into happy, sad, and neutral moods and asking them to rank their inclinations for future activities. Summarizing the dominant persuasion models in the literature, Petty and Wegener note:

> These models placed greater focus on the moderation and mediation of attitude change effects and explained how the same variable (e.g., source credibility, mood) could have different effects on attitude change in different situations, and how a given variable could produce the same persuasion outcome by different processes in different situations. A key idea in these new frameworks was that some processes of attitude change required relatively high amounts of mental effort, whereas other processes of persuasion required relatively little mental effort.
>
> (Petty & Wegener, 1998, p. 3)

Another related model of persuasion is the **Heuristic-Systematic Model (HSM)** (Chaiken, 1980; 1987; Chen & Chaiken, 1999). Systematic information processing focuses on the information provided in a comprehensive manner. This is essentially the same as the ELM's concept of the central route. Heuristic information processing involves the use of heuristics, which are "easily processed judgment relevant cues … rather than individualistic or particularistic judgment-relevant information" (Chen & Chaiken, 1999, p. 76). As noted in Chapter 3, people often use heuristics to reach judgments because they involve less cognitive effort than a careful assessment of information. The HSM takes this a step further through the *sufficiency principle*, which holds that people attempt to maintain a balance between their desire to expend as little cognitive effort as possible and their desire to be accurate in their judgments. If a person uses heuristics to evaluate a message, but is not confident they made one as correct or accurate as they like, the person will engage in systematic information processing (Chen & Chaiken, 1999). For example, take a person concerned about wildlife and interested in the issue of whether the introduction of a wolf population in the Rockies would restore a natural balance among species or cause a new imbalance, particularly a decline in the size of the elk population, a favorite wolf meal. If a wildlife biologist informs that person there is a decline in the elk population because of habitat loss, the person can use a heuristic to evaluate the message (wildlife biologists are experts; experts are usually correct). However, if the same person concerned with wildlife is informed by a hunter advocacy group that the decline in the elk population is because of wolves, and wolves should therefore be killed off, the person would engage in systematic information processing because he or she would be concerned about establishing an accurate position on the issue. Another approach is illustrated by the

Receive-Accept-Sample (RAS) Model (Zaller, 1992). Zaller (1992) argues that individuals have competing opinions on issues. The prevailing view results from what is on one's mind at a particular time.

If attitude persuasion occurs, how long does it last? Research indicates that while persuasion causes attitude change, it is not on a long-term basis. Many studies were conducted that sought to discover the conditions under which attitude change could be made less than fleeting (Hill, Vavreck, & Zaller, 2013). Research focused on multiple messages, source credibility, nature of the voice of the persuasive message, and peer pressure (e.g., Cook & Insko, 1968; Kelman & Hovland, 1953; Johnson & Watkins, 1971; Schopler, Gruder, Miller, & Rousseau, 1968). However, according to Hill et al. (2013), "Often these manipulations worked as expected to increase duration of change, but their strength and obtrusiveness underscore the difficulty of achieving lasting opinion change under ordinary circumstances" (p. 523). As the authors further explain:

> Laboratory studies show that persuasive communication tends to produce durable opinion change when subjects have been induced to engage in effortful processing. But most evidence also indicates that relatively few people habitually engage in effortful processing. Hence, we should expect that, under the uninvolving conditions of mass persuasion, some persuasive effects will be durable, but most will be short-lived. Field studies show rapid decay in the effects of mass communication but do not estimate the rate of decay or determine whether any long-term change occurs.
>
> (Hill et al., 2013, p. 527)

Therefore, the authors investigated the rate of decay and focused on advertising on broadcast television for candidates running for national and subnational office. They found that decay acts quickly because of memory-based processing. Alternatively, those who stored information in their long-term memory experienced a slower decay. They further found that "short-lived attitude change affects behavior in the period before it has decayed" (p. 541) and, interestingly, decay effects occur at a more rapid pace in races other than the presidential one.

PERSUASION AND POLITICAL CAMPAIGNS

Early studies of the effects of the media in political campaigns in the 1940s and 1950s (Berelson, Lazarsfeld, & McFee, 1954; Lazarsfeld, Berelson, & Gaudet, 1944) found partisanship was so solid for so many people that the media's effect on their attitudes was much less than anticipated. Instead, people attended to information in the media that supported their pre-existing preferences. Moreover, people who did not have candidate preferences early in the campaign tended to be influenced more by family and friends than by the media. Later studies reflecting societal changes, such as the advent of television, the general weakening of partisanship, and the diminished importance of extended families and communities as important influences on political attitudes, argued that the media had a stronger impact on the content and complexity of public attitudes (Milburn, 1991). People are influenced by opinions expressed by reporters (of whom there are more now than in the past), by experts, and by popular presidents. Glynn, Herbst, O'Keefe, and Shapiro summarize the perspective on media influence as follows:

> Most theories of media influence today generate from a view of audiences being largely active players in choosing what they hear, watch, or read, and responding accordingly. However, we cannot reject the notion that at times people are quite passive or reactive in attending to the media—or in everyday conversations for that matter, simply letting words or images wash over them, leaving themselves more open to influence or manipulation. This juxtaposition of more active versus more passive possibilities for audience involvement with media has led many researchers to look at media effects on public opinion as a more *interactive* or *transactional* process. The nature of the relationship between audiences and media likely changes and shifts across different personal traits, moods, contexts, and situations.
>
> (Glynn et al., 1999, p. 407)

In a democracy such as the United States, one of the most important times in which the media may influence public opinion is during election campaigns. Candidates use the media as part of their campaign strategy to deliver their campaign message, and the media also report on the candidates, issues, and campaign as independent observers. In addition, the media cover candidate debates. The media are also widely criticized for providing only lightweight coverage of issues during elections, focusing instead on the poll standings of candidates, character issues, and campaign gaffes, rather than core issues regarding policy positions and past performance in office (Ansolabehere, Behr, & Iyengar, 1993; Mayer, 1996; Sabato, 1991).

What about the effect of negative campaigning on attitudes? **Negative campaign ads** are ads in which one candidate criticizes another candidate by name (Krupnikov & Easter, 2013; Ridout & Franz, 2011). In a positive ad, the candidate promotes him or herself. This does not mean only negative ads are associated with negative emotions. Positive ads can provoke anger or fear. An example is Republican presidential candidate Mitt Romney's 2007 ads in which he promises to protect "freedom-loving" Americans from terrorists attempting to build a worldwide "jihadist caliphate" (Ridout & Franz, 2011, p. 79). This is a scary prospect, but Romney did not mention his opponent Barack Obama, so it is considered a positive ad. Ads that criticize the opponent while praising the candidate are called contrast ads (Krupnikov & Easter, 2013). As far as the effects of negative ads are concerned, the results are mixed. Some argue that negative campaigning decreases voter turnout. This may be because voters feel ineffective when they are exposed to negativity. Another possibility is that negative ads produce a negative response to the candidate being criticized, but are also a boomerang of negativity toward the candidate who sponsored the negative ad to begin with (Krupnikov & Easter, 2013). Others have demonstrated that negative ads can mobilize voters. Some possible explanations are that negative ads provide more useful information than positive ads, or people are tuned in more to negative information than positive information, and therefore are able to evaluate candidates quickly and confidently when exposed to negative information (Krupnikov & Easter, 2013). Krupnikov (2011) argues that the timing of negative ads may explain the mixed results. When they occur early in the election before voters have decided on the candidate they prefer, negative ads may be informative and help them make a choice. When they occur after the voter has decided, they may simply be discouraging, causing the voter to decide not to vote.

In other studies, negative messages from the sources were shown to be effective, while in others they were not (Carraro & Castelli, 2010). Carraro and Castelli (2010) argue that mixed findings are due to a number of factors, including murky definitions of negative campaigns and differences in evaluated dimensions and level of measurement. Thus, in their three studies, the authors investigated the impact of negative campaigning on attitudes, taking into account these three dimensions. In Study 1 (but not Study 2), they found that "not all negative messages led to comparable effects" (p. 626). In particular, voters were inclined to have more negative evaluations of a candidate when personal features (person-based evaluations) of the other candidate were attacked, as opposed to ideology or political programs. The authors also found that, in the evaluation of interpersonal qualities, negative person-based messages dampened evaluations, particularly if the member was part of the in-group. The messages had much less effect on evaluation of power and competence. They further found a discrepancy between explicit and implicit responses. As they explain,

> indeed participants expressed overt disliking toward the politician who relied on negative evaluations, but they were nonetheless forced to follow him in the spontaneous conformity task. This measure likely captures the tendency to consider the candidate as a reliable and powerful individual who is focused on his goals and is actively engaged in pursuing them. As a consequence, participants were more likely to follow his advice.
>
> (Carraro & Castelli, 2010, p. 637)

Participants in the study also felt less interpersonal closeness with candidates who used negative messages. Even so, conformity emerged. Finally, in Study 3, the researchers found individuals followed competent, as opposed to warm, politicians.

SOCIAL MEDIA

In the media and political context literature, social media are not as heavily examined as other types of mainstream media. Because of their importance, the literature to date warrants a separate discussion. Social media broaden the exposure of the message and increase "the speed, with networks of friends and associates sharing the information instantly" (Papic & Noonan, 2011). With Facebook, individuals are able to make posts to their specific page that can then be seen immediately by those friends in their network and can also be searched publicly. With Twitter, individuals can convey short 140-character messages in the form of tweets. With YouTube, individuals are able to upload videos in the hope that they may go viral, adding to their further dissemination. Social media can spread messages in a rapid manner, as the message can be transferred to individuals outside of one's own social network. With this new means of media communication proliferating throughout the world, the news media generated some momentum for phrases like "Twitter Revolution" and "Facebook Revolution" to convey the idea that social media have a major impact on how we communicate. Research also demonstrates that both Facebook and Twitter are particularly important forms of media and news for younger generations (Enjolras, Steen-Johnson, & Wollebaek, 2012). Later research showed 62% of adults in the United States get their news from social media (Allcott & Gentzkow, 2016).

How are social media being used in a political context? Not only do information cascades have an informational effect, but they can also have a motivational effect in that social media publicize people's decisions to join a group or sign up for an event (Enjolras et al., 2012). Social media are also a tool to rapidly spread protest information (see Chapter 11), getting individuals out of their houses and into the streets (Valenzuela, 2013). Tufekci and Wilson (2012) focused on the Tahrir Square protests in Egypt, and found individuals received protest information from electronic media such as Facebook, Twitter, and other internet blogs, in addition to print media. Outside of protests, in a recent study Groshek and Al-Rawi (2013) investigated the framing of social media with regard to the 2012 presidential election campaign. In particular, they examined social units from Facebook and Twitter to determine prevailing issues and themes. They found that, on opposing Facebook pages and nonpartisan election Twitter feeds, the presidential candidates were not framed in an overly critical manner. These were similar to what is found in mainstream media. In their study of live tweets during the 2012 Republican Primary, Hawthorne, Houston, and McKinney (2013) found that the views of elites spread faster than those of non-elites.

Social media is now widely used in political campaigns. Candidates have their own websites (the first was Senator Dianne Feinstein's 1994 website) containing their issue positions, campaign schedules, biographies, and contact information (Edgerly, Bode, Him, & Shah, 2013). The websites are also quite happy to take your donation. The early websites were basically electronic brochures and were not updated or particularly informational (Edgerly et al., 2013). As the political world became more familiar with the internet, the websites changed and campaigns became more adept at using social media to influence voters. As Buccoliero, Bellio, Crestini, and Arkoudas (2020) explain, "social media represents a new means of constructing and negotiating a candidate's image, and campaigns' social media strategies are important sources of information and perspective on a given year's election" (p. 91). Campaigns use Facebook, YouTube, Twitter, and Instagram. Commenting on the use of Twitter during the 2016 election, Buccoliero et al. (2020) argues that, "although it is hard to quantify the role Twitter played in the 2016 election, it was highly significant: it drove rather than merely followed the developments of the presidential elections" (p. 93). The importance of Twitter to Donald Trump's campaign communication strategy, and to his presidency afterward, was clear since he used it as his primary form of communication with 26,000 tweets.

In the 2006 election, Facebook created the "Election Pulse 2006" feature, which candidates used to create profiles. It enabled voters to learn about different candidates, and also let them know when their Facebook friends supported their candidate preference (Edgerly et al., 2013). In the years since 2006, candidates have developed Facebook pages that "allow campaigns the ability to post a variety of information (e.g., website links, YouTube videos, announcements, and photos)" (Edgerly et al., 2013, p. 83). Bronstein (2013) looked at the Facebook pages of candidates in the 2012 election three months before the election and found candidates used emotional and motivational appeals, revealed very little about their personal lives, and did not address controversial issues. The candidates used Facebook to raise money and for mobilization. They encouraged affective allegiances between themselves and the posters. These political watchers commented and produced "likes" and were influenced by the persuasion of the posts.

More generally, campaign practices adapted to the digital age. They can now specifically target particular potential voters with information they think will be important for them. For example, on the day one of this book's authors was writing this particular section of the book, she received emails from the Democratic National Headquarters (three of them), Barack Obama, Rich Cowan (not sure who he is, but he knows me by my first name), Bill Foster (not sure who he is either), and Debbie Wasserman Schultz, all with information and requests for action the Democratic Party thought she would want to receive (Joe Biden's email came yesterday). This kind of communication helps voters feel they can interact with political candidates. It also reflects the tendency to sustain engagement with potential voters rather than simply contacting them close to election day (Edgerly et al., 2013, p. 86). The emails sent to this author come every day, from a variety of sources, all providing information about current issues, who in Congress is supporting or opposing what, what the President needs in terms of political support, asking for money, or reporting the results of recent polls so the author recipient can gauge the pulse of the nation.

Internet Misinformation and Fake News

Given that social media are an important source for news, what happens when social media are not censored and lack veracity? After the 2016 election, the term "fake news" became a common phrase, particularly in the case of Facebook, where news stories were widely shared. Allcott and Gentzkow (2016) define fake news as "news articles that are intentionally and verifiably false, and could mislead readers" (p. 213). Vosoughi, Roy and Aral (2018) refer to the spread of this type of information more broadly as misinformation. According to them, "New social technologies, which facilitate rapid information sharing and large-scale information cascades, can enable the spread of misinformation (i.e., information that is inaccurate or misleading)" (p. 1146). The authors also point out that the term "fake news" was hijacked to refer to any claim made that did not support one's own view. For this reason, "the term has lost all connection to the actual veracity of the information presented, rendering it meaningless for use in academic classification" (p. 1146). The discourse on fake news impacts perceptions of the news in general. People are less able to see a difference between fake news and real news, and they have little trust in the news. In 2018, for example, "Only 12% of Americans surveyed said they had a 'great deal' of trust in the news media" (Tong, Gill, Li, Valenzuela, & Rojas, 2020, p. 3). This distrust of the news is stronger among Republicans than Democrats (Tong et al., 2020).

Garrett (2019) found with regard to misperceptions about Obama during the 2012 elections that social media had a "small but significant" influence, particularly among strong partisans. Part of misinformation is conspiracy theories spread on the internet (see also Chapter 8). For example, Alex Jones, a radio host and the creator of Infowars website, used his radio program, webshow, and website to spread conspiracy theories, by doing so ensuring that these beliefs were no longer confined to the fringes, but seeped into the mainstream. He was also a prolific user of social media platforms. However, Vosoughi et al. (2018) took a more comprehensive look at Twitter from 2006 to 2017, and found that news, defined as a claim made with an assertion, spread through rumor. Specifically, a rumor cascade is "when a user makes an assertion about a topic in a tweet, which could include written text, photos, or links to articles online" (p. 1), which is then spread by others. Through their data analysis they found falsehoods were 70% more likely to be retweeted by people, and much more quickly, than the truth. Alternatively, bots spread true and false information equally.

What are the implications? Supporters of Hillary Clinton argued that fake news propelled Trump to the presidency in 2016, and evidence suggests these stories did widely favor Donald Trump, and Russia's role in spreading false news stories was evident. But did it cost Clinton the election? While we cannot provide a definitive answer, Allcott and Gentzkow (2016) argue that the exposure to pro-Trump stories was greater than to pro-Clinton stories, but this still does not explain whether voter behavior was impacted enough to change the outcome of the election. However, what is concerning is how conspiratorial beliefs went from the fringes, to the mainstream, to individuals acting on these beliefs in violent ways. For example, Trump often parroted theories spread by Jones during his campaign and presidency. It took social media companies years to ban Jones, but he managed to carry on his message through his website, show, and social media, including disputing the 2020 election results, which materialized in the January 6, 2021 rally turned attack on the U.S. Capitol. Jones was also responsible for spreading the 2016 Pizzagate conspiracy, which pointed to a child-sex abuse ring connected to Democrats at Comet Ping Pong pizzeria in Washington, D.C. A North Carolina man traveled to the restaurant to investigate the ring, and fired a rifle inside to open a storage room lock during his search.

An additional pattern emerging during the Trump presidency was Trump's use of Twitter to communicate with his followers, often tweeting out obvious falsehoods. The most destructive of those tweets, believed by millions of Americans, was that he had in fact won the 2020 election. Thousands of people who believed this participated in the insurrection at the Capitol on January 6, 2021. Trump not only tweeted lies, but also falsely claimed mainstream media were producing fake news when reports on him were negative (Tong et al., 2020). The *Washington Post* (January 23,

2021) calculated that he told 30,573 lies during his term, half of which came in his last year in office. An important question is why people believe his lies. Millions of his supporters still believe he won the 2020 elections. There are some answers to this question. One obvious answer is that people silo their news sources. Trump supporters tend to watch Fox News, access Breitbart on the internet, and listen to Glen Beck or (the late) Rush Limbaugh, all of which support Trump and his statements. They are not exposed to contrary information, which they think is fake news anyway. Another argument is that hearing the same lies repeated—which Trump tended to do—evokes the "illusory truth effect" (Orr, 2019). This is related to the availability heuristic, because the more often people hear a statement of fact, even if it is a lie, the more they believe it, simply because it is easily accessible. A third explanation is that people know he lies, but they regard the political system to be in crisis or even illegitimate, so lies and norm violations are believed to be appealing and sincere (Hahl, Kim, & Sivan, 2018).

Clearly the study of how the internet and social media is used in the political context is receiving attention. The actual persuasion and attitude change from social media are still an emerging area of interest with the potential for more studies. Some academics argue that technological advances in communicating political information may result in an academic reexamination of conclusions about the media, particularly "the ways in which new technologies afford increasing selective exposure to political information, the fragmentation of audiences, and the decline of inadvertent citizen exposure to political information through the media" (Condor, Tileaga, & Billig, 2013).

CONCLUSION

This chapter has covered a number of approaches to studying the media. The major approaches included agenda-setting, priming, framing, and attitudes. We also addressed the literature on internet and social media effects. The literature on the media continues to evolve, contributing to more clarity regarding its impact.

Topics, Theories/Explanations, and Cases Covered in Chapter 7

Topics	*Theories/Explanations*	*Cases*
Media	Agenda-setting	Multiple
	Priming	Multiple
	Framing	Multiple
	Attitudes and persuasion	Multiple
	Social media	Multiple

Key Terms

agenda-setting
competitive frames
Elaboration Likelihood Model (ELM)
familiarity heuristic
framing
gatekeeping
Hedonic Contingency Model (HCM)
Heuristic-Systematic Model (HSM)
media bias
persuasion
priming
Receive-Accept-Sample (RAS) Model
satisfice
statement bias

Suggestions for Further Reading

Druckman, J. N. (2011). What's it all about? Framing in political science. In G. Keren (Ed.), *Perspectives on framing* (pp. 279–302). New York: Psychology Press.

Giles, D. (2010). *Psychology of the media*. London: Palgrave Macmillan.

Hobert, R. L., & Tchernev, J. M. (2013). Media influence as persuasion. In J. P. Dillar & L. Shen (Eds.), *The Sage handbook of persuasion: Developments in theory and practice* (2nd ed., pp. 36–52). Thousand Oaks, CA: Sage.

Ridout, T. N., & Franz, M. M. (2011). *The persuasive power of campaign advertising*. Philadelphia, PA: Temple University Press.

van Dijck, J. (2013). *The culture of connectivity: A critical history of social media*. Oxford: Oxford University Press.

Wallace, P. (2006). *The psychology of the Internet*. Cambridge: Cambridge University Press.

Chapter 8

The Political Psychology of Race

Racial prejudice and discrimination have been considered the "great American dilemma" (Myrdal, 1944) for decades. Yet on November 4, 2008, Barack Obama was the first African American elected to the office of the President of the United States. Racism was responsible for one of the most repressive regimes in modern history—the apartheid government of South Africa—yet South Africa had its first Black president, Nelson Mandela, in 1994. Understanding racial divisions and conflicts requires us to go beyond explanations that rely upon competition for resources as causes of these conflicts. From the political psychological perspective, we can understand the intransigence of group conflict as the result of the continual human drive to form in-groups and out-groups, and to compare one's group with others. Political psychology also enables us to understand how racial (and ethnic) groups can live together harmoniously for years, then erupt in horrific internecine violence. Identities can be manipulated by leaders, and emotions can rise to extremes of hatred and fear, when people are convinced by leaders and by rumors that their group is threatened by others. Political psychology also turns our attention to the ways in which issues are framed to produce particular anxieties in the minds of citizens. Stereotypes can be subtly or openly manipulated to produce stereotype-driven behaviors and attitudes.

Chapters 8 and 9 look at the underlying causes of political conflicts produced by racism and ethnocentrism. We begin with some concepts and definitions—some introduced in earlier chapters, others new—that enable us to have a common understanding of the perceptions and behaviors involved in race and ethnicity. These chapters explore most of the Political Being's personality, attitudes, cognition, emotions, and identities in relation to *us* (in-groups) and *them* (out-groups). In this chapter, we look at race and politics in the United States, Brazil, and South Africa. In the next, we examine cases of ethnic conflict, including Nigeria, Bosnia, Guatemala, and Syria, and we look at the most horrific form of inter-group violence: genocide.

Race and ethnicity are social constructs, not scientific distinctions. George Fredrickson notes:

> Throughout its history, the United States has been inhabited by a variety of interacting racial or ethnic groups. In addition to the obvious "color line" structuring relationships between dominant Whites and

DOI: 10.4324/9780429244643-8

> lower-status Blacks, Indians and Asians, there have at times been important social distinctions among those of White or European ancestry. Today we think of the differences between white Anglo-Saxon Protestants and Irish, Italian, Polish, Jewish Americans as purely cultural or religious, but in earlier times, these groups were sometimes thought of as "races" or "subraces"—people possessing innate or inborn characteristics and capabilities that affected their fitness for American citizenship.
>
> It can therefore be misleading to make a sharp distinction between race and ethnicity when considering intergroup relations ... Ethnicity is "racialized" whenever distinctive group characteristics, however defined or explained, are used as the basis for status of hierarchy of groups who are thought to differ in ancestry or descent.
>
> (Fredrickson, 1999, p. 23)

Having set forth this caution, we look at race in this chapter and ethnicity in Chapter 9 only as reflections of their social construction in real situations. In other words, when societies consider race to be race rather than ethnicity, so do we, in order to reflect the language used in these societies and the studies published about them.

This chapter is concerned with race because group differentiations in terms of race are so frequently associated with political inequalities. These patterns of political activity stem from stereotyping of, and prejudice toward, groups of different race (or ethnicity). What is **prejudice**? It is a commonly used term, but there are many definitions. Reviewing various interpretations of prejudice, Sniderman, Piazza, and Harvey (1998) note four components of prejudice that are generally agreed upon in the literature: a response to group members based on their membership in the group; a negative evaluative orientation toward a group and consequently an aversion to group members; an attribution of negative characteristics toward a group and its members that is incorrect; and, finally, consistency in the negative orientation toward the group and its members.

Prejudice is closely associated with a concept we introduced in Chapter 3: a *stereotype*, which we defined as "a set of beliefs about the personal attributes of a group of people" (Duckitt, 1994, p. 8). Stereotypes and prejudices that produce discriminatory behavior are filled with negative evaluations of the group and its members. Rothbart and Johns (1993) note that stereotypes have descriptive and evaluative components. The problem, they argue, "is that the evaluative component, which is a judgment that the observer makes about the group, is not perceived as a judgment *about* the group, but as an attribute *of* the group itself" (p. 40). This is called the **phenomenal absolutism error**. For example, a group that does not spend a great deal of money can be thought of as thrifty or stingy. Either characterization is an evaluation of a behavior, but that evaluation comes to be considered a characteristic of the group, not an evaluation or one of several possible evaluations of the behavior noticed. In a negative stereotype, a group whose members do not spend much money may be considered inherently stingy. The use of prejudices and pre-existing beliefs in evaluation of others also occurs in ambiguous situations, which is known as the **ultimate attribution error** (Pettigrew, 1979).

EXPLAINING RACISM AND ETHNOCENTRISM

Why do people stereotype others and engage in discriminatory behavior? One of the oldest explanations for prejudice and discrimination is **realistic conflict theory** (Bobo, 1983). According to this explanation, discrimination is a result of competition over scarce resources such as jobs, housing, and good schools. Thus, whenever such commodities are in short supply, the demand for them increases. Additionally, research suggests as competition becomes more severe, those involved tend to view the other in increasingly negative terms (White, 1977). For example, members of groups tend to solidify boundaries existing between them, derogate the other group, and believe their own group is superior. One of the earliest investigations of realistic conflict theory was conducted by Sherif, Harvey, White, Hood, and Sherif (1961). That study involved dividing a group of 11-year-old boys, who were attending a summer camp, into two groups. For one week, the boys in each group lived together, ate together, played together, and generally engaged in enjoyable activities. Then the boys in both groups were told they would be engaging in a number of competitions, the winners of which would receive valuable prizes (e.g., trophies). Over the next two weeks, as the boys competed with one another, tensions escalated. They taunted each other, attacked one another's cabins, overturned beds, and destroyed some of the other group's personal belongings. In only two short weeks, the boys, who were friends before the study, came to behave in hostile ways toward one another as a result of the competition.

In an attempt to restore the boys' friendships, Sherif and his colleagues (1961) created a series of *superordinate* goals—goals that both groups desired, which required the cooperation of both groups to achieve. When their water supply was severely reduced (as a consequence of being sabotaged by the researchers), for example, both groups of boys had to work together to restore it. Similarly, when the boys wanted to rent a movie, but could not afford to on their own, they pooled their money. The introduction of these superordinate goals worked to reduce the tensions created as a result of the competitions. Additionally, many of the boys, who were in different groups, were able to restore their friendships. This investigation is important in revealing how competition over scarce resources can quickly escalate into full-scale conflict.

A second explanation for prejudice and discrimination is **social learning theory**. According to this view, children learn negative attitudes and discriminatory behavior from their parents, teachers, family, friends, and others when they are rewarded for such behavior. Rewards can be in the form of praise, agreement, love, and so on. Children have a strong need to be accepted and loved by those who are important to them. One way to be accepted and loved is to adopt the same attitudes that valued others have toward certain groups. *Social norms* (rules governing appropriate and acceptable behavior) are also a powerful mechanism for learning prejudice. Most people choose to conform to their own group's norms. For example, a child might assume that if a member of their group does not like another group, then the child will also not like the other group. Recent research

(Towles-Schwen & Fazio, 2001) suggests that individuals' attitudes toward particular racial groups are determined by the attitudes of their parents, as well as by their childhood experiences with members of minority groups. Those with less-prejudiced parents and more positive experiences with minority group members have more favorable racial attitudes. The media also play a strong role in shaping our attitudes toward members of racial groups. When minority group members are portrayed (on television, in movies, in commercials) in stereotypical ways, media consumers tend to adopt stereotypical (prejudiced) attitudes.

Another explanation for the development of prejudice is **social identity theory,** first presented in Chapter 3. Social identity studies found that prejudice and stereotyping among groups occurs even in the absence of conflicting goals. Competition can occur even when the stakes are only psychological, and among groups that are arbitrarily formed by experimenters with no real interaction or conflicting goals (**minimal group paradigm**) (Tajfel, 1982; see Brewer & Brown, 1998, for a thorough review). In Chapter 4, we noted that social categorization and social identity are partially responsible for the initial process of group differentiation into in-groups and out-groups. With this process comes the accompanying perception of the superiority of the in-groups. In addition, psychologists found that people remember negative behaviors of out-groups far better than positive behaviors, and positive behaviors of in-groups far better than negative behaviors (Fiske, 1998; Rothbart & John, 1993). However, this kind of bias in favor of the in-group is not in and of itself stereotyping and prejudice. As Allport (1954) noted many years ago, "not every overblown generalization is a prejudice" (p. 9). Such generalizations become prejudices when they are resistant to disconfirming information—that is, when information indicating they are wrong is ignored, disbelieved, or rejected out of hand.

A core argument in social identity theory is that social categorization produces a basic motivation for intergroup social competition. Once social categories are formed, people strive for positive social identity, which in turn creates intergroup competition. This causes perceptual biases and discriminatory behavior patterns as people strive to view their in-group in a positive light, compared with out-groups. This explanation helps us understand general ethnocentrism; it directs our attention to the role of social cues that make salient intergroup distinctions and to the importance of status differentials—that is, the need to see one's own group as superior to others. But does it explain why prejudice toward some groups is so deep, but almost nonexistent for others? Not really. To do this, we must add in factors relating to the social context, the perceived legitimacy of intergroup relations, and individual personality characteristics.

Motivation and *personality traits* have also been examined in efforts to explain the causes of racism and ethnocentrism. One additional explanation that should be considered for racial and ethnic prejudice is related to studies of personality, discussed in Chapter 2. As mentioned in that chapter, there was a revival in the study of the authoritarian personality. Studies by Altemeyer (1981, 1988, 1996) and others argue that three central characteristics of the authoritarian personality co-vary across cultures and are directly related to ethnocentrism and prejudice. Those characteristics are authoritarian submission (to authority), aggression (against nonconformist groups), and conventionalism (blind acceptance of social norms). Altemeyer (1996) argues these characteristics are strongly linked to right-wing authoritarianism in particular, and his studies found them to be highly correlated with ethnocentrism. People who earn high scores in measures of authoritarianism tend to be more prejudiced toward low status out-groups than people whose authoritarianism scores are low (Altemeyer, 1996; Meloen, 1994). Those high-scoring individuals stereotype out-groups as inferior to their own groups. In general, despite ongoing debates about theory and methods, evidence indicates that individual differences account for degrees of racism, prejudice against out-groups (particularly those who are visible and low-status), likelihood of being ethnocentric, likelihood of being less cognitively complex, and being more likely to rely on stereotypes in ambiguous contexts (Perreault & Bourhis, 1999). Other personality traits have also been associated with ethnocentrism. Perreault and Bourhis (1999), for example, found that ethnocentrism and a personal need for structure predicted both in-group identification and discriminatory behavior. In later work, Duckitt, Bizumic, Krauss, and Heled (2010) refined Altemeyer's Right-Wing Authoritarian scale into the Authoritarianism-Conservatism-Traditionalism (ACT) framework.

Social Dominance Scale

The Social Dominance Scale is based on responses to the following statements. Along a seven-point scale, respondents are asked to disagree or to agree:

1. Some groups of people are just more worthy than others.
2. In getting what your group wants, it is sometimes necessary to use force against other groups.
3. Superior groups should dominate inferior groups.
4. To get ahead in life, it is sometimes necessary to use force against other groups.
5. If certain groups of people stayed in their place, we would have fewer problems.
6. It is probably a good thing that certain groups are at the top and other groups are at the bottom.
7. Inferior groups should stay in their place.
8. Sometimes other groups must be kept in their place.
9. It would be good if all groups could be equal.
10. Group equality should be our ideal.
11. All groups should be given an equal chance in life.
12. We should do what we can to equalize conditions for different groups.
13. Increased social equality.
14. We would have fewer problems if we treated groups more equally.
15. We should strive to make incomes more equal.
16. No one group should dominate in society.

(Sidanius et al., 2000, pp. 234–235)

Another explanation that examines personality characteristics, but is also group related, is **social dominance theory** (Pratto, Sidanius, Stallworth, & Malle, 1994; Sidanius, 1993; Sidanius & Pratto, 1993, 1999; Sidanius, Singh, Hetts, & Federico, 2000). Social dominance theory presents a social dominance orientation measure that differentiates those who prefer social group relations to be equal or hierarchical, and the extent to which people want their in-group to dominate out-groups. Social dominance orientation personality dimensions concern the degree to which a person favors an unequal, hierarchical, dominance-oriented relationship among groups. The Social Dominance Scale can be seen in the box. Clearly, those high in social dominance orientation would strongly agree with questions 1–8 and disagree with questions 9–16. The scale has produced results similar to the right-wing authoritarian measurements by Altemeyer (1998), although those high in social dominance are unlike authoritarians in that religion is not particularly important to them, and they "do not claim to be benevolent" (p. 61), whereas right-wing authoritarians do (Whitley, 1999).

Sidanius (1993) argues that, despite its strengths, social identity theory cannot explain experimental findings that demonstrate out-group favoritism, and it cannot predict how and along what dimensions discrimination against out-groups will occur. He argues that social identity theory expects out-group discrimination, yet studies have found evidence of low-status groups admiring high-status out-groups.[1] How can this be explained? Social dominance theory seeks to explain these behaviors as a product of social status and a human predisposition to form social groups that are arranged in a social hierarchy. There are three broad hierarchies in societies: gender (males dominate females); age (adults rule); and a third category, which varies from society to society, but that consistently includes socially constructed groups identified as differentiated in terms of race, ethnicity, class, clan, or nationality. These studies are concerned primarily with "the specific mechanisms by which social hierarchies are established and maintained and the consequences these mechanisms have for the nature and distribution of social attitudes and the functioning of social institutions within social systems" (Sidanius, 1993, p. 198). Those mechanisms are ideologies and political values that ascribe legitimacy to the social hierarchy. The people who support and promote such ideologies (e.g., the Protestant work ethic and liberalism/conservatism) are, of course, those who are at the top of the group hierarchy. They are able to use their dominance to perpetuate ideas and institutions to maintain their dominance. People accept inferiority because they are socialized to do so, and those at the top of the hierarchy survive; governments use coercion, when necessary, to defeat challengers. In essence, the theory attempts to look at individual, group, and social-structural variables to explain racism. People in dominant groups are socialized, as individuals, to have a social dominance orientation. They belong to groups on the top of the hierarchy, the social and political systems benefit them the most, and they use social and political structures to maintain the hierarchical relationships among groups (Sears, Hetts, Sidanius, & Bobo, 2000; see also Rabinowitz, 1999). The theory was also applied to groups in the United States and other countries (e.g., Levin & Sidanius, 1999), as well as the Canadian military (Nicol, Charbonneau, &

Boies, 2007), social policy (Pratto et al., 1998), and Whites' racial identity (Bai, 2020), among other topics.

Later theoretical research on SDO focused on refining the scale, and on subdimensions in particular (Ho, Sidanius, Kteily, Sheehy-Skeffington, Pratto, Henkel, & Stewart, 2015; Ho, Sidanius, Pratto, Levin, Thomsen, Kteily, & Sheehy-Skeffington, 2012; Kugler, Cooper, & Nosek, 2010). For example, in their SDO6 scale, which takes into account the dominance sub dimension (SDO-D), and egalitarian sub dimension (SDO-E), Ho et al. argue:

> SDO-D better predicted support for aggressive behaviors directed toward subordinate groups (e.g., immigrant persecution), endorsement of beliefs that would justify oppression (e.g., "old fashioned racism), and a strong focus on group competition and threat. Thus, SDO-D constitutes support for the active, even violent, maintenance of oppressive hierarchies in which high status groups dominate and control the prerogatives of low status groups…SDO-E better predicted political conservatism in the United States, support for ideologies that would justify inequality (e.g., the Protestant Work Ethic), and opposition to policies that would bring about more intergroup equality (e.g., affirmative action); in short, it manifested itself in an affinity for ideologies and policies that maintain inequality, especially those that have ostensibly different purposes (such as economic efficiency and meritocracy).
>
> (Ho et al., 2015, pp. 1004–1005)

This refined scale was used to examine social dominance in a cross-cultural context (Pratto et al., 2012).

Ho et al. (2015) created another refined scale, SDO7, reflecting SDO-D and SDO-E. They also looked at the role of personality. Here their findings were similar to their 2012 study. SDO-D strongly predicted racism, and therefore intergroup dominance, and SDO-E was linked to political conservatism and legitimizing inequality. The findings on personality aligned with previous studies. The validity of SDO7 and ACT were tested by Crowson and Brandes (2017) with regard to predicting voter intention in the 2016 election. Those with higher SDO-E and ACT-A (authoritarianism), and ACT-T (traditionalism) scores were more likely to vote for Donald Trump.

The why question—why racism and ethnocentrism occur—must be followed by the who question—what explains who the particular targets are. This is particularly perplexing when one considers the artificiality of race. As we noted earlier, people tend to think of race as denoting biological differences among people, but in fact it is largely socially constructed. Why is it that race is so important as an identifying marker for discrimination and prejudice in the United States, particularly when it comes to African Americans as perceived by Euro-Americans? Why were Jews the scapegoats in Nazi Germany, the Armenians in Turkey, the Tutsis in Rwanda, and the Maya in Guatemala and other parts of Central America? What determines who gets picked on in a society? In addition, perceptions of those who are targets for harsh treatment vary. Some, like the Maya in Guatemala or African Americans in the United States, are perceived to be inferior and have been victims of chronic and systematic discrimination. Others, like the Armenians, Jews, and Tutsis, are identified as the culprits to blame for bad things happening to society and as having far more than their fair share of the power and wealth.

The social dominance perspective provided one explanation about which groups receive the worst treatment: there are three potential hierarchies, and society maintains the status differential through legitimizing myths, institutions, and force if necessary. Likewise, realistic conflict theory cites competition for resources as a motivating factor producing prejudice. But does that hostility necessarily evolve into the view of the other group as inferior? For example, did the Nazis and Hutus perceive the Jews and Tutsis, respectively, as inferior, or was that perception preceded by a perception that they were in a superior position in society? If so, how and why does that perception occur?

Social identity theory provides some insights here. It maintains that **scapegoating** is a result of social causality assessments—finding an out-group to blame for bad things that happen to the in-group (Hogg & Abrams, 1988; Kecmanovic, 1996; Staub, 1989). It is sensible that out-groups identified as responsible for some problem the in-group is facing will have negative characteristics attributed to them. Whether the scapegoat begins in a superior position or not, they are ultimately described as inferior. Some analysts draw more from psychoanalytic concepts and argue that *projection*—that is, ascribing one's own unacceptable and repressed impulses or attributes to out-groups—explains why they are regarded as inferior. In particular, repressed anger is displaced on to the scapegoat, and that group is not only regarded with contempt, but reacted to with powerful emotions of anger, fear, and resentment (Milburn & Conrad, 1996). Experimental studies, such as those of Rogers and Prentice-Dunn (1981), demonstrate the importance of anger—for example, in studies that found that White subjects, when not angered, react with more hostility toward Whites than toward Blacks, but when White subjects were angered in the experiment, they reacted with more hostility toward Blacks than toward Whites.

The Political Psychology of Race

In the next section, we discuss the issue of race as portrayed in many academic studies on the United States that focus on this concept in particular. We also provide a discussion of the groups in the United States. Finally, we include some international examples and look at the cases of Brazil and South Africa.

RACE IN THE UNITED STATES, EUROPE, BRAZIL, AND SOUTH AFRICA

Race in the United States

American attitudes on race and race-related issues go right to the heart of democratic principles. Those attitudes changed greatly since the

1950s, and in a positive direction, in terms of the democratic principles of equality.[2] Nevertheless, the socioeconomic reality of Black and White American living standards indicates continuity in the wide disparity of wealth and power. Changing attitudes did not produce socioeconomic equality between Blacks and Whites in the United States. For example, in 1968, 8.4% of White families with children lived in poverty and 34.6% of Black families with children lived in poverty. In 1998, the figures were 6.1% and 30.5% respectively—an improvement, but still a great disparity in percentages of families living in poverty, when White and Black families were compared (Joint Center for Political and Economic Studies, 2001). The Great Recession of 2008 hurt people across the board, and by 2011, 10% of White Americans were living in poverty, while 28% of Blacks (as well as 25% of Hispanics and 12% of Asians) were living in poverty (Pew Research Center, 2016c).

More Blacks attend college today than in the 1940s, and more graduate from high school. In 1964, about 51% of Whites completed high school, compared with about 27% of Blacks. By 2012 the figures were 92% and 86% respectively (Pew Research Center, 2016c). In 2017, 87% completed high school or an equivalent (Bialik, 2018). College completion rates also improved, but a gap remains. In 1964, 10% of Whites completed college compared with 4% of Blacks. By 2012, the figures were 34% and 21% respectively (Pew Research Center, 2016c). College completion increased to 24% in 2017 (Bialik, 2018).

More Blacks are employed in white-collar jobs today, up from 5% in 1940 to 32% in 1990 (Sears et al., 2000). Still, Hoffman and Llagas (2007) note that "fewer Black and Hispanic men and women than White men and women held managerial or professional positions in 2000." Furthermore, Blacks still make less money than Whites, even with equal levels of education. In 1997, for example, Black women with high school diplomas earned $926 for every $1000 earned by a White female high school graduate. Black men with a high school education earned $723 for every $1000 earned by a White male high school graduate. The figures for Black and White male college graduates are $767 for every $1000, respectively (Shipler, 1997). Hoffman and Llagas (2007) noted that in 2000, Blacks at all educational levels had higher unemployment rates than both Whites and Hispanics. Figures from 2017 show the wealth gap between Blacks and Whites shrank for middle-income families, but decreased at lower incomes, a product of a decrease in White wealth (Bialik, 2018).

Racial attitudes have also changed dramatically in the United States, but not enough to eradicate racism. For the most part, White Americans no longer regard Blacks as biologically inferior to Whites, as they did during slavery and the Jim Crow era that followed. As late as 1942, survey data indicated that more than half of Whites believed Blacks to be less intelligent than Whites and opposed integration of schools and public transportation (Schuman, Steeh, Bobo, & Krysan, 1997). By the end of the century, those attitudes had changed dramatically, with over 90% of Whites favoring school integration and willing to vote for a Black political candidate, and only around 10% believing that Blacks are inherently unequal to Whites (Schuman et al., 1997).

Race and the Obama Election

Did racial prejudice influence the election of Barack Obama to the presidency? Generally, it did not. We saw in Chapter 6 that concerns about the Bradley effect were misplaced. Whites were truthful in saying they would vote for a Black candidate. But Whites did favor John McCain by 12%, while 95% of African Americans voted for Obama. Moreover, of the 7% of Whites who said race would affect their decision for whom to vote, two-thirds voted for McCain (Pew Research Center, 2008b).

Does this election of Barack Obama mean racism is a thing of the past in the United States? No. It signals progress, but this election alone did not undo the socioeconomic impact of the racism of the past.

Studies have found that racist attitudes in the United States diminished as education levels increased over the years. Those with more formal education are less likely to express racist attitudes. But their support for policies designed to address inequality between the races is another issue entirely, as we will see later (Jackman, 1978; Carmines & Merriman, 1993; Schuman et al., 1997). A 2007 Pew Research Center study found that by 2007, 82% of Whites had a favorable (57%) or very favorable (25%) view of Blacks. On the other hand, 80% of Blacks had a favorable (53%) or very favorable (27%) view of Whites (p. 50). Whites also tend to believe that Blacks and Whites share important values, and this grew from 62% of Whites in 1986 to 72% in 2007 (Pew Research Center, 2007, p. 20).

The Pew Research Center report (2016c) looked at intergroup relations and found majorities of Blacks, Whites, and Hispanics believe the groups "get along reasonably well" (2016c, p. 11). There are, however, considerable differences in perceptions of how well Blacks are treated in their communities. When asked whether Blacks are treated worse than Whites by the police, 37% of Whites, 70% of Blacks, and 51% of Hispanics agreed; when asked whether Blacks are treated worse than Whites in the courts, the figures are 27%, 68%, and 40% respectively; when asked the question about work, the figures are 16%, 54%, and 40% respectively; when asked the question about voting in elections, the figures are 13%, 48%, and 30% respectively (2016c, p. 12).

Nevertheless, vestiges of the past remain. Peffley and Hurwitz (1998), for example, found that a plurality of Whites have a positive perception of Blacks, but a surprisingly high proportion still see Blacks as lazy (31%), not willing to succeed (22%), aggressive (50%), and undisciplined (60%). At the heart of this is *affect*—negative feelings toward Blacks by Whites. But these perceptions are not just confined to Whites. In their study of Latinos in Durham, North Carolina, McClain et al. (2006) examined their perceptions of Blacks. Durham, according to the authors, had a significant increase in its Latino population.

> We found that 58.9% of the Latino immigrants in our study reported feeling that few or almost no blacks are hardworking; approximately one-third (32.5%) of the Latino immigrants reported feeling that few

> or almost no blacks are easy to get along with; and slightly more than a majority (56.9%) of the Latino immigrant respondents reported feeling that few or almost no blacks could be trusted.
>
> (McClain et al., 2006, p. 578)

However, the reverse was not true—that is, Blacks viewed Latinos much more favorably than Latinos viewed Blacks:

> Almost three-fourths (71.9%) of blacks feel most or almost all Latinos are hardworking, two-fifths (42.8%) believe most or almost all Latinos are easy to get along with, and only one-third (32.6%) indicate almost no or few Latinos could be trusted.
>
> (McClain et al., 2006, p. 579)

In the study, McClain et al. (2006) also examined what groups—Asians, Blacks or Whites—Latinos believed they had the most in common with. They found Latinos believed they had more in common with Whites (78.3%) and the least in common with Blacks (52.8%). Nearly 47% of Blacks felt they had the most in common with Latinos and 45.5% believed they had the most in common with Whites. A study by Cox and Jones (2017) asked similar questions of White survey respondents: How much do you have in common with Black, Hispanic and Asian people? They found nearly three-quarters of White Americans said they have either a "lot" (20%) or "some" (53%) in common with Black Americans. Similar numbers of Whites said they had a lot (17%) or some (54%) in common with Hispanic Americans. Fewer Whites reported the same with regard to Asian and Pacific-Islander Americans (14% said "a lot" and 48% said "some) (2017, p. 1). The Pew Research Center's 2016 report (2016c) looked at intergroup relations and found majorities of Blacks, Whites, and Hispanics believed the groups "get along reasonably well" (p. 11).

Needless to say, the topic of race relations in America today is enormously complex and it is no longer an issue of Black–White relations. Nearly 40% of Americans identify with some other race than White, and Whites are estimated to become the minority by 2045 (Frey, 2020). These trends, along with the 2008 election of the nation's first Black president, are producing change and backlash in White political psychology, which will be discussed in more depth below. We will look at different arguments and models that break race down into component parts and central questions. First, what is the relationship between attitudes toward race and positions on central political issues? This is a confoundingly difficult question to answer.

In the past, where White people stood on equal housing, busing, affirmative action, voting rights, equal access to public facilities, and so on, was determined by how they felt about African Americans. Sniderman and Piazza (1993) argue that today a distinction must be made among policies directed at equal treatment (e.g., in housing, schools, etc.); policy areas that are explicitly racially conscious, such as affirmative action, and social welfare-related policies. They argue that only equal treatment and race-conscious policies are uniquely related to racial attitudes. Social welfare policies involve programs for the poor, regardless of race or ethnicity. A person's positions on social welfare issues reflect their attitudes toward the role of the government, its size, its influence on the lives of citizens, and its role as agent of social change, rather than simply on race.

More generally, Schuman et al. (1997) examined trends in White racial attitudes regarding principles of equal treatment, implementation of equal treatment, social distance, beliefs about inequality, and affirmative action. Looking at survey results for several decades (when possible), they found a number of interesting patterns. There was an increase in White acceptance of the principles of equal treatment, but less change when Whites were asked about policies that would implement those principles. For example, White support increased for implementation of open access to public accommodation and housing, but a gap remained between those supporting the principle and those supporting policy to implement the principle, and the percentage supporting federal government efforts to integrate schools actually declined over time (Schuman et al., 1997). The social distance patterns were also mixed. Over the years, Whites expressed an increased willingness to send their children to schools with Black children in attendance, to the point where nearly 100% accepted integrated schools by the 1990s. But when they were asked about truly integrated schools, in which their children may be a minority (i.e. 51% of Black children), the picture changed. By 1996, 49% of White parents said they would not send their children to a school that was over 50% Black (Schuman et al., 1997). Looking at the issue from a different perspective, in 2007 only 23% of Whites believed it was more important to send their children to racially mixed schools than to neighborhood schools, whereas 65% preferred neighborhood schools. Blacks, in contrast, believed (56%) that it was more important to send children to mixed schools than neighborhood schools (33%) (Pew Research Center, 2007, p. 10). Acceptance of integrated neighborhoods showed a similar pattern, with 13% of Whites indicating that they would only live in an all-White neighborhood in 1994, compared with 28% in 1976, but with little change in those wanting to live in a mostly White neighborhood (Schuman et al., 1997).

In terms of beliefs about the causes of inequality, the percentage of Whites who believe that African American socioeconomic disadvantages are the product of slavery and discrimination has declined since the mid-1960s. Whites today prefer explanations that divide the blame between Blacks themselves and historical social discrimination against Blacks (Schuman et al., 1997). Finally, regarding affirmative action programs that explicitly attempt to compensate Blacks for past discrimination in housing, jobs, and access to education, White support remained at or below one-third (Schuman et.al., 1997). Sniderman and Piazza sum up the results of the various surveys with the following evaluation:

> With the exception only of citizens who are uncommonly well educated and uncommonly liberal, what is striking is the sheer pervasiveness throughout the contemporary American society of negative characterizations of Blacks—particularly the stereotype that most Blacks on welfare could get a job. Perceptions of Blacks as inferior were supposed to represent an archaic stock of beliefs that were in the process of dying out, and some indeed do appear to be fading out. But it completely misreads contemporary American culture to suppose that all negative characterizations of Blacks are dwindling away. On

> the contrary, images of Blacks as failing to make a genuine effort to work hard and to deal responsibly with their obligations is a standard belief throughout most of American society.
>
> (Sniderman & Piazza, 1993, pp. 50–51)

Nevertheless, there is a deep disagreement among political psychologists in their answers to questions of how prevalent and how deep racial prejudice is in the United States today. One camp is led by Sniderman, Piazza, Tetlock, Kluegel and others. They propose a model that they did not name, but that we call the **politics-is-complicated model** (also known as the principled objection model), wherein it is argued that White Americans vary in the degree to which they blame the inequalities between the races on structural factors (such as the historical legacy of slavery, and the current system-wide discrimination), as opposed to individual factors (individual acts of prejudice and discrimination, rather than system-wide factors). The other camp, led by Kinder and Sears, maintained that what we have in America today is **symbolic racism** disguised as traditional American individualist values. Let's take a look at each argument in some detail.

Data do not provide clear-cut evidence about the degree of racism among White Americans. For example, Sniderman and Piazza (1993) report that 81% of surveyed Whites agreed Blacks on welfare could find jobs; 43% agreed Blacks need to try harder, 36% agreed Blacks have a chip on their shoulder, but only 6% agreed Blacks are born with less ability.

Are people who agree with a negative description of another group of people necessarily prejudiced toward that group? The politics-is-complicated camp's answer is no. "Apart only from the characterization of Blacks as inherently inferior to Whites, [the negative characterizations] cannot be entirely reduced to bigotry, for these characterizations capture real features of everyday experience" (Sniderman & Piazza, 1993, p. 43). Moreover, they note that Blacks have an even harsher characterization of Blacks than Whites do: 59% of Blacks agree Blacks are aggressive, compared with 52% of Whites; 39% of Blacks agree Blacks are lazy, compared with 34% of Whites; and 40% of Blacks agree Blacks are irresponsible, compared with 21% of Whites (p. 45).

There are racists in America today, but scholars in this school of thought maintain true racists are people who express prejudicial attitudes toward Blacks, and who also systematically express anti-Semitic attitudes toward Jews and hostility toward other minorities. They accept stereotypes of Blacks as lazy, violent, and innately inferior to Whites, and of Jews as shady in business practices, arrogant, and concerned only with the wellbeing of other Jews, for example (Peffley & Hurwitz, 1998; Sniderman & Piazza, 1993). This indicates such people are broadly ethnocentric, hold a number of social stereotypes, and are generally socially intolerant. Advocates of the politics-is-complicated model argue that values related to authoritarianism, such as obedience to authority and hostility toward those different from one's own group, are more strongly correlated with negative attitudes toward Blacks than with values of individualism (e.g., the symbolic racism model) (Peffley & Hurwitz, 1998; Sniderman & Piazza, 1993).

An additional problem is a lack of consistency between support for equality between the races and a lack of support for policies to achieve that equality. The politics-is-complicated model maintains the inconsistency is not racism, but is attributable to changes in American politics, and attitudes about policies related to race and other political attitudes. Attitudes toward race, they argue, do not always dominate political choice. For example, if two people (one liberal and one conservative) both express support for equality, but only the liberal supports spending by the federal government to help Blacks, is the conservative then inconsistent and a closet racist? From the politics-is-complicated perspective, the answer is no because a conservative would believe that federal spending per se should be opposed. Conservatives would maintain that they support racial equality, but that less government is more important, and/or that government support for Blacks actually produces dependence on government, rather than giving a leg up. This point is extended to explain one of the paradoxes found among those with higher levels of education. The more educated White people are, the more likely they are to respond to political issues associated with race in terms of affect (liking or disliking Blacks) and cognition (understanding the broader political context and linking issues to ideological principles). The resulting cognitive complexity allows people to consider a variety of differentiated considerations in making a policy choice. Hence, more educated people are more likely to consider issues other than, or in addition to, race when deciding on their issue positions. Therefore, the conservative described earlier will consider race, but several other principles and policy characteristics, along with race, will also affect their decision, thus diminishing race-related principles in the overall decision-making process (Sniderman et al., 1991).

The politics-is-complicated model maintains that, in America today, there are "multiple agendas in racial politics, distinguishing the equal treatment agenda from the social welfare and the race conscious agendas" (Sniderman, Crosby, & Howell, 2000, p. 257). Some of these agendas, while having race-related implications, are not dominated by race-based attitudes when policy choices are expressed. The politics of race changed since the 1950s and 1960s, when they centered around legally sanctioned racial inequality—that is, Jim Crow laws—which created and enforced racial segregation and discrimination in schools, public facilities, housing, employment, and voting rights. Today's issues are more complex and include government enforcement of school integration through busing, affirmative action, assistance to Blacks to improve their economic situation, and government guarantees of equal opportunity.

Sniderman and Piazza (1993) assert that there are three issue agendas in the United States: the social welfare agenda, the equal treatment agenda, and the race-conscious agenda. The social welfare agenda is broadly defined to include governmental assistance to the disadvantaged, regardless of their race. However, because Blacks generally are at lower socioeconomic levels than Whites, race can become an issue in approving or rejecting social welfare policies. Sniderman and Piazza (1993) argue that "Whites tend to base their position on social welfare assistance for Blacks to a significant degree on judgments about effort and fairness" (p. 118). Whites are more likely to approve of social welfare policies if they believe Blacks have been the victims of prejudice and discrimination, regardless of the White person's level of education. Whites are more likely to oppose these policies if they believe that Blacks do not try hard enough, again, regardless of education.

Ideology influences judgments of social welfare policies as well, particularly among the more educated, who as noted, are more cognitively complex. Conservatives are more likely than liberals to believe Blacks do not try hard enough and less likely than liberals to believe that Blacks have been treated unfairly in the United States. Ideology plays a role for the more educated, but not for the less educated, in determining their support for social welfare policies. The implication here is that for the less educated, prejudice toward Blacks leads to the view that they have not been treated poorly and do not try hard enough, but for the more educated, ideology, rather than prejudice toward Blacks, produces opposition to welfare policies. Sniderman and Piazza (1993) explicitly note the "more prejudiced a person is, the more likely he or she is to perceive Blacks to be failing to make a genuine effort to deal with their problems on their own" (p. 120), and this attitude is a result of a general negative view of Blacks as lazy and irresponsible. They assert that, in statistical analysis, there is little correlation between prejudices (which they continue to assess not only by anti-Black attitudes, but also by anti-Semitic attitudes) and ideology. This means that conservatism and prejudice can statistically be pulled apart and don't hang together. Hence, ideology (liberalism and conservatism) plays a separate and distinct role in determining attitudes toward social welfare policies, not a general dislike of Blacks. This also affects White responses to the next issue agenda, equality (Sniderman & Hagen, 1985).

Looking at the equal treatment agenda, Sniderman and Piazza (1993) examine attitudes about antidiscrimination laws. Here they find that support or opposition to laws, such as fair housing, was only slightly related to the reasons why Whites favored or opposed social welfare support for Blacks by the federal government. In the issue area of fair housing, prejudiced opposition stemmed from social distance factors; prejudiced Whites do not want to live close to Black people. Again, Sniderman and Piazza (1993) found prejudice was low among those with higher levels of education. For those with higher education, opposition to fair housing laws came from the belief government power should not be used to enforce equality.

Finally, in their examination of the race-conscious agenda, Sniderman and Piazza (1993) examined attitudes toward affirmative action. There was generally strong White opposition to affirmative action, although the authors found about 40% willing to support set-asides (in which a certain portion of federal contracts are reserved for minorities). White opposition to affirmative action was profound, regardless of whether or not they liked or disliked Blacks. In a study by Sniderman and Carmines (1997), nine out of 10 prejudiced Whites opposed affirmative action, and eight out of 10 Whites who were neutral in their attitudes toward Blacks objected.

In short, this is the politics-is-complicated model. Different issue agendas related to attitudes toward race are also related to attitudes toward other principles in American politics. They are more complicated than race alone, and must be examined in terms of that complexity.

This school of thought is strongly opposed by the advocates of the symbolic or new racism model, led by Sears and Kinder (Sears & Kinder, 1971; Kinder & Sears, 1981) and a number of others who took the argument in different directions (e.g., Bobo & Smith, 1994; Gaertner & Dovidio, 1986; Kinder & Sanders, 1996; Mendelberg, 2001; Pettigrew & Meertens,

1995). Symbolic racism arguments suggest a new form of racism replaced that of the old pre-civil rights era racism and, rather than being rooted in self-interest or group competition, the new racism is founded in conservative political values and the moral values of the Protestant ethic. There is substantial White resentment of Blacks, a resentment embodied in and fueled by the campaigns and policies of Nixon and Reagan, along with other politicians (Kinder & Sanders, 1996). Kinder and Sanders (1996) asked the important question of whether racial resentment is associated with racial stereotyping and, looking at the results of surveys, they found racial resentment and stereotyping were closely related. However, the data indicated modern White prejudice toward Blacks was not based on the old notions of biological inferiority, but rather on the belief that Blacks fail to try hard enough.

Symbolic racism advocates maintained the lack of consistency between support for equality between the races and support for policies to achieve equality is evidence of underlying ongoing racism in White America (see Figure 8.1). Negative views of Blacks are still socialized into White Americans, who are conditioned to respond negatively to particular symbols regarding race-related issues, such as school busing (Sears, 1993). In terms of content, this new racism embodies the beliefs that "discrimination no longer poses a major barrier to the advancement of Blacks, that Blacks should try harder to make it on their own, that they are demanding too much, and that they are too often given special treatment by government and other elites" (Sears et al., 2000, p. 17). More specifically, symbolic racism is composed of a conviction that Blacks are no longer treated unfairly, do not have traditional American values, such as the work ethic and obedience to authority, continue to demand special treatment from the government, and get special treatment undeservedly (Sears, Henry, & Kosterman, 2000). These attitudes and beliefs account more powerfully for the attitudes on policy issues just discussed than does ideology.

The dispute between the two models centers mostly around the relationship between conservative values, particularly those ranking individualism very high, and racism. The role of individualism is particularly important because it emphasizes the importance of individuals "pulling themselves up by their boot straps," and not being reliant on government help to get ahead. Those who fail to do this are looked down upon.

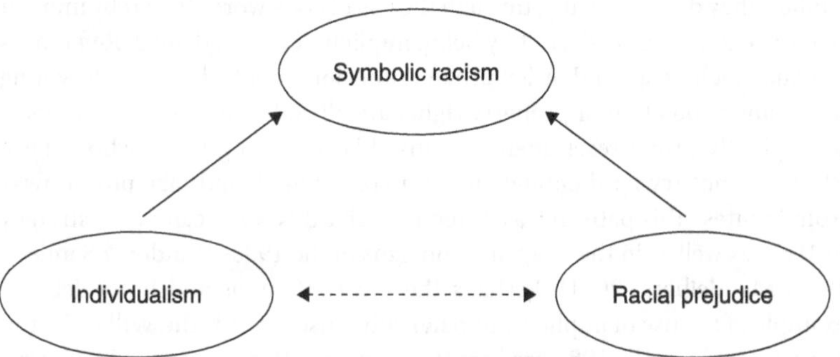

Figure 8.1 Model of constituent elements defining the new racism

Because many White Americans believe Black Americans do not work hard enough, they regard Blacks with disdain; this is a new form of racism, based upon American values. Those values giving primacy to individualism are held most strongly by conservatives, whereas liberals tend to value equality (of opportunity, under the law, etc.) more highly—hence the relationship between conservative values and the new racism. Thus, the symbolic racism school suggests hostile feelings toward Blacks blend with conservative values to produce a new form of racism. As discussed previously, the politics-is-complicated model claims conservative values are independent of prejudice.

Also of importance to the symbolic racism school is the use of race-related issues in electoral campaigns. In Chapter 7, we discussed the role played by *framing* and *priming* during campaigns in American politics. Those factors play a particularly important role in race-related issues during elections. The two dominant parties in the United States are deeply divided by the social cleavage of race. During the civil rights era, the Democratic Party moved left and the Republican Party moved right in positions on issues related to government intervention on behalf of racial equality for Blacks. The Democratic Party became the party to which most Blacks hold allegiance, and many Southern Whites left the Democratic Party (Kinder & Sanders, 1996; Mendelberg, 2001). Strategically, therefore, Democratic candidates want to mobilize Black votes without alienating White voters in the process. Democratic candidates are frequently accused of merely ignoring Black interests, assuming Blacks have little choice other than to vote Democratic. Republican candidates generally want to mobilize White voters who hold conservative views on race-related matters without alienating more moderate Whites. Added to the strategic problems is the advent of the norm of racial egalitarianism. The overwhelming majority of White Americans do not openly endorse racist ideas or practices, and embrace the norm of racial equality. However, as we saw, racial resentment remains a real part of race relations in the United States.

These trends in White attitudes and emotions produce a strategic dilemma, particularly for Republicans running for office. Democrats need only keep quiet on race to keep their coalition of Black and White voters together. Republicans, however, must appeal to racial conservatives while not alienating moderate Whites, and they must do that without violating the social norm of racial equality. In other words, they cannot get caught "playing the race card" openly. Consequently, according to symbolic racism studies, they do it implicitly, through the use of code words, whereby implicit reference to race is made, but by being implicit, it can be denied. References to issues such as law and order, urban crime, local control of schools, voting blocs, and protection of property rights are all code words or phrases used to implicitly prime resentments against Blacks among those who believe Blacks do not try hard enough and are lazy, violent, and take power away from Whites. This pattern was noted in Richard Nixon's campaign strategy in 1968, as well as in the Reagan campaigns in the 1980s (Kinder & Sanders, 1996; Mendelberg, 2001). Perhaps the most infamous and hotly debated example of the use of implicit campaign advertisements is the Willie Horton campaign during the 1988 presidential elections. This ad was run by George H. W. Bush's campaign (see box).

Willie Horton and the Race Card

In the 1988 presidential race, Vice President George H. W. Bush squared off against Massachusetts Governor Michael Dukakis. In an effort to demonstrate Bush was tougher on crime than Dukakis, a pro-Bush campaign organization, in collaboration with the Bush team, developed an ad showing the mug shot of Willie Horton, an African American convicted of murder in Massachusetts, who was allowed weekend furloughs from jail. During one of the furloughs, Horton ran away, ending up in Maryland, where he brutally beat a man and repeatedly raped a woman. Dukakis refused to revoke the furlough policy. The Bush team argued this was evidence that Dukakis was soft on crime. However, many argued the Willie Horton ad was an implicit effort to use the race card. Horton was shown on television with a big afro, scruffy beard, and scary scowl. He looked like a criminal and he was Black.

(Mendelberg, 2001)

This area of research is important for the symbolic racism argument because it digs through the layers of denial that these scholars believe cover latent racism in America (see also Milburn & Conrad, 1996). The denial is not difficult to understand because it is a way of avoiding painful conflict between competing ideas and emotions. The psychological processes are familiar, as Mendelberg notes:

> The conflict between negative racial predisposition and the norm of race equality can generate ambivalence; in turn, ambivalence creates a greater susceptibility to messages. A racial appeal thus has the capacity to affect public opinion about matters related to race. It is most likely to do so by making racial predispositions—stereotypes, fears, and resentments—more accessible. Once primed by a message, these predispositions are given weight when white Americans make political decisions that carry racial associations ... Racial priming can take place without the awareness of the individual, safeguarding the person's commitment to egalitarian conduct.
>
> (Mendelberg, 2001, p. 112)

The disagreement between the politics-is-complicated and symbolic racism camps about race in America cannot be settled here. Much of it rests on disagreements regarding the meaning and appropriate measurement of individualism. *Racialized Politics: The Debate About Racism in America* (Sears, Sidanius, and Bobo, 2000) contains informative discussions of both debates. Nevertheless, we can say there is a real conceptual disagreement here that is unresolvable. The politics-is-complicated school clearly believes people think in an additive way: they hold a number of distinct ideas (about policy, government's role, and Blacks); they unconsciously weigh those cognitive properties when making decisions; and, based on the priority they give them separately, they produce a policy position on race-related issues. They regard the cognitive process as complex and linear, moving from cognition to recognition of information regarding political realities and policy options among which the people must choose, to a choice. The symbolic racism camp takes more of a gestalt view of how people think, with ideas, values, information, and choice occurring in an ebb and flow, with complexity lying in their interaction and, most important, the idea that the mental system is a unique system different from the sum of its parts. The symbolic racism camp believes the interaction of portions of the race-related mind should not be separated, because that gives an inaccurate and artificial picture of the nature of modern racism.

While these debates are ongoing, others revisited some of the claims and focused on the measurement of certain concepts. For example, Federico and Sidanius (2002) set out to examine some measurement issues with regard to educational background and political sophistication. They first outlined the debate, already examined above, and then explain:

> While much of this debate has taken the form of a basic agreement about the relative explanatory power of racial and race-neutral predispositions and the degree to which concern for formal equality has become evenly diffused throughout the political spectrum, an additional—and perhaps more interesting—disagreement about the effects of education on the relationship between these variables has also arisen ... Several researchers argued that education may attenuate the relationship between racial hostility and opposition to affirmative action, as well as the relationship between racism and various race-neutral predispositions ... Since poorly educated individuals lack the expertise necessary for the comprehension and use of abstract political concepts, their racial policy attitudes—and more broadly, their general political outlook—should be more heavily colored by prejudiced considerations. In contrast, the knowledge possessed by well-educated individuals should allow them to bring complex ideological principles to bear on their racial policy attitudes ... Other analyses have offered less support for the hypothesis that education should attenuate the effects of racism and have instead suggested that education may simply allow individuals to better align their racial policy preferences—and broader political outlook—with a desire to protect the dominant position of the in-group.
>
> (Federico & Sidanius, 2002, pp. 147–148)

Federico and Sidanius concluded this had not been tested adequately by proponents and critics alike. The issue for them is the relationship between education and political sophistication; the latter does not necessarily mean the former:

> While education may very well provide individuals with the cognitive sophistication necessary for an advanced understanding of politics ... it does not guarantee attention to and comprehension of political ideas, as suggested by the relatively low correlation between education and various measures of interest in policies, such as media exposure to political information.
>
> (Federico & Sidanius, 2002, p. 149)

In their study of National Election Data from 1986–1992, the authors defined political sophistication as "actual political knowledge," and used this as a basis for their examination of "the relationships between affirmative action attitudes, prejudice, race-neutral political considerations, and beliefs about equality among white respondents with different political sophistication" (Federico & Sidanius, 2002, p. 169). The authors conclude:

> Our results provide little or no support for the notion that a better understanding of abstract political ideas and the norms of American political culture would attenuate the significance of racist and antiegalitarian motives. First of all, beliefs about racial superiority and inferiority were more strongly associated with affirmative action attitudes among the sophisticated than they were among relatively unsophisticated whites. Furthermore, rather than being less strongly related to superiority beliefs among sophisticates, political conservatism was, in fact, more strongly related to racism among these individuals. Perhaps more interestingly, we found little support for the notion that opposition to affirmative action may be driven by egalitarianism, particularly among sophisticated respondents. Not only was egalitarianism negatively (rather than positively) related to affirmative action opposition, but the magnitude of this relationship actually increased with political sophistication ... Rather than being embedded in support for egalitarian values, opposition to affirmative action shows every appearance of being driven by antiegalitarian values, particularly among those who should best understand the principles of the American Creed.
>
> (Federico & Sidanius, 2002, p. 169)

Federico and Sidanius also found that political conservatives were less supportive of equality of opportunity, and this was particularly so among those considered knowledgeable.

In addition to measurement and conceptual issues, there is another reason why it is difficult to determine which of these two models is best, and that is the difficulty today in knowing racism when we see it. Richard Ford (2008), for example, took a hard look at the issue of whether racism was involved in the terrible conditions faced by so many African Americans in the aftermath of Hurricane Katrina in 2005. Critics noted that the French Quarter, the heart of tourism, and the White parts of New Orleans were spared. The worst damage was done to the poorest parts of the city, which were largely Black. Was the lack of effective response by the federal government a result of racism and, if so, who were the racist decision-makers? Kanye West famously gave his answer to that question with the statement, "George Bush doesn't care about Black people" (quoted in Ford, 2008, p. 42). Many others criticized the press for racist coverage of the aftermath when Black people carrying supplies were "looting," while White people doing the same thing were "finding" necessities. But Ford makes a very interesting argument regarding this case in particular, and a general problem in evaluating racism in America today. Too often, we see racism without racists. The social, economic, and racist conditions that produced both the poverty and the segregation in New Orleans were the product of racists who are long dead, yet the legacy still exists. It is a "type of racism—or, more precisely, racial injury *without* racists—[that] accounts for a large and growing share of racial injustice in our society" (Ford, 2008, p. 58).

WHITE IDENTITY AND THE MYTH OF THE POST-RACIAL SOCIETY

When Barack Obama was elected to the presidency, many people rejoiced that the United States crossed the racial Rubicon and hoped it heralded the end of race as a factor in American life. His election followed positive trends over the years in White attitudes toward Blacks in general and the idea of a Black president in particular, according to the American National Election Studies, which have been gathering data on White attitudes toward Blacks since 1952 (Belcher, 2016). White attitude trends after Obama's election showed the continued complexity of those attitudes, a complexity that is one clue for the argument that the United States is far from becoming post-racial. In fact, the election of a Black man to the presidency, and the preceding decades of demographic change making Whites less and less of a majority in the United States, resulted in the intensification and mainstreaming of racism and the growth of White identity (the two are not necessarily the same). We can look at these trends from a variety of perspectives: first, White attitudes towards Blacks during Obama's administration, and the partisan differences therein; second, the growth of White identity; and third, the increase in right-wing racist extremism.

There are many examples of racist reactions to Obama as a candidate and as president, in a campaign Belcher (2016; see also Tesler, 2016) calls an attempt to "other" him. The "birther" movement claimed he was born in Kenya and was therefore not eligible to be president. His middle name, Hussein, and his father's religion were used by many to claim Obama was a Muslim, which is a euphemism for an alien outsider who by implication should not be a president of the United States. There were plenty of racist comments on social media as well. However, in general, Barack Obama's election did not immediately produce the feared White "backlash." ANES data show that out-group hostility did increase among Whites from 2004 to 2012, but it decreased from 2012 to 2016 (Fording & Schram, 2020). There was a significant increase in the number of racial extremists between 2004 and 2012, but that number too declined between 2012 and 2016 (although it was still higher in 2016 than 2004) (Fording & Schram, 2020). This is not to say that there was no growth in White racial resentment, and it was not just toward Blacks and an African American president. The emergence of the Tea Party is an important indicator of growth of White racial resentment in general. The Tea Party (see Chapter 11 for detail) began as a grassroots anti-tax, anti-government movement leading up to the 2010 interim election. As it grew, it was increasingly linked to White racial resentment toward Blacks, Latinos, Muslims, and immigrants (Fording & Schram, 2020; Jardina, 2019). Public opinion studies showed a link between racial hostility toward Black Americans and identification with the Tea Party (Fording & Schram). As Fording and Schram note:

> There were also numerous reports of racist rhetoric directed at President Obama and minorities by Tea Party leaders. One of the most publicized incidents involved an Arkansas Tea Party leader who eventually had to resign her position after making a racist joke at a Tea Party rally in 2012. A speaker at a Tea Party anti-immigrant rally also drew national attention when he advocated racial purity in breeding at an event near the Capitol in 2013, which was also attended by Senators Ted Cruz and Jeff Sessions.
>
> (Fording & Schram, 2020, p. 77)

Looking at the partisan divide and Obama's race, some studies showed that during the campaign, particularly among those with exposure to the campaign, there was a decrease in White aversion to Blacks across the board, among Democrats, Independents, and Republicans (Belcher, 2016; Parker, 2016). Optimism about race relations increased. Indeed, 52% of survey respondents believed the election of Barack Obama would improve race relations, and 66% said race relations were good (Pew Research Center, 2017). The optimism faded quickly. By the time Michael Brown was killed in Ferguson, Missouri in August 2014, 61% believed race relations were generally bad (Pew Research Center, 2017).

Despite the fact that Obama avoided running and governing with an emphasis on the fact that he was the first successful Black candidate for the presidency, the mere fact that he is Black made race inevitable in influencing attitudes toward the President (Tesler, 2016). By the midterm elections in 2010 (and the rise of the Tea Party), aversion toward Blacks had risen dramatically among Republicans and Independents, but not among Democrats (Belcher, 2016; Parker 2016). Negative stereotypes and affect toward Black people were a stronger influence on the 2012 election than in 2008 (Tesler, 2016).

Increasing White racial animosity during the Obama era was fortuitous for the presidential candidacy of Donald Trump. As mentioned in Chapter 6, Donald Trump's personal history shows clear evidence of racism, and he had no problem using racial animosity and White insecurity to help him win the Republican nomination for the presidency in 2016. As Ashley Jardina describes his ascent:

> What sets Trump further apart from the long line of politicians who have used race to win white votes is that he capitalized on more than white voters' animosity for racial and ethnic minorities. He also made pointed appeals that very well may have resonated with whites concerned about their group's status. Many journalists certainly proposed that support for Trump was motivated by whites' anxiety about their loss of status in an increasingly diverse nation. They suggested that Trump's campaign slogan—"Make America Great Again"—was really dog-whistle politics for restoring power to white Americans. Some even linked this slogan and Trump's political rhetoric more broadly to the language traditionally employed by the Ku Klux Klan. Troublingly, Trump even gained public support from bona fide white nationalists and white supremacists ...
>
> (Jardina, 2019, p. 232)

Many studies found evidence that Trump supporters were higher than Clinton supporters on animosity and resentment toward Blacks (Belcher, 2016; Fording & Schram 2020; Jardina, 2019; Luttig & Federico, 2017; Major, Blodorn, & Blascovich 2018; McElwee & McDaniel, 2017). Journalists and academic scholars, using a wide variety of methodologies, argued that Trump mainstreamed racism, making it acceptable to say and write offensive things about groups he targeted (Schaffner, 2018). Hate crimes increased during his administration and the evidence is strong that this was a direct result of Trump's rhetoric (Edwards & Rushin, 2018).

Another pattern evidenced in studies is the emergence of White identity. In the past there was little indication that White people had an identity as a racial group. This is normal for dominant and majority groups. As Sears and Savalei (2006) put it, Whites dominate American society politically, economically, socially, and numerically, and do not experience racial discrimination, so their "whiteness is usually likely to be no more noteworthy to them than is breathing the air around them. White group consciousness is therefore not likely to be a major force in whites' political attitudes" (p. 901). For many White people in America, this is changing because of the expectation that Whites will no longer be a numerical majority by about 2045. White people are beginning to see threats to their dominance and are developing a racial identity as Whites. White identity is not necessarily associated with racism (Fording & Schram, 2019; Jardina, 2019), but it can be. We know from social identity theory that attachment to, and support for, an in-group does not necessarily produce out-group antipathy. Indeed, about 38% of Whites identified strongly with whiteness, but are not resentful of other racial groups (Graham, 2019). What White racial identity does do is heighten perceptions of threat to the in-group, pride in the in-group, and in the case of identity with a dominant group, enhance the desire for that group to keep its privileges and position of power. However, people who identify strongly as White see themselves—their kind—as the prototypical or "real" Americans, which would indicate that they will not be as receptive to the idea of a multiracial American society. They are also likely to "express a sense of grievance over the apparent challenges to their status, expressing the belief that whites are in competition with other racial groups, that whites experience discrimination, or that whites are being treated unfairly" (Jardina, 2019, p. 44).

One reason it is difficult to separate White identifiers who are not racist and Whites who are racist is that both groups voted for Trump in 2016. However, there is a distinction when it comes to policy positions. White identifiers with low levels of racial hostility are not opposed to social welfare and Medicaid programs, which those with racial animosity associate with negative stereotypes of African Americans and other minorities, and traditionally oppose. White identifiers are strongly supportive of the social welfare safety net programs such as Social Security and Medicare, which provide big benefits for White people (Jardina, 2019). What does this increase in White racial identity portend for the future? It is unlikely to go away, and it is also likely to increase. Second, it is likely to increase intergroup competition rather than a growing acceptance of a diverse society in which all are considered American.

The Black American Perspective on Race and Politics

How do Black Americans view the politics of race relations in the United States? Black Americans are not a monolith. In terms of political ideologies, they—like White Americans—have differing perspectives. In some respects, there is a wider range of ideological systems in the Black community. Dawson (2001) argues that ideologies found in the community include Black nationalism, Black feminism, Black Marxism, Black conservatism, and disillusioned Black liberalism, with the latter being the most common ideology. He argues that Black liberals tend to desire a stronger state than other American liberals because it is needed to reinforce equality of opportunity and to prevent the exercise of power by White racists. Dawson also argues that for Black liberals, the "advancement of the self, the liberation of the self, is a meaningless concept outside the context of one's community" (p. 255), and therefore individualism is a less important concept. In Chapter 11, we discuss the Black Lives Matters movement. This organization seeks to promote inclusivity for the Black community. In a September 2020 survey of Black adults, 87% stated that they supported the movement; however, only 62% strongly supported it (Thomas & Horowitz, 2020).

Several studies found that Black identity is very strong for Blacks in the United States (e.g., Dawson, 2001; Sniderman & Piazza, 2002). There is a firm conviction that, for example, what happens to the community affects individual members. That strong identity as a group added some complexity, however, in that 37% of Blacks stated they no longer constitute a single race (Pew Research Center, 2007, p. 24). Blacks also strongly identify with the national community; however, unlike the White American opinion referred to above, only 54% of Blacks in 2007 believed White and Black Americans shared important values (Pew Research Center, 2007, p. 20).

Blacks differ markedly from Whites in terms of perceptions of the extent to which racial discrimination occurs. Comparing Black and White perceptions of discrimination against Blacks, 67% of Blacks believe they are faced with discrimination when looking for employment compared with 20% of Whites; 65% of Blacks believe they face discrimination when trying to find housing compared with 27% of Whites; 43% of Blacks believe they faced discrimination when applying to college compared with 7% of Whites; and 50% of Blacks believe they face discrimination when dining out or shopping compared with 12% of Whites (Pew Research Center, 2007, p. 30). At the same time, when asked why some Blacks failed to get ahead in life, the majority (53%) of Black respondents in the same study attributed this to individual responsibility rather than discrimination. Whites (71%) also attributed this to the individual rather than systematic discrimination, as did Hispanics (59%) (Pew Research Center, 2007, p. 33). In 2019, a majority of Blacks surveyed said they experienced discrimination because of race, but figures were higher (81%) among those with some college experience, as opposed to those with high school education or less (69%) (Anderson, 2019). Further, 59% of Black men, and 31% of Black women said they had been unfairly stopped by the police (Anderson, 2019). Overall, their outlook on race is not positive. Surveys show that:

> More than eight-in-ten black adults say the legacy of slavery affects the position of black people in America today, including 59% who say it affects it a great deal. About eight-in-ten blacks (78%) say the country hasn't gone far enough when it comes to giving black people equal rights with whites, and fully half say it's unlikely that the country will eventually achieve racial equality.
>
> (Horowitz et al., 2019)

In terms of some of the issues that are usually thought of as racial, Blacks tend to want more integration in housing than Whites do (62% compared with 40%), but they are basically equal in approving of school integration, with 96% of Whites and 95% of Blacks approving of it (Pew Research Center, 2007, p. 51). However, Blacks value going to integrated schools more than Whites do if a trade-off must be made between going to an integrated school versus going to a school in their community (56% vs. 23%) (p. 51). In terms of party identification, Blacks overwhelmingly identified with the Democratic Party (62%) in 2007, as opposed to only 6% identifying with the Republican Party (p. 62). This was down slightly from the early 1990s by 2% (p. 51). In 2020, 83% identified with or leaned toward the Democratic Party, and 10% identified or leaned toward the Republican Party (Pew Research Center, 2020).

One of the most important developments for the country and for the Black American populace was Barack Obama's 2007–2008 candidacy for the Democratic Presidential nomination. In the Pew Research Center's 2007 public opinion survey, Obama was viewed favorably by 89% of Blacks, but also by 65% of Whites, and 74% of Hispanics (p. 58). Obama's strong candidacy was a measure of changes in American racial attitudes, and the serious prospects for a successful run for the presidency by a Black American were reflected in opinions on the question of whether his race would help, hurt, or have no effect on his prospects. Overall, 18% believed it would help him, 26% that it would hurt him, and 44% that it would make no difference (p. 60). Blacks were more pessimistic than Whites, however, with 39% of Blacks, as opposed to 26% of Whites, believing his race would hurt him (p. 60).

The Hispanic Perspective on Race and Politics

The Hispanic community is the largest minority in the United States and also suffers from discrimination based upon racist stereotypes. In a 2007 report, the Hispanic population was about 46 million, or 15% of the U.S. population (Pew Research Center, 2007, p. i). However, in 2019, the number was over 60 million (Krogstad, 2020a). It is diverse. The largest group is of Mexican origin, followed by Puerto Rican and Cuban origin, but Hispanics in the United States may have ancestral origins in any of the Spanish-speaking countries. As we mentioned, race is socially constructed, and in the United States, Hispanics, or Latinos (from Latin America), were traditionally thought of as a racial classification. Nevertheless, this is really an in-between racial group, in part because Hispanics are racially diverse, with various combinations of indigenous, African, and European ancestries. White negative stereotypes of Hispanic Americans are primarily concentrated on Mexican Americans, as they are the largest Hispanic group. Conflict between Whites and Mexican Americans for resources and power occurred early on in the southwestern part of the United States. The White stereotype depicted Mexican Americans as lazy, violent, backward, poor, unskilled, and prone to committing crimes (Marger, 2003). On the positive side, they are also perceived as being religious and family oriented. There have been conflicts between Anglos and other Hispanic groups, including resentment about the strong Cuban American presence and power in the Miami area.

As Marger (2003) notes, "because of their 'in-between' minority status, Latinos have not been subjected to the dogged prejudice and discrimination aimed at African Americans; but neither have they been dealt with as European immigrant groups were" (p. 337). Nevertheless, like Black Americans they endure segregation in public facilities such as restaurants and schools (Mindiola, Flores Nieman, & Rodriguez, 2002) and their economic status is lower than that of Anglos. Of the Hispanic workforce, only 14% are white-collar professionals (National Society of Hispanic Professionals, 2008). The median income for Hispanic families in 2004 was $34,241, compared with non-Hispanic Whites' income of $48,977, and 22% of Hispanics lived below the poverty rate, compared with 8.6% of Whites in 2004 (U.S. Department of Commerce, 2005, p. 1).

In 2018, Hispanic identity in terms of race had many interesting patterns, and provides an example of the extent to which race is socially constructed and not a biological fact. The U.S. federal government does not consider Hispanics to be a separate race. Consequently, when asked which race they belong to on the census report, they can select White, Black or African American, American Indian or Alaska Native, Asian, Native Hawaiian and other Pacific Islander, or Some Other Race (SOR). The census does collect data on ethnicity with a category choice "Hispanic, Latino, or Spanish origin," or "No, not of Hispanic, Latino, or Spanish Origin." In the 2000 census, 48% of Hispanic identifiers considered themselves "White" and 42% checked "some other race" (Tafoya, 2004). Research found those who identified themselves as White had higher levels of education and income, and felt more enfranchised than those who selected SOR (Tafoya, 2004, p. 1). Moreover, those who selected SOR were more likely to be foreign born. Forty-six percent of foreign-born Hispanics selected SOR, compared with 40% of native Hispanics. Not surprisingly, 85% of the native-born Hispanics who considered themselves White were registered to vote, compared with 67% of native-born Hispanics who considered themselves SOR (p. 2). The author of this research concluded that, "The differences in characteristics and attitudes between those Hispanics who call themselves white and those who identify as some other race, suggests they experience racial identity as a measure of belonging: Feeling which seems to be a reflection of success and a sense of inclusion" (p. 3). It is not surprising, therefore, that 55% of the native-born Hispanics who considered themselves White identified first as Americans, while only 36% of the same population who considered themselves SOR did so (p. 18).

In terms of partisanship, 57% of Hispanics said they were Democrats or leaned toward the Democratic Party (Taylor & Fry, 2007, p. 1). Only 23% identified with the Republican Party. During the early 2000s, Hispanic voters moved toward the Republican Party, but this trend was reversed by late 2007. Hispanics have a number of values appealed to by President Bush in 2004. These included anti-abortion and anti-gay rights, as well as support for small business (Hutchison, 2007). Hispanic registered voters tend to believe the Democratic Party cares more for Hispanics (44%, although 41% say neither party cares) and that the Democratic Party has a better approach to the issue of immigration; they also showed a marked preference for Hillary Clinton in the 2008 contest for the Democratic Party presidential nomination (Taylor & Fry, 2007).

Of the many political issues under debate in the 2008 presidential contest, Hispanics pointed to education, followed by health care, the economy and jobs, crime, immigration, and the war in Iraq, in that order, as important to them (Taylor & Fry, 2007, p. 10). The Hispanic community differed from the general population in the United States in favoring bilingual education, and in terms of attitudes toward immigration. In the latter issue, the majority of Hispanics did not support open immigration, but they were more supportive of recent immigrants and amnesty for illegal immigrants (Sanchez, 2006). There was quite a bit of difference within the Hispanic community regarding immigration, depending upon their ancestral country of origin, whether they were native-born Americans or immigrants, and where they lived (see Sanchez, 2006). Hispanics did not favor open borders, but the immigration issue was also an indicator to many of vestiges of White prejudice. A 2008 poll conducted by the Pew Hispanic Institute found close to 10% of Hispanics were questioned by authorities about their residency status, 15% found it hard to get work because they were Hispanic, and 57% were concerned they or someone they cared about could be deported (Gaouette, 2008). The survey also found that 34% said immigration was extremely important to them and would affect their vote in the 2008 presidential race. The effect would benefit the Democratic Party, which about half of the respondents said was best on the immigration issue. Only 7% said the Republican Party was better on the issue (Gaouette, 2008). In 2016, election polls asked voters to rank a series of issues. The following were ranked as "very important" by percentage: education (83%), economy (80%), healthcare (78%), terrorism (73%), immigration (70%), how Hispanics are treated (69%), and gun policy (61%).

Do these trends still hold true? In 2020 election polling, voters were again asked to rank a series of issues. The top three ranked as "very important" to their vote included the economy (80%), healthcare (76%), and COVID-19 (72%), followed by racial and ethnic inequality (66%), and violent crime (63%). Immigration (59%) was eighth on the list after Supreme Court appointments and climate change (Krogstad & Lopez, 2020). There are, of course, differences found between men and women, with women seeing immigration, economic inequality, and abortion as more important. Clearly, issues such as the economy and healthcare were still top concerns, but immigration was less important. Trump's campaign promise was to build a wall on the Mexican border, and under him immigration was severely restricted, those without legal status rounded up, and children separated from families at the southern border and detained. Even so, Trump won a greater share of their vote in 2020 (32%) than in 2016 (29%) (Cadava, 2020), perhaps because other issues were more pressing. The economy and healthcare, followed closely by COVID-19, were more important to voters. While Cubans traditionally tend to lean Republican, and favor a hardline Cuban foreign policy, support has changed over time because of changing demographics. Still, in 2020, 58% identified as Republican, and 2016 data indicates that 58% of Cubans voted Republican, higher than all Latinos (Krogstad, 2020b). National trends still point to a Democratic Party advantage because 62% identify or lean toward the party, and 53% believe the Democratic Party has more concern for Latinos. Yet 32% say there is no difference. (Krogstad et al., 2020). Some point to a growing trend of more conservative Hispanic voters, and the fact that several Latino Republicans were also elected to Congress in 2020. Given the growing numbers of Hispanics and eligible voters, both parties realize their support is crucial.

Asian and Pacific Islander American Perspective on Race and Politics

Another minority racial group that has experienced tremendous prejudice and discrimination at the hands of the White society is the Asian American and Pacific Islander (AAPI) community. Beginning with the hostility toward Chinese immigrants in the 1840s, there was concern among Whites that Asians would take their jobs, and there were very negative stereotypes of Asians.

Historically, discrimination against Asians began when Chinese immigrants—mostly men—came to the United States after the gold rush started. They continued to work in difficult circumstances as laborers building railroad lines and in other areas. They were restricted in terms of occupation and where they could live, resulting in the ghettos we still identify as Chinatowns in major American cities, and particularly in the western part of the United States. The Chinese immigration was received with such hostility that the Chinese Exclusion Act was passed in 1882; it prohibited immigration from China altogether and was not repealed until 1943. After Chinese immigration stopped, immigration from Japan increased. They also engaged in labor occupations. The backlash against Japanese immigration produced the "Gentleman's Agreement" between the United States and Japan in 1908; the only Japanese who could enter the United States were relatives of those already here and those who were not laborers in occupation. This was followed by the Oriental Exclusion Act of 1924, which prohibited all Japanese immigration.

Accompanying these actions were strong negative stereotypes of Asians as inherently inferior to White people, inscrutable, dirty, and unassimilable. As a "yellow peril," they were forbidden to become citizens, were relegated to the lowest status jobs, were restricted in their movements and residency, and were socially excluded, making it impossible to learn English and American values (Kitano & Nakaoka, 2001; Marger, 2003). With the advent of Japanese power in the 1930s, the stereotype included an element of fear and suspicion.

These actions made it clear that Americans were hostile to immigration from Asia. But the most egregious act of prejudice and discrimination was the internment of Japanese Americans during World War II. People of Japanese ancestry—American citizens—all along the west coast were sent to camps with just one suitcase of belongings. Many lost businesses and land. A total of 120,000 were interned until the last waning months of the war.

After World War II, federal legislation changed and Asians were permitted to become citizens. There was an influx of Asians from other countries in addition to Japan and China, including the Philippines, Korea, Vietnam, India, American Samoa, Guam, and many other places.[3] There still are vestiges of the earlier stereotype and more. On the one hand, there were positive attitudes about Asian Americans (more specifically Chinese Americans) evident in a 2001 survey (Marilla Communications Group, 2001). They are believed to have strong family values (90% agreed), are honest in business (77% agreed), are patriotic Americans (68% agreed), and highly value education (67% agreed) (p. 21). On the other hand, 23% of Americans disliked the idea of an Asian president, 25% disliked the idea of intermarriage between a family member and an Asian person, and 17% did not want to live with a large number of Asians in their neighborhoods (pp. 44–46). The modern stereotype of Asian Americans can simultaneously be that of the "pollutant, the coolie, the deviant, the yellow peril, and model minority, and the gook" (Lee, 1999, p. 8). There was a considerable amount of resentment of the successes of Asians as well. The study of attitudes toward Chinese Americans, for example, found that 34% of respondents thought they had too much influence in high tech, 32% thought they liked to be at the head of things, and 26% thought they were aggressive in the workplace (Marilla, 2001, p. 22). In summarizing, the study divided Americans into three categories in terms of attitudes toward Chinese Americans: 32% had positive stereotypes, 43% somewhat negative stereotypes, and 25% very negative stereotypes (p. 24). Later studies reported the same mix of positive and negative stereotypes: on the one hand they are overachievers, intelligent, industrious, affluent, technologically savvy, talented at math, family orientated, law abiding; and on the other are "all work, no play," quiet, passive, and lack communication skills (Zhang, 2015). Zhang (2015) points out these studies focus on the cognitive, but not affective, component. In a study addressing affect, Zhang found:

> First, Asian Americans were perceived as more competent than warm, more of a realistic threat than of a symbolic threat, and elicited more admiration than envy, contempt, and pity. Second, perceived competence and warmth of Asian Americans have differing associations with perceived threats and emotions toward them. Third, perceived competence toward Asian Americans has only direct effects on emotions, whereas perceived warmth has only indirect effects on emotions mediated through perceived threats.
>
> (Zhang, 2015, p. 126)

This study informs the need for future research.

This stereotype lumps very diverse people together, ignoring the significant cultural and socioeconomic differences among Asian groups in the

United States. The diversity of the Asian American community can be seen in their identity patterns. Lien, Conway, and Wong (2004) conducted a study in which they sought to discover what percentages of Asian Americans identified as nonethnic (American), as ethnic American (e.g., Chinese American), as ethnic only (Chinese) or as pan-ethnic (Asian). They found a big difference between groups. Japanese Americans were those most likely to identify simply as American (41%), while Chinese and Vietnamese Americans were least likely to do so (1%). Chinese and Vietnamese Americans were most likely (42% each) to identify as ethnic only. Looking at other indicators of identity, they found only 10% of their survey respondents believed Asian groups in America were very similar culturally, but 41% thought they were somewhat similar (p. 47). The complexity of the identity patterns were summed up by the authors as follows:

> Ethnic self-identification varies greatly by ethnic origin. Japanese Americans are most likely to identify only as "American"; Chinese, Korean, and Vietnamese are most likely to identify only as "ethnic." While both Filipinos and South Asians are most likely to identify as "ethnic American," South Asians have the highest percentage of "Asian American" identifiers. When other conditions are controlled, South Asians, compared to Chinese, are more likely to self-identify not only as "Asian American" but also with the two other American-based identities. This is not the case with respondents of other ethnicities, except that a person of Japanese or Filipino descent is also more likely to identify only as "American" than as ethnic.
>
> (Lien, Conway, & Wong, 2004, p. 66)

Politically, they tended to be more liberal than conservative. The Lien, Conway, and Wong (2004) study found 8% surveyed considered themselves very liberal, 28% somewhat liberal, 32% middle of the road, 18% somewhat conservative, and 4% very conservative. Moreover, higher income Asian Americans were more likely to consider themselves very or somewhat liberal; lower income Asian Americans had a larger percentage who considered themselves somewhat or very conservative. Not surprisingly, this distribution blurred the distinctions among specific groups of Asian Americans and Pacific Islanders. Table 8.1 shows the differences.

In 2020, Asian Americans and Pacific Islanders represented 5.9% of the population, and they are clearly a diverse group. Like Hispanics, there are differences among them when it comes to political views and preferences. In 2016, there were 1.4 million more new voters than in 2012, but voting rates remained lower (49%) than other groups, and this varied by ethnicity with Chinese being lowest, and Japanese highest, and by state (Ramakrishnan, 2017). Generally speaking, they overwhelmingly backed Hillary Clinton (79%) as opposed to Donald Trump (18%) in the 2016 election, with the economy/jobs, immigration, refugees, healthcare, and education key issues (Asian American Policy Review, 2020). In 2020, Joe Biden received 63% of the vote, and interestingly, 31% still voted for Trump despite his xenophobic rhetoric and anti-immigration stance (Yam, 2020).

Despite the diversity and scope of this group, outreach efforts by candidates are not significant (Yam, 2020) and their views are not widely

Table 8.1 Percentage Distribution of Political Orientation by Ethnic Origin

	All	*Chinese*	*Korean*	*Vietnamese*	*Japanese*	*Filipino*	*South Asian*
Very liberal	8	4	4	12	9	8	18
Somewhat liberal	28	26	29	10	25	32	43
Middle of the road	32	42	28	47	37	18	16
Somewhat conservative	18	11	27	5	20	29	14
Very conservative	4	2	4	4	4	5	3
Not sure	10	15	8	21	4	6	6

Source: Lien, Conway, & Wong, J. (2004, p. 75).

reported (Kennedy & Ruiz, 2020). Kennedy and Ruiz explain that lack of information is a math problem. In national surveys, because so few are polled, it is difficult to reliably estimate their views. Furthermore, the variety of languages spoken in this diverse group sometimes presents language barriers. However, online polling is making it easier. One such poll found Asian Americans (and Blacks) had reported more negative experiences since the COVID-19 outbreak (Ruiz et al., 2020). This included slurs or jokes, people acting uncomfortable around them, and fears of attacks. Given it was widely reported that the coronavirus originated in China and Trump's regular references to it as the "China virus," this is not surprising.

RADICAL WHITE RACISTS AND THE RACIAL DIVIDE

The racial divide is apparent in the dialogue of a cluster of White groups in the United States (and other countries).[4] These groups include a wide variety of groups loosely organized through a circuit of leaders and lieutenants (Ezekiel, 1996).

The Southern Poverty Law Center (SPLC) (see box) is an organization that carefully tracks hate groups in the United States. As of 2006, it classified 884 groups into the Ku Klux Klan, Neo-Nazi, Racist Skinhead, Christian Identity, Neo-Confederate, and Black Separatist groups. In 2020, SPLC tracked 838 groups, broadening their descriptions to Anti-Immigrant, Anti-LGBTQ, Anti-Muslim, Christian Identity (see box), General Hate, Hate Music, Ku Klux Klan, Male Supremacy, Neo-Confederate, Neo-Nazi, Neo-Volkisch, Racist Skinhead, Radical Traditional Catholicism, and White Nationalist (see box). These groups are characterized in different ways as right-wing extremists, radical right, and alternative right (alt-right), a broad description invented by White Nationalist Richard Spencer, the head of the National Policy Institute. The alt-right made headlines with its 2017 Unite the Right rally in Charlottesville, VA where a counter protester was killed and several others injured (see box on Atomwaffen later in this chapter). The various components of the White Nationalist and alt-right movements will also be discussed in Chapter 11, where we look at social movements.

Southern Poverty Law Center Battles Racism

Morris Dees, a lawyer with the Southern Poverty Law Center, brought some high-level suits against the United Klans of America in 1991 and Aryan Nations in 2000. The case against the Klan involved a 1981 murder of a Black teenager. Dees won the suit against the United Klans and several of its members. The headquarters of the Klan was sold and the proceeds given to the mother of the victim.

The Klan was formed in 1866 by a group of Confederate soldiers in order to provide amusement. At first, the organization simply engaged in practical jokes, but soon it evolved into a group that would intimidate, harass, whip, and murder Blacks (Ridgeway, 1995). Several Klan groups still exist, but the organization was seriously weakened not only by the efforts of Dees, but also by the Federal Bureau of Investigation (FBI).

In the case of the Aryan Nations, Victoria Keenan and her son Jason were driving by the compound of the organization in North Idaho when their car backfired. The guards in the compound pursued them for two miles and shot at them. After their car went into a ditch, the guards assaulted them. Dees won $330,000 in compensatory damages and $6 million in punitive damages for the woman and her son against Saphire Inc., the corporate body of the Aryan Nations.

The estimates concerning membership size for these groups vary greatly. They are all vying for supporters from the same pool of people, and suffer from intragroup conflict and intergroup competition, efforts of law enforcement, and recently the effects of COVID-19. Thus, some groups lose members, or dissolve altogether, and reconstitute under different names, while others grow because they appear more appealing and successful (Abanes, 1996, p. 2).

There are numerous groups, and there is not one single view or philosophy to describe them, nor are they led, organized, and function in the same way. While classification of these groups by ideology is helpful, it is not perfect as they also share attributes and ideas. For example, White Nationalists can also include the Ku Klux Klan and Racist Skinheads, among others. A thorough discussion of each group is beyond the scope of this section, but we provide specific examples throughout and more detail in the boxes below.

Given the scope of these groups, what can we say about them here? Certainly, social identity theory explains why these groups form and then act. Social dominance theory studies demonstrate a link between White identity and attitudes, but does this explain participation in far-right extremism? Bai (2019) looked at this question and found the high White racial identity, in combination with high SDO, leads to far-right extremism. Therefore, identity alone may not be sufficient.

In general, these groups promote racist and anti-Semitic ideologies, rely on stereotypes, demonize out-groups, employ scapegoats, and most importantly preach hate. White identity is the cornerstone. Whites, they believe, have higher status than any other groups. These other groups should not have special status, and some suggest sending non-White immigrants back home to their original countries, while others are content to form their own White homelands within countries. They have a sense of injustice and victimization, of being deprived of their rightful status in society and being left behind. They are concerned about, and threatened by, social change, including influxes of immigrants, perceived special privileges given to minorities and women, changes in gender roles, race mixing, and other trends (Ezekiel, 1996; Green, Abelson, & Garnett, 1999; Langer, 1990). Among them, there is a distrust of government to be an advocate for Whites.

They glorify violence and reinforce group loyalty through rituals associated with religion and mythology, as well as through uniforms, banners, hierarchy, and symbols such as the swastika. They also promulgate conspiracy theories (see box). As George and Wilcox explain:

> The range of conspiracy theories may be almost encyclopedic, but they all have one thing in common: some kind of diabolical plot by the dark forces to do in the champions of righteousness and freedom. The details vary considerably, but they usually involve secrecy and deception, complicated scenarios by which the people are fooled, sometimes even by those claiming to oppose the plotters. All this ends with the control or enslavement of the masses by a self-appointed elite.
>
> (George & Wilcox, 1996, p. 266)

What is White Nationalism?

White nationalism rests on fears that White racial identity is threatened by changes in American society. The most extreme of these groups are White supremacists who believe that Whites are inherently superior to other races (Fording & Schram, 2020). Some groups include the American Freedom Party, American Patriots, National Justice Party, the Council of Conservative Citizens, the National Policy Institute, and the Patriot Front. The growth of non-White groups, and declining White birth rates are of paramount concern. Drawing inspiration from "studies" by Jared Taylor's New Century Foundation and others, White nationalists espouse the merits of eugenics, and Black criminality, and promote the "alt-right."

(SPLC, 2020c)

QAnon, which claims Satan-worshipping pedophiles are responsible for a global children's sex trafficking ring, is an example of this type of conspiracy theory. Interestingly, the number of hate groups rose 30% under Trump, after a decline toward the end of the Obama administration, suggesting individuals felt emboldened by the political climate (SPLC, 2019).

What is Christian Identity?

An unusual reading of the Bible is central to **Christian Identity**. It is the notion the true descendants of the Israelites are Whites. They also believe that White people descended from Adam and Eve, but non-Whites, whom they deem "mud people," came from another form of creation. Christian Identity believers also argue Jews are descendants of Satan (as a result of Eve mating with the serpent). The religious doctrine justifies, in their minds, their derogation of Blacks and their deep anti-Semitism (Bushart, Craig, & Bames, 1998). Not all right-wing extremist group members follow Christian Identity. However, racists and anti-Semites found common ground with the Christian Identity movement because both believe the end of the world will occur after a battle between good and evil. The difference lies in the former believing a race war will occur after the destruction of the Jews (government is a pawn of the Jews), with Whites emerging victorious; the latter "view Washington politicians as evil conspirators laying the foundation for the soon-to-be revealed Antichrist, whose reign of terror will end only when Jesus Christ returns to earth in glory" (Abanes, 1996, p. 3).

From Atomwaffen to the Nationalist Socialist Order

The Atomwaffen Division was a neo-Nazi group operating in the United States. The group believed a nationalist socialist government would be brought about through a violent revolution. Thus, society cannot be changed, only destroyed and reconstructed. Members met at camps to train for this purpose. The group attacked protesters in Charlottesville, VA in 2017. A series of arrests by the FBI resulted in the disbanding of the group, however, some members went on to form the Nationalist Socialist Order to continue their efforts.

The National Alliance

William Pierce was the founder of the National Alliance, a White nationalist group based in the United States. The ideology of the National Alliance is National Socialism, which had its roots in German Nazism. Before forming the National Alliance, Pierce was affiliated with the John Birch Society, the American Nazi Party, National Socialist White People's Party, and the National Youth Alliance. Pierce was not only the founder of the National Alliance, but a centerpiece in the group.

Pierce, a former physics professor who left his profession to work on the movement full time, was best known for his 1978 book *The Turner Diaries* (published under the pseudonym Andrew McDonald), which

(*Continued*)

(*Continued*)

is widely read by White supremacist groups, and was an inspiration to Timothy McVeigh. The book is supposed to be the diary of Earl Turner, a member of a White Patriot group called the Order, which is part of a larger group called "Organization." In his "diary," Turner describes an escalation of the war in which Jews, Blacks, and other people of color are killed by beatings, hangings, guns, and knives. Pierce also wrote *Hunter*, published in 1984, which is about a killer whose goal is to cleanse the United States of its "sickness" by murdering interracial couples and assassinating Jews.

The National Alliance was very popular and ran a radio program and a record label, released a video game, *Ethnic Cleansing*, produced publications, and ran a website. Annual income was estimated at US$1 million.

After Pierce's death in 2002, the National Alliance vowed to continue his work. The group was then run by Eric Gliebe, but splits within the group resulted in some members going on to form the National Vanguard, which also split in 2006, and dissolved a year later. It was replaced by European Americans United.

Conspiracy Theories

The song, "Evil, Filthy, Rotten Conspiracy" was written by Carl Klang and published in the patriot newspaper, *The Idaho Observer*, in February 1998. It encapsulates the beliefs and demonstrates the extent of conspiracy theories:

Now have you seen them flying saucers
Or some of them black helicopters
Flyin' down low and over my back yard recently?
Seen them foreign troops in ninja suits
Leavin' imprints of their combat boots
In the meadow down near the neighbor next to me?
Heard they're buildin' concentration camps
From the rate hike off our postage stamps
To protect and defend their great democracy
Though my vote in the last election
Didn't quite match the same projection
Made by those beautiful talking heads on my TV
When I called them to complain—and asked them to explain
They just said that it proves you're not in the groove
Of the new majority
Well just between you and me—can't you just feel the conspiracy?
Can't you sense the hypocrisy as they call it democracy
Well it's a threat to your sanity, not to mention your liberty
And it's all an evil filthy rotten conspiracy.
So as they redirect our mail

(*Continued*)

(*Continued*)

And all our incoming phone calls
To the Central Intelligence Agency
We'll just hope and pray someday they'll see
That you and me are not the enemy
Nor do we believe in cult theology
And as their police try to bust us
We'll keep tryin' to find some justice
Though it's hidden behind a wall of masonry
We'll keep working out our Salvation
With the feelin' and fear and tremblin'
Hopin' and praying someday that truth might set us all free
And just 'cause the media won't respond—don't mean there's nothin' going on
And brother what'll ya do if there's somethin' to
All the words inside this song?

Jared Taylor and the American Renaissance Group

Jared Taylor's views on race, as quoted in Swain and Nieli (2003, pp. 90–91):

> I think race relations are essentially unchanged for the last forty or fifty years. I think that the greatest set of problems having to do with race is simply inherent to multiracialism. There has never been a multiracial society on the face of the earth in which there was *not* racial friction, and in fact the most stable multiethnic or multiethnic societies that I can think of have been ones in which there was some kind of quite firm hierarchy of different groups, whether it be in the United States—if you're just speaking of blacks and whites, for example—or South Africa ... Race of course isn't the only source of group conflict.
>
> Probably language may be the most fertile source of conflict after that, but any kind of group identification, be it religion, language, race, culture, tribe, all of these things are sources of friction—far from being the kind of course of strength that we have been encouraged to take them to be. But as far as the United States is concerned, I think, well, there are many, many subsidiary aspects of this problem, but, as I say, the great source—the original problem, the original sin, if you will—is the attempt to try and construct a society of such disparate racial elements.

Leaders, Members, and Recruitment

There is no systematic analysis available of the leaders and members of these groups, although there are many case studies. Some studies, members of the media, and government officials classify or refer to these groups as domestic terrorists. Certainly, we can draw similar foundational conclusions based on the psychological literature on terrorism with regard to individuals and groups when it comes to motivation, intragroup dynamics, and intergroup conflict. We dedicate Chapter 12 to reviewing these terrorism studies and conclusions. Defining these domestic groups as terrorists in of itself is not problematic; however, it is when general conclusions about these groups and members are based on data from the terrorism literature, independent of analysis of these groups in particular. Thus, just because one is classified as a terrorist group, it does not mean data used to illustrate their ideas, organization, and behavior automatically apply to these domestic hate groups. Having said that, what can we say about these groups in particular?

It is clear that the leaders are men, and those with larger organizations run by charismatic leaders are more successful. Some leaders come from educated and professional backgrounds, while others don't. For example, William Pierce held a PhD and was a physics professor when he became part of the American Nazi Party, and before creating the National Alliance (see box). Erich Gliebe, his successor, was a professional boxer. Jared Taylor (see box), editor of the now defunct magazine *American Renaissance*, was a loan officer with a BA from Yale, and MA from Sciences Po in France.

Women participate and tend to be expected to maintain traditional roles (Ezekiel, 1996; Ryan, 2003). Groups perpetuate these norms, or even exclude women. For example, Proud Boys, which denies being part of the alt-right, is a male-only organization promoting western chauvinism. Its members promote anti-Semitic and racist views and participate in violence (see also the discussion in Chapter 11). At times, when women seek to play a more visible leadership role, they face backlash (Darby, 2020).

Membership of these groups tends to fluctuate, but committed leaders recruit constantly. Some studies indicate that in the United States, these groups draw from lower income sectors of society, are from rural areas, and have less formal education (Ezekiel, 1996; Hamm, 1993; Hewitt, 2003), or have suffered job losses (Blazak, 2001). Some smaller studies, case studies, and anecdotal evidence suggest members are drawn from different socioeconomic situations, educational backgrounds, professions, and geographical locations. They are not on the fringes of society. Former skinhead Christian Picciolini explained, "It's the average American,...It is our mechanics, it's our dentists, it's our teachers, lawyers, doctors, nurses" (CBS News, 2017). Members are part of the armed forces, and law enforcement. There are many members and supporters of these groups who do not make their affiliations public because of the stigma associated with it. Christian Picciolini described their participation as being "in the shadows" (CBS News, 2017). This suggests that general perceptions of these groups as uneducated, rural men may be filtered through our own stereotypes. In a study based on interviews with 47 former members, RTI International (2021) found:

- approximately 40% of interviewees grew up in middle-class or upper-middle-class families
- nearly 40% of females and 20% of males had been sexually assaulted as children or adolescents
- around 75% of interviewees said they were exposed to racist comments from family members (parents, grandparents, aunts, and uncles) as children.

In addition to holding public forums and meetings, these groups use a variety of methods to gain new recruits and disseminate information. They are very keen to recruit and have adapted their methods to meet needs of changing demographics. Their eclectic mix of propaganda tools help to indoctrinate potential recruits. Thus, in addition to magazines, books, newsletters, radio broadcasts, and television appearances, there are music production companies. White supremacist recording labels, such as Resistance Records, which was bought by the National Alliance, United Riot Records, linked to skinhead group 211 Bootboys, and bands with names such as Angry Aryans (with albums titled *Racially Motivated Violence* and *Too White for You*), and Nyogthaeblisz, spread their message through music CDs and live concerts. Video games such as *White Law*, *Freedom Fighters*, and *Ethnic Cleansing* are also used to entice recruits and entertain supporters.

The internet also serves as a way to disseminate information and, of course, to keep groups and members connected to each other, or to entice new recruits. They post and share their information to the internet for wide dissemination, promoting hate, conspiracies, misinformation, false depictions of events, and pseudo-science. Furthermore, they are able to organize protests and training, and fundraise. Websites are heavily used. For example, Stormfront, created by Don Black in 1996, was the first website dedicated to spreading the message of hate and community-building across ideologies and groups. According to Swain and Nieli (2003), "Stormfront is really a web junction box that provides the web surfer with links to literally hundreds of other white racialist websites ranging from fairly mainstream European heritage organizations to the outer fringes of neo-Nazi and white militia groups" (p. 152). There are Facebook pages, Gab, Parler, Tumblr, and Instagram accounts, Twitter feeds, YouTube videos, chat rooms, and commentary and message board threads such as the Daily Stormer. Known for promulgating conspiracy theories, Red Ice is a Swedish media company serving as a digital hub with talk radio, newscasts, and You Tube videos (Darby, 2020). YouTube, social media, and hosting companies began to crack down on these groups and content, making it more difficult to utilize these outlets, but groups find alternative and sympathetic hosting sites, and create new accounts.

Connections are made globally with like-minded people and groups (Lee, 1997). These connections may be personal, a result of movement entrepreneurs who want to spread the word in person or distribute materials abroad. However, the internet certainly facilitated these connections. For example, ties with the National Alliance extended beyond U.S. borders, notably to Europe. The National Alliance had ties to groups such as the British National Party (BNP) and the National Democratic Party (NPD) in Germany, among others. C18, a British neo-Nazi group, was said to be inspired by the work of William Pierce (Ryan, 2003), but his reach extended far beyond them. According to Ryan (2003), "he holds mythical status among white supremacists, running an international empire, which is particularly strong in northern Europe and Scandinavia" (p. 18).

RACE IN BRAZIL

The United States is not the only country in the Western Hemisphere with a history of slavery. Indeed, Brazil had the largest slave population in the hemisphere. Despite myths to the contrary (e.g., Freyre, 1956; Tannenbaum, 1947), slavery in Brazil was brutal. Slave death rates were so high that reproduction rates were low, the average mining slave lived for only seven to 12 years, and 80% of slave children did not live long enough to reach adulthood (Marx, 1998; Mattoso, 1986). Slaves died from disease and harsh working conditions, and, because of the terrible conditions in which they lived, there were numerous slave revolts. Finally, in 1888 slavery was abolished, but the Black former slaves were left in dreadful conditions, "lacking any means to advance themselves or to compete, isolated in rural areas or in the newly emerging urban slums, or favelas" (Marx, 1998, p. 161).

Despite the legacy of slavery, Brazil prides itself on having a nonracist society. This is also a myth—one that has increasingly been decried by Brazil's Afro-Brazilian community. The myth arises from the fact that, after the abolition of slavery, Brazil sought to avoid the kind of race-based conflicts that occurred in the United States. This was done through a conscious policy of miscegenation, encouraging the intermarriage of Black and White people in order to water down African heritage (in sharp contrast to the prohibition on race mixing in the United States after slavery).

There was certainly racial prejudice in Brazil, but inequality was socially, rather than politically, enforced. After slavery, for example, Whites were encouraged to immigrate from European countries and Africans were not allowed to, even though formal discrimination was prohibited by law. In addition, Brazilians appreciated and embraced many African cultural remnants in art, music, and dance. This, along with official encouragement of people to label themselves White, reduced Black racial group identity, and reduced the incentives of Blacks to mobilize politically. The average White income is twice that of Blacks; Afro-Brazilians have a higher unemployment rate than Whites; and, when employed, they are in lower skilled and lower paying jobs; Afro-Brazilians have shorter life expectancies than Whites; and race is correlated with poorer physical health (Hanchard, 1993; Marx, 1998).

Beginning in the late 1970s, in part as the result of the beginning of a gradual return to civilian government following 20 years of military rule, Brazil began to experience a newly mobilized Afro-Brazilian movement, particularly the Movimento Negro Unificado. Yet many Afro-Brazilians, including Black politicians, were still reluctant to challenge the myth of Brazil's racial democracy. The great irony in Brazil is that, without systematic and institutional racial discrimination, group identity and mobilization were limited, even though race matters in Brazil, and Afro-Brazilians have a great deal to say about the de facto inequality in Brazilian society.

South Africa

In 1948, the system of apartheid, which divided people according to racial categories, was instituted in South Africa. According to Eades (1999), "Apartheid was a radical and extreme extension of a system of segregation originating with colonial conquest and gradually evolving into complex sometimes uncoordinated institutions in the late nineteenth and early twentieth centuries" (p. 4). Within the system of apartheid were four racial categories: the Whites, the Coloreds, the Indians, and the Africans. Beginning with the Whites, each category was considered inferior to the one preceding it. In other words, Whites were considered superior to Coloreds, Indians, and Africans; Coloreds were superior to Indians and Africans, and so forth.

The Whites were made up of British English-speaking settlers and Dutch Afrikaner settlers. Even though they were considered part of the same White category, Afrikaners and English speakers were not a unified, homogeneous group. There were considerable clashes between these two distinct ethnic groups, exhibited mostly during the Boer War (1899–1902), as both tried to assert their power in South Africa (Marx, 1998). But as Eades explains:

> As Afrikaners came to dominate state power in South Africa, their sense of identity and destiny increasingly became more racial than cultural. A study carried out among Afrikaners in 1977 illustrated this shift. Before 1948 most of the Afrikaners' focus was on distinguishing themselves from the English-speakers. After 1948, however, the focus changed to race as apartheid based itself on racial distinction and had to be made legitimate.
>
> (Eades, 1999, p. 35)

The Coloreds were a broad racial category that included slaves from Madagascar, Indonesia, and tropical Africa, as well as Indigenous Khoisan people. They were Christians and Muslims, farm laborers and artisans, and had many cultural differences (Eades, 1999). The mostly Hindu Indians were descendants of workers who were brought to work on sugar plantations between 1860 and 1911. Another wave of Indian immigrants, who were mostly Muslim, came as British subjects beginning in the 1870s. Finally, the Africans were the largest category, making up 70% of the population of South Africa. This category encompassed many different tribes and clans, and was by no means a homogeneous group.

In addition to classifying individuals, other legislation was passed that prohibited the mixing of races by marriage or sexual contact between them. The Bantu Authorities Act also established "homelands," which were essentially independent states to which each African was assigned. Thus, Africans became citizens of a homeland and not South Africa, which meant they had no natural political rights. In essence, the apartheid system determined the political, social, and economic status of an individual because being in a certain group afforded one a certain status. In this system, Whites benefited the most. Thus, Afrikaners in particular had a vested interest in maintaining such a system. They did this through brutal repression of the non-White population.

The dismantling of the system began in February 1990, when President F. W. de Klerk announced sweeping changes in the country. The constitution was rewritten and elections were held, bringing Nelson Mandela, an African, to the presidency. Why, after all those years, did this system of institutionalized racism finally end? There was significant international pressure exerted on the South African government to end apartheid. In addition, domestic pressure became more intense. Possibly, de Klerk and many other Afrikaners realized they could not maintain such a system, given that the Black majority, in particular, would no longer accept their inferior status in society.

The end of apartheid is also understandable in the context of the political psychological theories set forth at the beginning of this chapter. White power-holders did not give up without a struggle. Perceptual change among Whites was gradual, and is attributable in part to a freer media, which showed the opposition as reasonable and organized, thereby pushing the "skeptical master race to the necessity of negotiations as equals" (Adam & Moodley, 1993, p. 230). Increased de facto integration in universities and churches also influenced a change in White values. But it was perhaps the strategy of inclusive national identity of the African National Congress (ANC), the umbrella opposition organization, that was crucial. By informing the South African Whites that they would be included as equals, not punished, in the post-apartheid South Africa, the ANC reduced the threat to the White identity group. Whites came to understand that things would change, but they would not face retribution. After apartheid ended, South Africa engaged in extensive efforts to heal the wounds. The truth and reconciliation process in South Africa lasted from 1996 to 1998. A more extensive discussion of the process can be found in Chapter 14.

The South African case is interesting because it demonstrates a pattern anticipated by both realistic conflict theory and social identity theory, and also by patterns of group formation discussed in Chapter 4. With regard to realistic conflict theory, the non-White groups competed with each other for resources (access to jobs, rights, etc.) until a superordinate goal—eliminating apartheid—united them. In terms of social identity, the South African case shows the malleability of race and ethnicity. The architects created a form of social categorization that would unite non-Whites. African ethnic groups ("tribes") had many conflicts among themselves and were divided from the Coloreds. However, apartheid gave them a common cause and enabled them to bridge their differences, thus changing ethnicity as a central political dividing point to race as a central factor in uniting these groups to oppose the apartheid regime (Marx, 1998).

Duckitt (1994) examined the political psychology of racism in South Africa and argues that getting to its roots is complicated when the system as a whole institutionalized racism. It offers the opportunity to explore the role of conformity pressures in producing prejudice, as well as arguments that authoritarian personality characteristics are associated with prejudice toward out-groups. After reviewing a number of studies, Duckitt (1994) related that studies of authoritarianism, using Altemeyer's right-wing Authoritarianism Scale, did find that authoritarianism was important in producing prejudice in South Africa. In addition, during the apartheid era in South Africa, there were differences in degrees of racism, with

English-speaking Whites being less racist than Afrikaans-speaking Whites. As in the United States, education made a difference, with prejudice falling as years of education increased. However, conformity pressures did not emerge as an important factor in prejudice in South Africa. Instead, racially prejudiced attitudes were learned through socialization.

Finally, South Africa offers a laboratory for the study of perceptions by the previously oppressed of their former oppressors, once the power tables are turned. Duckitt and Mphuthing (1998) examined this question. Studies from the apartheid era showed that Black Africans resented the power and privilege of Afrikaners more than that of English-speaking Whites. The supremacy of the Afrikaners was seen as illegitimate. Black Africans perceived themselves to be disadvantaged compared with Afrikaners, and were outraged. The Duckitt and Mphuthing study examined African attitudes toward Afrikaners before and after the first democratic election in South Africa in May 1994. The two studies were done just four months apart. Before the election, which was won by Nelson Mandela and ended the Afrikaner lock on political power, Africans saw themselves as less disadvantaged relative to Afrikaners. Duckitt and Mphuthing note that over a four-month period, the socioeconomic disadvantages of the African communities did not change significantly. What did change was the power they held and their sense that the political system was legitimate and just. Under those circumstances, "inequality in post-transition South Africa could be viewed as less unfair and less equitable than it was before the election" (1998, p. 827).

CONCLUSION

In this chapter, a number of theories have been used to look at different aspects of race. Although race in the United States received the lion's share of study in political psychology, we also looked at some cross-national examples in Brazil and South Africa. The theories used to examine different takes on race relations included realistic conflict theory, social identity theory, social learning theory, and social dominance theory. In our discussion of race, we entertained difficult arguments found in the literature about how much racism remains in the United States. As far as the literature on the United States is concerned, one camp argues that attitudes toward politics have changed in that race-related issues are not judged by many Whites in terms of racial attitudes, but no change, or even negative change, has occurred in terms of other attitudes. Hence, for example, White Americans who favor racial integration may oppose school busing not because they are closet racists, but because they do not want their children going to schools miles away from home. On the other side of the debate is the symbolic racism school, which maintains that racism is alive and well in America, but that people know it is considered inappropriate to be openly racist, so they hide their racist views behind traditional values such as the Protestant ethic and individualism. They say they disapprove of politics designed to help Black Americans not because the beneficiaries are Black, but because no one, White or Black, should get a government handout. Although not explicitly argued, there is a strong relationship between symbolic racism arguments and the arguments made in social learning theory that people learn racial attitudes from their families and societies. Racism in the United States and other countries is alive and well, as we also demonstrated with our discussion of the various White groups that exist and continue to perpetuate racist ideas.

Topics, Theories/Explanations, and Cases Covered in Chapter 8

Topics	*Theories/Models*	*Cases*
Race	Realistic conflict theory	United States
	Social learning theory	Brazil
	Social identity theory	South Africa
	Social dominance theory	
	Politics-is-complicated model	
	Symbolic racism model	

Key Terms

- Christian Identity
- minimal group paradigm
- phenomenal absolutism error
- politics-is-complicated model
- prejudice
- realistic conflict theory
- scapegoating
- social dominance theory
- social identity theory
- social learning theory
- symbolic racism
- ultimate attribution error

Suggestions for Further Reading

Citrin, J. & Sears, D.O. (2014). *American identity and the politics of multiculturalism.* Cambridge: Cambridge University Press.

DiAngelo, R. (2018). *White fragility: Why it's so hard for white people to talk about race.* Boston: Beacon Press

Duckitt, J. (1994). *The social psychology of prejudice.* New York: Praeger.

Fiske, S. (1998). Stereotyping, prejudice, and discrimination. In D. T. Gilbert, S. T. Fiske, & G. Lindzey (Eds.), *The handbook of social psychology* (4nd ed., Vol. *2*, pp. 357–411). New York: McGraw-Hill.

Ford, R. T. (2008). *The race card: How bluffing about bias makes race relations worse.* New York: Farrar, Straus, & Giroux.

Fording, R.C., & Schram, S.F. (2020). *Hard white: The mainstreaming of racism in American politics.* Oxford: Oxford University Press.

Jardina, A. (2019). *White identity politics.* Cambridge: Cambridge University Press.

Kinder, D., & Sanders, L. (1996). *Divided by color: Racial politics and democratic ideals.* Chicago, IL: University of Chicago Press.

Kitano, H., & Nakaoka, S. (2001). Asian Americans in the twentieth century. In N. Choi (Ed.), *Psychological aspects of the Asian-American experience* (pp. 7–18). New York: Hawthorn Press.

Marger, M. N. (2003). *Race and ethnic relations: American and global perspectives* (6th ed.). Belmont, CA: Thompson Wadsworth.

Marx, A. (1998). *Making race and nation: A comparison of the United States, South Africa and Brazil*. Cambridge: Cambridge University Press.

Sears. D., Sidanius, J., & Bobo, L (Eds.). (2000). *Racialized politics: The debate about racism in America*. Chicago, IL: University of Chicago Press.

Shipler, D. (1997). *A country of strangers: Blacks and Whites in America*. New York: Knopf.

Sniderman, P., & Carmines, E. (1997). *Reaching beyond race*. Cambridge, MA: Harvard University Press.

Tesler, M. (2016). *Post-racial or most-racial?: Race and politics in the Obama era*. Chicago: University of Chicago Press.

Tesler, M., & Sears, S.O. (2010). *Obama's race: The 2008 election and the dream of a post-racial America*. Chicago: University of Chicago Press.

Notes

1. It should be noted that social identity theory is simplified in this critique, in that it maintains that comparisons that result in out-group derogation are only made with relevant groups, not all groups. A university student, for example, would simply not compare his or her group's socioeconomic status with that of a professor's group, because that is not a relevant comparison group. On the other hand, if a student found students in a neighboring university to be generally more wealthy than his/her own group of students, that would be a relevant comparison group and it may be stereotyped as "a bunch of lazy rich kids who go to school to please their wealthy parents and who don't study." Moreover, social identity theory does maintain that people do not select social competition—that is, behaviors that seek to alter the social status relationship of their group—with those who have greater advantages unless they identify a clear alternative future.
2. There are many important methodological issues associated with getting and measuring an accurate picture of racial attitudes. Question wording; the nature of survey research, from which most of the data is drawn; race of the interviewer; and the use of telephone or person-to-person interviews, are all important in affecting the data. See Shuman et al. (1997, Ch. 3) for a review.
3. Koreans and Filipinos immigrated in the early twentieth century as well, many to provide cheap labor in plantations in Hawaii.
4. There are also Black separatist groups in the United States with anti-Semitic, anti-LGBT, and anti-White views responding to White Supremacy, such as Black Riders Liberation Party, Great Millstone, Nation of Islam, and the New Black Panther Party.

Chapter 9

From Ethnic Conflict to Genocide

What does it mean to be Italian American, or Swiss German, or Yoruba, or Azeri? These labels, which are used to delineate groups of people from each other all over the world, are actually ethnic identities. Ethnic groups have cultural, religious, and linguistic commonalities, as well as a shared view that the group has a common origin or a unique heritage or birthright (Smith, 1981; Young, 1976). As Rothschild (1981) explains, ethnic groups are "collective groups whose membership is largely defined by real or putative ancestral inherited ties, and who perceive these ties as systematically affecting their place and fate in the political and socioeconomic structures of their state and society" (p. 9). Ethnic groups are considered exclusive rather than inclusive: outsiders cannot join an ethnic group with which they do not share a common heritage. For example, a person from Zimbabwe could move to India, work, vote in national elections, and speak Hindi, becoming part of the Indian nation, but could not ever be accepted as an ethnic Indian, because that person does not possess a common ancestral heritage with other ethnic Indians.

Ethnicity is a particular focus of attention in political psychology because of the explosion of ethnic conflicts in various states within the past decade. However, interest in **ethnocentrism** can be traced back to William Graham Sumner's (1906) introduction of the term. He described it as "the view of things in which one's own group is the center of everything … and looks with contempt on outsiders" (p. 12). Ethnocentrism is singled out as the cause of ethnic conflict, political instability, and war (Hammond & Axelrod, 2006). Although ethnic conflict always existed, with the end of the Cold War the focus and attention of the international community shifted from conflict between the superpowers to ethnic conflicts within countries. In countries where internal conflict erupts, the state is no longer able to function as an authority over the groups. The conflicts are perplexing and surprising in many cases, because members of one ethnic group are now willing to kill members of another group who were formerly seen as neighbors, coworkers, people they went to school with, and perhaps even friends.

Ethnicity has an enormous impact upon group relations within countries and unfortunately resulted in many atrocities being committed by one group against another. Rwanda, Bosnia, Chechnya, Democratic Republic of the Congo, Liberia, Sierra Leone, Kosovo, and East Timor are only a few

DOI: 10.4324/9780429244643-9

of the countries or regions that experienced severe ethnic conflict and violence, some of which are ongoing. Even when an area seems to achieve peace, frequently no real political solution was found. As a result, conflict can resume at any time.

MULTIETHNIC OR MULTISECTARIAN STATES

Before looking at particular cases of ethnic conflict, it is important to describe some of the political characteristics of the countries that are most likely to experience ethnic conflict. In multiethnic or multisectarian states, there are at least two ethnic groups, neither of which is capable of assimilating or absorbing the other or of seceding and maintaining independence. This is an important definitional point. Multinational countries, which are discussed in the next chapter, do have national identity groups capable of existing as independent countries. However, by definition, multiethnic and multisectarian states are composed of ethnic groups that cannot realistically establish independent countries. People in multiethnic or multisectarian countries give primary loyalty to their ethnic or sectarian group, rather than to the broader community living in the country (see Figure 9.1). The ethnic groups frequently realize they do not have the resources to form their own state, but they may strive for the maximum autonomy possible and/or a large share of political and economic power in the state they share with other ethnic groups.[1] Often, members of the groups in multiethnic states maintain separate, geographically concentrated communities, but there are many instances in which ethnic group members are dispersed across the country. As is seen in the Bosnian case, ethnic groups sometimes have ethnic kin living close by in an independent country. In Bosnia, Bosnian Serbs and Croatians wanted to join Serbia and Croatia, respectively. To do that, however, required ethnic cleansing of one another, and of the Muslims living in Bosnia. This case is discussed in detail later. The disintegration of Yugoslavia, of which Bosnia was a part, is discussed more fully in the chapter on nationalism because, except for its republic of Bosnia-Herzegovina, Yugoslavia was a multinational state. Many of the multiethnic states found today are former colonies. As a result of colonialism, the ethnic groups became part of a state structure created by, and imposed upon them, by the colonial power. These are artificial states in the sense they were literally drawn on a map by an external power. In many cases, dominant ethnic groups within these colonial states took on the role as the local elite by serving the interests of the colonial power. Their political behaviors reflect their concern with matters such as the security, autonomy, and welfare of their ethnic group, rather than those of the country as a whole.

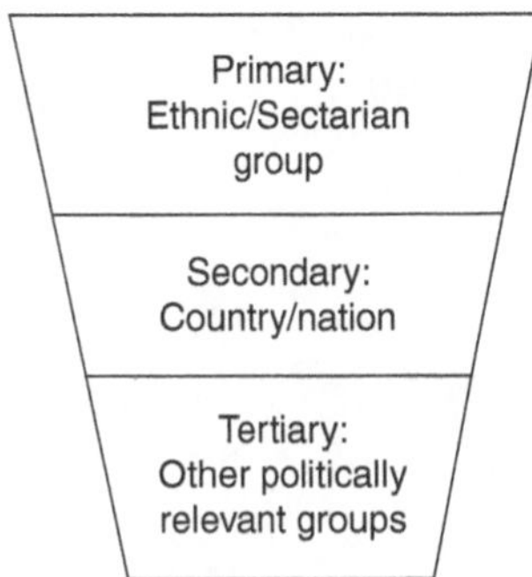

Figure 9.1 Political Identity and Loyalty in Multiethnic and Multisectarian States

To accommodate different ethnic groups' concerns, several structural options are employed by many multiethnic states, including consociationalism and federalism. These devices permit some degree of autonomy by offering some local political control, but they also allow for national governmental control to exist. Both consociationalism and federalism are particularly appealing to those states that have geographically concentrated communities. Consociationalism, or power sharing, has several features. Political parties representing the ethnic groups first form a **coalition** government and each group is represented in this coalition government through proportional representation. Rules are then implemented that are used to govern the public sector. Each group is also afforded a degree of autonomy over matters deemed important to them. Finally, there are constitutional vetoes for minority groups. Switzerland, with its strong German, French, and Italian ethnic groups, each of which has its own cantons, or governing regions, is a classic example of consociationalism.

In federal structures, there is a separation between a central government and provincial governments, with each having different spheres of influence. This type of government has a governing constitution and bicameral legislature. In constitutional matters, both levels of government must give their approval. As a rule, in the legislatures, smaller parties are overrepresented.

Even if either of these structures is put in place, there is no guarantee they will completely solve the conflict between groups within multiethnic states. In former colonies in particular, groups that engage in conflict do not have short memories of the acts perpetrated against them. For this reason, it is very difficult to foster a sense of community between the groups. An examination of some cases of ethnic conflict will demonstrate how quickly they can become inflamed, how violent they can be, and how difficult they are to stop. Many multiethnic states employ federalist institutional structures. Russia is one, and Nigeria—a case described shortly—is another.

EXPLANATIONS OF CONFLICT

The same psychological explanations of racial conflicts can be used to explain ethnic conflict. There is some basis for realistic conflict and competition among these ethnic groups for power, influence, and autonomy in a political system. In good times, cooperation in pursuit of common goals is possible. In bad times, competition for resources and power can be fierce. But these conflicts are not simply contingent upon good or bad times. The roots are psychological, and so deep that conflicts easily erupt when an opportunity or threat is perceived by one ethnic group *vis-à-vis* another and when at least one group is mobilized—often by political leaders—to challenge the perceived threat or seize the opportunity. From social identity theory, we know groups engage in social comparison. When the outcome of that comparison is negative, groups are motivated to change their status. An insecure social comparison results in a conclusion that an out-group has an unfair advantage and the relationship among the groups is conceived of as unfair, among other perceived inequities. One strategy for changing a group's status is social competition, which takes place when a subordinate group engages in direct competition with the dominant group. The group in the dominant position will feel threatened by the challenge to its status by a subordinate group. When this occurs, competition can lead to conflict. Even without conscious social comparisons, social identity theory suggests that the mere presence of different groups is sufficient to cause conflict and competition.

Many of the ethnic conflicts that have occurred in the post-Cold War era have been shockingly brutal and could devolve into genocide. The discussions of group behavior in Chapters 3 and 4 provide some insights into how violence can become so severe. These are situations in which the group perceives an intense threat, which in turn increases cohesion; dehumanization of other groups; deindividuation, so people see the group as responsible for events, not their own actions as individuals; and strong pressures for conformity and unanimity in the face of threat. Strong emotions associated with out-groups, discussed in Chapter 4, erupt and add to the violence. The emotions emanating from ethnic out-group stereotypes are often extremely powerful. They can change from simmering bitterness and resentment to rage and hatred toward other ethnic groups when underlying conflicts increase in intensity. At the same time, people experience increased love and attachment to their own ethnic group. In addition, in ethnic conflicts, one is unlikely to find the reticence evident in American racial politics, in which political elites resort to implicit code word references to race in race-related issues. In ethnic conflicts, such as those discussed in the next section, political leaders actively manipulate the stereotypes and emotions in order to mobilize their ethnic brethren against other ethnic groups. They use stereotypes and emotions to arouse intense feelings of hatred and anger toward other ethnic groups. As Kaufman (2001) notes, "If emotional appeals to ethnic themes are simultaneously appeals to ideas that lead one to blame another group, those appeals are apt simultaneously to arouse the feelings of anger and aggression most likely to motivate people to want to fight" (p. 9). Leaders play an important role in defining a threat or an opportunity, in sharpening perceptions of ethnic identity, and in furthering conflict by obstructing diplomatic solutions. In the process, committing acts of violence against others for the sake of the in-group becomes more likely, even if the victims once were friends.

In recent years, another psychological explanation, *evolutionary psychology*, was offered for ethnic conflict and ethnocentrism; this explanation sought to contribute to our understanding of the degree of violence that can erupt (Hammond & Axelrod, 2006; Shaw & Wong, 1989; Tooby & Cosmides, 1990; Waller, 2002). The evolutionary psychology perspective on human behavior is that it is "driven by a set of *universal reasoning circuits* that were *designed by natural selection* to solve *adaptive problems* faced by our *hunter-gatherer ancestors*" (Waller, 2002, p. 145). Universal reasoning circuits refer to the information-processing and problem-solving functions of the brain. These work to enable people to adapt to changes in their environments over time, including changes in communication, warfare capabilities, and economic production. Throughout this evolution, there is competition among groups for resources and other essentials of survival. Some groups win and others lose, and in the long run, as Waller (2002) argues, "all of us today owe our existence to having 'winners' as ancestors, and each of us today is designed, at least in some circumstances, to compete" (p. 150). The legacy of the evolutionary process is in-group favoritism, and a predisposition to compete with out-groups. To not compete was and is, according to this perspective, a recipe for extinction of the group. Hence, ethnocentrism is universal (Shaw & Wong, 1989; Waller, 2002).

At the same time, the evolutionary psychology perspective attempted to explain in-group solidarity, cooperation, and altruism as a result of the evolutionary need for adaptation. Why, they ask, do individuals in a group cooperate with each other, work together to achieve a common goal, and even sacrifice their lives for one another when a self-interested individual would never do something so seemingly irrational? It is done for the survival and benefit of the group. Hunting together, cooperating in group-benefit related tasks all increase the resources, including safety, available for the group, and thus for its individual members (Shaw & Wong, 1989).

THE PERPETRATORS OF VIOLENCE: POLITICAL EXTREMISTS

In many of the cases to be considered below and in the following chapters, horrific violence occurs. It is worth looking at some general arguments about the people who commit these acts. These people can be considered political extremists.

One of the central themes of this chapter is that political psychological studies of such people demonstrate that under the right circumstances the most ordinary people can be the perpetrators of extremist actions, or they can be passive bystanders who watch while such acts are carried out and do nothing to stop them. What is an **extremist** and what makes a person an extremist? According to Taylor, an extremist is a person who is:

> Excessive and inappropriately enthusiastic and/or inappropriately concerned with significant life purposes, implying a focused and highly personalized interpretation of the world. Politically, it is behavior that is strongly controlled by ideology, where the influence of ideology is such that it excludes or attenuates other social, political or personal forces that might be expected to control and influence behavior.
>
> (Taylor, 1991, p. 33)

Extremists, then, are concerned only with the logic of their own behavior and their ideological construction of the world. Extremists tend to disregard the lives of others and disregard alternatives. It follows that extremists are very resistant to change.

Political psychologists have some thoughts on why people are extremists. There are several explanations, ranging from personality attributes to the need for group conformity. Let's examine these insights more closely. People who commit extremist acts are typically lacking in empathy for others and tend to dehumanize their victims; however:

> "You can have people who have a well-developed capacity for empathy, relating, who are very close to their friends, but who have been raised in an ideology that teaches them that people of another religion, color, or ethnic group are bad," says psychologist Bruce Perry ... "They will act in a way that is essentially evil based upon cognition rather than emotion." But the heart and the head interact. People who grew up amid violence and cruelty are more susceptible to ideologies that dehumanize the other in favor of the self (Begley, 2001, p. 33).

There is disagreement in political psychology as to whether there are personality traits commonly found among political extremists. Studies of torturers in Greece and Latin America did not find any particular personality syndrome that differentiates them from people who do not torture. For example, Haritos-Fatouros (1988) did not find evidence of sadism or extreme authoritarianism in Greek torturers before they entered the armed forces. Rosenberg's (1992) studies of torturers in Argentina, although journalistic rather than scientific, described quite normal, career-minded officers who were in charge of the Argentine torture unit. Claudia Reyes-Quilodran (2001) argues that there appear to be two types of torturers—those motivated by ideology, training, and loyalty to the military, and those who are simple criminals—but she also found no particular personality type.

Although there does not appear to be a particular personality associated with political extremists, personality is not unimportant. One characteristic that is arguably quite important in explaining the actions of extremists is their response to authority. As we explained in Chapter 2, in his work on the authoritarian personality, Altemeyer discussed the attributes of submission to authority, aggression against nonconformist groups, and conventionalism, which are strongly linked to right-wing authoritarianism. Other studies demonstrated it is not only people who are high in authoritarianism who can respond very strongly to instructions from authority: people with more education tend to at least *say* they would resist authority. The **locus of control** personality trait influences susceptibility to authority. **Internals**—that is, people who believe they have considerable control over their fate—are more likely to resist authority than **externals**—people who believe the external environment strongly determines what happens to them (Blass, 1991; Kressel, 1996). Also, people who do not care much about the impression they make on others (low self-monitors) are less susceptible to authority's demands (Kressel, 1996). The experiments by Stanley Milgram (1974) are among the most often-cited studies demonstrating the power of authority.

In the Milgram experiments, subjects were told they were going to participate in an experiment on learning. They were instructed by an experimenter in a laboratory setting to deliver shocks to a "learner" when he made a mistake. (The learner was in fact a confederate in the experiment.) With each mistake, the subjects were told to increase the electrical voltage. When the learner started to moan and claim a bad heart, the subjects were told to keep delivering the shocks, with instructions such as "the experiment requires you to go on," and "you have no other choice." More than 62% of the subjects delivered the highest level of voltage, ignoring the printed warnings of danger and the screams and protestations of the learner. Most of the subjects who persisted in delivering the shocks did so with great reluctance and asked for permission to discontinue the shocks or called the experimenter's attention to their learner's suffering, demonstrating that the subjects didn't hate the learners, nor did they even dislike them.

Examining the results of his study, Milgram argued that the subjects were not sadistic because the context of the action had to be considered—that is, there is an important person–situation interaction effect. The experimenter appeared to have the legitimate authority to know what could be done—that is, how much electrical voltage the subject could endure. The subjects became integrated into a situation that carried its own momentum. The problem for individuals is how to become disengaged from a situation that has moved in an apparently terrible direction. In subsequent experiments, Milgram found obedience diminished rapidly if one person in a group refused to obey. In addition, distance from the experimenter reduced compliance. If the experimenter sat next to the subject, compliance was high. The farther away he was physically, the more likely people were to refuse to continue administering the shocks. Personality plays a role as well. Elms and Milgram (1966) found people higher in authoritarianism were more likely to be obedient to authority.

Examining extremists from a group perspective also yielded some interesting insights into their behavior. As Baumeister notes, extremist acts of violence are

> nearly always fostered by groups, as opposed to individuals. When someone kills for the sake of promoting a higher good, he may find support and encouragement if he is acting as part of a group of people who share that belief. If he acts as a lone individual, the same act is likely to brand him as a dangerous nut.
>
> (Baumeister, 1997, p. 190)

In earlier chapters, we discussed the importance of belonging to groups and seeing those groups positively in comparison to others. When this is not possible, people look for some out-group to blame. Under normal conditions, conflicts among groups can occur over scarce resources, territory, values, ideology, status, security, power, and many other things (Fisher, 1990; Stroebe & Insko, 1989). In conditions of severe socioeconomic and political despair and depression, the environment is often conducive to the identification of one group as a *scapegoat*, a group that is blamed for all of society's ills. During hard times, the groups people are particularly attracted to are those that "provide an ideological blueprint for a better world and an enemy who must be destroyed to fulfill the ideology" (Staub, 1989, p. 17). This is called **social causality** (Hogg & Abrams, 1988). Typically, a negative stereotype of that group is promulgated on a society-wide scale. Next, **social justification** occurs, wherein that group's poor treatment is justified. The most extreme version of this is **dehumanization** of the scapegoat, whereby the group members are regularly described as less than human and therefore deserving of treatment one would not administer to a human being. In Germany during the Hitler era, Jews were regularly vilified and called rats. In Rwanda, before that genocide, the Tutsis were called insects and cockroaches by the Hutu extremists. Under these conditions, hating the enemy becomes a noble and righteous cause in the minds of group members.

The identification of an out-group to place blame upon is important for groups and their members to provide an explanation for their own circumstances. But, as was noted in Chapter 4, the group also offers individual members important psychological benefits. While there are certainly many reasons why a person may join a group, such as ideology and a sense of social support among others, once they become members, uniform views tend to reinforce the conformity of individuals. In addition, members face so-called psychological traps and the group experiences the escalation of commitment pattern discussed in Chapter 4 (Taylor, 1991). People find themselves in circumstances that require a great amount of time and effort toward the accomplishment of the group's goals. It follows that the more investment a person makes in a goal, the harder it becomes to abandon the group, regardless of actual accomplishment of that goal. Commitment to a group—especially one that requires the use of violent behavior—is very psychologically demanding. The more acts of violence one commits, the more psychologically entrapped a person becomes.

At this point, we can pull together some of the patterns we have reviewed in individual and group behavior with the obedience to authority patterns present in the Milgram experiments. People are obedient not only to individual authority figures, but also to groups and their authority structure. Why? In Chapter 4, we presented several reasons for conformity in groups, including informational social influence, wherein people conform to group norms because they wish to be correct, and conforming enables people to gather information. Normative social influence was also mentioned, wherein people conform in order to be liked. Situational factors such as group size and unanimity also affect conformity. Commitment to the group is also an important situational factor. Consider what will happen if you are not loyal and obedient to a group. If you do not conform to group norms and goals, the most likely outcome is that everyone in the group will dislike you. In fact, you may even be expelled from the group, which can be very threatening, particularly when the group is cohesive, when members are isolated from other groups, and when the group is an important component of a personal identity. Yet, there is a caveat because how you conduct your deviance from a group makes a significant difference. For example, *heretics*, who do not disavow their membership but deviate from the group, fare better than *renegades*, who denounce their membership in a group. This is because a renegade is questioning the core values of a group as opposed to questioning group tactics.

An individual can be obedient to a group even when the group acts in a way contrary to an individual's values. However, when an individual is obedient depends on the social context in which the authority is being used, the character of the authority holders, and the nature of the demands they make. They are more likely to obey when the action is authorized by authority, when the action is routinized, making it mechanical and possible to do with little thought, and when the victim is dehumanized. Obedience is also more likely when individuals want to comply, not because they necessarily agree with the activity, but because of the positive impression gained from compliance (Kelman & Hamilton, 1989; Sabini & Silver, 1993; Staub, 1989). Often the most fanatical members become group leaders, and they act strongly to prevent dissension within the group.

Groups and their members interact in a symbiotic fashion, and being obedient to group norms and the demands of authority is not simply the product of fear or rejection. Groups often indoctrinate members through initiation rites, training, and providing a feeling of being part of a family. These are the forming and norming stages of group development discussed in Chapter 4. The process can be extremely dramatic. Group members who undergo severe initiations or who endure harsh pain and suffering to become a member tend to be more committed to the group than group members who do not have to suffer to join the group (Aronson & Mills, 1959; Wicklund, Cooper, & Linder, 1967). Indoctrination and initiation rites can be brutal, giving the member who survives and becomes a member of the group a strong sense of belonging, having passed the test of strength and will. Indoctrination presents the member with a worldview. Torturers in Guatemala, for example, were often given horrifically brutal training and indoctrination in anti-communist ideology and the idea that they were saving the country by torturing deviants (Conroy, 2000; Reyes-Quilodran, 2001).

People do not want to let the group down. Staub (1989, 1999, 2000) and Kelman (1990), among others, argue that human needs must also be introduced to fully understand this type of phenomenon. Generally, the point is people are not just cogs in these groups' machinery. The perception of hard times is deeply threatening to the extremists, and this activates basic survival needs. They join groups they think will satisfy those fundamental survival needs. The groups are more than social. Obedience and compliance with group norms that demand extremism and violence are done out of more than fear of rejection or punishment. They are undertaken willingly. The group makes it easier, true enough. The group makes it possible for people to distance themselves from the violence by distributing and diffusing responsibility for it. The group provides the moral authority for the actions the individual takes. Groups with this type of cohesion and dedication to a cause are more likely to experience groupthink, introduced in Chapter 4, particularly if their leaders are charismatic and/or narcissistic, and unwilling to hear disagreement or critical information.

Finally, research on how perpetrators of acts that are condemnatory perceive their own actions provides important insights into why people do things that cause great suffering and harm. Baumeister's (1997) research found that perpetrators see their actions as much less wrong than the victims do. They minimize the harm done, and often explain their actions as justified by the evil nature of the victim. This is an example of patterns of perception described by attribution theory.

The following illustrations of ethnic conflict and genocide will enable us to flesh out some of these political psychological patterns.

CASE ILLUSTRATIONS OF ETHNIC CONFLICT

Ethnic Clashes in Nigeria

Nigeria is a multiethnic state that was a product of colonialism by the British. Three main ethnic groups make up two-thirds of the population: the Hausa/Fulani (who are Muslim); the Yoruba (who are Christian and Muslims); and the Ibo (who are Christian). Within these three groups, there are many subdivisions, so that, as a whole, Nigeria has more than 248 distinct ethnic groups (Diamond, 1988). The Hausa/Fulani are found in the north, the Yoruba in the west, and the Ibo in the east. However, each region does contain other ethnic groups.

Social stereotypes, group conflict, and social comparison processes are important factors in understanding ethnic conflict in Nigeria. Under British colonialism, Nigeria was partitioned into three regions, each dominated by an ethnic group. The Hausa were chosen by the British to be their administrative representatives. Although the Hausa were permitted to keep their traditional class hierarchy, social structure, and educational system based upon the Koran, the British imposed their own education system and made the common language English in the areas dominated by Yoruba and Ibo. This set forth the basis for ethnic competition after independence: an outside power, the British colonizers, had already established the basis for Hausa superiority, in terms of political power; the other groups' self-comparison with the Hausa would be negative, at least from the standpoint of political power.

Nigeria achieved its independence from Britain in 1960, and the colonial regional structuring based on ethnicity was initially left in place in a federated political system. Ethnic competition preceded independence and quickly became a central factor in Nigerian politics after independence. The Ibos, in the southeast, were tired of the domination by the north. In the early colonial era, the British had considered the Ibo to be the most backward and inferior of Nigeria's ethnic groups. By the 1930s, however, the social and economic position of the Ibo had improved. The perception by the British of the Ibo as backward shifted to view them as "dynamic, aggressive, upwardly mobile" (Young, 1983, p. 206).

During the 1950s, the Ibo became strongly nationalistic, desiring a role in the existing national institutions. The Ibos also tended to be very entrepreneurial and moved into Hausa and Yoruba regions. Their economic success, as well as their desire for greater participation and political power, was perceived as threatening to other groups. Increasingly, the Ibo were seen, through an anti-Semitic type of stereotype, as insular, elitist, devious, and power- and wealth-acquisitive. Thus, stereotyping and social identity patterns appear in this case. The Ibos were downtrodden, and sought to alter their social, economic, and political roles in Nigeria. This was threatening to the other groups, which had a strong stereotype of Ibos as bad in a variety of ways, and they were not about to let change occur.

In January 1966, Ibo military officers led a successful coup, overthrowing the government. They, in turn, were ousted later that year by northerners, bringing Lieutenant Colonel Yakubu Gowon to power. Ethnic clashes followed, and many Ibos were killed, particularly in the north. Continued persecution prompted the Ibos to declare independence in the region of the country where they were the numerical majority, which they called Biafra. The federal government refused to let them secede, and in 1967 a civil war broke out between the Ibos, seeking to establish an independent Biafra, and the federal government of Nigeria. The war, which lasted for three years, ended in a loss for the Ibos and claimed the lives of over one million people, mostly Ibos. After the war, the federal government developed a very important approach to the defeated Ibo: reincorporation into the country, opportunities in education, and reconstruction. This type of policy is crucial to the future of any multiethnic state that contains a defeated breakaway group. And it worked in Nigeria. Despite the one million Biafran deaths, the war is not a topic of discussion and continued resentment in Iboland today.

After the war, ethnic divisiveness continued to plague Nigerian politics. General Gowon was overthrown in a coup in 1975 (Ihonvbere, 1994). General Olusegun Obasanjo, a Yoruba, took power and adopted measures to pave the way for democratic reform and a return to civilian rule. Those reforms included the creation of a new constitution, with provisions that would accommodate ethnic diversity. A new federal state structure was introduced, with 19 states. In order to win the presidency, a candidate would have to receive at least one-third of the popular vote and at least one fourth of the vote in two thirds of the 19 states (Shively, 1993).

Since the end of the first 13 years of military rule in 1979, Nigeria has only had a few years of intermittent civilian rule, and ethnic conflict and competition have been instrumental in inhibiting the establishment of stable democracy. For example, elections were finally held in 1979, as promised by Obasanjo, bringing the northerner, Shehu Shagari, to power. However, he was overthrown in 1983, amid accusations of corruption, a failing economy, and his inability to deal with ethnic divisions (Shively, 1993). In 1993, Chief Moshood Abiola, a Yoruba, won the election. However, General Ibrahim Babangida, a northerner who had been in power since 1985, nullified the results. Babangida finally stepped down, naming Ernest Shonekan, a civilian, as interim leader for a few months, until the defense minister, General Sani Abacha, took control. In June 1994, Abacha arrested Abiola and charged him with treason. When Abacha suddenly died in June 1998, an interim leader, General Abdulsalami Abubakar, succeeded him. After years of promises, elections were finally held, and Olusegun Obasanjo took office once again on May 29, 1999. However, Obasanjo took office amid election irregularities such as inflated turnout, the stuffing of ballot boxes, intimidation and bribery of election officials and voters, and alteration of results (Human Rights Watch, 2000). Obasanjo won reelection in 2003, again amid accusations of irregularities in the electoral process. The Nigerian National Assembly appointed Vice President Goodluck Jonathan acting president in February 2010 because President Umaru Yar'Adua was seeking medical treatment for an extended period. Goodluck Jonathan was sworn in as president following the death of Yar'Adua in May. His support lies mainly in the Christian south.

In each case of regime change, the ethnicity of the old and new powerholders is centrally important to the people of Nigeria. Each group continually compares itself with the others, and the propensity to identify some basis for a negative social comparison is strong. The power and economic pie in Nigeria is small. Nigeria is a poor country despite its oil, and each group fears the others will get more than their fair share.

The Nigerian case shows how ethnicity and national identification can become mutually exclusive. In Nigeria, control of the state was associated with ethnicity, so extensively that each of the three dominant ethnic groups was susceptible to ethnicity-based political parties and issues. They were constantly fearful that the essence of being Nigerian would be captured by one of the other ethnic groups, and their own group would lose out on power and security. In fact, the Biafran war served as a catalyst for a struggling Nigerian identity to gain momentum. According to Oyovbaire:

> The quantum or quality of national consciousness generated by [federal efforts during the war] is impossible to assess, but there is no doubt that a new public consciousness of the role of the centre previously

> unknown in the politics, economics and management of the federation had been generated by the civil war... If before the Biafran occupation, Nigeria was just a name—lacking meaning, attachment and symbolism to the literate and nonliterate, the urban unemployed and rural dwellers—after that experience Nigeria became a fact of existence, the federal government being regarded as protector and benefactor.
>
> (Oyovbaire, 1984, pp. 132–133)

Nevertheless, ethnicity continues to be a dominant factor in Nigerian politics, and it continues to cause frequent outbreaks of violence, resulting in hundreds of deaths on a regular basis. For example, a state of emergency was declared in central Nigeria in 2004 due to attacks on Muslims by Christian militias. The Muslim Boko Haram movement perpetrates attacks and has killed thousands in its drive to establish control in Nigeria. To satisfy ethnic demands, the country was divided repeatedly into more and more states, currently standing at 36. In the process, the three largest and most dominant ethnic groups are distributed among several states. Thus, Nigerian identity remains secondary to ethnic identities and is unlikely to be enhanced by the ongoing corruption, political instability, poverty, and repression of ethnic discontent, such as the execution in 1995 of nine ethnic Ogoni leaders who protested government policies in Ogoniland. This leaves the glaring question of how Nigeria as a state survives, and the answer must be that no group sees an alternative.

ETHNIC CLEANSING IN BOSNIA

Yugoslavia was a multinational and multiethnic country. For many years, the people from different ethnic groups lived together harmoniously. After World War II, Yugoslavia's government was headed by a very charismatic leader, Josip Broz Tito, who encouraged a common Yugoslav political identity. Tito died in 1980, and over the next decade the unity and brotherhood encouraged by Tito gradually unraveled. The final disintegration of Yugoslavia began on June 25, 1991, with the declaration of independence of Croatia and Slovenia. The Yugoslav republic of Bosnia-Herzegovina was declared an independent country on April 5, 1992, and was subsequently recognized as such by the international community. Yugoslavia was composed of what was left—Serbia and Montenegro.

The powerful pull of in-groups, as well as the impact of negative threatening images, is useful in explaining the conflict that erupted in Bosnia. Bosnia has three main ethnic groups: the Serbs (who are Eastern Orthodox), the Muslims, and the Croatians (who are Roman Catholic). The Serbs and Croatians in Bosnia were part of larger ethnic groups in the Croatian and Serbian republics of Yugoslavia. As Thomas explained, during the days of Yugoslavian unity,

> in Bosnia-Herzegovina, whether Muslim, Orthodox Christian or Roman Catholic Serbs, Croats and Muslims were all comfortable

> being labeled "Bosnian" even if they believed themselves to be Bosnian Serb, Croat or Muslim. This was because Bosnia was a smaller and narrower representation of the larger concept of multi-ethnic Yugoslavia, a country voluntarily created in 1918 for the South Slav peoples ... Bosnia-Herzegovina, like Yugoslavia, denoted territorial space and not ethnic identity.
>
> (Thomas, 1996, p. 30)

The 1991 census demonstrated the importance of ethnic identity, however: 44% self-identified as Muslim, 31.5% Serb, 17% Croat, and only 5.5% Yugoslav. As a republic in Yugoslavia before it disintegrated, Bosnia-Herzegovina could and did provide these groups with opportunities for social mobilization and social creativity. The Yugoslav state prevented one group from being dominant and provided opportunities for all ethnic groups. In fact, the state created the concept of Bosnian Muslims as a distinct ethnic identity in the 1960s, which was more preferable to the Muslims than their previous identities as Croat or Serb Muslims (Thomas, 1996). Intergroup competition was held in check by the Yugoslav government while efforts were made to forge a common identity.

As Yugoslavia fell apart, the three ethnic communities in Bosnia faced a real dilemma. Should they remain part of Yugoslavia or attempt independence? None of the three had the power to dominate an independent Bosnia. The ethnic populations were territorially dispersed, and there was significant intermarriage among the groups. Therefore, the groups could not simply be divided up geographically, providing each its own state in a multi-ethnic country. Nor, given the distribution of ethnic populations and the complexity of their intermixture, could Bosnia simply be divided up, with its Croatian and Serbian ethnics annexed to their respective national states, Croatia and Serbia. The dilemma by 1991, therefore, became whether to stay with Yugoslavia, which now consisted primarily of Serbs, or attempt independence. Staying in Yugoslavia was threatening to the Muslim and Croat populations. Bosnian Serbs, on the other hand, had every reason to want to remain in what was left of Yugoslavia, where Serbs would be the dominant group. It was in this context that a referendum was held to decide upon independence. The Serbs boycotted the referendum, and the Muslims and Croats voted for independence from Yugoslavia. Bosnian leaders quickly developed a power-sharing arrangement among the parties representing all three ethnic groups in an autonomous Bosnia. That arrangement was doomed to failure, however. The Croatian and Serb communities in Bosnia each saw an opportunity to join their ethnic brethren in Croatia and Serbia. The strong pull of group identity made this option very attractive for the Bosnian Croats and Bosnian Serbs. This destroyed any basis for power-sharing. The Bosnian Serbs declared themselves part of the Serb nation. The Bosnian Croats insisted that they would not remain in Bosnia if Bosnia remained in Yugoslavia (Woodward, 1995). Eventually, Bosnian Croats marked for themselves a Croat state in western Bosnia-Herzegovina. The Muslim community, recognizing its inability to maintain sovereign independence for long in this setting, was faced with the options of emigration or accepting minority status in Croatia or Serbia.

In Their Own Words: Radovan Karadžić on the Situation of the Bosnian Serbs

Below are some excerpts from a speech given by Radovan Karadžić to the Parliament of Bosnian Serbia, (Republika Srpska) in 1996. Karadžić was the President of Republika Srpska at the time.

> Five years have passed since the first multiparty elections in the former Bosnia-Herzegovina, four years and three months since the founding of the Republic and four years since the beginning of the war. There are few nations in the world who were exposed to such trials and suffering in such a short period as our people have been. Centuries and decades which our enemies had spent working on the denationalization of the Serbs west from the Drina and on their separation from the mother Serbia. Regardless of whether those guilty for this war will be tried, we shall always hold them responsible and will never forget what they did to us ... Three weeks after the recognition of our state we were forced to defend it with arms. Our armed struggle and the defense of the state and the people are among the brightest examples of knightly self-sacrifice... . We fought against huge powers. Against a more numerous and better equipped enemy ... The people was on our side, and the God was on our side... Our goal was, and remains, the united state of all Serbs ... We saved our people from a genocide and secured a significant proportion of its historic territories. Some precious territories we didn't include in our state, and we will never accept that that loss is definitive.
>
> (Karadžić, 1996, pp. 1–2)

Threat perceptions in all three communities were very high. Croatians traditionally saw Serbs as barbarians—that is, through the barbarian image (see Chapter 3). Serbs were horrified at the prospect of being separated from the Serb population that dominated the old Yugoslavia, at least in size and presence in the military. Moreover, the Serbs recalled the slaughter of Serbs by Croatians during World War II. The Muslims feared both Croatians and Serbs, with good reason. They too received brutal treatment from the Croatians during World War II, and the Serbs maintained an historical animosity toward the Muslims that went back hundreds of years.

Ethnic Hatreds

Journalist Anthony Loyd's (1999) report from the battlegrounds of Bosnia provides a first-hand illustration of ethnic stereotyping and hatred:

> I had left Citluk at dawn and after walking a few miles had been picked up by a heavily built middle-aged Bosnian Croat woman ... Naively I had imagined having to listen to tales of grandchildren

(*Continued*)

(*Continued*)

or cats for the next leg of my journey. Instead she had launched into a tirade against Islam that gathered momentum with each dragging mile. There were thousands of Arab *mujahidin* swarming through the hills, she told me. They had radicalized the minds of the Bosnian Muslims who were now waging a jihad, a holy war, upon the beleaguered Croat people who for so long had been persecuted by the filth of the Ottoman Empire. Bosnia was now Europe's frontier against the fundamentalist legions of Allah, the Croatian people the brave hajduk vanguard in the battle for Christianity. As for the Serbs, not one of them would find salvation ... Spittle began to fly like sparks from the edge of her mouth.

Describing his next lift, Loyd writes:

Within five minutes I was hearing the same story: *mujahidin*, fundamentalism, the Ottoman empire, jihad, Turks, Christ... . It was the key to so much of what was happening in Bosnia. If I, a relatively impartial foreigner ... could be frightened by local scaremongering and propaganda, imagine what it was doing to the minds of isolated rural communities with no access to outside news, no experience of media impartiality ... You could pop common sense from the minds of villagers in Bosnia like a pea from a pod. Make them afraid by resurrecting real or imagined threats, catalyse it with a bit of bloodletting, and you were only two steps from massacre and mayhem.

(Lloyd, 1999, pp. 70–71)

The ensuing war was brutal. All three ethnic communities were mobilized and galvanized by leaders (Serbian President Slobodan Milošović, Croatian President Franjo Tudjman, and Bosnian Muslim leader Alija Izetbegovic) in the years preceding Bosnia's war, while Yugoslavia as a whole disintegrated (Kaufman, 2001). Local Bosnian Serb, Croatian, and Muslim leaders also contributed to the slandering and dehumanization of the other ethnic groups. The means selected by all three groups for solving the question of the future of Bosnia-Herzegovina was ethnic cleansing. If living with the other groups was too threatening, they would just get rid of the others. In the spring of 1992, Serb-dominated Yugoslav forces, together with Bosnian Serbs, began a campaign to ethnically cleanse the other groups from the country. In addition to forcing Muslims and Croats to flee the country, the list of atrocities committed by the Serbs against the other groups included mass killings, rape, and the creation of concentration camps. The other groups also committed atrocities, but not on the same scale as the Serbs.

In November 1995, the United States brokered talks that resulted in the Dayton Peace Accord. Bosnian Serbs did not negotiate for themselves but were represented by Slobodan Milošević. Under the agreement, a Bosnian Serb Republic and Muslim–Croat federation were established. A federal government, with a presidency that rotates among the groups, was also created. North Atlantic Treaty Organization (NATO) peacekeeping troops were also brought in to ensure a peaceful transition.

This war claimed the lives of an estimated 200,000 people (Power, 2002). Hatred in this conflict erupted quickly, in part because of the efforts of leaders to provoke it. It cannot be expected to disappear overnight, particularly after so many died. Ethnic cleansing in Bosnia is a classic example of the group patterns leading to violence discussed earlier. Without the Yugoslav state to manage ethnic group competition, concerns began to arise about the domination by one ethnic group. Wrongs done by each group to the others in the past were recalled, threat perceptions increased, stereotyping increased, the salience of group attachments increased, and eventually war erupted. Once the fighting started, it was increasingly possible to dehumanize the others and to divest oneself of personal responsibility for violence; ethnic cleaning, ethnic rape, and thousands of deaths were the result.

THE MAYA OF GUATEMALA

The case of ethnic conflict in Guatemala also involves various aspects of social identity theory and group competition. In this case, the indigenous Maya of Guatemala were downtrodden people kept in an inferior socioeconomic situation and lacking in political power. The dominant group, the *ladino* (non-Indigenous) population in general, and the military in particular, looked at them with contempt. During the worst years of the conflict there, they were dehumanized by the military, who slaughtered thousands of Maya. In Guatemala, 60% of the 12.5 million citizens are Maya; the rest are *ladinos*. The two differ in language and custom, but not in appearance, because most *ladinos* have Mayan ancestry. *Ladinos* speak Spanish, wear western clothing, and engage in capitalist enterprise. The Maya of Guatemala, however, are composed of 23 subgroups and languages, some of which are mutually unintelligible. Many Maya do not speak Spanish, and many are bilingual (Warren, 1993). They often wear traditional colorful clothing and maintain a traditional communal lifestyle.

Since the Spanish conquest of the Maya in the sixteenth century, the central direction of change has been toward the assimilation of the Maya into Spanish culture. One was *ladino* or one was Maya. The two identities were not complementary. Being *ladino* meant one was Guatemalan, whereas being Maya meant one was not. The Indigenous Maya were stereotyped as racially and culturally inferior. Their socioeconomic characteristics and political powerlessness reflected this perception of them by the *ladino* society.

Over the centuries since conquest by Spain, the Maya remained at the bottom of the social and economic ladder in Guatemala. The first stage of the mobilization of the Maya to change this situation began in 1944, with the establishment of a reform-minded government, and ended with the 1954 overthrow of that government and the brutal repression that followed. But, by the late 1970s, the Indigenous people were politically and socially mobilized again. This is an illustration of the efforts people make when they perceive a realistic opportunity exists to change their group's status. At that point, they were participating in political party activities, running for office, and had established a Mayan-led labor organization, the Committee of Peasant Unity. This took place in the context of broader social and political discontent in Guatemala, which included sectors of the *ladino* population. The period also witnessed the emergence of left-wing guerrilla groups intent on overthrowing the government. The guerrilla military offensive reached its height in 1980–1981, with 6000–8000 armed fighters and 250,000–500,000 active collaborators and supporters operating in most parts of the country (Schirmer, 1998).

This movement was seen as threatening to the dominance of the *ladinos* in general, and of the wealthy landowner *ladinos* in particular. The military government's response was a scorched-earth assault on all opposition, including the Mayan communities in rural areas, which were suspected of supporting the guerrillas. The violence was horrific, and the intention was to eliminate as many guerrillas and their supporters as possible and to terrorize the Mayan communities into submission. The tactics used were very brutal. Witness accounts such as the following were common:

> A North American priest described how this process took place in an isolated northern province where he worked during the early years of the violence:
>
> "Between 1975 and 1997, 47 project leaders were assassinated or disappeared. One returned. He suffered torture and witnessed the murder of some 30 members of his community... In March, 1981, 15 members of our co-op were dragged from their homes and murdered by the military. In December 1981, assassins in army uniforms and with government trucks entered a remote village and assassinated several co-op leaders. Five others were found later, crucified with sharp sticks to the ground and tortured to death."
>
> Another respondent ... a Peace Corps volunteer, described the following situation in the Indian town where she worked:
>
> "I was working in one town which was trying to organize a bread-baking and shirt-making co-op to raise funds for community projects such as a pharmacy. Several of the members were murdered in an attack by uniformed government soldiers. I did not witness this, but I saw the effects on the project and the source was truthful beyond any doubt. I later read an account in a U.S. publication that said that these 'terrorists' (bread makers) had been roasted alive in the schoolyard in front of their friends and families."
>
> (Davies, 1992, pp. 22–23)

Moreover, the military were unabashed about their conduct. They admitted to the tactics they used and felt quite justified in using them. The press secretary for General Ríos Montt, who took control of the dictatorship after a coup in 1983, stated:

> The guerrillas won over many Indian collaborators. Therefore, the Indians were subversives. And how do you fight subversion? Clearly you had to kill Indians because they were collaborating with

> subversion. And then it would be said that you were killing innocent people. But they weren't innocent; they had sold out to subversion.
> (quoted in Carmack, 1992, p. 57)

Villages were routinely attacked, many suspected subversives were killed, women were gang raped, victims were tortured, and the soldiers even engaged in ritual cannibalism in order to terrorize the civilians (Stoll, 1992).

For the Maya, the consequences of this "dirty war" were disastrous, approaching a "demographic, social and cultural 'holocaust'" (Davies, 1992, p. 21). More than 150,000 people were killed, depending on when one starts the count, 150,000 went into exile in Mexico, and half a million became internal refugees. Guatemala ended up with more than 40,000 disappearances. Eighty-three percent of the victims of the scorched-earth policy were Maya. Ninety-three percent of human rights violations were attributed to the military or paramilitaries. If the Maya fled the army's assaults by going into the mountainous highlands or Mexico, they faced hunger and misery. When they tried to return, they were imprisoned in "poles of development" (*pollos de desarrollo*)—internment camps for Mayan returnees where they were to be indoctrinated in anti-communism, and where their way of life was systematically destroyed. The campaign was not simply directed at the Maya, but was an ideologically based internal security campaign that combined with ongoing ethnocentrism to devastate the Indigenous population.

The military turned the reins of government back to civilians in 1985, but this was only a cosmetic democracy. The military was free to continue to run its counterinsurgency program, and the Mayan people continued to suffer. Although the guerrillas had a resurgence in the late 1980s, by then they recognized that the war could not be won by either side. They suggested peace talks, but it was not until December 1996 that the final peace agreement was reached. The United Nations (UN) brokered the talks and the subsequent reforms of the political system. After the war, the Mayan communities again mobilized, this time to ensure their participation in the establishment of a new Guatemala. Of central importance is the fact that their mobilization appears to be toward achieving a new definition of the national community, and what it means to be Guatemalan. During the early 1990s, many *ladinos* began to accept and prize aspects of Maya culture, the teaching of Mayan languages in schools, and the participation of Maya political organizations in the political system (LaBaron, 1993). In and of itself, that did not mean the *ladino* community was interested in the creation of a new common third identity incorporating elements of Maya culture; however, there were signs that this too might be changing: the 1995 Accord on the Identity and Rights of Indigenous Peoples, a goal of the peace accord, and constitutional changes agreed to by the government, was supposed to turn Guatemala into a multiethnic, multicultural, and multilinguistic society, and protect the rights of the Indigenous. However, these changes in favor of indigenous people were put to popular vote, which failed in 1999. Significant reform did not take place (Campos, Brannum, & Mastors 2021). It appears, then, that Guatemala had a chance to reconcile competing Indigenous versus *ladino* identities, so they may still be different, but both would be Guatemalan; in reality, though, important reform failed to take place. We return to this process in our discussion of conflict resolution.

ETHNICITY AND SECTARIANISM IN IRAQ

Ethnic and sectarian differences are a cause of the instability and civil violence that has rocked Iraq since the overthrow of the Baathist regime of Saddam Hussein in 2003. The identity profile of Iraqis is quite complex. The Iraqi population is 75–80% Arab in ethnicity and 15–20% Kurd; the remaining population includes Turkomen, Assyrian, and "other" (CIA World Factbook, 2008). In terms of religious sectarian identity, 97% of Iraqis are Muslims. But that percentage does not reflect the important division within Islam between the Sunni and Shia sects, a division that is the cause of serious hostility, stereotyping and, in Iraq, violence. In Iraq the majority are Shia, about 60–65%, with 32–37% Sunni, and 3% Christian. Although the Sunnis are the overwhelming majority in the Arab world, Iraq is unique in having a Shia majority. Moreover, Iraq's neighbor, Iran, is majority Shia as well, but Iranians are not Arabs, and there is a great deal of stereotyping and animosity between Iranians and Arabs.

Added to this complex identity is tribal identity. It is estimated that 75% of Iraq's people belong to one of the 150 tribes in Iraq (Hassan, 2008). The tribes, in turn, are composed of smaller clans, possibly as many as 2000, with extended families being central elements. The tribes form confederations, called *qabila*. Tribal sheiks traditionally had extensive political and economic power. Tribal identity was and is powerful and served to diminish identification with both the Arab community and the Iraqi state (Hassan, 2008). While Saddam Hussein was in power, tribal identity was initially suppressed, but then used and rewarded during the Iran–Iraq war of the 1980s. After the Gulf War of 1991, Saddam Hussein gave tribal leaders more power and authority because he had lost control of the country. He exchanged greater autonomy for their willingness to secure parts of the country (Hassan, 2008).

Much of the post-Saddam Hussein violence in Iraq, as well as questions about Iraq's future viability as a country, can be understood by looking into the Sunni-Shia-Kurdish identities. First, consider the fate of the Sunnis. Britain took control of what is now Iraq after World War I with the defeat of the Ottoman Empire, which had previously controlled this land. As they did in many places, British authorities chose one ethnic/sectarian group, the Sunnis, to be the politically dominant group in Iraq. Remember, the Sunnis were and are the numerical minority as a sectarian group, yet they emerged as the institutionalized power-holders when Iraq became independent. This continued when the Baathists took over in 1968. Saddam Hussein was a Sunni and their political dominance was maintained under his regime. This, along with the brutality of the regime, fueled deep resentment by Shia and Kurds towards the Sunnis.

After Saddam Hussein was overthrown in 2003, the Coalition Provisional Authority (CPA) was established. Ambassador Paul Bremer III became the civilian adviser in Iraq. Bremer would also become head of the CPA. Under CPA tutelage, the "de-Baathification" process commenced (Diamond, 2005).

Given that the Sunnis dominated positions of power in Saddam's government, and a position of authority required membership in the Baath Party, the reasoning behind this was that the immediate destruction of the Sunni power base was necessary. The CPA also dismantled the Iraqi armed forces and police and Sunni strongholds.

The Sunnis, who had dominated Iraq for decades, now found themselves out of power and unemployed, and many had plentiful arms caches. It seemed to the Sunnis that the Coalition was ensuring their marginalization in post-Saddam Iraq. An insurgency was born, and much of it revolves around identity and humiliation of that identity. As Hashim articulates:

> people fight to gain more ... resources. It is equally true that people also fight not only to maintain or advance things they value materially, but also for a set of *nonmaterial* values that are subsumed under the rubric of identity ... For the Sunni Arabs the downfall of the regime in April 2003 was not only or even primarily the collapse of power and privileges—indeed, many of them had little power and few, if any, privileges—but the entire nationalist edifice that has been in existence for more than eight decades and that had *identified* Iraq with them.
> (Hashim, 2006, pp. 67–68)

The Sunni were humiliated, and we saw in Chapter 3 the power of humiliation as an emotion. As one Sunni told Hashim (2006), "We were on top of the system. We had dreams. Now we are the losers. We lost our positions, our status, the security of our families, stability. Curse the Americans. Curse them" (p. 69). Moreover, the Sunni have a very negative stereotype of the Shia, which has only exacerbated their sense of humiliation. Their stereotype depicts the Shia as dirty, inferior aliens who secretly act as puppets of Iran and the Persians there. Hashim, (2006) quotes one Iraqi Sunni who expresses this stereotype: "They [Shia] cannot rule Iraq properly. They cannot take charge of Iraq in the same manner as the Sunni. The Shiites are backwards. They are barbarian savages, they do not know true religion, theirs is twisted, it is not the true religion of Muhammad" (pp. 71–72). As suggested by this quotation, we can reasonably argue that the image the Sunni hold of the Shia is one of the barbarian. The barbarian image is very threatening, and holds the prospect of the annihilation of the perceivers' group.

Given this loss of power and the crushing humiliation the Sunnis perceived as the majority Shia took power—particularly considering the image they have of the Shia—it is not surprising the Sunni joined insurgent groups trying to oust the Coalition and return the Sunni to their previous position. Moreover, the Sunni did not have effective political leaders who could represent them effectively in the political arena. Insurgency may have seemed their only hope to return to power. The New Baath Party, the 1920 Revolutionary Brigade, and Jaysh Muhammad became the most prominent Sunni insurgent groups. The insurgency also opened opportunities for al-Qaeda to acquire a presence in Iraq. Al-Qaeda in Iraq (AQI) was established and led by Abu Musab al-Zarqawi. Certainly, Iraqis were part of the group, but many foreign fighters filled the ranks for a chance to defend their fellow Muslims against what they believed to be an infidel invader. Alliances were made between the various groups that had a common goal of fighting the Americans, but these relationships were strained. For example, members of the 1920 Revolution Brigades, Army of the Mujahedeen and Ansar al-Sunna were killed by AQI. The killing of Sunnis, in turn, "warranted retaliation under the prevailing tribal code" (Simon, 2008, p. 63). Some tribal leaders soon decided to work against al-Qaeda and formed the new Sunni Awakening groups. While the United States welcomed and rewarded this development, it posed the danger of increasing tribal identity, which worked contrary to the establishment of a new Iraq with a superordinate common Iraqi identity (Simon, 2008).

The other two major sectarian/ethnic groups in Iraq, the Shia and the Kurds, have little sympathy for the Sunnis. The Kurds as a people were originally nomadic and are distributed across Turkey, Iraq, Syria, Iran, and Armenia. They never had their own nation, despite their size (23–28 million) and the fact that they speak their own language. When the Ottoman Empire dissolved after World War I, the Kurds were not given an independent state. Stirrings of nationalism began in the early twentieth century, but efforts to forge an independent state were crushed. The Iraqi Kurds were treated brutally by the Saddam Hussein regime. The regime initiated an "Arabization" effort to increase the Arab population in Kurdistan, effectively a policy of ethnic cleansing. During the Iran–Iraq war of the 1980s, the Kurds were severely repressed by the regime, and civil disturbance on the level of civil war broke out. In March 1988, the regime attacked the Kurdish town of Halabja with chemical weapons, killing thousands. Years later, the Kurds were still affected by the regime's use of chemical weapons. In 1992, for example, BBC News ran a story on Halabja.

> The chemical after-effects of the attack are still affecting people. "Traces of the chemical agents are still residing in the water, air and food," said one surgeon. Since the chemical attacks, the number of various forms of cancer, birth deformities, still-born babies and miscarriages is reported to have dramatically increased.
>
> (BBC News, 2002)

In 1989, some 180,000 Kurds were killed during the Anfal campaign, and a Kurdish uprising in 1991 was also crushed. After the 1991 Gulf War, the Kurds were protected by the international community. Their region in Iraq was designated a no-fly zone and they had de facto autonomy. They began to develop institutions and military forces, the *peshmerga*. The region became governed by the Kurdistan Regional Government (KRG). Needless to say, this autonomy was not something they are willing to give up.

The real question for the Kurds was whether they would ultimately remain in post-Saddam Iraq. For most Kurds, their identity is Kurdish, not Iraqi. Fewer young Kurds speak Arabic today than during the Saddam years, and there is a strong negative stereotype of Iraqis. Hashim argues the stereotype verges on racist, and depicts Iraqi Arabs as vastly inferior people (2006, p. 216). Reporting indicated the Kurds were reversing the Arabization campaign by driving Arabs and Turkmen out of towns where they dominated (Arab News, 2008; Hashim, 2006). At this time, Kurdish authorities did not move toward independence, despite the temptation, largely because the United States did not want to see that develop. The reasons were numerous, ranging from the issue of how to distribute the wealth generated from the oil that lies under Kurdish soil, and Turkish fears an independent Kurdistan would motivate further efforts by Turkish Kurds for independence. Indeed, Turkey bombed Iraqi Kurdistan several times in 2008 in an effort to attack members of the Turkish Kurd independence insurgency, the Kurdistan Workers' Party (PKK).

Finally, the Shia community in Iraq is the majority community historically kept from having a proportionate share of political power. They were influenced by the revolution in Iran and called for the elimination of the secular Baathist government. As Hashim (2006) notes, "the politicization of the Shia via the vehicle of religion constituted a national security threat, a threat to the construction of a seemingly progressive and modernizing Arab power—whose despicable acts and corruption were well-hidden as were its victims—and to the national identity of the country as defined by the Ba'th" (2006, p. 239). The retaliation was predictably brutal, and many Shia were killed or went into exile in Iran. They naturally welcomed the demise of Saddam Hussein's regime.

Post-Saddam Iraq is divided on a number of issues, including the role of Islam in the state as well as the issue of power-sharing with the Sunnis. Some, like Muqtada al-Sadr, are nationalistic, and do not want to share power with the Sunnis. Others, like Ayatollah Ali al-Sistani, are less amenable to the idea of subordination of the Sunni to the Shia majority (Simon, 2008). Supporters of al-Sadr tend to be the poorest residents of the Sadr City slum in Baghdad. Shia divisions reflect differences of opinion on national unity, the role of religion in politics, the presence of the United States, and class-based issues.

There are many different political and paramilitary Shia organizations. Among the most important are the Islamic Dawa Party (the party of Prime Minister Nouri al-Maliki), the Supreme Council of the Islamic Revolution in Iraq (SCIRI), and Jamat al-Sadr al-Thani. The SCIRI is associated with the Badr militia and Jamat al-Sadr al-Thani, led by Muqtada al-Sadr, is associated with the Mahdi militia. There were very serious disputes between these organizations and their followers regarding constitutional issues and the presence of the United States in Iraq, among other things. In 2005, there were violent clashes between the Badr Brigade and the Mahdi army over constitutional issues. Sadr objected to the SCIRI objective of giving the Kurdish north and Shiite south semi-autonomy (*Christian Science Monitor*, 2005). In 2008, fighting broke out again, this time between Sadr's supporters and the Iraqi security forces in the southern port city of Basra. Al-Maliki had asked all political parties to disband their militias before provincial elections were held, and Sadr and his supporters viewed this as an effort to weaken his movement before those elections (Raghavan, 2008, p. A01).

The United States withdrew troops in 2011, and instability in Iraq continued. The Islamic State in Iraq, renamed Islamic State of Iraq and Syria (ISIS), remained a destabilizing force, and expanded its scope of activities into Syria in a violent campaign (see discussion on Syria below). ISIS captured Fallujah in 2013, and in 2014, its leader Abu Bakr al-Baghdadi established an Islamic state in Mosul and called himself caliph. Iraq was in crisis, and mobilization across groups and countries took place.

> The rise of ISIS further split Iraqi society. Grand Ayatollah Ali al-Sistani, the Shia world's top marja, responded to the Sunni jihadis movement with a fatwa calling Iraqis to take up to [sic] arms. Tens of thousands of men, mostly Shia, joined new and old militias, many supported by Iran. More than 60 armed groups eventually merged under the umbrella of the Popular Mobilization Forces (PMF).
>
> (Hamasaeed & Nada, 2020)

The United States also created the Global Coalition to Defeat ISIS, which was a coalition of international institutions and countries; airstrikes ensued. Al-Maliki was ousted amidst allegations of perpetuating sectarianism, and a government that included Sunnis and Kurds was formed by Haider al-Abadi in September 2014. Iraqi forces, together with the Kurdish Peshmerga and U.S.-led coalition, were able to seriously wound ISIS by the end of 2017. Tensions continued to mount between the Kurds and the Iraqi government. In a September 2017 referendum for independence, almost 93% voted for independence, which was rejected by the government of Iraq as not legally binding. President Masoud Barzani and the governing political parties disagreed. Conflict with the Iraqi government ensued, and the KRG lost the Kirkuk oil fields and almost half of its territory. The president resigned. In 2020, KRG Prime Minister Masrour Barzani accused Arab settlers of forcibly evicting Kurdish families.

In May 2018, the country held national elections, and a coalition group of secular Sunnis, Shias and communists won the most seats; however, by October 2019, protests erupted because of perceived lack of change and reform. Hamasaeed and Nada (2020) explain this unusual political coalition, and subsequent protests:

> Shia cleric Moqtada al-Sadr led an unlikely coalition with secular Sunnis and communists that won the largest number of seats while an Iran-backed block came second. Parliament elected veteran Kurdish politician Barham Salih as president and Muhammad al-Halbusi, a 37-year-old Sunni lawmaker, as speaker. Salih designated Adil Abdul al-Mahdi, a 76-year-old economist and veteran Shia politician to be prime minister. Although both have long been desired by Iraqis and international interlocutors to lead in those positions, they were unable to usher the changes in governance and reform that Iraq needed. In October 2019, hundreds of thousands of protestors took to the street to demand change and reform. However, the response from government forces and armed groups was lethal, leaving over 20,000 people injured and more than 450 people killed.

The continued violence and uncertainty carried into 2020 and 2021. In January 2020, in retaliation for the U.S. killing of Qassem Soleimani, leader of Iran's Quds Force, Iran launched missiles at two Iraqi bases occupied by U.S. troops, followed by an attack on the U.S. Embassy. While no deaths were reported, over 100 soldiers were reported to have brain injuries (Hamasaeed & Nada, 2020). ISIS and Hezbollah continued to launch attacks, while the Iraqi government pressured the United States to withdraw troops.

Iraq demonstrates some of the most complex identity-based problems in the world. The resolution of identity-group conflicts, withdrawal of outside forces, and defeat of terrorist groups is essential if Iraq has any hope of finding stability and cohesiveness.

Syria

In Chapter 11, we discussed the Arab Spring. The current conflict in Syria is considered part of that movement. Syria also is considered an ethnic conflict. The country is governed by Baathist President Bashir al-Assad, who succeeded his father, Hafez al-Assad, with the same authoritarian brutality. "What is evident is that Bashar al-Assad, once heralded as a new type of leader in Syria; one who was schooled as an ophthalmologist, and reluctant to lead, is exhibiting the same behavior as his father" (Hesterman & Mastors, 2001). Assad is an Alawite, a sect of Shia Islam. Alawites, or Alawis, are the minority in the country, with Sunnis as the majority. But as far as ethnic groups are concerned, the situation is much more complicated.

Syria is composed of Kurds (mostly Sunni), Arab and Turkmen Alawites, Arab Druze and Ismalis, Arab Syrian, Lebanese, and Iraqis and Iranian Shias (Twelvers), Sunni and Christian Palestinians, Sunni and Alevi Turkmens, and Sunni Circassians. As we demonstrate below, this explains the issues inherent in satisfactorily solving the civil war in which all groups are represented because of shifting alliances, infighting, and outside interference by countries and terrorist groups. Furthermore, these ethnic groups are mixed throughout the country. But is Syria only about ethnic conflict between Sunni and Shia and alliances with other groups and countries? This was not the case at first.

The current conflict in Syria began in March 2011 when protests erupted after teenagers who painted graffiti on the wall in support of the Arab Spring were arrested and tortured. According to Osseiran (2018):

> The Syrian conflict is not only sectarian. It should not be understood solely as a war between Shiites and Sunnis. It is also a class conflict between a wealthy ruling elite and marginalized communities. This is why early protests in 2011 started in peripheral areas that were neglected by the state for years.

Instead of heeding calls for his resignation, Assad responded with force, which only served to fuel more protests and led to the formation of armed rebel groups. Commenting on the initial violence, which eventually resulted in fully fledged civil war, Hesterman and Mastors (2011) explained:

> Syrian President Bashar al-Assad now finds himself in a situation similar to that of his father, with mass civil unrest and demonstration. He has made no noticeable concessions, handling the uprisings with violent suppression. The levels of brutality associated with the current confrontations are startling; eyes of protestors have been gouged, refugee camps have been shelled, and government agents opened fire on mourners at a funeral for their dead children, victims

> of the violence. In October, the government began a campaign of executions aimed at eliminating dissidents and prominent spokesmen for the opposition. Since the unrest began in March, more than 1,700 civilians have been killed in Hama, with another 10,000 arrested or missing. Undeterred, the protests seem to have grown larger. On July 1, over 300,000 people reportedly gathered for a protest in Hama, overwhelming tanks and militia, forcing them to withdraw.

To carry out his repressive campaign, the president relied on the Syrian army, the Shabiha, armed plain-clothes militiamen who were integrated into army units, the Syrian intelligence branch, Mukhabarat, and his personal protection body, the Republican Guard (Hesterman & Mastors, 2011). His regime is mostly composed of Alawite loyalists. Assad's primary support comes from Iran, Hezbollah (see Chapter 12), and Russia.

The Free Syrian Army (FSA), which opposes the regime, is composed of groups drawn from the Sunni majority. But it was not an organized command structure. Thus, as the war progressed, Assad also faced defections from his forces, and the FSA missed the opportunity to coopt them into an organized force (Sary, 2015). The Free Syrian Army fractured, and groups competed with each other. As Sary explained, "the FSA was constantly splintering into competing factions. And as the war in Syria became more atrocious, it began to be reshaped along sectarian lines. A rise in the number of jihadists—both Syrian and foreign—soon followed."

In addition to local jihadist Sunni groups such as Ahrar al-Sham and Jaesh al-Islam, outside terrorist groups such as ISIS and al-Nusra saw an opportunity to gain territory in their quest to establish a caliphate. For example, in 2013 ISIS made headway in the country by seizing territory, prompting the United States, along with some allies and partners, to carry out airstrikes. But these groups also fought among themselves. Added to this mix was the alliance of Kurds, Christians, and Arabs known as the Syrian Democratic Forces (SDF) (Sary, 2015). Therefore, while it can be said that a Syrian opposition existed, it was fractured, composed of different ethnic groups, and pursued its own political and territorial goals, adding to the violence in the country.

Outside material support and intervention by a variety of countries only served to exacerbate the situation. For example, in April 2017 the Syrian government used Sarin gas against the opposition in Idlib province, and the United States responded with airstrikes. Then, in 2019, Turkey invaded the northeastern part of Syria (Operation Spring Shield) and subsequently occupied it because President Tayyip Erdogen claimed that the SDF, dominated by the Kurdish Yekineyen Parastina Gel (YPC), was a terrorist group with ties to the Kurdistan Workers' Party (PKK), which is opposed to the Turkish government. Turkey was already providing support to the Free Syrian Army. The invasion happened a few days after President Trump pulled U.S. troops out of the area.

At the start of the civil war, Assad gave the SDF control of this area to fight the FSA groups. The United States, however, backed SDF, and by early 2021 the group began to gain control of areas in the northeast, where most of the country's oil and wheat production existed, and expelled ISIS. This prompted a siege by the Syrian army, but with Russian mediation there were signs of it being lifted. By 2021, Assad, with strong Russian military support, took back control of most of the country (Nebehay, 2021).

During all this conflict and devastation, the UN sought a political solution with the formation of the Syrian Constitutional Committee, composed of the government and opposition groups. Several rounds of talks, led by the U.N. Special Envoy for Syria, have taken place since 2019, but no solution has been found. Since it appears that Assad managed to gain significant territorial ground, it is not surprising that in 2021, "Representatives of Bashar al-Assad rejected proposals by the Syrian opposition as well as the envoy's own ideas for moving the process forward" (Nebehay, 2021).

Commenting on the situation in Syria after years of civil war, the United States Institute of Peace said in 2020:

> Now in its 10th year, the Syrian conflict has led to more than 500,000 deaths and displaced an estimated 13 million—over half of Syria's pre-war population. Over 6.2 million Syrians are internally displaced, and 5.6 million are refugees, predominantly in Lebanon, Jordan, and Turkey.

What will happen in Syria remains to be seen. But it appears that, after years of conflict and destruction, the situation returned to being dominated by Assad, with no redress for opposition groups. Further, what will happen in the northeastern part of Syria controlled by SDF remains to be seen, especially since it is an important resource area.

The Rohingya of Myanmar

The Rohingya are an ethnic minority of about 3.5 million people, one million of whom lived in Myanmar (Burma), in Rakhine state. They are Muslims and migrated from India and Persia to what was then the Arakan Kingdom in the twelfth century (Wade, 2019). The Rohingya of Myanmar are (or were, as we explain below) a Muslim ethnic minority in a predominantly Buddhist Myanmar. They faced persecution, exclusion and, beginning in August 2017, ethnic cleansing.

Social identities and threats are important for understanding what has happened to the Rohingya. Initially they lived in harmony with the Buddhists. In the 1000s, King Anawratha used Buddhism to unite the people, which "provide[d] a sense of unity and security in times of war and len[t] a moral justness to the defence of borders, but also narrow[d] the spectrum of identities that people can express and still rightly claim membership in the nation" (Wade, 2019, pp. 20–21). When the British colonized the whole area (1824–1948), "Burma," as it was then called, became a province of British India. The British opened the border so more people moved into the area from India, which changed the demographics of the region. Now Indian Muslims and Hindus were the majority, which angered the Barma ethnic group, the majority in the rest of Burma (Wade, 2019). The British also deposed the king, which undermined the political power of the Buddhist clergy.

Burma became independent in 1948 and initially the Rohingya received identity cards. After the 1962 military coup, however, they were not considered citizens and instead of national identity cards they received foreign identity cards. The military and succeeding military government was almost entirely Barma Buddhist, and they called for national unity, a return to a noble past, which meant national identity coincided with Buddhism, and the clergy would once again have political power (Wade, 2019). The situation became worse in 1982 when a new citizenship law declared 135 ethnic groups native to Myanmar, and the Rohingya were not among them. This meant they were essentially stateless, despite the fact their people had lived there for centuries. As a result, they could not vote, travel outside of their village, marry without permission, get an education, work, or enjoy any of the rights conferred by citizenship. They were basically illegal immigrants with no legal documents (CFR, 2020). They were clearly considered inferior and stereotyped as "black skinned (Kalar)" with "big bellies", and the men were accused of trying to marry Barma women (Wade, 2019, p. 101). The UN stated that the perception "demonstrates the hateful, widespread and mainstream perception by Myanmar's Bamar majority of the 'sub-human' status of the Rohingya. Their continued segregation from the rest of Myanmar society through the continued imposition of movement restrictions cements this perception. It is a visible sign of their continued persecution" (p. 176). Rakine state, where most Rohingya Muslims lived, had a poverty rate of 78% compared with the national average of 37.5% (CFR, 2020).

As the military junta loosened its control in a move toward democratization, a freer press and pro-democracy movement actually made things worse for the Rohingya. The press inflamed feelings about the Rohingya and anti-Rohingya rhetoric was spewed by Buddhist monks. They formed the 969 movement, which was very hostile toward the Rohingya, and when it was dismantled it was replaced by the Organization for the Protection of Race, Religion, and Sasana (Ma Ba Tha), which had the same leadership as 969 (Wade, 2019). The monks were politically powerful. Even some in the pro-democracy movement, such as Ko Ko Gyi, regarded the Rohingya as illegals, and the Nobel Laureate who won the honor for her work in human rights, Aung Sun Suu Kyi, remained silent. Buddhists sympathetic to the Rohingya were considered traitors (Wade, 2019).

In 2012, the rape and murder of a Buddhist woman by Muslims increased ethnic conflict in Rakine state. Then, in August 2017, Rohingya militants attacked police and army posts. The government and Buddhist militias began a violent campaign against the Rohingya. Killings, arson of villages, and rape ensued; 1000 people were killed and 300,000 began an exodus, fleeing the area. The United States called the military action "disproportionate" and Myanmar's treatment of the Rohingya a "textbook example" of ethnic cleansing (Ratcliff, 2017). By 2019, over 900,000 Rohingya made the dangerous journey to squalid, overcrowded refugee camps in Bangladesh (UNOCHA, 2019a, p. 1). The Rohingya have been called the most persecuted people in the world, and are clearly the victims of hyper identity-based hostility and negative stereotyping by the Buddhist majority in Myanmar. They continue to live in misery.

The Perpetrators of Genocide

The cases of ethnic conflict described in this chapter ranged from somewhat to very violent, including the pursuit of ethnic cleansing. But in a few cases, the violence perpetrated against an ethnic group went to the extreme of genocide, and we will look at three cases of genocide below. In some cases, such as Rwanda, genocide is planned by an organized group of political extremists. But in other cases, such as the Holocaust in Europe during World War II, it is the product not only of a group (the SS), but also of a large, complex bureaucratic system. In addition, the discussion in this chapter should not mislead readers into thinking that genocide is only the product of extremist groups. In theory, the conditions that produce genocide can occur anywhere, and genocide can be committed by very ordinary people.

What is genocide? The UN defines **genocide** as "acts committed with the intent to destroy in part or in whole a national, ethnic, racial, or religious group as such," which Staub (2000) has objected to on several grounds. First, it does not include political groups as specific possible targets of genocide. Second, it groups killing the group in whole or in part as constituting genocide, whereas Staub argues that killing in part is mass killing. Mass killing may kill many people, as does genocide, but genocide as an act is designed to eliminate the group from the face of the Earth.

Genocide is a result of an intense feeling of frustration and threat, produced by a combination of many of the psychological patterns discussed in Chapters 3 and 4—social identity factors, stereotyping, and group loyalties—usually operating in the context of extremely difficult social economic and political circumstances. As Staub (1989) explains, "powerful self-protective motives then arise: the motive to defend the physical self (one's life and safety) and the motive to defend the psychological self (one's self-concept, values, and ways of life). There is a need to both protect self-esteem and to protect values and traditions. There is also a need to elevate a diminished self" (p. 15), which some argue can be the result of a harsh childhood upbringing (Milburn & Conrad, 1996; Miller, 1983). If an enemy is not readily identified as the cause of the condition, one is created—becoming a scapegoat. Similarly, in interviews with Nazi perpetrators, Monroe (2008) found a strong sense of victimization. They felt they were victims, and needed to get rid of the threat before it could intensify. The perception of victimization gives rise to intense emotions, including shame, anger, humiliation, and hatred for the victimizer (Chirot & McCauley, 2006).

Why Not Kill Them All?

In their 2006 book with this title, Daniel Chirot and Clark McCauley address this important question. They argue that one simple explanation is that mass killing is very costly, and it is very dangerous in that threatened groups will react with violence to protect themselves. Killing others may mean getting killed yourself. They also note that many societies throughout history have had codes of conduct that limit the

(*Continued*)

(*Continued*)

scope of killing during conflict. A third factor they identify is the practice of marrying outside of one's group, known as exogamy. This has many origins and is common across cultures and time. It enhances the potential to build alliances, and this leads to an incentive to limit violence. Modern manifestations of these practices include arms control agreements, the establishment of strong states that can prevent violence within societies, and assimilation in ethnically and racially mixed countries. Chirot and McCauley also note that "those who have studied modern genocides have noted that the major ones in the twentieth century took place after periods of great social and economic instability. The old rules no longer seemed to apply."

(Chirot & McCauley, 2006, p. 111)

Although some argue that certain cultures are more disposed to this than others (e.g., Staub, 1989), the potential for violence of this magnitude exists in most cultures. The more cohesive a group is, the more likely the potential, particularly when it is accompanied by a sense of superiority. This is especially evident when nationalism is strong in a country. Other predisposing characteristics for mass killing and genocide include strong respect for authority and strong inclination for obedience. Those characteristics make it more likely that personal responsibility will be relinquished, and leaders will be followed without question. In addition, people are susceptible to the foot-in-the-door technique, wherein they respond positively to a small request and then become much more likely to respond positively to subsequent requests. Freedman and Fraser (1966) maintain that in the process of complying to first one, and then another, request, people change their attitudes about what they are doing, and they may also change their attitudes about themselves (from, for example, "I'm not the kind of person who hits others" to "I am the kind of person who hits others, and hitting is not a bad thing to do").

Genocides are also facilitated by organizations. Organizations overseeing and promoting genocide enable the perpetrators to divest themselves of responsibility for their actions. Organizations also impose norms and group loyalties so those individuals who do not like the tasks they are supposed to fulfill will be made to feel guilty for not adhering to the groups' norms, and for not carrying out their fair share of the work (Chirot & McCauley, 2006; Waller, 2002).

In the twentieth century, there were a number of horrific cases of genocidal violence. Genocide occurred in Turkey, where approximately one and a half million Armenians lost their lives from 1915 to 1917, and in Cambodia, where two million died from 1975 to 1979. The greatest loss of life in a genocide case took place in the Holocaust during World War II, but the genocide in Rwanda, which took the lives of around one million, occurred in the space of a mere three months, from April through June of 1994, a kill ratio five times greater per day than during the Holocaust. Genocide in the Darfur region of Sudan resulted in close to 500,000 deaths and the displacement of over 2.8 million people. The three cases of genocide we consider below offer evidence of all the political psychological patterns discussed above.

THE HOLOCAUST

As we have seen in the previous chapter, Germans were strongly nationalistic, devoted to the nation as a group. Germany suffered terribly from the demands of the Treaty of Versailles and the Great Depression of the 1930s. The Weimar Republic was seen as a government imposed by the victors of World War I and there was considerable political instability on top of the social and economic problems. In 1933, Adolf Hitler achieved his goal of being appointed Chancellor of the German Reichstag, or parliament, and was able to capture the mantle of German nationalism. Once established, his regime, the Third Reich, instituted a repressive political system that made dissent increasingly dangerous. The SS (*Schutzstaffeln*, i.e., security echelon), which began in 1922 as Hitler's personal security force, later became the organization responsible for most of the genocide. When Hitler came to power, he established control over the entire police system in Germany and used it to repress dissent. The concentration camps were set up in 1933, but initially they were used to detain political enemies from leftist political parties, the clergy, liberals, and "undesirables" such as homosexuals (Dicks, 1972).

Thus, the German nation held the in-group quality discussed above, the political and economic situation contained the ingredients that motivate the search for a scapegoat in order to bolster positive group esteem, and Jews were an easy target for vilification and dehumanization by the Nazis. Political repression made resistance difficult and passive acquiescence easy. For those who complied, resistance was far more difficult than under the conditions of the Milgram experiment, and we saw how many complied under those weak conditions. Finally, the Holocaust did not occur overnight. It was a gradual process beginning in 1933 with relatively mild (compared with what was to come) forms of discrimination against Jews in areas such as employment and rights. Later they were prohibited from owning businesses and were forced to wear a yellow six-pointed star to identify themselves as Jews. The deportation of Jews to concentration camps began in 1938, but mass extermination in the concentration camps did not come until the order was given by Hitler in 1941, by which time the maltreatment of, and discrimination against, Jews became "normal." These characteristics of German politics and political psychology help us understand both the willingness to identify with the nation, to vilify a scapegoat, and for those who did not agree with the government, to become passive bystanders.

Still, there are other important ingredients in this case that help us understand how Germany went from a condition of intolerance, repression, and scapegoating to the establishment of a giant death machine that sought ultimately to annihilate the Jewish population of Europe. A look at the characteristics of the Nazi leadership and the followers who carried out the genocide is important. Many Nazi leaders claimed they did what they did because they were following orders, behaving like good citizens and soldiers. But this is far too simple an explanation of their deeds. They did not just follow orders, but willingly carried out and developed enormous acts of cruelty designed not only to kill, but to also to make victims suffer terribly before they died. Studies conducted on leaders in the SS report both significant elements of authoritarian personality in many, and also fanatical loyalty to the SS, which then led to a refusal to disobey orders, or admit to qualms about carrying out genocide (Dicks, 1972; Staub, 1989). SS training techniques were similar to those described in other extremist groups—harsh discipline, ideological indoctrination, glorification of the group, and fanaticism. In addition, belonging to the SS provided career opportunities, something that was reportedly important for many. The people who participated in the killings of Jews did so under the auspices of authorities that they viewed as legitimate. By obeying these legitimate governmental authorities, perpetrators' judgment was subordinated to them. Thus, they were able to participate in the murder of Jews, despite personal misgivings, and even feelings of guilt in some cases. Norman Dicks (1972), a psychiatrist who interviewed SS officers imprisoned for their crimes against humanity, provides an interesting assessment of these men. He notes their ordinariness, but also the fact that they

> at some point crossed the line between their previous "law abiding" lives and their subsequent killer careers. And—their SS roles ended or interrupted—these same "fiends incarnate" in various ways disappeared quietly into civilian life, in some instances resumed orderly and normal careers, and are in prison "the easiest convicts to handle."
>
> (Dicks, 1972, p. 234)

Dicks (1972) and Lifton (1986) both believe they were able to oversee and participate in the extermination of millions of people because they could split or compartmentalize those actions from the rest of their lives. Hence, they could be loving fathers at home, yet murderers at work. They varied in personality, of course, with some coming to the extermination of Jews reluctantly, others with enthusiasm. But, they were not "Mad Nazis" (Waller, 2002). After years of controversy regarding the interpretation of personality tests called Rorschachs, a definitive reexamination in the 1980s found Nazi leaders who stood trial at Nuremberg were essentially normal people, albeit above average in intelligence (Waller, 2002).

Additional personality characteristics were noted by Monroe (2008), who found that Nazi sympathizers had strong values integral to their self-identity. These values included "a passionate commitment to the Nazi cause, racial purity, [and] cultural separatism" (p. 723). In terms of their categorization of the world around them, they saw a strong distinction between themselves and Jews, which included a sense of racial difference and superiority. One generalization that can be made is that these perpetrators were not insane, but were for personal reasons susceptible to the SS indoctrination, and thereafter group dynamics and fanaticism took over.

In addition to the group dynamics, the Nazi political system had some important elements that facilitated the size of the genocide. Much of this was done in concentration camps, but the political police and *Einsatzgruppen* (special mission groups) in the SS units followed the German army as it swept eastward through eastern Europe, and executed thousands of "undesirables"—Jews, Gypsies, communists, homosexuals, and so on. Typically, they were rounded up, a big ditch was dug, and they were shot and thrown into the ditch, dead or alive. The task was extremely difficult, even for the most dedicated Nazis. Personal contact with those who were to be executed proved to be a major problem. The *Einsatzgruppen* men were actually told they did not have to participate in the executions because the officers understood that compelling them to do so could backfire and break the units (Browning, 1992). They were also given plenty of alcohol and were required to work only for short periods of time.

Depersonalization was also important in facilitating the genocide. The camps were organized in such a way that personal identification with the victims did not need to occur. Gas chambers were constructed to kill on a massive scale, and to eliminate personal responsibility for the killing. Some Jews were spared so that they, not the SS, could remove gold from the mouths of victims, collect their clothing, and so on. Then there was the massive bureaucracy that divided the entire process, provided bureaucratic rules guiding the process, and permitted people who participated in the process of exterminating the Jews to deny personal responsibility (Sabini & Silver, 1993). The engineer who drove the cattle cars filled with people destined for the gas chambers could avoid responsibility because he just drove the train—he did not kill anyone. Different ministries handled different portions of the destruction of the Jewish population, with one taking their property, another firing them from their jobs, another rounding them up, and another sending them off to die.

This situation parallels the Milgram obedience experiments described earlier. In those experiments, the "learner" (the person who was supposedly receiving electric shocks) was out of view of the teacher (the person administering the shock). In some ways, this situation allowed the learners to be depersonalized, making it easier for the teacher to administer such high levels of shock. This situation also parallels the Milgram experiments because the teacher did not feel responsibility for shocking the learner. This **diffusion of responsibility** occurs when there is more than one person present in the situation to take all or some of the responsibility for the outcomes. In the Milgram experiment, many of the participants asked the experimenter whether he was going to take responsibility for whatever happened to the learner. When the experimenter responded that he would, this gave the participants a green light to continue shocking the learner. In most cases, however, the diffusion of responsibility is perceived rather than actually distributed among actors in the situation.

RWANDA

For roughly three months in the spring of 1994, the international community witnessed, and did nothing to stop, the genocide of Tutsis and moderate Hutus by more extremist Hutus in Rwanda. In public view, Tutsis were systematically rounded up and shot, stabbed, beaten, or hacked to death with machetes. The *New York Times* reported on April 10, 1994, just four days after the violence started, "that 'tens of thousands' were dead, 8000 in Kigali [the capital city] alone, and that corpses were in the houses, in the streets, everywhere" (quoted in Power, 2002, p. 256). How could this have happened?

Rwanda, like many African countries, was colonized by Europeans—first Germany and then Belgium. Before colonialism, the Hutus and Tutsis lived in relative harmony. They spoke the same language, practiced the same religion and were economically interdependent. Tutsis were herders and Hutus usually were farmers. As Peterson (2000b) notes, the "caste system was largely apolitical: Tutsi came to mean 'rich,' someone with many long-horned cows; Hutu, or 'servant' came to mean someone with fewer than ten cows" (p. 258). Under certain circumstances, a Hutu could become a Tutsi. Over time, the Tutsi, along with a few Hutu, became the economic and political elite.

When the Belgians arrived in Rwanda after World War I, they sought to impose their own colonial administration. Even though Hutus were the majority, the Belgians chose to put Tutsis in positions of power. The Belgians selected the Tutsis because they had aquiline features, and thus looked more similar to the Belgians than did than Hutus; therefore, the Belgians reasoned, the Tutsis must be the superior group (Human Rights Watch, 1999). The Belgians created a system of colonial administration in which the Tutsis were favored in jobs and education. Ethnic identity cards were issued. Tutsis became the administrative elite for Belgian colonial rule. Because they were able to benefit from the colonial system, Hutus considered Tutsis an elitist class and an arm of the colonial state. Ethnicity was thereby politicized by colonialism, and would return to haunt Rwanda many times. Rwanda gained its independence from Belgium in 1959 when the Hutus overthrew the colonizers. During this drive for independence, many Tutsis were driven into exile.

By the late 1980s, the Tutsis in exile desired a permanent home, and wanted to return to Rwanda. However, in 1986 the Hutu government, led by General Juvenal Habyarimana, argued that Rwanda was overpopulated, and could not accommodate the refugees. By July 1990, the government seemed to be making progress toward their accommodation. However, according to the Rwandan Patriotic Front (RPF), a Tutsi-led rebel army operating from neighboring Uganda, Habyarimana not only needed to facilitate the return of the Tutsi refugees, but also establish a democratic government that replaced a one-party state dominated by him (Human Rights Watch, 1999). On October 1, 1990, hoping to overthrow Habyarimana, the RPF left Uganda and attacked a small detachment of the Rwandan military. From there they made their way to Kigali, the capital. In response, Habyarimana falsely claimed the RPF attacked the capital, hoping to mobilize Hutus against the RPF and gain the support of the international community. The government cracked down, and 13,000 people were arrested and detained (Human Rights Watch, 1999). Habyarimana's strategy was to divide the Hutus who supported him from those Tutsis and Hutus who collaborated with the enemy. This resulted in the deaths of many Tutsis and moderate Hutus who were attacked and killed.

By 1991, support for Habyarimana was waning as opposition parties demanding change began to emerge. Habyarimana and his supporters created a militia known as the Interahamwe, whose members were allowed to attack Tutsis without any repercussions. Civilian defense groups were also created. But the RPF continued to make advancements and forced the Habyarimana government to enter into negotiations. The RPF and the government finally signed a ceasefire in Arusha, Tanzania, in July 1992 and a series of agreements that became known as the Arusha Accords were finally signed in August 1993. This was a power-sharing agreement wherein military commanders would be 50/50 Tutsi/Hutu and troops would be 40% Tutsi and 60% Hutu. This clearly did not reflect the distribution of the Tutsi and Hutu population in Rwanda, which was 14% and 85% respectively. In an attempt to monitor the implementation of the accords, on October 5, 1993, under the name of the U.N. Assistance Mission in Rwanda (UNAMIR), the UN finally allocated 2548 peacekeeping troops. Despite the accords, the killing of Tutsis continued, but Hutu extremists were planning much worse to come.

On April 6, 1994, Habyarimana was returning from Tanzania when his plane was hit by two surface-to-air missiles. Even though the identity of those responsible is not certain, after the news of his death broke, the Hutus mobilized. A well-organized and systematic campaign to rid Rwanda of Tutsis and Hutus who were suspected of not supporting the government-backed campaign to eradicate the Tutsis was begun by the armed forces, including the police, and the paramilitaries, the Interahamwe and the Impuzamugambi. This campaign lasted roughly three months, and over one million people are estimated to have been killed. By April 21, after the murder and mutilation of 10 Belgian peacekeepers, the UN withdrew the rest of its forces from the country. The slaughter of Tutsis continued unabated for three months. When it ended, as one Hutu told a journalist, "It's not out of kindness ... but because there are so few Tutsis left alive" (Peterson, 2000b, p. 288).

In July 1994, the RPF defeated the Hutu government. Paul Kagame, the leader of the RPF, installed Pasteur Bizimungu as President. A Hutu, Bizimungu was chosen to reflect the diversity of the new administration although it is widely believed that Kagame was running the government from behind the scenes (Simpson, 2000b). In March 2000, Bizimungu resigned and Kagame was chosen by Parliament to officially become the President of Rwanda.

For the first time since independence, the Tutsis were the governing ethnic group. Yet the conflict does not seem to be over because the Interahamwe militia has regrouped and is now waging a war against the government from the Congo. This has prompted Rwandan and Ugandan troops, together with the Congolese rebel group the Congolese Rally for Democracy (RCD), to wage a war against the Congolese President Laurent Kabila's (Kabila was assassinated on January 17, 2000, and his son Joseph became president) government troops and the Rwandan and Burundian militia fighters (Talbot, 2000). Because ethnicity is the primary basis for group loyalty, and served as a basis for the conflict, the question remains: How long will Tutsis remain in power?

The Rwanda genocide shares many of the characteristics of the Holocaust, but there are some important differences as well. Social and economic conditions in Rwanda before the massacre were difficult, as was the case in Germany when Hitler came to power. Rwanda was overpopulated and one of the poorest countries in Africa. All but 5% of its land was under cultivation, the average woman had nine children, and hunger was rampant (Peterson, 2000b). The majority Hutus had suffered significant strategic losses to the Tutsi rebel forces and faced the prospect of having to share power with them. Germany, too, had experienced the loss of World War I, a factor in setting the stage for that genocide. In addition, as in Germany, there was a legacy of Hutu–Tutsi stereotyping, mutated by the influence of the colonial powers. By the time this holocaust took place, Tutsis were dehumanized by the Hutu, who called the Tutsis *inyenzi* (cockroaches). The Hutu extremists were organized in a political party, the Mouvement Révolutionnaire National pour le Développement (National Revolutionary Movement for Development, MRND), which, in turn, had the paramilitary organization, the Interahamwe. The Impuzamugambi were associated with the hardline Hutu organization the Coalition pour la Défense de la République (Coalition for the Defense of the Republic, CDR). The party and its leaders promoted an ideology of "Hutu Power" complete with a document of anti-Tutsi "principles," such as "every Hutu should know that every Tutsi is dishonest in business. His only aim is the supremacy of this ethnic group ... All strategic positions ... should be entrusted to Hutus ... The Hutu should stop having mercy on the Tutsi" (quoted in Power, 2002, p. 339). Any Hutu who did not agree was considered a traitor. Again, this resembles Germany's Nazi Party and Nazi ideology.

As in Germany, this genocide was planned in advance by the Hutu political and military leaders. The Rwandan army began to train the Interahamwe in 1990, which resembled the Nazi SS in that it offered members strong psychological and material rewards. Prominent Hutu leaders began publicly to call for the elimination of the Tutsis as early as 1992. For example, Leoin Mugeser, a member of the MNDR, stated in 1992 that, "The fatal mistake we made in 1959 was to let [the Tutsi] get out ... They belong in Ethiopia and we are going to find them a shortcut to get there by throwing them into the Nyabarongo River. I must insist on this point. We have to act. Wipe them all out!" (quoted in Power, 2002). And finally, as in the case of the German commanders of the Holocaust, who claimed to be only following orders, the perpetrators of this violence demonstrated little remorse.

But there are differences in these genocides. Rwanda's was not as technical, depersonalized, and hidden as Germany's. There was no complex bureaucracy that carried out the genocide in bits and pieces. Here every Hutu was either involved in the killing, or in hiding. Although this permitted diffusion of responsibility, as was the case in Germany, the average citizen took a hand in the direct killing in Rwanda—that is, publicly hacking Tutsis with machetes and clubs, stabbing them, or—if merciful—shooting them. As a *Frontline* documentary stated,

> the main agents of the genocide were the ordinary peasants themselves ... [E]ven in the cases where people did not move spontaneously but were forced to take part in the killings, they were helped along into violence by the mental and emotional lubricant of ideology. We can see it for example in the testimony of this seventy-four year-old "killer" captured by the RPF: "I regret what I did ... I am ashamed,

> but what would you have done if you had been in my place? Either you took part in the massacre or else you were massacred yourself. So I took weapons and *I defended the members of my tribe against the Tutsi.*"
>
> (*Frontline*, 1998, p. 4; italics added)

DARFUR

Darfur is a region in western Sudan that abuts Chad. Fighting started there in February 2003. In September 2004, Colin Powell, who was then U.S. Secretary of State, called the situation in Darfur genocide. Nevertheless, the UN did not formally deem Darfur genocide and was heavily criticized. It is estimated that close to half a million people were killed in the conflict and almost three million became refugees (Cotler, 2008). The conflict in Darfur was described as a conflict between Arabs and Africans but, as discussed below, this is a gross oversimplification.

There are numerous groups or tribes in Darfur, with the estimate ranging from 40 to 90 (Flint & de Waal, 2005). Darfur was an independent Sultanate from 1600 to 1916, with the exception of a period from 1874 to 1898. The Darfur Sultanate was quite powerful, trading within the Mediterranean. In 1917, it was taken over by the British.

Darfur's population and ethnic mixture are a result of centuries of migration. If there is an Indigenous ethnic group, it is the Fur, but it is difficult to know for certain about the population in Darfur before the fourteenth century because of the lack of a written history (Prunier, 2005). Other ethnic groups include the Zaghawa, the Berti, the Bidayat, who came from the northwest, the Birgid, and the Meidob, who came from the northeast (Prunier, 2005). Arab ethnic groups began to migrate into the region in the fourteenth century and include the Ziyadiyya, Ta'aisha, Beni Halba, Habbaniya, and Rizzeqat (Prunier, 2005). There are also many other ethnic groups.

The Sultanate was a Fur Muslim Sultanate. As the Sultanate expanded southward, it spread Islam (people had to convert or leave), and the Fur language; over time, people became Fur themselves (Flint & de Waal, 2005; Prunier, 2005). But the nature of the Sultanate evolved as time passed. As Prunier explains:

> The Fur has produced the Sultanate (and the other way around) but it soon stopped being exclusively or even mainly theirs. Since the kingdom's population was largely multi-ethnic (even after the Fur "assimilation" of the first years), it was held together by a complex system of Arabo-Islamic legitimacy and Sudanic sacred ritual.
>
> (Prunier, 2005, p. 11)

The Sultanate's land ownership system was called the *hakura*. *Hakura* holders collected dues from people living in their *hakura*, and over time gathered family members in the *hakura*. These would then form a "tribe" (Flint & de Waal, 2005). The land-holding rights and patterns are important because they influence the crisis in Darfur in later years.

Arab migration into Darfur took place largely between the fourteenth and eighteenth centuries. They included individuals and the Juhayna Bedouins. These ethnic groups raised cattle and became sedentary. They were known as the Baggara. The four main Baggara groups, Ta'aisha, Beni Halba, Habbaniya, and Rizeigat, were given large *hakuras* by the Sultan. The other Arabs, the Abbala Arabs, did not get land and remained nomads in the northern provinces (Flint & de Waal, 2005).

In typical British colonial style, they selected local authorities to administer the area. They chose the Arab tribes. The Darfur region of Sudan was largely ignored under British colonialism. In 1935, they had "one elementary school, one 'tribal' elementary school, and two sub-grade schools" (Flint & de Waal, 2005, p. 15). Only the sons of chiefs were allowed to be educated in order to protect their power and privilege. There was no investment or development in Darfur.

Darfur won independence on January 1, 1956. This was followed by a military dictatorship from 1958 to 1965, led by Brigadier-General Ibrahim Abboud. Darfur continued to be neglected. The first post-dictatorship elections were held in May 1965, but there was another coup in 1969, and Colonel Jaafor al-Nimiery came to power. He relied on the backing of the Communist Party, and other political parties were marginalized. Throughout, the country was dominated by the so-called Blue Nile Arabs, the people who lived along the Nile. The people of Darfur remained powerless.

During the 1960s, Darfur was also affected by events in Chad. In 1965, Chad embarked on a civil war between the north and the south. Darfur borders Chad, and because the border is an artificial one, there were many members of the same ethnic group on both sides of the border. Complicating this was the interest of Colonel Gaddafi of Libya in the Chad conflict. Gaddafi supported the revolutionaries (northern and Muslim). Gaddafi was an Arab nationalist and overt racist. In 1976, a Libyan-trained militia of Sudanese attacked the Sudan capital of Khartoum in an effort to overthrow Nimieri. As a result, Nimieri gave his support to the Chad faction most hostile to Libya. The impact of these machinations on Darfur, particularly on the inter-ethnic group relationships, was strong. As Prunier describes below, stereotypes and inter-group hostilities were imported into Darfur:

> This rough handling of Darfur by Libyans, the Chadians, and the Khartoum forces decisively worsened the regional ethno-political landscape. Tribes which had seen themselves primarily in local terms were suddenly catapulted into a broader artificial world where they were summoned to declare themselves as either Arab or *zurqa*. The Arabs were "progressive" or "revolutionary" while the Africans were "anti-Arab" and "reactionary."
>
> (Prunier, 2005, p. 46)

Meanwhile, Darfur had years of drought, which produced severe hardships and, by 1984, famine. Lack of rainfall forced the semi-nomadic tribes to become completely nomadic, moving their herds farther and farther in search of food. This led them to encroach on the land of farming peasants. The farmers naturally did not like this because it interfered with their traditional way of life, and they blocked nomadic passage. To make things worse, the government of Sudan did not want to admit a famine was occurring.

The identities politicized by Darfur's role in the Chad civil war, and the resentments produced by the drought and famine, combined to cause negative stereotypes among "Arabs" and "Africans" in Darfur. According to Prunier,

> The "Arabs" did not care about the famine which the "African" governor had tried to prevent. Now that it was over, the "Africans" were trying to make the "Arab" victims pay and to cut them off from available pastureland. The "Arabs" were thieves who were trying to steal the livestock which remained in "African" hands. The selfish "Africans" shot at the "Arabs" who were then just recuperating from the famine. The "Arabs" were killers who got weapons from Libyan troops and the Chadian insurgents to steal what they could from the "Africans."
>
> Prunier, 2005, p. 58)

The next important development on the path to genocide was the Sudanese civil war between the North and the South. In 1983, Nimieri introduced Islamic Sharia Law to Sudan, which caused the Christian south to revolt. Many of the northern soldiers came from Darfur. In April 1985, Nimieri was overthrown. There was a civilian government that struggled for a time. A military coup led by General Omar al-Bashir overthrew that government in 1989, and brought the Islamic National Front, whose leader was Hassan al-Turabi, to a position of political power. Bashir declared himself the head of the Revolutionary Command Council. He then became the President when the Revolutionary Command Council dissolved itself in 1993. The Blue Nile people, however, continued to dominate.

The civil war between north and south ended in a negotiated peace in 2002 amidst a new bonanza of oil, in the southern part of the country. Things seemed to be going well for Sudan, but the situation in Darfur was deteriorating quickly. There was a great deal of resentment about the lack of resources coming into Darfur, particularly in light of the contribution the region had made to the north during the civil war. In 1996, three Fur activists established a clandestine organization. They then began to try to organize the scattered resistance activities that were merging all over Darfur. Eventually, the Fur and Masalit ethnic groups formed an alliance with one of the Zaghawa clans, and established the Sudan Liberation Army. A second rebel organization also formed, called the Justice and Equality Movement (JEM). The rebellion began in February 2003. The rebels' demands were not for independence, but for better treatment, a bigger share of the country's resources, decentralization, and more self-determination (Flint & de Waal, 2005; Prunier, 2005). They launched attacks against villages and government offices.

The response of the Bashir government was to attack the "African" villages of Darfur. They bombed and launched ground attacks. The government forces and the Janjaweed militias who supported the government have been accused of mass slaughter, rape, the destruction of entire villages, and other human rights violations. Of particular importance is the Janjaweed. The word means "devil on horseback" and these militias are literally that. They were initially formed during the north–south war and it is alleged that the government encouraged their actions. The Janjaweed recruited from demobilized soldiers from the army, young members of Arab tribes having land conflicts with neighboring African tribes, common criminals who were pardoned and released from jail on condition they join the militia, members of the Tajammu al-Arabi (Union of Arabs, a militant racist organization), and young, unemployed "Arab" men and bandits (Prunier, 2005, p. 97).

The Darfur Peace Agreement (Doha Agreement) was signed by the government and Sudan Liberation Movement in 2006, but not by the Justice and Equality Movement, and the conflict continued. At the beginning of March 2009, Bashir was indicted by the International Criminal Court for the atrocities committed in Darfur. The Liberation and Justice Movement emerged to represent several rebel groups. In 2010, JEM agreed to the Doha Agreement. In July 2011, Sudan split into two countries, to form Sudan in the north, and South Sudan.

BYSTANDERS AND ALTRUISTS

In New York City one night in 1963, a woman named Kitty Genovese was stabbed to death. Her assailant beat and stabbed her for close to an hour while dozens of people heard her screams and saw her being attacked, but did nothing. This tragic story is often used to illustrate the bystander phenomenon—when people do nothing to help others. Why does this happen? There is a tendency to blame the bystanders as being apathetic or uncaring, but researchers Latane and Darley (1970) argue that situational factors can explain the lack of help given to Kitty Genovese. When people are bystanders in an emergency situation, they sometimes experience *pluralistic ignorance*. They do not know how to respond, so they look to others to see how to respond (as in informational social influence, described in Chapter 4). The problem is, everyone is looking at everyone else to figure out how to respond. Unfortunately, the result is that bystanders become paralyzed and do not respond at all. A second situational determinant that can explain the lack of help often given to those in emergency situations is diffusion of responsibility. If you were the only person available to help, then you would have 100% of the responsibility to give help. But if just one other person is present, then your sense of responsibility drops to 50%. The more people who are present in a situation, the more diffused is the responsibility. It is partly due to group characteristics. When people are part of a group, there is a diffusion of responsibility, and people feel less compelled to intervene and help. Many analysts believe that the **bystander phenomenon** is a crucial component in genocide.

Bystanders know, at least implicitly, that something wrong is happening, and they do nothing about it. A bystander can be a person, a group, an organization, or a country. Indeed, the entire international community knew about the genocide unfolding in Europe and, 50 years later, in Rwanda, and we did nothing. We engaged in denial. Stanley Cohen maintains that denial "includes *cognition* (not acknowledging the facts); *emotion* (not feeling, not being disturbed); *morality* (not recognizing wrongness or responsibility) and *action* (not taking steps in response to knowledge)" (Cohen, 2001, p. 9). Milburn and Conrad (1996) argue that at the individual and social levels, denial is a product of an unwillingness to face a horrifically painful reality. This, they contend, stems from childhood denial of punitive parental treatment. Denial is also often a subtle social pressure. Everyone knows and no one admits what is happening. Those who do are condemned or ostracized by the group. To admit something bad is happening is often threatening to the group's self-image, so avoiding or ignoring information is necessary to maintain the positive self-image and to be complicit in the general denial. Hence many Germans could ignore the evidence that Jews and others were being exterminated in death camps because Germans, by definition, are good people, and good people do not do such things. It is often extremely difficult for individuals *not* to be bystanders in the face of political violence. They are often threatened with severe punishment if not death, they do not know what to do or how to act, and they know as individuals they have little power to do anything. Yet still some individuals do act, hiding a Jew or a Tutsi, managing to save lives, one at a time.

Denial comes in many forms. People deny inflicting pain (it was an accident), that an injury occurred (no one was really hurt), that the victim is a victim (he or she deserved it), and that they had no knowledge about atrocities. Denial also comes in degrees, from knowing about but refusing to believe information, to knowing but maintaining only a vague awareness of the facts, to knowing, being aware, and choosing to do nothing (Cohen, 2001; Monroe, 2008). For example, to this day arguments abound as to how much ordinary Germans knew about the Holocaust, and those arguments will inevitably continue because many Germans did not then, and cannot now, recognize the extent to which they knew, but did not attend to, information about the extermination of Jews and others. As Walter Laqueur wrote, "It is, in fact, quite likely that while many Germans thought that the Jews were no longer alive, they did not necessarily believe that they were dead" (Laqueur, 1980, p. 201).

The likelihood that people will engage in denial and refuse to help victims of violence is augmented when there are many people involved (as in a crowd surrounding an accident victim), when the situation is ambiguous, and when people are fearful of the reaction of others. People are also influenced by a belief in a just world. They believe the world is benevolent, and that bad things only happen to bad people. Therefore, if the SS hauls someone off, that person must have done something wrong. This belief comforts people by letting them think the world is stable, certain, and predictable (Cohen, 2001; Staub, 1989). These patterns can be seen in Germany and in Argentina during the "dirty war" (1976–83), where bystanders abounded. In both cases the information was, for many, very ambiguous. In both cases there was no free press that provided concrete and undeniable information that atrocities were occurring. To speak out against regime policies was dangerous and deadly, and certainly discouraged by others who did not want to rock the boat. And, as in so many cases of genocide and state terror, there was pride in a civilization that led people to believe nothing so horrible could happen.

In cases of state terror and genocide, there are always some who help others and speak out. In Europe during the Holocaust, 90% of the Jewish population in Latvia, Lithuania, Poland, and Hungary died. But 90% survived in Denmark, and in Belgium, where there was resistance to German dictates for rounding up Jews, 53% survived (Staub, 1989). Studies of **rescuers** or **altruists**, as these brave people are called, found that one central characteristic is an ability to empathize with others, to imagine themselves suffering in the same way (Beck, 1999; Cohen, 2001; Monroe, 2008). **Empathy** is defined as "an 'other centered' emotion which is produced by observing another individual in need and taking that individual's perspective" (Batson, 1975; Rumble, 2003, p. 8). Rumble (2003) cites numerous studies of empathy and noted evidence indicated people will be empathetic when they see another person in need, *and* when they can adopt that person's perspective. In addition, rescuers tend to have an ability to identify with humanity at large, rather than only with their families, local community, or country (Monroe, 2008). Oliner and Oliner (1988) determined in a study of 406 people who attempted to rescue Jews during the Holocaust that they also had a strong sense of personal responsibility. Finally, Cohen (2001) notes that "these people reacted instinctively: they did not look for accounts or neutralizations for why *not* to help" (p. 263).

CONCLUSION

In this chapter, a number of theories are used to look at different aspects of ethnic conflict. We examined ethnic conflicts with various levels of violence, including the phenomenon of genocide. In addition, we explored the political psychology of bystanders and altruists. Ethnic conflicts are often bubbling under the surface of multiethnic societies. We examined cases with considerable amounts of mass violence and killing. Governments of many multiethnic/multisectarian states, particularly those that are poor and where resources are the object of tough competition, are constantly forced to fight against upsurges of ethnic conflict.

Topics, Theories/Explanations, and Cases Covered in Chapter 9

Topics	*Theories/Explanations*	*Cases*
Ethnic conflict	Realistic conflict theory Social identity theory Group conflict Evolutionary psychology	Nigeria Bosnia Guatemala Iraq Syria Myanmar
Genocide		The Holocaust Rwanda Darfur

Key Terms

- altruists
- bystander phenomenon
- coalition
- dehumanization
- diffusion of responsibility
- empathy
- ethnocentrism
- externals
- extremist
- genocide
- internals
- locus of control
- Mujahedeen
- rescuers
- social causality
- social justification

Suggestions for Further Reading

Chirot, D., & McCauley, C. (2006). *Why not kill them all? The logic and prevention of mass political murder.* Princeton, NJ: Princeton University Press.

Duckitt, J. (1994). *The social psychology of prejudice.* New York: Praeger.

Fiske, S. (1998). Stereotyping, prejudice, and discrimination. In D. T. Gilbert, S. T. Fiske, & G. Lindzey (Eds.), *The handbook of social psychology* (4nd ed., Vol. *2*, pp. 357–411). New York: McGraw-Hill.

Gourevitch, P. (1998). *We wish to inform you that tomorrow we will be killed with our families.* New York: Picador.

Hashim, A. S. (2006). *Insurgency and counter-insurgency in Iraq.* Ithaca, NY: Cornell University Press.

Horowitz, D. (1985). *Ethnic groups in conflict.* Berkeley, CA: University of California Press.

Ihonvbere, J. O. (1994). *Nigeria: The politics of adjustment and democracy.* New Brunswick, NJ: Transaction Books.

Loyd, A. (1999). *My war gone by, I miss it so.* New York: Penguin.

McGarry, J., & O'Leary, B. (Eds.). (1993). *The politics of ethnic conflict.* New York: Routledge.

Power, S. (2002). *A problem from hell: America and the age of genocide.* New York: Basic Books.

Prunier, G. (2005). *Darfur: The ambiguous genocide.* Ithaca, NY: Cornell University Press.

Staub, E. (1989). *The roots of evil: The origins of genocide and other group violence.* Cambridge: Cambridge University Press.

Wade, F. (2019). *Myanmar's enemy within: Buddhist violence and the making of a Muslim "other."* London: Zed Books.

Waller, J. (2002). *Becoming evil: How ordinary people commit genocide and mass killing.* Oxford: Oxford University Press.

Note

1. When a multiethnic state has one or more ethnic communities desirous of independence that have the capability to achieve independence, conflict can best be avoided when those communities are territorially homogeneous, by granting them the right of national self-determination. As long as such communities perceive a real option for independence, they are unlikely to respond to efforts to attract a primary attachment to the territorial community.

Chapter 10

THE POLITICAL PSYCHOLOGY OF NATIONALISM

For the past 200 years or so, **nationalism** has been an important driving force in political behavior. Nationalism is not universal and not everyone is a nationalist, but it lies dormant until the populace perceives a threat or opportunity to the nation. Following the French Revolution, nationalism first emerged in Europe with the development of the modern state. Nationalism is considered one of the most dangerous sources of political behavior in the twentieth century. For example, German nationalism is blamed for causing World War II, and it certainly played a major role. The nationalisms of various communities in Yugoslavia tore the country apart in the 1990s. Conflict between the United States and its Latin American neighbors often rested upon nationalistic indignation of one at the behavior of the other. The causes of nationalism and the impact of nationalism on political behavior are the topics of this chapter. They are illustrated with many examples from different regions of the world. Various conflict-resolution strategies, which can be used to ameliorate these conflicts, are then addressed in Chapter 14.

We begin with a general discussion of nationalism, its definition, the patterns of nationalistic behavior, the psychological roots of nationalism, and a description of different kinds of states with varying arrays of nationalists and nationalism. This is followed by a discussion of the political psychological causes of nationalist passions and behavior. From there, we present case illustrations of patterns of behavior. We begin with a look at nationalists' responses to perceived threats to national values and the case of Western European responses to immigrants. Next, we look at nationalism and the strong desire nationalists have for unity and independence for their people. This is illustrated in the cases of Northern Ireland, Yugoslavia's breakup, the Albanian revolt in Kosovo, the conflict in Cyprus, German unification, the Ukraine, the revolt in Chechnya, and the Kurds' drive for independence from Turkey. Then we turn to the impact of nationalism on foreign policy behavior, and look at World War II and the contemporary war on drugs in U.S.–Mexico relations.

DOI: 10.4324/9780429244643-10

AN OVERVIEW OF NATIONALISM

Definition and Patterns of Behavior

Before beginning any discussion of nationalistic behavior, a definition of the concept is necessary. In this chapter, Emerson's definition of nationalism is used:

> The nation is a community of people who feel they belong together in the double sense that they share deeply significant elements of a common heritage and that they have a common destiny for the future ... The nation is today the largest community which, when the chips are down, effectively commands ... loyalty, overriding the claims both of the lesser communities within it and those which cut across it or potentially enfold it within a still greater society ... In this sense the nation can be called a terminal community with the implication that it is for present purposes the effective end of the road for man as a social animal.
>
> (Emerson, 1960, pp. 95–96)

As Emerson explained, nationalists give their primary loyalty to their perceived nation, which can be considered a political identity in-group—a concept introduced in Chapter 3. For example, people can call themselves Irish, and see themselves as part of that nation of people. A **nation-state** exists when the average citizen of a country is a nationalist. Those who see themselves as part of the Mexican nation would consider the territorial boundaries of Mexico the nation-state. Alternatively, those in Ireland who see themselves as part of the Irish nation, would consider the territorial state of Ireland the nation-state. Countries in which people are generally not nationalistic are countries in which primary political loyalty is directed elsewhere, such as to an ethnic group, rather than to the community living within the territorial boundaries of the state. Nationalist identity patterns are illustrated in Figure 10.1.

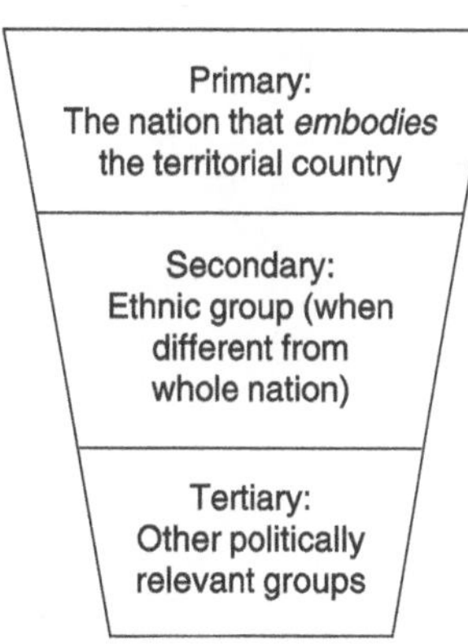

Figure 10.1 Political Identities and Loyalty in Nation-states

Being strongly attached to their nation, nationalists are committed to the unity, independence, dignity, and wellbeing of the national community and the nation-state. Even when they dislike their government, they love the nation itself. The concept of nationalism is similar to social identity, which was discussed in detail in Chapter 3. Recall that social identity refers to the identification people perceive with groups and organizations. People strive to maintain a positive sense of self-esteem from their memberships in social groups (Tajfel & Turner, 1986). People are motivated to feel good about their groups. Nationalists are group members who are motivated to have a strong, positive attachment to their nation.

Several patterns of behavior occur in nation-states and by nationalists, as opposed to those who are not nationalistic in non-nation-states. First, nationalists tend to be more sensitive than non-nationalists to threats to the nation-state, and the image through which they view the threatener is extreme. Research (see Dietz-Uhler, 1999) suggests people who identify strongly with a group react strongly when their sense of positive social identity is threatened. Similarly, nationalists—particularly nationalistic leaders—are very sensitive to opportunities to advance their country's influence, and are more likely than non-nationalists to seriously consider the option to expand state influence at the expense of others. Third, there will be a greater tendency among the public of nation-states to be deeply concerned with the objective of gathering together communities existing outside the borders of the state, who they regard as a part of their national community. Generally, nationalists desire a territorial state for their people, and they want all of the community to live in that state. This is referred to as **irredentism**—the desire to join together all parts of a national community within a single territorial state. Those members of the nation who live outside the territory of the country are called a **diaspora**. Irredentism was an important factor in Bismarck's wars for German national unification in the late nineteenth century, and in the German conquest of Poland and Czechoslovakia, where millions of ethnic Germans lived, at the beginning of World War II. Fourth, nationalists are more concerned with their country's prestige and dignity than non-nationalists, and they are more willing to take action to rectify perceived affronts. Fifth, there is more likelihood that the public of a nation-state will be susceptible to grandeur interests, and will therefore want to see national prestige and status enhanced and recognized globally. Sixth, leaders of nation-states, compared with non-nation-states, are better able to make effective appeals to the citizens to make great sacrifices to enhance the power of the state. Seventh, members of the public are more willing to serve in the military, and have a more intense commitment to the defense of that state. Finally, the citizens of a nation-state are more likely to grant leaders considerable freedom to take risks in defending the country's interests. However, leaders who fail will be punished by nationalistic people. They will not grant those leaders the freedom to accept defeats or the loss of face.

Given these patterns of behavior, we can begin to generalize about governance in nation-states. All governments have certain tools available to them to keep their populations stable and supportive. They can and must satisfy the utilitarian needs of the population through a functioning economy and political system. They also have at their disposal coercive instruments such as the police and the military, which can be used to keep order, prevent instability and, if necessary, force the society to comply with the government's decisions. Many governments combine these tools, and have a public accustomed to compliance and political stability. The habit of the public is to obey the laws of the government and accept governmental authority.

However, the governments and leaders of nation-states have an added instrument that helps them govern and, when necessary, mobilize the population to make great sacrifices for the country: they can use nationalistic symbols to arouse passionate feelings of devotion to the nation—symbols such as the flag; historic events, such as success in a great battle; or the idea of the motherland or fatherland. Because nationalists deeply value the independence, unity, dignity, and wellbeing of their national community, they respond readily to the use of symbols to mobilize them to achieve national goals. Experimental research in social psychology examined the effectiveness of group symbols in arousing and making salient one's group (or national) identity. For example, Wilder and Shapiro (1984) found the mere presence of an out-group symbol was sufficient to make one's in-group identity salient. Specifically, participants were exposed to a pennant of either their own university (in-group condition) or a rival university (out-group condition). Participants were asked to review a list of words, and were later given a word-recognition test. The words in the recognition test included words related to either the in-group or the out-group. The results showed participants were more likely to falsely recognize in-group-related words when an out-group symbol was present. More importantly, the presence of an out-group was sufficient to increase group members' adherence to their own group's norms. Thus, nationalistic symbols can be powerful motivators of pro-nation behavior.

Nationalism in Non-nation-states

Some countries are **multinational states**, in which several groups of people, who think of themselves as separate nations, and are capable of establishing viable independent states, live together in a single country. They do not see the populations of the country as their primary identity group. Instead, their primary identity group is the nationality to which they belong (see Figure 10.2). Examples include the Russians and Ukrainians who lived in the Soviet Union. Their primary identity was with the Russian or Ukrainian national community, not the Soviet Union. In these cases, no nation completely controls its own destiny, and has its own independent state. The dynamics of nationalism are likely to be directed toward striving for independence. Thus, multinational states have chronic disintegrative forces they must try to prevent from exploding. Northern Ireland is a case in point, as we will see later.

Finally, a third type of state, which is not strictly speaking a nation-state, but whose leaders often behave like nationalists, is called a **core community non-nation-state**. These are countries with a dominant ethnic or sectarian community that believes it is the primary nation embodied in the country, and that identifies with that nation in the strongest terms. In addition, that community tends to be politically dominant and controls the political system. However, also present within the territorial state are other communities, which give primary loyalty to their ethnic groups. These secondary groups desire autonomy or independent statehood, but they do not have sufficient resources to sustain it. A good example of a core community non-nation-state is Russia. Russians are clearly the dominant group, and Russians tend to be quite nationalistic, yet there are many other ethnic groups living in Russia who speak Russian, are part of the country's political system, but have a different ethnic identity.

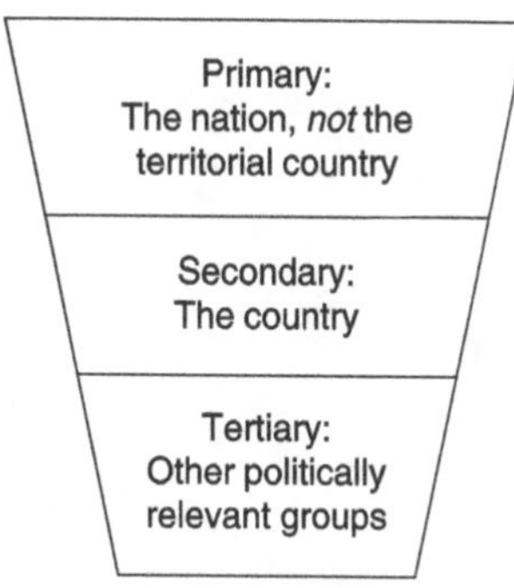

Figure 10.2 Political Identities and Loyalty in Multinational States

In many of these cases, the core community advocates the integration and assimilation of the other groups, encouraging the minorities to speak the dominant group's language, abandon their customs, identify with the country as a whole, and perhaps intermarry. Under these circumstances, minority groups can use social mobility as an option and assimilate into the core community. Social mobility is one of the strategies suggested by social identity theory to cope with a threatened or negative social identity. When the social identity of a group member (especially a low-status group member) is at risk, one option is to leave the group and join a group that is positively valued. Of course, this option is only available when group membership is achieved, rather than ascribed. However, the option of assimilation or social mobility is not always welcome if assimilation requires the complete abandonment of group identity; and, if the existence of the group is threatened, political conflict may occur. Resistance to assimilation may also come from members of the core community who view these other groups as undesirable. Under some circumstances, such as the events leading up to the Albanian revolt in Kosovo and the Chechen revolt in Russia, those small communities may identify a chance to break free and go for independence, despite the prospect of tremendous loss of life.

CAUSES OF NATIONALISTIC BEHAVIOR

We have already mentioned the importance of social identity theory as an explanation for the power of nationalism. To review, social identity theory notes that people need to belong to groups, and ideally they see their groups (in-groups) as better than other groups (out-groups). Nations are groups, and for nationalists they are a deeply important in-group. Central to in-group–out-group relations is the concept of social categorization. Members of a group see themselves as similar, sharing common attributes, and this group identification inspires behavior consistent with the norms of the group. Members of a group also tend to accentuate their positive attributes when they compare their in-groups with relevant out-groups, which they do regularly. When engaging in social comparison, the self-esteem of group members is enhanced when that comparison is positive for the in-group. Sometimes, conflict is a result of engaging in social comparison.

As noted in Chapter 3, the social comparison process is a complicated one. When the comparison is unsatisfactory, people can switch to a new group; they can engage in social creativity strategies, which change the comparison process itself, so that people can find a positive basis for comparison to replace a negative one; or they can engage in competition. The important thing to remember about nationalists is that the first option is out: they are committed to their nation as a group. The second and third options are acceptable, but the potential to engage in the third option (competition with other countries or nationalities within a single country) is high when they perceive a threat to the nation, or an opportunity to achieve some important goal. Nationalists reach this point faster, and with greater intensity, than non-nationalists. Members of a nation or nation-state—an in-group—will perceive themselves as better than their social comparison groups. They are highly cohesive and very willing to sacrifice for the nation. They are also more likely to be sensitive to things such as insults, frustrations, and aggressive behavior by out-groups (Cottam & Cottam, 2001; Searle-White, 2001). As Cottam and Cottam (2001) further explain, "The nation as an identity group is highly salient for nationalist citizens, indicating that the intensity of emotional responses to threats or opportunities for the nationalist will be strong and volatile" (p. 95).

Nationalism involves very strong positive emotions associated with the nation, as well as a propensity for heightened negative emotions associated with the out-group. If the nation is considered an in-group—which it is for nationalists—we can expect a range of positive emotions to be associated with the nation, such as pride in the achievements of one's group or country, or happiness when an opportunity to achieve an important goal occurs. As mentioned in Chapter 3, positive emotions tend to make people more flexible, and also more creative in problem-solving. They are able to see more nuances and have more complex evaluations of other people when feeling positive emotions. Clearly, these emotions, such as pride in your country, and joy and happiness when the country does well in things such as economic development and growth, or in international athletic competitions, are associated with politics. There is a potential downside to this, however. Commonly observed in the behavior of nationalists is an inability to look critically at one's own country's behavior. If pride is strong, then recognition of one's own inadequacies is less likely. When things go wrong, someone else is responsible. One's own policies cannot be to blame. This refusal to look at the country's own role in national difficulties also encourages a search for scapegoats upon whom to place the blame for the poor circumstances. This, in turn, can produce behaviors ranging from violation of civil and human rights to genocide. More generally, Kecmanovic (1996) and Searle-White (2001) argue that, in terms of affective properties, nationalistic behavior resembles crowd behavior, in that there is low tolerance for differing views, oversimplification, diminished personal responsibility, a reluctance to consider alternate views, a readiness to act out, a sense of being endowed with unrivaled power, which makes people less critically minded, intensified emotional reactions, and feelings of persecution.

In addition, group factors such as group loyalty and obedience (discussed in Chapter 4) come into play in terms of conformity to the in-group's position toward the out-group. There are tremendous internal and social pressures on people to conform when nationalism is aroused. One either faces ostracism and condemnation by friends, neighbors, the community, and even family, or one participates in the flag waving or becomes a passive bystander. This was certainly evident in the United States after 9/11.

Exactly how nationalists will respond to other countries depends upon the image (see Chapter 3) of other countries or nationalities within a single multinational country. They will confront an enemy with different tactics than a barbarian or an imperialist, for example. The emotions attached to the image will be supercharged among nationalists because they are so intensely attached to the nation. To refresh the reader's memory, Table 10.1 outlines the images and their attributes.

Let us turn now to some case studies. Given the previous description of patterns of nationalistic behavior, and the use of social identity theory to explain the underlying psychological causes of nationalism, we use nationalism as the political psychological concept in explaining the cases, rather than repeating the elements of social identity theory over and over again. We also point out the operative images that accompany nationalism and affect the exact nature of behaviors.

Table 10.1 Images and Their Attributes from Image Theory

Image	*Capability*	*Culture*	*Intentions*	*Decision-makers*	*Threat or opportunity*
Enemy	Equal	Equal	Harmful	Small elite	Threat
Barbarian	Superior	Inferior	Harmful	Small elite	Threat
Imperialist	Superior	Superior	Exploitive	A few groups	Threat
Colonial	Inferior	Inferior	Benign	Small elite	Opportunity
Degenerate	Superior or equal	Weak-willed	Harmful	Confused, differentiated	Opportunity
Rogue	Inferior	Inferior	Harmful	Small elite	Threat
Ally	Equal	Equal	Good	Many groups	Threat/opportunity

CASE ILLUSTRATIONS OF NATIONALISM

Nationalism and Perceived Threats to National Values: Western Europe and Immigrants

We mentioned above that, as a group, nationalists see themselves as distinct and better than others. They are strongly devoted to the identity of the group as it stands, and view any perceived contamination of the group through the imposition of alien values as extremely threatening. During the 1990s and into the new century, much attention was devoted to the growth in hostility toward non-European immigrants in Western European countries. This is an illustration of what happens when nationalists perceive a threat to their group identity (Brader & Valentino, 2007). The hostility was particularly intense toward immigrants from developing countries whose cultures (as well as racial makeup) are distinctly different from those of European cultures.

This pattern is manifested in the acceptance of falsehoods about the impact of immigrants on European societies, and in a fear of cultural contamination and change. Many Europeans, for example, believe myths such as the idea that immigrants take jobs from citizens. In fact, countries such as Germany, Italy, and Denmark need immigrant laborers because their own birth rates are falling (Fijalkawski, 1996). Immigrants are also believed to be responsible for increased levels of crime, and surveys showed Europeans feared immigrants would change their European culture. Many Europeans explicitly rejected multicultural practices that would allow immigrants to retain aspects of their culture. Hence, they do not believe immigrants can enrich the culture of their nation, and they reject instruction of immigrants in native languages.

Surveys have demonstrated this pattern. For example, in 1992, two-thirds of Italians surveyed explicitly rejected the possibility their culture could benefit from the influence of immigrants, and two-thirds of Danes objected to educating immigrants in their native languages. In 1990, 45% of Austrians agreed foreigners were a threat to Austrian identity and way of life (Fijalkawski, 1996). Indeed, by 1999, hostility toward immigrants was so strong in Austria that the anti-immigrant Freedom Party, led by Joerg Haider, had enough political power to be part of the governing coalition in Austria. Although the controversial Haider stepped down as party leader, the party held the vice chancellor's office and the ministries of justice and defense. Moreover, in coalition with the right-wing People's Party, the governing coalition held 104 of the 183 seats in parliament. Other European countries, as well as the United States, reacted strongly and negatively to these events. Although most Europeans condemn violence committed against foreigners, this is an example of the rise of anti-foreigner nationalism in Europe, resulting from perceived threats to the nation as a group and the values associated with that group.

Nationalism vs. Populism

What is the difference between nationalism and **populism**? In common speech, the two terms are often used interchangeably, but they are different phenomena. Populism is defined by Norris and Inglehart as:

> A style of rhetoric reflecting first-order principles about who should rule, claiming that legitimate power rests with 'the people' not the elites. It remains silent about second order principles, concerning what should be done, what policies should be followed, what decisions should be made. The discourse has a chameleon-like quality which can adapt flexibly to a variety of substantive ideological values and principles, such as socialist or conservative populism, authoritarian or progressive populism, and so on.
>
> (Norris & Inglehart, 2019, p. 4)

Norris and Inglehart go on to note that populists challenge the legitimacy of the establishment, including the power of elected representatives, and believe legitimate and authority power only resides with "the people" (2019, pp. 4–5). The people are thought to know more than experts (e.g., scientists, legal scholars), intellectuals, the media, international organizations, and most particularly politicians. Furthermore, "populist leaders knock-down safeguards on executive power by claiming that they, and they alone, reflect the authentic voice of ordinary people and have the capacity to restore collective security against threats" (Norris & Ingelhart, 2019, p. 6). Populism is accompanied by authoritarian values that demand conformity of thought and obedience to the leader. They also identify outsiders—the "other"—as a threat to the in-group, which often translates to resentment toward minorities and immigrants.

One of the most important elements of populism is that the "establishment" is the enemy. What is the establishment? It is the institutions, laws, elected representatives, and the political norms and values people follow. It is "the swamp" Donald Trump, and before him Benito Mussolini, the fascist leader of Italy and ally of Adolf Hitler, vowed to "drain" (Albright, 2018).

This chapter is about nationalism, so the differences between nationalism and populism may be self-evident. Nationalism is the primary identity with the national community, and all of the smaller communities within the nation. Nationalists give legitimacy to the institutions of their country and abide by the laws and principles of the state because they think they should. Like populists, nationalists are highly sensitive to threats, but those threats are identified as directed at the national community as a whole. Nationalists may not like or approve of a given government in time, but that does not change their attachment to the nation as a whole. Nationalism may be, but is not necessarily, associated with authoritarianism. Many liberal democracies have nationalistic populations—including the United States, Germany, and France. As the

(*Continued*)

(*Continued*)

discussion above indicates, nationalists may also resemble populists in being resistant to immigration, not wanting to see challenges of change to the national culture. Donald Trump is a populist (despite coming from the financial elite), and his movement took over the Republican Party in the United States during his administration, and possibly long after.

There has been a resurgence of nationalist parties in Europe since the 2010s, and this trend continued into 2020 (see Table 10.2 with figures from 2019). While their long-term success is different within countries, and level of support waxes and wanes, as Table 10.2 shows, there is evidence of support for these parties across Europe.

NATIONALISM AND THE DESIRE FOR UNITY AND INDEPENDENCE

Following are several case studies illustrating the importance nationalists attach to independence and unity. Given a perceived opportunity, a perceived realistic chance of achieving independence and unity, or a sense that the deprivation of independence and unity is unacceptably unjust, nationalists will make great sacrifices to achieve those goals. The cases covered are

Table 10.2 Support for Right-Wing Nationalist Parties in Europe

European country	*Party and percentage of vote*
Hungary	Fidesz 49%, Jobbik 19%
Austria	Freedom Party 26%
Switzerland	Swiss People's Party 25.8%
Denmark	Danish People's Party 21%
Belgium	New Flemish Alliance 20.4%
Estonia	Conservative People's Party 17.8%
Finland	The Finns 17.7%
Sweden	Sweden Democrats 17.6%
Italy	The League 17.4%
Spain	Vox 15%
France	National Rally 13%
Netherlands	Freedom Party 13%
Germany	Alternative for Germany 12.6%
Czech Republic	Freedom & Direct Democracy 11%
Bulgaria	United Patriots 9%
Slovakia	Our Slovakia 8%
Poland	Confederation 6.8%
Greece	Greek Solution 3.7%
Cyprus	ELAM 3.7%

Source: www.bbc.com/news/world-europe-36130006

Northern Ireland, the breakup of Yugoslavia, the Albanian revolt in Kosovo, the conflict in Cyprus, the revolt in Chechnya, the Kurds' drive for independence from Turkey, German unification, and the Ukraine.

Northern Ireland

Historical Background

Northern Ireland is a region within the United Kingdom, which since its creation in 1920 has been immersed in nationalism and national identity-based conflict. The Northern Ireland conflict is over national identity, involving several groups, notably British Protestant unionists/loyalists (the majority) and Irish Catholic nationalists/republicans (the minority). Until 1972, Northern Ireland enjoyed devolved status, meaning that the regional parliament enjoyed a great deal of autonomy, except in fiscal and foreign affairs. The regional parliament was dominated by the unionist majority, and allegations soon surfaced of discrimination in areas such as elections, housing, and employment. As a result of the perceived discrimination against Irish Catholic nationalists, the Northern Ireland Civil Rights Association (NICRA) formed in 1967 (Mastors, 2000). The association intended to protest discrimination using nonviolent means such as marches, meetings, and sit-ins. NICRA held its first march on August 24, 1968, but the Orange Order, a Protestant organization formed during the late 1700s, had also planned a march for the same day. To avoid clashes, the Royal Ulster Constabulary (RUC) police force attempted to reroute the Catholic marchers. When some Catholics resisted, the march was broken up by the police and the B Specials—a unit established in 1920 to augment the Ulster police (disbanded in 1969)—resulting in rioting by nationalists. The treatment of the marchers by the police sparked allegations of brutality. By 1969, the violence between unionists and nationalists had escalated, which prompted the British government to send 6000 troops to quell the disturbances. The British Army assumed responsibility for restoring public order and directing internal security, and the RUC was reserved the authority to investigate criminal activity.

At first, the nationalist population welcomed the troops, but soon they resented their presence because the army was viewed as biased in favor of the Protestants. On July 3, 1970, the army raided a Catholic area of Belfast in search of illegal arms. When the army encountered resistance from the Irish Republican Army (IRA), they imposed a curfew. After subsequent clashes between members of the IRA, other nationalist civilians, and the army, internment was introduced on August 9, 1971. Internment is a practice of detaining people without formal arrest and is often associated with brutal treatment or torture, including forcing people to stand for long hours with their hands against a wall, putting a hood over their heads for sensory deprivation, continuous noise, deprivation of food and sleep, beatings, and terror, produced by making prisoners believe they will be tossed out of helicopters alive (Conroy, 2000). Of the 342 men interned that same day, only two were Protestants.

Perhaps the most significant incident that enraged the nationalist community occurred in Derry in January 1972. The army decided to block the exit from the Catholic area to contain the marchers, some of whom rioted in response. The army then fired upon the marchers, killing 13 people. That day became known as Bloody Sunday. The army claimed they were provoked, although the allegation was not substantiated.

After the Bloody Sunday incident, the British government proposed assuming total responsibility for the maintenance of order. The RUC reserved the authority to investigate criminal activity. When the unionist government rejected the proposal, the British government dissolved the Northern Irish parliament and imposed direct rule on the region. The six counties were then represented in the British Parliament at Westminster by 12 members elected within the North. Thus, legislation involving Northern Ireland was to be debated in London. However, there were fundamental disagreements over the British solution. There have been many attempts at political solutions over the years, culminating in a 1998 peace agreement—the Belfast Agreement—which created a devolved Northern Ireland Assembly, a North–South Ministerial Council, and an Executive Committee of Ministers, with executive power shared by parties representing the British and Irish identity groups. As Goldie and Murphy explain:

> The Agreement rested on the legal and normative principles of equality of opportunity, human rights and respect for diversity … leading both the British and Irish governments to legislate to ensure impartiality, human rights, equality, respect for diversity, and a series of civil, political, social, cultural and human rights. Achieving a fair society based on reaching—reconciliation, tolerance and mutual trust required new law that addressed the constitutional status of Northern Ireland, power sharing, police reform, and protections for equality and human rights.
>
> (Goldie & Murphy, 2010, p. 36)

Peace was finally achieved—or was it? The answer to this question depends on how the concept of peace is characterized. If peace is the absence of open conflict, the goals were achieved. But Northern Ireland, as discussed below, still suffers from intercommunal violence and sectarianism.

The Political Psychology of the Conflict

There are many ways to characterize the Northern Ireland conflict, but social identity factors and the images the players hold of one another are crucial. In terms of social identity, one way is to delineate and define the groups in the conflict by religion, notably as Catholics and Protestants. However, this characterization simplifies the conflict as one over religious preference. In doing so, it does not indicate Catholics and Protestants were part of two distinct national groups—British and Irish—with differing national identities and aspirations. Distinct groups within these national groups had their own political parties and paramilitary groups. The Protestant factions identified with Great Britain and considered themselves British. The Catholic factions identified with Ireland and considered themselves Irish. The terms "unionist" and "loyalist" describe British national groups who are pitted against their Irish counterparts, known as nationalists/republicans. While unionists/loyalists had different perceptions of the appropriate tactics to use in the conflict (specifically, differences about the utility of force and paramilitaries vs. working in the political system), they were both British in national identity. Nationalists/republicans also had different preferences regarding how the conflict was to be fought and won, but they were both Irish in national identity. The underlying conflict over national identity has not changed since the inception of the state, even though, over the years, political parties and armed groups under unionist/loyalist and nationalist/republican auspices emerged, changed names, or reconstituted.

Unionists/loyalists believe they are British, and that Northern Ireland is rightfully part of the United Kingdom and should remain that way. They perceive their counterparts as threatening. Any discussion of the images they hold must also include their perceptions of the Irish government, because they perceived the country to be a looming enemy with threatening intentions. This enemy had designs on Northern Ireland, and nationalists/republicans were merely the dependent arms (colonial image) of the enemy. Together, they made up a pan-nationalist front, whose intent was to break apart the United Kingdom. Unionists/loyalists both proclaimed their "Britishness," but they were not a united front because they were divided over the use of violence to ensure their union with Britain. Unionists worked through the political process, and some loyalists, although participating in the political process through the Progressive Unionist Party, also had corresponding armed groups—the Ulster Volunteer Force/Red Hand Commandos. Thus, their images of each other further complicated the intergroup relationships in Northern Ireland. Loyalists, for example, were seen by unionists as their dependent children—a **colonial image**—who needed guidance from the unionists. Loyalists, however, saw the unionists as weak allies because, in their view, loyalist parties and armed groups formed to represent the working-class Protestants, a group that unionists had overlooked.

The Right to March: Demonstrations of Nationalism

Marching season in Northern Ireland generally takes place between April and August. Marching parades are a way for both unionists/loyalists and nationalists/republicans to commemorate their heritage and celebrate their identity. Thousands of marches take place (the majority of which are unionist), but at times the marches result in violent clashes between the police and the marchers, as well as between the two communities. Each year before the parade on July 12 commemorating King William of Orange's defeat over Catholic King James at the Battle of the Boyne, the Irish flag is burned in a bonfire in the loyalist areas. In July 2000, several areas of the region were again paralyzed by ten days of rioting, the catalyst for which was the decision by the police, fearing a confrontation between the two communities, to refuse to allow the unionists to march through a nationalist section of Portadown, located outside of Belfast. In subsequent years, outbreaks of violence during marching season have continued to take place.

Nationalists/republicans believe they are Irish and that Britain should relinquish its illegal rule over the region. Their goal is to see both parts of Ireland reunited. Nationalists/republicans see the British government as an imperialist power holding the North hostage. The British were responsible for partitioning Ireland and creating an artificial majority who were essentially the colonial elite. Like their British counterparts, nationalists/republicans were divided over the acceptable use of tactics. Nationalists, like unionists, worked through the political process; republicans, like loyalists, had both political parties and corresponding armed group. Sinn Fein had the Provisional Irish Republican Army (PIRA), and the Irish Republic Socialist Party (IRSP) had the Irish National Liberation Army (INLA). However, even though they disagree on tactics, and want votes from the same community, nationalists/republicans essentially see each other using an **ally image**—as allies who have represented the same communities, are the same people culturally, and shared the same problems of discrimination.

Even after the peace agreement, sectarianism continued to persist because of competing identity groups. Further, dissident armed republican groups such as the RealIRA and ContinuityIRA formed to carry on the struggle against the British and the colonial children. The old guard sold out to the British. According to Dixon:

> Republican dissidents tend to argue (there are both violent and non-violent dissidents) that the IRA has surrendered and lost the war. They attack the Sinn Féin leadership for "selling out" republican principles and cynical realism in deceiving the grassroots of the movement. Dissidents have argued that the Sinn Féin leadership should admit that the IRA has lost the war because it failed to achieve a united Ireland.
>
> (Dixon, 2012, p. 265)

Governance also proved to be problematic, with the Democratic Unionist Party and Sinn Fein dominating the executive and assembly. There were a number of unresolved issues, and the parties could not agree. The assembly was suspended from 2002 to 2007, and again from 2017 to 2020. Even though the Alliance Party exists, and seeks to cross the identity divide by promoting inclusiveness, these identity parties continue to dominate politics.

Yugoslavia

Historical Background

One of the most often mentioned cases in which nationalists of different nationalities took great risks and committed great acts of violence in pursuit of national independence is found in what used to be Yugoslavia. There were six nationalities in Yugoslavia before it fell apart: Serbians, Croatians, Macedonians, Slovenians, Montenegrans, and Bosnian Muslims, who were recognized as a national identity group in the 1970s. Except for Slovenians and Bosnian Muslims, each of these peoples once existed as a medieval state. Some of the nationalities had also been conquered by, and incorporated into, great empires: first the Ottoman Empire and then the Austro-Hungarian

Empire. The people of each nation identified with a defined territory, and they differed in language, alphabet, culture and, most importantly, religion. However, the majority were ethnically South Slav.

After centuries of conquest by different empires, Yugoslavia was formed as a single South Slav state in 1918. The government was a compromise among the strongest nations, particularly Serbia and Croatia, and reflected their national symbols, religions, and the Cyrillic and Latin alphabets used in Serbia and Croatia, respectively. Their union was motivated primarily by political and security concerns (Crnobrnja, 1994).

Yugoslavia was decimated during World War II, and horrible atrocities were committed during that time by the nationalities against one another. Germany invaded Yugoslavia and found allies in the Croatian fascists, whose military forces, the Ustashe, slaughtered Serbs by the thousands. Serbian royalists formed a military force, the Chetniks, who fought against the German Nazi forces, as well as against the Ustashe and the partisans. The partisan forces, led by Josip Broz Tito, were the only military forces whose members considered themselves Yugoslavs, and who fought for the federation (Crnobrnja, 1994). Tito was also the head of the Yugoslavian Communist Party. The war cost an estimated one million lives in Yugoslavia, half of them Serbs.

After the war, Tito's partisan forces quickly took control of the country and Tito became head of state. He developed a program for governing Yugoslavia that directly addressed the nationalities problem. His strategy included a brotherhood and unity campaign that promoted a common Yugoslav identity among all nationalities in the country, but not at the complete expense of the national identities. The brotherhood and unity campaign attempted to transform national identities, such as Serbian or Croatian, into ethnic identities, leaving Yugoslav identity as the national identity of all. He hoped to make Yugoslavia the nation to which all gave primary loyalty and with which people identified most strongly. Instead of being a multinational country, he intended to have Yugoslavia become a multiethnic federation. Yugoslavia was divided into six republics, or federal units, which were nationally based in terms of territory (with the exception of Serbs, many of whom lived outside of the Serb Republic): Serbia, Croatia, Bosnia-Herzegovina, Slovenia, Macedonia, and Montenegro. In addition, there were two autonomous provinces in Serbia: Kosovo and Vojvodina. For a communist country, the Yugoslavian state was unusually decentralized. Tito carefully avoided using the largest nation, Serbia, as a foundation for a common Yugoslav identity. In fact, Serbian power, which was in part a result of the fact that the Serb population was the largest of the nationalities in Yugoslavia, was purposefully reduced by Tito. The 1974 constitution is an example of this reduction of power. In that constitution, Tito gave Kosovo and Vojvodina more power and autonomy (their own assembly, representation in the Serbian assembly, and a turn in the rotating presidency), Serbian power was reduced, and the other republics were reassured that Serbia would not be able to control the federal government.

In addition, the Communist Party and ideology were used to counteract periodic upsurges of nationalist sentiment, as well as too-liberal reform movements. Tito believed the communist ideology would bring the country together as Yugoslavia and ultimately reduce nationalism to a cultural artifact, rather than remain a political element in Yugoslavia (Schöpflin, 1993). Nationalism was a crime, and those found guilty were punished with long prison terms. In particular, the nationalists in Croatia were severely punished in the 1970s. Tito himself became a unifying symbol. He was charismatic, and very popular among the citizens of Yugoslavia. While he was alive, the international behavior of Yugoslavia appeared to be quite nationalistic. This was enhanced by the existence of an external threat to Yugoslav independence. Shortly after World War II, Yugoslavia was pressured by the Soviet Union to follow the Soviet model, which it strongly resisted. In later years, Tito became one of the founders of the nonaligned movement, which was an organization of countries that rejected being pulled into either the U.S. or Soviet camp in the Cold War. Yugoslavs enjoyed the grandeur acquired by having this leadership role in an international movement. Yugoslavia also achieved considerable economic success.

Ironically, the successes of Tito's strategy produced forces that ultimately caused the country to fall apart. With economic success came further economic liberalization in the 1960s, which in turn made the republics more autonomous and weakened the central state. Constitutional changes in 1974 gave each republic and the two provinces a central bank, police, and educational and judicial systems. By the time Tito died in 1980, the economy was on a downward spiral, and no political leader emerged who could fill Tito's role as national unifier. Tito's importance in keeping Yugoslavia whole was evident in the failure of the federal presidency after his death. He did not promote a successor, but instead developed the peculiar idea of a rotating federal presidency, which would rotate among the republics annually. This made it virtually impossible for any single political figure to emerge as a national leader, and it fueled the rise of nationalism among the separate nationalities in Yugoslavia. The presidency was used as a bargaining tool by the different republics. In 1986, for example, Slovenia gave its turn in the presidency to Bosnia in exchange for concessions on economic reforms (Woodward, 1995).

Leader Manipulation of Nationalism

In the post-Tito era, Serbian nationalism was inflamed by a memorandum produced by the Serbian Academy of Sciences and Arts in 1986. It focused on Kosovo, where the situation was described as the "physical, political, legal and cultural genocide of the Serbian people" (quoted in Doder & Branson, 1999, p. 37). The document was crafted by Dobrica Cosic, an important author and a leader of intellectual nationalists in Serbia. Slobodan Milošević recognized early on the potential opportunity for his own political ambitions embedded in the arousal of nationalism by the intellectual nationalist camp. In 1987, Milošević, by then leader of the Communist Party, was sent by the president of the Serb Republic to Kosovo to address concerns of the Serb minority about mistreatment by the Albanian majority. In response to protesters' assertions that they were being beaten by Albanians, Milošević stated: "No one will ever dare beat you again … You must stay here. Your land is here … You are not

(*Continued*)

(Continued)

going to leave them, are you, because life is hard and because you are subject to injustice and humiliation? It was never in the spirit of the Serb … people to succumb before obstacles, to quit when one has to fight, to be demoralized in the face of hardship" (quoted in Doder & Branson, 1999, pp. 43–44). With this statement, and others that followed, Milošević manipulated Serb nationalist symbols, mobilized Serb nationalists, and won the mantle of the defender of Serb nationalism.

The Political Psychology of the Conflict

Within Yugoslavia, the Serbs were the most numerous and were dominant in the military officer corps (Silber & Little, 1996). After Tito's death, Serbia's role and position in the federation became increasingly galling to Serbian nationalists. They believed that they were unfairly deprived of their just deserts. First, unlike the other nationalities, Serbs were not unified in a single republic. Second, they believed Serbs should control Kosovo and Vojvodina, but particularly Kosovo, a central symbol of Serbian nationalism and the cradle of Serbian civilization. The symbolic importance of Kosovo made irrelevant the fact that only 10% of its residents were ethnic Serbs and the rest were Albanian. Meanwhile, as Serbian nationalism surged, Slobodan Milošević maneuvered his way to the top of the Communist Party in Serbia by defeating party rivals less inclined toward radical nationalism (Silber & Little, 1996). He then managed to gain de facto control of the votes of Kosovo, Vojvodina, and Montenegro in the federal government.

The upsurge of Serbian nationalism follows the patterns described earlier, which occur when nationalists believe they have the capability for autonomous statehood and, when comparing themselves with other out-groups, believe they were mistreated and deprived of natural rights. The case also demonstrates the important role of leaders in manipulating nationalism to mobilize people to fight against other national groups in defense of their own nation (see box). As Kaufman (2001) notes, "Yugoslav politics makes sense only in the context of the nationalist myths and symbols that the peoples of Yugoslavia found so moving. The power of Milosevic had everything to do with his ability to appropriate and manipulate [those symbols]" (p. 199).

Meanwhile, nationalist passions were on the rise in the other republics, particularly Slovenia and Croatia. The Slovenes considered themselves to be culturally superior to their fellow Yugoslavs, particularly the Serbs (they were Roman Catholic; the Serbs were Eastern Orthodox). The Slovenes saw themselves as more like Western Europeans, and their economy was more advanced than those of the other nationalities in Yugoslavia. This also enhanced their self-image. The Slovene nationalists wanted greater autonomy from the rest of the republics and more decentralization in the country. Although Serb nationalists wanted more centralization, not decentralization, they tended not to have severe conflicts with the Slovenes in this regard because they were far apart geographically, and there were very few Serbs living in the Slovene republic. Eventually, Slovenia pushed for greater and greater autonomy, rejected the legitimacy of federal control, and appeared to be heading toward secession, which the Serbs would not agree to. Conflict between the two republics was then inflamed in 1988 when the Slovenian government supported a strike by ethnic Albanian miners in Kosovo and condemned Serbian efforts to revoke Kosovo's status as an autonomous province and simply make it part of the Serb republic. Slovenian Communist Party leader Milan Kucan "portrayed Serbia as the enemy of Slovene democracy, as witnessed by its repression of Albanian rights" in Kosovo (Remington, 1996; Woodward, 1995, p. 98). Serb nationalists were infuriated that the Slovenes would side with the Albanians in Kosovo, who they believed were preventing Serbians from having their own national territory.

The growth of Serbian power in Yugoslavia, as well as the upsurge in Serb nationalism, contributed to the rise of nationalism in Croatia. Croatians, like the Slovenians, viewed themselves as culturally superior to the Serbs (Silber & Little, 1996). In other words, Serbs were peasants, Croatians were sophisticated; Serbs were Orthodox, Croatians were Roman Catholic. Because the Serbs were also powerful, having a strong presence in the military, the Croatian leadership quickly developed a **barbarian image** of Serbia. Recall from Chapter 3 that this image is described as one of people who are perceived to be superior to the perceiver in capability, inferior in culture, and aggressive in intentions. This image was reinforced by statements such as this one, regarding the breakup of Yugoslavia: "If we have to, we'll fight. I hope they won't be so crazy as to fight against us. Because if we don't know how to work and do business, at least we know how to fight" (quoted in Silber & Little, 1996, p. 129).

Croatia had pockets of Serbs in Krajina, who revolted from the newly forming Croatian state. Given the legacy of World War II, they naturally would not want to live in an independent Croatia. Additionally, the Serbs of Serbia would not want this. The rebellion spread to other Serbian-dominant communities in Croatia in the first half of 1991. The Yugoslav army was dominated by Serbs, but was still the army of the federation, and it intervened when the Croatian police tried to crush the Krajina Serb revolt. Although the Yugoslav army did not support the rebels, both Slovenia and Croatia interpreted the intervention as an ominous sign that the Yugoslav army was a tool of the Serbs. This was the final straw in their decisions to secede from Yugoslavia. Milošević's official position was that both Croatia and Slovenia had the right to secede from Yugoslavia, but that Serbs living in either one, meaning Croatia, had the right to live in Serbia. Therefore, borders would have to be redrawn, and portions of Croatia where Serbs lived would have to stay in Yugoslavia, but this was unacceptable to Croatian nationalists.

The impact of the Croatian barbarian image of Serbia, on both the mobilization of Croatian nationalism and its movement toward secession, can be seen in late 1990 and early 1991. We noted in Chapter 3 that when this image is dominant, people will look for alliances rather than take on the barbarian directly. Croatia, under President Franjo Tudjman, initially advocated a confederation with the rest of Yugoslavia rather than complete independence, indicating it did not want a direct confrontation with Serbia or the Yugoslav army. Croatia did look for allies—which is what one would expect when the barbarian image is operative—and it found one in

Slovenia. As Slovenia moved toward a bid for independence, Croatia was faced with two options: isolation in the federation, along with a rebellious Serb population in the eastern regions; or declaring independence, as Slovenia did, and searching for international support as an independent sovereign state. Slovenia had a referendum on independence in December 1990, and Croatia did in May 1991. Both declared independence on June 25, 1991. Violence escalated in the regions of Croatia where Serbs were in rebellion.

The difference in Serbia's response to Slovenian and Croatian independence is evident in the differences in the wars that followed. The Yugoslav army tried to prevent Slovenia from leaving the federation in a two-week conflict, which ended with few dead, and a ceasefire agreement. Slovenia seceded from the Yugoslav federation. This heralded the end of Yugoslavia as a multinational federation, and it became merely another name for Serbia. The Yugoslav army was no longer the military force of the federation, but was Serbia's army, which would be used in a much more destructive war to prevent Croatia from seceding. The difference in these wars is attributable to a number of perceptual factors. Slovenians and Serbians did not have the history of ethnic genocide that Croatians and Serbs did. The Serbian nationalists believed their own national kindred must be protected from a repeat of the slaughter of World War II, and that they should be incorporated into the territory the nation deserved and was denied for so long. This was not an issue with Slovenia.

Kosovo and Albanian Independence

Historical Background

Kosovo was a province within the Serb Republic of Yugoslavia. Of the two million people who inhabit Kosovo, 90% are Albanian and 10% are Serbian. In 1974, when Yugoslavia changed its constitution, the province was granted autonomous status within the Serb Republic of Yugoslavia, angering many Serb nationalists. Over the next 15 years, the Albanian majority engaged in ethnic discrimination against the minority Serb population. Kosovo's autonomy was taken away in 1989 by Yugoslav President Slobodan Milošević. In doing this, he abrogated provisions in the constitution that allowed for such things as the Albanian language to be used in schools, as well as for the observance of Islamic holy days. Milošević also sent troops and police to the region. In the view of Milošević and other Serb nationalists, Kosovo was an integral part of Serbian history, and a cradle of their civilization. Serbs trace this history to 1389, when they fought and lost the province to Ottoman rule under the Turks.

The Albanians did not want to abide by their loss of autonomy, and in effect created a shadow government in 1992, led by Ibrahim Rugova. By 1996, the Kosovo Liberation Army (KLA) formed in order to gain independence for the region. It began with attacks on Serb forces. Over the next few years, clashes between the Serbian forces and the KLA increased. Albanians were divided in their loyalties, with some supporting the KLA and others, such as Rugova who was not an advocate of armed resistance to the Serbs, and who preferred a negotiated settlement to the conflict. While the fighting escalated, the Serbs were strongly resistant to outside interference. In a referendum held in April 1998, 95% of Serb voters rejected foreign mediation of the conflict (Judah, 2000). Sanctions were imposed on Serbia in late April, and in May Milošević and Rugova agreed to talk. However, Rugova had no influence over the KLA, and lacked the authority to end the fighting.

Concerned about the fighting and the number of refugees fleeing the fighting, in September 1998, the UN Security Council voted in favor of a resolution that called for a cease-fire in Kosovo. The council also warned the Yugoslav government it would take additional action if they did not comply. In addition to the cease-fire, the UN demanded the withdrawal of Serbian troops from the region, peace talks, a return of the refugees, full access by aid agencies, and cooperation with the International War Crimes Tribunal at The Hague. In October, Richard Holbrooke, the U.S. nominee for ambassador to the UN, met with Milošević. After a series of talks, an agreement was settled on. In that agreement, Serb forces were to be withdrawn, a force of 2000 troops from the Organization for Security and Cooperation in Europe (OSCE) would verify compliance with the agreement tasks on the ground, and NATO would be permitted to perform air verifications. Finally, elections were to be held in nine months' time.

By mid-October, Milošević was not complying with the guidelines negotiated with Holbrooke. For example, he did move the largest army battalion out of Kosovo, but just over the Kosovo border. NATO warned again that if Milošević did not comply, airstrikes would ensue. On October 25, the UN Security Council passed another resolution, which implicitly indicated that military action would take place, again, if Milošević did not abide by the negotiated agreement. Russia and China, however, opposed any unilateral action against Serbia.

By January 1999, it was apparent that, despite negotiations, the fighting had not ceased. Among the incidents were the capture of eight Serbian soldiers by the KLA and the murder of 45 Albanians in the village of Racak. In addition, OSCE observers, who were unarmed, encountered resistance from the Serb forces. Serbia, represented by Minister of Foreign Affairs Milan Milutinovic, once again began to participate in negotiations in Rambouillet, France, on February 6. In that meeting, Milutinovic agreed to autonomy for Kosovo, as well as a ceasefire. However, also proposed in the so-called Rambouillet Agreement was not only that NATO forces be placed in the region, but also they "shall enjoy ... unrestricted passage and unimpeded access throughout the FRY [Federal Republic of Yugoslavia] including airspace and territorial waters" (p. 47). This proposal was unacceptable to the Serbian government—which is not surprising, considering Serbs are very nationalistic and this was a direct threat to the unity and independence of Serbia. As we have seen, unity and independence are core nationalistic values. Essentially, what was proposed was an occupation force in all of Serbia. At this point, Holbrooke reemerged, but was not successful in trying to convince the Serbs to accept this aspect of the accord. NATO responded with a bombing campaign on March 24, 1999, which lasted 78 days. On June 12, UN forces (Unmik) and NATO forces (K-for) entered the region, at which point Kosovo was considered an international protectorate.

The Political Psychology of the Conflict

The strength of Serbian nationalism enables us to understand why the Serbs were so determined to keep Kosovo as part of Serbia. This is an outcome of their attachment to the symbols of the country, and the people, and the desire for unity. Kosovo Albanians, on the other hand, saw an opportunity for independence, and for their own unity, and took advantage of that opportunity. They knew the history of international (UN and NATO) involvement in Bosnia as Yugoslavia broke up, and they had reason to believe that if the international community intervened to support the Bosnian Muslims' effort to split from Yugoslavia and Serb domination, which it did, then the international community would help them too.

The question remains, why would Slobodan Milošević take on the greatest military powers on Earth? Here, images play an important role in helping us understand his behavior. Evidence indicates that Milošević held a **degenerate image** of NATO countries, and he simply did not believe they would carry out their threats to attack Serbia: his previous experiences in negotiating with Holbrooke; the fact that threats were made before and not carried out; his belief that, even if NATO did attack, Serbs were strong enough to resist; his knowledge of disagreements on the use of force within NATO; and many other factors all supported a degenerate image of NATO countries (Cottam, Mahdasian, & Sarac, 2000). With that image, he could have concluded that risking resistance to NATO's demands was worth the gamble to achieve goals driven by nationalism.

A related question is why the Albanians would rise up and fight for independence from Serbia? *Social identity theory* and its implications for nationalism also provide a plausible answer to that question. People will try to change their group's status and position—in this case, a change toward independence—when they identify a realistic cognitive alternative. In the case of the Albanians, there can be no doubt that they too watched as the UN and NATO came to the aid of the Muslims in Bosnia, and they figured that the same could realistically happen for them. Hence, the chances of actually achieving independence would have seemed better in the late 1990s than at any time in history.

Although the bombing succeeded in forcing Milošević to withdraw Serb forces from the region, and restored the autonomy of the region, it did not mend the hatred between the still-segregated Serbs and Albanians. The desire for independence by Albanians and the Serbian view that Kosovo is part of Serbia both remain unchanged. Furthermore, it was not until the October 2000 elections that Milošević was ousted from power and succeeded by Vojislav Kostunica. At first it did not seem that Milošević would accept the outcome of the election, but widespread protests helped convince him to step down. Milošević remained a face in Serbian politics. Another blow, however, was dealt to his party when Kostunica's alliance, the Democratic Opposition of Serbia, won two-thirds of the seats in the December 24 parliamentary elections. Milošević, who was considered an international war criminal, went on trial in the International Court of Justice, but died in prison before the trial was finished.

Kosovo was under UN supervision after 1999, and security was provided by NATO forces. In February 2008, the parliament voted for independence.

Serbs strongly protested this, but the United States and many other European countries supported it. Unrest between the two groups continues, however.

Cyprus

Historical Background

Like Northern Ireland, the Cypriot conflict involves two countries, Greece and Turkey, whose people believe they are rightful owners of Cyprus. However, unlike Northern Ireland, ethnic Greek and Turkish Cypriots coexist on the island as part of two separate nation-states: the Turkish Republic of Northern Cyprus and the Republic of Cyprus. Cyprus was a colony of the British by 1925. In 1955, the Greek majority (about 80%) decided they did not want to be under British rule, and started a campaign known as Enosis (union). Greek Cypriots wanted to be unified with Greece. In 1959, the British reluctantly granted unification, and the following year the Republic of Cyprus was established. The parties signed the Treaty of Guarantee, which established the independence and territorial integrity of the island. Thus no country would attempt to unify with Cyprus (UN Peacekeeper, n.d.). The Greeks, Turks, and British settled on a Greek president and a Turkish vice president, as well as on proportional power-sharing within the legislature. The British were also given two sovereign military bases. The three powers also left themselves as guarantors, meaning that if there was any constitutional disruption, they would have the right to intervene.

Before long, communal violence between the two national groups broke out. In 1964, the UN sent in peacekeeping troops to deal with the violent situation. By this point, the Turks and the Greeks had established their own enclaves. The situation was further exacerbated by the toppling of the Greek Cypriot president by what Turks argued was a pro-Enosis Greek government. As a result, in 1974 the Turkish government invaded the island, arguing that it had the right under the Treaty of Guarantee. The Turks established a partition line, known as the Attila Line, resulting in the creation of two countries on the island. The Greeks govern the southern part of the island, the Republic of Cyprus. The Turks control the northern part of the island, and in 1983 declared it the Turkish Republic of Northern Cyprus. It is not recognized by the international community.

The Political Psychology of the Conflict

The Cyprus dispute is problematic because of the conflict between two nationalistic groups. However, the situation is further compounded by the involvement of Greece and Turkey, both of which are highly nationalistic countries that have a long and historical animosity towards each other. They are essentially enemies whose perception of each other is highly threatening. The island of Cyprus represents a battleground for these enemies, much like many developing countries were for the United States and the Soviet Union during the Cold War. The Greeks and Turks desire to protect, and ultimately bolster, the power of their own people. And, because of their long-standing historical animosity, both countries have a strategic interest in the island, ultimately not wanting the other to control the island. The national groups on the island, the Greek and Turkish Cypriots, are Greek and Turk *diasporas*. They do not see themselves as Cypriots with a common heritage and common goals. In essence, there is no conception of a common Cypriot nation (Fisher, 2001). Their view of each other is highly threatening, each perceiving the other to be an arm of the Greek or Turkish government. This is especially problematic for nation-building, which would require them to overcome their perceptions of each other and begin to see themselves as one nation whose aim is to build a country beneficial to both groups.

Chechnya

Historical Background

The nationalist uprising in Chechnya is an ongoing problem for the Russian government. Chechnya is one of six republics in Russia. Chechens are an Indigenous group, descendants of herdsmen and farmers, who speak their own distinct language (Kline, 1998). Chechens have a long history of nationalist resistance to Russian rule. As Pavin and Popov explain regarding the early nineteenth century:

> Russian imperialism in the Caucasus lasted several centuries and met its most determined and well-organized resistance on [in] the territory of Chechnya and the bordering regions of Dagestan. There, for a quarter of a century, Shamil's Islamic proto-state fought the Russian army until 1864. The Republic of the North Caucasus, that included Chechnya, declared independence soon after the Bolshevik revolution in May 1918 ... and fought a brutal war against the Tsarist army, commanded by General Denikin ... After Denikin's defeat, the Red Army entered Chechnya in early 1920, and a new rebellion erupted, this time against the Bolsheviks. This revolt was not suppressed until fall 1921 ... Over the ensuing three years, Chechnya, Ingushetia, and a number of other autonomous oblasts of the Northern Caucasus became independent. A brief period of relative tranquility was cut short by the mass political repression of the collectivization campaign during the late 1920s and early 1930s. This sparked a new wave of anti-Soviet uprisings in Chechnya that continued for the next ten years, gradually taking on the character of guerilla warfare.
>
> (Payin & Popov, 1996, p. 2)

In 1944, Soviet leader Joseph Stalin banished the Chechens to Kazakhstan after he accused them of collaborating with the Germans. Chechens were permitted to return to their homeland by Nikita Khrushchev in 1957.

The most recent conflict with Russia began in October 1991 when Chechen General Dzhokhar Dadaev declared independence for Chechnya. Subsequently, Chechnya created an independent secular government with a constitution, president, and parliament. As in the case of Kosovo's

Albanians, it is very likely that the Chechen rebels saw the disintegration of the Soviet Union, and the subsequent independence of neighboring countries, as an indication that a realistic opportunity existed for them to make a successful break from Russia. As we noted in the case of Kosovo, this is something social identity theory would lead us to expect. Similarly, nationalism explains the Russian response: *Nyet!* Russia had already experienced numerous humiliations, such as loss of territory, severe economic problems, and loss of international status as a superpower. There was no way a nationalistic people would tolerate the further humiliation of losing Chechnya. Consequently, the Russians, who claimed the republic was rightfully part of the Russian Federation, did not recognize an independent Chechnya. In December 1994, Russia sent 40,000 troops to the republic. Even though the Russians were able to occupy the urban centers, they were unable to defeat the guerrillas in the south. The guerrillas were able to retake Grozny, the capital (Grozny was later renamed Djohar by Chechens). Although the Russians anticipated a quick victory, this was not to be. In July 1996, after an estimated 100,000 people died, 40,000 homes were destroyed, and an estimated 300,000–400,000 people were displaced, the war-torn Russian army was forced to withdraw its forces (Kline, 1998).

Dudeyev died in a Russian missile attack and was succeeded by Zemikhan Yandarbiyev. Within the peace agreement signed in August 1996 by Russian General Alexander Lebed and Chechen Chief of Staff Aslan Maskhadov (elected president of Chechnya in January 1997), there was a provision that independence would be addressed in five years, in 2001. Russia subsequently recognized Maskhadov's presidency. In August 1999, the Chechens invaded neighboring Dagestan to assist Islamist forces there to gain independence. Clashes between the Russians and Chechens continued.

Russia once again invaded Chechnya with 100,000 troops, and was accused of human rights abuses, from torture, summary executions, kidnappings and disappearances to looting and extortion (Peterson, 2000a). Russian President Vladimir Putin initially saw the solution as direct rule from the Kremlin, which is obviously a different outcome of national liberation than envisioned by the rebels (Weir, 2000). He put Akhmat Kadyrov in place to oversee Chechnya. Russia continued to claim that victory over the rebels was imminent. In 2002, Chechens took around 900 people hostage in a Moscow theater. After Russian soldiers stormed the theater, 120 hostages died, and most of the Chechens.

In March 2003, a referendum was called for by the Russian government, which would provide Chechnya with a new constitution and limited autonomy, although it was clearly to remain a part of Russia. That same year, Akhmat Kadyrov was elected president, but was killed almost a year later by a bomb, with Chechen rebel leader Shamil Basayev claiming responsibility. Basayev was also responsible for commanding the subsequent three-day Beslan school siege, which resulted in over 300 deaths, including schoolchildren. Attacks by Basayev continued, but he was killed in 2006. Chechen leaders made overtures for peace talks in 2005, but these were rejected by the Chechen government instituted by Russia. Russia maintains its control over Chechnya and its local leadership, and holds and wins control in elections, but these are seen as a farce by the opposition. Attacks in Russia and Chechnya continued, despite Russian claims of normalization. The

Islamic State of Iraq and Syria (ISIS) joined the fight against the government in 2015. Russian-backed President Ramzan Kadyrov has been widely criticized by human rights organizations for human rights abuses.

The Political Psychology of the Conflict

The position taken by the Russian government, and its actions, sheds light on the image it holds of the Chechens. The nationalistic Chechens represent a threat to the Russians, but they are also perceived by them to be inferior in terms of capability and culture, which explains the Russian view that this rogue group needs to be taught a lesson and must be defeated by force. The Russians are also highly nationalistic, and granting the demands of the Chechens would compromise the territorial integrity of a greater Russia. On the other hand, the Chechens clearly view the Russians as imperialists, and this **imperialist image** includes believing they have superior capability. However, the relationship between them is seen by the Chechens as unjust, explaining why they have repeatedly challenged Russian rule, despite the country's perceived strength. Negotiating an end to the conflict would certainly require the perceptions of one group to change: either the Russians would have to accept that the Chechens are a unique national/ethnic group, relinquishing control over the region, or the Chechens would have to see themselves as part of a greater Russia, thus not perceiving themselves as distinct within the country.

Turkey and the Kurdish Revolt

Historical Background

Since 1984, over 30,000 people have died as a result of the conflict between the Kurds and the Turkish government. The Kurds, a minority group of 12 million people concentrated in southeastern Turkey, are predominantly Sunni Muslims who speak two distinct dialects: Kurmanji and Zara. This minority expressed demands ranging from complete independence to autonomy. The Turkish government, however, believes the Kurds should assimilate into Turkish society, and has banned the Kurdish language, television, and the arts.

The conflict between the Kurds and the Turks did not begin with the Kurdish offensive of 1984, nor is it a problem situated solely in Turkey. The Kurds are a nation of around 25 million people without a state. Their traditional homeland is in the area where Turkey, Iraq, and Iran share borders. The majority of the Kurds live in those three countries, with smaller Kurd populations in Syria and Azerbaijan. They revolted against the governments of Iran and Iraq in recent years, and their aspirations for nation-statehood were repressed, often brutally (the role of the Kurds in Iraq is addressed in Chapter 11). The conflict in Turkey can be traced to the creation of the post-Ottoman Empire Turkish state in 1923. At the end of World War I, the Ottoman Empire was defeated and the Treaty of Lausanne in 1923 divided the multinational holdings of the empire. The Republic of Turkey was established, but the Kurds were left without a homeland. There were three major revolts against the Turkish government between 1925 and 1939, in the southeastern part of the country where the Kurds resided, and the Turkish government responded with brutal repression, attempting to assimilate the minority group. Martial law remained in effect until 1946.

The Kurdistan Workers Party (PKK) was formed in 1978. Defining its struggle as one of anticolonialism, the group demanded independence. With the military coup of 1980, and a campaign of repression against the Kurds by that regime, many members of the PKK fled to Iran, Iraq, and Syria. In Syria, members of the PKK were supplied with money, weapons, and training. In 1987, the Syrians agreed to no longer support the PKK and claimed its bases were closed. However, in reality the PKK simply moved its bases to an area in Lebanon controlled by Syria and continued its campaign (Graham-Brown & Suckur, 1995).

Beginning in 1984, the campaign was responded to with a declaration of a state of emergency in 10 of Turkey's southeastern provinces. The following year, Prime Minister Turgut Ozal created a system of village guards, whereby local citizens were recruited to help the armed forces fight the PKK (Graham-Brown & Suckur, 1995). In recent years, with the weakening of the movement, the leader of the PKK, Abdullah Ocalan, has claimed he was willing to discuss a political settlement, possibly including autonomy rather than independence (O'Toole, 2000). Ocalan was arrested in Kenya in February 1999, and was given a death sentence. After his arrest, he called for a ceasefire with the Turks. Most of the guerillas retreated to Northern Iraq and Iran. The PKK claims it is no longer at war with the Turks (BBC News, 2000); however, in the spring of 2000, Turkish troops crossed into Northern Iraq in an offensive against them, signaling the Turkish government did not believe the conflict was over. The Turkish government was still threatened by Kurdish nationalist sentiments, referred to them as terrorists, and still driven by the perception this rogue group was not to be negotiated with, but defeated. Turkey also bombed Iraqi Kurdistan several times in 2008 in an effort to attack members of the PKK.

The Political Psychology of the Conflict

This conflict can be explained in terms of conflicts about the meaning of national identity, as well as images. The Kurds had a nationalist awakening fairly late in the game, after their nation had already been divided among other countries (Gunter, 1990). During the time when nationalism was sweeping through Turkey and Iran, the Kurds were still divided into parochial communities—that is, communities where the strongest identities were with the clan or tribe, rather than with the Kurdish nation. Those identities remain very strong in the Kurdish population, and there are significant animosities among the Kurds. As Gunter (1990) notes, in "all of the Kurdish revolts of the twentieth century ... whether in Turkey, Iraq, or Iran ... significant numbers of Kurds have supported the government because of their tribal antipathies for those rebelling" (p. 6). Kurds also have linguistic divisions. The language has two major dialects (Kurdi and Kurmanji), as well as sub-dialects, and some are mutually incomprehensible. As national identity grew, however, they came to see the Turks as oppressive imperialists. Kurds in other countries saw their governing regimes in the same manner.

By the late 1900s, they had reached the conclusion a favorable international environment would improve their chances of attaining an independent Kurdistan. Their hopes were reinforced by the autonomy of the Iraqi Kurds. We will return to this point later.

The Power of National Identity

Bruni (2003) wrote the following story about a 15-year-old Kurdish boy, Bayram, which illustrates the extent to which Turkey is determined to force the assimilation of the Kurds:

> On a school day last November, his teachers in this remote, poor, densely Kurdish area of southeastern Turkey asked him to lead his classmates in the customary Turkish pledge of allegiance, which includes the line "Happy is one who calls himself a Turk." Bayram ... balked ... [The teachers] insisted that he press ahead. So he did, and what they heard him say was this: "Happy is one who calls himself a Kurd." The teachers not only sent him home from school for the day, but also summoned the police. Bayram now stands accused of "inciting hatred and enmity on the basis of religion, race, language or regional differences" ... Bayram's case provides a glimpse into the extreme vigilance of Turkish government officials against any possible flicker of Kurdish separatism, a watchfulness that continues to shape the country's response to the war in Iraq. (Bruni, 2003, p. A3)

Bayram faced up to five years in prison if convicted.

Turkish nationalists, on the other hand, do not want the Kurds to have either independence or autonomy within Turkey. They attempted to force assimilation of the Kurds through repressing their language and culture. But this is not just the determination of one group to suppress another. When modern Turkey emerged from the ashes of the Ottoman Empire, whose heart was in Istanbul, it was not precisely clear who was a Turk. Islam provided a common link between the Turks and Kurds, but the new Turkey was to be a secular state. In the process of repressing the revolts between 1925 and 1939, Turks increasingly denied the existence of an ethnic or national group of Kurds. Instead, they began to refer to them as "mountain Turks" and attempted to force them to assimilate into Turkish society. Speaking the Kurdish language was illegal until 1991. In 1999, after the capture of Ocalan and 15 years of war against the PKK, one member of parliament refused to acknowledge there was a "Kurdish" problem in Turkey. He was quoted as saying, "We call it the southeast problem. We don't separate any ethnicity in Turkey in our hearts and minds" (Freeman, 1999). With Turkey pushing to be considered a member of the European Union, it is coming under increasing pressure from members to grant rights to the Kurdish minority. Turkey argues that granting rights, such as allowing education in the Kurdish language, and lifting the ban on broadcasting, could foster separatism (Bruni, 2003). However, the most significant opportunity for the Kurds of Turkey may come from the Kurds in Iraq. With the Gulf War of the first President Bush, they rebelled against the Iraqi Republican Guard, and the United States decided to protect them from retaliation by creating a safety zone in northern Iraq. This in essence established a rump Kurdish state. Then came the second Gulf War, the product of decisions made by the second President Bush, which presented a spectacular opportunity for the Iraqi Kurds to establish a larger and fully independent state. They moved quickly against the Iraqi military.

As mentioned in the chapter on ethnicity, Kurdish military forces took over Mosul and Kirkuk and the rich oil wells there. Their status as an autonomous entity is secure. The whole prospect of instability (i.e., war) in Iraq is deeply worrying to the Turkish government, because they understand full well the impact for the Kurdish community in Turkey of an independent Kurdistan in portions of what used to be Iraq—particularly portions with oil wealth. It would present them with a clear-cut opportunity to try to revolt and unite with the Iraqi Kurds. The United States insisted the Kurds in Iraq will be asked to pull back, but the future remains very unclear. In 2008, Turkish planes bombed camps of the PKK inside Iraqi Kurdistan, so the problem clearly remains an extremely serious one. The next case demonstrates full well the power of nationalism when the opportunity for unity of a national identity group appears.

German Unification

Our last example of the power of the desire nationalists have to live together in a unified, independent country is a more positive one—German unification in 1990. Germans are commonly considered to be very nationalistic, and German nationalism is considered a primary cause of World War II. German political behavior is historically replete with examples of popular sacrifice for the sake of the country and the German people. This is a pattern of behavior from strong attachment to the nation as an in-group. After World War II, however, Germany was divided into the Federal Republic of Germany (commonly referred to as West Germany), and the German Democratic Republic (commonly referred to as East Germany). The East became a Soviet ally and the West became an American and Western European ally. During the Cold War, the option of unification did not exist, despite Soviet statements to the contrary. This led to uncertainty as to the composition of the German national community. Was it the territorial community of both Germanies, or were there two German national communities—West and East? If the latter, then both West and East Germany could be considered distinctive nation-states. If not, then the desire for national unification would still exist, even if only in a dormant state, because of the constraints imposed on the possibility of unification by the Cold War. The answer to the question of how many German nations there were was dramatically apparent as the Soviet Union relinquished its control in East Europe. The German people moved quickly to take up the new option of reunification.

One of the most interesting aspects of German unification is its appeal to Germans, who had in the preceding years demonstrated less and less interest in reunification. West Germany was prosperous and closely identified with the NATO alliance. In 1969, the West German government began a process of neutralizing conflict with Eastern Europe, which in effect signaled acceptance of the status quo (Grosser, 1992; Mahncke, 1992). Public opinion polls conducted in West Germany also demonstrated the diminution of hope for unification, and the low expectation that it would ever materialize. A 1986 survey found one-third of the West Germans polled believed East Germany was a foreign land. This was particularly the case among those aged 14–29 years: 51% of this age group regarded the East as foreign (Plock, 1993). Only 9% of respondents believed Germany would be united in their lifetimes, but Germans still approved of the idea of reunification, as shown in a 1987 poll, in which 70–80% of respondents were advocates of reunification (Plock, 1993). When the opportunity finally came, it took only one year from the disintegration of the East German government, in October 1989, to formal unification, on October 3, 1990, even though the German government had to convince the United States, Britain, France, and the Soviet Union that a newly unified Germany would not be aggressive, and would commit to undertaking the enormous financial commitment and sacrifice unification would require.

Ukrainian or Russian? Who are We?

The Cold War ended in 1989, so it was something of a surprise when bloody conflict erupted in eastern Ukraine in November 2013. Looking at the political psychology of Ukraine, however, it probably should not have been a surprise. Ukraine is a country without much history as an independent country. Nevertheless, Ukrainian identity and nationalism can be very strong. It was part of the Russian empire until the Russian Revolution in 1917, after which it became independent. Independence was followed by a civil war among rival factions wanting to govern the new country. By 1921, the Russian Red Army had conquered two-thirds of Ukraine, and the western third became part of Poland. Government by Stalin's Soviet Union was extremely brutal in Ukraine as approximately seven million peasants died during the campaign to collectivize agriculture (BBC News, 2015). Stalin also purged political dissidents. Then, in 1941, the Third Reich invaded and occupied Ukraine until 1944. Nazi rule was also extraordinarily brutal. Nevertheless, Ukrainian nationalists did collaborate with the Nazis in 1941, and when they tried to get their anticipated reward—independence—the Nazis arrested or killed the Ukrainian nationalist leadership (Snyder, 2014). As the war progressed, Ukrainian nationalists formed the Ukrainian Insurgent Army (UIA), which they hoped would defeat the Soviets once the Soviets drove the Germans out, thus establishing an independent Ukraine. The UIA was vicious, ethnically cleansing Poles in 1943 and fighting a brutal conflict with the Soviets, which the Soviets won (Snyder, 2014). However, many more Ukrainians fought against, rather than collaborated with, Germany and most collaborators were part of the Soviet Red Army (Snyder, 2014).

After World War II, the Soviet Union brought Ukraine back into the Soviet Union. Russian was the common language taught in schools, and the Ukrainian language remained in the home. In 1954, Soviet Premier Nikita

Krushchev gave the Crimean Peninsula to Ukraine. Crimea was Russian speaking and Russian in identity, except for the 200,000 Tatars, who the Soviets deported to Siberia as punishment for collaboration with the Nazis in 1944. After the collapse of the Soviet Union in 1991, Ukraine declared independence, and 250,000 Tatars returned to Crimea (BBC News, Ukraine Profile, 2015).

Ukraine's politics after independence were tumultuous, with major developments occurring in 2004. By that time, the European Union (EU) and NATO were both stretching east, and included more members of the former Soviet Union's political bloc. Divisions between those who favored a closer association with the EU and the West, and those who favored a closer association with Russia, began to crystalize in Ukraine. In 2004, it was time to elect a new president, and the candidates were Viktor Yanukovich, the prime minister at the time, who was supported by the outgoing president and Russia, and Viktor Yushchenko, who favored a closer association with the West and eventual membership in the EU. Yanukovich narrowly won the election, but there were massive protests against the results, with allegations of vote rigging. These demonstrations were part of a political movement called the Orange Revolution, which demanded greater transparency and democracy in Ukrainian politics. Eventually the election results were thrown out by the Supreme Court, and new elections resulted in Viktor Yushchenko's election to the presidency. Yanukovich resigned as prime minister. In 2010, Viktor Yanukovich won the presidential election and returned to the office. In 2012, parliamentary elections were held, and Yanukovich's Regions and Community Party, as well as the far-right Freedom Party, did well.

Throughout these years, Ukrainian economic problems, corruption, and continuing political turmoil, including the arrest and imprisonment of political figures, prompted criticism from Western European countries and the European Court of Human Rights. Meanwhile, Russia launched its own Eurasia campaign, which sought to form an economic and political alliance among former Soviet Republics, including Ukraine. Russia applied economic pressure to Ukraine, encouraging it to move closer to Russia, while Europe and the United States applied pressure to Ukraine to move closer to the EU. By November 2013, pressures to lean East or West reached a climax when Yanukovich decided not to pursue the option of an association agreement with the EU, and accepted a Russian offer of US$15 billion (Mearsheimer, 2014). Massive protests erupted in Kiev and other cities in Ukraine, with thousands of demonstrators protesting the decision as well as corruption (BBC News, 2015). These protests grew and continued until February 20, 2014, when 88 protesters were killed by government snipers. President Yanukovich then signed a ceasefire with the opposition, according to which he would stay in office until elections could be held. The agreement broke down, and he fled to Russia (Mearsheimer, 2014). The opposition put Olexander Turchynov in office as acting president. Russia refused to recognize the new government, calling the demise of Yanukovich's presidency a coup. Elections were held in May 2014, resulting in Petro Poroshenko's election to the presidency. The new government was "pro-Western and anti-Russian to the core, and it contained four high-ranking members who could legitimately be labeled neofascists" (Mearsheimer, 2014, p. 80).

Protests continued to spread, but began to take a different direction, as protesters in the eastern part of Ukraine—particularly Crimea, where most people spoke Russian and identified with Russia—demanded to join Russia. In late February 2014, pro-Russian separatists seized the Crimean parliament and raised the Russian flag. In March, with Russian help, they seized power in Crimea, and Russia annexed the peninsula. Pro-Russian separatists then moved into other sections of eastern Ukraine, including the Donetsk and Luhansk areas. Russians were involved as leaders of separatist forces and paramilitaries, and Russian troops entered Ukraine in August 2014. Both sides stood accused of human rights abuses as the conflict pressed on. Russia claimed to withdraw many of its troops, which was disputed by NATO and the United States, and they continued to supply separatist forces. Russia also had almost 18,000 troops on the border. A truce was signed on September 5, but fighting continued in the east. By 2018, over 10,000 people were killed (Amadeo & Boyle, 2020). Volodymyr Zelensky, a former comedian, became president in May 2019, and his Servant of the People party also won the majority in parliament in July. This was followed by a prisoner exchange between Russia and Ukraine, but fighting and human rights abuses carried on until it subsided in July after a ceasefire.

The Political Psychology of the Conflict

This is a very complicated case because it has been aggravated by international political competition. Yet, at its heart, it is a case of nationalism and conflicting political identities. Even though Ukraine is a new country, Ukrainian nationalism and nationalists are not new, and they have sought an independent Ukraine for generations. For most of the twentieth century, that meant being free of Russian (or Soviet) domination. Consequently, the desire to affiliate with the EU and Europe is a natural outgrowth of Ukrainian nationalism.

As noted above, images tend to be strongly held in nationalism-based conflicts. Ukrainian President Petro Poroshenko was pragmatic and understood that some sort of tolerable relationship would ultimately have to be developed with Russia. Even so, he described Russian motivation and behavior as that of a barbarian. For example, in a speech before the United States Congress on September 18, 2014, he stated that Russian aggression would have to be stopped: "If they are not stopped now, they will cross European border(s) and they will absolutely spread throughout the world ... The choice is simple: it is between civilization and barbarism" (quoted in Shinkman, 2014). His actions also reflect that image. In a search for allies he told the European Union leadership that Ukraine must be part of the EU, and in doing so would "collapse" the idea that Ukraine belonged in the Russian sphere of influence (Harding, 2014). He also asked the United States for aid and support in Ukraine's resistance to Russian actions in eastern Ukraine.

The desire of the "pro-Russian separatists" to join Russia is also a natural outcome of their nationalism. As Ukraine territory moves east, an increasing portion of the population speaks Russian as the first language and identifies with Russia. This is part of the legacy of Stalin's movement of people across the Soviet Union. Many Russians moved into the Ukrainian

Republic of the Soviet Union. When the Soviet Union disintegrated, they suddenly found themselves citizens of a new country, Ukraine. The relationship between Ukraine and Russia was uncertain for several years after Ukraine's independence. There was still significant economic interaction, and many of Ukraine's political leaders were pro-Russian. The question of how strong that relationship would be came to a head in November 2013. At that point, people decided they wanted to be either Ukrainian or Russian, and the country began to split.

The pro-Russian nationalists in Ukraine were not the only Russian nationalists involved in this crisis. Putin is a Russian nationalist, and nationalism is strong throughout Russia (Hale, 2014). Russian nationalists experienced many losses in the past 20-plus years, including a dramatic decline in territory, prestige, and influence. Moreover, while Russia has declined, its former Cold War adversaries expanded both the EU and NATO into countries that used to be part of the Soviet Union's sphere of influence. Putin tried to restore some of the former grandeur and influence, and supporting a Russian diaspora in Ukraine, and annexing Crimea, are part of restoring Russian nationalism. In fact, in taking on Ukraine, Putin's popularity rating rose to 80% (Amadeo & Boyle, 2020). At the same time, Russian action increases security, which has been threatened by the expansion of the EU and NATO. There was also an economic aspect as the EU and United States companies sought to develop natural gas.

Russian stereotyping of the pro-Europe Ukrainian leaders, and the protesters who put them in power, is also related to Russian nationalism. Russians derogated them as "fascists" and "Nazis," a reference back to the days of World War II when some Ukrainian nationalists hoped collaboration with Hitler's regime would win them freedom. While it is true the anti-Russian Ukrainian opposition included some radical right nationalists, it also included center and left-leaning nationalists. As noted earlier, nationalism is not an ideology, and it can associate with any ideology of the left, right, or center. The reality is nationalism on both sides is standing in the way of a negotiated settlement.

Nationalism and Foreign Policy[1]

Nationalism also impacts foreign policy behavior. The heightened propensity to identify threats and opportunities, the importance of national grandeur, and the tendency to be quicker and more extreme in using stereotypical images of others all influence foreign policy predispositions among nationalists. In addition, nationalists are more easily mobilized by their governments, through the manipulation of symbols important to them, to make sacrifices for foreign policies designed to respond to threats or take advantage of opportunities. Here, we examine a few cases of nationalism and foreign policy.

World War II

World War II is considered possibly the most horrendous illustration of the impact of nationalism on the foreign policy behavior of nation-states. But if we look at the policies of two of the major nation-states in the conflict—Germany and the United States—we can see that, although nationalism drove Germans to embark on a policy of expansion that ultimately cost 50 million lives, it also enabled the United States to mobilize the American population to prevent Hitler from achieving his goals.

Germany in the 1920s was in a terrible condition. The country had been defeated in World War I, and the settlement ending the war, the Versailles Treaty, imposed onerous war reparations and peace conditions upon the country. There was severe inflation in the early 1920s, which wiped out much of the savings of the middle class. The government of the post-war state, known as the Weimar Republic, could not meet the basic needs of the public. Moreover, the Weimar Republic was imposed by the victors of World War I, and was politically alien to Germans, who never previously lived under democratic rule. The institution of the monarchy was overturned when Germany was defeated in World War I, and there was an uncertain attachment to the new republican institutions. In short, Germany was not politically stable. The Weimar government could not guarantee Germans would obey its decisions or support it out of principle or habit, and it did not have the ability to provide conditions of economic prosperity for the people. Because of its lack of legitimacy, the government could not mobilize the nationalistic German people by manipulating national symbols to encourage them to make the sacrifices necessary to rebuild and get through the hard times. Any serious effort to manipulate German national symbols would most likely have led the public to insist on the rectification of German national humiliation, and to a questioning of the nationalist legitimacy of the Weimar Republic, which had submitted to this humiliation. The Weimar Republic was a consequence of military defeat; thus, it was a symbol of national humiliation (Cassels, 1975; James, 1989).

Under the circumstances, it is not surprising that a right-wing nationalist leader such as Adolf Hitler would appear on the scene to challenge the Weimar Republic, and would be attractive to the German people. Hitler's ability to manipulate national symbols was a major factor in his rise to power in Germany. His defiant nationalism both silenced his opposition and increased his support base (James, 1989). Nevertheless, when he actually came to power, Hitler not only lacked majority support, but was viewed by large sections of the public with a mixture of fear and loathing (Steinert, 1977). Thus, he developed a system of coercive control that would ensure his authority by intimidating his opposition through violence. It started with street violence during electoral campaigns, even before he came to power, and continued with the development of institutionalized coercion and terror after he came to power. Opponents of the regime were threatened simultaneously with brutal coercion and with appearing unpatriotic by opposing a government that wrapped itself in the flag, declaring itself the savior of the German nation.

By using nationalistic symbols, condemning the humiliations and territorial losses Germany had experienced after World War I, and instituting a strong coercive control system, Hitler was able to mobilize the German people to make the sacrifices necessary to construct a military machine so strong that the Nazi leadership could embark on a plan that not only recovered land lost after World War I, but also included a goal of vast expansion. He saw an opportunity to achieve nationalist goals, the rectification of the punishment of Versailles, the expansion of Germany into much-needed territory (*lebensraum*), and the reunification of Germans living in Poland, Czechoslovakia, and Hungary with the broader German nation. German nationalists supported these goals, and the threat of coercive retribution prevented opponents from objecting to those policies. As World War II progressed, the same tactics produced an acceptance of a terrible loss of life and devastating destruction, even as it became increasingly clear that the goal could not be achieved. The German people became resigned to war (Steinert, 1977). Meanwhile, Germany's opponents were demonized, and Jews were identified as the scapegoats upon whom the blame for Germany's problems was placed.

We often think of U.S. involvement in World War II as simply the fight of good against evil and a normal response to the attack by the Japanese, Hitler's ally, on Pearl Harbor. But American behavior is also attributable to American nationalism. By the 1920s, the United States was a country whose populace was nationalistic. This explains in part why the country made it through the Great Depression without serious instability. The economic crisis of the depression years was a shock to the stability of the system, but the government did not have to respond to instability with coercion. Instead, President Franklin Roosevelt was able to call upon American nationalism to generate a willingness to accept the sacrifices necessary to deal with the economic crisis.

Roosevelt recognized the dangers to the United States emanating from the crisis developing in Europe in the 1930s, but the American public did not yet see events in the same way that Roosevelt did (Dallek, 1983). Instead, the public was concerned with the threat to the nation caused by the economic crisis. Many Americans were isolationists during these years, and believed that the national interest lay in avoiding another involvement in European squabbles. Roosevelt was clearly aware of the public's preference and acquiesced to it, despite his concerns as early as 1935 about the possibility of German aggression in Europe (Dallek, 1979). The Japanese attack on Pearl Harbor on December 7, 1941 erased American isolationism. After the attack, Roosevelt found it easy to mobilize the country. He announced a program to use America's industrial base, resources, and people to create an overwhelmingly powerful military force. He asked for and received enormous material sacrifices, personal sacrifices, and a willingness to risk lives to deal with this threat to the security of the nation. His request was received with approval and even enthusiasm and with little dissent. Americans did not have to be forced to fight for the nation; they were willing to die for it.

This case illustrates one of the most important features of nationalistic behavior: the willingness of a national community to make enormous sacrifices in order to construct the military, diplomatic, intelligence, and economic instruments necessary for dealing with an external threat. This ability to generate a willingness to make sacrifices is the most important impact of nationalism on a country's foreign policy. Nationalism makes a state more powerful because people are willing to make great sacrifices for it. These cases show nationalists can be mobilized by the identification of opportunities to achieve a desired goal, as in Germany, as well as by threats to the nation, as in the United States.

The United States, Mexico, and the War on Drugs

U.S. domestic and international counter-narcotics policy, known as the "war on drugs," and the responses of other countries to that policy, is another arena bearing the mark of nationalism. Both the United States and Mexico are nation-states, and Mexican and American nationalism influenced the war on drugs (Cottam & Cottam, 2001; Cottam & Marenin, 1999). Typical of nationalists, American policy-makers had difficulty believing Americans were responsible for their own drug use. Instead, U.S. policy-makers viewed the drug war predominantly in supply-side terms. In other words, drugs are a problem because they are produced in other countries and sold to Americans, and, although demand for drugs is also seen as a problem, the central solution to drug abuse has been identified as cutting off the supply. To deal with the supply of drugs coming into the country, U.S. policy-makers adopted an interdiction campaign on U.S. borders, at ports of entry, on the high seas, and on major foreign trans-shipment routes and production sites. Other methods include crop eradication in source countries, as well as money for training and supplies for source countries.

The first conflict between Mexico and the United States regarding drugs occurred in the early 1970s, with Operation Intercept. The idea behind Operation Intercept, initiated by the United States, was in effect to close the borders by slowly searching border traffic for illicit drugs, snarling traffic, and dissuading millions of American and Mexicans from trying to cross the borders on regular business and tourist activities. The Mexicans did comply with U.S. demands to improve its drug interdiction efforts, resulting in increased U.S. aid to Mexico, the establishment of Mexico's Northern Border Response Force, and increased collaboration between the Mexican military and police with U.S. military counter-narcotics officials and civilian law enforcement agencies (Dunn, 1996). However, because the United States unilaterally launched Operation Intercept, it placed a great strain on U.S.–Mexican relations. Later, the United States adopted a more bilateral approach through Operation Cooperation, but that operation was still a result of U.S. demands for improvement in drug interdiction.

U.S. policy toward Mexico concerning drug interdiction continually strained relations between the two countries through the 1980s and 1990s, evoking nationalist resentment in Mexico. International narcotics matters offer plenty of opportunities for threats to nationalist sensitivities because cooperation requires, at a minimum, an overlap of law enforcement activities. Mexicans were very cautious about that interaction. From their perspective, if you give the United States an inch, they may take a mile. If concessions are made on Mexican sovereignty, the United States will soon be making similar demands in other areas such as immigration. Mexicans were highly suspicious about the intentions of the United States and strongly resisted any effort to give American law enforcement officials free reign on Mexican soil. The United States added credence to that perspective by demanding a certain amount of freedom to operate as law enforcement agents on Mexican soil. In the late 1980s, for example, in response to the murder of a DEA agent in Mexico, U.S. agents participated in the kidnapping of a Mexican national, who was then taken to the United States to stand trial for his role in the murder. The U.S. Supreme Court upheld this action, which infuriated

Mexican nationalists. Mexico argued that the United States could not send agents to Mexico and kidnap Mexican nationals to stand trial for a crime committed in Mexico.

Another U.S. policy inflaming nationalist sentiments was the decertification process, whereby U.S. monetary funds (as well as international funds, because of U.S. pressure) were withheld if a country was not seen as cooperating with the United States in narcotics control. Every year, the executive branch must "certify" other countries before the U.S. Congress. Any country evaluated as not cooperating with was denied assistance from the United States in matters unrelated to drugs. In addition, the United States would recommend against the granting of funds from international aid sources. This was deeply insulting to nationalistic Mexicans, who refused to recognize certification, arguing that it is a violation of international law and a certain illustration of American ignorance and imperialism. Who is the United States to grade other countries, they ask? Moreover, Mexican nationalism was inflamed when the United States argued Mexico should control the flow of drugs into the United States. Americans view drugs as a supply problem, but when Mexican authorities complained illegal firearms flood into Mexican criminals' hands from the United States, American officials say it is Mexico's demand at fault. They maintain that this too is an illustration of American imperialism and hypocrisy.

By the late 1990s, American policy-makers at the executive level finally realized the battling nationalisms between the United States and Mexico were counter-productive. The executive level could do nothing about Congressional power to require certification hearings, but they did change the tone from decertification to certification hearings. The Clinton administration started executive level High Level Contact Group meetings in which officials of equal rank from both countries would meet to plan strategies for dealing with the drug problem.

Meanwhile, political change came to Mexico in 2000 when competition among political parties became real. In 2000, the nationalistic Institutional Revolutionary Party (PRI) lost power at the presidential level for the first time in 71 years to the conservative National Action Party (PAN). Cooperation between the United States and Mexico in the war on drugs improved. Both PAN Presidents (Vicente Fox, 2000–2005, and Felipe Calderón, 2006–2012) were less nationalistic than politicians in the PRI typically had been. These administrations coincided with U.S. President George W. Bush's two terms, also conservative. Bush initiated an aid program called the Mérida Initiative in 2008, which provided $1.9 billion for military training and equipment (Archibald, Cave, & Thompson, 2013). However, the situation in Mexico became dire, with competition between the drug cartels resulting in ever-increasing levels of violence. Between 2006 and 2013, an estimated 60,000 people were killed as a consequence of this violence (Seelke & Finklea, 2014). By the time Calderón became president in late 2006, the situation was so bad Calderón asked for assistance from the United States, which resulted in the Mérida Initiative. When President Obama took office, the emphasis of the initiative changed from supplying training and equipment to disrupting the operational capabilities of the cartels and building stronger institutions, particularly in justice and criminal justice in Mexico (Seekle & Finklea, 2014). The Calderón administration also took the unusual step of using the Mexican military to combat the drug cartels. This was not very successful.

In late 2012, the PRI returned to power when Enrique Peña Nieto was elected President of Mexico. Initially, it appeared the level of cooperation achieved in the previous six years would come to an end (Archibald, Cave, & Thompson, 2013) due to a return of intense nationalism that protected Mexican sovereignty. Peña Nieto did plan to make changes to the Calderón approach, and some—such as creating five regional intelligence fusion centers, which Americans will not be allowed into—should give Mexico greater control of its anti-cartel program. Nevertheless, Presidents Obama and Peña Nieto reaffirmed the commitment to the Mérida Initiative in May 2013. Does this mean that nationalism was no longer a source of conflict between the two countries? Not necessarily. Two developments impacted the willingness to cooperate. First, for the last decade Mexico paid an ever-increasing cost for drug consumption by Americans. The cartels killed thousands of people, corrupted the Mexican security system, and threatened to turn Mexico into a failed state. This is much more dangerous for Mexico than the drug trade of the 1970s, 1980s, and 1990s. Survival of the country will always come first for nationalists, and Mexican political leaders' willingness to let the United States have a more direct role in Mexico's war on drugs is a reflection of this concern.

Second, American political leaders, particularly at the executive level, finally became more sensitive to Mexican nationalism and made an effort to treat Mexican leaders with respect and equality. As Seelke and Finklea put it:

> U.S. and Mexican officials have described the Mérida Initiative as a "new paradigm" for bilateral security cooperation. As part of Mérida, the Calderón government put sovereignty concerns aside to allow extensive U.S. involvement in Mexico's domestic security efforts. The two governments increased cooperation through the establishment of a multi-level working group structure to design and implement bilateral security efforts that included annual cabinet-level meetings.
>
> (Seelke & Finklea, 2014, p. 6)

While past conflicts were inflamed by an American tendency to tell Mexicans what to do as though they were children, meetings among equally high-ranked officials with a mind to mutual planning helps reduce potential for conflict. But did this continue?

Donald Trump and the War on Mexico

During his campaign for the presidency, Donald Trump promised to build a wall and make Mexico pay for it. His beliefs about the U.S.–Mexico border were part of a wider xenophobic perception of Mexico and Mexicans. According to Trump:

> When Mexico sends its people, they're not sending their best. They're not sending you. They're not sending you. They're sending people that

> have lots of problems, and they're bringing those problems with us. They're bringing drugs. They're bringing crime. They're rapists.
>
> (Cooper, 2018, p. 235)

Trump assured Americans he was the man to solve the Mexican problem. As Trump whipped up nationalist fervor, and perceptions of threat, he set a course to divert government funds, and raise private money to build his wall. Further, he promised to deport the "illegals." They were "bad hombres." He renegotiated NAFTA into the United States–Mexico–Canada Agreement (USMCA) after declaring the United States had got a bad deal from the original agreement.

Trump depicted the drug issue simply as one where the United States got drugs, and the dealers across the border got cash (Cooper, 2018). Like all Mexicans coming over the border, these criminals operating drug cartels had highly threatening intentions. It was a supply issue to be solved by a wall, but equally an immigration issue because once in the United States they needed to be destroyed. The two were interconnected for Trump (Cooper, 2018).

Drug violence in Mexico was on the rise as cartels took their violence to the streets, and the State Department warned Americans who traveled to popular tourist destinations:

> Gun battles between rival criminal organizations or with Mexican authorities have taken place on streets and in public places during broad daylight. The Mexican government dedicates substantial resources to protect visitors to major tourist destinations and has engaged in an extensive effort to counter criminal organizations that engage in narcotics trafficking and other unlawful activities throughout Mexico. There is no evidence that criminal organizations have targeted U.S. citizens based on their nationality. Resort areas and tourist destinations in Mexico generally do not see the level of drug-related violence and crime that are reported in the border region or in areas along major trafficking routes.
>
> (Cooper, 2018, p. 244)

Many promises were made, and some partially carried out, but never actualized despite his continued comments that he was successful.

In July 2020, the response from Mexican President Andres Manuel Lozez Obrador to Trump's characterization of Mexico after a White House visit was not virulent but instead noted that the president had showed "kindness and respect" to Mexico (Reuters, 2020). Thus, he saw a change from previous rhetoric. Why? According to Rodriguez (2020):

> López Obrador, a lifelong populist and face of Mexico's left, actually has a lot in common with Trump. They've built a relationship based on their respect for each other's nationalist, authoritarian tendencies and their ability to stay out of each other's way on domestic issues.

Even so, in a poll taken in June of perceptions of Trump, 70% of Mexicans disagreed with Obrador and viewed Trump negatively, but 58% did support the visit (Reuters, 2020).

CONCLUSION

This chapter has examined the role of nationalism as a political psychological factor affecting a variety of political conflicts. It looked at nationalistic desires for unity and independence in a number of civil conflicts, from Europe (Northern Ireland, Yugoslavia, Kosovo) to Russia and Ukraine, and the Middle East (Turkey and the Kurds, Cyprus). We also examined German unification, where the power of nationalism to promote the peace and unity required substantial sacrifices. Fear of contamination of national unity and values were discussed in the case of Western European concerns about immigrants. Finally, the impact of nationalism on foreign policy was discussed by examining World War II and U.S.–Mexican relations.

Nationalism is popularly condemned as a force for great violence, and it has indeed been the cause of millions of deaths and tremendous suffering. However, it can also inspire people to make great sacrifices for others. From the standpoint of political psychology, nationalism is normal in-group behavior. It is therefore going to be a factor in politics as long as nations exist. Understanding that it is neither good nor bad, but simply a reality that produces particular patterns of behavior, is much more constructive than condemning it.

Topics, Theories/Explanations, and Cases Covered in Chapter 10

Topics	*Theories/Explanations*	*Cases*
Nationalism defined		
Nationalistic behavior described		
Nationalism explained	Social identity theory Image theory	
Nationalism and the drive for unity and independence		Northern Ireland Yugoslavia Kosovo Cyprus Chechnya Turkey German unification Ukraine
Nationalism and foreign policy		World War II Drug war U.S.–Mexico border

Key Terms

ally image
barbarian image
colonial image
core community non-nation states
degenerate image
diaspora
imperialist image
irredentism
multinational states
nation-state
populism

Suggestions for Further Reading

Carnegie Commission on Preventing Deadly Conflict. (1997). *Preventing deadly conflict: Final report*. New York: Carnegie Corporation.

Cottam, M., & Cottam, R. (2001). *Nationalism and politics: The political behavior of nation states*. Boulder, CO: Lynne Rienner.

Farnen, R. (Ed.). (1994). *Nationalism, ethnicity, and identity*. New Brunswick, NJ: Transaction Books.

Fijalkowski, J. (1996). Aggressive nationalism and immigration in Germany. In R. Caplan & J. Feffer (Eds.), *Europe's new nationalism: States and minorities in conflict*. Oxford: Oxford University Press.

Kecmanovic, D. (1996). *The mass psychology of ethnonationalism*. New York: Plenum Press.

Norris, P.& Inglehart R. (2019). *Cultural backlash: Trump, Brexit, and authoritarian populism*. Cambridge: Cambridge University Press.

Searle-White, J. (2001). *The psychology of nationalism*. New York: Palgrave.

Silber, L., & Little, A. (1996). *Yugoslavia: Death of a nation*. New York: Penguin.

Note

1. Many of the cases that follow are developed in greater detail in Cottam & Cottam (2001).

Chapter 11

The Political Psychology of Social Movements

In the 1950s and 1960s, the United States experienced a massive social movement, the Civil Rights Movement, which changed the American political, legal, and social systems. In 2008, the Tea Party made a major splash in American politics, and in 2011, the Occupy Wall Street movement began. Years later, other movements emerged, such as Black Lives Matter, #MeToo, and alt-right. However, social movements are not seen only in America. In recent years, Europe has experienced the rise of the radical right, and in the Middle East the "Arab Spring" resulted in the overthrow of dictatorial regimes in Tunisia, Egypt, Libya, and Yemen.

What are **social movements**, and why do some people join them enthusiastically while others sit the movement out? We can understand a lot about social movements by studying the political psychology underlying them. First, a definition:

> Social movements are collective challenges by people with common purposes and solidarity in sustained interaction with elites and authorities.
>
> (Klandermans, 1997, p. 2)

Klandermans and van Stekelenburg (2013) note that social movements have three essential characteristics. First, they are collective endeavors that challenge existing authority structures, elites, and/or cultural norms. Second, they have a "common purpose and solidarity," which means they have a shared message and claims, and a common identity. Finally, they engage in "sustained collective action" (p. 775). In other research, van Stekelenburg (2013) describes collective action broadly as the political psychology of protest.

Researchers frequently ask why social movements arise. What conditions are necessary for social movements to organize? Klandermans and van Stekelenburg (2013) call this the **dynamics of demand**. The dynamics of demand includes grievances, social comparisons, and a lot of emotion. It also involves the development of collective identity that becomes politicized. Van Stekelenburg (2013) argues antecedents of protest participation include grievances, efficacy, identity, emotions, and social embeddedness.

DOI: 10.4324/9780429244643-11

A second important question the authors ask is why some people join social movements and participate actively while others do not? Logically, if a group is a beneficiary of a social movement, it can easily sit back and be a free-rider. If the movement succeeds, the group benefits, and if it does not, there is no invested time and/or resources in a failed movement. Moreover, since social movements are outside of the normal political, economic, and social systems, they have no power other than their message. They can expel group members, who may then establish competing groups, and they cannot force people to join the movement. So why do people join? Individuals join due to the **dynamics of supply or mobilization** (Klandermans & van Stekelenburg, 2013; Walgrave, 2013). This involves variables at the individual and organizational levels.

In this chapter, we will examine these questions and related sub-questions. There are many variables involved in answering these questions, and they lie at the individual, group, organizational, and political levels. After reviewing the research on these levels, we turn to some case studies. The first is a classic: the American Civil Rights Movement. Others are more recent and illustrate the impact of current social media capabilities on social movements. They include the Arab Spring, the Tea Party, Occupy Wall Street, Black Lives Matter, and the #MeToo movement.

BACKGROUND: CHARACTERISTICS OF SOCIAL MOVEMENTS

Social movements have been around for a long time. For example, the movement to eliminate slavery, the movement for women's rights, and the temperance movement all started in the nineteenth century. Social movements are not simple protests. They require some form of minimal organization, including identifiable leaders. Some social movements have **social movement organizations (SMOs)**, which are institutions designed to further the goals of the social movement. The social movement itself tends to be broader than the SMO, and is sometimes quite factionalized in terms of its goals, strategies, and tactics. Examples of SMOs include the National Organization of Women (NOW), the Ku Klux Klan (KKK), and the National Association for the Advancement of Colored People (NAACP). Often social movements have several SMOs that may be competitive, thus representing competing visions of social movement goals (e.g., the NAACP vs. the Student Nonviolent Coordinating Committee, or SNCC, the latter being more radical). These SMOs are usually not institutionalized, although some are—such as the American Federation of Labor and the United Auto Workers, which started as SMOs in the labor movement and became legal representatives of organized labor over time (Stewart, Smith & Denton 2012). Social movements and the SMOs that become part of them are not part of the political, economic, or social establishment.

Social movements are organized in very different ways. Some are hierarchical, while some are loose gatherings. The **structure** of the movement affects recruitment and the preferred form of collective action. Dieter Rucht (2013) developed the following typology of the components of social movements and their environments (see Table 11.1):

Table 11.1 Structural Components of Social Movements and Their Immediate Environments

Component	*Main characteristic*	*Examples*
Basic action groups	Small, local; informal, face-to-face interaction	Local antinuclear groups, feminist consciousness-raising groups, citizen initiatives
Movement organizations	Greatly varying in size, from local to international levels; importance of formal rules	Robin Wood, National Organization for Women, Campaign for Nuclear Disarmament, Greenpeace
Networks • campaign network • enduring network	Non-hierarchical relationship; components can be basic action groups, organizations, task forces, service structures	Climate Alliance, Preparatory Assembly of the European Social Forum, Global People's Movement
Service structures • material • nonmaterial	Run by volunteers and/or employees, usually offering political instead of market prices for their goods and services in support of social movements	Halfway houses, Ruckus training center for civil disobedience, press houses, informal advisory groups for social movements
Social relations	Open access, not oriented toward movement activity but populated to some extent by activists	Parental group running a kindergarten, educational center for adults, factories, universities
Social milieus	Marked by similar lifestyles and cultural and political tastes	Left-alternative milieu of the 1970s, politicized urban Black communities, rural communes, rural farmer communities, worker communities

Source: Rucht (2013).

Size is also important in determining whether a social movement is effective in achieving its goals. The larger a social movement is, the less likely it is to be dismissed as unimportant or irrelevant. Stewart et al. (2012) argue that social movements are "large in terms of geographical area, life span, events, organizations, leaders, participants, goals, strategies, and adaptations. Scope distinguishes them from pressure groups, lobbies, PACs, campaigns, and protest acts" (p. 10). Further, social movements can promote or resist change, and any social movement may have participants who differ in the nature of that change. For example, some members of the environmentalist social movement may encourage the development of wind farms to reduce reliance on carbon-generated power, while others may oppose wind farms because they result in the deaths of many birds.

Some researchers differentiate between old and new social movements (Kriesci, Koopmans, Duyvendak, & Guigni, 1997). They maintain new social movements appeared after World War II, and they are "more spontaneous, informal, and loosely organized network of supporters around a single issue" (Stewart et al., 2012, p. 4). Social movements are also influenced by globalization, the internet, and social media, all of which have made it easier for social movements to have a global scope. These developments made participation in social movements easier and less time-consuming, and they dramatically increased the dissemination of information available to social movement members. Their impact on recruitment and mobilization will be discussed later in the chapter. Another distinction made among social movements concerns the types of disadvantages they address. Some groups in social movements face structural disadvantages such as racism, sexism, or ethnocentrism, while others face incidental disadvantages such as an industrial plant polluting the air, or tuition hikes for college students. According to van Zomeren, Postmes, and Spears (2008), "*structural* disadvantage includes structural low group status or discrimination based on membership in a social group or category ... In contrast, *incidental* disadvantage revolves around issue-based or situation-based disadvantages" (p. 509).

Collective action is another crucial part of social movements. Collective action is defined in the literature as "any action that aims to improve the status, power, or influence of an entire group, rather than that of one or a few individuals" (van Zomeren & Iyer, 2009, p. 646). Collective action can also be designed to stop or prevent harmful actions against a group. The civil disobedience of Civil Rights-era activism is an example of nonviolent collective action. Many of the violent protests against the regimes in Tunisia, Libya, Yemen, and Egypt in 2011 and 2012 were examples of violent collective action. Collective action can be ad hoc, occurring suddenly and stopping quickly, or it can be long term and continuous. It can also be costly in terms of time and commitment, or easy to do (Klandermans & van Stekelenburg, 2013). For example, being a member of the humane treatment of animals social movement can involve participating in People for the Ethical Treatment of Animals (PETA), and demonstrating at every fashion show where furs are worn, or sitting at the computer and clicking on the link to send money to the American Humane Society.

THE POLITICAL PSYCHOLOGY OF SOCIAL MOVEMENTS

Why do people create and/or join social movements? Clearly, they join because they perceive a wrong that needs to be righted. However, while many people have real and imagined grievances, not all do something about them. Thus, the issue is more complex than simply having grievances. One of the earliest arguments regarding why people join was the *rational actor approach*, which claims people join after completing a cost/benefit analysis of the likelihood they will gain something through participation. Many reject this argument for a variety of reasons, including findings that people are actually not very good at calculating costs and benefits or probabilities (see van Zomeren, 2013 for a discussion). Thus, participation in social movements is more complex than depicted by the rational actor model.

Another school of thought, **relative deprivation theory**, suggests more complex answers and variables to flesh out an explanation for why people participate in collective action and join social movements (Crosby, 1976; Davies, 1962; Folger, 1986; Gurr, 1970). Relative deprivation is a situation in which people look at their group's condition compared with a socially accepted standard of comparison, and find that their group is not faring as well as it should (Klandermans & van Stekelenburg, 2013). People then feel they are not getting what they deserve and feel deprived compared with others. Although not put in terms of social identity theory initially, later research showed that group-based inequality is more likely to promote action than individual inequality. In other words, people are more likely to take action when a group with which they identify strongly suffers inequality or injustice than when they as individuals suffer the insult (van Zomeren, Postmes, & Spears, 2008). In addition, further research demonstrated that the *emotional component* perceiving relative deprivation is more powerful as a motivator for action than the *cognitive component* (van Zomeren, Postmes, & Spear, 2008). As discussed in Chapter 3, specific emotions lead to specific action-tendencies. When people get angry because they feel their group is experiencing some form of deprivation, they are motivated to confront those responsible for the grievance. From the standpoint of relative deprivation theory, these arguments did not satisfy some critics, who continued to argue that relative deprivation occurs everywhere and often, but social movements do not. Theorists such as Klandermans (1984) argue that people's willingness to engage in collective action in a social movement must have some subjective expectation that by doing so they will achieve some important goals. This, in turn, grew into the argument that in order to expect that participation in social movements will achieve some goals, people have to feel a *sense of efficacy* (Corcoran, Pettinicchio, & Young, 2011; Mummendey et al., 1999; van Zomeren, Postmes, & Spear, 2008). They need to believe they can resolve their grievances through collective action. This also relates back to social identity theory as discussed in Chapter 3. In the discussion of social comparisons, we noted when people make social comparisons, and they are negative for the in-group, one strategy to change this is social competition, which can produce major political and social change. However, people only do this when they see a "cognitive alternative"— that is, an achievable better future. This is a sense of efficacy. Van Stekelenburg (2013) connects group-based anger to efficacy: "people who perceive the ingroup as strong are more likely to feel fearful and to move away from the outgroup" (p. 227).

A final component in people's decision to form or join a social movement is the development of a **politicized collective identity** (Drury & Riecher,

2009; van Doorn, Prins, & Welschen, 2013; van Zomeren, Postmes, & Spear, 2008; Taylor, 2013). In Chapter 3, we discussed social identity in general. Some identities are naturally political, such as nationalism or ethnic identity. These identities may or may not be politicized. They can be activated and produce the types of political behaviors discussed in other chapters in this book when threat or opportunity is posed to the identity group. Identity in social movement groups is politicized in terms of the grievances the group has, but also in terms of a call to collective action. As van Zomeren, Postmes, and Spears put it,

> politicized identity focuses on the political struggle for power with the authorities in the public domain ... which allows the political to become a (personal) identity project ... that transforms individuals' identity from one defined by social circumstance [as in ethnic or national identity] into a more agentic one.
>
> (van Zomeren, Postmes, & Spears, 2008, p. 507)

The identities associated with collective action and social movements take work, and activists endeavor to persuade followers to adopt the identity and join the movement (Taylor, 2013). The work is different for structural and incidental disadvantages. Identities are created and sustained when the disadvantage is incidental, but structural identities are already in existence (van Zomeren, Postmes, & Spears, 2008). Further, individuals have multiple identities, and these may produce conflict as in the case of union members and the decision to go on strike (van Stekelenburg, 2013).

Researchers on the politicization of identities found it occurs through several stages. The first is the creation of boundaries that clearly delineate the dominant groups from the subordinate groups with grievances (van Doorn, Prins, & Welschen, 2013). The second is the process of the development of political consciousness or awareness. Groups are not automatically able to see their issue as a political one, and their position in the social order as unjust. Being accustomed to poor treatment does not automatically produce an effort to change that treatment, as we saw in our discussion of the belief in a just world. People come to the realization they are being treated unfairly. In addition, some issues actually have to be defined as political issues for the identity to form and expand. Domestic violence was once considered a private matter between couples, whereas today it is considered a crime. The legalization of same-sex marriage was once not an issue, whereas now it is a widely recognized social movement.

The creation of a politicized identity also has an emotional side. Groups with grievances often are socially and politically stigmatized and discriminated against. Their primary feelings about this reality can be shame and fear, particularly if they are strongly repressed. Part of the politicized identity process includes replacing those emotions with pride and anger (Taylor, 2013), thereby making people more inclined to engage in collective action. This can be done through consciousness-raising campaigns, as occurred in the civil rights and the feminist movements (Taylor, 2013). The third element in the politicization of identity is called negotiation (van Doorn, Prins, & Welschen, 2013). Negotiation involves redefining the symbolic meaning of the subordinate group's position in society, and the relationship between the dominant and subordinate group. This is an example of social creativity, a social identity strategy discussed in Chapter 3. In part, this can involve name changing. The Civil Rights Movement changed the common name of Black people from *Negro* to *African American*. Social creativity also involves convincing the group and its members to change their defensive posture to a more combative one *vis-à-vis* the dominant portions of society (Stewart, Smith, & Denton, 2012).

Finally, the formation of social movements and collective action is not a linear process. The act of participation in collective action empowers people even if the outcome is not a success. It increases the strength of the identity and the willingness to engage in further action (Drury & Riecher, 2009).

Mobilization

The mobilization of people to support a social movement is another crucial element. Mobilization brings the demand for action and the supply of participants together. Social movements are dependent upon social networks to develop group-based collective action. Klandermans and van Stekelenberg (2013) argue that **social capital** plays an extremely important role in the quality of those social networks. Social capital is an old concept, with varying definitions, but it is generally a set of relationships and resources in a community that can be mobilized for the common good. Klandermans and van Stekelenberg (2013) note that it is structural, relational, and cognitive. Social capital provides a basis for social embeddedness through structural elements such as social networks. The richer the social networks, the more people are reached and able to interact. The relationship component refers to relationships in the group—the friendships, trust, and confidence members hold in one another. Finally, according to Klandermans and van Stekelenberg (2013), the cognitive component "is defined as those resources providing shared representations, interpretations, and systems of meaning" (p. 790). This is essentially raised consciousness. The nature of these three components of social embeddedness strongly affects the ability of social movements, and the organizations they build, to mobilize followers. In order to be mobilized to take collective action, people need to be sympathetic to the cause, identify with it, know about upcoming events, and be willing and able to participate (Klandermans & van Stekelenberg, 2013). Social movements provide people with a sense of connectivity to a community, even if that community is at a distance.

The structural aspect of social embeddedness certainly changed with the advent of the internet. The internet vastly widens the number of people who can be instantly communicated. Social movements no longer depend on standard media to cover their issues. Social movement activists also use the internet to hack into the websites of organizations they oppose, overwhelm them, and cause them to collapse. For example, this was done in 1999 during the World Trade Organization meetings in Seattle, Washington, when protesters shut down the server for the conference (Stewart et al., 2012). The ease of internet communication also means social movements attract followers who are less able and willing to participate in collective action than in pre-internet days. It makes mobilization with minimal organization more feasible (Klandermans & van Stekelenberg, 2013, p. 793). Finally, the internet improves the prospects of mobilizing people for collective action in repressive political systems where collective protest is most dangerous.

Social movements have strategies to mobilize members for collective action. Among their tactics are campaigns to encourage collective action and donate to the organization. One progressive political social movement, called MoveOn, makes extensive use of the internet to inform people of upcoming political actions, events, votes, and so on. They use persuasive tactics to shore up the identification of adherents with the movement, emphasizing commonalities among members and using phrases and themes that promote the idea that they constitute "a people" and "unity" (Stewart, Smith, & Denton, 2012). Movements make use of symbols such as suffering animals (American Society for the Prevention of Cruelty to Animals [ASPCA]) or a cup painted with red, white, and blue stripes with a tea bag hanging out of it (Tea Party). Along with symbols are slogans (e.g., "We are the 99%" from Occupy Wall Street) and songs (e.g., "We Shall Overcome" from the Civil Rights Movement). Social movements also make heavy use of *framing*, a concept addressed in other chapters. They develop "collective action frames" that give meaning to facts, defining who has committed an injustice to whom (Klandermans & van Stekelenburg, 2013). Snow, Rochford, Worden, and Benford (1986) argue that the development of an "injustice frame," wherein the actions of authority are seen as unjust and resistance to those actions are seen as legitimate, is necessary for social movements to acquire support and mobilize adherents. Frames often link independent beliefs by "bridging ... ideologically congruent but structurally unconnected" frames in SMOs or individuals (Snow et al., 1986, p. 467).

Leaders

Researchers on social movements do not focus much on leaders. Leaders of social movements are in a relatively weak position because these organizations are voluntary, so they have little direct authority (Wilson, 1973). Leaders who form fledgling social movements establish networks and relationships with potential members and effectively communicate a common identity. A leader expresses the injustice of the commonly felt grievance, but in a way that inspires potential members to believe they have the efficacy to change their circumstances through collective action (Ganz, 2010). The leaders are responsible for establishing the symbols and framing the problem to increase solidarity among members. Leaders also strategize to mobilize resources and people, gain attention from potential followers and authorities, and deal with inevitable dissent over beliefs, strategies and tactics, and the use of resources.

Stewart, Smith, and Denton (2012) argue that successful leaders of social movements have at least two of three personality traits: **charisma**, **prophecy**, and **pragmatism**. Charisma comes from an ability to articulate action to achieve an imagined future. It "enables persons to lead fellow activists in direct actions that stir things up, supply vigor to social movements, and make people believe in the impossible" (Stewart et al., 2012, p. 123). Prophets are the purveyors of the movement's beliefs, doctrines, and morality. Pragmatic leaders have organizational skills, are good negotiators and resource mobilizers, and they are inclusive, expanding group membership (Stewart et al., 2012). These traits are useful in different contexts and enable leaders to handle the various roles and conflicts they face across the activities of the social movement. Charisma attracts new members, prophecy creates a politicized identity with meaning, and pragmatism achieves goals.

THE CIVIL RIGHTS MOVEMENT IN AMERICA

One of the most remarkable social movements was the American Civil Rights Movement. Below we will look at some of the most important events of the Civil Rights Movement from 1954 to 1968, and then turn to an analysis of it using the concepts developed regarding social movements. The Civil Rights Movement is commonly thought to have started in the 1950s. However, Black people struggled for equality continually after the end of slavery in 1865, with boycotts, protests, and the formation of the National Association for the Advancement of Colored People (NAACP) in 1909–1910. This was the first national organization in the struggle against Jim Crow laws and regulations (Morris, 1999). In World War II, 900,000 Black Americans enlisted in the armed forces to fight fascism, yet they were denied the opportunity to fight alongside their White countrymen. After the war, Black Americans were even more determined not to be denied participation in a democracy for which they had risked their lives during the war (Takaki, 2008). Many of the first victories in the post-World War II Civil Rights Movement came through the courts. In 1954, the Supreme Court struck down the "separate but equal" doctrine from the 1896 *Plessy v. Ferguson* ruling in the famous *Brown v. Board of Education* decision. This made segregation in public education illegal, which in principle mandated school integration. The ruling did not result in desegregation because many Southern states simply refused to implement the decision. In 1957, three years after the Supreme Court decision and two years of planning, nine Black students attempted to enter the all-White Central High School in Little Rock, Arkansas. Arkansas Governor Orval Faubus deployed the Arkansas National Guard to prevent the school's integration. The Eisenhower administration responded by sending federal troops to Little Rock to implement the integration and protect the students.

Another important event that stimulated mobilization in the Civil Rights Movement was the lynching of Emmett Till. In August 1955, the 14-year-old Chicago boy went to visit relatives in Money, Mississippi, and made the mistake of whistling at a White woman. Four days later, he was kidnapped and murdered. His murderers were acquitted of the crime, which they later admitted to committing. Emmett Till's murder caused national outrage and his funeral received widespread attention. This galvanized the Black American community for further action.

By the end of 1955, the Black community had turned to mobilization. On December 1, 1955, in Montgomery, Alabama, Rosa Parks, a Black woman, refused to give up her seat on a bus to a White person and was arrested for violating city law. Her actions were not those of a tired seamstress, but an activist member of the National Association for the Advancement of

Colored People (NAACP). Her arrest was followed by a massive protest and a 381 day boycott of the bus system in Montgomery. This too was planned, and it started on the day Parks went on trial. Black school children were sent home with flyers informing their parents of the boycott. By the end of the boycott, Reverend Dr. Martin Luther King, Jr., a member of the NAACP with great oratorical skills, had risen to prominence in the Civil Rights Movement.

The boycott ended when the Supreme Court ruled that segregation on buses was illegal on November 13, 1955. During the boycott, King's house and the house of E. D. Nixon (president of the Montgomery chapter of the NAACP) were bombed. Martin Luther King, Jr. was an advocate of non-violence and civil disobedience, and as he emerged as a leader of the Civil Rights Movement, these were the tactics adopted by the movement. King also became the president of a new civil rights organization in 1957, the Southern Christian Leadership Conference (SCLC), which was regional in focus and clergy led (Foner & Garraty, 1991).

Following the events in Montgomery, a group of four students from the North Carolina Agricultural and Technical College staged a sit-in at a segregated lunch counter in Greensboro, North Carolina on February 1, 1960. This ignited sit-ins elsewhere in the South at segregated eateries, and spawned the Student Nonviolent Coordinating Committee (SNCC). As its name implies, this was a student-led group and, although nonviolent, it was more aggressive and had a different strategic approach to protest than did the SCLC. It advocated autonomous local activity rather than a coordinated local-to-national approach (Foner & Garraty, 1991).

The next major activity of the Civil Rights Movement was the "freedom rides," which began a year after the Greensboro sit-in. The freedom rides were "acts of civil disobedience to integrate interstate buses and bus terminals of the South" (Takaki, 2008, p. 391). The freedom rides were led by the Congress of Racial Equality, a largely White organization, but they involved Black and White people riding buses together. The buses were attacked by White racists and the riders beaten (Takaki, 2008). In 1963, nonviolent protests were held in Birmingham, Alabama, led by the SCLC (the NAACP and SNCC were not very active in Birmingham). Birmingham was a logical choice for protest because its police chief, "Bull" Connor, was an avowed racist, the Ku Klux Klan was very strong there, and many of the freedom rider beatings took place there. Connor behaved in character, and the protesters, many of whom were children, were bitten by police dogs, beaten by policemen, and blasted with water from fire hoses. Martin Luther King, Jr. was arrested and not permitted to see his lawyer. The events made national news and drew a lot of sympathy for the protesters.

The years 1963, 1964, and 1965 were a time of triumph and tragedy for the Civil Rights Movement. In June 1963, Mississippi NAACP field secretary Medgar Evers was murdered. August saw the March on Washington where 200,000 people gathered at the Lincoln Memorial and heard Dr. Martin Luther King, Jr.'s famous "I Have a Dream" speech during a massive interracial support for equality (see box). In September, four little girls were killed when the Sixteenth Street Baptist Church, where many civil rights meetings were held, was bombed in Birmingham, Alabama.

"I Have a Dream": An Excerpt from Dr. Martin Luther King, Jr.'s Speech on August 28, 1963

Let us not wallow in the valley of despair, I say to you today, my friends—so even though we face the difficulties of today and tomorrow, I still have a dream. It is a dream deeply rooted in the American dream.

I have a dream that one day this nation will rise up and live out the true meaning of its creed: "We hold these truths to be self-evident, that all men are created equal."

I have a dream that one day on the red hills of Georgia, the sons of former slaves and the sons of former slave owners will be able to sit down together at the table of brotherhood.

I have a dream that one day even the state of Mississippi, a state sweltering with the heat of injustice, sweltering with the heat of oppression, will be transformed into an oasis of freedom and justice.

I have a dream that my four little children will one day live in a nation where they will not be judged by the color of their skin but by the content of their character.

I have a dream today.

I have a dream that one day down in Alabama, with its vicious racists, with its governor having his lips dripping with the words of *interposition* and *nullification*—one day right there in Alabama little Black boys and Black girls will be able to join hands with little White boys and White girls as sisters and brothers.

I have a dream today.

I have a dream that one day every valley shall be exalted, and every hill and mountain shall be made low, the rough places will be made plain, and the crooked places will be made straight, and the glory of the Lord shall be revealed and all flesh shall see it together.

This is our hope. This is the faith that I go back to the South with. With this faith, we will be able to hew out of the mountain of despair a stone of hope. With this faith, we will be able to transform the jangling discords of our nation into a beautiful symphony of brotherhood. With this faith, we will be able to work together, to pray together, to struggle together, to go to jail together, to stand up for freedom together, knowing that we will be free one day.

This will be the day, this will be the day when all of God's children will be able to sing with new meaning, "My country 'tis of thee, sweet land of liberty, of thee I sing. Land where my fathers died, land of the Pilgrim's pride, from every mountainside, let freedom ring!"

And if America is to be a great nation, this must become true. And so let freedom ring from the prodigious hilltops of New Hampshire. Let freedom ring from the mighty mountains of New York. Let freedom ring from the heightening Alleghenies of Pennsylvania.

Let freedom ring from the snow-capped Rockies of Colorado. Let freedom ring from the curvaceous slopes of California. But not only that; let freedom ring from Stone Mountain of Georgia. Let freedom ring

(*Continued*)

(*Continued*)

from Lookout Mountain of Tennessee. Let freedom ring from every hill and molehill of Mississippi. From every mountainside, let freedom ring.

And when this happens, and when we allow freedom ring—when we let it ring from every village and every hamlet, from every state and every city, we will be able to speed up that day when all of God's children—Black men and White men, Jews and Gentiles, Protestants and Catholics—will be able to join hands and sing in the words of the old Negro spiritual: "Free at last! Free at last! Thank God Almighty, we are free at last!"

The summer of 1964 came to be known as the Freedom Summer. SNCC activists confronted the barriers to voting that Blacks faced in Mississippi during their work there. SNCC leaders formed the Council of Federated Organizations (COFO), which brought the other major civil rights SMOs and organized a huge drive to help Blacks in Mississippi register to vote. SNCC had networks of college-age volunteers that they mobilized to go to Mississippi to register Black voters, to teach prospective Black Americans the literacy level required to register to vote, and other fundamental subjects that the segregated Mississippi schools failed to teach. Most of the 1,000 volunteers were White (McAdam, 1988). Shortly after the first volunteers arrived in Mississippi, three civil rights workers, Andrew Goodman, Michael Schwerner, and James Chaney, disappeared. Six weeks later, their bodies were discovered. They had been murdered, beaten to death by segregationists, including law enforcement officers, because of their civil rights work (McAdam, 1988). Many of the other volunteers also experienced violence and arrests. Finally, in July 1964, President Johnson signed the Civil Rights Act, which gave the federal government powerful capabilities to punish segregation and discrimination in schools, housing, hiring, public facilities, and elsewhere.

The next year, 1965, began with the assassination of Malcolm X on February 21. Malcolm X was a Black nationalist who converted to Islam while in prison in the late 1940s. He was part of a more radical portion of the Civil Rights Movement, and was associated with the Nation of Islam, led by Elijah Mohammad. Malcolm X was responsible for a huge upsurge in membership in the Nation of Islam, but eventually split with Elijah Mohammad and founded Muslim Mosque, Inc. During his activism, he faced several attempts on his life, but was assassinated by members of the Nation of Islam.

A second major event in 1965 was a series of marches for voting rights between Selma and Montgomery, Alabama. There were three marches, and the first was on March 7, 1965. The march was 600 strong and was led by John Lewis and Hosea Williams (CNN Library, 2015). The marchers were attacked by law enforcement officers with tear gas and billy clubs, and they never made it out of Selma. The day was dubbed "Bloody Sunday" because of the violence. Two days later, another march was led by Martin Luther King, Jr., up to the Edmund Pettus Bridge where the earlier march had been halted. Demonstrations in support of the marches occurred in many other cities. After legal maneuvers and other efforts by Alabama Governor

George Wallace to stop the marches, President Johnson authorized federal troops to protect the marchers. On March 21, 1965, 3200 people started to march from Selma to Montgomery. By the time they arrived, there were 25,000 people in the march (CNN Library, 2015). The final major events in 1965 came on August 6 and September 24, when President Johnson signed the Voting Rights Act of 1965, and issued an executive order establishing affirmative action. This required government contractors to make proactive measures to hire minorities.

By 1966, serious divisions over strategies and ideologies had begun to affect the Civil Rights Movement. Dissatisfaction with the results of the Civil Rights Movement's accomplishments motivated Stokely Carmichael to leave the SNCC and form the Black Power movement; Huey Newton and Bobby Seale formed the Black Panther Party. They advocated separatism rather than integration and rejected nonviolence in favor of self-defense, a reaction to the violence against civil rights activists and Blacks in general. The reality was that it was easier to eliminate the legal segregation of Jim Crow in the south than to eliminate the poverty and inequality Black Americans everywhere in the United States experienced as a long-term result of discrimination. Additional pieces of legislation and court rulings strengthened the government's enforcement powers in civil rights over time, but that did not change the conditions in which Black Americans lived. Indeed, Martin Luther King, Jr. shifted his attention to the issue of Black American poverty after the passage of the Civil Rights and Voting Rights Acts. On April 4, 1968, Martin Luther King, Jr. was assassinated, and the Civil Rights Movement lost its greatest leader.

The Civil Rights Movement is remarkable for many reasons, not least the willingness of Black Americans to confront the violent oppression of the Jim Crow system. However, the movement has all the elements discussed above that make social movements possible. First, there was a strongly politicized collective identity in the Black American population, with all three criteria mentioned above as important to the establishment of a politicized collective identity. Second, there were clear boundaries to group membership, particularly in the Jim Crow South. A person was White or Black. Further, Black Americans had worked for equality long before the big movement of the 1950s and 1960s. The historically Black churches were important in politicizing and mobilizing the people, and they provided relatively safe gathering places. In addition, the segregationists were more likely to overlook these activities, given their image of Blacks as inferior and unable to mount an effective opposition to their subordination (Morris, 1999). Finally, there was a concerted effort to redefine the symbolic meaning of the group's position. Black was no longer inferior, but beautiful.

The pre-1950s protests and other efforts to get segregation eliminated achieved many successes. Additionally, the formation of the NAACP early in the twentieth century provided a sense of efficacy despite continued repression. Participation in the movement increased that sense of efficacy. Takaki (2008) quotes several participants who expressed their sense of pride and efficacy. For instance, after participating in the Woolworth sit-in, Franklin McCain said, "I probably felt better that day than I've ever felt in my life. I felt as though I had gained my manhood, so to speak, and not only gained it, but had developed quite a lot of respect for it." Another said, "I myself desegregated a lunch counter, not somebody else, not some big man, some powerful man, but me, little me." Martin Luther King, Jr. generalized about the sense of efficacy: "a generation of young people ... has come out of decades of shadows to face naked state power; it has lost its fears, and experienced the majestic dignity of a direct struggle for its own liberation" (all quotes from Takaki, 2008, p. 391).

The Civil Rights Movement certainly had the social embeddedness necessary for mobilization. There were local and national networks of volunteers and supporters. The movement had several major SMOs, including the NAACP, SLCL, SNCC, and CORE, with national and local chapters, as well as very local organizations and churches. Moreover, as Morris (1999) notes, the migration of Blacks from the South to the North in the first half of the twentieth century affected the structural component of embeddedness. It "led to institution building especially within the Black Church and community organizations. These were the kinds of institutions through which protest could be organized and supported. The urban setting also provided the Black community with dense social networks through which social protest could be organized rapidly" (p. 523). In addition, there was the impressive development of television during the Civil Rights Movement era. By 1958, more than 83% of American homes had TVs which, along with communication satellites, "were capable of providing a window through which millions could watch Black protest and become familiar with the issues it raised" (Morris, 1999, p. 522). Finally, the Civil Rights Movement was extremely capable of creating an injustice frame, and it was not limited to Black Americans. Inequality and discrimination were at the heart of the frame, bridging the many divides among minorities and women.

The Civil Rights Movement had a variety of leaders, with combinations of the leader characteristics discussed above—charisma, prophecy, and pragmatism. Certainly, Martin Luther King, Jr. had all three, but there were also many other leaders at the national, church, and local levels with these characteristics. For example, at the national and church levels, there were Rosa Parks, Ralph Abernathy, James Meredith, Bernard Lee, Andrew Young, Malcolm X, Daisy Bates, Charles Evers, James Lawson, and so forth. Student leaders included John Lewis, Julian Bond, Hosea Williams, Stokely Carmichael, Diane Nash, Bob Moses and many others. There was competition and disagreement among the leaders of the movement about goals, ideology, and strategy, but they were effective.

THE TEA PARTY

The Tea Party appeared on the American political scene in 2009 after a commentary by CNBC reporter Rick Santelli. Criticizing President Barack Obama's stimulus package response to the Great Recession of 2008, Santelli said, "The government is promoting bad behavior ... This is America. How many of you people want to pay for your neighbor's mortgage ... we're thinking of having a Chicago Tea Party in July. All you capitalists that want to show up to Lake Michigan ..." (quoted in Williamson, Skocpol, & Coggin, 2011, p. 37). The Tea Party is a reference to the Boston Tea Party of December 16, 1773, when Bostonians, dressed like Native Americans, tossed tea into the harbor in protest of the British colonial Tea Act, which forced them to buy tea from the British East India Company. On April 15, 2009, hundreds of Tea Party protests were held across the United States, and some had thousands of participants. One of the Tea Party's earliest concerns was the health reform proposals of newly elected President Obama. This concern expanded to focus on the size of government and the Tea Party supporters' perceived need to follow an interpretation of the Constitution they believed should replace the current, and in their view, distorted interpretation. Four years later, the Tea Party penetrated the House of Representatives and used its power to advance its view of the proper role of government.

The Tea Party is often described as a grassroots or populist social movement composed of people fed up with politics as usual. Some disagree, believing the Tea Party is not a social movement. Early on, the Tea Party phenomenon was considered nonpartisan and anti-establishment (Street & DiMaggio, 2011). When it first emerged after the 2008 election of Barack Obama and the Republican defeats in the House and Senate, the Tea Party was described as helpful for the Republican Party, but equally problematic. Because Tea Party ideology demands small government, a reduction in the deficit, and lower taxes even if it means fewer jobs, its positions were clearly in opposition to that of the Democratic Party. However, because members rejected many of the compromises that traditional Republicans were willing to make, they were also seen as a challenge to the Republican old guard, and a force moving the Republican Party to the right, or kicking traditional Republicans out of office, replacing them with Tea Party supporters (DiMaggio, 2011). Tea Parties were locally organized, and there was no national Tea Party formal organization, although a number of local organizations joined a federation called the Tea Party Patriots in 2009 (McCarthy, Rafail, & Gromis, 2013). The Republican National Committee and state Republican organizations did not control the Tea Parties (Williamson et al., 2011). Local organizations made use of the internet to organize meetings and activities. Local Tea Parties also differed in their agendas and issues. The idea that government was too big and intrusive was widely shared, but some took positions on social issues such as abortion and gay marriage, while others did not. They opposed the stimulus, the Affordable Care Act (Obamacare), and amnesty for illegal immigrants. The Tea Party also contained members who were explicitly racist toward Black and Muslim people, and the Latino community, particularly immigrants.

After Obama won a second term, the Tea Party lost its steam and membership fell off, leaving only a few groups. The House Tea Party Caucus no longer exists (Haupt, 2020). When Donald Trump was elected, he made a budget deal with Congress undermining Tea Party efforts because it lifted defense spending and domestic spending constraints for two years, and the debt ceiling through July 2021 (Cillizza, 2019). The Tea Party went from a Democratic adversary to a Republican group that didn't share their ideals. As we discussed in Chapter 6, Trump's movement gave people a platform to follow outside of mainstream society. The Tea Party could not compete. Given this series of events, it is no surprise the movement faded away. But while the Tea Party appears to be a description of a social movement, is it?

Looking at some of the qualities of the Tea Party several years after it emerged on the scene, many observers concluded that it was not a social movement. In determining the answer, the first consideration is whether there was a mobilized political identity with a clear grievance. Montopoli (2012) argues Tea Party members were not those who suffered from relative deprivation, although they were angry. Tea Party supporters tended to be rural or suburban dwellers, better educated and wealthier than the average American. They were male (59%), middle-aged (75% are 45 or older), and White (89%) (Street & DiMaggio, 2011, p. 48). It is also unclear whether they had a distinct collective identity. Most Tea Partiers were Republicans. In a CBS News/*New York Times* survey in 2010, a majority of Tea Party supporters described themselves as conservative Republicans (Williamson et al., 2011). Fifty-four percent had a favorable view of the Republican Party, and 92% had an unfavorable view of the Democratic Party (Street & DiMaggio, 2011). Moreover, "[f]ewer than 1 in 5 TPS [Tea Party Supporters] thought there was 'a lot of difference between the Republican Party and the Tea Party Movement'" (Street & DiMaggio, 2011, p. 63). In a 2012 CBS News poll, 54% identified as Republican, 41% as Independent, and only 5% as Democrats. Seventy-five percent called themselves conservative and 39% very conservative. Sixty percent said they usually or always voted Republican, and only 40% agreed that the United States needed a third party, while 52% of Tea Party supporters did not agree with that idea (Montopoli, 2012). Only Tea Party activists wanted greater independence from the Republican Party, and there were not a lot of Tea Party activists. For example, the same poll found that only 20% of those who considered themselves Tea Party supporters ever sent in a donation or attended a Tea Party activity (Williamson et al., 2011). In a different poll in 2010, 80% of Tea Party supporters who intended to vote in the November 2010 election said they would vote for Republicans, and this included Independents who leaned Republican (Street & DiMaggio, 2011). Consequently, it cannot be argued they had a distinct and separate political identity. They were overwhelmingly Republicans. They were a faction within the Republican voting community with a Tea Party identity. Does this constitute the kind of politicized identity associated with social movements?

Another question is whether they were challenging authority and seeking to change the political system. This is a difficult question to answer definitively. On one hand, the Tea Party was a vocal movement of protesters who engaged in grassroots lobbying, creating opportunities for people with grievances to protest (McCarthy, Rafail, & Gromis, 2013). They were effective in challenging long-term politicians. Tea Party candidates defeated mainstream Republicans such as Lisa Murkowski and Richard Lugar, long-serving Republican Senators from Alaska and Indiana, respectively, in primary contests in 2010, and House Majority Leader Eric Cantor in the 2014 Republican primary. Tea Party Republicans in Congress tried to use the 2013 debt ceiling crisis to force the repeal of Obamacare. They effectively shut down the government for 15 days by refusing to vote for a solution to the debt ceiling problem. In the end, they were defeated, but they demonstrated political muscle by stalemating the establishment.

On the other hand, the Tea Party benefited from the political establishment, and most social movements are not associated with institutional support structures. Fox News consistently placed the Tea Party front and center in reporting on its activities. Several of its most prominent reporters,

Glenn Beck, Sean Hannity, Greta Van Susteren, and Neil Cavuto, broadcasted from Tea Party actions (Williamson et al., 2011). The Tea Party had early support from several grassroots organizations such as Freedomworks, an organization associated with the activities of former Congressman Dick Armey, the American Family Association (AFA), and Americans for Prosperity (AFP), an organization established by the billionaire Koch brothers in 2003. The Tea Party also benefited from having sympathetic current or former elected officials at the national level when it was formed, including Sarah Palin, Michelle Bachmann, Ron Paul, and other prominent members of the Republican Party. These characteristics led some scholars to argue that the Tea Party was not a social movement, but rather a "fundamentally top-down, elite-directed affair" (Street & DiMaggio, 2011, p. 127).

OCCUPY WALL STREET

The winter and spring of 2011 were politically dramatic. The Arab Spring began, ending in the demise of dictatorships in Tunisia, Libya, and Egypt. There were protests across Europe against economic cuts by recession-drained European governments. Inspired by these events, the Occupy Wall Street social movement began in the United States. A predecessor of Occupy Wall Street in the United States was an extended protest by the group New Yorkers Against Budget Cuts, who settled in on the sidewalk near New York City Hall to protest Mayor Bloomberg's plan to lay off 4,000 teachers and shut down 20 firehouses. They brought their sleeping bags and dubbed their camp Bloombergville (Sledge, 2011). They started in the middle of June, and by the end of June Bloombergville was gone. However, it helped give birth to the Occupy Wall Street idea. On July 13, 2011, a magazine called AdBusters called for an occupation of Wall Street in New York City. Despite initial difficulties, the idea began to grow, and around 200 veteran activists and organizers from protests such as the Seattle WTO protests in 1999 began to work toward the development of ground rules that would get people mobilized (Sledge, 2011). On September 17, 2011, protesters occupied Zuccotti Park in New York City, and Occupy Wall Street began. By early October, demonstrations had spread to other cities across the United States and many other countries. Camps were set up and people settled in with their tents and sleeping bags. Word spread through Facebook, Twitter, media coverage, and electronic communication.

The central grievance of the movement was the economic inequalities and injustices perceived in the capitalist economic system. They noted that 1% of American households owned between 30% and 40% of the nation's wealth, and therefore deemed themselves the 99% who were the have-nots (Gautney, 2011). Initially, other than protesting the growing income inequality in the United States, the Occupy movement did not have specific demands. This served the movement at the time because their desire was to be inclusive and democratic. Specific demands early on would have to come from someone, and Occupiers did not believe in top-down directives from authorities. Their identity was that of the outsiders, the "un-mainstream." They were "deeply committed to a radical departure from political norms" (Gitlin, 2012, p. 105). They perceived themselves as practitioners of direct democracy. All viewpoints deserved a hearing, and decisions would be made by consensus. Because of these views, they eschewed support for any candidate in the upcoming 2012 elections, were ambivalent about support from labor unions and celebrities, and were disappointed in Barack Obama. As Todd Gitlin notes:

> It ought to have been obvious what the movement stood for. Anyone with an ear could have figured out the essentials. The loudest, most frequently chanted slogans on the largest marches were "We are the 99 percent" and "Banks got bailed out, we got sold out." The first meant: The Plutocracy that controls the commanding heights of the economy and politics needs to be curbed. The second meant: The federal government under both George W. Bush and Barack Obama caved into the big banks while failing to relieve householder debt or stop foreclosures.
>
> (Gitlin, 2012, p. 82)

In accordance with the principle of direct democracy, the Occupy Wall Street movements were local, not national, organizations, and they were only loosely organized. Encampments were horizontally organized and not hierarchical (Gitlin, 2012). They each had General Assemblies (GA) where all issues were discussed, but there were no institutions, because none were perceived necessary. The General Assemblies had "people's mics" so everyone could take the microphone and speak. Minutes were taken and shared. While this was democratic, it also meant decision-making was glacial in pace. The Occupiers also formed "Working Groups" to carry out specific tasks such as food, outreach, and security.

Another important characteristic of the Occupy movement concerned leaders: there were none. The GA, for example, would have the daily meetings led by rotating facilitators and anyone could be trained as a facilitator (Gautney, 2011). The Working Groups were also open to anyone, and they reported to the GA. To build a consensus on decision-making, proposals were discussed, questions posed and answered, and votes would be cast through hand signals; proposals were recast until 90% agreed with the proposal (Gautney, 2011). The GA had the only legitimate voice for the Occupiers. This manner of governance had its problems. It was very difficult to deal with concrete issues such as how to spend donated money. A solution was developed through setting up "Spokes Councils" (as in the spoke of a wheel). Spokes Councils began to be organized in October 2011. They were made up of members of Working Groups, who would meet three times weekly to deal with technical issues like how to use donations. The representatives of the Working Groups were to be backed up by other members of the Working Group, and they would be rotated weekly on the Spokes Councils (Gitlin, 2012, p. 73). After considerable discussion, the Spokes Councils began meeting on November 7, but they did not work well and the meetings became chaotic and hostile (Gitlin, 2012).

The Occupy Wall Street camps lasted until early 2012, when police began to force the camps to disperse (McCarthy, Rafail, & Gromis, 2013). Three months after it started, the Occupy movement had about the same number of supporters as the Tea Party movement, which had started three years earlier (Gitlin, 2012). The two movements were both polarizing and very different. Occupy Wall Street was clearly a grassroots movement, while the Tea Party was not. The Occupy movement lacked leaders, and the Tea Party started with leaders and created more as time went on. The Tea Party had clear electoral goals, and the Occupy movement did not. Unlike the Tea Party, which became a movement within the Republican Party, the Occupy movement rejected the political parties as part of the problem and refused to become part of the Democratic mainstream. The Tea Party impacted the functioning of the American political system. The effect of the Occupy movement more likely impacted culture and values, as it called attention to economic injustice, rather than policy (McCarthy, Rafail, & Gromis, 2013).

THE ME TOO MOVEMENT

The phrase "Me Too" was popularized in 2006 by Tarana Burke in the United States to raise awareness of sexual violence. Burke was a women's advocate in New York. However, in 2016 actress Alyssa Milano used the phrase on Twitter to accuse producer Harvey Weinstein of sexual assault. The tweet went viral, leading to an investigation into his conduct. Weinstein was convicted of sexual crimes against his assistant, and also an actress. After Milano, other actresses came forward too, shedding light on the issues pervasive in the film industry. Even though Me Too went from grassroots to more popular in scope, this was not all about Hollywood. Milano's tweet sparked a movement where all people became empowered to come forward and share their stories, not only with her, but publicly. #MeToo started trending on Twitter and Instagram. Tarana Burke runs a website dedicated to helping survivors and providing education and resources. Through various platforms connecting people, the movement is a way to facilitate the sharing of stories, discuss issues, and support and empower others with regard to sexual violence—not only in the United States, but around the world.

Ultimately, the goal of the movement is to show how widespread the problem is, which may bring about social and political change. Certainly there have been high-profile investigations and prosecutions, along with resignations from public officials (Beitsch, 2018), but as mentioned above, this is also a problem that goes beyond high-profile elites. And here is where law-makers need to bring about necessary change to better protect individuals from sexual violence, and support them if it takes place. To that end, there are examples of changes state legislatures made in 2018 under the banner of supporting the movement, such as limits on nondisclosure agreements, improvement of testing of rape kits, and extending the statute of limitations for civil suits (Beitsch, 2018). A review by the Associated Press found mixed results. As Lieb (2020) explains:

> The AP review found mixed indications of progress and problems as the #MeToo movement enters its third legislative year. Over the past two years, states have enacted more than 75 laws and resolutions targeting sexual harassment, abuse and assault within government or the private sector.

> Some of those laws have required regular training intended to prevent harassment, established clear channels for reporting allegations, granted greater legal protections to whistle blowers, shed public light on secretive settlements and extended the deadline for prosecuting or suing over past instances of sexual abuse. At least two-thirds of all states have enacted some sort of new law in the #MeToo era.
>
> The AP review found that at least 43 state Senate chambers and 45 House or Assembly chambers require sexual harassment training for their members. That's up significantly from January 2018, when the AP's initial survey found that about a third of all legislative chambers did not require lawmakers to receive training about what constitutes sexual harassment, how to report it and what consequences it carries.
>
> Two years ago, the AP found that only a minority of legislative bodies conducted external investigations into complaints, with most others entrusting lawmakers or staff to look into allegations against colleagues. Today, the AP found that about half of all state legislative chambers have procedures for external investigators to look into sexual misconduct complaints involving lawmakers— a process that experts say can instill greater confidence for people to come forward with complaints.

Since 2017, at least 101 state lawmakers have publicly been accused of sexual harassment or misconduct, even in the face of training programs (Lieb, 2020).

With the aid of social media and high-profile advocates, the phrase "Me Too" went from a grassroots effort to a global movement. It is likely that this movement will continue to remain a force for change as lawmakers grapple with this high-profile and sustained movement for change.

Black Lives Matter

Black Lives Matter was founded in 2013 by Alicia Garza, Patrisse Cullors, and Opal Tometi in response to the acquittal of George Zimmerman for the murder of Trayvon Martin. Since that time, it has become a global member-led network with over 40 chapters. According to the organization, "Black Lives Matter is an ideological and political intervention in a world where Black lives are systematically and intentionally targeted for demise. It is an affirmation of Black folks' humanity, our contributions to this society, and our resilience in the face of deadly oppression" (https://blacklivesmatter.com/herstory). The stated mission of the movement is to:

> Eradicate white supremacy and build local power to intervene in violence inflicted on Black communities by the state and vigilantes. By combating and countering acts of violence, creating space for Black imagination and innovation, and centering Black joy, we are winning immediate improvements in our lives.
>
> (https://blacklivesmatter.com/about)

The movement is also based on Black inclusivity, pointing out that it welcomes queer, trans, and undocumented people, women, all spectrums of gender, disabled people, and folks with records. The movement organizes protests, educates and supports people in their communities, and advocates for political and social change. It also celebrates the important contributions made by Black Americans. Black Lives Matter has a large internet and social media profile with a website, Twitter, Facebook, and Instagram accounts.

Years after 2013, President Donald Trump was elected on the promise of restoring America to its greatness. He was a president unapologetic for the ongoing incidents of racism and police brutality against minorities, and refused to condemn the actions of White supremacists. In fact, as Serwer (2020) puts it:

> Instead of ushering in a golden age of prosperity and a return to the cultural conservatism of the 1950s, Trump's presidency has radicalized millions of white Americans who were previously inclined to dismiss systemic racism as a myth, the racial wealth gap as a product of Black cultural pathology, and discriminatory policing as a matter of a few bad apples.

In 2020, Ahmaud Arbery was shot and killed by three men in Georgia because he looked suspicious, but they were let go. This was followed by the fatal shooting by police in Louisville of Breonna Taylor while they were serving a no-knock warrant on her boyfriend. Only one of the officers was fired. Following this, George Floyd died after a Minneapolis police officer kneeled on his neck (Serwer, 2020). In May, protests erupted in Minneapolis, but also spread to other towns and cities across the United States, some including rioting and looting. Some cities responded with tear gas, rubber bullets, and pursued arrests. The National Guard was activated. Instead of a message of unification, Trump responded with threats to crack down on and punish the protesters. He called them "thugs" and "terrorists" (Serwer, 2020). This undermined the gravity and importance of the protests, in particular those peaceful protesters who came in the spirit of unity in support of Black Lives Matter and other organizations. Protests continued and, by June, data from Civis Analytics estimated at least 15–26 million people had participated in protests in cities across the United States since George Floyd's death, making it the largest movement in the country's history (Buchanan et al., 2020). Even with the election of President Joe Biden, Black Lives Matter will continue to play an important role as the country continues to grapple with systemic racism, and individuals emboldened by Trump who perceive this movement as an ongoing threat to their White identity.

FROM THE TEA PARTY TO WHITE NATIONALISM AND THE ALT-RIGHT

The White Nationalist Movement (WNM) and the Alternative Right Movement (referred to as the alt-right) are related in some core elements. The WNM includes White supremacists as well as those who are not obsessed with ideas pertaining to White racial superiority, including some of the groups in the alt-right. These include the American Freedom Party, Identity Europa (which is now the American Identity Movement), and the National Policy Institute led by Richard Spencer. These organizations tend to have younger members, also advocate for White men, have fascistic ideas, and make extensive use of internet sites to communicate with members and recruit new members (Fording & Schram, 2020; Griffin, 2017). There is a fine line differentiating these groups from White supremacist groups, since both types want to maintain the power and political control of White people in the United States.

The number of White supremacist groups increased from 2000 to 2010, then began to decline in numbers. The number of other White nationalist groups increased from 2015 to 2018, although the total number of these groups decreased after 2010. Obama's election fueled their fears that Whites were losing political power, so the increases make sense. The decline, however, is a surprising pattern. Fording and Schram (2020) explain that the number of White nationalist groups decreased because White nationalists identified an opportunity to enter mainstream politics because of the Tea Party movement and the entrance of Donald Trump into national politics. Both the Tea Party and Trump mainstreamed racism toward both Black and Latino immigrants, White identity politics, and White nationalism. Fording and Schram (2020) argue that conventional channels of participation, such as party politics and electoral mobilization, were shut off for these people. Neither the Democratic Party nor the Republican Party wanted avowed racists and related White nationalists in their ranks until the Tea Party and Donald Trump changed that for the Republican Party. In effect, Trump became the leader of a social movement that included White nationalists, racists, and members of the alt-right. As Fording and Schram write:

> Not all white nationalists embraced Trump straight away as their natural leader even if they shared his sense of resentment toward mainstream society. Yet by 2016 most white racial extremists had come around and overwhelmingly swung their support solidly in his direction ... From its inception, Trump's campaign was indebted to the WNM. It built on the resentment the movement was articulating regarding how whites saw themselves as under assault in a changing society. This resentment crystalized in reaction to Obama's presidency, and Trump shared that resentment. While as a candidate he opportunistically chose to align himself with this movement to give himself a needed base of support, it was a base he felt at home with given his own personal racist past and proclivity to increasingly express hostility to outgroups he saw as threatening to the position of whites in American society.
>
> (Fording & Schram, 2020, pp. 98–99)

As discussed in Chapter 8, but elaborated on here, the alternative right, or alt-right, is a term introduced by Richard Spencer of the National Policy Institute to describe people who belong to loose groups who believe in neo-reactionary ideals and decry what they describe as the undermining of White civilization. Like Occupy Wall Street, this movement is not organized, has no institutions (although there are some organizational publications), and no recognized leadership (Hawley, 2017). They make heavy use of the internet for communication. Up until 2017, they were generally nonviolent. They are anti-egalitarian, hostile to traditional conservatism, and associated with White nationalism (Griffin, 2017; SPLC, 2020a). They tend to disavow racism but, as Griffin (2017) argues, the "new white nationalist professionalism practiced by Richard Spencer and others cannot always skirt the obvious association with fascist ideology and the long history of hate groups in the United States whose lineage they court, despite attempts to tamp down KKK and Neo-Nazi visibility within the movement itself" (p. 8). They also vary in terms of anti-Semitism, with some regarding Jews as White people, and others being explicitly hostile toward Jews (SPLC, 2019). Feminists are also a target, and the movement supports a patriarchy where women stay home and serve the needs of their men. The alt-right organizations protest political correctness and found a soulmate in Donald Trump. Like Trump, they have no interest in traditional conservatism in American politics. Hawley summarizes them in this way:

> Using the loosest definition, we could say that the Alt-Right includes anyone with right-wing sensibilities that rejects the mainstream conservative movement. But there are certain, perhaps universal attitudes within the Alt-Right. The Alt-Right is fundamentally concerned with race. At its core, the Alt-Right is a white nationalist movement even if many (perhaps most) of the people who identify with the Alt-Right do not care for that term. The most significant and energetic figures of the movement want to see the creation of a white ethnostate in North America.
>
> (Hawley, 2017, p. 9)

Members of the alt-right tend to be young and computer savvy, using the internet to recruit and to promote neo-reactionary themes, particularly through blogs by Nick Land and Curtis Yarvis, also known as Mencius Moldbug. The movement is composed of various loosely organized groups and is fluid, filled with disagreements, competition for leadership, and conspiratorial thinking. The various groups associated with the alt-right may or may not accept that association. Unlike the White identity and nationalist movement discussed above, the alt-right is not moving into mainstream politics. The alt-right turned to violent tactics when Richard Spencer and others organized the Unite the Right rally in Charlottesville, Virginia in August 2017. The demonstration turned violent and counter-protester Heather Heyer was hit and killed by a car driven by alt-right activist James Fields.

In addition to the alt-right there is the alt-light, or alt-lite. The chief difference between the two is the rejection by the alt-lite of White supremacy. They agree with the alt-right on many issues, including disdain for liberals, Black Lives Matter, and opposition to immigration. The alt-lite calls for "Western chauvinism," which espouses American nationalism and glorifies western civilization, particularly at the expense of Islam. Among their leaders are Milo Yiannopoulos, Gavin McInnes, founder of vice media and the Proud Boys in 2016, and Steve Bannon, former Trump adviser and Breitbart News head. Confrontations between the alt-right and alt-lite have been tense, as in a Houston demonstration when alt-lite activists from the Oath Keepers tried to expel an alt-right advocate.

There are several militias associated with the alt-right and alt-lite. As mentioned, the Proud Boys were organized by alt-liter McInnes in 2016. Despite their claims to be non-racist, they are associated with racist memes and were present at the Charlottesville rally with other hate groups. In fact, former Proud Boy Jason Kessler was one of the organizers of the rally (he was later expelled from the organization). Although they later condemned the killing of Heather Heyer, they regularly engage in violent clashes with anti-fascist (antifa) demonstrators (SPLC, 2020b).

Another militia organization associated with the alt-lite is the Oath Keepers, founded in 2009 by Stewart Rhodes. The group recruits at events and through the internet, and heavily from the police and the military in the United States. The Oath Keepers strongly support Donald Trump and many participated in the insurrection at the U.S. Capitol building on January 6, 2021. Several were indicted on charges related to that attack. The central issues with which the Oath Keepers are concerned are gun rights and the New World Order. The latter includes the fear that liberals will use their demographic advantage to take away the rights of others, that the Green New Deal will threaten agriculture, and that Black Lives Matter, and other "Marxists," along with immigrants and Muslims, will destroy western values (Giglio, 2020). In addition to the insurgency at the Capitol in 2021, the Oath Keepers participated in the 2014 standoff between supporters of Cliven Bundy and federal authorities over cattle grazing rights, and went to Ferguson, Missouri to protect businesses from rioters following the killing of Michael Brown. There, pictures "of Oath Keepers standing guard on rooftops with semi-automatic rifles became symbols of an America beginning to turn on itself" (Giglio, 2020, p. 65). The Oath Keepers are preparing for civil war and intend to use the skills they learned in the military or police to fight.

The Arab Spring

The phrase "Arab Spring" is a western term used to describe the dynamic political social movements that began in early 2011, and spread across Tunisia, Egypt, Libya, Yemen, Bahrain, Algeria, and Syria. The outcomes varied, and some are still undetermined, but the movement reflected widespread desires for economic, social, and political change in the Arab countries in North Africa and the Middle East. Protests occurred in several different countries during the decade preceding the events of 2011. These protests expressed grievances about the rising prices of basic food needs, corruption, unemployment, and political repression. Nevertheless, the protests that started in 2011 gained a great deal of traction and spread across the region. These social movements were calls for revolutionary change. In this section, the overall causes of the movement will be discussed, then attention will turn to four cases with very different outcomes: Tunisia, Egypt, Libya, and Yemen.

What caused the social movement called the Arab Spring? There were many causes, and the Arab Spring was not a sudden and unprecedented series of events. The countries in the Arab world are diverse. The oil-producing countries have a great deal of wealth and can provide their citizens with enough benefits to prevent economic discontent. Those without oil resources have high levels of poverty. Some have relatively well-educated populaces; others do not. Many have high unemployment, particularly among the legions of young people under the age of 30. Some, like Saudi Arabia, Jordan, the United Arab Emirates, and Morocco, are monarchies, while others had dictators from various walks of life. Some countries are homogeneous in terms of religion, ethnicity, and tribal loyalties; others are heterogeneous. Thus, the factors causing the Arab Spring were different in each country, but some generalizations can be made about conditions important in many countries.

The grievances driving the Arab Spring movement were economic and political in nature. Economic growth in the region was not robust despite the implementation of some neoliberal reforms. Gross Domestic Product (GDP) was only 3% on average for the region during the preceding three decades. Oil and gas were the only exports that grew, and nearly 60% of the region's exports went to Europe, meaning there was little penetration of the huge new market potential in China and India (Gelvin, 2012). Moreover, the high oil prices of the 1970s, which benefited oil producers and nonproducers alike, began to fall in the 1980s. States could no longer provide the benefits of the past. Unemployment remained high in many countries, and with 60% of the region's population under the age of 30, this could only get worse (Gelvin, 2012). One important sector suffering from unemployment and dashed expectations was the large number of university graduates trying to enter the job market. They ended up being unemployed or under-employed.

The neoliberal reforms of the 1970s and 1980s so strongly supported by the International Monetary Fund also affected the economies of the region. States in the region began to privatize industry, liberalize economically, and invite in foreign investors. This improved the economies for the economic elite and some jobs and resources trickled down to the rest of society, but some of the reforms increased hardship for the poor, as subsidies for important items such as wheat (bread) and heating fuel were cut. Moreover, the economic benefits from increased foreign investments "were diluted by crony capitalist systems that ensured the benefits of foreign investment went to a small clique of businesses owned or controlled by key regime figures" (Noueihed & Warren, 2013, p. 27). The corruption was no secret in any of these countries. In addition to corruption, the average citizen faced constant demands for graft. Salaries paid to public servants were low, and the states employed large portions of the working population so people were forced to pay bribes for most transactions. Meanwhile, people who could not get work in oil-poor countries could find work in oil-rich countries, and they sent money home. This caused an increase in housing prices in the home countries, making it difficult or impossible for people without relatively high-paying jobs to find affordable housing (Noueihed & Warren, 2013).

Another important characteristic of the region was the persistence of aging dictatorships and traditional monarchies. For example, Egypt's President Hosni Mubarak was in office for 31 years, Tunisia's President Zine el Abidine Ben Ali was in office for 24 years, Libya's leader Muammar al-Qaddafi ruled for 42 years, and Yemen's President Ali Abdullah Saleh for 21 years when the movements began. The dictatorships were repressive, and by 2010 it looked as if they were going to turn into corrupt dynasties. Hosni Mubarak's son Gamal was widely believed to be his father's designated successor, and Ben Ali in Tunisia was grooming his son-in-law for the role. In Syria, Hafez al Assad's son Bashar took over after his death in 2000. The dictatorships cemented their rule with state of emergency laws, which suspended constitutional rights, empowered security agencies to detain people, and censored news coverage in the name of security. In addition, these dictatorships used formal and informal intelligence agencies that arrested people, kept them in secret prisons, and tortured them, all to prevent political dissent. Spies were everywhere, and people would engage in self-censorship in order not to violate known or unknown rules. The most repressed political groups were Islamists, but anyone could come under the scrutiny of the intelligence forces.

All of this produced an "Arab malaise," particularly among the young, well-educated portions of the populations. A new *politicized collective identity* emerged that included concern for justice, the ability to participate in a transparent political system, and human rights as central themes. As mentioned, protests occurred during the decade before the Arab Spring, but by 2010 there began a "battle for the identity of the region … a battle for satisfying jobs, decent housing, and the right of young people to grow up and build families and futures of their own" (Noueihed & Warren, 2013, p. 7). Added to this was the growth of social media, which made a huge difference in awareness of conditions in and among the countries in the region, despite regime efforts to quash information and knowledge. Al Jazeera, which started broadcasting in 1996, was the first news-oriented channel in Arabic, and it offered not only news, but debate about the news (Noueihed & Warren, 2013). Viewers were also able to call in and express their own opinions. Further, the internet and mobile phones had a big impact on the activists of the Arab Spring. They could communicate and organize for action through the internet and cell phones. Cell phones were available in remote areas where landlines had never existed, which broadened the politically aware community.

Given these circumstances, it is not surprising the Arab Spring was largely leaderless. The movement was not an ideological one, but represented general concerns for justice and human rights. It was not a movement based upon political organizations, although political organizations such as labor and Islamist organizations supported it on a case-by-case basis. As Noueihed and Warren put it:

> Lacking the hierarchical structures of traditional organizations, the loose and leaderless networks flummoxed police, who could not identify the ringleaders and did not see the young Internet-savvy activists as a serious threat. Focusing on a single demand with general appeal, protesters would build coalitions that brought together the Islamist and secular, the trade unionist and the businessman, the young and the old. Those coalitions would be broad, but they would necessarily be loose and easily divided. The online networks that were formed were able to grow very large, very quickly, but they lacked the cohesion

> of smaller, tight-knit networks based on face-to-face interactions over a long period, and they could vanish as quickly as they appeared.
>
> (Noueihed & Warren, 2013, p. 59)

Tunisia

Tunisia was ground zero of the Arab Spring. On December 17, 2010, a street vendor named Muhammad Bouazizi set himself on fire in front of municipal buildings in the rural Tunisian town Sidi Bouzid. He had operated his fruit stand without a legal permit and it was confiscated by police, who also humiliated him. Bouazizi was the sole provider for his widowed mother and siblings. This act sparked protests, which quickly spread to Tunis, the capital of Tunisia.

Tunisia was not the obvious first candidate for the Arab Spring. It had a relatively small population of 10 million, 98% of whom were Sunni Arabs. It had a large middle class, the best educational system in the Arab world, and organized labor through the Tunisian General Union of Labor (UGTT), although it was not particularly strong or effective in representing labor interests. Tunisia had a robust tourist business and was a popular destination. President Zine el-Abidine Ben Ali cultivated an international reputation as a technocratic ruler (Anderson, 2011). Nevertheless, once one left the developed and relatively prosperous coastal area, poverty and despair were evident.

Ben Ali had been in office since 1987 after he deposed Habib Bouguiba, who took power after independence in 1956. Tunisia had many of the characteristics of the countries affected by the Arab Spring. When Ben Ali took over, his predecessor, who declared himself president for life, became mentally incompetent. Ben Ali initially looked as though he would not follow Bouguiba's footsteps, limiting presidential terms to three years, and eligibility to serve up to age 75. However, he soon reversed these restrictions and ran for office five times, each time winning 89–98% of the vote (Gelvin, 2012). He allowed his family and extended relatives access to the economy and was notoriously corrupt. More than half of the country's commercial elites were related to them (Anderson, 2011). Islamists were considered the biggest threat to the regime, and the Tunisian Islamist movement, called Ennahda (Renaissance), was severely repressed (Noueihed & Warren, 2013). Ben Ali also established a security force separate from the army and the police, over which he had personal control. By the time of Bouazizi's self-immolation, Ben Ali had alienated the business community through corruption, undermined his ruling political party, and displeased the armed forces and police, who resented the power of his separate security force (Noueihed & Warren, 2013). In short, he was vulnerable.

The protests that started after Bouazizi's death started in Sidi Bouzid, and included vendors like Bouazizi as well as his friends and family, young activists, lawyers, teachers, labor activists, and even some politicians (Gelvin, 2012; Noueihed & Warren, 2013). They set up a Popular Resistance Committee to keep the demonstrations going. The protests were encouraged by labor strikes. As Anderson (2011) notes, "the protests also revealed a sharp generational divide among the opposition. The quick-fire demonstrations filled with angry youth made the generation of regime dissidents from the 1980s, primarily union activists and Islamist militants ... appear elderly and outmoded" (p. 4). Because this was the first Arab Spring event, it was less organized than those that followed. As the demonstrations spread, clashes with police in the town of Thala resulted in five protesters being shot.

Ben Ali attempted to placate the protesters by offering to create 50,000 new jobs, hold parliamentary elections, end censorship, and step down when he turned 75 (Gelvin, 2012). In order to prevent young people from gathering, he closed down the schools, which of course left them free to gather elsewhere. Although the army refused to fire on protesters, 21 people were killed by government snipers in a town near the capital. News of the uprisings spread through social media and al Jazeera. By January 13, the armed forces chief of staff told the army to stand down, and the next day Ben Ali fled for Saudi Arabia (Gelvin, 2012). His departure was not enough, and people demanded an end to the old regime in its entirety. "The regime must go" became their slogan. In October 2011, the country held elections to form a constituent assembly to create a new constitution. The Islamist party Ennahda won, and formed a coalition with two other secular parties. More protests erupted from those who either wanted a more conservative, or more secular government. Then in 2013, two secular politicians were killed. For some the blame fell on Ennahda. New elections were organized and took place in 2014 with secular parties, particularly Nidaa Tounes, gaining more seats. Beji Caid Essebsi, leader of Nidaa Tounes, became president. Unfortunately, stability in the government did not follow, with a split in Nidaa Tounes in 2016 and a change in platform by Ennahda when it dropped political Islam. After a no confidence vote removing the prime minister, a new one from Nidaa Tounes settled in: Youseef Chahed.

Adding to an already tenuous situation was an attack in 2015 on the Bardo Museum in Tunis by al-Qaeda in the Islamic Maghreb (AQIM), one in the city of Sousse, and an attack on a bus carrying the Presidential Guard perpetrated by the Islamic State of Iraq and Syria (ISIS). Security forces and local residents managed to push back ISIS during another attack on the border town of Ben Guerdane (Lounnas, 2019). As we will also see in the case of Libya, foreign fighters in Iraq, Libya, and Syria were drawn from Tunisia. Returnees had experience and would support ISIS back home.

At first, Tunisia appeared to be heading toward a stable democratic political system. However, organized protests emerged, and they are still taking place because of issues such as inflation, tax hikes, unemployment, police repression, and corruption.

Egypt

Egyptian activists watched the unfolding events in Tunisia with great interest. They planned their first protests for January 25, 2011, shortly after Ben Ali left Tunisia. They got their nonviolent tactics, their "the regime must go" slogan, and their determination to bring down the regime of Hosni Mubarak from the Tunisian movement (Gelvin, 2012). They also relied heavily on social media to mobilize people from across the political, economic, and social spectrum. The Egyptian movement, like the Tunisian movement, was also leaderless.

This does not mean the Egyptian uprising would not have occurred without Tunisia's example. Egypt was similar to Tunisia in terms of factors leading to susceptibility to the Arab Spring movement, and there were many events leading up to the downfall of the Mubarak regime in Egypt. Between 2006 and 2011, there were 3000 strikes in Egypt (Noueihed & Warren, 2013). A movement called Kefaya formed in 2004 and called for the end of Mubarak's rule. Activists from Kefaya formed another resistance organization called the April 6th Movement, and arose in solidarity with textile strikers in Mahalla in 2008. They were very adept at using the internet to spread its goals of justice and human rights (Iskander, 2013). Egypt had its equivalent to Muhammad Bouazizi as well, Khaled Said, a 28-year-old political activist who was beaten to death by police in June 2010 in front of many witnesses. His death led to a Facebook-based group calling itself "We are all Khaled Said" (Iskandar, 2013). It attracted more than a million followers (Shehata, 2011). Thus, the potential for much larger mobilization was clearly there before Tunisia bloomed.

Egypt's structural and political characteristics also revealed many of the factors discussed above as important in causing the Arab Spring. In the 1990s, Egypt implemented neoliberal reforms in an agreement with the World Bank, necessitated by unsustainable debt. The reforms involved reduced spending on social services, liberalized trade, privatization of state-owned enterprises, and the end of guaranteed employment for university graduates (Shehata, 2011). Privatization dramatically increased the gap between rich and poor, creating enormous wealth for some, while 44% of Egyptians were poor or extremely poor (Gelvin, 2012, p. 35). By 2010, the only development indicators in Egypt not falling were education and access to cell phones, television, and the internet (Iskandar, 2013). Unemployment was also a problem and, as in Tunisia, it was particularly severe for the most educated young people. Corruption, always present in Egypt, was galvanized by privatization, and the people who gained the most were those closest to the Mubarak regime, particularly the associates of his son Gamal. The "governing" party, the National Democratic Party (NDP), was basically an association whose elite members used the state and their positions to amass fortunes. It was "an unholy alliance between the ruling elite and the business elite" (Shehata, 2011, p. 27).

There have been three presidents since the 1952 coup that put Gamal Nasser in office. Nasser and each of his successors came from the military. The governments varied in terms of ideology, but all were dictatorships. Mubarak, who had been in office since 1981, had an extensive system of formal and informal security agencies gathering information on potential troublemakers. Like Ben Ali, Mubarak had a personal security detail, called the Central Security Services. A state of emergency law was in effect in Egypt from 1981, when Mubarak's predecessor Anwar al-Sadat was assassinated. Political repression increased in recent years as well. One of the most brutally repressed groups in Egypt was the Muslim Brotherhood. Under Sadat, there was a period of political reform allowing contested elections as long as the NDP held a majority in the nation's parliament. Mubarak followed this formula until 2006, when he started to impose constraints on opposition parties (Shehata, 2011). The 2010 parliamentary elections were fraudulently manipulated to ensure victory by the NDP, causing the Muslim Brotherhood and the New Wafd Party, in particular, to doubt the utility of continuing to participate in electoral contests (Shehata, 2011). The purpose of these maneuvers was to ensure that Mubarak's son Gamal could take the reins of power in the future (Shehata, 2011).

Young activists called protests for January 25, 2011. They trained in non-violent tactics before the protests, and employed tactics such as having marchers start from 20 different places, rather than converging as one large group on Tahrir Square in Cairo (Noueihed & Warren, 2013). Many of the activist groups joined in the demonstrations on January 25; others, such as the Muslim Brotherhood, waited until January 28 to formally join in the protests (some of the younger members were already participating). The groups participating in the uprising were secular, Islamist, and from all over the political spectrum. As the three weeks of protest went on, more and more sectors of the polity joined. By uniting behind the goal of ousting the regime, their differences did not splinter the movement. The protests spread to Alexandria and other areas across Egypt.

Thousands of people entered Tahrir Square and, not surprisingly, the police responded with tear gas and rubber bullets. The police disappeared after a day of battling with the protesters, and the protesters took the square. Mubarak ordered the military to restore order, but the protesters welcomed them. The military in Egypt had a much better reputation than the police, and were respected as an institution of the state. They were also economically and politically powerful and avoided any involvement in political repression over the years. Over the next two weeks, protesters were attacked by hired thugs, some riding on horses and camels.

Mubarak refused to make concessions, although he did remove Gamal and his associates from power, thus addressing Gamal as his successor. As violence against the protesters from irregular forces continued, and Mubarak indicated he would stay in office until September, the military became increasingly concerned. According to Shehata, "it took new groups joining the protests and the rising prospect of confrontation between the protesters and the presidential guard for the military to finally break with Mubarak" (2011, p. 31). Mubarak left office on February 18, 2011, and the military took control of the country, suspended the constitution, and dissolved parliament.

A new constitution was approved on March 19, 2011, and elections for a new parliament were held at the end of November, giving a majority of seats to Islamists. Muhammad Mursi from the Muslim Brotherhood won the presidential election on June 24, 2011. He lasted little more than a year before being overthrown by the military. Egypt suffered considerable inter-communal conflict among Christians and Muslims, Islamists, and secularists during this time. Egypt held another presidential election in 2014, with a very popular former military general, Abdul Fatah al-Sisi, winning the election. He was reelected in March 2018. Unfortunately, al-Sisi has followed the path of previous leaders by consolidating power and clamping down, arresting and imprisoning political opposition members and human rights advocates, calling them terrorists and traitors (Mansour, 2021).

Libya

Muammar al-Qaddafi came to power in Libya in 1969 as a result of a military coup that overthrew the Libyan monarchy. Although when he came into office Qaddafi was part of the Nasser-era Arab nationalist and socialist camp, his rule was based on a cult of personality, rather than on building a state with strong institutions and a clear set of political principles. After the coup, he became the chairman of the Revolutionary Command Council, which was the new governing body. As time progressed, he did not take a normal title such as President of Libya, but preferred dramatic titles such as "King of Kings of Africa" and "Brotherly Leader and Guide of the Revolution" (Gelvin, 2012, p. 71). In 1977, he announced his "Third Universal Theory" of governance, which was a theory of direct democracy. Instead of a representative democracy, which Qaddafi thought led to rule by the elite, he called for "people's congresses," which were supposed to operate at the local and national levels. There was no private ownership of business as the economy was nationalized, no free press or dissent permitted, no labor unions, no public sector bureaucracies, and no political parties. The military and security apparatus were vicious, and human right abuses were pervasive. Qaddafi's notion that Libya could be ruled by the masses (*jamajiriya*) was a functional impossibility, so people retreated to kinship networks for access to goods and services, and for security (Anderson, 2011). Meanwhile, Qaddafi's own kinship network of family, friends, and associates benefited from oil profits in an extremely corrupt system.

In addition to internal repression, Qaddafi's security apparatus went after dissident Libyans abroad, intimidating and sometimes assassinating them. Qaddafi's regime was responsible for international acts of terrorism, including the bombing of a club in West Berlin in 1986 and the downing of Pan Am flight 103 over Lockerbie in Scotland in 1988, killing all aboard and 11 people on the ground. His regime also involved itself in a brutal civil war in neighboring Chad. Nevertheless, by the 1990s Qaddafi had embarked on various steps to improve his relationship with the United States and Europe. By the 2000s, foreign investment began to flow into Libya, resulting in new rules on private investment. Nevertheless, within a decade investors were very disappointed by the constant unpredictability of the government's policy and the pervasive corruption (Noueihed & Warren, 2013).

Qaddafi's son Said al-Islam Qaddafi emerged at this time as both a potential heir (which he repeatedly declined to consider) and as an advocate for reform. He advocated a more open society and engaged in some human rights work as well as international diplomacy. He also faced strong opposition from the old guard, who wanted the political system and distribution of spoils to stay as they were (Noueihed & Warren, 2013). When the Arab Spring came to Libya, he stood by his father.

The Arab Spring arrived in Libya on February 15, 2011, when protests broke out in Benghazi, a city in eastern Libya. The capital, Tripoli, was in western Libya, where the regime had greater control. Protests spread around the country, and a National Transition Council was established as the political arm of the revolt and temporary interim government. The regime responded with the most violence seen thus far in the Arab Spring.

Live ammunition was used against the protesters, and helicopter gunships sought to quash the demonstrations. Qaddafi's forces remained loyal:

> Elite units under the command of four of Qaddafi's seven sons remained loyal, of course, as did the twenty-five-hundred Islamic Pan-African Brigade, made up of mercenaries from Chad, Sudan, and Niger. Most of the air force, whose leaders were affiliated with Qaddafi's tribe, and the security forces, which consisted of members of Qaddafi's family and tribe and members of allied tribes, also remained loyal. Qaddafi had lavished his special units with military hardware while starving the regular army of resources to prevent a coup.
>
> (Gelvin, 2012, p. 82)

As time went on, the protests became a civil war, with armed combatants facing Qaddafi's forces. The opposition forces drew in militias, both Islamist and secular. The battleground shifted back and forth during February and March 2011, with the rebels taking land to the west, followed by Qaddafi's forces pushing them back to the east. On March 17, 2011, the United Nations Security Council passed Resolution 1973, which authorized the establishment of a no-fly zone over Libya and the use of any means necessary other than a land invasion to protect civilians. The operation was eventually taken over by NATO.

The opposition forces eventually won. Muammar Qaddafi was found in Sirte and killed on October 20, 2011. The National Transitional Council became the de facto government for the next 10 months until elections were held. A new Islamist-dominated General National Congress (GNC) based in Tripoli was elected in July, and took over in August 2012. After some maneuvering, Ali Zeidan became Prime Minister, only to be replaced. The government's hold on the country was weak, as demonstrated by the 2012 attack by Islamist militants known as Ansar al-Sharia (Ansar al-Sharia formed after the uprising against Qaddafi in 2011, a coalition of two different groups) on the U.S. consulate in Benghazi, in which the ambassador, information officer, and two Central Intelligence Agency (CIA) agents were killed. The GNC was supposed to dissolve, and when it didn't protests took place in February 2014. General Khalifa Haftar of the Libyan National Army launched a military action, Operation Dignity, against Ansar al-Sharia and other groups in Benghazi. Haftar also attempted to seize parliament, and the next month the supreme court declared Prime Minister Maiteg's appointment illegal, and he resigned. Elections took place in June, but civil war ensued between GNC loyalists and the new House of Representatives government, located in Tobruk. At this point, Libya, with two rival governments vying for control, was abandoned in July, with foreigners, including United Nations personnel leaving the country, followed by the capturing of Benghazi by Anshar-al Sharia.

During this time, another player, ISIS, entered the scene. Many Libyan fighters went to Syria, and other countries to fight with ISIS, and were now returning to spread the internationalized caliphate message (Anaizi, Dotolo, & Lakehal-Ayat, 2015). However, this was not well-received by established groups such as al-Qaeda in the Islamic Maghreb (AQIM), and the tribal militia the Libyan Shield Force, who backed the Tripoli government (Anaizi, et. al, 2015).

A Government of National Accord (GNA) supported by the United Nations was established in 2016, but was not recognized by the two sides (Glenn, 2017). Fighting continued, and efforts by General Haftar to expel ISIS, and gain ground, were launched. In April 2019 Hafter's forces clashed with GNA forces as he moved toward Tripoli. Ultimately, Hafter's forces were pushed back by the GNA.

There are ongoing efforts to repair the damage of the civil war and establish a unified government. A ceasefire was negotiated in October 2020. However, despite this, it is not fully actualized. The conflict is not just about warring factions, but a "proxy war" with multiple countries backing different parties mainly because of ideological and economic (oil), and some migration concerns (Weise, 2020). Current Prime Minister Fayez al-Sarraj, who heads the GNA, is supported by the United Nations, militia groups, the Muslim Brotherhood, Western European countries and the United States, "but mainly relies on Turkey, Qatar and Italy" (Weise, 2020). On the other hand, General Haftar, and the LNA are backed by Egypt, the United Arab Emirates (UAE), Russia, Saudi Arabia, Jordan and France (Weise, 2020).

Yemen

The civil war in Yemen was a result of long-standing internal issues in the country. In 2011, protests took place, and long-time authoritarian leader Ali Abdullah Saleh was forced to turn over power to his deputy, Abdrabbuh Mansour Hadi, in 2012. Hadi inherited multiple issues, including attacks by al-Qaeda in the Arabian Peninsula (AQAP), separatists in the south, security members still loyal to the former president, corruption, unemployment, and food insecurity (BBC, 2020). The transition of power was viewed by many as problematic. Saleh, and those loyal to him, sought to undermine the transition. The Houthi Movement, which represented the Shia Muslim minority in the country, together with sympathetic Sunnis, and support from Saleh, took the opportunity in 2014 to begin taking over Saada province and surrounding areas in the north, eventually seizing the capital, Saana (BBC, 2020). Hadi, who unveiled a new constitution not supported by Saleh or the Houthis, was arrested by them, but escaped and was pursued by the Houthis. This event, coupled with the success of the Houthis, supported by Iran, prompted Saudi Arabia and other Sunni Arab states to intervene militarily with an air campaign, while the United States, Great Britain, and France provided logistical and intelligence support (BBC, 2020). The coalition tried to reinstate Hadi while fighting Saleh and Houthis. Meanwhile, amidst the chaos, AQAP attempted to establish a foothold in Mukalla, only to be driven out by forces supported by the United Arab Emirates (UAE).

The Houthi Movement was not the only internal issue facing the government. From 1967 to 1990, the South Yemen Republic was a country backed by communist countries. With the collapse of communism, the country was unified under Saleh. An attempt at secession by the south resulted in a civil war in 1994, and then occupation by the north. It joined the anti-Houthi coalition. After a dispute between the governor of Aden and the president, the governor was removed from power, sparking protests, and as a result, in 2017, the Southern Transitional Council (STC) was formed to establish independent rule. It is backed by the UAE.

Amidst the chaos, AQAP and ISIS continued to carry out attacks, while the Houthis turned their attention to attacks on Saudi Arabia, which found working with the UAE difficult. Concerned with his own power, Saleh attempted to turn on the Houthis, who killed him. In 2018 parties agreed to the Stockholm Hodeidah truce, but the Houthis pressed forward with capturing land, and the UAE continued its air campaign in the south in support of the STC.

The devastation to the population is tremendous. According to Human Rights Watch, "six years into an armed conflict that has killed over 18,400 civilians, Yemen remains the largest humanitarian crisis in the world. Yemen is experiencing the world's worst food security crisis with 20.1 million people—nearly two-thirds of the population—requiring food assistance at the beginning of 2020" (Human Rights Watch, 2021). Issues such as destruction of critical infrastructure, lack of fuel, loss of businesses and employment, health, and COVID-19 spread, malnutrition, abuse by security forces, landmines, a weak state, and flooding illustrate the dire situation (Human Rights Watch, 2021).

CONCLUSION

As we pointed out, issues were present in countries already, and the movements were not necessarily connected. At the same time, there were rolling effects. In 2011, civil war broke out in Syria in 2011, and in Yemen in 2014. In 2019, Omar al-Bashir, the dictatorial leader of Sudan, was overthrown, and protests emerged in Lebanon, Algeria and Iraq (Safi, 2020). Positive changes undoubtedly took place after the Arab Spring, yet certain countries became embroiled in new civil conflicts, and now had leaders consolidating power at the expense of human rights and political participation. A poll conducted by the *Guardian* (Safi, 2020) 10 years after the Arab Spring in nine Arab countries showed the majority of people did not regret the protests, with the exception of countries where it led to civil war (Libya, Syria, and Yemen) (Safi, 2020). In these countries, people also indicated that they were worse off than before: Syria (75%), Yemen (73%), and Libya (60%), while in Sudan it was 51%, and Tunisia 50% (Safi, 2020). In many countries, people also believed there was a widening gap between rich and poor: Syria (92%), Yemen (87%), Tunisia (84%), Egypt (68%), Sudan (51%), and Tunisia (50%). Interestingly, Egyptians were described as ambivalent (Safi, 2020). In Egypt, 57% supported the protests, while 43% did not, and 38% believed their lives were worse after the Arab Spring, while 39% selected neither, and 23% believed life was better. With regard to the future of children, 41% of Egyptians felt they were worse off, while 33% selected neither, and 26% believed they were better off.

Social movements will undoubtedly continue to arise. In this chapter, we have reviewed the political psychology of the social movement phenomenon and examined several different cases. As the cases demonstrate, social movements have many similarities: grievances, a politicized identity, mobilization strategies, and collective action. They differ extensively in leadership, with the American Civil Rights Movement having the most identifiable leaders, and the Arab Spring, Occupy Wall Street, Black Lives Matter, and Me Too movements being largely leaderless. Perhaps future research will reveal the extent to which the internet made these movements possible without leaders. The movements examined here also differed in outcomes. The American Civil Rights Movement had many successes, but inequalities and discrimination persist. The Tea Party had many electoral victories, but faded away for a series of reasons. Occupy Wall Street faded as a movement, but made an impact in other ways. The outcome of the Arab Spring is an ongoing development, especially in light of civil wars, terrorist attacks, and persistent political, social, and economic problems, as are the Me Too and Black Lives Matter movements.

Topics/Theories and Case Studies in Chapter 11

Topics	*Theories*	*Cases*
Social movements	Relative deprivation	Civil Rights Movement
	Dynamics of supply	Tea Party
	Dynamics of demand	Occupy Wall Street
	Sense of efficacy	Arab Spring
	Politicized collective identity	– Tunisia
		– Egypt
	Social capital	– Libya
	Leaders	

Key Terms

- charisma
- collective action
- dynamics of demand
- dynamics of supply or mobilization
- politicized collective identity
- pragmatism
- prophecy
- relative deprivation theory
- social capital
- social movements
- social movement organizations (SMOs)
- structure

Suggestions for Further Reading

DiMaggio, A. (2011). *The rise of the Tea Party*. New York: Monthly Review Press.

Fording, R.C., & Schram, S.F. (2020). *Hard white: The mainstreaming of racism in American politics*. Oxford: Oxford University Press.

Gelvin, J. L. (2012). *The Arab uprisings: What everyone needs to know*. Oxford: Oxford University Press.

Gitlin, T. (2012). *Occupy nation: The roots, the spirit, and the promise of Occupy Wall Street*. New York: HarperCollins.

Gurr, T. (1970). *Why men rebel*. Princeton, NJ: Princeton University Press.

Hawley, G. (2017) *Making sense of the alt-right*. New York: Columbia University Press.

Klandermans, B. (1997). *The social psychology of protest*. Oxford: Blackwell.
McAdam, D. (1988). *Freedom summer*. Oxford: Oxford University Press.
Noueihed, L., & Warren, A. (2013). *The battle for the Arab Spring: Revolution, counter-revolution and the making of a new era*. New Haven, CT: Yale University Press.
Street, P., & DiMaggio, P. (2011). *Crashing the Tea Party: Mass media and the campaign to remake American politics*. Boulder, CO: Paradigm.

Chapter 12

THE POLITICAL PSYCHOLOGY OF TERRORISM

A WORLD OF TERRORISM

Terrorism is not a new subject by any stretch of the imagination. "Each year, terrorist groups commit hundreds of acts of violence." This is the sentence with which the authors started the section in terrorism in the first edition of this book six months before the attack on the World Trade Center in New York City and the Pentagon in Washington, DC on September 11, 2001. That day was the single most brutal and coordinated attack by a foreign terrorist group on U.S. soil, far worse than the first strike on the World Trade Center in 1993, led by Ramzi Yousef. The 9/11 attack was, for many, unimaginable. After this date, Americans were bombarded with information and images of al-Qaeda, the group that perpetrated the attack. September 11, 2001 changed the way Americans psychologically dealt with terrorism. Americans were on a steep learning curve and suddenly had a higher threat perception of al-Qaeda, and the U.S. government stepped up its counterterrorism initiatives and policies. Terrorism, no matter where it is perpetrated, can have a profound effect on the mindset of a targeted population.

Before the 9/11 attack, volumes of research and case studies on terrorist groups had already been produced. The media and academics tended to focus particularly on groups found in Europe and Latin America. There were, however, limited books and articles on al-Qaeda, even though it had long been active before September 11, 2001. In fact, the United States was the target of several al-Qaeda attacks, such as the bombings of the U.S. embassies in Tanzania and Kenya in 1998, and the bombing of the *USS Cole* in Yemen in 2000, among others. This threat was not perceived by the U.S. government as important enough to gain its full attention. The importance of such attacks, and the existence of intelligence information, coupled with Osama bin Laden's explicit promise of future threats to come, now seem obvious enough to have predicted 9/11. However, these events and information were overlooked, ignored, and discounted.

This chapter covers a lot of different topics on the political psychology of terrorism. It draws on many psychological concepts and theories already covered in the book to discuss terrorism at the individual and group levels. Thus, there are both group-level and individual-level concepts relevant to

DOI: 10.4324/9780429244643-12

the discussion of terrorism. At the individual level, we examine issues such as personality—that is, we talk about whether there is a terrorist personality. We also address specific personality attributes, such as individual traits and motivations for joining terrorist groups. At the group level, we highlight intra-group level factors such as radicalization and disengagement, recruitment, indoctrination, conformity, obedience, conflict, role, and social control. Throughout the chapter, we use many studies and examples to illustrate both individual- and group-level factors.

Before delving into these aspects of terrorism, it is necessary to first define terrorism. We then look at why individuals and groups turn to terrorism.

DEFINING TERRORISM

There are many different definitions of terrorism in the academic and policy communities. In fact, many different government agencies choose to rely on their own definitions to suit their goals and objectives. Essentially, we are left with different perceptions of what it takes to be a terrorist group. Martha Crenshaw captures the essence of this debate:

> The problem of defining terrorism has hindered analysis since the inception of studies of terrorism in the early 1970s. One set of problems is due to the fact that the concept of terrorism is deeply contested. The use of the term is often polemical and rhetorical. It can be a pejorative label, meant to condemn an opponent's cause as illegitimate rather than describe behavior. Moreover, even if the term is used objectively as an analytical tool, it is still difficult to arrive at a satisfactory definition that distinguishes terrorism from other violent phenomena. In principle, terrorism is a deliberate and systematic violence performed by small numbers of people, whereas communal violence is spontaneous, sporadic, and requires mass participation. The purpose of terrorism is to intimidate a watching popular audience by harming only a few, whereas genocide is the elimination of entire communities. Terrorism is meant to hurt, not to destroy. Terrorism is preeminently political and symbolic, whereas guerilla warfare is a military activity. Repressive "terror" from above is the action of those in power, whereas terrorism is a clandestine resistance to authority. Yet in practice, events cannot always be precisely categorized.
>
> (Crenshaw, 2000, p. 406)

Crenshaw goes on to argue that the wide-ranging tactics used by terrorists further complicate the problem. For example, some use methods such as kidnapping and hostage taking, others bomb, some use assassination, some may use all of these, and some mix and match. When independent nonstate terrorist organizations are supported by states, terrorism is state sponsored. It is also organized differently, ranging from hierarchical and centralized to anarchical and decentralized. Finally, classification of terrorist groups is complicated because terrorist groups have many different identities, which includes their definition of the enemy, group norms, and leadership. We cannot settle the definitional debate here. Suffice to say that for the purposes of this chapter, we have taken elements from existing definitions and include groups composed of small numbers of people who use, or threaten to use, systematic violence in order to accomplish a political goal. Acts of terrorism are symbolic—that is, the targets of terrorists are symbols of the state or of social norms and structure.

TERRORIST GROUPS

There are numerous terrorist groups in the world. There are also many terrorist groups that are proscribed by the U.S. State Department. Of note is that the proscribed list grew exponentially after the United States became involved in Iraq. Al-Qaeda in Iraq formed as a response, and the group gained significant popularity, eventually expanding to the regional Islamic State of Iraq and Syria (ISIS). Inspired by the successes of ISIS, multiple offshoots of the group were formed around the world. If we examine the number of different groups on the proscribed list, we get an idea of how many groups the United States perceives through the **rogue image**. Recall that rogues are considered bad children—those one does not negotiate with and those who must be punished. These groups are not seen as formidable, but they threaten U.S. national security and interests. Some of the groups we mention in this chapter are no longer found on the U.S. proscribed list. The psychology behind the decisions to proscribe is interesting. If the threat is no longer perceived, if we agree with the goals of the groups or believe they are acting in good faith, they are not put on the list, or they are removed, even if they remain participants in terrorist or criminal activities. In Chapter 3, we introduced the concept of selective interpretation of information—that is, inconsistent information is ignored or distorted to appear consistent with attitudes or cognitive categories. Remember, ignoring information is why 9/11 happened in the first place.

Let's look at some specific groups to underscore the general similarities and differences between them. Groups such as the Kurdish Kongra-Gel, the Basque Fatherland and Liberty (ETA) oppose the national identity of the existing state and strive for independent rule (Byman, 1998). Palestinian groups such as Hamas, al-Aqsa Martyrs' Brigade, the Popular Front for the Liberation of Palestine (PFLF), and others, dispute the existence of Israel. In the long run, they seek to reclaim the land Israel occupies, but at this time they cannot defeat Israel. The situation is complicated, with multiple actors involved, including other countries and groups in the region and internationally, coupled with perceptions of threat, scapegoating, and intransigence. In 2006, Hamas stood for elections in the Palestinian Authority and won 70 seats. This led to a conflict between Fatah, which holds the presidency of the Palestinian Authority (PA), and Hamas. The PA, under President Mahmoud Abbas, dissolved the government and Hamas took control of Gaza. Supported by Iran, Lebanese Hezbollah, and outside aid, Hamas poses a threat to Israel, through its use of rocket attacks, suicide bombings, cyber warfare, and other tactics. The group does not recognize Israel's right to exist, and Israel will not negotiate with a terrorist group. The United States has thrown its support behind Fatah and President Abbas, who stated that there will be no negotiations with Hamas unless it gives up control in Gaza (Assadi, 2007).

Mentioned earlier was Hezbollah's support for Hamas. Hezbollah is a Shia group in Lebanon and is supported by Iran. The group states it wants to destroy Israel, and often confronts the country in a variety of ways. However, Hezbollah also holds elected seats in the Lebanese parliament. On July 12, 2006, Hezbollah confronted Israel by firing thousands of rockets at an Israeli border town, and launching anti-tank missiles on a border patrol. Israel responded with a bombing campaign and ground incursion into southern Lebanon. The conflict ended on August 14 with several thousand deaths, and the displacement of an estimated 1.5 million people.

The Red Brigades

The left-wing Red Brigades was formed in 1970 by sociology students in Italy. "A group with its roots in the sociology department in the University of Treto in northern Italy evolved into the Red Brigades. Highly secretive, they counted 5,000 members, many with training in explosives, firearms and forging documents" (Crane, 2007, p. 18). The Red Brigades has committed many acts since its formation. "Their attacks were brazen, including bank heists and prison breaks, and hit factory owners, politicians, journalists, police and military officers" (Crane, 2007, p. 18). By 1988, security forces were successful at debilitating the Red Brigades. However, in March 1999, a group claiming to be the "new" Red Brigades killed Massimo D'Antona, a professor and government adviser. In February 2007, Italian authorities arrested 15 people who were accused of being part of a terrorist cell.

Other groups such as the Real Irish Republican Army (RIRA) and Continuity Irish Republican Army (Continuity IRA) are fighting against British control of Northern Ireland and these groups want to become part of another country, the Republic of Ireland. Historically, loyalist (Protestant) groups—the Ulster Defense Association/Ulster Freedom Fighters (UDA/UFF) and the Ulster Volunteer Force/Red Hand Commandos (UVF/RHC)—also operated in Northern Ireland. They formed because of the activities of the Provisional Irish Republican Army (PIRA), which fought to liberate the territory of Northern Ireland from British rule and reintegrate Ireland. With a peace process in Northern Ireland signed in 1998, the British government maintained that all groups should decommission, including the Protestant paramilitary groups. After many years, the Provisional IRA did decommission its weapons, and in May 2007 the UVF announced it had put its arms beyond reach. While the relationship between Protestant paramilitaries and the state and its security forces was at times seen as collusion, the perception on the part of these groups was that they were doing their duty as part of the defenders of Britain, and thus the state.

In South Asia, Pakistani groups are fighting for regional control of the disputed region of Kashmir on behalf of the state of Pakistan, and against the Indian government. However, many of these groups also cooperate with outside groups, and thus are also a threat to Pakistan.

Gush Emunim Underground

Gush Emunim Underground was formed in 1979 by members of Gush Emunim (Block of the Faithful), a group of Jewish settlers that used squatter tactics in the West Bank. The group conducted attacks in the early and mid-1980s, including car bombings of five Arab mayors in the West Bank and a machine gun and grenade attack on Hebron Islamic College in which three Arab students were killed and 33 wounded.

Finally, Al-Qaeda, "the Base," was originally formed in 1988. Its leader, Osama bin Laden, drew his support base from those that had fought in the Afghan war against the Soviets. Fighters from all over the world participated in this war. Ayman al-Zawahiri, a member of the Egyptian Islamic Jihad (IJ) formed an alliance with Bin Laden in 1998. Until Bin Laden's death in 2011, al-Zawahiri was a key influencer of Bin Laden. Al-Zawahiri took control of the organization several months after Bin Laden's death. The al-Qaeda of today is a transnational network composed of many groups operating in countries throughout the world. Thus, as the original group of 1988 expanded, it drew in more groups, and new ones were created on its behalf. For example, AQI only formed after the U.S. invasion in 2003. The Algerian Salafist Group for Preaching and Combat (GSPC) is a long-standing group, which merged with the al-Qaeda network. The group subsequently changed its name to al-Qaeda Organization in the Lands of the Maghreb (AQIM). As Lav explains:

> On January 24, 2007, with the blessing of Osama bin Laden, the Algerian Salafist Group for Preaching and Combat (GSPC) changed its name to The Al-Qaeda Organization in the Islamic Maghreb. Thus was cemented a union that had been announced several months previously; this union is the fruit of long standing relations between the GSPC and Al-Qaeda and represents a further stage in the globalization of the jihad movement. Shortly after joining al-Qaeda, the GSPC, whose operations had for the most part been limited to Algeria and the Sahara, began to attack foreign interests and threaten attacks in Europe.
>
> (Lav, 2007, p. 1)

AQIM is no longer just a national group committed to overthrowing the Algerian regime. AQIM works to envelop other North African-affiliated al-Qaeda groups into a larger consortium, and has expanded its influence in many African countries. In addition to these, there are many other groups operating in different countries claiming membership or some affiliation with the network. These groups have their own leadership structure, norms, and goals—they have distinct identities.

Osama bin Laden and Ayman al-Zawahiri were heralded as the true leaders of al-Qaeda. However, while they may have commented, given advice, and submitted operational guidance, the original group blossomed far beyond their personal reach and total control. That being said, there is still a core al-Qaeda group, led by Ayman al-Zawahiri.

As mentioned earlier, AQI changed its name to the Islamic State of Iraq and the Levant (ISIL), to reflect its broader goals in the region. However, the group is now commonly referred to as the Islamic State of Iraq and Syria (ISIS). The success of ISIS, however, resulted in its own expansion as affiliates formed and cooperation was established with other groups. Fighters traveled across the globe to help the group establish its caliphate, and operate its own network out from under al-Qaeda.

State-Sponsored Terrorism

State-sponsored terrorism occurs when a state supports a terrorist group either directly or indirectly. In its report on state-sponsored terrorism, the U.S. government has identified Cuba, Iran, Iraq, Libya, North Korea, Sudan, and Syria as governments that support or engage in terrorism.

Libya, led by Colonel Muammar Qaddafi, is an example of a country that not only engaged in terrorist activity, but also backed terrorist groups. Libyan agents were accused of the 1988 bombing of Pan Am flight 103, which exploded over Lockerbie, Scotland. United Nations sanctions were imposed on Libya until 1999, when Qaddafi surrendered two men. They were tried in a Scottish court, and in January 2001, one was found guilty and the other acquitted. In the past, Qaddafi was also accused of supplying many terrorist groups with weapons and training, including the Provisional Irish Republican Army and various Palestinian groups.

Like Libya, the North Korean government was accused of engaging in, and backing terrorist activity. For example, in 1983, a bomb exploded, killing 17 South Korean officials visiting Myanmar. Two North Korean officers were caught and confessed to their role in the act. In another incident in 1987, Korean Airlines flight 858 was the target of the North Korean regime. All 115 people on board were killed in that midair bombing. North Korea has also provided a safe haven for members of the Japanese Communist League-Red Army Faction that hijacked a Japanese Airlines flight to North Korea in 1970.

Perhaps the most publicized state supporter of terrorism is Iran; this undoubtedly demonstrates the ongoing identity conflict that exists between the United States and Iran. Iran is at the forefront of U.S. policy concerns, especially because Iran is seeking to build a nuclear program, and supports groups in contravention to U.S. stated values. Hezbollah is at the core of conflict between the two countries, and the creation of the group can be traced to Iran. In fact, Iranians have seats on Hezbollah's governing council. Hasan Nasrallah, the leader of Hezbollah, has a very close relationship with Iran's Supreme Leader Khamenei. The Iranians provide arms, equipment, and training to Hezbollah. Additionally, the group is awash with money, compliments of Iran. This was evident in the aftermath of the Israeli campaign in Lebanon in which Hezbollah took

(*Continued*)

(*Continued*)

the opportunity to use their money to rebuild the community (Bejjani, 2006). Syria is a transshipment point for the movement of Iranian equipment to Hezbollah. Therefore, both the Syrians and Iranians are state-supporters of terrorism with regard to this group. The elite Iranian Revolutionary Guard Corp (IRGC) is also heavily involved in Iraq and Syria and works squarely against U.S. goals. Finally, the Iranians also provide financial support and weapons training to members of militant Palestinian groups.

WHY DO GROUPS TURN TO TERRORISM?

Recall that in Chapter 3, we introduced *social identity theory*. We classify ourselves as part of groups; groups we belong to are characterized as in-groups, and other groups are considered out-groups. Social identity theory rests on the principle of intergroup comparison. When a group compares itself to another relevant out-group, and is faced with a threatened identity, group members have three options. They can leave the group and join the higher status group (social mobility), they can change the basis for comparison (social creativity), or they can seek to compete with the higher status group (competition). This competition can lead to conflict. It is at this point where we find an explanation for why groups turn to terrorism. Groups find themselves threatened by the status of a superior group, usually the state apparatus of a country. One way to equalize the status between groups is to engage in activities that harm the high-status group. Explanations are also found in other theories. In Chapter 3, we introduced *image theory*. While an individual can hold many different images of an out-group, one image, the *imperialist image*, involves a perception that another group is superior in capability and culture. At times, the subordinate group perceives this relationship is not legitimate and may seek to change the relationship. Of course, the flip side to this is the superior status group views this as threatening to their survival. They likely will view the group through the *rogue image*. Rogues are inferior in capability, but are threatening in their intentions. Rogues are not negotiated with; they are taught a lesson. Thus, numerous counterterrorism strategies are put in place to deal with rogue terrorist groups.

PSYCHOPATHOLOGICAL VIEWS

Terrorists suffer from deep psychological problems; they are psychopaths or cold-blooded killers. They are not only crazy—they are evil. This line of thinking is still very widespread, particularly in the media and among some academics. In the academic community, this perspective was popular in earlier research when terrorism researchers were few and far between. In fact, the literature was dominated by the case study approach and those who broadened the scope of the research to include the study of personality can be considered pioneers of the field of terrorism research (see Corrado, 1981; Crenshaw, 2004; Post, 1984 for reviews).

Some focused on psychopathological causes such as sociopathy/psychopathy. This personality disorder was outlined in the American Psychiatric Association's *Diagnostic and Statistical Manual of Mental Disorders III (DSM-III).* In the next versions, DSM-IV and DSM-V, sociopathy/psychopathy fall under antisocial personality disorders, although there is refinement in thinking in DSM-V. Individuals with these disorders tend to disregard and violate the rights of others and fail to feel empathy for their victims. Using the DSM-III classification (relevant at the time), Cooper (1977) and Pearce (1977) argue that terrorists are sociopaths. Lasch (1979) examined individuals in the Weathermen and the Symbionese Liberation Army and found evidence of narcissistic personality disorder. In his work, Kaplan (1981) traced terrorist behavior to psychopathology—namely a defective personality stemming from childhood experience of humiliation by an aggressor. Pearlstein (1991) also identified narcissistic personality disorders among terrorists as central. Post (2004) maintains that although there is not a specific terrorist personality type or constellation or major psychopathologies, "individuals with particular personality traits and personality tendencies are drawn disproportionately to terrorist careers" (p. 128). Post notes the psychological mechanisms of externalization and splitting, a defense mechanism of individuals with a damaged self-concept, are found among those with narcissistic and borderline personality disorders. These are prevalent in terrorists. He argued terrorists have a special psycho-logic they construct "to rationalize acts they are psychologically compelled to commit" (p. 128):

> It is not the intent ... to imply that all terrorists suffer from borderline or narcissistic personality disorders, or that the psychological mechanisms of externalization or splitting are utilized by every terrorist. It is my distinct impression, however, that these mechanisms are found with extremely high frequency in the population of terrorists, particularly among the leadership, and contribute significantly to the uniformity of terrorists' rhetorical style and their special psycho-logic.
>
> (Post, 2004, p. 129)

Whether or not there are personality disorders prevalent amongst terrorists is still a subject of debate. As Post (2004) points out, access to terrorists is difficult and therefore they are not particularly well studied. To really understand them, access is key and then we may shed light on their "psycho-logic." However, research on terrorists has grown and other perspectives reflect a different line of thinking on the terrorist personality. Many now argue there is no such thing as a terrorist personality, especially one that is considered deviant. According to many academics and practitioners alike, there is simply not enough evidence to support this particular viewpoint, and many studies indicate quite the opposite. For example, Silke (2004) argues that "research on the mental state of terrorists has found that they are rarely mad or crazy; very few suffer from personality disorders. But the body of research confirming this state of affairs has not prevented a steady and continuing stream of 'experts,' security personnel, and politicians from freely espousing and endorsing views to the contrary" (p. 177). In addition, McCauley (2002) maintains "thirty years of research has found psychopathology and personality disorder no more likely among terrorists than nonterrorists from the same background" (p. 1). More specifically, Mastors and Deffenbaugh (2007) argue that "there is no compelling evidence found in the research for this book that Osama bin Laden is a psychopath. Granted, he may be a product of his own power designs, like many leaders, but that is a very different matter, and one that does not lend credence to him being a psychopath" (p. 20).

Why is this still a popular view? We suspect that in dismissing terrorists as crazy, we don't have to look much further for an explanation of why they take human life, often in mass numbers. This is not to suggest people with severe psychological problems are not part of the terrorist mix. Any group can recruit them, even unknowingly. These individuals often go on some very brutal killing sprees because they are fulfilling their own need to kill, and not a group need to adhere to the beliefs, values, goals, and tactics of the group. Often, groups deal with these individuals, as we shall see later in our discussion of conformity. As a general rule, terrorist groups are careful not to recruit those with pathologies (Crenshaw, 2004).

PERSONALITY TRAITS AND MOTIVATION

What about personality traits? Are there specific traits found in the terrorist population? Earlier we discussed the work of Adorno and his colleagues on the **authoritarian personality**. Later criticisms of the work included the notion that those high in this personality trait were assumed to have syndromes. Thus, in light of this criticism, further work was carried out and refined by other scholars, and it did not rely on the psychoanalytical school. Recall that Altemeyer (1996) discussed the attributes of submission to authority, aggression against nonconformist groups, and conventionalism, all strongly linked to right-wing authoritarianism. Altemeyer saw right-wing authoritarianism as a product of personality predispositions and life events.

Other trait-based approaches include looking at certain constellations of traits important to understanding leadership (Hermann, 1980b). Specifically, they include cognitive complexity, self-confidence, ethnocentrism, distrust of others, and motivation (task, power, affiliation). Mastors (2000) applied this trait-based approach to Gerry Adams, leader of Sinn Fein in Northern Ireland. Jacquier (2012) looked at the **operational code** in the case of Ayman al-Zawahiri and found he characterizes the world as black and white—a struggle between good and evil.

In Chapter 4, we discussed motivations in the context of joining a group. Joining a group can satisfy the *need for affiliation* or *need for power.* Additionally, the **Fundamental Interpersonal Relations Orientation (FIRO)** claims that joining a group can satisfy three basic needs: inclusion, control, and affection. Festinger (1950, 1954) argues that individuals join groups in order to provide standards with which to compare their own beliefs, opinions, and attitudes. Rubenstein and Shaver (1980) suggest groups can also satisfy interpersonal needs. Mastors and Norwitz (2008) examined motivation in the case of Ayman al-Zawahiri and found he was motivated by power. In another line of research, Taylor and Louis (2004) note individuals are looking for individual meaning and join terrorist groups to engage in meaningful behavior. In his discussion of self-esteem, Baumeister (1997) argues that having high self-esteem can lead to violence, as threats to self-esteem will be met with aggression. Other authors suggest motivations such as frustration, economic misery (Victoroff, 2005), moral disengagement (Bandura, 2004), moral reasoning (Ginges, Atran, Sachdeva, & Medin, 2011), excitement, ultimate meaning, and glory (Cottee & Hayward, 2011), humiliation-revenge (Juergensmeyer, 2000), need for belonging (Borum, 2004), a personal crisis (Silber & Bhatt, 2007; Wiktorowicz, 2005), a quest for personal significance (Kruglanski, Chen, Dechesne, Fishman, & Orehek, 2009), moral outrage (Sageman, 2008), and perceived injustice (Moghaddam, 2007).

Individual motivations for joining a terrorist group are often very complex. Psychologists provide some understanding, but it is important to note that there may not be just one characteristic explaining the motivation of individuals. For example, in their study of al-Qaeda recruits and motivation, Mastors and Deffenbaugh (2007) argue that motivations are complex and varied. By examining the personal stories of many al-Qaeda recruits, they discerned many specific motivations for recruitment. They found that individuals had joined the network for a variety of social, political, economic, and personal reasons. In particular, the authors found personal motivations such as absent fathers, boredom, camaraderie, the desire to fit in, disputes with parents, fame, family influence, lack of purpose, marital problems, parental divorce, peer pressure, poor academic performance, poor job performance, adventure seeking, status/recognition, a traumatic event, and vengeance. Social motivations were also evident. Here, elements such as alcohol abuse, cultural alienation, drug abuse/addiction, societal alienation, and wanting a cause were evident. Economic motivations included criminal activity, financial problems, a lack of motivation to seek employment/work, underemployment, and unemployment. Finally, political motivations can be traced to acts by another country, cultural imperialism, a country's support for a defined enemy, objectionable government policies, and oppression of an identity group. These motivations are not mutually exclusive, and individuals can be impacted by more than one motivating factor, even across categories. For example, in their study of Omar al-Hammami, an American who joined al-Shabaab, Mastors and Siers (2014) found his motivation "complex and personal," involving his need for adventure/excitement, personal significance, and a personal conflict with his father.

In her research, Stern conducted interviews with Muslim, Jewish, Christian, Sikh, and Hindu "radicals." According to Stern, individuals are humiliated and angry, and then act:

> My interviews suggest that people join religious terrorist groups partly to transform themselves and to simplify life. They start out feeling humiliated, enraged that they are viewed by some "other" as second class. They take on new identities as martyrs on behalf of a purported spiritual cause. The spiritually perplexed learn to focus on action. The weak become strong. The selfish become altruists, ready to make the ultimate sacrifice of their lives in the belief that their death will

> serve a supposed public good. Rage turns to conviction. They seem to enter a kind of trance, where the world is divided neatly between good and evil, victim and oppressor. Uncertainty and ambivalence, always painful to experience, are banished. There is no room for the other side's point of view. Because they believe their cause is just and that God is on their side, they persuade themselves that any action—no matter how heinous—is justified. They know they are right, not just politically, but morally.
>
> (Stern, 2004, p. 1)

There is also a body of literature that examines the attractiveness of violence and the role of aggression. However, here the findings are mixed. Some studies on the attraction to violence demonstrated an attraction to violence amongst some (e.g., Merkl, 1980); however, other studies could not provide definitive conclusions (Knutson, 1981). In an examination of children in Northern Ireland, Fields (1979) argues exposure to violence can drive children to become terrorists later. Fields received criticism for this approach. Taylor (1988) notes Fields looked only at children and not actual terrorists, and maintains the work suffers from a lack of validation.

The role of frustration is another area of investigation. Generally, this literature promotes the idea that when individuals are frustrated from achieving a goal, the result is aggression (Dollard, Doob, Miller, Mowrer, & Sears, 1939). According to Borum (2004), the basic premise of the frustration-aggression (FA) hypothesis is twofold: (1) aggression is always produced by frustration, and (2) frustration always produces aggression (p. 12). This is a controversial area of study, and it has been heavily criticized. According to Kruglanski and Fishman:

> But in scientific psychology the simple frustration-aggression has long been questioned. Just because one is frustrated does not necessarily mean that one would aggress against others. Frustration could lead to withdrawal, depression, escape, or aggression against the self rather than against others. Frustration could also motivate the search for alternative means to one's objectives, not necessarily violent means. Indeed, studies have shown that terrorism does not appear to constitute a strategy of last resort, used when all other means have been exhausted.
>
> (Kruglanski & Fishman, 2006, p. 196)

This body of literature did evolve over time. Those such as Berkowitz (1989), for example, refined the basic notion. Berkowitz contended that frustration alone does not cause aggression, but also depends on environmental cues. According to Borum (2004), "in an important reformulation of the FA hypothesis, Berkowitz (1989) claimed that it was only 'aversive' frustration that would lead to aggression. The newly proposed progression was that frustration would lead to anger, and that anger—*in the presence of aggressive cues*—would lead to aggression" (p. 12). In some cases, terrorists recognize the consequences of their angry behavior. For example, McCauley (2004) and Wagner (2006) suggest that terrorists sometimes commit an act so the enemy responds with extreme anger. Of course, this is the reaction that the terrorists hoped for in the first place. In addition to anger, frustration can be further inflated by engaging in social comparison. When they compare themselves to others (e.g., salary, number of possessions), the result may not be favorable. If that is the case, then they might experience *relative deprivation*, which refers to the belief that one is less well off than others. Research (Hagerty, 2000) showed happiness is lower and crime rates higher in nations with large disparities in income. Relatedly, Kampf (1990) argues that intellectuals and affluent youth are frustrated with the conditions of the social climate and therefore want to change their societies. However, Silke (2003) notes that, "although the explanation appears attractive (certainly at least in the context of revolutionary notions), the level of integration is weak, not only from being rather too context specific, but also because the ideological control is not considered within a developmental process of involvement" (p. 11).

The study of women and terrorism is often overlooked; however, there is a growing body of literature focused on this area (Alexander, 2017; Bloom, 2011; Herath, 2012). Often in the popular media, women are depicted as cruel, fanatical, or "bad" if they participate in terrorism, or raise their children to be part of the movement. Ultimately, they are judged through *stereotypes* as mothers, daughters, wives, and sisters. Therefore, women do what husbands, brothers, and fathers say, as if they have no will of their own, no decision-making capability, and are always victims. This certainly presents an inaccurate account of why women participate in terrorism.

SUICIDE BOMBERS

Since 9/11, and considering the ongoing violence in Israel/Palestine, **suicide bombers** received considerable attention, especially in the media. Yet suicide terrorists are not new and unique to al-Qaeda, ISIS, and Palestinian groups. Indeed, this tactic was used by the Tamil Tigers in Sri Lanka for a few decades, and is a noted tactic of the Turkish PKK, Chechens and other groups. Suicide bombers were and are still only a small part of many groups. Unfortunately, suicide terrorism is a growing tactic and remains a weapon of choice. According to Zedalis:

> Suicide bombers are today's weapon of choice. An action that was once so surprising, horrific, and terrifying has now become the daily fare of the nightly news. From Jerusalem to Jakarta and from Bali to Baghdad, the suicide bomber is clearly the weapon of choice for international terrorists. The raw number of suicide attacks is climbing; suicide bombs are now used by 17 terror organizations in 14 countries. In terms of casualties, suicide attacks are the most efficient form of terrorism. From 1980 to 2001, suicide attacks accounted for 3 percent of terrorist incidents but caused half of the total deaths due to terrorism even if one excludes the unusually large number of fatalities of 9/11.
>
> (Zedalis, 2004, p. 1)

Groups that use terrorism vary in the extent to which suicide attacks are institutionalized as a strategy. Some use this form of attack regularly, while others use it only occasionally and as a temporary tactic. According to Sprinzak (2000), neither Hamas nor Hezbollah has permanent suicide units, but each group recruits bombers on an ad hoc basis.

As with much of the literature, there are different perspectives on the personality of suicide bombers, what motivates them to join a terrorist group with the goal of killing themselves, and whether these individuals suffer from pathologies. Ariel Merari, a psychologist, looked at groups such as Hezbollah, Amal, Hamas, the Palestinian Islamic Jihad, and secular groups in Syria, but could not identify a psychological nor demographic profile of suicide terrorists (Sprinzak, 2000). Another study on Hamas argued suicide bombers deeply value the identity of the group, and want to join and do their part for the cause:

> The recruits do not fit the usual psychological profile of suicidal people, who are often desperate or clinically depressed. Hamas bombers often hold paying jobs, even in poverty-stricken Gaza. What they have in common, studies say, is an intense hatred of Israel. After a bombing, Hamas gives the family of the suicide bomber between three thousand dollars and five thousand dollars and assures them their son died a martyr in holy jihad.
>
> (Council on Foreign Relations, 2007)

Fields, Elbedour and Hein argue that the motivations of Palestinian suicide bombers are varied:

> Eight of the nine bombers were described by family and friends as very religious. Five expressed the desire at one time or another to meet God and defend their land through martyrdom. Eight bombers were described as very likable guys, devoted to their communities, or noted for helping friends and other community members and, in one case, defending and helping the community's weaker members.
>
> Three bombers were described as peaceful, nonaggressive and/or calm, and were clearly not pathological. Neither did they suffer from psychological or educational problems. Three were especially described as average, normal guys, one of whom loved life, another of whom was generally happy, and two of whom loved to work.
>
> Five bombers were described as being frustrated and depressed at times. One was described as usually serious. And one was described as especially depressed because his family had no money for him to pursue graduate studies and because the Israeli army did not permit him to leave Gaza to pursue his education in the West Bank. None of the bombers drank, took drugs, or engaged in antisocial behavior against the community.
>
> (Fields, Elbedour, & Hein, 2002, p. 214)

The authors note that depression is part of the equation for some. The role of depression has also been brought up by others. Mahmud Sehwait, a psychiatrist in Ramallah, noted the prevalence of post-traumatic stress disorder among those who can potentially or eventually become suicide bombers (Perina, 2002).

A special issue of *Political Psychology* in 2009 addressed suicide terrorism. The first article was presented by Kruglanski, Chen, Dechesne, Fishman, and Orehek (2009). They advanced the notion of the quest for personal significance involving a collective crisis situation that includes a perceived threat to the in-group, the presence of an ideology supporting terrorism, and attachment to the hero status of martyrdom. There were a range of responses from scholars in the field, reflecting different perspectives on the study of the same phenomenon. Some will be reviewed here. In response, Bloom maintained:

> There are significant problems with the case they construct as well as how as [sic] they construct it. The arguments and evidence used to support the authors' claims betray a limited understanding and narrow interpretation of terrorist psychology, a failure to acknowledge the severe limitations with the evidence identified to support their premise, and a failure to acknowledge that complexity of how motivation is conceptualized in contemporary psychology.
>
> (Bloom, 2009, p. 387)

Further, as in any body of research, Mintz and Brule (2009) cautioned that there are methodological issues in the study of suicide terrorism, including selection bias, selection effects, contradictory anecdotal evidence, small sample size, and lack of measurement validity. Further, while Kruglanski and co-authors advanced a promising theory, it lacked data and evidence. Others, such as Crenshaw (2009), suggest there is a complex social process involved.

Others join the group for the various reasons we highlighted above, but are later convinced through group pressures that suicide is something demonstrating ultimate commitment. Here the recruiters use propaganda tactics and *conformity* pressures to gain the ultimate sacrifice from an individual. Either way, when individuals join such a group, they become part of a "special" subgroup of suicide bombers. They are treated separately from the rest of the group and pressure focuses exclusively on reinforcing the person's willingness to die for the group.

Not only men, but also women, participate in suicide terrorism. According to Zedalis (2004), "female suicide bombers were used in the past; however, the recent spate of them in different venues, in different countries, and for different terrorist organizations forces us to study this terrorist method" (p. 1). More specifically, research on various groups indicates that:

> About 15 percent of suicide bombers have been women. Most of them belonged to the Tamil LTTE or the Turkish PKK; almost two thirds of the PKK's suicide bombers were female. In both of these groups, their charismatic leaders assured the female volunteers that by participating in the suicide campaign, they would support the group cause while proving that they were as brave as their male peers. Until recently, female suicide bombers were unique to the LTTE, PKK, and other non-religious terror organizations, but this trend has changed recently; some religious leaders have sanctified women's participation

> in such acts under their "loose" interpretation of Islamic tradition. (Ironically, the same men claim "strict" readings of the Koran to justify terrorism.) Thus, the Palestinian Hamas and PIJ as well as Chechen separatists have started utilizing female bombers. Importantly, those organizations have been operating in very conservative and traditional societies where women have not enjoyed equal rights with men.
>
> (Schweitzer, 2004, p. 1)

In another study looking at support for suicide terrorism, Victoroff, Adelman and Matthews (2012) examined psychological factors relevant to support for suicide bombings in the Muslim diaspora. Looking at Pew Attitude Surveys of Muslims in Great Britain, France, Germany, Spain, and the United States, the authors concluded that perceived discrimination and younger ages were correlated with support for suicide bombings within the diaspora.

DEMOGRAPHIC PROFILING

Another line of research looks for demographic profiles of terrorists. The idea behind this research is that it can lead to identification of notable commonalities among terrorists. When discussing demographics, a number of factors need to be taken into consideration—for example, economic, gender, age, religion, occupation, and education (Mastors & Deffenbaugh, 2007).

However, it is very difficult to generalize about the backgrounds of terrorists. Terrorists come from a variety of socioeconomic classes, age groups, gender groups, occupations, educational backgrounds, and in the case of transnational networks such as al-Qaeda, countries of origin/citizenship/residency (Mastors & Deffenbaugh, 2007). In many terrorist groups, the initial leadership tends to be held by middle-class and upper middle-class people. But as the group evolves over time, new leaders obviously emerge. These are usually drawn from the ranks and are not necessarily from the social classes of the old cadre. The masses tend to be drawn from those with lower- or working-class backgrounds, but not always. For example, Silber and Bhatt (2007) examined five cases and found that individuals were young, often educated, middle-class males operating in male-dominated societies. Some were immigrants, but not first generation and not radical or even devout Muslims. Furthermore, the demographics of a recruit may not be indicative of motivation. There is a line of research in both academia and the government looking at demographic attributes and then likening these attributes to motivation (Ehrlich & Liu, 2006). Often, these claims about demographics rely on stereotypes rather than research. For example, a blanket statement often made is that recruits are economically disenfranchised. As such, we just need to fix the economic problems of the country and individuals will not be attracted to terrorism. However, for some economics is not even an important motivating factor. Furthermore, even if a person is economically disadvantaged, there may be another motivating factor that is the determinant of why an individual sought to join a terrorist group in the first place (Mastors & Deffenbaugh, 2007). As more and more data are gathered on the backgrounds of such individuals, it may be possible to make more definitive judgments about where certain characteristics may be coalescing, or shed more light on particular subsets. For example, in their study of 71 American ISIS recruits, Vidino and Hughes (2015) found that the average age was 26 and 86% were male. While a demographic profile alone does not provide a picture of why people join, it does illuminate their backgrounds.

Individuals and Groups

The relationship between individuals and groups is something not totally agreed upon among social psychologists and those from other disciplines conducting terrorism research (Brown, 2000). Is there such a thing as group behavior that can influence individual behavior, or is group behavior really just a reflection of individuals acting in groups? Allport (1962) argues that it is the psychology of individuals that matters. There is no such thing as a "group mind" (Brown, 2000, p. 5). On the other hand, Sherif (1936), Asch (1952) and others maintain that group processes influence individuals (Brown, 2000). Others such as Tajfel (1978) claim that we need to distinguish between interpersonal behavior and group behavior. "Group behavior is typically homogenous or uniform, while interpersonal behavior shows the normal range of individual differences" (Brown, 2000, p. 6). Further, "Tajfel saw all social behavior as lying on a continuum where at one end the interaction is seen as being determined by the membership of various groups and relations between them, while at the other it is more decided by personal characteristics and interpersonal relationships" (Brown, 2000, p. 7). Along the same lines, Turner (1982) explained that individuals have both personal and social identities. Personal identities are self-descriptions, and are more personalistic and idiosyncratic (Brown, 2000). Social identity, however, is defined in terms of category memberships (Brown, 2000). When individuals define themselves as part of a group, they identify with the norms and attributes of the group.

As highlighted earlier, personality attributes are also important. Groups are made up of individuals with different personalities, even though they subscribe to the same group identity. The group can influence the individual, and the individual can influence the group.

RECRUITMENT AND RADICALIZATION

Recruitment plays a central role in any terrorist group. Without a flow of new members, the existence of the group comes under threat. Within secretive terrorist groups, significant measures are taken to vet recruits. Letting through one person into the group who is a foreign government agent or source can be potentially devastating to a terrorist group. Vetting is a continual process that takes place throughout the recruit's tenure. Once a member is trusted, some suspicion is alleviated, but groups tend to continually watch their members for potential betrayers. Thus, terrorist groups create their own counterintelligence wings to not only stop penetration from the outside, but to find betrayers. For example, the Provisional Irish

Republican Army (PIRA) investigated any potential breaches or events that could have happened because of potential penetration (O'Callaghan, 1998). Diamond and Locy note the vigorous vetting tactics used by al-Qaeda. They argue:

> Becoming a member of al-Qaida is just as tough, in its own way, as getting into the CIA, an elite American university or even the Mafia. There are no SATs or lie-detector tests, but talent hunters for the group that carried out the Sept. 11 attacks use rigorous vetting techniques that include background checks, interviews with relatives and friends and one-on-one meetings to test a recruit's commitment.
>
> (Diamond and Locy, 2002, p. 1)

Those who join terrorist groups do so gradually, through a series of steps removing them from their old lives and leading them to new ones. As we highlighted earlier, some social identity theorists argue that social identity is "intimately bound up with our group memberships." Therefore, joining a group requires a form of self-redefinition (Brown, 2000, p. 28). Other social psychologists argue that when individuals join groups, processes of depluralization and *deindividuation* take place. Depluralization is when previous group identities are stripped away. Deindividuation refers to a loss of self-awareness and evaluation apprehension that can occur when individuals join groups and become anonymous (Zimbardo, 1971, 2007). Personal accountability and responsibility are shifted away from the individual to the group. Zimbardo (1971, 2007) argues it is at this point that individuals commit heinous acts against others on behalf of groups. Individuals, as part of groups, can commit acts they wouldn't have done as individuals. Some subsequent research challenged Zimbardo's perspective. For example, Diener (1976, 1979) and Johnson and Downing (1979) maintain individuals do not automatically engage in such destructive ways just because they are part of a group. Instead, behavior depends on "which norms are salient in each particular situation" (Brown, 2000, p. 16). Bandura (2004) suggests individuals who participate in harmful activities toward others go through a process of **moral disengagement**. Thus, they will not participate in such behaviors unless there is a moral justification to do so.

Adding to the body of literature are numerous models seeking to explain the radicalization process through a series of stages. For example, Sageman (2004) proposes a four-stage process beginning with moral outrage and ending with mobilization through networks. Borum (2003) suggests four stages resulting in legitimizing violence against another group. These are based on social psychology and the notion of group comparison. First, individuals reflect on their circumstances and determine "it's not right," compared with other groups. They then use comparative judgments regarding the conditions of others who are in more favorable positions. Borum describes this stage as "it's not fair." The next stage is "it's your fault," in which blame is assigned to the out-group and vilification and dehumanization occur. Finally, negative stereotyping takes place, leading to the legitimized violence directed at the out-group. In their model, McCauley & Mokalenko (2008) propose 12 mechanisms and three levels: individual, group, and mass-public. In his work, Moghaddam (2005) describes his framework as having five staircases of the radicalization process. On the ground floor, deprivation drives group comparison, and then the societal factors of social mobility and procedural justice come into play. If the situation is not rectified, individuals progress to the second floor, where the outgroup is blamed for deprivation; those with aggressive behavior pass onto the third floor where they interact with like-minded people and consider options. The fourth floor is where individuals join the group and ideas are solidified. On the fifth floor, individuals are ready to commit a terrorist act and are fully committed to the group.

In their examination of radicalization, Silber and Bhatt (2007) look at five cases and suggest four stages of radicalization. They talk about pre-radicalization. As already noted, they found that in their cases, individuals were young, often educated, middle-class males operating in male-dominated societies. Some were immigrants, but not first generation and not radical or even devout Muslims. Individuals engage in self-identification: there is a personal crisis causing them to turn to Islam to deal with that crisis. They are also exposed to radical literature and seek out like-minded individuals. During indoctrination, the radicalized Salafi-worldview is accepted. This is where the individual goals are supplanted by larger considerations for Muslims and interaction with like-minded people occurs. Finally, jihadization occurs when individuals commit to violent jihad, train, and plan attacks.

In his study, Wiktorowicz (2005) focuses on individuals joining a group and, in particular, the case of al-Muhajiroun. He contends that there is not enough focus on individuals' role in the literature—that is, why they are attracted to the group and the role of socialization. In response to the other social psychology-based approaches, he argues that there is a "cognitive opening" requiring a willingness on the part of individuals to expose themselves to the message. While many would outright reject the claims, the experience of a personal crisis can cause individuals to question their beliefs and open themselves up to alternative views. This crisis can be economic, social, cultural, political, or personal. Further, the cognitive opening is facilitated by outreach, which occurs as activists in the current social network or new contacts generate discussions, appealing to Muslims and educating them on crises around the world. A common tactic, Wiktorowicz (2005) argues, is "moral shock" to generate a cognitive opening. This leads to religious seeking, where individuals explore religious worldviews "to interpret and resolve his discontent." During this time, individuals seek out religious institutions to provide solutions to the issues they are facing. This generally does not occur in a vacuum: individuals typically look to friends and family for direction and sources. Individuals are also led to events and activities so they can shop around for what appeals to them. Personal ties can also be made with strangers and bonds developed. Activists have at their disposal many social organizations, including charities, professional organizations, cultural societies, mosques, political parties, religious lessons, and study circles, as well as informal institutions.

Determining the validity of religious arguments, Wiktorowicz (2005) maintains, is a difficult task, especially in the face of competing perspectives. To determine the validity of arguments, individuals seek out religious authorities (community leaders, mosque imams, self-taught charismatic leaders, trained Muslim scholars). Finally, there is a progression to high-risk activism. "Socialization *redefines* self-interest, and helping produce the collective good is a means, not an end, toward fulfilling individual spiritual goals" (p. 28). There can also be material incentives. In the world of radical Islam, individuals are inculcated with views that violence is God's will and the failure to act will impact salvation. Intrinsic to this is the work on the part of the activists to educate individuals about responsibilities and proper behavior. All of it must be accepted to be a good Muslim.

The frameworks proposed above were developed seemingly in isolation from each other (King & Taylor 2011). They are not in total agreement on how radicalization happens, or at what level of analysis, but there is a general understanding that motivation is relevant, and some type of indoctrination occurs, leading to an individual joining the group. However, many are not supported with replicable empirical case studies. Wiktorowicz (2005) focused on one case study of al-Muhajiroun; Silber and Bhatt (2007) looked at five cases of homegrown terrorism. Thus, their frameworks are born of these limited cases. Other frameworks were general proposals and not based on empirical case studies. This suggests the need for cross-talk among academics, more replicable empirical studies to test the assumptions of the frameworks, and cooperation in the future development of theory.

Moving from the theoretical into the realm of examples of recruitment demonstrates how individuals join these groups can be a difficult problem to unravel. Stories from recruits from different terrorist groups paint a complicated picture of how they come to join a terrorist group. There is not one path to recruitment, and groups employ different recruitment strategies. It is also important to keep in mind that a group can employ many different recruitment strategies at one time: groups are not necessarily beholden to one type of recruitment strategy. Individual motivation, as we have already addressed, has some role to play.

Taking this into account, we can only talk generally about what occurs during initial recruitment, and we also use specific examples to illustrate these recruitment strategies. First, terrorist groups have "spotters"—that is, potential recruits are spotted and assessed, and the recruiter tries to bring this individual into the group. The places where individuals are spotted are plentiful. For example, an individual can be attending a lecture, or be in a library, at school, in prison, at an internet café, and so forth. In their discussion of recruitment by Islamic terrorist groups in the United States, Silber and Bhatt (2007) describe recruitment venues as "radicalizing incubators" (p. 20). As they further note, "generally these locations, which together comprise the radical subculture of the community, are rife with extremist rhetoric. Though the locations can be mosques, more likely incubators include cafes, cab driver hangouts, flophouses, prisons, student associations, non-governmental organizations, hookah (water pipe bars), butcher shops and bookstores" (p. 20).

The internet boom has given spotters an additional opportunity to radicalize, recruit (and mobilize existing members). As Weimann illustrates:

> The Internet can be used to recruit and mobilize supporters to play a more active role in support of terrorist activities or causes. In addition to seeking converts by using the full range of website technologies (audio, digital video, etc.) to enhance the presentation of their

> message, terrorist organizations capture information about the users who browse their websites. Users who seem most interested in the organization's cause or well suited to carrying out its work are then contacted. Sophisticated methods are used by terrorists to refine or customize recruiting techniques on the Net: "Using some of the same marketing techniques employed by commercial enterprises, terrorist servers could capture information about the users who browse their websites, and then later contact those who seem most interested. Recruiters may also use more interactive Internet technology to roam online chat rooms and cyber cafes, looking for receptive members of the public—particularly young people. Electronic bulletin boards and Usenet discussion forums can also serve as vehicles for reaching out to potential recruits. Interested computer users around the world can be engaged in long term 'cyber relationships' that could lead to friendship and eventual membership."
>
> (Weimann, 2004, p. 60)

In a study of propaganda and dissident Irish Republicanism, Bowman-Grieve (2010) found that virtual communities don't just create opportunities to disseminate information, but also forge online and offline engagement. ISIS, al-Shabaab, and Boko Haram, among others, have internet and social media presence. In the Philippines, groups use Facebook, Twitter, and YouTube to disseminate propaganda, and connect with supporters, other network members, and recruits (Asia Foundation & Rappler Inc., 2018).

Some individuals are brought in by existing members through a personal or social connection (Sageman, 2004). At other times, an individual finds the message (propaganda) of the group appealing and seeks out members of the group or a way to join, such as via the internet, and a variety of other places where groups and individuals are known to operate. Here personal and social ties are also important because these individuals can facilitate introductions to the terrorist groups (Mastors & Deffenbaugh, 2007; Sageman, 2004). Some members of terrorist groups are also forcibly conscripted. The Tamil Tigers in Sri Lanka, for example, use forced conscription of children in their recruitment (UTHR, 2003). This is also true of the Maoists in Nepal, who carry out forced recruitment of children (Human Rights Watch, 2007).

Those who do the recruiting focus on the mindset of the potential recruit. Therefore, pitches are tailored to the demographic characteristics of the individual. Emotional appeals are especially important. The threat portrayed is imminent and action is necessary. Appealing to an individual's emotions helps to not only draw in new members, but to also sustain old ones (Mastors & Deffenbaugh, 2007). Recruiters are also looking for individuals they can indoctrinate, and those who conform to the rules of the group. We discuss conformity in more detail below.

INDOCTRINATION

Recruits also go through a significant indoctrination process, and propaganda is central to this. Propaganda is defined by Jowett and O'Donnell (1999) as "the deliberate attempt to shape perceptions, manipulate cognitions, and direct behavior to achieve a response that furthers the desired intent of the propagandist" (p. 6). Propaganda can shape beliefs or bolster a belief system. Earlier we noted that individuals are motivated to join groups for various reasons. However, not all individuals will join a group simply because of an existing motivation unless there is also a willingness to seek alternative views. It is here that propaganda is an important tool for recruitment because those who do the recruiting focus on the message of the group as much as they do the mindset of the recruit. Once recruits are assessed (where propaganda is used to draw the member in) they are then further indoctrinated with illustrations of group propaganda. The group central messages are constantly reinforced. When recruits (and members) are faced with conflicting information or question the group's stance, alternative views are conveniently explained away. If a recruit being indoctrinated or a member of the group questions the messages and explanations given to them, they are offered rationalizations to explain away doubt. Here the recruiters can draw upon the aforementioned sources of information bolstering the group's views. Gartenstein-Ross (2007) provides an excellent depiction of this in his autobiographical account of his work with a Saudi charity that had many radical members. The author takes the reader on his journey of working with those who subscribed to the Salafi view of Islam. He described how at first he would question the explanations provided to him on a variety of issues, but these questions were always answered with the Salafi way of thinking. For example, he would be given an "authoritative" book on the subject at hand. Eventually, Gartenstein-Ross internalized those views, did not seek out alternative information, and became more radicalized over the course of a year.

Propaganda serves several purposes for the group. As already mentioned, it can be used as a recruitment tool. Propaganda can also be used as a conformity measure, and to popularize a group's message. Thus, the use of propaganda can serve to entice recruits, exemplify group norms and goals, reinforce these for existing members, and keep existing supporters such as financial donors and the diaspora informed.

PROPAGANDA MESSAGES

Terrorist groups disseminate their propaganda message through a variety of media. There are many different examples, including video and audio tapes, leaflets, pamphlets, books, lectures/sermons, poetry, video games, music videos, songs, CDs, and cassettes, among others. The internet boom has given terrorist groups new ways to disseminate their messages and gain potential recruits. Through websites and chat rooms, blogs and other social media tools, they are able to reach a wider audience. Terrorist groups can and do learn from each other, and they often adopt the successful strategies of other groups. We now turn to specific examples of propaganda efforts by terrorist groups.

Through media outlets such as al-Manar Television, a website, and al-Nour radio station, Hezbollah has been able to sustain an effective campaign promoting its message—for example, when Hezbollah captured two Israeli soldiers in 2006 and the Israelis responded with a limited, but very destructive campaign in Lebanon. Even though the Israeli campaign was prompted by Hezbollah's actions and, to an extent the perception was that Hezbollah was responsible for provoking the Israelis, through a concerted propaganda effort Hezbollah managed to win the war of perceptions and come out on top. Dickey and Norland point out that the Israeli operation had a positive impact on Hezbollah's recruitment efforts:

> No one denies that Hezbollah started the fight, with its unprovoked incursion into Israel, and no one doubts that Israel can win it, at least in conventional terms. But that's not what matters as much as public perceptions, and the impact those perceptions have from Tehran to Cairo. These conflagrations in Gaza, Lebanon and Iraq risk converging, if not on the ground, then in that virtual reality—on satellite television and the Web—where Al Qaeda and Hezbollah find recruits for their global networks. Israel can bomb Lebanon's infrastructure all it wants, but Hezbollah, which operates beyond the limits of a state, ultimately has no infrastructure. Hezbollah's own rockets and missiles can miss nearly all their targets, with comparatively little loss of life, but so long as they keep firing, they shatter the myth of Israeli invincibility and win friends and admirers in a radicalized Muslim world. "The Zionist enemy has not been able to reach military victory," said Hezbollah leader Hassan Nasrallah in a speech Friday on his organization's Al-Manar TV, still broadcasting despite Israeli Air Force strikes that obliterated its studios and transmission towers.
>
> (Dickey & Norland, 2006, p. 1)

Like Hezbollah, al-Qaeda and ISIS have very sophisticated propaganda efforts, and promote core messages explaining their goals and successes. As Mastors and Deffenbaugh explain of al-Qaeda:

> A spectrum of themes is associated with these methods. Generally, some of the more consistent themes are anti-American, anti-Western, anti-Christian, anti-Israeli, and anti-Jewish in character. Notably, the United States is depicted as an imperial power, while the Israelis are the enemy supported by them. Both are accused of committing atrocities against Muslims. Other Western governments are added into the mix, especially because of the Iraq war. Many of these themes take aim at what are deemed to be corrupt Arab and Muslim governments, and which the United States stands accused of supporting. In addition, jihad is often referred to as an honorable duty. Some of the methods openly call for jihad against the United States and Americans, as well as their allies, such as other western countries or corrupt Arab and Muslim regimes, and the network makes Muslims aware of how they can participate in jihad. Other information simply broadcasts events impacting Muslims, such as United States involvement in Iraq. Finally, a dedicated propaganda effort informs the public of the network's nature and pursuits.
>
> The network also clearly informs individuals that it is responding to the ills perpetrated on Muslims throughout the world. Thus, activities are not so much offensive as they are defensive in nature. The

> imperial West, as well as corrupt Arab regimes, Israel, and many other enemies, started the fight. By these methods, al-Qaida can provide their spin on, or interpretation of, behavior, events, policies, and so forth, while offering violence as the principal solution. Thus, these sources of information are influential in shaping the views of others, and can cause those on the receiving end of the message to act in support of such views. It is in this way that al-Qaida can provide an outlet for pursuing this solution of violence.
>
> (Mastors & Deffenbaugh, 2007, p. 90)

Groups in the Philippines, such as Abu Sayyaf and Islamic State-Ranao, focus on connecting local grievances in their messaging (Asia Foundation & Rappler Inc., 2018).

Another interesting example of how groups get their messages out is through music videos. The use of music videos demonstrates the adaptability of the network, especially with regard to recruitment. In other words, they have realized they need to expand propaganda efforts to draw in more segments of society. For example, early on, "Dirty Kuffar," aimed at Pakistani Muslims, was a rap music video performed by Shaykh Terra and the Soul Salah Crew, while ISIS uses hip hop music to entice supporters.

Iraqi insurgent groups in particular demonstrated a notable propaganda machine. For example, they often filmed and then disseminated videos of their attacks on U.S. soldiers. According to Kimmage and Ridolfo:

> At the heart of each video clip is the field record of an actual insurgent operation. The most commonly recorded operation is an IED attack on U.S. forces, usually in a Humvee or Bradley fighting vehicle. In these video clips, a stationary camera films a stretch of road and captures the moment when an IED destroys a passing vehicle. Other frequently recorded operations include sniper and mortar attacks. The most prized videos, judging by download statistics, are the downing of U.S. helicopters and sniper attacks in which a U.S. soldier is seen falling to the ground.
>
> (Kimmage & Ridolfo, 2007, p. 27)

Filming operations have been used successfully by Chechen groups for many years. Again, groups learn from each other about what works in propaganda. While affiliates of al-Qaeda and ISIS networks support the overall thrust of core arguments, they do have their own distinct propaganda efforts tailored to their own regional concentrations.

Dehumanization and Scapegoating

Dehumanization of the enemy is an extremely effective tool in getting potential recruits to understand the importance of the defined enemy. Dehumanization also serves to reinforce the beliefs of existing members (Staub, 1989; Zimbardo, 2007). In group propaganda, and in the language of members, the enemy is demonized and defined as subhuman and threatening. Violence against this enemy is acceptable. As Zimbardo explains:

> Dehumanization is the central construct in our understanding of "man's inhumanity to man." Dehumanization occurs whenever some human beings consider other human beings to be excluded from the moral order of being a human person. The objects of this psychological process lose their human status in the eyes of their dehumanizers. By identifying certain individuals or groups as being outside the sphere of humanity, dehumanizing agents suspend the morality that might typically govern reasoned actions toward their fellows ... Dehumanization stigmatizes others, attributing to them a "spoiled identity." Under such conditions, it becomes possible for normal, morally upright, and even usually idealistic people to perform acts of destructive cruelty.
>
> (Zimbardo, 2007, p. 307)

We have already highlighted Bandura's (2004) discussion of moral disengagement. To reiterate, individuals have moral standards that are a product of socialization. Individuals sanction themselves to prevent their inhumanity toward others. However, these self-regulatory mechanisms are not fixed and static, and individuals and groups can disengage this sense of morality in order to commit inhumane acts. Zimbardo (2007) argues that anyone can morally disengage from destructive conduct. For example, an individual disengages by redefining harmful behavior as honorable, thus creating moral justifications for violence. Another option is to "minimize our sense of a direct link between our actions and harmful outcomes by diffusing or displacing personal responsibility." Individuals can also "ignore, distort, minimize or disbelieve any negative consequences of our conduct." Finally, individuals can reconstruct perceptions of the enemy by blaming them for the consequences and by dehumanizing them (pp. 310–11).

There are numerous examples of dehumanization and moral disengagement. For example, amongst many radical Muslim groups, Israel is portrayed as the enemy. Jews are demonized and have even been described as descendants of pigs. Deeds against the evil enemy are portrayed as necessary and justifiable. O'Callaghan (1998) describes this type of thinking by members of the IRA about the British and its Protestant supporters in Northern Ireland.

The enemy is also a scapegoat for the problems of the members of the terrorist group. As Staub (1989) states, "finding a scapegoat makes people believe their problems can be predicted and controlled; and it eliminates one's own responsibility, thereby diminishing guilt and enhancing self-esteem" (p. 48). In al-Qaeda, for example, the United States and Israel are the enemies, responsible for the suffering of Muslims worldwide, and they are vilified. Many of the problems that Muslims face throughout the world, recruits are told, are because of the actions of the Israeli and American tyrants.

CONFORMITY

Groups often have rituals for newcomers, whether a ceremony or some other form of initiation (Moreland & Levine, 1982). For example, some al-Qaeda members were asked to take a *bayat* (oath of allegiance) to Osama bin Laden. In his court testimony, Zacarias Moussaoui admitted to being a member of al-Qaeda, and claimed he took a *bayat* to Osama bin Laden (Shenon, 2002). A *bayat* was also used by the Afghani Taliban, and by ISIS.

New recruits are put through a variety of measures to ensure their conformity. They are taught the way of the group, and pressured to buy into the group norms. Once in a group, a recruit is expected to conform to the norms of the group. Individuals do incorporate these norms into their own behavior (Brown, 2000). Group norms must be constantly reinforced. Even with committed recruits, there are a number of measures that groups have to employ to keep them in line. Usually, this task falls on the more experienced members of the group.

As discussed in Chapter 4, individuals conform for two reasons: to be liked (normative social influence) and to be right (informational social influence). Individuals tend to change their beliefs or behaviors so that they are consistent with the standards set by the group. Recall the moving light experiments of Mazur Sherif (1936), discussed in Chapter 4. Sherif found a great deal of convergence when it came to the judgments within the group of participants. Because the situation was so ambiguous, group members actually used the judgments of others to modify their own judgments about what they saw. Those individuals who want to be seen as distinct from other members are less likely to conform. Those highly committed to a group are more likely to conform. Finally, conformity in a group drops even if there is just one dissenter in the group.

Another line of research focuses on obedience to authority in groups. Recall the series of electric shock experiments done by Stanley Milgram (1963) discussed in Chapter 9. The results indicated that when people are told to do something by someone they view as an authority, most will obey—even if it violates their values. Zimbardo (2007) argues that there are several lessons to be learned from the Milgram experiments about gaining compliance from others. We note a few of them: prearranging a form of contractual obligation; giving participants meaningful roles; presenting basic rules to follow; offering an ideology to justify use of any means to achieve a goal; and creating opportunities for the diffusion of responsibility or abdication of responsibility for negative outcomes (pp. 273–274).

Deviant group members are problematic because when they don't conform, they threaten the cohesiveness of the group and the conformity of other members. Additionally, they often bring negative and unwelcome attention to the group. Deviants are dealt with by the group through conformity measures. They can also be expelled or killed, usually after other conformity measures have been tried. For example, the UVF, a group we highlighted earlier, had to contend with several group members who became known as the "Shankill Butchers." These members went on a sadistic killing spree in the 1970s. Eventually, the PIRA killed Lenny Murphy, the Butchers' notorious leader, and the UVF did not stand in the way. His behavior was no longer containable (Dillon, 1989). When faced with problematic members within the group, the UDA in Northern Ireland made moves to contain the behavior, and at times decided to have these members expelled. Others were killed (Mastors, 2008; Wood, 2006). Taylor and Quale (1994) illustrate in interviews with Irish Republican Army (IRA) activists that those who betray the organization are killed.

Another example of pressure to conform is found in the al-Qaeda network. In 2005, Ayman al-Zawahiri, a core leader of al-Qaeda, wrote a letter to Abu Musab al-Zarqawi, the now deceased leader of al-Qaeda in Iraq. In the letter, Ayman al-Zawahiri wanted to gain conformity from al-Zarqawi, who ultimately brought negative attention to the network by killing Muslims. Al-Zarqawi, however, ignored al-Zawahiri's directive and continued on his own path, setting the stage for the rise of ISIS and a new network. A different example of control and conformity was seen in the Abu Nidal Organization. The leader of the organization was Sabri al-Banna. He was extremely feared, paranoid and distrustful, and micromanaged everything in the group to ensure his safety and the conformity of members (Siers & Mastors, 2017).

Group Conflict

As we noted in Chapter 4, there are conflicts that occur in groups, and there are reasons why conflict erupts between group members. Scholars argue problems such as attributions, harsh criticism, nay-saying, and the aggression hypothesis can provoke conflict. Typically, the disaffected in one group take on the leadership role of another group. For example, the Armed Islamic Group (GIA) in Algeria formed in 1991, arising from the more militant side of Islamic Salvation Front (FIS). From there, even the GIA split, and the Salafist Group for Call and Combat (GSPC) emerged as a new group in 1992:

> The GSPC splintered from a rival Algerian organization, the Armed Islamic Group (GIA) over a disagreement on whether civilians constitute legitimate targets. Since its inception in 1992, the GIA has killed thousands of Algerian civilians, including women and children in targeted massacres.
>
> (Daly, 2005, p. 1)

Again, even after this, the GSPC merged with al-Qaeda to form yet another group, AQIM, although not all members supported this merger. The case of American-born jihadi Omar al-Hammami illustrates inability to conform. While he joined the Somali group al-Shabaab, he fell out with the leadership because they did not follow true Islamic doctrine. He left the group, but was eventually killed by al-Shabaab because he was a vocal and visible critic.

Related to group conflict is the work on disengagement. Horgan (2009) suggests some exploratory propositions about disengagement. Psychological disengagement can take on many forms, such as burnout, conflicting personal priorities, internal disagreements, disagreements over strategy, tactics, politics or ideology, and a "mismatch between the fantasy and the reality" (p. 31). There are also physical disengagement factors related to exiting the movement voluntarily or involuntarily, and involuntary or voluntary movement to a new role. Psychological disengagement can also precede physical engagement.

ROLES

Recruiters tend to be sophisticated and assess recruits for specific roles in the group. Some people are seen as valued for key roles, while others are not. Thus, some recruits are more coveted than others.

Let's consider the case of José Padilla. Padilla was seen as ultimately expendable and therefore not a valued long-term member of al-Qaeda. First, Padilla was pliable and he was easily taught to conform. But he was not an Arab, a very important ethnic trait in the group. As such, he would never move into the trusted circle. Al-Qaeda wanted him because he followed directions and also held American citizenship, which allowed him to move freely throughout the United States. The haphazard nature of his plan to carry out terrorist operations on U.S. soil was further evidence that Padilla's operation was not thoroughly vetted, or seen as of high importance. To put it plainly, the operational planners sent him off to just do something against the United States.

The same can be said for Richard Colvin Reid, the notorious "shoe bomber." Reid is a British citizen and son of an English mother and Jamaican father, and he converted to Islam while in prison in Great Britain for robbery. After his release, he attended London mosques, notably a key recruitment center, the Finsbury Park Mosque. Eventually, he traveled to Afghanistan to participate in al-Qaeda's training camps. Reid's plan to blow up an airliner by lighting his explosive laden-shoes on fire during the flight wasn't particularly well thought out or tested. But, down and out on his luck, Reid was expendable to the organization. He may or may not have succeeded, but he was sent out to cause chaos as Americans were reeling in the aftermath of 9/11. In another case, because al-Hammami was American, al-Shabaab put him in charge of American recruitment.

SOCIAL CONTROL

One of the tactics used by groups is social control of the communities in which they operate. Thus, their view of proper behavior is extended to the wider populace and the communities are often held hostage by fear of the terrorist groups. In a sense, the group wants the wider community to conform. Often these measures are coercive in nature, and terrorist groups can and do operate unfettered in their communities. Not everyone in these communities supports the groups, but they are still subject to the domination of these groups and their rules. A good example comes from Northern Ireland and the PIRA. In 2005:

> The IRA offered to shoot the men involved in the murder of Robert McCartney, but his family refused the use of violence, republicans said Tuesday night. In a five-page statement, the Irish Republican Army gave its most detailed account yet of McCartney's brutal murder, saying four men were behind the killing, two of whom were its members ... That the IRA felt forced to make such a macabre offer shows the pressure it feels within its own communities, which it

> effectively polices, and where there has sometimes been tacit support of punishment beatings of local criminals.
>
> McCartney was stabbed and beaten to death outside a Belfast bar on Jan. 30 after a row broke out over an allegedly rude gesture made at a woman. His family, who has launched an international campaign for justice, has blamed IRA members and said there were up to 70 witnesses in the bar but many were too frightened of republicans to give evidence.
>
> The IRA Tuesday night stated that after "voluntary admissions by those involved," it knew four men were involved—two were IRA volunteers and two were not—and "the IRA knows the identity of all these men." The statement described how after a "melee" in the bar, a crowd spilled out onto the street and Robert McCartney and his friend Brendan Devine and two other men were chased. One attacker fetched a knife from the pub's kitchen. A second man used the knife to stab McCartney and his friend. A third man kicked and beat McCartney after he was stabbed. A fourth hit Devine and another of McCartney's friends across the face with a steel bar. The IRA said: "The man who provided the knife also retrieved it from the scene and destroyed it."
>
> The IRA said it had had two meetings with the McCartney family in the presence of an independent observer. In the first five-and-a-half-hour meeting last month, an IRA representative had "stated in clear terms that the IRA was prepared to shoot people directly involved in the killing of Robert McCartney." But the statement added: "The family made it clear that they did not want physical action taken against those involved. They stated that they wanted those individuals to give full account of their actions in court."
>
> The IRA stopped short of declaring whether its offer to shoot those involved in the murder meant they were to be killed, or punished with a kneecapping or "six pack," where victims are shot in the ankles, knees and elbows. The IRA has already expelled three volunteers, and Sinn Fein has suspended seven members over the murder.
>
> (Chrisafis, 2005, p. 1)

The following story illustrates social control on a number of levels. Terrorist group members are feared and operate "above the law." However, they also have measures in place to punish those who bring them bad press or violate acceptable behavior. Here it is important to realize that despite decommissioning, the PIRA and the other Protestant paramilitary groups still commit acts of violence, are engaged in criminal activity, and exercise social control.

Social control measures are adopted by groups to keep control of the diaspora as well. Here the tactics of the Tamil Tigers are noteworthy. Individuals in the diaspora were monitored for cooperation and compliance. According to a Human Rights Watch report in 2006:

> Since the ceasefire between the Sri Lankan government and the LTTE in February 2002, increasing numbers of Tamil expatriates have taken advantage of the relative peace to visit family and friends who

> remained in the North and East of Sri Lanka, areas that are largely under the control of the LTTE. Increasingly, these visits have become a source of revenue for the LTTE as the LTTE has begun to systematically identify visiting expatriates and pressure them to contribute to the "cause."
>
> Visitors to the North of Sri Lanka may travel by one of two routes: fly to Jaffna from Colombo, or travel north by bus or car on the main A9 highway that stretches from Kandy in the south to Jaffna at the northern tip of Sri Lanka. North of Vavuniya, travelers reach the Omanthai and Muhamalai crossing points that separate government- and LTTE-held territory. Leaving government-held territory, they must exit their vehicles and show documentation at a government checkpoint before crossing several kilometers of no-man's land that is monitored by the International Committee of the Red Cross (ICRC). On the other side, visitors stop again at an LTTE checkpoint where they must show documentation before proceeding into LTTE-held territory. At the checkpoint, travelers are directed by signs into separate queues depending on whether they are Sri Lankan nationals, or whether they carry foreign passports.
>
> Recent expatriate visitors to the North report that foreign Tamil visitors are given a pass at the checkpoint, for which they must pay 1,000 rupees (approximately U.S.$10). They are told that within three days of reaching their destination, they must take the pass to the local LTTE office in Jaffna or Kilinochchi.
>
> At the LTTE office, visitors must give detailed personal information, such as their name, home phone and address, employer, salary information, whether or not they own their home, and how long they have lived there. They are also asked for information about their past contributions to the LTTE. If visitors cannot verify a history of regular contributions, they then may be told an amount of money that they "owe" to the LTTE. The amount varies but is often calculated on the basis of \$1, £1, or €1 per day, for each day that they have lived in the West. For expatriates who have lived in the West for long periods of time, the amount can be substantial. For example, a Tamil who has lived in Toronto for twenty years might be expected to pay Cdn\$7,300. Alternatively, they may be pressured to sign a pledge to pay a monthly amount once they return home.

Thus, the Tamil Tigers not only expected support from the diaspora, they demanded it.

State Terror and Cultures of Fear

Another form of terror consists of systematic efforts by a government to terrorize the population of the country through torture, political murder, genocide, and other atrocities (Rummel, 1994; Sluka, 2000). The goal is to terrorize the population into political submission and obedience while opponents of the government are being violently repressed or killed. This occurs frequently and across the globe. Amnesty International reported in

1996 that of 150 countries examined, 55% used torture and 41% had politically motivated murders of opponents of the governing regimes (Sluka, 2000). In Latin America during the 1970s and 1980s, this occurred in Brazil, Chile, Argentina, and Uruguay, among other countries. They came to be known as "dirty wars," and a new term was coined for victims of repression: *desaparecidos*, or the "disappeared." Although the exact number of deaths is not known, and probably never will be, approximately 30,000 people were killed or disappeared in Argentina, and between 9000 and 30,000 people suffered similar fates in Chile. Torture was a common instrument used to extract information out of "subversives," anyone expressing opposition to the government or associated with those expressing opposition to the government (relatives, friends, neighbors, students, etc.). Anyone was a potential target.

The populations of these countries were terrorized into submission through the gradual establishment of a **culture of terror**. As Sluka describes it:

> A culture of terror ... is an institutionalized system of permanent intimidation of the masses or subordinated communities by the elite, characterized by the use of torture and disappearances and other forms of extrajudicial death squad killings as standard practice. A culture of terror establishes "collective fear" as a brutal means of social control. In these systems there is a constant threat of repression, torture, and death for anyone who is actively critical of the political status quo.
>
> (Sluka, 2000, pp. 22–23)

In these situations, people have little access to substantiated information. Rumors abound but, not surprisingly, there is little concrete information about what is happening, to whom, and how. Lack of concrete information does two things; it increases fear of the unknown, and makes it easy for the average person to ignore what is going on, to not even try to find out, for if one knows, one may be the next victim. Knowledge is dangerous in these situations, so people hunker down, attend to their own personal situations and try not to make waves. This facilitates the state's control of the population by making political killings and passive acceptance by the population possible. In these cases, the entire population becomes a massive bystander.

THE DIRTY WAR IN ARGENTINA

In 1976, the Argentine military overthrew President Isabela Perón after a period of economic and political turmoil. During the preceding years, the military had begun a campaign against a leftist guerrilla organization, the Montoneros. The Montoneros engaged in various acts of political violence, such as blowing up banks and kidnapping wealthy people in the late 1960s and early 1970s. In response, right-wing death squads were formed, which then proceeded to kill even more people than the Montoneros killed. By the time the military took power in 1976, it had already suppressed the Montoneros. It then turned to any other apparent dissidents. Those not executed immediately were taken to various locations for the extraction of information. Among the most notorious was the Navy Mechanics School, ESMA, where people were tortured and killed. Not all prisoners were killed: some were turned into informants, and some survived by performing important functions for the unit—similar to how some prisoners worked in the concentration camps in Nazi Germany. Others, after being tortured, were drugged, stripped naked, placed upon an airplane, and thrown alive into the Atlantic Ocean. These were some of the many who simply disappeared. In response, Argentine society became silent. The major exception was the mothers of some of the disappeared. These brave women assembled every Thursday at the Plaza de Mayo wearing white scarves bearing the names of their missing children. Known as the Madres de la Plaza de Mayo, they still assemble every Thursday, still seeking to know what became of their children.

The behavior of the torturers was reflective of the patterns discussed above. They were a tight unit composed of carefully selected men committed to the idea that they were saving Argentina from its own worst enemies, political activists. The torturers were isolated, living in the ESMA building and permitted to see their families only three times per month (Rosenberg, 1992). They were well rewarded with money and other perks, such as the personal belongings of those they disappeared. They dehumanized their victims and joked about them, referring to two French nuns who were tossed into the ocean as "the flying nuns," for example. The torturers used euphemisms for their actions. When prisoners were thrown out of planes into the ocean, they were "transferred" or "sent up." Torturers referred to the administration of electric shocks as "giving the machine" (Rosenberg, 1992, p. 90). Many of the torturers believe to this day that they were only doing their duty, and victims were to blame for their treatment. In the words of one torturer:

> At first, I'll be honest, it was hard to accustom ourselves to put up with torture. We're like everyone else. The person who likes war is crazy. We all would have preferred to fight in uniforms, a gentlemen's fight where you all go out to have dinner afterward. The last thing we wanted to do was interrogate ...
>
> In the first phase of the war everyone who was captured was executed ... We knew if we put them into the courts they would ask for all the guarantees of the system they were attacking. They'd have been freed ... Let's say that ten thousand guerrillas disappeared. If we hadn't done it, how many more people would have died at the hands of the guerrillas? How many more young people would have joined them? It's a barbarity, but that's what war is.
>
> (quoted in Rosenberg, 1992, pp. 129–130)

This particular torturer simply saw it as another justifiable battle, not something to be ashamed of.

In addition, the silence of Argentinian society, as in so many other cases, encouraged the implementers of state repression to continue on with it. They did, indeed, have support for their actions. The same individual quoted above also stated, "We had the backing of the church ... Not that priests would say 'go ahead and torture,' but that the church said there were two groups here and we were the ones who were right. I really feel that any armed forces with a decent level of culture and human feeling would do the same as we did" (quoted in Rosenberg, 1992, p. 130). This form of terror was extremely effective in silencing Argentinian society. Indeed, when the military left power, it did so because it lost a war with Great Britain over the Falklands/Malvinas Islands, not because of popular protests about the brutality of the regime.

PARAMILITARIES/DEATH SQUADS

Violence can also be committed by organized groups, paramilitaries, or death squads on behalf of a state, whether sanctioned by that state or not. The state will either turn a blind eye to the actions of these groups or drag its feet when it comes to apprehending them. Paramilitaries and death squads are difficult to define distinctly. Sluka (2000) defines **death squads** as "progovernment groups who engage in extrajudicial killings of people they define as enemies of the state" (p. 141). Cubides (2001) defines **paramilitaries** as "organizations that resort to the physical elimination of presumed auxiliaries of rebel groups and of individuals seen as subversive of the moral order ... They mostly operate through death squads" (p. 129). They often act as a close-knit clandestine organization, which many know about but whose members try to hide their association with the group—although the leader of the largest paramilitary in Colombia was well known and the group had a website. They kidnap, torture, and kill victims identified as belonging to a political group that they believe is undermining them and their country. Thus, the element of intensely perceived threat to the group operates in these cases, as in the others discussed in this chapter.

Death squads and paramilitaries are effective in that they not only destroy the opposition, but terrorize those who object to their activities into silence. Death squads and paramilitaries appear in many countries experiencing severe political instability, and they are not confined to developing countries. The Protestant-loyalist groups in Northern Ireland, such as the UDA, and UVF, and death squads such as the UFF/RHC and Protestant Action Force, killed around 700 Catholic civilians (Sluka, 2000). There were many paramilitaries and death squads operating in Latin America during the era of repressive military regimes in the 1960s and 1970s, and in the civil wars in Central America during the 1970s and 1980s. In El Salvador, for example, the government fought a civil war with leftist rebels called the Farabundo Martí Liberation Front (FMLN), who wanted to gain control of the government. The ARENA Party was the most militant of the right-wing parties in El Salvador and became associated with death squads. Many people from political parties, labor organizations, peasant organizations, universities, and the clergy died at the hands of these squads if they were even thought to have been colluding with the enemy.

The Colombian government was battling the leftist Revolutionary Armed Forces of Colombia (FARC) and the National Liberation Army (ELN) for over 30 years. Baltodano (2008) developed a typology of membership in the FARC. He argued that there were three levels, the *Liderazgo*, or top leadership level, composed of men and women who made a life-time commitment; the *Guerrilla*, armed insurgent members who were full-time fighters; and the *Milicias*, members who supported and fought with the organization, but who left for months at a time to make a living and support their families. While the army was deeply engaged in this war, some Colombians defended their country from the FARC and the ELN. On December 22, 2000, the paramilitary group called United Self-Defense Forces of Colombia (AUC) declared war on these groups and their supporters (Wilson, 2001a). The AUC became infamous for brutal acts of violence used in its counterinsurgency campaign. For example, in April 2001 in the village of Naya, at least 40 civilians were killed with machine guns, machetes, and chainsaws (Wilson, 2001b). Allegations of army collusion led to questions of whether or not they really wanted to put an end to their activity. Sixty-two members of the AUC were finally apprehended in April, and the Colombian President at that time, Andres Pastrana, argued that despite international and domestic criticism, this signaled that the government was not tolerating their activities. The Final Agreement to End the Armed Conflict and Build a Stable and Lasting Peace was signed in November 2016. However, a new government came to power in August 2018, effectively obstructing progress. Since that time, the FARC has demobilized, but other issues such as land access and protection of human rights remain. Further, reintegration of fighters remains partially unfulfilled. Because of the perceived inadequacy of government follow-through, some FARC members returned to violence (Campos, Brannum, & Mastors, 2021).

CONCLUSION

In this chapter, we have briefly covered a wide variety of topics on terrorism. We noted differences among terrorist groups and provided an overview of the basis for intergroup conflict, traits, motivation, recruitment, demographics, propaganda, conformity and obedience to authority, group conflict, role, and social control. The chapter also examined state terror. There is currently a lot of research on terrorism; however, given the plethora of topics and groups, there is definitely more work to be done. It is here that psychology can provide additional interesting insights.

Topics, Theories/Explanations, and Cases Covered in Chapter 12

Topics	*Theories/Explanations*	*Cases*
Terrorism	Personality	Al-Qaeda
Suicide bombers	Social identity theory	Hamas
Recruitment	Image theory	Hezbollah
	Psychopathology	Al Qaeda in Iraq
	Authoritarian personality	IRA
		UDA
	FIRO	PIRO
	Interpersonal needs	LTTE
	Dehumanization	
	Scapegoating	
State terror	Culture of terror	Argentina
Paramilitaries/death squads		Colombia

Key Terms

- authoritarian personality
- culture of terror
- death squads
- Fundamental Interpersonal Relations Orientation (FIRO)
- moral disengagement
- paramilitaries
- rogue image
- suicide bomber
- terrorism

Suggestions for Further Reading

Alexander, A. (2016). Cruel intentions: Female jihadists in America. Program on Extremism, George Washington University. Retrieved from https://extremism.gwu.edu/sites/g/files/zaxdzs2191/f/downloads/Female%20Jihadists%20in%20America.pdf

Bjorgo, T., & Horgan, J. (2009). *Leaving terrorism behind: Individual and collective disengagement.* London: Routledge.

Borum, R. (2003). Understanding the terrorist mindset. *FBI Law Enforcement Bulletin, 72,* 7–10. Retrieved from www.ojp.gov/pdffiles1/nij/grants/201462.pdf

Horgan, J. (2014). *The psychology of terrorism.* London: Routledge.

King, M., & Taylor, D. M. (2011). The radicalization of homegrown jihadists: A review of the theoretical models and social psychological evidence. *Terrorism and Political Violence, 23,* 602–622.

Mintz, A., & Brule, D. (2009). Methodological issues in studying suicide terrorism. *Political Psychology, 30,* 365–380.

Silke, A. (2011). *The psychology of terrorism.* London: Routledge.

Victoroff, J., Adelman, J. R., & Matthews, M. (2012). Psychological factors associated with support for suicide bombing in the Muslim diaspora. *Political Psychology, 33,* 791–809.

Chapter 13

THE POLITICAL PSYCHOLOGY OF INTERNATIONAL SECURITY AND CONFLICT

Throughout history, people have seemingly been embroiled in violence, conflict, and war. And for an equally long period of time, writers from numerous disciplines have sought to understand the causes of such strife (Brown, 1987; Nieburg, 1969). While a discussion of this subject could reasonably be seen to require a review of the voluminous research into violence and aggression conducted in psychology and sociology, this is beyond the limited scope of this chapter. In fact, much of this literature is already discussed in our other chapters dealing with ethnic nationalism, violence, and genocide. Instead, this chapter uses international security and conflict as an example to illustrate how political scientists have applied political psychological approaches to better understand such problems as the causes of war, the security dilemma, and deterrence. In doing so, our hope is that students will better appreciate how psychological concepts are usefully applied to real-world political problems. The portions of the Political Being focused on in this chapter are cognition, emotion, and perceptions of *them*.

WHY VIOLENCE AND WAR?

There are many competing explanations for violence and war proposed by scholars across numerous disciplines (Brown, 1987). Some, for example, looked to biology to suggest humankind is genetically predisposed to be innately violent (Freud, 1932, 1950, 1962; Lorenz, 1966; Scott, 1969; Shaw & Wong, 1989; Wilson, 1978). Others suggested human aggression was more of a socially learned response (Bandura, 1973, 1977, 1986; Skinner, 1971, 1974). Over time, a general consensus emerged. As Brown (1987) notes, "most serious students of human violence recognize some mixture of innate predisposition (which may vary with individuals) and situational conditions" (pp. 8–9). Often, explanations of conflict in political science have suggested psychological factors as a key component. For example, the role of perception and misperception between the leaders of states in causing or avoiding international conflict was described at length across historical crisis cases

DOI: 10.4324/9780429244643-13

(Jervis, 1976; Lebow, 1981). Similarly, problems of successful crisis management given leader psychology or organizational limitations as a factor in avoidance of war have been discussed by a number of scholars (Allison & Zelikow, 1999; George, 1991).

The dynamics and composition of policy-making groups play a major role in averting or causing conflict (Janis, 1972; Janis & Mann, 1977; Boin & 't Hart, 2003). Finally, the personalities and characteristics of leaders play a role in causing or preventing conflicts (Birt, 1993; Post, 1991; Preston, 2011; Stoessinger, 1985). Indeed, there is a growing literature focused on how leaders' own individual, unique risk propensities influence their willingness to use force, or accept high degrees of risk when pursuing their policy objectives (Boettcher, 2005; Keller & Foster, 2012; Kowert & Hermann, 1997; Vertzberger, 1998).

One of the earliest expositions of the causes of political violence is found in Thucydides' *History of the Peloponnesian War*, which chronicles the events surrounding the bloody conflict between the neighboring Greek city-states of Sparta and Athens over 3000 years ago. Although an ancient Greek historian, Thucydides was often described as the first "realist" due to his attention to the anarchic, self-help nature of the ancient Greek international system; his emphasis on how the Spartans and Athenians competed with one another in their pursuit of power, alliances, and influence ("power politics"); and his clear depiction (captured in the Melian Debate) of the lack of morality in the affairs of states ("might makes right"). This perspective is also depicted by the famous statement "the strong do what they will and the weak suffer what they must" by the Athenians to their weaker Melian neighbors (see Morgenthau, 1948 for an overview of realist, power politics arguments). Yet, while much of Thucydides' history clearly expressed realist, power politics notions of state behavior, including the notion that competition for power between states often leads to conflict, Thucydides could also be considered one of the first political psychologists.

Far from using only state characteristics or power motivations to explain the war, Thucydides suggested (much as a modern-day political psychologist might) that the *main spark* igniting this bloody conflict between Sparta and Athens was fear on both sides of one another: fear by the Spartans of what they perceived as the growing power of Athens and its increasingly expansionist policies, and fear by the Athenians of what they perceived as a ruthless, militaristic power bent on competing with them for control of Greece. During the councils of war that followed on both sides, speeches by the leaders of Sparta and Athens were replete with immensely negative stereotypes and caricatures of one another, as well as strong **enemy images** (Cottam, 1994). Driven by these perceptions (and misperceptions) of each other, war became inevitable. Yet the end result of this 23-year struggle was not supremacy over Greece, but rather the weakening of both combatants to such an extent that they were easily conquered by the Persians almost immediately afterwards! Objectively, if we were to speak the language of realists, the balance of power in that region of the world, it would *never* be in the broader interests of either Sparta or Athens to go to war. They needed to be allies and pool their military power to offset the might of Persia, as they had in earlier conflicts. But as Thucydides demonstrated, neither side was making such coolly rational calculations of the regional power balance.

Instead, *the psychology of fear and misperception* were at work, leading both nations to a disastrous bloodbath. Indeed, as Thucydides made clear, to ignore the psychological factors at work between Sparta and Athens would be to miss a crucial underlying cause of the war.

Similarly, the events leading up to World War I (1914–1918) provide another powerful illustration of the importance of psychological variables in explaining conflict. While many factors contributed to the speed with which war engulfed Europe in the summer of 1914 (e.g., military alliances, great power competition over colonies and naval forces, etc.), clearly misperception by leaders played a major role (Farrar, 1988). Indeed, the Great War was not desired by the political leaders of the time. Certainly, the Austrians did not envision their dispute with Serbia igniting a world war, nor did the German Kaiser when he (unwisely) gave support to his Austrian ally. Once again, *fear* played a major role among both political and military leaders of the time. It was accepted by all that technological advancements in warfare and the rapid mobilization capabilities provided by modern railway systems had fundamentally altered the nature of warfare. Not only would a major war be so immensely destructive as to last at best three months (a widely held belief prior to 1914) but, more importantly, the state that succeeded in mobilizing (getting its armies organized and transported to the front lines) first would automatically be the victor (see Keegan, 1998; Tuchman, 1962). In crisis management terms, this was a highly unstable security environment analogous to a country during the Cold War having the capability of launching a completely disarming nuclear first-strike upon an opponent (Jervis, 1976; Levy, 1991). It gave policy-makers precious little time to manage a crisis, and did not allow for defensive moves (since these would automatically be perceived to be offensive by their opponents). In 1914, a mobilized army at the front line was necessary to either defend yourself from attack or invade your neighbor. Offensive and defensive capabilities were indistinguishable from one another. As a result, even though statesmen on all sides tried to reassure one another that their mobilizations were purely for defensive purposes, each fell into what Jervis (1976) later described as the *security dilemma*, a situation in which the actions taken by each state to increase its own security had the effect of simultaneously decreasing the security of its neighbors. Since the true motivations of their neighbors could not be determined with certainty, each state was left to make decisions based solely upon its beliefs about its neighbors' motivations and capabilities. By the end of August, Europe was in flames in a conflict that would eventually claim over 15 million lives.

The Security Dilemma

The basic notion of the security dilemma is a simple one. Faced with what is *perceived* to be (either correctly or incorrectly) a threatening international security environment, national leaders take actions they *perceive* to be defensive ones (such as arms buildups, increased defense spending, fortification of borders, development of national missile defenses, etc.) to protect themselves from these external threats. Knowing their own motivations are peaceful, these leaders tend to make the assumption that their true (peaceful) intentions are equally clear to all their neighbors (Jervis, 1976). However, unlike the relatively unthreatening steps (at least to law-abiding neighbors) that homeowners might take to enhance the security of their own house from burglars (such as installing alarms or better locks, putting bars on windows, or buying a guard dog), equivalent actions taken by states to enhance their security *vis-à-vis* other states require the building of more imposing militaries or defenses, actions that inevitably undermine the security of their neighbors.

What distinguishes offensive and defensive weapons from one another are the *motivations* of their owners, not the basic characteristics of the arms; hence the long-standing joke among security specialists that the true difference between an offensive and defensive weapon is which end of the barrel you are looking down! Indeed, the problem for policy-makers struggling to understand the psychology of their potential opponents (and their real policy intentions) is that they become trapped in a cycle of trying to divine intentions based solely upon visible indicators of behavior—such as size of militaries, where they are located, what political disputes arise between them, and so on. Unfortunately, as Jervis (1976) ably points out with the notion of the "security dilemma," in the real world of security, one cannot judge an opponent's true military intentions based solely upon their capabilities. Any military weapon—whether it be guns, tanks, planes, nuclear weapons—can be employed either offensively or defensively (to attack a neighbor or to defend the homeland). The military strategy adopted determines how the characteristics of the weapons will be used, not vice versa. Weapons themselves are agnostic. Further, almost any action taken by a state for defensive purposes could also support offensive military strategies.

For example, national missile defense (NMD) programs that seek to provide states with the ability to intercept and destroy an opponent's incoming missiles (thereby shielding their countries from attack) are often described as purely defensive by their advocates. And clearly some uses of NMD would be purely defensive (say by a non-nuclear country without an offensive military that sought only to prevent another country from attacking it with nuclear weapons in war). However, as other countries facing proposed NMD defenses vehemently argue (as Russia and China have against U.S. missile defense plans), a shield can also be offensive in nature. A country that suddenly became invulnerable to nuclear retaliation by other states could use that invulnerability to its own military advantage. It could launch a nuclear-first strike of its own with impunity, or invade the other country militarily and not fear retaliation. In this sense, an effective NMD would provide its owner with actual military superiority over all other states and vastly increase its options across the board for using both nuclear and conventional forces (since no retaliation would need to be considered). Thus, NMD can be both offensive *and* defensive. It is how it is used, and not its characteristics, that makes it one or the other. Regardless of the *true motivations* of a country's policy-makers (of which other states can never be absolutely certain), the basic security reality is that by strengthening their military postures, states obtain more offensive options to be prepared should they ever *choose* to become aggressors. In an international system characterized by anarchy, neighboring states must consider all the possibilities behind their opponents' actions and assume the worst (see Jervis, 1976; Richardson, 1960).

As a result, policy-makers pursuing what they believe to be purely defensive military buildups often fail to understand how their actions are likely to be perceived (or misperceived) by neighboring states. Since defensively motivated policy-makers know their own motivations for their military buildups are peaceful, they sometimes assume (incorrectly) that these peaceful intentions are obvious and self-evident to all interested observers. Unfortunately, this is often not the case. For example, during the Cold War, the United States and the Soviet Union saw the actions of each other in a threatening light. The formation of the great military alliances of the period—the North Atlantic Treaty Organization (NATO) in the West and the Warsaw Pact in the East—were seen by their creators as defensive in nature, but viewed as evidence of hostile intent, and a desire to possibly launch an armed invasion by their opponents. Similarly, Soviet military doctrine of the time held that to defend against Western attack, one needed massive, numerically superior conventional forces to offset issues of quality with sheer quantity—a strategy employed effectively against the Germans in World War II (Legvold, 1988). However, for the West, the massive size of the Red Army, its forward deployment in Eastern Europe, and the buildup of such large numbers of tanks, artillery, and combat aircraft were seen as clearly having offensive potential. The Cold War became a classic example of the security dilemma in action. Although we now know neither side seriously contemplated invading the other during the Cold War, these motivations or intentions were not accurately perceived or understood by their opponents (see Gaddis, 1992, 1997).

Contributing to these problems of perception are issues of attribution, or how we tend to psychologically assign cause-and-effect relationships in our environment—for example, the *fundamental attribution error*, which, as we have seen in previous chapters, involves our tendency to explain (or attribute) another person's behavior or actions to their dispositional qualities (their personalities, motivations, etc.) rather than to situational factors in the environment that may have caused the behavior (Heider, 1958). In the security dilemma example above, U.S. policy-makers during the Cold War tended to explain the Soviet Union's military buildup and forward deployment of forces in Eastern Europe by the dispositional qualities of Soviet leaders (i.e., Stalin or Khrushchev's aggressive, expansionist intentions towards Western Europe), and not due to situational factors (such as the formation of NATO, concerns about another invasion from the West, etc.) that actually motivated the behavior. A similar dynamic was demonstrated by Russian President Vladimir Putin's actions in Crimea and Ukraine, which are often portrayed by policy-makers and media in the West as being driven by his authoritarian personality or ambitions for expansionism, instead of the many situational factors that could also be at work (i.e., the threat opposition coup in Kiev against a democratically elected, pro-Russian leader, perceptions that Russia's legitimate security interests were ignored by the West post–Cold War, etc.).

A somewhat similar process of misattribution during the Cold War was described by Ole Holsti's (1967, 1969) work describing the ways in which American policy-makers perceived the behavior and motivations of their Soviet counterparts. For example, in describing the belief system of John Foster Dulles, who served as Dwight Eisenhower's secretary of state during the 1950s, Holsti observed that his world view was characterized by an **inherent bad-faith** perspective of the Soviets. Simply stated, if Soviet behavior in the world was *good* (i.e., not threatening to U.S. interests), it was not because Soviet intentions *were* benign, but rather because their good behavior was only due to overwhelming U.S. military strength. On the other hand, when Soviet behavior in the world was bad (i.e., threatening U.S. interests in Berlin or Cuba), this was a true reflection of their real policy intentions. In other words, when the Soviets were good, it was only because, posed by NATO/EU expansion eastward, the active Western support of the United States made them be good, and when they were bad, it was because they really were bad. American policy-makers throughout the Cold War routinely shared this perspective on the Soviets (as did many Soviet policy-makers of the United States). Further illustrations of this belief system included Paul Nitze's formulation of Soviet intentions in NSC-68 (perhaps the most important U.S. foreign policy document of the Cold War), and Ronald Reagan's depiction of the Soviet Union as "the evil empire" and his "peace through strength" arguments of the 1980s to justify the largest peace-time military buildup in American history. Obviously, this belief system made it very difficult for either side to show good faith toward the other, since this would often be interpreted as further evidence supporting the effectiveness of pursuing a tough policy line towards them. Policy-makers effectively preserved their existing enemy images or negative stereotypes of one another, since the selective perception involved allowed them to discount any cooperative behavior by their opponents as coerced, and focus on the examples of negative behavior that better reflected their existing views of the other side.

The Cold War relationship between the United States and Soviet Union was also described as being characterized by a malignant (spiral) process of hostile interaction (Deutsch, 1986). According to Deutsch, the key elements contributing to the development and perpetuation of a protracted, malignant interaction process included:

> (1) an anarchic social situation, (2) a win–lose or competitive orientation, (3) inner conflicts (within each of the parties) that express themselves through external conflict, (4) cognitive rigidity, (5) misjudgments and misperceptions, (6) unwitting commitments, (7) self-fulfilling prophecies, (8) vicious escalating spirals, and (9) a gamesmanship orientation which turns the conflict away from issues of what in real life is being won or lost to an abstract conflict over images of power.
>
> (Deutsch, 1986, p. 131)

The malignant process escalates as these elements interact with one another to gradually worsen ongoing conflicts, causing them to spiral towards more hostile interactions over time. Thus, according to Deutsch (1986), the basic security dilemma problem for the superpowers and their fear of becoming militarily inferior created an anarchic social situation characterized by extreme competitiveness (a win–lose orientation). As a result, gains in military capability by one side were viewed as threatening losses to the security of the other. Adding to this problem was the use of the external enemy to serve as justification for internal conflicts in both superpower societies (i.e., the need for Stalin's harsh rule at home or the need for internationalist policies in the United States). The cognitive rigidity of policy-makers in how they viewed the other side led to misjudgments and misperceptions of opponents, unwitting commitments to rigid policy positions, and escalating spirals of conflict. The hostility and suspicion expressed towards the other side became a self-fulfilling prophecy when hostility was returned in kind (Deutsch, 1986).

The Psychology of Deterrence

During the Cold War, the superpowers sought to deter extreme threats to their national interests (e.g., invasions of their homelands or attacks upon vital allies) through nuclear deterrence—or the threat to retaliate for such aggression by using nuclear weapons. A simple definition of **deterrence** is the threat by one political actor to take actions in response to another actor's potential actions that would make the costs (or losses) incurred far outweigh any possible benefits (or gains) obtained by the aggressor. Of course, definitions of deterrence vary across the literature. Schelling (1966, 1980), for example, defined deterrence as the use of threats to prevent someone from doing something (or starting something) (p. 195). Stein (1992), on the other hand, defined it as threatening punishment or denial to prevent an adversary from taking unwanted action (p. 147). A classic Cold War example of deterrence is that even if the Soviets could have successfully invaded and occupied Western Europe and obliterated the United States in a nuclear first strike, the United States would still have had enough surviving forces to respond with a retaliatory nuclear attack that would have utterly destroyed the Soviet Union. Thus, no matter how great the potential gains were, the consequences (utter destruction of the home nation in retaliation) would have far exceeded any gains from the original aggression. As a result, once both superpowers possessed comparable abilities to attack and destroy the other with nuclear weapons by the late 1960s, the famous Mutual Assured Destruction (MAD) nuclear doctrine was established, recognizing this deterrent relationship.

But the most fundamental element to this deterrence formula is *perceptual*. Both sides during the Cold War recognized that the *credibility* of their nuclear retaliatory threats was only effective if the other side truly *believed* they would carry them out if suitably provoked. In the final analysis, whether deterrence would fail or succeed depended not on how many weapons each side possessed, but on the perceptions each side possessed regarding the willingness of their opponents to really "push the button." Thus, deterrence (whether nuclear or conventional) is, at its heart, a psychological relationship between the deterrer and the deterred. In order for deterrence to function successfully (e.g., prevent any aggression from taking place to begin with), the actor seeking to deter an opponent must be able to effectively communicate to the opponent (and the opponent must accurately perceive) that the deterrer has both: (1) the physical capability to carry out a threat (nuclear weapons, survivable delivery systems, etc.); and (2) the threat has credibility (the deterrer truly has the resolve (or willingness) to carry out their promised retaliation, no matter how horrific the consequences). If your opponent does not believe in the credibility of your threat, regardless of real intentions, then you will not be able to effectively deter them. This is part of the inherent peril of deterrence—that it can unravel due to an opponent's misperception of *either* your substantive military capabilities *or* the credibility of your threats to use these capabilities.

Consider the example of Saddam Hussein's calculations prior to the invasion of Kuwait. Although truly one of history's worst generals, even Hussein understood that the United States enjoyed vast, overwhelming military superiority over Iraq in terms of numbers and quality of equipment. That much was no mystery to him. What he fundamentally misunderstood was the extent to which an immense technological gap opened up between the U.S. armed forces and those of less advanced states. Indeed, this revolution in military affairs was not fully appreciated, even by U.S. analysts, until after the war was over (Cohen, 1996; Biddle, 1998; Freedman & Karsh, 1993; O'Hanlon, 2000). Yet, for Saddam, the calculation was never one of pure military capabilities; rather, his calculations were governed by his *perception* (as it turned out, an incorrect one) of the credibility of the U.S. threat to intervene in the region and reverse his invasion. Indeed, he told both U.S. officials and reporters prior to the Gulf War that after Vietnam, Iraq only needed the ability to cause lots of American casualties to deter the United States from becoming militarily involved in a conflict. Saddam believed the United States would not accept casualties and could never sustain substantial losses of troops politically at home. This perception is indicative of the *degenerate image* discussed in Chapters 3 and 10. Recall this is an image wherein a country of equal or greater power is seen as confused and lacking the will to respond to the actions of another country. The image was supported by previous actions by the United States, particularly communication from the American ambassador that the United States would not oppose his position on the dispute with Kuwait on the oil fields. In order to use that perceived lack of will to his advantage, Hussein and his spokesmen spent much time making pronouncements to the world's press regarding the tens of thousands of body bags that would be required to send the Americans back home if they attacked him. Once inside Kuwait, the Iraqi forces dug in and attempted to create, for Coalition forces, the choice of accepting his invasion, or fighting a long, bloody *war of attrition* like the one he had recently waged with Iran (Freedman & Karsh, 1993).[1] This degenerate image-based perception by Saddam—both of actual U.S. credibility (our willingness to accept casualties or use force to reverse the Kuwaiti invasion) and actual U.S. military capabilities *vis-à-vis* the Iraqi forces in Kuwait (the technological gap)—made the Iraqi leader unwisely accept the risk (which he viewed as slight) that the United States would intervene in the Gulf, and be willing to pay the price in blood to reverse his invasion (Freedman & Karsh, 1993; Stein, 1992, 1993; Woodward, 1991). His perceptions of the situation mattered more than calculations of U.S. military capabilities (which he didn't believe Washington would be able to fully exploit).

There exists tremendous debate and disagreement within the political science literature about how to test deterrence theory, with the debate usually revolving around how differing camps of scholars chose to operationalize the concept, or interpret historical events (cf. Huth & Russett, 1984, 1988, 1990; Lebow & Stein, 1987, 1989, 1990). As Eric Herring (1995) observes, "virtually all aspects of how to test deterrence and compellence theory are disputed" (p. 33). The use of historical cases purporting to represent successes or failures of deterrence by these authors was problematic to say the least, since there are seldom universally accepted, objective interpretations of historical events or records of exactly what was on the minds of the policy-makers during the crises (rather important when motivation matters as much as it does for deterrence questions). Although it is beyond the scope of this chapter to delve into these debates at length, a number of excellent overviews and critical analyses of these methodological debates exist (Harvey, 1997a, 1997b, 1997c, 1998; Herring, 1995). As Harvey briefly explains:

> Case selection and coding immediate deterrence encounters remains a key area of difficulty for researchers who test deterrence theory using the dominant success-failure strategy. The approach recommends identifying cases of immediate deterrence, coding these cases as instances of success or failure, isolating conditions that were present or absent during failures, and, based on these differences, drawing conclusions about why and how deterrence works. The problem, as Huth and Russett acknowledge, is that a single crisis frequently encompasses several different types of interactions and outcomes ... carefully separating the threat/counter-threat sequence that would allow the researcher to pinpoint those aspects of behavior that conform to a direct or extended, immediate deterrence or compellence military encounter is often difficult, if not impossible, to accomplish with any degree of empirical precision, especially if the entire crisis is the unit of analysis.
>
> (Harvey, 1997b, p. 13)

Harvey (1997b) sought to avoid some of the pitfalls of seeking to judge historical cases as a whole (as did Huth & Russett, 1984, 1988, 1990; Lebow & Stein, 1987), by employing the **protracted crisis approach**. Explicitly rejecting the assumption crises should be counted as a "single, dominant encounter," Harvey (1997b) argues that, much like the frames of a motion picture film, crises should be viewed as a long series of "separate and distinct deterrence and compellence exchanges" running throughout the crisis from the beginning until the end of any episode (p. 13). As Harvey notes:

> Dissecting each crisis to reveal different encounters allows for multiple interpretations of any one foreign policy crisis and, therefore, can help to account for discrepancies across existing case lists; it forces the researcher to specify the precise time frame and exact sequence within which the appropriately designated threats, counter-threats and responses are made.
>
> (Harvey, 1997b, p. 13)

In adopting this approach, Harvey followed in the tradition of George and Smoke (1974), who also argued for viewing deterrence cases as involving multiple exchanges in a protracted crisis. As a result, an individual case, such as Bosnia-Herzegovina (1993–1994), moves from being a single case of one primary exchange between the parties to one with 14 total exchanges between the parties (Harvey, 1997c). Indeed, much of the disagreement between Huth/Russett and Lebow/Stein centers on what stage of a historical crisis they focused upon for their analysis of deterrence failure or success, a problem eliminated through the adoption of Harvey's more nuanced approach.

Of course, in order to determine whether or not an actor was deterred from taking a specified action (or compelled to change course from an already adopted course of action) due to credible threats (military, economic, or political), one has to know the motivations of that actor. In other words, did they actually intend to take the course of action that is the subject of the deterrent or compellent action? You cannot deter an action that was not being considered by your opponent in the first place, nor can you judge an effort at deterrence or compellence as a success or failure in the absence of information about your opponent's intentions. As many scholars note, the target actor's motivations, calculations of costs-benefits, ability to accurately perceive their environments (whether that be military or political ones), and their own particular judgments regarding the correlation of these elements must drive any discussion of deterrence or compellence success or failure (see George, 1991; George & Smoke, 1974; Jervis, Lebow, & Stein, 1985; Schelling, 1966, 1980; Stein, 1992).

A good illustration of this point is found in Stein's (1992) analysis of U.S. deterrence and compellence attempts prior to the Gulf War of 1990–1991. While the historical record provided a great deal of data to support any number of hypotheses regarding why deterrence or compellence efforts failed in this case, in the end it is the motivations and calculations of Saddam Hussein that drove Stein's analysis of these efforts. Stein suggested three possibilities for the failure of U.S. deterrence and compellence efforts against Iraq: (1) the United States failed to mount an effective strategy of deterrence in the period preceding the Kuwaiti invasion; (2) Saddam Hussein systematically miscalculated the capabilities and resolve of the United States; or (3) Saddam could not be deterred regardless of the strategy employed (p. 148). At the heart of the question, however, was the issue of Saddam Hussein's motives and intentions—was he an "opportunity-driven aggressor" or a "vulnerable leader motivated by need" (Stein, 1992, p. 155)? Stein also points out that many of Saddam's strategic calculations prior to the Gulf War may have led him to discount the credibility of U.S. threats to use force—that is, the likelihood of a major U.S. intervention, American willingness to take heavy casualties, and the difficulties facing Arab leaders in maintaining public support for a war against another Arab state were not necessarily irrational. Although traditional realists like Morgenthau (1948) would argue imbalances of power between states are often a cause of war, Stein (1992) notes that "overwhelming local military superiority does not, however, necessarily lead to crisis and war unless the motive and the intention to use force are also present" (p. 156). In the case of the Gulf War, Stein makes a strong case that it was the psychology of Saddam Hussein—his motives, calculations, and perceptions of his environment—that determined the outcomes of all of the U.S. influence attempts.

Another important issue to consider when testing deterrence theory is how the analyst will view limited uses of force by one or both parties in a deterrence relationship. This touches upon the distinction between general and immediate deterrence. As Herring (1995) explains, "general deterrence is the use of a standing threat in order to prevent someone from seriously considering doing something, while immediate deterrence is the use of specific threats to prevent someone from doing something which is being seriously considered" (p. 18). Although any use of force could be argued to represent a failure of general deterrence, George and Smoke (1974) argue that limited force can be used to probe a general deterrence commitment without compromising deterrence itself. For example, in Kashmir, India and Pakistan have had numerous crises and military clashes, which threatened to escalate into major wars, perhaps even nuclear ones, over a 12-year period. Yet, to argue these brief, though intense, military incursions, or the periodic shelling going on along the borders represent a failure of general deterrence misses the point that it was likely the fear of nuclear escalation that prevented these skirmishes from growing (Hagerty, 1995/1996, 1998). At the most, such probes should be seen only as "a partial failure of immediate deterrence," and not failures of general deterrence (Herring, 1995/1996, p. 26).

Of course, the strongest criticisms of deterrence theory always had a psychological basis. In particular, critics noted the retaliatory threats required by deterrence often demand a state to make arguably irrational decisions (i.e., commit national suicide by launching a retaliatory nuclear strike upon an opponent that would invite an equally devastating retaliation in return by the victim). While one can easily make the argument that an opponent might be deterred by a state if it promised nuclear retaliation in response to aggression (since the costs would outweigh the benefits), it is equally the case that for the state actually carrying out this threat, *the costs would also outweigh the benefits*! The need to make such a fundamentally irrational decision into a rational one for states has led security analysts to rely upon "meta-rational" solutions to game-theory approaches in their search for a logic to support the credibility of some of the more extreme deterrent threats required of nuclear states.

For example, the **game of chicken** (see Figure 13.1) is often used by scholars to represent the nature of the deterrence problem facing the superpowers during the Cold War (Brams, 1985; Freedman, 1981; Jervis, 1976). In that game, one imagines a long, deserted stretch of highway with two cars facing each other at opposite ends of the road. The object of chicken, predictably, is to get the other driver to chicken out first (i.e., swerve out of the way of your oncoming vehicle) while you continue to drive straight down the highway. Thus, both drivers (assuming they were not suicidal maniacs) would need to not only demonstrate their capability of causing a horrific, fatal accident by driving straight down the road as fast as possible, but would also need to somehow communicate the credibility of their threat to continue to do so (regardless of the consequences) to the opposing driver in the hopes of making him or her swerve out of the way first! Obviously, for both drivers, the rational solution is to swerve out of the way of the other car every time, since to carry out the threat would carry a cost greater than any conceivable benefit a victory might bring to the driver.

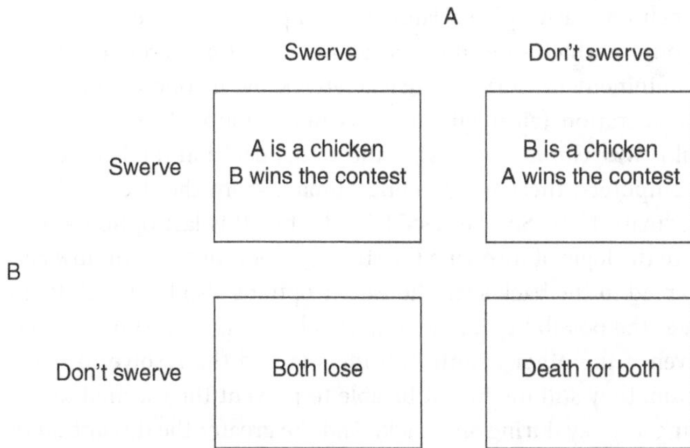

A
Swerve
Don't swerve
B
Swerve
A is a chicken
B wins the contest
B is a chicken
A wins the contest
Don't swerve
Both lose
Death for both

Figure 13.1 The game of chicken. Each driver wants the other to believe that they will not swerve, thereby forcing the other to chicken out and swerve first. Whoever swerves first is a chicken. But the dilemma for both drivers is just that: Will the other really swerve first? If neither do, both die.

However, if the drivers insist upon playing chicken (or states to rely upon MAD nuclear doctrines for their security), and for some reason must play the game to win, then it becomes imperative for them to be able to make an irrational threat credible. For if the threat is not credible, neither driver will swerve and both will die (Brams, 1985).

Making such a threat credible could be accomplished in several ways. For instance, one driver might put the car on cruise control, throw the steering wheel out of the window, and crawl into the back seat to read a good (hopefully short) book. Seeing such behavior and recognizing it for what it was, an irrevocable commitment, the other driver would have no further cause to doubt the credibility of the opponent's threat and would recognize *that only the driver now had control* over whether the cars crashed or not. At this point, the rational decision would be to swerve in the face of this irrevocable commitment by the opponent to this inherently irrational action (Powell, 1990). Similarly, countries relied upon what Schelling (1966) describes as "the threat that leaves something to chance" to make irrational threats credible (Freedman, 1981; Powell, 1990). In other words, even if you really don't believe your opponent would actually go through with a retaliatory strike that would result in their own self-destruction, these threats retain some credibility if your opponent became a "contingently unsafe actor" in the context of a crisis (Rhodes, 1989). Simply put, the country's leaders might not be able to control all their military forces in the event of a war, especially if nuclear weapons began going off, interrupting command-and-control functions between the nation's leaders and its armed forces. As a result, the leaders would lose positive control over their forces and lack the ability to prevent retaliation from occurring (Feaver, 1992, 1993; Sagan, 1994).

During the Cold War, both superpowers adopted strategic postures roughly equivalent to climbing into the back seat of the speeding vehicle in the game of chicken. Subordinates such as submarine commanders were given preauthorization to launch weapons in the event of permanently losing contact with the nation's leadership during a crisis. Similarly, both sides adopted "launch-on-warning" or "launch-on-impact" doctrines regarding nuclear weapons, in which subordinates had authorization to retaliate upon evidence of imminent or current nuclear attack by an opponent. There was even consideration (although this was never adopted except in the Hollywood film *War Games*) of leaving the actual decision (and ability) to retaliate to computers, thereby removing humans from the decision loop entirely (Freedman, 1981; Smoke, 1987). And while this last option would come closest to the logic of throwing the steering wheel out the window and curling up to read in the back seat, the earlier options also held with them (and increased) the possibility that an objectively irrational response could still occur. Even if the other country's leaders lacked the resolve to really push the button, they still might not be able to prevent their armed forces from retaliating anyway during an attack. And the greater the disruption of command-and-control as the result of an attack, or the greater the stress of an ongoing crisis between two nuclear-armed states, the greater the likelihood (or possibility) that the state could become *contingently unsafe* and respond irrationally to a provocation.

In addition, critics of reliance on deterrence for maintaining peace between nuclear states also noted the many psychological or information-processing challenges that deterrence must master to function properly (Dunn, 1982; Feaver, 1992, 1993; Feaver & Niou, 1996; Lebow & Stein, 1989, 1990; Sagan, 1994). For example, they observe that history is replete with cases in which decision-makers *misperceived* either the nature of their security environments (i.e., the Peloponnesian War or World War I), or the intentions and motivations of their opponents (i.e., Chamberlain of Hitler at Munich, or the superpowers of each other during the Cold War). Given the potential consequences of a breakdown in deterrence (nuclear war), these critics argued that it was dangerous, given the enormous difficulties facing policy-makers in seeking to rely on deterrence, to depend on it to maintain the peace. Not only did deterrence require policy-makers to rationally take irrational actions to support the strategy, but it also required them to accurately perceive both their own (and their opponent's) capabilities and intentions, and be able to maintain positive control over their subordinates and arsenals during extremely challenging crisis contexts. Further, by focusing principally on the use of threats, deterrence theory tended to ignore the role rewards and concessions might play in defusing or preventing conflicts (Jervis, 1976). One possible consequence of relying on threats rather than more positive inducements is that it reinforces the perception of policy-makers of the opposing state as hostile or aggressive. As a result, **cognitive rigidity** among policy-makers can exacerbate the tensions between states as neutral or friendly behavior is ignored or reinterpreted to better fit a preexisting negative stereotype (Holsti, 1967; Jervis, 1976). Because foreign policy beliefs are highly resistant to change (George, 1980), once a particular image or stereotype of a neighboring state is adopted (e.g., as aggressive and likely to attack; or as weak and unlikely to attack), belief perseverance serves as a barrier to the successful transmission of either warnings of credible threats or the gathering of information diverging from the accepted belief systems of policy-makers (Tetlock et al., 1991).

In contrast to deterrence theory, Jervis (1976) laid out a spiral model that incorporates many of the concerns critics had about assumptions of

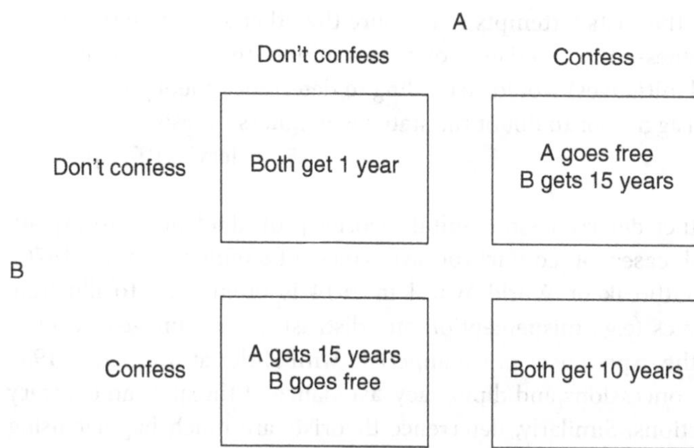

Figure 13.2 The Prisoner's Dilemma. In this classic game, two prisoners, A and B, accused of a crime, have the options of confessing or not confessing. If they maintain their alliance and neither confesses, both get short sentences. If each of them confesses, they each get a heavy sentence. But if one confesses and the other does not, the prisoner who confessed is rewarded with freedom, and the one who did not confess gets a severe sentence. The dilemma for each prisoner is that, if he trusts the other not to confess, his best option is to rat out his partner in crime.

deterrence. Indeed, spiral theorists focus on many of the same dynamics previously described by Deutsch's (1986) *malignant spiral process of hostile interaction*. As Jervis (see also Figure 13.2) observes:

> If much of deterrence theory can be seen in terms of the game of Chicken, the spiral theorists are more impressed with the relevance of the Prisoner's Dilemma ... if each state pursues its narrow self-interest with a narrow conception of rationality, all states will be worse off than they would be if they cooperated ... A second point highlighted by the Prisoner's Dilemma is that cooperative arrangements are not likely to be reached through coercion. Threats and an adversary posture are likely to lead to counteractions with the ultimate result that both sides will be worse off than they were before.
>
> (Jervis, 1976, p. 67)

Thus, spiral theorists emphasized reducing the degree to which rival states overestimate the hostility of each other, countering the dynamics of the security dilemma through confidence building measures, and using concessions to both reduce tensions and induce a less hostile, aggressive perception of the state's intentions by neighbors. Jervis notes that the two theories contradict each other at every point:

> Policies that flow from deterrence theory (e.g., development of potent and flexible armed forces; a willingness to fight for issues of low intrinsic value; avoidance of any appearance of weakness) are just those that, according to the spiral model, are most apt to heighten tensions and create illusory incompatibility. And the behavior advocated by

> the spiral theorists (attempts to reassure the other side of one's non-aggressiveness, the avoidance of provocations, the undertaking of unilateral initiatives) would, according to deterrence theory, be likely to lead an aggressor to doubt the state's willingness to resist.
>
> (Jervis, 1976, p. 84)

Further, neither deterrence nor spiral theories proved adequate to explain all historical cases of conflict or avoidance of conflict (Jervis, 1976). While the outbreak of World War I in 1914 is often used to illustrate spiral dynamics (e.g., misperception and distrust, enemy images, security dilemmas), the experiences of Chamberlain with Hitler at Munich in 1938 (e.g., use of concessions and diplomacy, avoidance of threats) ran contrary to its predictions. Similarly, deterrence theorists are much happier using the example of Munich's appeasement and the aggressive states of the 1930s to illustrate the importance of not appearing weak to opponents through concessions, and maintaining credible threat postures. As Jervis (1976) observes, "given the histories of these two conflicts, it is not surprising that deterrence theories have little to say about World War I and that the spiral theorists rarely discuss the 1930s" (p. 95).

As the ongoing debates over deterrence effectiveness between Huth and Russett (1984, 1988, 1990) and Lebow and Stein (1987, 1989, 1990) illustrate, proving empirically that deterrence works through examining past historical cases of deterrence successes and failures is exceedingly difficult. Indeed, since successful deterrence would often be invisible due to the fact it prevented a state from ever taking an action in the first place, what would be visible in the historical record would generally be only deterrence *failures* that led to war, not successful examples of deterrence that maintained the peace. And, despite decades of research and debate about deterrence, scholars still greatly dispute whether deterrence is generally successful or not, or what historical cases legitimately represent one or the other outcome. Indeed, the "long peace" of the Cold War and the absence of a World War III between 1947 and 1991 is hotly debated among scholars, who see it as either: (1) a powerful example of how deterrence can maintain international peace and stability; or (2) a case of extraordinary good luck in which war was avoided for other reasons (see an excellent overview of this debate in Gjelstad and Njolstad, 1996).

The Effects of Problem Representation or "Framing" Upon Perception and Decision Making in the Security Context

How policy-makers "frame" or "represent" (structure or assign meaning to) a given policy problem, option, or situation—in other words, how they perceive it, or see it as similar or dissimilar to previous events—can be critically important in determining how they will behave when making decisions in a security setting (see Tetlock & Belkin, 1996; Sylvan & Voss, 1998). At the simplest level, limitations on the ability of decision-makers to *accurately perceive* the entirety of their policy environments (or the true range of options available to them in dealing with a given policy problem) may result in decisions based on either a distorted or incomplete understanding of the situation (Jervis, 1976; Preston, 2011; Vertzberger, 1990). In security studies, for example, when assessing military balances of power it is important to recognize that while there is an *objective reality* regarding a nation's military capabilities (i.e., an actual number of tanks, aircraft, soldiers; specific qualitative characteristics of weapons systems that govern their performance on the battlefield; explicit military doctrines or strategies that will govern the use of a nation's armed forces in battle, etc.), it is *how policy-makers perceive their opponent's military forces and capabilities* that governs how they view them, and what decisions they make *vis-à-vis* that country.

Recall the earlier example of Saddam Hussein's calculations prior to the Gulf War, in which his misperceptions regarding his own military's abilities to create a war of attrition dilemma for American policy-makers were coupled with his mistaken belief that the United States was unwilling to absorb large numbers of combat casualties, leading him to discount the credibility of American military threats over Kuwait (Stein, 1992). Indeed, after the 2003 U.S. invasion of Iraq, former Foreign Minister Tariq Aziz noted Saddam was so convinced the Americans would simply bomb him heavily for a period of time and then go away (as had happened before) that he ordered his frontline units to take no action as the Coalition columns crossed into Iraq (Preston, 2011). His prior experiences with the First Gulf War, where President G. H. W. Bush was unwilling to assume the costs of occupying Iraq, Operation Desert Fox during the Clinton administration (consisting solely of a cruise missile campaign), and the no-fly zone policy without ground troops all framed his view of the environment as being one in which the Americans would not want to conquer and occupy Iraq—a view completely divorced from the new reality of how George W. Bush and his advisers saw the world.

Similarly, while there was an *objective military reality* in 1914 (at that point unknown to Europe's military leaders) regarding how military strategies emphasizing the "cult of the offensive" and infantry assaults would fare against the advent of the heavy machine-gun, more precise and powerful artillery, and their use to defend fortified positions (Tuchman, 1962; Keegan, 1998), decisions were made based upon policy-makers' mistaken perceptions of reality (Snyder, 1984; Van Evera, 1984). How policy-makers frame their strategic environments can shape what they believe to be their options. For example, it was universally accepted military doctrine prior to 1914 that technological advances (quantified in terms of machine-guns, numbers of divisions, ability to mobilize and transport these forces to the fronts using railroads, etc.) made modern warfare so destructive it could only last a matter of months. Further, the first nation to fully deploy its forces, given this revolution in military technology, would automatically win (Keegan, 1998; Tuchman, 1962). This representation of the problem by decision-makers contributed to their sense of a security dilemma and the failure to recognize a new military reality in which weapons technology rendered the offensive strategy inferior to the defensive one.

To illustrate this point about how our subjective perceptions of the situation are not necessarily driven by objective reality, imagine your professor advises your class that there is a giant pit in the floor in the middle of your classroom, filled to the brim at its great depths with sharp iron spikes. With the room's lights on, and the warnings about its existence given, it is highly unlikely students would inadvertently stumble into it. Thus, the objective reality was observable (students could see the pit), the credibility of the threat (falling into the pit would cause serious, if not fatal, injury) was believable, and students' behavior was impacted (no one attempted short-cuts across the center of the room after class). However, if the lights were off and no warnings were given, then many students would likely fall into the pit. In neither case were the students' behaviors irrational, and whether the light was on or off, the pit continued to exist. Simply put, individuals respond to the reality they perceive, and their behavior is unaffected by what they either don't believe to be true or do not observe directly. This illustrates the nature of the problem for policy-makers in effectively communicating deterrent threats to their opponents (who subjectively perceive reality), and how powerful framing effects might be once policy-makers accept a particular formulation of reality as the truth.

For example, a growing literature focuses on how policy-makers use **analogical reasoning** to frame (or understand) policy problems, and the kinds of policy options that might be appropriate to address their problem (Dyson & Preston 2006; Khong, 1992; May, 1973; Neustadt & May, 1986). An **analogy** is essentially a decision-making heuristic, or shorthand, in which policy-makers see a current event or situation as similar to (or sharing many of the same characteristics as) a previous historical event. When U.S. policy-makers consider intervening militarily in almost any situation—whether it be sending the military to the Persian Gulf to liberate Kuwait after the Iraqi invasion, sending peacekeepers to Bosnia to keep the warring factions apart and maintain regional stability, or even engaging in humanitarian relief efforts to prevent starvation in Somalia—the **Vietnam analogy** is frequently heard (Preston, 2001, 2011). This analogy suggests that any U.S. military intervention will likely result in the same outcome as did American intervention in Vietnam during the 1960s–1970s: an open-ended commitment to a losing cause that results in tremendous bloodshed for our troops and political unrest at home. To say that something will be another Vietnam is to essentially say, "we should not become involved because of how bad our experience in Vietnam was," and that we will be inviting a political disaster.

Of course, while the Vietnam analogy works against policy-makers intervening militarily abroad, other analogies encourage such intervention. The **Munich analogy**, for example, argues that if you do not stand up to an aggressor, and instead seek to appease them or make concessions to them in the hopes of keeping the peace, the end result will be to only encourage them to be even more aggressive, and likely bring on the very war you sought to avoid (Khong, 1992; May, 1973; Neustadt & May, 1986; Preston 2001). Obviously, this analogy grew out of an earlier historical experience, that of British Prime Minister Neville Chamberlain's efforts at Munich in 1938 to appease Adolf Hitler's territorial demands and achieve "peace in our time" through these concessions. Chamberlain's appeasement, many argued, emboldened Hitler more, and encouraged further actions on his part (such as the invasion of the rest of Czechoslovakia in 1938 and Poland in 1939), which subsequently led to World War II. Clearly, how policy-makers perceive the situation, and what kind of analogies they use to understand the problems they face, have a tremendous impact upon the ultimate policy decisions for war or peace. As Khong (1992) illustrates in *Analogies at War*, President Lyndon Johnson and his advisers were most influenced by the Munich analogy in their decision-making on whether or not to intervene militarily in Vietnam in 1965. Seeing the North Vietnamese as aggressive expansionists in the Hitler mold, perhaps as mere surrogates for a general pattern of Soviet-led communist aggression worldwide (the dominant U.S. policy view, given containment policy), the choice was clear for Johnson. Intervening in Vietnam, it was believed, was the only thing standing between maintaining regional stability and a row of falling dominoes throughout Southeast Asia, as country after country eventually fell to continuing communist aggression after South Vietnam was conquered. Johnson chose to send more and more U.S. troops to Vietnam (Preston, 2001). Similarly, during the lead-up to the Gulf War, Bush frequently invoked the Munich analogy to explain the need to send U.S. forces to oppose Saddam Hussein and liberate Kuwait. In this case, the analogy suggested Hussein would continue his aggression into Saudi Arabia and beyond if left unchecked in Kuwait (Preston, 2001). In contrast, John F. Kennedy's use of the **Guns of August analogy** during the Cuban Missile Crisis of 1962—an analogy based upon the experience of the events leading up to the outbreak of World War I, a war which none of the policy-makers desired or intended to occur—led him to be far more cautious and mindful of his actions during the tense days of that crisis (Preston, 2001; Schlesinger, 1965; Sorensen, 1965). In this case, one could argue that analogy served a war-avoidance function for Kennedy, and sensitized him to how easily the crisis could spin out of control and into war.

That analogies are always gross simplifications of reality, and that two historical situations are seldom identical, is beside the point. Policy-makers use analogies in their decision-making, sometimes well and sometimes poorly, and their use can (as illustrated above) often have significant consequences in terms of the ultimate decisions for war or peace (Neustadt & May, 1986).

Another growing body of framing literature in political science seeks to apply **prospect theory** to foreign policy decision-making and security issues (Berejikian & Early, 2013; Goertz, 2004; Haas, 2001; Kahneman & Tversky 2000; Lebow & Stein, 1987; Levy, 1997; McDermott, 1998; Mintz, 2004, 2005). Building upon a psychological model developed by Kahneman and Tversky (1979), prospect theory predicts that individuals will tend to be risk averse in the domain of gains and risk seeking in the domain of losses (Tetlock et al., 1991). Further, what determines whether something is considered to be a gain or a loss is determined relative to the original starting, or reference, point. In other words, "change is evaluated relative to that position, but value itself derives from the difference between that starting, or reference, point and the amount of any positive or negative shift away from it" (McDermott, 1998, p. 28). As McDermott observes:

> In theoretical terms ... people tend to be risk averse in the domain of gains and risk seeking in the domain of losses; this is the crux of prospect theory. In short, prospect theory predicts that domain affects risk propensity ... losing hurts more than a comparable gain pleases ... Loss aversion is exemplified by the endowment effect, whereby

> people value what they possess to a greater degree than they value an equally attractive alternative. This endowment bias makes equal trade unattractive. It also presents a bias toward the status quo in almost any negotiating context.
>
> (McDermott, 1998, p. 29)

This determination of domain is inherently a subjective one, since individual policy-makers may value certain outcomes (e.g., policy success, popularity, poll numbers) differently from one another—but prospect theory only needs to have knowledge of how policy-makers perceive the domain (gains or losses) in order to predict their risk propensity (McDermott, 1998). In addition, prospect theory takes into account the fact that people assign different weights to the likelihood of certain probability outcomes. As McDermott observes, highly vivid yet low probability events (e.g., being in a plane crash) tend to be over-weighted by people, while high or medium probability events (e.g., being in a car wreck) are subjectively under-weighted:

> The classic examples of this are lotteries and insurance. In lotteries, people are willing to take a sure loss, however small, for the essentially nonexistent chance of a huge gain. In this way, people can be risk seeking in gains when the probability of gain is low. In insurance, people are willing to take a sure loss in the present to prevent the small likelihood of a larger loss in the future. In this situation, people can be risk averse in losses when the probability of loss is small. In both these situations, expected utility models might not consider such behavior to be normative. However, prospect theory accounts for these discrepancies by noting the extreme (over)weight and attention that individuals give to small probabilities that potentially involve either huge gains (winning the lottery) or huge losses (losing your house in a fire). This phenomenon helps account for worst-case scenario planning.
>
> (McDermott, 1998, pp. 31–32)

Translated to questions of international conflict and war, one would expect policy-makers in nations to take far greater chances (and risk war far more often) to protect their current resources (e.g., national territory, economic relationships, etc.) than they would be to gain additional resources beyond what they currently control. In other words, they would be expected to be risk averse in the domain of gains and risk acceptant in the domain of losses. For deterrence, this suggests that the credibility of a threat made by a nation faced with losing its national sovereignty, territory, or very existence is far higher (and more believable) than threats made by states just seeking aggrandizement (more territory). Further, in crisis management terms, this suggests the danger of war is greatest, and the risks likely to be taken by states more extreme, when a crisis threatens the current resources of the state (the status quo). At the same time, prospect theory poses a serious challenge to traditional realist power politics formulations of international politics (Morgenthau, 1948), since it questions their main assumptions about power maximization as the primary goal of states in their interactions with one another (McDermott, 1998). Instead, while states may seek to increase their own power resources when risks are low, they will focus first and foremost upon maintaining what they currently have (the status quo). Further, they will be less likely to go to war to obtain gains from other states when potential risks are high (be risk averse in the domain of gains), and be far more likely to go to war with other states when their own resources are threatened (be more risk acceptant in the domain of losses).

Accountability

Another interesting psychological concept that has implications for understanding international conflict is **accountability** (Tetlock, 1985). Specifically, accountability argues that political leaders will take greater risks and be more likely to engage in conflict the more they lack accountability to a higher power (i.e., a ruling coalition, a voting public, a military junta). Saddam Hussein, for example, answered (and was accountable) to no one domestically, and could essentially do as he liked in terms of foreign or domestic policy. Since there was no accountability internally, one would expect him to engage in much riskier, more conflictual behavior towards other nations (such as Kuwait) than we would expect of leaders of more democratic nations who are more accountable to others (such as a voting public, a parliament or Congress). This basic notion of accountability underpins much of the current "democratic peace" argument—that democracies are inherently more peaceful (and less warlike) than autocracies—and is clearly useful in terms of understanding the psychology of international conflict (Hermann & Kegley, 1995).

Group Dynamics and Malfunctions of Process

Finally, malfunctions of group process or decision-making under stress are often suggested to increase the likelihood of bad decisions or conflict (Janis 1972; Janis & Mann, 1977; Hermann, 1979; 't Hart 1990/1994). Perhaps the most familiar argument regarding such group malfunctions under stress was that of Irving Janis (1972) and his **groupthink** concept, presented in Chapter 4. As noted there, Janis argued governmental policy groups, particularly at high levels, tended to be smaller groups that over time developed a pattern of interactions between group members that emphasized the maintenance of group cohesion, solidarity, and loyalty. While not necessarily a bad thing, this emphasis on group cohesion can lead to faulty group decision processes, or **group malfunctions**. These faulty processes, which become far more pronounced and prevalent during the high-stress conditions of crises, can lead groups to become even more insular, and fall into patterns of decision-making that increase the chances of conflict. As mentioned in Chapter 4, among the eight symptoms of groupthink listed by Janis are:

1 **The illusion of invulnerability**—where group members find a comfort zone within the group because of the psychological belief that there is safety in numbers. Ultimate responsibility for group decisions or actions is dispersed among the entire group, making no one individual ultimately *accountable* for the outcomes. Janis notes that this leads to a tendency towards the **risky shift**, or pattern in which groups tend to take riskier decisions (and more chances) than do individuals.
2 **Rationalization**—where group members rationalize (or explain away) information or opinions that do not support the dominant preexisting beliefs held by the group members.
3 **Belief in the inherent morality of the group**—where group members share with one another the belief that they are making the best decisions possible, that they are trying to do the right thing, that they have a solid moral compass.
4 **Active use of stereotypes**—group members simplify reality and their information-processing through reliance upon use of stereotypes and other simplifying heuristics.
5 **Use of direct pressure on dissenters**—where group members pressure individual group members who may disagree with the dominant view of the group not to rock the boat and go along with the group.
6 **Self-censorship**—where dissenting group members, over time, cease to challenge or question the dominant group views due to the application of direct pressure upon them and a concern for group cohesion.
7 **Use of mind-guards**—self-appointed individuals within the group who seek to maintain the group's cohesion and morale by applying direct pressure to dissenters and preventing access of information or views to the group that might challenge its existing beliefs.
8 **The illusion of unanimity**—where group members come to believe that everyone in the group agrees with the dominant group view and supports their policy decisions because no one vocally objects. It is an illusion because of the use of direct pressure and the self-censorship of group members, who may well disagree with the group, but lack the will to object.

Janis (1972) argues that these group malfunctions, leading to groupthink by senior decision-making groups, resulted in a number of historical **policy fiascoes**, or failures of policy. Examples include: U.S. naval leaders' decision-making prior to Pearl Harbor; the Kennedy administration's decision-making surrounding the Bay of Pigs; the decision by General Douglas MacArthur to approach the Yalu River during the Korean War (thereby provoking Chinese intervention); and the decision by the Johnson administration to intervene in Vietnam in 1965. That Janis identifies only cases of war, or resort to force, as "policy fiascoes" in his book illustrates his strong normative bias against war ('t Hart, Stern, & Sundelius, 1997). However, regardless of the subjectivity of his overall analyses, Janis does make a useful point in observing the interactional and decision dynamics within groups can sometimes lead policy-makers to war. A more detailed discussion of group dynamics is presented in Chapter 4.

Applications of Political Psychology to Modern Security Studies: Deterrence as a Psychological Relationship and the Credibility of Threats

With the continuing proliferation of nuclear capabilities to states in the international system (i.e., Iran's increasingly advanced nuclear program and fissile material producing infrastructure, North Korea's continued nuclear testing, Pakistan and India's expanding arsenals), discussions about the resulting security environment inevitably turn toward whether nuclear deterrence increases or decreases interstate security and stability (Preston, 2007, 2009). What insights does political psychology offer regarding how we think about such modern security problems?

One example of the application of political psychology to security involves looking at a critical dimension of deterrence—the credibility of nuclear threats to opposing decision-makers. Moreover, it involves the need to understand deterrence as a psychological relationship between individual policy-makers. It requires us to recognize the *constraints* placed upon psychological variables by the *simplicity of the strategic situations* created by nuclear weapons across various contexts. It is an area that has received only cursory attention within the security studies literature, and one previously utilized only by deterrence skeptics to criticize the concept. However, a more nuanced application of political psychology to the issue of deterrence can be equally useful in fleshing out the possible interactional dynamics within nuclear security relationships between states—especially since policy-maker perceptions regarding the nature of the situation, the type of interests (central or peripheral) at stake, their view of how opponents perceives their threats, and so on are likely to be key to whether deterrence relationships will be effective or not.

As suggested earlier, the debate between deterrence advocates and skeptics has often centered on epistemological disagreements between scholars over their rival's chosen theories or methodological approaches to studying deterrence. Critics have pointed to the less than satisfactory treatment of psychological factors relating to deterrence within the security literature (Jervis, 1976; Lebow & Stein, 1989, 1990), which was primarily due to the dominance of rational-choice and game theory approaches in this scholarship (e.g., Zagare & Kilgour, 1993). Others note the dependence of much of the rational deterrence theory literature upon neo-realist, system-level arguments that tend to leave out subsystem or psychological factors—leading critics to note that a more useful theory would incorporate both systemic and sub-systemic factors (Feaver, 1992, 1993).

In fact, real-life behavior by decision-makers varies greatly from the rational model, and is neither as consistent nor as predictable as implied by game theory approaches. Indeed, a typical definition of *perception of threat* as "the product of the estimated capability of the opponent's forces multiplied by the estimated probability that he will use them" fits nicely into rational-choice or game theory models, but is a poor approach to understanding or defining policy-maker perceptions (cf. Legault & Lindsey, 1974; Singer, 1958). To understand the behavior of policy-makers, one must develop an understanding of the psychological factors affecting the ways in which individuals perceive the world, process information, respond to stress, and make decisions (e.g., Burke & Greenstein 1991; Helfstein, 2012; Hermann 1980b; Jervis 1976; Khong 1992; 't Hart, Stern, & Sundelius 1997; Preston 2001, 2011; Vertzberger 1990; Wohlstetter, 1962). Research by O'Reilly (2012), for example, shows the importance of understanding policy-maker perceptions about their surrounding environments (and perceived strategic context) in explaining decisions to pursue development of nuclear weapons. Similarly, Hymans (2006) focuses on the role of identity and emotions in influencing nuclear proliferation decisions taken by policy-makers. Only through understanding the subjective perceptions of decision-makers does it become possible to both determine the effectiveness of deterrent threats and ascertain the nature of security relationships between states. As Johnson et al. observe:

> Deterrence, like all coercion, occurs in the mind of the adversary. Reality matters in deterrence only insofar as it affects the perceptions of those who will choose whether or not to be deterred ... [Thus] assessments of the adversary's capabilities are of only limited predictive value unless accompanied by sound understanding of what the enemy values, how it perceives the conflict, and how it makes decisions—to name but a few of the critical variables.
>
> (Johnson et al., 2002, p. 12)

Since this involves exploring the complex realm of decision-maker perceptions, characterized by substantial interplay between objective and subjective reality, much of the security studies literature has been content to avoid the issue, assume rationality, and emphasize bean-counting approaches instead. As a result, the primary focus has mistakenly been placed on the objective characteristics of the situation (i.e., size of forces, actual military balance, political situation, etc.) as seen by observers, rather than upon the subjective characteristics of the situation as perceived by the decision-makers themselves—which actually governs their behavior. These subjective perceptions of reality held by leaders have provided the basis for strategic decisions and shaped their beliefs regarding the credibility of opponents' nuclear threats or forces. And, despite Lebow and Stein's (1989) contention that rational deterrence theories are theories "about nonexistent decision makers operating in nonexistent environments" (p. 224), and other epistemological critiques made by political psychologists regarding rational choice, neo-realist, or game theory approaches, one can make very strong psychological arguments in favor of deterrence and why it should work as well.

For example, Tetlock et al. (1991) provides a useful overview of many of the psychological factors that had a bearing on the issue of nuclear deterrence and found their impact on deterrence effectiveness or success was variable, and not predictably negative in all contexts. Moreover, one does not need to adopt the same conception of rationality employed in rational choice models for deterrence to remain a valid concept. As Johnson et al. note:

> Because coercion depends on the adversary weighing the expected results of several courses of action and then choosing the more attractive one, it presumes that policy decisions are made with some degree of rationality. However, the adversary need not behave with perfect rationality for coercion to be applicable, its behavior simply must not be totally irrational ... In practice, no state acts perfectly rational, stemming from such factors as incomplete information, limited time to make decisions, bureaucratic politics and organizational processes, and leaders' personalities. Yet states (and significant non-state political entities) rarely act in ways that appear truly unreasoning on close analysis. It is far more common for states' actions to be branded as irrational when they are actually being driven by logical and consistent sets of preferences, but these are not well understood by others.
>
> (Johnson et al., 2002, pp. 17–18)

In fact, deterrence is best understood as a *psychological relationship* (between deterrer and deterree), in which notions like the "credibility of the threat," "attentiveness to signaling," "resolve," "willingness to take risks," "degree to which central or peripheral interests are challenged," or even the basic "awareness of the overall security environment (or military situation) in a given situational context" are almost completely dependent upon the individual psychologies of the rival policy-makers. As such, deterrence becomes a contingent variable, the effectiveness of which is dependent upon both the psychological characteristics of the policy-makers involved and the structural clarity of the situation created by the absolute nature of the destructiveness of nuclear weapons. This latter element serves as a constraint on the impact of individual psychologies on decision-making, and serves to clearly distinguish nuclear from conventional deterrence contexts.

Thus, while nuclear deterrence relationships, if properly structured, can be expected to be highly robust and reliable in preventing conflicts—because it is a *psychological* relationship between human beings, it can never be expected to function perfectly across all situational contexts. Rather than use this argument—as many political psychologists have done—to suggest that deterrence is an unsound or ineffectual policy approach, we need to place this concept into its proper perspective. Just because something could potentially fail doesn't mean it will, especially with any frequency. In the case of nuclear deterrence, the empirical evidence to date suggests a highly reliable and robust system. The same psychological problems or malfunctions routinely associated by deterrence critics apply equally to any other policy approach (e.g., conventional deterrence, diplomacy, sanctions, etc.), all of which are linked in the last century alone to recourse to very costly wars.[2] Yet human beings do generally make reasonably sound, rational decisions—especially when the stakes are high and there is little room for ambiguity regarding situational outcomes. In this regard, nuclear deterrence relationships represent special cases that are not easily compared with fundamentally different kinds of policy contexts (such as conventional deterrence). Indeed, extrapolating conventional deterrence processes and outcomes to hypothetical nuclear ones (as many deterrence skeptics have done) is as useful for determining the taste of an orange as eating an apple.

Instead of placing unrealistic and unfair performance standards upon deterrence, we should recognize it is like any other policy or strategy—dependent upon the perceptions of policy-makers and the constraints on their actions for its success.

On a practical level, one reason why the importance of the psychological characteristics of individual policy-makers in determining the effectiveness of deterrence (or other types of security relationships) was given short attention by scholars is that one cannot (in the absence of unrealistic assumptions about "rational-choice"-type actors) develop broad, general security frameworks that apply to all possible decision-makers across all country and cultural contexts. Although it is laudable to seek grand, general theories on security and simple formulations of deterrence relationships, given the central importance of individual policy-makers in the process, they are simply unworkable and inappropriate in this context. It would be problematic, for example, to assume Kim Jong-Un, Bashar al-Assad, George W. Bush, Angela Merkel, Barack Obama, Vladimir Putin, Ayatollah Khameini, or any number of other world leaders perceive the world, process information, possess belief systems, face political constraints, or make decisions in the same manner (Hermann et al., 2001). Who the leaders are and what they are like as individuals makes a tremendous difference in determining what a nation's security policies will be, how they will perceive risk and threat, and what limitations they might believe exist in either their own capabilities or in the environment itself. Indeed, Keller (2005) observed, for example, that strongly nationalistic leaders who were distrustful of others were far more likely to ignore domestic constraints against the use of force than leaders with the opposite characteristics. Mumford (2006; Mumford et al., 2007) found the more ideological leaders were, in terms of their exercising influence based on the articulation of distinct, powerful ideologies, the greater their propensity for resorting to extreme violence. From group effects to individual characteristics, many factors influence how policy-makers perceive their threat environments and their willingness to take risks or resort to violence. Clearly, political psychology has much to say about international conflict and resorting to war. In Figure 13.3, the importance of these individual policy-maker filters are emphasized, along with the notion that actual security relationships between states rest in the nexus between the objective capabilities/characteristics of the arsenals, and the subjective perceptions of this reality by the policy-makers.

CONCLUSION

Throughout this chapter, we have provided numerous examples of how political psychological approaches were applied to the study of international security and conflict in political science, ranging from the security dilemma, to deterrence and prospect theories, to the impact of group dynamics. Obviously, this brief review merely scratches the surface of this wide-ranging security literature, and is by no means exhaustive. Our task was not to replicate a national security textbook, but to provide students with a useful insight into how psychological approaches were employed to study important political questions. Further, literature discussed elsewhere in this

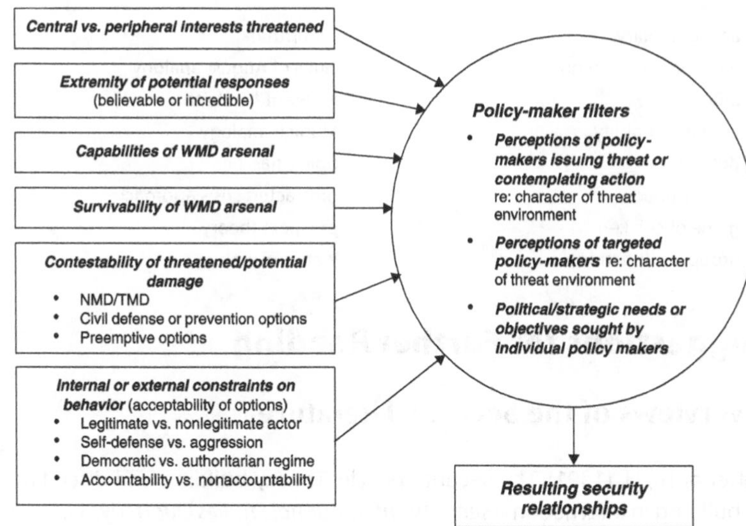

Figure 13.3 Individual Policy-Maker Filters

textbook, such as the development of social identity, stereotypes, ethnic conflict, etc., can also usefully be applied to the study of international security and conflict. Indeed, psychological approaches have much to offer as we continue to advance our understanding of this important subject.

Topics, Theories/Explanations, and Cases Covered in Chapter 13

Topics	*Theories/Explanations*	*Cases*
Why war?	Psychology of fear and misperception Security dilemma	Peloponnesian War World War I
Security dilemma	Fundamental attribution error Inherent bad-faith Spiral process	Cold War
Psychology of deterrence	Cognitive rigidity Belief perseverance Spiral model	Cold War, Iraq protracted crisis; general and immediate deterrence; game of chicken
Problem representation	Framing Analogical reasoning Prospect theory	Vietnam analogy Munich analogy Guns of August analogy
Accountability		
Groupthink	Group malfunctions Stress Eight symptoms of groupthink	

Key Terms

accountability
analogical reasoning
analogy
cognitive rigidity
deterrence
enemy image
game of chicken
group malfunctions
groupthink
Guns of August analogy
inherent bad faith
Munich analogy
policy fiascoes
protracted crisis approach
prospect theory
Vietnam analogy

Suggestions for Further Reading

Overviews of the Security Literature

Haftendorn, H. (1991). The security puzzle: Theory-building and discipline-building in international security. *International Studies Quarterly*, *35*, 3–17.

Krause, K., & Williams, M. C. (1996). Broadening the agenda of security studies: Politics and methods. *Mershon International Studies Review*, *40*, 229–254.

Walt, S. M. (1991). The renaissance of security studies. *International Studies Quarterly*, *35*, 211–239.

Rational-Choice or Game Theory Approaches

Bilgin, P. (2003). Individual and societal dimensions of security. *International Studies Review*, *5(2)*, 203–222.

Brams, S. J. (1985). *Superpower games: Applying game theory to superpower conflict*. New Haven, CT: Yale University Press.

Lantis, J. S. (2002). Strategic culture and national security policy. *International Studies Review*, *4(3)*, 87–113.

Walt, S. M. (1999). Rigor or rigor mortis? Rational choice and security studies. *International Security*, *23*, 5–48.

Other Treatments of Security or Deterrence

Brody, B. (1973). *War & politics*. New York: Macmillan.

Mearsheimer, J. J. (1983). *Conventional deterrence*. Ithaca, NY: Cornell University Press.

Powell, R. (1990). *Nuclear deterrence theory: The search for credibility*. New York: Cambridge University Press.

Preston, T. (2007/2009). *From lambs to lions: Future security relationships in a world of biological and nuclear weapons*. Boulder, CO: Rowman & Littlefield.

Schelling, T. (1960/1980). *The strategy of conflict*. Oxford: Oxford University Press.

Schelling, T. (1966). *Arms and influence*. New Haven, CT: Yale University Press.
Sun Tzu. (1910). *The art of war*. London: Luzac and Company.
Thucydides. (2009). *The history of the Peloponnesian war*. Oxford: Oxford University Press.
Von Clausewitz, C. (2010). *On war*. Princeton, NJ: Princeton University Press.

Notes

1. See Mearsheimer (1983) for more on wars of attrition and other military strategies.
2. Some of the critics of nuclear deterrence using political psychological arguments at times seem to be using a logic that would equally suggest one shouldn't fly on passenger airplanes (because of the potential for catastrophic failure), but rather drive cars everywhere (since the potential for large loss of life in any one incident is smaller). Yet, as we know, flying is far and away the statistically safer means of travel—despite its technical and organizational complexity and potential for catastrophic failure. Indeed, the fatalities from automobile accidents each year dwarf even the very worst years for aviation crashes. Nuclear deterrence (no wars or use at all over last 50 years) versus conventional deterrence (60–70 million killed over last 50 years) are empirically even more dissimilar.

Chapter 14

Conflict Resolution and Reconciliation

In the previous chapters on race, ethnicity, and nationalism, we discussed the psychological underpinnings of conflict and illustrated these with numerous case studies. This chapter focuses on conflict avoidance and resolution strategies. It covers conflict resolution strategies that can be used to reconcile groups engaged in various forms of conflict.

Reconciliation after mass violence and killing is very difficult. **Reconciliation** is defined as "mutual acceptance by groups of each other. The essence of reconciliation is a changed psychological orientation toward the other" (Staub, 2006, p. 868). Reconciliation and **forgiveness** are interrelated. Forgiveness involves the restoration of a positive relationship between perpetrator and victim wherein negative emotions toward the perpetrator are replaced with positive emotions and prosocial behavior (Cehajic, Brown, & Castano, 2008; Staub, 2006). Unlike reconciliation, forgiveness is regarded as one-sided in that the victim forgives the perpetrator. Staub (2006) argues that forgiveness without regret on the part of the perpetrator can have harmful effects: "Victimization creates wounds, as well as an imbalance in the relationship between victims and perpetrators. It diminishes the status of the former in relation to the latter, and also in relations to other, non-victimized people" (p. 886). In other words, perpetrators get away with what they did. On the other hand, forgiveness may make perpetrators less likely to justify their victimization of others (Cehajic, Brown, & Castano, 2008).

By definition, victims, perpetrators, and bystanders must be involved in the reconciliation process. Each group has its own difficulty reaching the point where it is amenable to reconciliation. Victims have been traumatized, abandoned, and often brutalized by people they considered neighbors, friends, even relatives. Many victims suffer from the chronic effects of trauma. Studies of trauma-induced stress show a number of different patterns of psychological and behavioral reactions. Trauma produces hypervigilance, chronic anxiety, insomnia, nightmares when sleep is possible, and a variety of tension-related physical problems (Gilligan, 1997; Herman, 1992). People are both numbed and angered by violence and, when persistent, both reactions can lead to Post Traumatic Stress Disorder (PTSD) (Weingarten, 2004). Life is constricted in the sense that daily survival is the focus of victims of trauma, and their sense of the future is surviving until

DOI: 10.4324/9780429244643-14

tomorrow. People who have survived genocide have also experienced a loss of their past. Isolation and fear make an acknowledgment of their past lives intolerably painful, so they disassociate themselves from them (Herman, 1992). Chronic trauma also disempowers people so they become incapable of planning actions that would change their circumstances, take advantage of opportunities, make opportunities, and offer an alternative future. The trauma of experiencing violence can distort memory to the extent that experiences are remembered "without reference to time and place. Thus when they are retrieved, it is as if they are happening in the present. They are experienced as a contemporary terror" (Weingarten, 2004, p. 49). Given these wounds, it is easy to see how victims would be reluctant to enter into reconciliation contexts. Having strong institutional support to make them feel safe is crucial.

Meanwhile, although one would expect perpetrators to feel guilty, they often do not. They often continue to see their victims through the negative, dehumanizing stereotypes that led them to commit the violence in the first place. They often continue to believe what they did was the right thing to do, and they minimize the victims' suffering (Baumeister, 1997; Cohen, 2001; Staub, 2006). Ironically, perpetrators of violence also can experience trauma, and suffer similar ill-effects (MacNair, 2005; Staub, 2006). Bystanders often turn away from victims, refusing to acknowledge what happened, and distancing themselves from those who suffered (Cohen, 2001; Staub, 2006). Some perpetrators and bystanders do feel guilt and remorse. Neither are pleasant emotions, and they often result in a desire to compensate the victims in some manner (Klandermans, Werner, & van Doorn, 2008).

In post-conflict situations, punishment for crimes against humanity was always part of the reconciliation process. The trials of the Nazi leadership, the identification of Bosnian Serbs guilty of mass murder, the trials of Rwanda's killers, and the execution of Timothy McVeigh all illustrate the importance attached to punishment by the international community and victims of violence. Punishment is also supposed to act as a deterrent to others who would commit such acts. But at some point punishment stops, and conflict resolution and reconciliation require returning to the source of the conflict to begin with.

Many studies of conflicts, such as those discussed in the previous chapters, draw on social identity and human needs theories to explain the conflicts, and propose methods of prevention, resolution, and reconciliation. From this perspective, conflict arises in societies because basic human needs aren't being met, whether those needs are physical and objective, or psychological and subjective. If one's primary identity groups are threatened, then a basic need for safety, through higher needs such as self-esteem, is not being met. As Staub argues:

> Economic problems, political conflict, and disorganization, and intense and rapid social change (separately or in combination) not only have material effects, but also profoundly frustrate basic human needs ... To satisfy needs for identity and connection, people often turn to a group. They elevate the group ... by psychologically or physically diminishing other groups. They scapegoat another group for life problems, which protects their identity, strengthens connection

> within the group, and provides a psychologically useful (even if false) understanding of events.
>
> (Staub, 2000, pp. 369–370)

Every group we considered in the previous chapters reflects these dynamics. Recognizing that these groups are not always going to be stopped before they commit violent actions, what can be done to promote reconciliation afterward? A crucial first step in conflict resolution in the aftermath of violence is for people to feel safe. Once the fighting has stopped, people still have highly charged emotions about other groups, and they will quite reasonably fear that their own safety is still in jeopardy. Even after the fighting has stopped, individuals and groups do not simply forgive and move on. There is usually distrust of intentions of the other groups involved in the conflict. This makes peace-building—that is, reconstructing a new peaceful society—very difficult. The healing process can be long and tenuous. Leaders who have skills are crucial to this effort, enabling them to build coalitions and calm fears.

WAR TRIBUNALS

Reconciliation is necessary to prevent violence from becoming cyclical, with one group seeking violent revenge against another. In addition to punishment, reconciliation requires recognition of the humanity of one another, forgiveness, and the reestablishment of trust. Victims must have an audience that acknowledges their trauma. Perpetrators must explain their actions, which often results in a description of the perceptions of their reality, their sense of mistreatment. They must express contrition. There is an outlet for understanding for the victims, however unpalatable that understanding may be. In the process, victims recognize that what happened to them is not a result of their own inhumanity (Staub, 2000).

A number of methods are used in the aftermath of conflict to promote resolution and reconciliation. No approach is perfect, and as Minow (1998) notes, "at best they can only seek a path between too much memory and too much forgetting" (p. 4). In fact, many societies choose not to confront the past, try to forget the horrors they experienced, and move on. But for others this is too much forgetting, and they employ approaches ranging from trials and purges, wherein at least some of the perpetrators are put on trial for crimes against humanity, and others are removed from positions of authority. This is what happened in Nuremberg after World War II, when Nazi leaders were tried. It took nearly 50 years for another round of international trials for crimes against humanity to take place. In 1993 and 1994, the United Nations established war crimes tribunals for Yugoslavia and Rwanda, respectively. The International Court at the Hague indicted 76 people for human rights abuses during the war in Bosnia. The most famous person was Slobodan Milošević, who was indicted in 1999 and finally surrendered in 2004. He died in 2006 before a verdict was delivered. Those accused of committing acts of genocide in Rwanda were tried in Arusha, Tanzania, at the International Crimes Tribunal for Rwanda. Eighty-five people were indicted for the Rwandan genocide. The United Nations also established a permanent International Criminal Court in 2002, which the

United States did not support. The International Criminal Court is different from the International Court of Justice, which settles disputes between countries. The court opened up investigations into the situations in Northern Uganda, the Democratic Republic of Congo, the Central African Republic, Darfur, Sudan, the Ivory Coast, Kenya, and Myanmar (the Rohingya in exile in Bangladesh). The trials of Saddam Hussein and other members of his regime were handled by the Iraqi government. Saddam Hussein and many other individuals were put on trial by the Iraqi Higher Tribunal (Iraqi Higher Criminal Court) for crimes committed during his rule. In November 2006, he and two other defendants were sentenced to death by hanging for their role in the 1982 murder, torture, and incarceration of individuals in the Shiite town of Dujail. Hussein was executed in December 2006.

War crimes trials are not without criticism. The Nuremberg trials, conducted by the International Military Tribunal, were criticized for being little more than vengeance by the victors of World War II. The laws, procedures, and judges were all selected by the allies, and the victorious allies, who committed some horrifying acts of violence against civilians, including the firebombing of Dresden and the atomic bombing of Hiroshima and Nagasaki, were not held accountable for their own actions. Defendants were accused of retroactive crimes; they were not clearly crimes at the time of their commission. The Nuremberg trials were criticized for going too far and for not going far enough. There were 85,882 cases prosecuted, but only 7000 convictions. Some argued these individuals should not be held accountable for actions conducted by a state government; others noted that putting only 185 people on trial could hardly be considered enough.

War crimes trials being held today are less susceptible to the criticism that the laws and procedures are arbitrary because, in the years since the establishment of the United Nations, there have been international agreements concerning what constitutes genocide and violations of human rights. The United Nations built on the Nuremberg trials and used them as precedents for the codification of international laws. The Hague and Geneva Conventions are also important legal statements. These developments help address the retroactivity issue. Now, certain actions are deemed crimes in accordance with international laws agreed to by an international organization and its members. The International Court also establishes procedures for trials. Nevertheless, the complaint remains that participants in violence are not treated equally. For example, many Serbs maintained Croats and Muslims who committed atrocities against Serbs during the Yugoslavian wars were not pursued as vigorously as Serbs. In addition, the ongoing war crimes trials only sought to indict and try the commanders who gave orders, not those who actually committed the violence, reasoning that the latter were only following orders and would have been shot if they had disobeyed. This gives little satisfaction to victims' families, however.

In addition to international trials, individual governments held trials to bring to justice people who participated in atrocities and state terror. Trials were held in Argentina, Chile, Brazil, and in several Eastern European countries after the fall of communist regimes there. However, it is not always easy to carry out effective trials. In both Chile and Argentina, for example, the return to democracy was done under the watchful gaze of the military. Governments seeking to punish those who commit politically motivated crimes must be in control of the situation and, in both of these cases, the military could conceivably act again to overthrow the civilian governments. Therefore, in Argentina after the return to civilian rule in 1982, the newly elected president, Raul Alfonsin, ordered nine top-level military officers to be tried, five of whom were convicted. Middle and junior ranking officers were not tried. His successor, President Carlos Menem, fearful of the military and wanting officers to close the past, pardoned the officers and forbade future trials, but efforts to bring these officers to accountability did not stop. In 1997, for example, an Argentine lawyer, representing 13 families of disappeared victims, used the courts to bypass that prohibition by maintaining the pardons of officers were illegal because the kidnapping of the victims was continuing, and they were never found. In March 2001, an Argentine judge struck down the amnesty laws that protected middle-level and junior officers from prosecution. In addition, Spain and France were both trying to use legal means to punish Argentine perpetrators of violence against their citizens, such as the "flying nuns," who were captured and disappeared by the military regime. To carry out trials, governments and societies must have the power and will to punish those responsible. However, the trials will never be sufficient to punish everyone in every case, particularly in situations like Rwanda, where so many people were involved in the slaughter of Tutsis. Moreover, trials do not produce reconciliation. To achieve this, people must admit their wrongdoing, but often during trials people do not admit wrongdoing. For example, both Slobodan Milošević and Saddam Hussein both claimed they were innocent of any crimes.

DIALOGUE AND TRUTH AND RECONCILIATION COMMISSIONS

There are different techniques for recovering from violence. Two of these techniques are **dialogue** and the **truth and reconciliation commission**.

Dialogue is a process by which individuals engage with each other in an open forum to speak about their side of the story, and to hear the other side. Dialogue can be used to promote understanding between racial groups. In 1998 President Clinton released *One America in the 21st Century: The President's Initiative on Race*. In this document, dialogue is described as "a forum that draws participants from as many parts of the community as possible to exchange information face-to-face, share personal stories and experiences, honestly express perspectives, clarify viewpoints, and develop solutions to community concerns" (Clinton, 1998, p. 1). There are four phases "that have proven useful in moving participants through a natural process from sharing individual experiences to committing to collective action. Whether meeting for one dialogue session or a series of sessions, participants move through all four phases, exploring and building on shared experiences" (p. 11).

The first phase sets the tone and explores the question "Who are we?" through the sharing of personal stories. The second phase helps participants understand "Where are we?" through a deeper exploration of personal and shared racial history in the community. During the third phase, participants develop a vision for the community, in response to the question "Where do we want to be?" In the fourth phase, participants answer the question, "What will we do as individuals and with others to make a difference?" Often, they discover shared interests and start working together on specific projects (p. 11).

Truth and reconciliation commissions are designed to reveal the truths of political violence, to let the revelation of truth allow the victims or their survivors to grieve, and to achieve some measure of reconciliation and forgiveness. Truth commissions gather evidence, determine accountability, and often recommend policies for the treatment of victims and perpetrators. As Rigby notes:

> Whereas trials and purges are aimed at punishing the perpetrators of crimes against their citizens, the prime concern of the truth commission approach is with the victims. The aim is to identify them, to acknowledge them and the wrongs done to them, and to arrive at appropriate compensation.
>
> (Rigby, 2001, p. 6)

Truth and reconciliation commissions were established in a number of countries following periods of massive violations of human rights. Argentina, Chile, El Salvador, and South Africa all used truth and reconciliation commissions. Truth commissions are often used in situations in which the government replacing the power-holders who committed the acts of violence is not powerful or stable enough to challenge all of those agents. This was the case in Argentina, where the new civilian government could not prosecute all of the military officers responsible for the repression. The military made it clear that this would not be tolerated. Argentina's truth commission was established in 1983 and was called the National Commission on Disappeared People. Its primary mission was to discover what happened to those who disappeared and where their remains could be found. It ultimately produced a 50,000-page report called *Nunca Mas* (Never Again), as well as a documentary. However, as Rigby argues:

> To many of the relatives and friends of the victims, who were what can be termed secondary victims of the military junta, the report was a whitewash. They know who the victims were: what they wanted was the names of those who had tortured, raped, and killed them.
>
> (Rigby, 2001, pp. 69–70)

Another reason for the use of truth and reconciliation commissions is that often the number of people involved in one way or another with the commission of violence is so great that the prosecutorial approach would only serve to make reconciliation and the reconstruction of a working political and social system impossible. Guilt and blame are also often difficult to discern. How does one condemn a person who breaks under torture, turns into an informant, and then, in that role, causes someone else to be tortured? Truth and reconciliation commissions are also useful in trading amnesty for information about what happened to whom. In many cases, families of victims have no idea what happened to their loved ones and, when perpetrators of violence are granted amnesty, they are more likely to produce vital information about the fates of victims. They may also provide details about the conduct of violence, including who had what kind of decision-making authority. Finally, truth and reconciliation commissions do serve the fundamental needs of victims and their families to have an audience willing to listen to their accounts, and acknowledge publicly the wrongs done to them.

The South African Truth and Reconciliation Commission (TRC), which lasted from 1996 to 1998, is perhaps the most famous example. During apartheid, tremendous violations of human rights took place, as Whites attempted to suppress the desires of Black South Africans for equality. As shown in Chapter 8, after years of struggle, the White power structure finally dismantled the apartheid state through a negotiated process, and free elections were held. The last apartheid-era White president, F. W. de Klerk, made it clear during the negotiations that a peaceful transition from apartheid to democracy would not be possible if trials were conducted to punish members of the apartheid establishment. Nelson Mandela, who was the leader of the ANC resistance movement, and was held prisoner by the government for 27 years, was elected to hold the office of the president in the new democratic government. The new government approved a law called the Promotion of National Unity and Reconciliation Act in 1995, thus establishing the TRC. The TRC was headed by another hero of the anti-apartheid resistance, Archbishop Desmond Tutu. The TRC aspired for transparency in its deliberations and attempted to be very public and open in procedures, gathering of testimony, and decision-making. The TRC gathered testimony from thousands of victims, and included testimony from those abused by the resistance, as well as by the regime. It was also empowered to grant amnesty to perpetrators of violence who applied for amnesty and confessed about what they did. In this way, information was obtained about victims and the chain of command, and often perpetrators apologized to victims. Not all victims testified publicly, but those who were willing to do so had their testimonies broadcast on radio and television, and they are also available on the TRC website. For victims, the experience can be very therapeutic (Minow, 1998).

A centrally important element in the South African TRC was the amnesty condition. Unlike Argentina, there was no blanket amnesty. Instead, perpetrators applied for amnesty and admitted their actions. Amnesty was not granted until the admission of guilt was evaluated, to determine whether the actions were politically motivated, rather than personal or criminal. They had a limited time in which to do this, and those who refused were susceptible to criminal prosecution. In the end, over 8000 people asked for amnesty.

In South Africa, the human rights abuses were mostly carried out by members of the government's security forces. There were also many bystanders—White people who benefited from the apartheid system, but who had not committed human rights abuses. In order to enable these people to admit guilt and shame for indirect complicity, "and to extend the domain of truth telling beyond the confines of the Commission hearing, a Reconciliation Register was opened, with books kept at various locations where people could go and sign them as a personal symbol of regret for their past culpability and commitment to a new beginning" (Rigby, 2001, p. 130).

Truth and reconciliation commissions can be used to address historical wrongs to people which may have gone unnoticed for years. Canada, for example, established one active commission from 2008–2015. That commission was devoted to the examination of the Canadian residential school system, where Canada's indigenous, or "First Nation," children were sent over decades, starting in the 1870s. The last one closed in 1996. Children were not allowed to speak their Indigenous languages, or wear traditional clothes, and they were mistreated, underfed, and forced to work rather than learn. The treatment amounted to cultural genocide, according to the commission's final report (TRCC, 2015). Survivors' stories were collected, and 30,000 survivors were compensated financially by the Canadian government. The government formally apologized for the schools in 2008, and the final report has 94 calls to action for reconciliation.

Do truth commissions accomplish their goals? In some respects, they do. Victims get an opportunity to express their outrage, and it is heard. Families find out what happened to their lost loved ones, and a country learns about the systems of abuse—that is, who ordered what, when and why. But many victims and their relatives object to amnesty for perpetrators and resent the fact that those individuals are free to go on with their lives. Then there is the question of what the truth is. It is not always clear-cut, nor is it immune to wide variations in perceptions. In fact, the South African TRC's final report discussed four truths; factual, personal, social, and healing. Factual is just that—objective, measurable truth; personal is the victims' stories; social is the discussion of conflicting interpretations of what happened; and healing is reconciliation and compensation (Cohen, 2001; Tepperman, 2002).

There is also the question about what reconciliation really is, and whether truth commissions can achieve it. Reconciliation is usually thought to occur when there is a willingness to forgive, to tolerate one another, and to live together in harmony in the future. Yet, in South Africa, public opinion polls taken after the TRC finished found "two thirds of South Africans felt the commission's revelations had only made them angrier and contributed to a worsening of race relations" (Tepperman, 2002, p. 134). It is also necessary to question who considers who to be a victim. Normally, we think of those who suffered the abuse as victims, and the perpetrators need to accept responsibility to make amends. But it is quite likely that, although perpetrators apologize, other perpetrators see themselves as victims, persecuted by truth commissions, persecuted for only doing their jobs, or persecuted for having tried to save the country. As Minow (1998) puts it, "perhaps acknowledgement of wrongs is most helpful to the victimized and the entire society when it comes from perpetrators, yet no sincere acknowledgement can be ordered or forced" (p. 76).

In Rwanda, a combination of tactics was used to advance punishment and reconciliation. The United Nations International Criminal Tribunal for Rwanda (the ICTR), based in Arusha, Tanzania, handled the cases of those accused of the most horrific actions, particularly those who planned the genocide. However, there was much criticism of the ICTR for incompetence, lack of adequate progress and resources, and corruption. Other cases were brought to trial through the Rwandan national criminal justice system.

This too was problematic. After the genocide, estimates indicated that there were just 10 lawyers left in the country (Zorbas, 2008). The legal system had to be rebuilt and, as a result, many thousands of accused languished in miserable conditions in prison awaiting trial.

A third strategy used in Rwanda was the revival of a traditional, grassroots court called *Gacaca*. The *Gacaca* system is similar to the South African Truth and Reconciliation system in that victims and perpetrators gather in a public forum—often a village center—and the victims tell their stories; the accused then express an admission of guilt, and an apology. However, there were some provisions in the process that were criticized. As Zorbas notes,

> under these provisions, if someone confesses before being denounced, he or she is liable for a substantial decrease in length of the sentence. However, confessions are only acceptable if they include 1) all information about the crime, 2) an apology, and 3) *the incrimination of one's co-conspirators*. This system of incrimination creates rife conditions for vendetta settling; some estimate that an additional 200,000 people could see themselves accused and imprisoned for genocide-related crimes.
>
> (Zorbas (2008), pp. 36–37)

Nevertheless, the public response to the *Gacaca* courts appeared to be positive (Zorbas, 2008). There were approximately 10,000 of these courts in Rwanda, and they were the sites of reconciliation for most Rwandans. By the end of 2007, these courts had tried over one million cases, beginning with property-related cases, torture, and incitement, and then in 2007 taking on rape, attempted murder, and murder. About 30% of the accused were acquitted (Global Security, 2008).

The Rwandan government also established a Unity and Reconciliation Commission and encouraged the development of an overarching Rwandan identity. Other local-level efforts to promote reconciliation are widespread, such as coffee cooperatives that bring Tutsi and Hutu together in collaboration in an economic project that carries financial rewards to all (Tobias, 2008). But the government also used repressive measures, in particular forbidding people to call themselves Tutsi or Hutu, and making "divisionism," or the discussion of differences between Tutsis and Hutus, a crime. This is contrary to the dialogue goals of talking through identity issues.

INTEGRATION STRATEGIES

Over the long term, whether discussing racial or ethnic/national separation and conflict, integration and the elimination of inequalities and their causes are essential to conflict resolution and avoidance. Integration without discrimination is really the only practical solution in many cases because separation is not an option. In the following sections, we discuss two types of integration strategies: shared sovereignty and utilitarian. A central feature of these conflicts is fear—the development of the security dilemma wherein different identity groups (racial, ethnic, national) fear they will lose out in competition for power and justice, fear the destruction of their group as an identity group, or even fear for their very existence. People mobilize to defend themselves against perceived threats by other groups. A good example of this was in Northern Ireland. The Ulster Defense Association, a Protestant armed group, refused to decommission its weapons at first. The leaders of the organization believed they still faced threats from the groups they formed to fight against after the beginning of the "Troubles" in 1969. While some Republican groups were still active, the UDA's biggest competitor, the Provisional Irish Republican Army (PIRA), decommissioned its weapons and entered the peace process. In fact, Martin McGuiness, a key leader in the group, was second minister in the Northern Ireland Assembly. This heightened the threat even more because the UDA perceived the Republican goal of a united Ireland could be orchestrated from within the government. The identity of the UDA was being threatened because they were being asked to disarm from the very state they sought to remain a part of. This created an identity crisis within the group, and their response was to dig in their heels and refuse to become a political player in the post conflict process.

Ultimately, the best long-term solution to these conflicts is the development of an overarching common identity among the groups: "Yes, I am White and you are Black, but we are both Americans first and can live together harmoniously" or "I am Ibo and you are Hausa, but we are both Nigerians first and can live together harmoniously." An ideal integration strategy to achieve this end would be a plan for developing a population-wide, first-intensity identification with the territorial community—for example, with America, or Nigeria, or Guatemala. Indeed, this was the goal of the peace process in Guatemala: to establish a common and multifaceted Guatemalan identity that incorporated both *ladino* and Mayan culture, rather than *ladino* alone. But in some cases, the development of an overarching identity, which receives all groups' primary and most intense loyalty, is neither desirable nor possible. Often, distrust is too high, or people do not want to be assimilated into a dominant culture and lose their cultural uniqueness. Nevertheless, integration strategies can be developed to resolve conflict in those cases as well. To be successful, an integration strategy requires eliminating racial or ethnic prejudice, and the accompanying structural (legal, social) factors that maintain it.

Successful integration strategies require a number of political and psychological components. Psychologically, integration strategies would provide different identity groups in a polity with options for **social mobility** and **social creativity**. In this way, the different groups can maintain their primary identity and do not need to rely on having a common third identity in order to get along. Integration strategies need to establish an environment in which groups feel secure their identities are not threatened. The greater the disparity in cultural, religious, and racial characteristics, the more complicated the problem. A multifaceted formula is needed here, in which different group characteristics are looked at positively when comparisons are made. When **social comparisons** are different, but equally positive, conflict can be avoided (van den Heuvel & Meertens, 1989). For example, in the United States, the "Black is beautiful" campaign during the Civil Rights Movement, and other more current efforts to promote multiculturalism, attempt to recognize cultural and racial differences and to celebrate those differences as equally valuable and equally American.

A second psychological element involves a need to address stereotypes and social distance among groups. Possibly most important in this process is addressing perceptions of group inferiority and superiority. Breaking such stereotypes and images is central to a workable integration strategy. The objective should be the replacement of a highly simplified and negative view of the other group with a far more complex and non-judgmental view. This requires acceptance of, and respect for, group differences and changed expectations about other group members' behavior (Hewstone, 1989; van den Heuvel & Meertens, 1989). An early idea about how to do this was the **contact hypothesis**, which proposed increasing intergroup contact and exposing people to the complexity of group members, thereby providing information that breaks down stereotypes. But the contact hypothesis works only in an environment or institutional context that is supportive, where contact can be ongoing, and in which groups are equal in status (Allport, 1954; Brewer & Brown, 1998; Fiske, 1998). A number of studies noted that increased contact may merely lead people to assume that the member of another group who appears to be different from the stereotypical members is simply atypical of the group, meaning the stereotype of the group will stand, but a particular known individual will be seen as different, not like the others (Brewer & Miller, 1984; Hewstone & Brown, 1986; Mackie & Hamilton, 1993).

The political or policy aspect of integration strategies would have to meet these psychological requirements. Policies would have to address the particular needs, demands, and alternatives regarding conflicting groups' capability, power, and rewards accrued within the political system. Mechanisms used for this part of an integration strategy include supplying multiple channels for acquiring power, so no group dominates limited channels; promoting intragroup, rather than intergroup, conflict; policies that promote intergroup cooperation; policies that encourage cross-group alignments based on interests, rather than on group identity; and policies that reduce various kinds of disparities between groups, thereby reducing dissatisfaction (Horowitz, 1985). Politically, the strategy has to be tuned to the distribution of power among groups. Identity groups often vary greatly in terms of perceived power and influence in their political systems. Those who see themselves as strong enough to possibly achieve independence would only be satisfied with institutional and social conditions offering broad autonomy just short of independence. At the other end of the scale are groups far too weak to achieve independence; for these groups, integration in the form of assurances of equality with other groups, rather than autonomy, would be satisfactory.

Shared sovereignty and utilitarian strategies are good examples of the importance of blending political structures, institutions, and distribution of power with psychological patterns. The strategies recognize that identities are not negotiable, but interests are (Burton, 1990; Gurr, 1994; Rothman & Olson, 2001).

SHARED SOVEREIGNTY STRATEGIES

The first type of integration strategy considered here is one in which a group is given some degree of self-rule. It accommodates a group's desire to maintain its integrity as an identity group and the primacy of that identity for group members. People must be confident that the integrity—indeed, the very continuity of their primary identity groups—will be secure, for these groups to be resolvable. **Shared sovereignty strategies** usually provide for some degree of regional autonomy or statewide confederation or federation—that is, some form of shared homeland (Rabie, 1994). Autonomy, confederation, and federation all involve the devolution of power. Which of these arrangements works best depends greatly on the specific characteristics of group interaction and settlement patterns—for example, whether ethnic and national groups are clearly divided territorially or are dispersed and intermixed. In the cases we reviewed in this chapter, shared sovereignty strategies incorporating some form of autonomy or self-rule designed to reduce threat perceptions were attempted in Nigeria, Bosnia, and Guatemala.

Autonomy may be preferred by a group that understands it does not have the capability necessary to achieve independence. In this type of situation, the option of autonomy can set into motion a gradually intensifying identification with the broader national community. Unfortunately, as the Nigerian case shows, these efforts often fail. As Horowitz notes:

> Most such agreements are concluded against a background of secessionist warfare or terrorist violence. When central authority is secure ... the appropriate decisions can be made and implemented by the center. But, where the very question is how far the authority of the center will run, devolution is a matter of bilateral agreement, and an enduring agreement is an elusive thing.
>
> (Horowitz, 1985, p. 623)

These forms of integration strategy address the important political issues of providing groups' increased capability and decision-making power in their region or state, and with competitive power in the broader country government.

These institutional arrangements can accommodate identity needs of groups, particularly when a group's identity is threatened. However, reducing stereotypes and promoting equality in group comparisons is very difficult to realize. Often, policy-makers rely upon the contact hypothesis, wherein, as mentioned previously, it is assumed that if people get to know members of groups against which they discriminate, the interaction will disprove those stereotypical ideas, and tolerance and acceptance will result. But, in reality, contact is limited in countries where shared sovereignty strategies are employed because groups tend to be geographically concentrated. Moreover, failure to identify group variability increases with emotions (Mackie et al., 2000; Park & Banaji, 2000; Stroessner & Mackie, 1993), and shared sovereignty integrative strategies often come into play after serious violent clashes between groups have occurred. Thus, intense emotion is likely to prevail in these situations, making the breakdown of preexisting stereotyped images extremely difficult.

Integration strategies should explicitly address intergroup perceptions. Some steps can be taken, through policies that prevent systematic integration against groups even in autonomous regions in which they are minorities, or that ensure that national institutions, such as the military, are not dominated by one particular ethnic or racial group. Such control can easily cause resentment because it often involves the reduction in power of dominant groups. However, over time, learning nonstereotyped responses to others is crucial to a change in image. People change perceptions of others by acting differently, not just thinking differently (Pettigrew & Martin, 1989). In other words, people can be trained not to stereotype (Kawakami, Dovidio, Moll, Hermson, & Russin, 2000). In fact, change in American racial attitudes may be a good example of just this. From a policy standpoint, this requires the explicit promotion of tasks that require intergroup cooperation to achieve goals and interdependence at equal status levels. Equal status in group member interaction is important for disconfirming stereotypes (Allport, 1954; Bizman & Amir, 1984; van Oudenhoven, 1989).

Emotions are involved in changing stereotypes, too. Perceptions that the elite of another group is inferior tend to generate anger among those considered inferior, as well as anger and guilt among those considered superior (Duckitt, 1994; Swim & Miller, 1999). This, as was mentioned, can be counterproductive, because strong emotions tend to inhibit the identification of group variance, and thus the breaking down of stereotypes. On the other hand, emotions can also be used to reduce stereotyping. **Perspective-taking**, for example, involves empathizing with others, experiencing their perspective and the emotions it generates in them. Galinsky and Moskowitz (2000) argue that perspective-taking "appears to diminish not just the expression of stereotypes but their accessibility. The constructive process of taking and realizing another person's perspective furthers the egalitarian principles themselves" (p. 722). Other studies found people adopt and change stereotypes when given information about how other in-group members think about the out-group (Sechrist & Stangor, 2001; Stangor, Sechrist, & Jost, 2001).

UTILITARIAN INTEGRATION STRATEGIES

The institutional options of independence or autonomy are not available when the groups are geographically intermingled across a country or minorities are low in power and capabilities. Social distance factors are very important in these cases, as is the nature of existing stereotypes or images. The contact hypothesis probably will be relied upon by policy-makers to naturally reduce group stereotyping images because contact is more likely to occur in countries where groups intermingle and can be more easily promoted by government agencies as a solution to group stereotyping. Of the cases reviewed here, this type of strategy would be prominent, for example, in conflict resolution in the United States, Brazil, and South Africa.

An essential feature of a **utilitarian integration strategy** is to satisfy the population's needs, and this requires removing any obstacles to equality of access to important political positions in the country. This most immediately involves unimpeded access to state educational institutions and the elimination of any state-sponsored social discrimination, but the speed with which integration develops varies with the social distances between groups. The greater the distances, the harder and slower integration will be. Memories of historical relationships, such as slavery, and the depth of institutional discrimination also affect the speed of integration.

One of the greatest difficulties in this type of integration strategy is changing traditional perceptions of groups regarded as inferior. The task is complicated when the self-imagery within the subordinate minority is also negative. This kind of imagery is the imperial-colonial pattern referred to in Chapter 3. As mentioned there, conquered people can, through years of repression, come to accept as just the conditions and position in which they live. In countries with histories of this kind of repression, in which one or more of the identity communities is perceived, and perceives itself, as underachieving, there is likely to be a strong, persisting inclination toward the colonial and imperial images. Our earlier discussion of racism in America illustrated this as well. Breaking these stereotypes requires making opportunities for those in the minority community and persuading them that they can and should try to take advantage of those opportunities.

A key aspect of the utilitarian strategy in this case is attracting qualified individuals in the minority community or communities into positions that exceed their expectations, and those of the majority. Affirmative action programs are designed to do this. These achievements should help break stereotypes of inferiority, eventually, as people from minority groups increasingly come to be associated with high achievement. A study by Sinclair and Kunda (1999), for example, showed that American subjects high in prejudice did not activate their racial prejudice when motivated to have high regard for a Black person. In their experiments, when subjects were induced to have high regard for a Black doctor, they invoked the doctor stereotype, not the racist anti-Black stereotype.

The American affirmative action program illustrates both the promise and problems associated with this component of the strategy. Inevitably, those perceiving minority groups through the contemptuous colonial image will make the case that the program is ideologically driven and individuals who benefit from affirmative action lack the requisite qualifications. The program, they argue, is damaging both in the placement of inherently unqualified individuals into positions in which they will not perform adequately and in causing serious hardship among those who are qualified in achieving communities. Additionally, Brown, Charnsangavej, Keough, Newman and Rentfrow (2000) offer experimental evidence that affirmative action programs may be self-defeating if they become "reminders of people's stigmatized status," which can "have dramatic, detrimental effects on their performance. A phenomenon referred to as 'stereotype threat'" (p. 737). Thus, the stereotype of inferiority can become a self-fulfilling prophecy, with people who are considered inferior given fewer opportunities, and thus remaining inferior in education, income, social standing, and so on—and knowing this is the case. Meanwhile, the high-achieving members of the minority group will see integration as an unattractive prospect.

Clearly, dominant groups that are numerical minorities can be pushed from power, but not all dominant groups are numerical minorities, as in the case of White Americans, and it would be hoped violence can be avoided. What is also clear is for utilitarian strategies to occur, and for violence to be avoided, dominant groups—whether numerical majorities or minorities—must choose to accept equality with subordinate groups. As both the United States and South African cases show, perceptual change must accompany internal and external pressures for structural change. Stereotypes are shaken when expectations are consistently disconfirmed. If successful, the utilitarian strategy applied to subordinate groups should do this. As subordinate groups achieve more, the dominant group's expectations, noted in the colonial image, would not be realized, and the image would be challenged. The impact should be a decline in opposition to further expanding access to opportunities and, gradually, a diminution of the colonial image of the disadvantaged groups. Image disconfirmation in this direction also can occur through the direct efforts of the subject of the colonial image to alter it by disconfirming it. This occurs through group mobilization and organization, demonstrating power and control unexpected from those perceived through the colonial image.

Let us conclude this discussion on a practical note, with a look at one component of conflict resolution in divided societies that illustrates the importance of using political institutions to tackle the political psychology of conflict. One of the central elements in conflict resolution and reconciliation in divided societies that have experienced intense violence is the training of a new, impartial professional police force. Political science is only now learning this lesson, but from a political psychology standpoint it is not surprising. One of the most important elements of the governance process in a country is the criminal justice system, particularly the police. They can ameliorate competition and perceptions of inequality, or they can exacerbate those perceptions. They are the representatives of government with whom people interact on a daily basis; as such, they are the central source of perceptions of justice, or lack thereof, in the political system. They must be seen as impartial and unbiased in the treatment of citizens, regardless of ethnicity. They are crucial in conflict resolution because, although military peacekeepers may disarm combatants, police provide the order necessary for people to feel secure. Without this, political reconstruction cannot occur.

In **multiethnic and multisectarian states**, too often the police force becomes a tool of one ethnic or national group. Often, the police in these deeply divided countries are characterized by bias in law enforcement. They are politicized and identified with the repressive regime, the dominant group monopolizes top positions, they are not held accountable by authorities for abuses of power, and they have extraordinary power to control the subordinate populations (Call & Barnett, 2000; Mani, 2000). When this pattern occurs, it erodes state legitimacy, increases resentment against the state by unrepresented groups, and increases the possibility of conflict, as well as the need of the state to employ coercion to quell the conflict.

The importance of impartial policing in conflict resolution was recognized in the cases discussed earlier. Let us return to the Guatemalan case for illustration. Guatemala's Mayan population suffered violence on the scale of mass killing, if not genocide, although cultural genocide was certainly intended. There were death squads operative and a campaign of state terror. Mass murder took place indiscriminately in Mayan villages committed by the military and the police force. Nevertheless, despite many difficulties, Guatemala is trying to undergo political reforms attempting to dismantle the counterinsurgency state.

During the war, the military and police committed numerous and appalling human rights violations. One of the most important aspects of reform is the separation of the police and military institutions. Before the peace accords, the police in Guatemala were part of the military. This is the case in most Latin American countries. Now the police are a separate institution and have the authority in internal security matters. The military's domain is left to external security. The enabling legislation and the regulations for the new National Civilian Police were designed primarily by the Spanish police, who also took the lead in training and advising the new Guatemalan policy force. The reform of the police was actually part of the peace accords themselves, and the government—particularly then President Alvaro Arzu—was committed. The accord provided the broad outlines for the police, including the provisions it would be under the authority of the ministry of the interior, rather than under the military; that there would be established a separate academy for police training; and that the police force would take into account the multiethnic nature of the society and would form specialized agencies in that regard. This was to be done in the context of a reformed and impartial justice system.

Progress has been slow. On the negative side, the policing portion of the peace accords was very general and lacked important details. There were no provisions made regarding the inclusion of police officers from the old order; no provisions for vetting officers, to eliminate those involved in human rights abuses during the dirty war years (imagine having your local police officer be the same person who tortured you during the civil war); and no details about the content of training, organization, or disciplinary measures, including no education level requirements, which is an issue in countries with high levels of illiteracy.

The law that went into effect, implementing the government's agreement with the rebels, had no requirement that the new police include members of the different Mayan groups in Guatemala. Only about one-fifth of the new recruits were Indigenous. And former military personnel, who are prohibited from joining the police, managed to get in. Guatemala experienced a tremendous increase in crime, and the government permitted joint military-police patrols to combat it, which is a dangerous practice. Finally,

> the constitutional reforms that would have consolidated the separation of police and military functions ... was defeated in May 1999 in a nation-wide referendum ... [so] the ... military continues to have constitutional authority to be involved in internal security, and the future division of roles remains unclear.
>
> (Byrne, Stanley, & Garst, 2000, p. 5)

On the positive side, the government was clearly committed to this reform. By October 1999, the new police force was 17,339 strong and 36.5% of those employed were new recruits. The force is more service-oriented and was positively received by the public. Complaints about human rights violations and corruption have diminished. However, in 2019 Guatemala began the process of amending the law to provide amnesty to those who committed human rights violations during the civil war. This would be a setback on the country's road to recovery.

INTRACTABLE CONFLICTS

Some conflicts are prolonged and are considered intractable. By definition, **intractable conflicts** last a long time, and those involved in them cannot win, and will not agree to a settlement. According to Bar-Tal and Halperin (2013), intractable conflicts have seven characteristics:

1. *They are total,* being perceived as concerning essential and fundamental goals, needs, and/or values that are regarded as essential for the group's existence ...
2. They involve *physical violence* in which people are killed in either wars, small scale military engagements or terrorist attacks.
3. They are *zero sum,* those involved see no possibility of compromise and perceive any loss by the other side as their own gain.
4. They are perceived as *irresolvable.*
5. They occupy a *central place* in the lives of individual groups' members and the group as a whole.
6. Parties engaged in an intractable conflict make *material and psychological investments* in order to cope successfully with the situation.
7. *They are protracted* in that they persist for a long time, at least a generation.

(Bar-Tal and Halperin, 2013, p. 924)

Examples of intractable conflicts include the Israeli–Palestinian conflict, Kashmir, Bosnia, Cyprus, and until recently Northern Ireland. Intractable conflicts tend to occur in contexts of threatened identities, and we have seen throughout this book the extent to which threatened identities provoke violence. When identities are associated with relative deprivation, conflict over territory, and restrictions on the expression of cultural characteristics including religion, language and heritage, intractable conflicts follow (Bar-Tal & Halperin, 2013; Kriesberg, 2010). The situation is worse when some identity groups consider themselves to be superior to others.

Not all identity conflicts or competitions turn into intractable conflicts. Those that do often have leaders who manipulate fears and mobilize group members (Bar-Tal & Halperin, 2013) and governments unwilling or unable to prevent intercommunal conflict (Kriesberg, 2010). Once violence erupts, perceptions of threat increase and the violence escalates. In some cases, a particular event, such as Bloody Sunday in Northern Ireland, will serve as a call to action for the broader community. Conflicts are sustained as participants become "entrapped": they cannot back down because they have already lost so much (Kriesberg, 2010). The enemy is demonized and dehumanized so it is impossible to negotiate with "those people." Members of the group who disagree and advocate negotiations are deemed traitors.

Intractable conflicts can be transformed to tractable conflicts. Some suggestions include "unfreezing" the psychological mindset by spreading new beliefs about the conflict, its goals, the need to resolve it, and the nature of the opponents (Bar-Tal & Halperin, 2013). Another idea is to mediate the conflict when the combatants have reached a point of exhaustion, a "hurting stalemate" (Zartman, 1989). Other approaches suggest pitting the conflicting parties against a common enemy, implementing confidence building measures, eliminating external actors who may be promoting the conflict, and using neutral mediators (Kriesberg, 2010).

A recently developed approach to resolving intractable conflicts is *dynamical systems.* This draws from chaos theory and proposes these types of conflicts are unique in their propensity to overcome simple motivations for a good life. These are conflicts where everyone suffers for a long time. Normally, motivations for peace and security drive people to resolve conflicts, but that does not happen in intractable conflicts. In the dynamical systems approach the root of the conflict is called an *attractor.* Attractors are deeply entrenched in the conflict system and strongly resistant to efforts to change them. They "*provide a coherent view of the conflict,* including the character of the ingroup, the nature of the relationship with the antagonistic party, the history of the conflict, and the legitimacy of claims made by each party" (Vallacher, Coleman, Nowaki, & Bui-Wrzosinska, 2010, p. 268, italics in original). They also "provide *a stable platform for action,* enabling each party to a conflict to respond unequivocally and without hesitation to a change in circumstances or to an action initiated by the other party" (Vallacher et al., 2010, p. 268, italics in original). Attractors affect all levels of a social system. They become linked in the system by reinforcing feedback. Needless to say, attractors are difficult to change. According to Vallacher et al. (2010) they can be changed by "reverse engineering," wherein some of the feedback loops are changed "from reinforcing to inhibitory" (p. 273); the system is moved "out of its manifest attractor into a latent attractor that is defined in terms of benign or even positive thoughts, actions, and relationships" (p. 273); finally (and here is where they draw on chaos theory), small changes in a nonlinear system can bifurcate and produce "qualitative changes in the system's attractor landscape" (p. 274). In the latter case, it is necessary to identify the "control parameters" or variables that can potentially alter the system in a positive way. The authors give the example of the police. Transforming them may produce greater coercion, or greater confidence among the populace that their human rights will be respected.

CONCLUSION

In this chapter, we have explored political psychology and conflict resolution. Drawing on previously addressed theories and concepts, we discussed the role of reconciliation, and some approaches and examples of resolving conflict. These included war tribunals, truth and reconciliation commissions, and integration strategies, concluding with a discussion of intractable conflicts. Throughout the world, different approaches are tried to resolve conflict. The success of these strategies depends on the particular circumstances of the conflict, then finding solutions to address them appropriately.

Topics, Theories/Explanations, and Cases Covered in Chapter 14

Topics	*Theories/Explanations*	*Cases*
Reconciliation		Bosnia
Forgiveness		Rwanda
Post-Traumatic Stress Disorder (PTSD)	Long-term mental health issues	
War tribunals		Rwanda Nazi Germany Yugoslavia Argentina
Truth and Reconciliation Commissions		Northern Ireland South Africa Chile Argentina
Integration strategies	Social identity Contact hypothesis	Guatemala
Shared sovereignty strategies	Perspective-taking	

Key Terms

- contact hypothesis
- dialogue
- forgiveness
- intractable conflicts
- multiethnic and multisectarian states
- perspective-taking
- reconciliation
- shared sovereignty strategies
- social comparison
- social creativity
- social mobility
- truth and reconciliation commission
- utilitarian integration strategies

Suggestions for Further Reading

Burton, J. (1990). *Conflict: Its resolution and prevention*. London: Macmillan.

Coleman, P. (2011). *The five percent: Finding solutions to seemingly impossible conflicts*. New York: Public Affairs.

Coleman, P. (2021). *The way out: How to overcome toxic polarization*. New York: Columbia University Press.

Minow, M. (1998). *Between vengeance and forgiveness: Facing history after genocide and mass violence*. Boston: Beacon Press.

Rigby, A. (2001). *Justice and reconciliation after the violence*. Boulder, CO: Lynne Rienner.

References

Abanes, R. (1996). *American militias: Rebellion, racism and religion*. Downers Grove, IL: InterVarsity Press.

Abelson, R. P. (1986). Beliefs are like possessions. *Journal of the Theory of Social Behavior, 16*, 223–250.

Abramowitz, A. I. (2018). How race and religion have polarized American voters. In D. Hopkins & J. Sides (Eds.), *Political polarization in American politics* (pp. 80–87). New York: Bloomsbury.

Adam, H., & Moodley, K. (1993). South Africa: The opening of the apartheid mind. In J. McGarry & B. O'Leary (Eds.), *The politics of ethnic conflict regulation* (pp. 226–250). New York: Routledge.

Adorno, T., Frenkel-Brunswick, E., Levinson, D., & Sanford, P. (1950). *The authoritarian personality*. New York: Harper.

Albright, M. (2018). *Fascism: A warning*. New York: HarperCollins.

Aldag, R. J., & Fuller, S. R. (1993). Beyond fiasco: A reappraisal of the groupthink phenomenon and a new model of group decision processes. *Psychological Bulletin, 113*, 533–552.

Alexander, A. (2016). Cruel intentions: Female jihadists in America. Program on Extremism, George Washington University. Retrieved from https://extremism.gwu.edu/sites/g/files/zaxdzs2191/f/downloads/Female%20Jihadists%20in%20America.pdf

Alexander, A. (2017). Mass media misconceptions of female terrorists. In E. Mastors, & R. Siers (Eds.), *The theory and practice of terrorism: Alternative paths of inquiry* (pp. 123–147). New York: Nova Science.

Alexander, M. G., Brewer, M. B., & Herrmann, R. K. (1999). Images and affect: A functional analysis of out-group stereotypes. *Journal of Personality and Social Psychology, 77*, 78–93.

Alfonsi, C. (2006). *Circle in the sand: Why we went back to Iraq*. New York: Doubleday.

Allcott, H., & Gentzkow, M. (2016). Social media and fake news in the 2016 election. *Journal of Economic Perspectives, 31*, 211–236.

Allen, M. (2005, September 19). Living too much in the bubble? A bungled initial response to Katrina exposed the perils of a rigid, insular White House. *Time*. Retrieved from http://content.time.com/time/subscriber/article/0,33009,1103581,00.html

Allen, V. L., & Wilder, D. A. (1979). Group categorization and attribution of belief similarity. *Small Group Behavior, 10*, 73–80.

Allison, G. (1971). *The essence of decision: Explaining the Cuban missile crisis*. Boston, MA: Little, Brown.
Allison, G., & Zelikow, P. (1999). *The essence of decision: Explaining the Cuban Missile Crisis*. New York: Longman.
Allport, F. H. (1962). A structuronomic conception of behavior: Individual and collective. *Journal of Abnormal and Social Psychology, 64*, 3–30.
Allport, G. (1937). *Personality: A psychological interpretation*. New York: Holt, Rinehart, and Winston.
Allport, G. (1954). *The nature of prejudice*. Cambridge, MA: Addison-Wesley.
Allport, G. (1961). *Pattern and growth in personality*. New York: Holt, Rinehart and Winston.
Allport, G. (1968). *The person in psychology*. Boston, MA: Beacon Press.
Altemeyer, B. (1981). *Right-wing authoritarianism*. Winnipeg: University of Manitoba Press.
Altemeyer, B. (1988). *Enemies of freedom: Understanding right-wing authoritarianism*. San Francisco: Jossey-Bass.
Altemeyer, B. (1996). *The authoritarian specter*. Cambridge, MA: Harvard University Press.
Altemeyer, B. (1998). The other "authoritarian personality." *Advances in Experimental and Social Psychology, 30*, 47–92.
Amadeo, K., & Boyle, M. (2020, August 21). Ukraine crisis summary and explanation. *The Balance*. Retrieved from www.thebalance.com/ukraine-crisis-summary-and-explanation-3970462
American Patriot Network. (2002). Retrieved from www.patriotnetwork.info
Anaizi, A., Dotolo, F.H., & Lakehal-Ayat, M. (2015). Confronting ISIS in Libya. *Small Wars Journal*. Retrieved from https://smallwarsjournal.com/jrnl/art/%E2%80%98confronting-isis-in-libya-the-case-for-an-expeditionary-counterinsurgency%E2%80%99
Anderson, J. (1983). *The architecture of cognition*. Cambridge, MA: Harvard University Press.
Anderson, L. (2011). Demystifying the Arab Spring: Parsing the differences between Tunisia, Egypt, and Libya. *Foreign Affairs, 90*, 2–7.
Anderson, M. (2019, May 2). For Black Americans, experiences of racial discrimination vary by education level, gender. *Pew Research*. Retrieved from www.pewresearch.org/fact-tank/2019/05/02/for-black-americans-experiences-of-racial-discrimination-vary-by-education-level-gender/IN
Annenberg Public Policy Center. (2019). Americans' civic knowledge increases but still has a way to go. Retrieved from www.asc.upenn.edu/news-events/news/appc-civics-survey-2019
Ansell, C., Boin, A., & 't Hart, P. (2014). Political leadership in times of crisis. In R. A. W. Rhodes & P. 't Hart (Eds.), *The Oxford handbook of political leadership* (pp. 418–433). Oxford: Oxford University Press.
Ansolabehere, S., Behr, R., & Iyengar, S. (1993). *The media game*. New York: Macmillan.
Anti-defamation League (ADL). (n.d.). William Pierce. Retrieved from www.adl.org/learn/ext_us/Pierce.asp
AOL News. (2008, September 20). Racial views may cost Obama election. Retrieved from http://news.aol.com
Arab News. (2008, September 29). Kurds reverse Saddam's ethnic cleansing. Retrieved from www.arabnews.com

Archibald, R. C., Cave, D., & Thompson, G. (2013, May 1). Mexico's curbs on U.S. role in drug fight spark friction. *New York Times*. Retrieved from www.nytimes.com/2013/05/01/world/americas

Aronson, E., & Mills, J. (1959). Effect of severity of initiation on liking for a group. *Journal of Abnormal and Social Psychology, 59*, 177–181.

Asch, S. E. (1952). *Social psychology*. Englewood Cliffs, NJ: Prentice Hall.

Asch, S. E. (1955). Opinions and social pressure. *Scientific American, 19*, 31–35.

Asch, S. E. (1956). Studies of independence and conformity: A minority of one against a unanimous majority. *Psychological Monographs, 70*, 416.

Asia Foundation, & Rappler Inc. (2018). *Understanding violent extremism: Messaging and recruitment strategies on social media in the Philippines*. Retrieved from https://asiafoundation.org/publication/understanding-violent-extremism-messaging-and-recruitment-strategies-on-social-media-in-the-philippines

Asian American Policy Review. (2020). *The Asian American vote 2016: A report by the Asian American legal defense and education fund*. Retrieved from https://aapr.hkspublications.org/2018/11/06/the-asian-american-vote-2016-a-report-by-the-asian-american-legal-defense-and-education-fund

Assadi, M. (2007, October 12). Fatah rules out talk with Hamas. *Boston Globe*.

Bai, H. (2020). Whites' racial identity centrality and social dominance orientation are interactively associated with far-right extremism. *British Journal of Social Psychology, 59*, 387–404.

Baker, J. A., & Hamilton, L. (2006). *The Iraq Study Group report: The way forward—a new approach*. New York: Vintage Books.

Baker, P. (2007, July 2). A president besieged and isolated, yet at ease. *Washington Post*.

Bales, R. F. (1951). *Interaction process analysis*. Boston, MA: Addison-Wesley.

Bales, R. F., & Strodtbeck, F. L. (1951). Phases in group problem solving. *Journal of Abnormal Social Psychology, 46*, 485–495.

Baltodano, B. (2008). Becoming an insurgent in Colombia: Images at war in the Putumayo (Unpublished master's thesis). Washington State University.

Bamford, J. (2005). *A pretext for war: 9/11, Iraq, and the abuse of America's intelligence agencies*. New York: Anchor Books.

Bandura, A. (1973). *Aggression: A social learning analysis*. Englewood Cliffs, NJ: Prentice Hall.

Bandura, A. (1977). *Social learning theory*. Englewood Cliffs, NJ: Prentice Hall.

Bandura, A. (1986). *Social foundations of thought and action: A social cognitive theory*. Englewood Cliffs, NJ: Prentice Hall.

Bandura, A. (2004). The role of selective moral disengagement in terrorism and counterterrorism. In F. Moghaddam & A. Marsella (Eds.), *Understanding terrorism*. Washington, DC: APA.

Barber, J. D. (1965). *The lawmakers: Recruitment and adaptation to legislative life*. New Haven, CT: Yale University Press.

Barber, J. D. (1972). *The presidential character: Predicting performance in the White House*. Englewood Cliffs, NJ: Prentice-Hall.

Barkow, J. Cosmides, L., & Tooby, J. (Eds.). (1992). *The adapted mind: Evolutionary psychology and the generation of culture.* New York: Oxford University Press.

Barley, S. R., & Bechky, B. A. (1994). In the backrooms of science: The work of technicians in science labs. *Work and Occupations, 21,* 85–126.

Barlow, K. M., Taylor, D. M., & Lambert, W. E. (2000). Ethnicity in America and feeling "American." *Journal of Psychology, 134,* 581–600.

Barnes, R., & Shear, M. (2008, November 5). Obama makes history. *Washington Post.* Retrieved from www.washingtonpost.com/wp-dyn/content/article/2008/11/05

Baron, R. A. (1989). Applicant strategies during job interviews. In G. R. Ferris and R. W. Eder (Eds.), *The employment interview: Theory, research, and practice* (pp. 204–216). Newbury Park, CA: Sage.

Baron, R. S., Vandello, U. A., & Brunsman, B. (1996). The forgotten variable in conformity research: Impact of task importance on social influence. *Journal of Personality and Social Psychology, 71,* 915–927.

Barrera, M., Jr. (1986). Distinctions between social support concepts, measures, and models. *American Journal of Community Psychology, 14,* 413–422.

Bar-Tal, D. & Halperin, E. (2013). The psychology of intractable conflicts: Eruption, escalation, peacemaking. In L. Huddy, D. O. Sears, & J. S. Levy (Eds.), *The Oxford handbook of political psychology* (pp. 923–956). Oxford: Oxford University Press.

Bartels, L. (1996). Uninformed votes: Information effects in presidential elections. *American Journal of Political Science, 40,* 194–230.

Bartels, L. (2000). Partisanship and voting behavior, 1952–1996. *American Journal of Political Science, 44,* 35–50.

Bartle, J. (1998). Left-right position matters but does social class? Causal models of the 1992 British general election. *British Journal of Political Science, 28,* 501–529.

Barton, S. L., Duchon, D., & Dunegan, K. J. (1989). An empirical test of Staw and Ross's prescription for the management of escalation of commitment behavior in organizations. *Decision Science, 20,* 532–544.

Bass, B. M. (1955). Authoritarianism or acquiescence? *Journal of Abnormal and Social Psychology, 51,* 616–623.

Bassili, J. N., & Provencal, A. (1988). Perceiving minorities: A factor-analytic approach. *Personality and Social Psychology Bulletin, 14,* 5–15.

Bastien, D., & Hostager, T. (1998). Jazz as a process of organizational innovation. *Communication Research, 15,* 582–602.

Batson, C. D. (1975). Rational processing or rationalization? The effect of disconfirming information on a stated religious belief. *Journal of Personality and Social Psychology, 32,* 176–184.

Baumeister, R. F. (1997). *Evil: Inside human violence and cruelty.* New York: Freeman.

Baumeister, R. F., Vohs, K. D., & Tice, D. M. (2006). Emotional influences on decision making. In J. P. Forgas (Ed.), *Affect in social thinking and behavior* (pp. 143–159). New York: Psychology Press.

Bayulgen, O., & Arbatli, E. (2013). Cold war redux in US–Russia relations? The effects of U.S. media framing and public opinion of the 2008 Russia–Georgia war. *Communist and Post-Communist Studies, 46,* 513–527.

Bazerman, M. H., Beekun, R. I., & Schoorman, F. D. (1982). Performance evaluation in a dynamic context: A laboratory study of the impact of a prior commitment to the ratee. *Journal of Applied Psychology, 67*, 873–876.

Bazerman, M. H., Giuliano, T., & Appelman, A. (1984). Escalation in individual and group decision making. *Organizational Behavior and Human Performance, 33*, 141–152.

BBC News. (2000, April 1). Turkish troops pursue Kurds.

BBC News. (2002, March 17). Iraqi Kurds recall chemical attack. Retrieved from http://news.bbc.co.uk/1/hi/world/middle_east/1877161.stm

BBC News. (2015). Ukraine profile. Retrieved from www.bbc.com/news/world-Europe-1801012

BBC News (2020, November 2). *Yemen, crisis: Why is there a war?* Retrieved from www.bbc.com/news/world-middle-east-29319423

Beck, A. (1999). *Prisoners of hate: The cognitive basis of anger, hostility and violence.* New York: HarperCollins.

Beck, P., Dalton, R., Greene, S., & Huckfeldt, R. (2002). The social calculus of voting: Interpersonal, media, and organizational influences on presidential choices. *American Political Science Review, 96*, 57–74.

Beeler, J. D. (1998). Effects of counter-explanation on escalation of commitment: An experimental assessment of individual and collective decisions. *Advances in Accounting Behavioral Research, 1*, 85–99.

Beeler, J. D., & Hunton, J. E. (1997). The influence of compensation method and disclosure level on information search strategy and escalation of commitment. *Journal of Behavioral Decision Making, 10*, 77–91.

Begley, S. (2001, May 20). The roots of evil. *Newsweek*. Retrieved from www.newsweek.com/roots-evil-152587

Beitsch, R. (2018). #MeToo has changed our culture. Now it's changing our laws. *Stateline.* Retrieved from www.pewtrusts.org/en/research-and analysis/blogs/stateline/2018/07/31/metoo-has-changed-our-culture-now-its-changing-our-laws

Bejjani, E. (2006, August 23). *Funding Hezbollah: The Iranian connection.* Retrieved from www.frontpagemag.com/Articles/Read.aspx?GUID={4D8A52F8-9B8D-4131-8DA0-1884F7C6C4E2

Belcher, C. (2016). *A Black man in the White House: Obama and the triggering of America's racial-aversion crisis.* New York: Water Street Press.

Bennis, W. G., & Shepard, H. A. (1956). A theory of group development. *Human Relations, 9*, 415–437.

Benoit, W. L., & Benoit-Bryan, J. M. (2013). Debates come to the United Kingdom: A functional analysis of the 2010 British prime minister election debates. *Communication Quarterly, 61*, 463–278.

Bentler, P. M., & Speckart, G. (1981). Attitudes cause behaviors: A structural equation analysis. *Journal of Personality and Social Psychology, 40*, 226–238.

Berejikian, J. D., & Early, B. R. (2013). Loss aversion and foreign policy resolve. *Political Psychology, 34*, 649–671.

Berelson, B., Lazarsfeld, P., & McPhee, W. (1954). *Voting: A study of opinion formation in a presidential campaign.* Chicago: University of Chicago Press.

Berent, M., & Krosnick, J. (1995). The relation between political attitude importance and knowledge structure. In M. Lodge & K. McGraw (Eds.),

Political judgment: Structure and process. Ann Arbor, MI: University of Michigan Press.

Berger, J., Rosenholtz, S. J., & Zelditch, M. (1980). Status organizing processes. *Annual Review of Sociology, 6*, 479–508.

Berkowitz, L. (1989). Frustration-aggression hypothesis: Examination and reformulation. *Psychological Bulletin, 106*, 59–73.

Berscheid, E. (1987). Emotion and Interpersonal communication. In M. Roloff & G. Miller (Eds.), *Interpersonal processes: New directions in communication research.* Thousand Oaks, CA: Sage.

Bertram, B.C.R. (1978). Living in groups: Predators and prey. In P. G. Bateson & R. A. Hinde (Eds.), *Behavioral ecology: An evolutional approach.* London: Blackwell.

Bettenhausen, K., & Murnighan, J. K. (1991). The development of an intragroup norm and the effects of interpersonal structural challenges. *Administrative Science Quarterly, 36*, 20–35.

Bialik, K. (2018). 5 facts about black Americans. Pew Research. Retrieved from www.pewresearch.org/fact-tank/2018/02/22/5-facts-about-blacks-in-the-u-s

Biddle, S. (1998). The past as prologue: Assessing theories of future warfare. *Security Studies, 8*, 1–74.

Bilali, R., & Vollhardt, J. R. (2013). Priming effects of a reconciliation radio drama on historical perspective-taking in the aftermath of mass violence in Rwanda. *Journal of Experimental and Social Psychology, 49*, 144–151.

Billig, M., & Tajfel, H. (1973). Social categorization and similarity in intergroup behavior. *European Journal of Social Psychology, 3*, 27–52.

Birt, R. (1993). Personality and foreign policy: The case of Stalin. *Political Psychology, 15*, 607–626.

Bizman, A., & Amir, Y. (1984). Integration and attitudes. In Y. Amir & S. Sharan (Eds.), *School desegregation.* Hillsdale, NJ: Lawrence Erlbaum.

Blanton, S. L. (1996). Images in conflict: The case of Ronald Reagan and El Salvador. *International Studies Quarterly, 40*, 23–44.

Blascovich, J., Nash, R. F., & Ginsburg, G. P. (1978). Heart rate and competitive decision making. *Personality and Social Psychology Bulletin, 4*, 115–118.

Blass, T. (1991). Understanding behavior in the Milgram obedience experiment: The role of personality, situations, and their interactions. *Journal of Personality and Social Psychology, 60*, 398–413.

Blay, A. D., Kadous, K., & Sawers, K. (2012). The impact of risk and affect on information search efficiency. *Organizational Behavior and Human Decision Processes, 117*(1), 80–87.

Blazak, R. (2020) White boys to terrorist men. *American Behavioral Scientist, 44*, 982–1000.

Blight, J. G. (1992). *The shattered crystal ball: Fear and learning in the Cuban missile crisis.* Boulder, CO: Rowman & Littlefield.

Bloom, M. (2009). Chasing butterflies and rainbows: A critique of Kruglanski et al.'s "Fully committed: Suicide bombers' motivation and the quest for personal significance." *Political Psychology, 30*, 387–395.

Bloom, M. (2011). *Bombshell.* Philadelphia, PA: University of Pennsylvania Press.

Bobo, L. (1983). Whites' opposition to busing: Symbolic racism or realistic group conflict? *Journal of Personality and Social Psychology, 45*, 1196–1210.

Bobo, L., & Smith, R. (1994). From Jim Crow racism to *laissez-faire* racism: An essay on the transformation of racial attitudes in America. In W. Katkin & A. Tyree (Eds.), *Beyond pluralism: Essays on the conceptions of groups and identities in America.* Stanford, CA: Stanford University Press.

Boettcher, W. A. (2005). *Presidential risk behavior in foreign policy: Prudence or peril?* New York: Palgrave.

Boin, A., & 't Hart, P. (2003). Public leadership in times of crisis: Mission impossible? *Public Administration Review, 63*, 55–564.

Boin, A., 't Hart, P., McConnell, A., & Preston, T. (2010). Leadership style, crisis response, and blame management: The case of Hurricane Katrina. *Public Administration, 88*, 706–723.

Bond, C. F., Jr., & Titus, L. J. (1983). Social facilitation: A meta-analysis of 241 studies. *Psychological Bulletin, 94*, 265–292.

Bond, R., & Smith, P. B. (1996). Culture and conformity: A meta-analysis of studies using Asch's line judgment task. *Psychological Bulletin, 119*, 111–137.

Bone, P. (1999). Rwanda: The children's return. Retrieved from http://theage.com.au/news/agenews/pbrwanda.htm

Borkenau, P., Riemann, R., Angleitner, A., & Spinath, F. M. (2001). Genetic and environmental influences on observed personality: Evidence from the German observational study of adult twins. *Journal of Personality and Social Psychology, 80*, 655–668.

Borum, R. (2003). Understanding the terrorist mindset. *FBI Law Enforcement Bulletin*, 7–10.

Borum, R. (2004). *Psychology of terrorism.* Tampa, FL: University of South Florida.

Bos, A.L., Schneider, M.C., & Utz, B.L. (2017). Navigating the political labyrinth: Gender stereotypes and prejudice in U.S. elections. In V. Travis & J. White (Eds.), *APA handbook of the psychology of women.* Washington, DC: American Psychological Association.

Bowen, M. G. (1987). The escalation phenomenon reconsidered: Decision dilemmas or decision errors? *Academy of Management Review, 12*, 52–66.

Bowman-Grieve, L. (2010). Irish republicanism and the internet: Support for new wave. *Perspectives on Terrorism, 4*(2), 22–34.

Boyd, R., & Richerson, P. J. (1985). *Culture and the evolutionary process.* Chicago, IL: University of Chicago Press.

Brader, T., & Valentino, N. A. (2007). Identities, interested, and emotions: Symbolic versus material wellsprings of fear, anger, and enthusiasm. In W. R. Neuman, G. E. Marcus, A. N. Crigler, & M. Michael (Eds.), *The affect effect: Dynamics of emotion in political thinking and behavior.* Chicago: University of Chicago Press.

Brams, S. J. (1985). *Superpower games: Applying game theory to superpower conflict.* New Haven, CT: Yale University Press.

Brändström, A., Bynander, F., & 't Hart, P. (2004). Governing by looking back: Historical analogies and crisis management." *Public Administration, 82*, 191–210.

Brauer, M., Judd, C. M., & Gliner, M. D. (1995). The effects of repeated expressions on attitude polarization during group discussions. *Journal of Personality and Social Psychology, 68*, 1014–1029.

Brawley, L. R., Carron, A. V., & Widmeyer, W. N. (1988). Exploring the relationship between cohesion and group resistance to disruption. *Journal of Sport and Exercise Psychology, 10*, 199–213.

Brehm, J. W. (1976). Responses to loss of freedom: A theory of psychological reactance. In J. W. Thibaut, J. T. Spence, & R. C. Carson (Eds.), *Contemporary topics in social psychology* (pp. 51–78). Morristown, NJ: General Learning Press.

Brewer, M. B. (1979). Ingroup bias in the minimal intergroup situation: A cognitive–motivational analysis. *Psychological Bulletin, 86*, 307–324.

Brewer, M. B. (1988). A dual process model of impression formation. In T. Srull & R. Wyer (Eds.), *Advances in social cognition* (Vol. 1, pp. 1–36). Hillsdale, NJ: Lawrence Erlbaum.

Brewer, M. B., & Brown, R. J. (1998). Intergroup relations. In D. T. Gilbert, S. T. Fiske, & G. Lindzey (Eds.), *The handbook of social psychology* (4th ed., Vol. 2, pp. 554–594). New York: McGraw-Hill.

Brewer, M. B., & Kramer, R. M. (1986). Choice behavior in social dilemmas: Effects of social identity, group size, and decision framing. *Journal of Personality and Social Psychology, 50*, 543–547.

Brewer, M. B., & Miller, N. (1984). Beyond the contact hypothesis: Theoretical perspectives on desegregation. In N. Miller & M. Brewer (Eds.), *Groups in contact: The psychology of desegregation*. New York: Academic Press.

Brickner, M. A., Harkins, S. G., & Ostrom, T. M. (1986). Effects of personal involvement: Thought-provoking implications for social loafing. *Journal of Personality and Social Psychology, 51*, 763–770.

Bridgeman, B. (2003). *Psychology and evolution: The origins of mind*. Thousand Oaks, CA: Sage.

British National Party. (2007). Manifesto. Retrieved from www.bnp.org.uk/?page_id+51

Brockner, J. (1992). The escalation of commitment to a failing course of action: Toward theoretical progress. *Academy of Management Review, 17*, 39–61.

Brockner, J., Rubin, J. Z., & Lang, E. (1981). Face-saving and entrapment. *Journal of Experimental Social Psychology, 17*, 68–79.

Brockner, J., Shaw, M. C., & Rubin, J. Z. (1979). Factors affecting withdrawal from an escalating conflict: Quitting before it's too late. *Journal of Experimental Social Psychology, 15*, 492–503.

Brodie, F. M. (1981). *Richard Nixon: The shaping of his character*. New York: W. W. Norton.

Brody, R. A., & Rothenberg, L. S. (1988). The instability of partisanship and analysis of the 1980 presidential election. *British Journal of Political Science, 18*, 445–465.

Bronstein, J. (2013). Like me! Analyzing the 2012 presidential candidates' Facebook pages. *Online Information Review, 37*, 173–192.

Brown, R. (1974). Further comment on the risky shift. *American Psychologist, 29*, 468–470.

Brown, R. (2000). *Group processes: Dynamics within and between groups*. Oxford: Blackwell.

Brown, R. (2010). *Prejudice: Its social psychology.* Chichester: John Wiley & Sons.

Brown, R. P., Charnsangavej, T., Keough, K. A., Newman, M. L., & Rentfrow, P. (2000). Putting the "affirm" into affirmative action: Preferential selection and academic performance. *Journal of Personality and Social Psychology, 79,* 736–747.

Brown, S. (1987). *The causes and prevention of war.* New York: St. Martin's Press.

Brown, V., & Paulus, P. B. (1996). A simple dynamic model of social factors in group brainstorming. *Small Group Research, 27,* 91–114.

Browning, C. (1992). *Ordinary men: Reserve police battalion 101 and the final solution in Poland.* New York: HarperCollins.

Browning, R. P., & Jacob, H. (1964). Power motivation and the political personality. *Public Opinion Quarterly, 28,* 75–90.

Bruni, F. (2002). *Ambling into history: The unlikely odyssey of George W. Bush.* New York: Harper Collins.

Bruni, F. (2003, April 11). What's in a name? For a Turkish youth, maybe jail. *New York Times,* p. A3.

Buccoliero, L. Bellio, E., Crestini, G., & Arkoudas, A. (2020). Twitter and politics: Evidence from the US presidential elections 2016. *Journal of Marketing Communications, 26,* 88–114.

Buchanan, L., Bui, Q., & Patel, J.K. (2020, July 3). Black Lives Matter may be the largest movement in US history. *New York Times.* Retrieved from www.nytimes.com/interactive/2020/07/03/us/george-floyd-protests-crowd-size.html

Bullock, A., & Stallybrass, O. (1977). *The Harper dictionary of modern thought.* New York: Harper and Row.

Burke, J. P. (1992). *The institutional presidency.* Baltimore, MD: Johns Hopkins University Press.

Burke, J. P. (2004). *Becoming president: The Bush transition, 2000–2003.* Boulder, CO: Lynne Rienner.

Burke, J. P., & Greenstein, F. I. (1991). *How presidents test reality: Decisions on Vietnam, 1954 and 1965.* New York: Russell Sage Foundation.

Burnett, D. G. (2001). *A trial by jury.* New York: Alfred A. Knopf.

Burns, J. M. (1978). *Leadership.* New York: Harper and Row.

Burnstein, E., & Vinokur, A. (1977). Persuasive arguments and social comparison as determinants of attitude polarization. *Journal of Experimental Social Psychology, 13,* 315–332.

Burton, J. (1990). *Conflict: Its resolution and prevention.* London: Macmillan.

Bushart, H. L., Craig, J., & Barnes, M. (1998). *Soldiers of God: White supremacists and their holy war for America.* New York: Pinnacle.

Butler, D. E., & Stokes, D. (1974). *Political change in Britain* (2nd ed.). New York: Macmillan.

Buzbee, S. (2001, September 18). Bush's use of word "crusade" a red flag. *Seattle Post-Intelligencer,* p. A1.

Byars, R.S. (1972). The task/affect quotient. *Comparative Political Studies, 5,* 109–120.

Byars, R.S. (1973). Small group theory and shifting styles of political leadership. *Comparative Political Studies, 5,* 443–469.

Byman, D. (1998). The logic of ethnic terrorism. *Studies in Conflict and Terrorism, 21*, 149–169.

Byrne, H., Stanley, W., & Garst, R. (2000). *Rescuing police reform: A challenge for the new Guatemalan government.* Washington, DC: Washington Office on Latin America.

Cadava, G. (2020). The deep origins of Latino support for Trump. *The New Yorker*, Retrieved from www.newyorker.com/news/the-political-scene/the-deep-origins-of-latino-support-for-trump

Caldwell, D. F., & O'Reilly, C. A. (1982). Response to failure: The effects of choice and responsibility on impression management. *Academy of Management Journal, 25*, 121–136.

Call, C., & Barnett, M. (2000). Looking for a few good cops: Peacekeeping, peacebuilding, and CIVPOL. In T. T. Holm & E. B. Eide (Eds.), *Peacebuilding and police reform* (pp. 43–68). Portland, OR: Frank Cass.

Camacho, L. M., & Paulus, P. B. (1995). The role of social anxiousness in group brainstorming. *Journal of Personality and Social Psychology, 68*, 1071–1080.

Campbell, A. Converse, P., Miller, W., & Stokes, D. (1960). *The American voter*. New York: John Wiley and Sons.

Campbell, C. S. (1986). *Managing the presidency: Carter, Reagan, and the search for executive harmony.* Pittsburgh, PA: University of Pittsburgh Press.

Campbell, D. T. (1958). Common fate, similarity, and other indices of the status of aggregates of persons as social entities. *Behavioral Science, 3*, 14–25.

Campos, J., Brannum, K., & Mastors, E. (2021). *The fetish of peace: The myth of transformational peace.* Lanham, MD: Lexington Books.

Carmack, R. (1992). The story of Santa Cruz Quiché. In R. Carmack (Ed.), *Harvest of violence: The Maya Indian and the Guatemalan crisis.* Norman, OK: University of Oklahoma Press.

Carmines, E., & Merriman, R. (1993). The changing American dilemma: Liberal values and racial policies. In P. Sniderman, P. Tetlock, & E. Carmines (Eds.), *Prejudice, politics and the American dilemma* (pp. 237–255). Stanford, CA: Stanford University Press.

Carnegie Commission on Preventing Deadly Conflict. (1997). *Preventing deadly conflict: Final report.* New York: Carnegie Corporation.

Carraro, L., & Castelli, L. (2010). The implicit and explicit effects of negative political campaigns: Is the source really blamed? *Political Psychology, 31*, 617–645.

Carsey, T, & Layman, G. (2018). Our politics is polarized on more issues than ever before. In D. Hopkins & J. Sides (Eds.), *Political polarization in American politics* (pp. 23–31). New York: Bloomsbury.

Carson, R. C. (1969). *Interaction concepts of personality.* Chicago, IL: Aldine.

Cassels, A. (1975). *Fascism.* New York: Thomas Crowell.

Cassese, E.C. (2019). Partisan dehumanization in American politics. *Political Behavior*, 43, 29–50.

Cassino, D., & Lodge, M. (2007). The primacy of affect in political evaluations. In W. R. Neuman, G. E. Marcus, A. N. Crigler, & M. MacKuen (Eds.), *The affect effect: Dynamics of emotion in political thinking and behavior* (pp. 101–123). Chicago: University of Chicago Press.

Cattell, R. B. (1964). *Personality and social psychology*. San Diego, CA: Knapp.

Cattell, R. B. (1965). *The scientific analysis of personality*. Baltimore, MD: Penguin.

Cattell, R. B., & Child, D. (1975). *Motivation and dynamic structure*. New York: Wiley.

CBS News. (2017). Who are the members of white supremacist groups in America? Retrieved from www.cbsnews.com/news/people-behind-white-supremacist-groups-america

Cehajic, S., Brown, R. J., & Castano, E. (2008). Forgive and forget: Antecedents and consequences of intergroup forgiveness in Bosnia and Herzegovina. *Political Psychology, 29*, 351–367.

Central Intelligence Agency. (2008). Iraq. Retrieved from www.cia.gov/library/publications/the-world-factbook/geos/iz.html

Chaiken, S. (1980). Heuristic versus systematic information processing in the use of source versus message cues in persuasion. *Journal of Personality and Social Psychology, 39*, 752–766.

Chaiken, S. (1987). The heuristic model of persuasion. In M. P. Zanna, J. M. Olson, & C. P. Herman (Eds.), *Social influence: The Ontario symposium* (Vol. 5, pp. 3–39). Hillsdale, NJ: Lawrence Erlbaum.

Chen, S., & Chaiken, S. (1999). The heuristic-systematic model in its broader context. In S. Chaiken & Y. Trope (Eds.), *Dual-process theories in social psychology* (pp. 73–96). New York: Guilford Press.

Chirot, S., & McCauley, C. (2006). *Why not kill them all? The logic and prevention of mass political murder*. Princeton, NJ: Princeton University Press.

Choma, B.L. & Hanoch, Y. (2017). Cognitive ability and authoritarianism: Understanding support for Trump and Clinton. *Personality and Individual Differences, 106*, 287–291.

Chrisafis, A. (2005, March 9). Ready to shoot. *Salon*. Retrieved from www.dir.salon.com/story/news/feature/2005/03/09/irish/index.html

Christian Science Monitor. (2005). Moqtata al-Sadr's militia clashed with Badr fighters, revealing a Shiite divide over the new draft charter. Retrieved from www.csmonitor.com

Cialdini, R. B., & Trost, M. R. (1998). Social influence: Social norms, conformity, and compliance. In D. T. Gilbert, S. T. Fiske, & G. Lindzey (Eds.), *Handbook of social psychology* (pp. 151–192). Boston, MA: McGraw-Hill.

Cillizza, C. (2019, July 23). The day the Tea Party died. CNN. Retrieved from www.cnn.com/2019/07/23/politics/debt-deal-budget-ceiling/index.html

Citrin, J. & Sears, D.O. (2014). *American identity and the politics of multiculturalism*. Cambridge: Cambridge University Press.

Clarke, H.D., Goodwin, M., & Whiteley, P. (2017). *Why Britain voted to leave the European Union*. Cambridge: Cambridge University Press.

Clark, R. D. (1990). Minority influence: The role of argument refutation of the majority position and social support for the minority position. *European Journal of Social Psychology, 20*, 489–497.

Clarke, R. (2004). *Against all enemies: Inside America's war on terror*. New York: Free Press.

Clinton, W. (1998). *One America in the 21st century: The president's initiative on race*. Washington, DC: The White House.

CNN (2018, March 6). The pledge to halt missile tests comes after a busy year of launches by North Korea. *CNN.* Retrieved from www.cnn.com/2018/03/06/asia/north-korea-missile-tests-2017-intl/index.html

CNN Library. (2015, March 2). 1965 Selma to Montgomery March fast facts. Retrieved from www.cnn.com/2013/09/15/us/1965-selma-to-montgomery-march-fast-facts

Coe, K. (2013). Television news, public opinion and the Iraq war: Do wartime rationales matter? *Communication Research, 40,* 486–505.

Cohen, B. (1963). *The press and foreign policy.* Princeton, NJ: Princeton University Press.

Cohen, E. (1996). A revolution in warfare. *Foreign Affairs, 75,* 37–54.

Cohen, S. (2001). *States of denial: Knowing about atrocities and suffering.* Oxford: Blackwell.

Coleman, P. (2011). *The five percent: Finding solutions to seemingly impossible conflicts.* New York: Public Affairs.

Coleman, P. (2021). *The way out: How to overcome toxic polarization.* New York: Columbia University Press.

Condor, S. Tileagă, C., & Billig, M. (2013). Political rhetoric. In L. Huddy, D. Sears, & J. S. Levy (Eds.), *The Oxford handbook of political psychology* (2nd ed., pp. 262–300). Oxford: Oxford University Press.

Conlon, E. J., & Parks, J. M. (1987). Information requests in the context of escalation. *Journal of Applied Psychology, 72,* 344–350.

Conover, P., & Feldman, S. (1991). Where is the schema? Critiques. *American Political Science Review, 85,* 1364–1369.

Conroy, J. (2000). *Unspeakable acts, ordinary people.* New York: Alfred A. Knopf.

Converse, P. E. (1964). The nature of belief systems in mass publics. In D. Apter (Ed.), *Ideology and its discontents* (pp. 206–261).New York: Free Press.

Converse, P. E. (1966). The concept of a normal vote. In A. Campbell, P. E. Converse, W. E. Miller, & D. Stokes (Eds.), *Elections and the political order* (pp. 9–39). New York: Wiley.

Cook, M. (1977). The social skill model and interpersonal attraction. In S. Duck (Ed.), *Theory and practice in interpersonal attraction* (pp. 239–258). New York: Academic Press.

Cook, T. D., & Insko, C. (1968). Persistence of induced attitude change as a function of conclusion reexposure: A laboratory-field experiment. *Journal of Personality and Social Psychology, 9,* 322–328.

Cooper, H.H.A. (1977). What is a terrorist: A psychological perspective. *Legal Medical Quarterly, 1,* 16–32.

Cooper, J. M. (2018). The United States, Mexico, and the war on drugs in the Trump administration. *Faculty Scholarship, 239.* Retrieved from https://scholarlycommons.law.cwsl.edu/fs/239

Cooper, M. (2005, September 12). Dipping his toe into disaster. *Time.*

Corcoran, K. E., Pettinicchio, D., & Young, J.T.N. (2011). The context of control: A cross-national investigation of the link between political institutions, efficacy, and collective action. *British Journal of Social Psychology, 50,* 575–605.

Corneille, O., Yzerbyt, V. Y., Rogier, A., & Buidin, G. (2001). Threat and the group attribution error: When threat elicits judgments of extremity and homogeneity. *Personality and Social Psychology Bulletin, 27,* 427–446.

Corrado, R. R. (1981). A critique of the mental disorder perspective of political terrorism. *International Journal of Law and Psychiatry. 4*, 293–310.

Coser, L. A. (1956). *The functions of social conflict*. Glencoe, IL: Free Press.

Costa, P. T., & McCrae, R. (1992). *Revised NEO Personality Inventory (NEO PI-R) and NEO Five-Factor Inventory (NEO-FFI): Professional manual*. Odessa, FL: Psychological Assessment Resources.

Costa, P. T., Jr., Terracciano, A., & McCrae, R. R. (2001). Gender differences in personality traits across cultures: Robust and surprising findings. *Journal of Personality and Social Psychology, 81*, 322–331.

Cotler, I. (2008, September 30). Forgetting Darfur. *Montreal Gazette*. Retrieved from www.canada.com/montrealgazette

Cottam, M. (1986). *Foreign policy decision making: The influence of cognition*. Boulder, CO: Westview Press.

Cottam, M. (1994). *Images and intervention*. Pittsburgh, PA: University of Pittsburgh Press.

Cottam, M. (2020). Foreign policy decision making in the Trump administration. In S. Renshon & P. Seudfeld (Eds.), *The Trump doctrine and the emerging international system* (pp. 129–153). London: Palgrave Macmillan.

Cottam, M., & Cottam, R. (2001). *Nationalism and politics: The political behavior of nation states*. Boulder, CO: Lynne Rienner.

Cottam, M., Mahdasian, S., & Sarac, M. (2000, March). The degenerate and the rogue: War in Kosovo. Unpublished paper presented at the International Studies Association, Los Angeles.

Cottam, M., & Marenin, O. (1999). International cooperation in the war on drugs: Mexico and the United States. *Policing and Society, 9*, 209–240.

Cottam, M., & Preston, T. (2007, February 28–March 3). Building stronger images of leadership: A framework for integrating image theory and leadership trait analysis (LTA) into a more powerful tool for analyzing leaders-at-a-distance. Paper presented at the 48th Annual Meeting of the International Studies Association, Chicago.

Cottam, R. (1977). *Foreign policy motivation*. Pittsburgh, PA: University of Pittsburgh Press.

Cottee, S., & Hayward, K. (2011). Terrorist (E)motives: The existential attractions of terrorism. *Studies in Conflict & Terrorism, 34*, 963–986.

Cottrell, N. B. (1972). Social facilitation. In C. G. McClintock (Ed.), *Experimental social psychology* (pp. 185–236). New York: Holt, Rinehart, and Winston.

Cottrell, N. B., Wack, D. L., Sekerak, G. J., & Rittle, R. H. (1968). Social facilitation of dominant responses by the presence of an audience and the mere presence of others. *Journal of Personality and Social Psychology, 9*, 245–250.

Council on Foreign Relations. (2007). *Hamas*. Washington, DC: Author. Retrieved from www.cfr.org/publication/8968/#10

Council on Foreign Relations. (2020). *The Rohingya crisis*. Washington, DC: Author. Retrieved from www.cfr.org/backgrounder/Rohingya-crisis

Cox, D., & Jones, R. (2017). *Attitudes on child and family well-being: National and southeast/southwest perspectives*. Retrieved from www.prri.org/research/poll-child-welfare-poverty-race relations

Crabb, C. B., Jr., & Mulcahy, K. V. (1986). *Presidents and foreign policy making: From FDR to Reagan.* Baton Rouge, LA: Louisiana State University Press.

Crane, S. (2007, December 13). In Europe, some still cling to dreams. *Wall Street Journal.* Retrieved from www.online.wsj.com/article/SB119751147863255567.html?mod=googlenews_wsj

Crenshaw, M. (2000). The psychology of terrorism: An agenda for the 21st century. *Political Psychology, 21,* 405–420.

Crenshaw, M. (2004). The political psychology of terrorism. In J. Jost & J. Sidanius (Eds.), *Political psychology: Key readings* (pp. 379–413). New York: Taylor & Francis.

Crenshaw, M. (2009). Intimations of mortality or production lines? The puzzle of "suicide terrorism." *Political Psychology, 30,* 359–364.

Crnobrnja, M. (1994). *The Yugoslav drama.* Montreal: McGill-Queens University Press.

Cronin, T. E. (1980). *The state of the presidency* (2nd ed.). Boston: Little, Brown.

Cropanzano, R. (Ed.) (1993). *Justice in the workplace* (pp. 79–103). Hillsdale, NJ: Lawrence Erlbaum.

Crosby, F. J. (1976). A model of egotistical relative deprivation. *Psychological Review, 83,* 85–113.

Crowson, H.M., & Brandes, J.A. (2017). Differentiating between Donald Trump and Hillary Clinton voters using facets of right-wing authoritarianism and social-dominance orientation: A brief report. *Psychological Reports, 120,* 364–373.

Cubides, F. C. (2001). From private to public violence: The paramilitaries. In C. Berquist, R. Peñaranda, & G. Sánchez (Eds.), *Violence in Colombia, 1990–2000.* Wilmington, DE: Scholarly Resources.

Curry, T. (2008, November 7). Young voters not essential to Obama win. *MSNBC.* Retrieved from www.msnbc.com/id/27582147/page2

Daghagheleh, A. (2018). Ambivalent voting behavior: Ideology, efficacy, and the socioeconomic dynamic of voter turnout in Iran, 1997–2005. *Sociological Forum, 33,* 1023–1044.

Dallek, R. (1979). *Franklin D. Roosevelt and American foreign policy, 1932–1945.* New York: Oxford University Press.

Dallek, R. (1983). *The American style of foreign policy.* New York: Alfred A. Knopf.

D'Alessio, D., & Allen, M. (2000). Media bias in presidential elections: A meta-analysis. *Journal of Communication, 50,* 133–156.

Daly, S. (2005, March 11). The Algerian Salafist group for Call and Combat: A dossier. Jamestown Foundation. Retrieved from www.jamestown.org/terrorism/news/article.php?articleid=2369399

Darby, S. (2020). *Sisters in hate: American women on the front lines of White nationalism.* New York: Little, Brown.

Dasgupta, N., Banji, M. R., & Abelson, R. P. (1999). Group entitativity and group perception: Association between physical features and psychological judgment. *Journal of Personality and Social Psychology, 75,* 991–1005.

Davies, J. (1962). Toward a theory of revolution. *American Sociological Review, 27,* 5–19.

Davies, S. (1992). Introduction: Sowing the seeds of violence. In R. Carmack (Ed.), *Harvest of violence: The Maya Indian and the Guatemalan crisis*. Norman, OK: University of Oklahoma Press.

Davis, W. L., & Phares, E. J. (1967). Internal-external control as a determinant of information-seeking in a social influence situation. *Journal of Personality, 35*, 547–561.

Dawes, C. T., & Fowler, J. H. (2009). Partisanship, voting, and the dopamine D2 receptor gene. *Journal of Politics, 71*, 1157–1171.

Dawkins, R. (1976). *The selfish gene*. New York: Oxford University Press.

Dawson, M. (2001). *Black visions: The roots of contemporary African-American political ideologies*. Chicago: University of Chicago Press.

Day, D. V., Schleicher, D. J., Unckless, A. L., & Hiller, N. J. (2002). Self-mentoring personality at work: A meta-analytic investigation of construct validity. *Journal of Applied Psychology, 87*, 390–401.

Dean, J.W., & Altemeyer, R. (2020). *Authoritarian nightmare: Trump and his followers*. New York: Melville House.

Deaux, K., Reid, A., Mizrahi, K., & Ethier, K. A. (1995). Parameters of social identity. *Journal of Personality and Social Psychology, 68*, 280–291.

Delli-Carpini, M. X., & Keeter, S. (1993). Measuring political knowledge: Putting first things first. *American Journal of Political Science, 37*, 1179–1206.

Delli-Carpini, M. X., & Keeter, S. (1996). *What Americans know about politics and why it matters*. New Haven, CT: Yale University Press.

Denton, R. E., & Kuypers, J. A. (2008). *Politics and communication in America: Campaigns, media and governing in the 21st century*. Long Grove, IL: Waveland Press.

Denver, D. (1994). *Elections and voting behaviour in Britain*. London: Harvester Wheatsheaf.

Denver, D. (1998). The government that could do no right. In A. King, D. Denver, I. McLean, P. Norris, P. Norton, D. Sanders, & P. Seyd (Eds.), *The new Labour triumphs: Britain at the polls*. Chatham, NJ: Chatham House.

Desportes, J. P., & Lemaine, J. M. (1988). The sizes of human groups: An analysis of their distributions. In D. Canter, J. C. Jesuino, L. Soczka, & G. M. Stephenson (Eds.), *Environmental social psychology* (pp. 57–65). Dordrecht: Kluwer.

Deutsch, M. (1969). Socially relevant science: Reflections on some studies of interpersonal conflict. *American Psychologist, 24*, 1076–1092.

Deutsch, M. (1973). *The resolution of conflict*. New Haven, CT: Yale University Press.

Deutsch, M. (1986). The malignant (spiral) process of hostile interaction. In R. K. White (Ed.), *Psychology and the prevention of nuclear war* (pp. 131–154). New York: New York University Press.

Deutscher, I. (1973). *What we say/what we do: Sentiments and acts*. Glenview, IL: Scott Foresman.

Devine, P. G., & Elliot, A. J. (1995). Are racial stereotypes really fading? The Princeton trilogy revisited. *Personality and Social Psychology Bulletin, 21*, 1139–1150.

Diamond, J., & Locy, T. (2002, September 22). Al-Qaida recruits undergo rigorous checks, initiation. *USA Today*. Retrieved from www.intellnet.org/news/2002/09/22/11890-1.htm

Diamond, L. (1988). *Class, ethnicity, and democracy in Nigeria: The failure of the first republic*. Syracuse, NY: Syracuse University Press.
Diamond, L. (2005). *Squandered victory*. New York: Henry Holt.
Dickey, C., & Norland, R. (2006, August 7). The wider war. *Newsweek*.
Dicks, H. V. (1972). *Licensed mass murder: A socio-psychological study of some SS killers*. New York: Basic Books.
Diehl, M., & Stroebe, W. (1987). Productivity loss in brainstorming groups: Toward the solution of a riddle. *Journal of Personality and Social Psychology, 53*, 497–509.
Diener, E. (1976). Effects of prior destructive behavior, anonymity, and group presence on deindividuation and aggression. *Journal of Personality and Social Psychology, 33*, 497–507.
Diener, E. (1979). Deindividuation, self-awareness and disinhibition. *Journal of Personality and Social Psychology, 37*, 1160–1171.
Dietrich, B. J., Lasley, S., Mondak, J. J., Remmel, M. L., & Turner, J. (2012). Personality and legislative politics: The big five trait dimensions among U.S. state legislators. *Political Psychology, 33*, 195–210.
Dietz-Uhler, B. (1996). The escalation of commitment in political decision-making groups: A social identity approach. *European Journal of Social Psychology, 26*, 611–629.
Dietz-Uhler, B. (1999). Defensive reactions to group-relevant information. *Group Processes and Intergroup Relations, 2*, 17–29.
Dijksterhuis, A., Aarts, H., & Smith, P. K. (2005). The power of the subliminal: On subliminal persuasion and other potential applications. In R. R. Hassin, J. S. Uleman, & J. A. Bargh (Eds.), *The new unconscious* (pp. 77–106). New York: Oxford University Press.
Dillon, M. (1989). *The Shankill butchers: A case study of mass murder*. London: Arrow Books.
DiMaggio, A. (2011). *The rise of the Tea Party*. New York: Monthly Review Press.
Dion, K. L. (1979). Intergroup conflict and intragroup cohesion. In W. G. Austin & S. Worchel (Eds.), *The social psychology of intergroup relations* (pp. 211–224). Pacific Grove, CA: Brooks/Cole.
DiRenzo, G.J. (1974). Perspectives on personality and political behavior. In G. I. DiRenzo (Ed.), *Personality and politics* (pp. 3–28). Garden City, NY: Anchor Books.
Dirilen-Gumas, O. (2017). Cross-cultural comparison of political leaders' operational codes. *International Journal of Psychology, 51*, 35–44.
Dixon, P. (2012). In defence of politics: Interpreting the peace process and the future of Northern Ireland. *The Political Quarterly, 83*, 265–276.
Doder, D., & Branson, L. (1999). *Milosevic: Portrait of a tyrant*. New York: Free Press.
Doise, W. (1969). Intergroup relations and polarization of individual and collective judgments. *Journal of Personality and Social Psychology, 12*, 136–143.
Dollard, J., Doob, L., Miller, N., Mowrer, O., & Sears, R. (1939). *Frustration and aggression*. New Haven, CT: Yale University Press.
Dowd, M. (2001, July 4). The relaxation response. *New York Times*, p. A1.
Dowd, M., & Friedman, T. (1990, March 6). The fabulous Bush and Baker boys. *New York Times Magazine*, 58–64.

Dragojlovic, N. I. (2011). Priming and the Obama effect on public evaluations of the United States. *Political Psychology, 32*, 989–1006.

Draper, R. (2007). *Dead certain: The presidency of George W. Bush*. New York: Free Press.

Dreben, E., Fiske, S., & Hastie, R. (1979). The dependence of item and evaluative information: Impression and recall order effects in behavior-based impression formation. *Journal of Personality and Social Psychology, 37*, 1758–1768.

Driver, M. J. (1977). Individual differences as determinants of aggression in the inter-nation simulation. In M. G. Hermann (Ed.), *A psychological examination of political leaders* (pp. 337–353). New York: Free Press.

Druckman, J. N. (2004). Priming the vote: Campaign effects in a U.S. senate election. *Political Psychology, 25*, 577–594.

Druckman, J. N., & Chong, D. (2007). A theory of framing and opinion formation in competitive elite environments. *Journal of Communication, 57*, 99–118.

Druckman, J. N., & Holmes, J. W. (2004). Does presidential rhetoric matter? Priming and presidential approval. *Political Science Quarterly, 34*, 755–778.

Druckman, J. N., Jacobs, L., & Ostermeier, E. (2004). Candidate strategies to prime issue and image. *Journal of Politics, 66*, 1180–1202.

Drury, J., & Reicher, S. (2009). Collective psychological empowerment as a model of social change: Researching crowds and power. *Journal of Social Issues, 65*, 707–725.

Duckitt, J. (1994). *The social psychology of prejudice*. Westport, CT: Praeger.

Duckitt, J., Bizumic, B., Krauss, S. W., & Heled, E. (2010). A tripartite approach to right-wing authoritarianism: The authoritarianism-conservatism-traditionalism model. *Political Psychology, 31*, 685–715.

Duckitt, J., & Mphuthing, T. (1998). Political power and race relations in South Africa: African attitudes before and after the transition. *Political Psychology, 19*, 809–832.

Duelfer, C. A., & Dyson, S.B. (2011). Chronic misperception and international conflict: The U.S.–Iraq experience. *International Security, 36*, 73–100.

Duffy, M. (2002, May 6). Trapped by his own instincts. *Time*, pp. 24–29.

Dunn, L. A. (1982). *Controlling the bomb: Nuclear proliferation in the 1980s*. New Haven, CT: Yale University Press.

Dunn, T. (1996). *The militarization of the U.S.-Mexico Border, 1978–1992*. Austin, TX: University of Texas, Center for Mexican American Studies.

Durand, V. M. (1985). Employee absenteeism: A selective review of antecedents and consequences. *Journal of Organizational Behavior Management, 7*, 135–167.

Durkheim, E. (1966 [1938]). *The rules of sociological method*. New York: Free Press.

Dyer, W. G. (1987). *Team building: Issues and alternatives* (2nd ed.). Reading, MA: Addison-Wesley.

Dyson, S. B. (2001). Drawing policy implications from the "operational code" of a "new" political actor: Russian president Vladimir Putin. *Policy Sciences, 34*, 329–346.

Dyson, S. B., & Preston, T. (2006). Individual characteristics of leaders and the use of analogy in foreign policy decision making. *Political Psychology, 27*, 265–288.

Eades, L. M. (1999). *The end of apartheid in South Africa.* Westport, CT: Greenwood Press.

Eagly, A. H., & Carli, L. (2007). *Through the labyrinth: The truth about how women become leaders.* Boston, MA: Harvard Business School Press.

Eagly, A. H., & Chaiken, S. (1998). Attitude structure and function. In D. T. Gilbert, S. T. Fiske, & G. Lindzey (Eds.), *The handbook of social psychology* (4th ed.). New York: McGraw-Hill.

Easton, D., & Dennis, J. (1973). Governing authorities. In J. Dennis (Ed.), *Socialization to politics* (pp. 59–81). New York: John Wiley and Sons.

Edgerly, S., Bode, L., Kim, Y. M., & Shah, D. (2013). Campaigns go social: Are Facebook, YouTube, and Twitter changing elections? In T. Ridout (Ed.), *New directions in media and politics* (pp. 82–99). New York: Routledge.

Edwards, G. S., & Rushin, S. (2018). The effect of President Trump's election on hate crimes. *SSRN.* Retrieved from https://papers.ssrn.com/sol3/papers.cfm?abstract_id=3102652

Ehrlich, P., & Liu, J. (2006). Socioeconomic and demographic roots of terrorism. In J. Forest (Ed.), *The making of a terrorist: recruitment, training, and root causes* (pp. 160–171). Westport, CT: Praeger.

Eiser, R. J., & Stroebe, W. (1972). *Categorization and social judgment.* New York: Academic Press.

El Gazzar, N. (2013). The role of social media in the formation of public opinion towards Islamists: A content analysis. *Journal of Arab & Muslim Media Research, 6*, 35–49.

Elms, A. C., & Milgram, S. (1966). Personality characteristics associated with obedience and defiance toward authoritative command. *Journal of Experimental Research in Personality, 2*, 282–289.

Emerson, R. (1960). *From empire to nation.* Boston, MA: Beacon Press.

Emmons, R. (1997). Motives and goals. In R. Hogan, J. Johnson, & S. Briggs (Eds.), *Handbook of personality psychology* (pp. 485–512). New York: Academic Press.

Enders, A.M. & Armaly, M.T. (2019). The differential effects of actual and perceived polarization. *Political Behavior, 41*, 815–839.

Enjolras, B., Kari Steen-Johnsen, K., & Wollebæk, D. (2012). Social media and mobilization to offline demonstrations: Transcending participatory divides? *New Media and Society, 15*, 890–908.

Entman, R. (1993). Framing: Toward clarification of a fractured paradigm. *Journal of Communication, 43*, 293–300.

Epstein, S. (1979). The stability of behavior: I. On predicting most of the people most of the time. *Journal of Personality and Social Psychology, 7*, 1097–1126.

Erikson, E. H. (1950). *Childhood and society.* New York: W. W. Norton.

Erikson, E. H. (1958). *Young man Luther.* New York: W. W. Norton.

Erikson, E. H. (1969). *Gandhi's truth.* New York: W. W. Norton.

Esses, V. M., & Dovidio, J. F. (2002). The role of emotions in determining willingness to engage in intergroup contact. *Personality and Social Psychology Bulletin, 28*, 1202–1214.

Etheredge, L. S. (1978). *A world of men: The private sources of American foreign policy*. Cambridge, MA: MIT Press.
Ewen, R. (1998). *An introduction to theories of personality* (5th ed.). Mahwah, NJ: Lawrence Erlbaum.
Eysenk, H. J. (1975). *The inequality of man*. San Diego, CA: Edits.
Eysenk, H. J. (1979). The conditioning model of neurosis. *Behavior and Brain Sciences, 2*, 155–199.
Ezekiel, R. (1996). *The racist mind: Portraits of American neo-Nazis*. New York: Penguin.
Falbo, T. (1977). The multidimensional scaling of power strategies. *Journal of Personality and Social Psychology, 35*, 537–548.
Fallows, J. (2006). *Blind into Baghdad: America's war in Iraq*. New York: Vintage Books.
Farrar, L. L., Jr. (1988). The limits of choice: July 1914 reconsidered. In M. Small & D. Singer (Eds.), *International war: An anthology* (pp. 264–287). Homewood, IL: Dorsey.
Fazio, R. H., & Williams, C. (1986). Attitude accessibility as a moderator of the attitude-perception and attitude-behavior relations: an investigation of the 1984 presidential election. *Journal of Personality and Social Psychology, 51*, 505–514.
Feaver, P. D. (1992/1993). Command and control in emerging nuclear nations. *International Security, 17*, 160–187.
Feaver, P. D., & Niou, E. (1996). Managing nuclear proliferation: Condemn, strike, or assist? *International Studies Quarterly, 40*, 209–234.
Federico, C., & Sidanius, J. (2002). Sophistication and the antecedents of Whites' racial policy attitudes. *Public Opinion Quarterly, 66*, 145–176.
Feldman, D. C. (1984). The development and enforcement of group norms. *Academy of Management Review, 9*, 47–53.
Festinger, L. (1950). Informal social communication. *Psychological Review, 57*, 271–282.
Festinger, L. (1954). A theory of social comparison processes. *Human Relations, 7*, 117–140.
Festinger, L. (1957). *A theory of cognitive dissonance*. Evanston, IL: Row, Peterson.
Festinger, L., Schachter, S., & Back, K. (1950). *Social pressures in informal groups*. New York: Harper.
Fields, R. (1979). Child terror victims and adult terrorists. *Journal of Psychohistory, 7*, 71–75.
Fields, R., Elbedour, S., & Abu Hein, F. (2002). The Palestinian suicide bomber. In C. Stout (Ed.), *The psychology of terrorism: Clinical aspects and responses* (pp. 193–223). Westport, CT: Praeger.
Fijalkowski, J. (1996). Aggressive nationalism and immigration in Germany. In R. Caplan & J. Feffer (Eds.), *Europe's new nationalism: States and minorities in conflict*. Oxford: Oxford University Press.
Fiorina, M. P. (1981). *Retrospective voting in American national elections*. New Haven, CT: Yale University Press.
Fishbein, M., & Ajzen, I. (1972). Attitudes and opinions. *Annual Review of Psychology, 23*, 487–544.
Fishbein, M., & Ajzen, I. (1975). *Belief, attitude, intention, and behavior: An introduction to theory and research*. Reading, MA: Addison-Wesley.

Fishbein, M., & Ajzen, I. (1980). Predicting and understanding consumer behavior: Attitude-behavior correspondence. In I. Ajzen & M. Fishbein (Eds.), *Understanding attitudes and predicting social behavior* (pp. 130–147). Englewood Cliffs, NJ: Prentice Hall.

Fisher, R. J. (1990). Needs theory, social identity and an eclectic model of conflict. In J. Burton (Ed.), *Conflict: Human needs theory* (pp. 89–112). New York: St. Martin's Press.

Fisher, R. J. (2001). Cyprus: The failure of mediation and the escalation of an identity-based conflict to an adversarial impasse. *Journal of Peace Research, 38,* 307–326.

Fiske, S. (1998). Stereotyping, prejudice, and discrimination. In D. T. Gilbert, S. T. Fiske, & G. Lindzey (Eds.), *The handbook of social psychology* (4th ed., Vol. 2, pp. 357–411). New York: McGraw-Hill.

Fiske, S., & Pavelchak, M. (1986). Category-based vs. piecemeal-based affective responses: Developments in schema-triggered affect. In R. Sorrentino & E. Higgings (Eds.), *Handbook of motivation and cognition* (pp. 167–203). New York: Guilford Press.

Fiske, S., & Taylor, S. E. (1991). *Social cognition*. New York: McGraw-Hill.

Fleeson, W. (2004). Moving personality beyond the person-situation debate. *Current Directions in Psychological Science, 13,* 83–87.

Flint, J., & de Waal, A. (2005). *Darfur: A short history of a long war.* London: Zed Books.

Fodor, E. M. (1985). The power motive, group conflict, and physiological arousal. *Journal of Personality and Social Psychology, 49,* 1408–1415.

Fodor, E. M., & Farrow, D. L. (1979). The power motive as an influence on the use of power. *Journal of Personality and Social Psychology, 37,* 2091–2097.

Fodor, E. M., & Smith, T. (1982). The power motive as an influence on group decision making. *Journal of Personality and Social Psychology, 42,* 178–185.

Folger, R. (1986). A referent cognitions theory of relative deprivation. In J. M. Olson, C. P. Herman, & M. P. Zanna (Eds.), *Relative deprivation and social comparison: The Ontario Symposium* (Vol. 4, pp. 217–242). Hillsdale, NJ: Lawrence Erlbaum.

Foner, E., & Garraty, J. A. (1991). *The reader's companion to American history*. Boston: Houghton Mifflin. Retrieved from www.history.com/topics/black-history

Ford, R. T. (2008). *The race card: How bluffing about bias makes race relations worse.* New York: Farrar, Straus & Giroux.

Fording, R.C., & Schram, S.F. (2020). *Hard white: The mainstreaming of racism in American politics.* Oxford: Oxford University Press.

Forsyth, D. R. (1990). *Group dynamics*. Pacific Grove, CA: Brooks/Cole.

Foschi, M., Warriner, G. K., & Hart, S. D. (1985). Standards, expectations, and interpersonal influence. *Social Psychology Quarterly, 48,* 108–117.

Fowler, J. H., Baker, L. A., & Dawes, C. T. (2008). Genetic variation in political participation. *American Political Science Review, 102,* 233–248.

Fox, F., & Staw, B. M. (1979). The trapped administrator: The effects of job insecurity and policy resistance upon commitment to a course of action. *Administrative Science Quarterly, 24,* 449–471.

Fowler, J., & Dawes, C. (2008). Two genes predict voter turnout. *Journal of Politics, 70,* 579–594.

Francis, A. (2017). *Twilight of American sanity: A psychiatrist analyzes the age of Trump.* New York: HarperCollins.

Franklin, C. H. (1992). Measurement and dynamics of party identification. *Political Behavior, 14,* 297–309.

Franklin, C. H., & Jackson, J. E. (1983). The dynamics of party identification. *American Political Science Review, 77,* 957–973.

Fredrickson, G. (1999). Models of American ethnic relations: A historical perspective. In D. Prentice & D. Miller (Eds.), *Cultural divides: Understanding and overcoming group conflict.* Thousand Oaks, CA: Sage.

Freedman, J., & Fraser, S. (1966). Compliance without pressure: The foot-in-the-door technique. *Journal of Personality and Social Psychology, 4,* 195–202.

Freedman, L. (1981). *The evolution of nuclear strategy.* London: Macmillan.

Freedman, L., & Karsh, E. (1993). *The Gulf conflict, 1990–1991: Diplomacy and war in the new world order.* Princeton, NJ: Princeton University Press.

Freeman, A. (1999, June 11). Turkish Kurds endure conditions "just like Kosovo." *Globe and Mail,* p. A1.

French, J. A., Smith, K. B., Alford, J. R., Guck, A., Birnie, A. K., & Hibbing, J. R. (2014). Cortisol and politics: Variance in voting behavior is predicted by baseline cortisol levels. *Physiology & Behavior, 133,* 61–67.

French, J.R.P., & Raven, B. (1959). The bases of social power. In D. Cartwright (Ed.), *Studies in social power* (pp. 150–167). Ann Arbor, MI: Institute for Social Research.

Freud, S. (1950/1932). Letter to Albert Einstein, September 1932. Reprinted in W. Ebenstein, Ed., *Great political thinkers: Plato to the present* (pp. 804–810). New York: Rinehart.

Freud, S. (1950). *Beyond the pleasure principle.* New York: Liveright.

Freud, S. (1962). *Civilization and its discontents.* New York: W. W. Norton.

Frey, D. (1986). Recent research on selective exposure to information. In L. Berkowitz (Ed.), *Advances in experimental social psychology* (pp. 41–80). New York: Academic Press.

Frey, W. (2020). The nation is diversifying even faster than predicted according, to new census data. Brookings. Retrieved from www.brookings.edu/research/new-census-data-shows

Freyre, G. (1956). *The masters and the slaves (Casa-Grande and Senzala): A study in the development of Brazilian civilization* (S. Putnam, Trans.). New York: Alfred A. Knopf.

Friedland, N. (1976). Social influence via threats. *Journal of Experimental Social Psychology, 12,* 552–563.

Frijda, N. (1986). *The emotions.* Cambridge: Cambridge University Press.

Fromm, E. (1941). *Escape from freedom.* New York: Holt, Rinehart, and Winston.

Fromm, E. (1955). *The sane society.* New York: Holt, Rinehart, and Winston.

Fromm, E. (1964). *The heart of man.* New York: Holt, Rinehart, and Winston.

Frontline (1998, March 25). *100 days of slaughter: The triumph of evil.* PBS.

Fuller, S. R., & Aldag, R. J. (1997). Challenging the mindguards: Moving small group analysis beyond groupthink. In B. Sundelius, P. 't Hart, & E.

Stern (Eds.), *Beyond groupthink: Group decision making in foreign policy*. Ann Arbor, MI: University of Michigan Press.

Funder, D. C. (2010). *The personality puzzle*. New York: W. W. Norton.

Funk, C. (1999). Bringing the candidate into models of candidate evaluation. *Journal of Politics, 61*, 700–720.

Funk, C. (2013). Genetic foundations of political behavior. In L. Huddy, D. O. Sears, & J. S. Levy (Eds.), *The Oxford handbook of political psychology* (2nd ed., pp. 237–261). New York: Oxford University Press.

Funk, C. L., Smith, K. B., Alford, J. R., & Hibbing, J. R. (2010, September 2–5). Toward a modern view of political man: Genetic and environmental transmission of political orientations from attitude intensity to political participation. Paper presented at the Annual Meetings of the American Political Science Association, Washington, DC.

Funk, C. L., Smith, K. B., Alford, J. R., Hibbing, M. V., Eaton, N. R., Krueger, R. F., ... Hibbing, J. R. (2013). Genetic and environmental transmission of political orientations. *Political Psychology, 34*, 805–819.

Gaddis, J. L. (1992). *The United States and the end of the Cold War: Implications, reconsiderations, provocations*. New York: Oxford University Press.

Gaddis, J. L. (1997). *We now know: Rethinking Cold War history*. New York: Oxford University Press.

Gaertner, S., & Dovidio, J. (1986). The aversive form of racism. In J. F. Dovidio & S. L. Gaertner (Eds.), *Prejudice, discrimination and racism* (pp. 61–89). Orlando, FL: Academic Press.

Gage, N., Leavitt, G., & Stone, G. (1957). The psychological meaning of acquiescence set for authoritarianism. *Journal of Abnormal and Social Psychology, 55*, 98–103.

Galinsky, A., & Moskowitz, G. (2000). Perspective-taking: Decreasing stereotype expression, stereotype accessibility, and in-group favoritism. *Journal of Personality and Social Psychology, 78*, 708–724.

Gallagher, M. E., & Allen, S. H. (2014). Presidential personality: Not just a nuisance. *Political Psychology, 10*, 1–21.

Gallup Center. (1999). Gay and lesbian rights. Retrieved from www.Gallup.com/poll/1651/gay-lesbian-rights

Gallup Poll. (2000). One in five Americans unaware that either Bush or Gore is a likely presidential nominee. Retrieved from www.gallup.com

Gamson, W. A. (1961). An experimental test of a theory of coalition formation. *American Sociological Review, 26*, 565–573.

Gamson, W. A. (1964). Experimental studies of coalition formation. In L. Berkowitz (Ed.), *Advances in experimental social psychology* (Vol. 1, pp. 82–110). New York: Academic Press.

Gamson, W. A. (1992). The social psychology of collective action. In A. D. Morris & C. M. Mueller (Eds.), *Frontiers in social movement theory* (Vol. 1, pp. 82–110). New York: Academic Press.

Gangestad, S. W., & Snyder, M. (2000). Self-monitoring: Appraisal and reappraisal. *Psychological Bulletin, 126*, 530–555.

Ganz, N. (2010). Leading change: Leadership, organization, and social movements. In N. Nohira & R. Kharana (Eds.), *Handbook of leadership: Theory and practice* (pp. 507–526). Cambridge, MA: Harvard Business School.

Gaouette, N. (2008, September 19). Hispanics souring on situation in U.S. *Idaho Spokesman Review*, p. A4.

Gardner, W., & Martinko, M. (1996). Using the Myers-Briggs type indicator to study managers: A literature review and research agenda. *Journal of Management, 22*, 45–83.

Garrett, R.K. (2019). Social media's contribution to political misperceptions in U.S. presidential elections. *PloS ONE, 14*, doi:10.1371/journal.pone.0213500.

Gartenstein-Ross, D. (2007). *My year inside radical Islam*. New York: Penguin.

Gautney, H. (2011, October 10). What is Occupy Wall Street? The history of leaderless movements. *Washington Post*. Retrieved from www.washingtonpost.com/national/on-leadershp/what-is-occupy-wall-street

Gazzaniga, M., Ivry, R., & Mangun, G. (Eds.). (2014). *Cognitive neuroscience V*. Cambridge, MA: MIT Press.

Geiger, S. W., Robertson, C. J., & Irwin, J. G. (1998). The impact of cultural values on escalation of commitment. *International Journal of Organizational Analysis, 6*, 165–176.

Gellman, B. (2008). *Angler: The Cheney vice presidency*. New York: Penguin.

Gelvin, J. L. (2012). *The Arab uprisings: What everyone needs to know*. Oxford: Oxford University Press.

George, A. L. (1969). The "operational code": A neglected approach to the study of political leaders and decision making. *International Studies Quarterly, 13*, 190–222.

George, A. L. (1979). The causal nexus between cognitive beliefs and decision making behavior: The "operational code" belief system. In L. Falkowski (Ed.), *Psychological models in international politics* (pp. 95–123). Boulder, CO: Westview Press.

George, A. L. (1980). *Presidential decisionmaking in foreign policy: The effective use of information and advice*. Boulder, CO: Westview Press.

George, A. L. (1991). *Forceful persuasion: An alternative to war*. Washington, DC: U.S. Institute of Peace.

George, A. L. & George, J. L. (1964). *Woodrow Wilson and Colonel House: A personality study*. New York: Dover.

George, A. L., & George, J. L. (1998). *Presidential personality and performance*. Boulder, CO: Westview Press.

George, A. L., & Smoke, R. (1974). *Deterrence in American foreign policy*. New York: Columbia University Press.

George, A. L., & Stern, E. (2002). Harnessing conflict in foreign policy making: From devil's advocate to multiple advocacy. *Presidential Studies Quarterly, 32*, 484–508.

George, J., & Wilcox, L. (1996). *American extremists: Militias, supremacists, Klansmen, communists and others*. New York: Prometheus Books.

Gifford, R., & O'Connor, B. (1987). The interpersonal circumplex as a behavior map. *Journal of Personality and Social Psychology, 52*, 1019–1026.

Giglio, M. (2020). Civil war is here, right now. *The Atlantic*. Retrieved from https://longreads.com/picks/civil-war-is-here-right-now

Gilligan, J. (1997). *Violence: Reflections on a national epidemic*. New York: Vintage Books.

Gitlin, T. (2012). *Occupy nation: The roots, the spirit, and the promise of Occupy Wall Street*. New York: HarperCollins.

Ginges, J., Atran, S., Sachdeva, S., & Medin, D. (2011). Psychology out of the laboratory: The challenge of violent extremism. *American Psychologist.* Retrieved from http://artisresearch.com/articles/Ginges_Atran_Sachdeva_Medin_Violent_Extremism.pdf

Gjelstad, J., & Njolstad, O. (Eds.) (1996). *Nuclear rivalry and international order.* London: Sage.

Glad, B. (1980). *Jimmy Carter: In search of the great White House.* New York: W. W. Norton.

Glad, B. (1983). Black-and-white thinking: Ronald Reagan's approach to foreign policy. *Political Psychology, 4,* 33–76.

Glad, B. (1989). Reagan's midlife crisis and the turn to the right. *Political Psychology, 10,* 593–624.

Glenn, C. (2017). Libya's Islamists: Who they are – and what they want. *Wilson Center.* Retrieved from www.wilsoncenter.org/article/libyas-islamists-who-they-are-and-what-they-want

Gliebe, E. (2007, May/June). The people that shall dwell alone: An explanation of Jewish behavior. National Vanguard. Retrieved from www.natwan.com

Global Security. (2008). Sustainable peace key to post-genocide reconciliation. Retrieved from www.globalsecurity.org/military/library/news/2008/08/mil-080826-irin01.htm

Glynn, C., Herbst, S., O'Keefe, G., & Shapiro, R. (1999). *Public opinion.* Boulder, CO: Westview Press.

Goertz, G. (2004). Constraints, compromises, and decision-making. *Journal of Conflict Resolution, 48,* 14–38.

Goldberg, J. (2005, October 31). Breaking ranks: What turned Brent Scowcroft against the Bush administration? *New Yorker,* pp. 54–65.

Goldie, R., & Murphy, J. (2010). Embedding the peace process: The role of leadership, change and government in implementing key reforms in policing and local government in Northern Ireland. *International Journal of Peace Studies,* 15, 33–58.

Goltz, S. M. (1992). A sequential learning analysis of decisions in organizations to escalate investments despite continuing costs or losses. *Journal of Applied Behavior Analysis, 25,* 561–574.

Goltz, T. (2012). The successes of the spin doctors: Western media reporting on the Nagorno Karabakh conflict. *Journal of Muslim Minority Affairs, 32,* 186–195.

Goodwin, M.J. (2017). Brexit: Causes and consequences. *Japan Spotlight.* Retrieved from www.jef.or.jp/journal/pdf/216th_Recent_JEF_Activity_02.pdf

Graber, D. (1984). *Processing the news: How people tame the information tide.* New York: Longman.

Graham, D.A. (2019, August). Trump's white identity politics appeals to two different groups. *The Atlantic.* Retrieved from www.theatlantic.com/ideas/archive/2019/08/who-does-trumps-white-identity-politics-reach/595189

Graham-Brown, S., & Sackur, Z. (1995). The Kurds, a regional issue. Retrieved from www.unhcr.ch/refworld/country/writenet

Grant, A. (2013, September 18). Goodbye to MBTI: The fad that won't die. *Psychology Today.* Retrieved from www.psychologytoday.com/blog/give-and-take/201309/goodbye-mbti-the-fad-won-t-die

Green, D. P., Abelson, R. P., & Garnett, M. (1999). The distinctive political views of hate-crime perpetrators and white supremacists. In D. A. Prentice & D. T. Miller (Eds.), *Cultural divides: Understanding and overcoming group conflict* (pp. 429–464). New York: Sage.

Greenstein, F. I. (1969). *Personality and politics: Problems of evidence, inference, and conceptualization.* Chicago, IL: Markham.

Greenstein, F. I. (1982). *The hidden-hand presidency: Eisenhower as leader.* New York: Basic Books.

Greenstein, F. I. (1988). *Leadership in the modern presidency.* Cambridge, MA: Harvard University Press.

Greenstein, F. I. (2000). *The presidential difference: Leadership style from FDR to Clinton.* New York: Free Press.

Greer, C. R., & Stephens, G. K. (2001). Escalation of commitment: A comparison of differences between Mexican and U.S. decision-makers. *Journal of Management, 27,* 51–78.

Griffin, J. (2017). Motley fringe: The moral and political psychology of the altright's radicalization pipeline. Unpublished doctoral dissertation, Washington State University.

Griffith, J., & Greenlees, J. (1993). Group cohesion and unit versus individual deployment of U.S. Army reservists in Operation Desert Storm. *Psychological Reports, 73,* 272–274.

Groeling, T., & Kernell, S. (1998). Is network news coverage of the president biased? *Journal of Politics, 60,* 1063–1087.

Groff, B. D., Baron, R. S., & Moore, D. L. (1983). Distraction, attentional conflict, and drive like behavior. *Journal of Experimental Social Psychology, 19,* 359–380.

Groshek, J., & Ahmed Al-Rawi, A. (2013). Public sentiment and critical framing in social media content during the 2012 U.S. presidential campaign. *Social Science Computer Review, 31*(5), 563–576.

Gross, K. (2008). Framing persuasive appeals: Episodic and thematic framing, emotional response, and policy opinion. *Political Psychology, 29,* 169–192.

Gross, K., & D'Ambrosio, L. (2004). Framing emotional responses. *Political Psychology, 25,* 1–29.

Grosser, D. (1992). The dynamics of German reunification. In D. Grosser (Ed.), *German unification: The unexpected challenge* (pp. 1–20). Oxford: Berg.

Gruenfeld, D.H. (1995). Status, ideology, and integrative complexity on the U.S. Supreme Court: Rethinking the politics of political decision making. *Journal of Personality and Social Psychology, 68,* 5–20.

Gulati, G. J. (2011). News frames and story triggers in the media's coverage of human trafficking. *Human Rights Review, 12*(3), 363–379.

Gunter, M. (1990). *The Kurds in Turkey.* Boulder, CO: Westview Press.

Gurr, T. R. (1970). *Why men rebel.* Princeton, NJ: Princeton University Press.

Gurr, T. R. (1994). Peoples against states: Ethnopolitical conflict and the changing world system. *International Studies Quarterly, 38,* 347–377.

Haas, M. L. (2001). Prospect theory and the Cuban missile crisis. *International Studies Quarterly, 45,* 241–270.

Hackman, J. R., Brousseau, K. R., & Weiss, J. A. (1976). The interaction of task design and group performance strategies in determining group effectiveness. *Organizational Behavior and Human Performance, 16,* 350–365.

Hackman, J. R., & Lawler, E. (1971). Employee reactions to job characteristics. *Journal of Applied Psychology, 55,* 259–286.

Hackman, J. R., & Morris, C. G. (1975). Group tasks, group interaction process, and group performance effectiveness: A review and proposed integration. In L. Berkowitz (Ed.), *Advances in experimental social psychology* (Vol. 8, pp. 47–99). New York: Academic Press.

Hagan, J. D. (2001). Does decision making matter? *International Studies Review, 3,* 5–46.

Hagerty, D. T. (1995/1996). Nuclear deterrence in South Asia: The 1990 Indo-Pakistani crisis. *International Security, 20,* 79–115.

Hagerty, D. T. (1998). *The consequences of nuclear proliferation: Lessons from South Asia.* Cambridge, MA: MIT Press.

Hagerty, M. R. (2000). Social comparisons of incomes in one's community: Evidence from national surveys of income and happiness. *Journal of Personality and Social Psychology, 78,* 764–771.

Hahl, O., Kim, M., & Sivan, E. (2018). The authentic appeal of the lying demagogue: Proclaiming the deeper truth about political illegitimacy. *American Sociological Review, 83,* 1–33.

Hale, H. (2014, August 29). Russian nationalism and the logic of the Kremlin's actions on Ukraine. *The Guardian.* Retrieved from www.theguardian.com/world/2014/aug/29/russian-nationalism-kremlin-actions-ukraine

Hall, C., & Lindzey, G. (1970). *Theories of personality* (2nd ed.). New York: John Wiley and Sons.

Hamasaeed, S., & Nada, G. (2020). *Iraq timeline: Since the 2003 war.* Washington, DC: United States Institute for Peace. Retrieved from www.usip.org/iraq-timeline-2003-war

Hamm, M.S. (1993). *American Skinheads: The Criminology and Control of Hate Crime.* Westport, CT: Praeger.

Hammond, R. A., & Axelrod, R. (2006). The evolution of ethnocentrism. *Journal of Conflict Resolution, 50,* 1–11.

Hanchard, M. (1993). Movimento negro in Brazil. In Kay Warren (Ed.), *The violence within: Cultural and political opposition in divided nations* (pp. 83–106). Boulder, CO: Westview Press.

Handley, I. M., Lassiter, G. D., Nickell, E. F., & Herchenroeder, L. M. (2004). Affect and automatic mood maintenance. *Journal of Experimental Social Psychology, 40,* 106–112.

Haney, P. J. (1997). *Organizing for foreign policy crises: Presidents, advisers, and the management of decision making.* Ann Arbor, MI: University of Michigan Press.

Hantula, D. A. (1992). The basic importance of escalation. *Journal of Applied Behavior Analysis, 25,* 579–583.

Harding, L. (2014, September 12). EU would be safer with Ukrainian president. *The Guardian.* Retrieved from www.theguardian.com/world/2014/sep/12

Hardy, C., & Latane, B. (1986). Social loafing on a cheering task. *Social Science, 71,* 165–172.

Hargrove, E. C. (1988). *Jimmy Carter as president: Leadership and the politics of the public good.* Baton Rouge, LA: Louisiana State University Press.

Haritos-Fatouros, M. (1988). The official torturer: A learning model for obedience to the authority of violence. *Journal of Applied Social Psychology, 18,* 1107–1120.

Harkins, S. G. (1987). Social loafing and social facilitation. *Journal of Experimental Social Psychology, 23,* 1–18.

Harkins, S. G., & Petty, R. E. (1982). Effects of task difficulty and task uniqueness on social loafing. *Journal of Personality and Social Psychology, 43,* 1214–1229.

Harper, N. L., & Askling, L. R. (1980). Group communication and quality of task solution in a media production organization. *Communication Monographs, 47,* 77–100.

Harvey, F. P. (1997a). Nuclear deterrence: The record of aggregate testing. New directions for aggregate testing. In F. P. Harvey (Ed.), *The future's back: Nuclear rivalry, deterrence theory, and crisis stability after the Cold War* (pp. 19–46). Montreal: McGill-Queen's University Press.

Harvey, F. P. (1997b). Deterrence and compellence in protracted crises: Methodology and preliminary findings. *International Studies Notes, 22,* 12–23.

Harvey, F. P. (1997c). Deterrence and ethnic conflict: The case of Bosnia-Herzegovina, 1993–1994. *Security Studies, 6,* 181–210.

Harvey, F. P. (1998). Rigor mortis, or rigor, more tests: Necessity, sufficiency, and deterrence logic. *International Studies Quarterly, 42,* 675–707.

Harvey, P. H., & Greene, P. J. (1981). Group composition: An evolutionary perspective. In H. Kellerman (Ed.), *Group cohesion.* New York: Grune and Stratton.

Hashim, A. S. (2006). *Insurgency and counter-insurgency in Iraq.* Ithaca, NY: Cornell University Press.

Haslam, S. A. (2001). *Psychology in organizations: The social identity approach.* London: Sage.

Haslam, S. A., & Platow, M. J. (2001). The link between leadership and followership: How affirming a social identity translates vision into action. *Personality and Social Psychology Bulletin, 27,* 1469–1479.

Haslam, S. A., Reicher, S. D., & Platow, M. J. (2011). *The new psychology of leadership: Identity, influence, and power.* New York: Psychology Press.

Hassan, H. D. (2008). Iraq: Tribal structure, social, and political activities. *CRS Report for Congress.* Washington, DC: Congressional Research Service.

Hastie, R. (1986). Review essay: Experimental evidence on group accuracy. In G. Owen & B. Gofman (Eds.), *Information pooling and group decision making* (pp. 129–157). Westport, CT: JAI Press.

Hastie, R., & Park, B. (1986). The relationship between memory and judgment depends upon whether the task is memory-based or on-line. *Psychological Review, 93,* 258–268.

Hatemi, P. K., Funk, C. L., Medland, S. E., Maes, H. M., Silberg, J. L., Martin, N. G., & Eaves, L. J. (2009). Genetic and environmental transmission of political attitudes over a life time. *Journal of Politics, 71,* 1141–1156.

Haupt, W. (2020). Op-ed: What happened to the Tea Party? *The Center Square.* Retrieved from www.thecentersquare.com/opinion/op-ed-what-happened-to-the-tea-party/article_3c1825a8-cf4f-11ea-991c-afdb6483c1a7.html

Hawley, G. (2017) *Making sense of the alt-right.* New York: Columbia University Press.

Hawthorne, J., Houston, J. B., & McKinney, M. S. (2013). Live-tweeting a presidential primary debate: Exploring new political conversations. *Social Science Computer Review, 31*, 552–562.

Heclo, H. (2003). The political ethos of George W. Bush. In F. I. Greenstein (Ed.), *The George W. Bush presidency: An early assessment* (pp. 17–50). Baltimore, MD: Johns Hopkins University Press.

Heider, F. (1946). Attitudes and cognitive organization. *Journal of Psychology, 21*, 107–112.

Heider, F. (1958). *The psychology of interpersonal relations.* New York: Wiley.

Heim, K. (2013). Framing the 2008 Iowa democratic caucuses. Political blogs and second level intermedia agenda setting. *Journalism & Mass Communications Quarterly, 90*, 500–519.

Helfstein, S. (2012). Backfire: Behavioral decision making and the strategic risks of successful surprise. *Foreign Policy Analysis, 8*, 275–292.

Herath, Tamara. (2012). *Women in Terrorism: The Case of the LTTE.* Thousand Oaks, CA: Sage.

Herman, J. (1992). *Trauma and recovery: The aftermath of violence from domestic abuse to political terror.* New York: Basic Books.

Hermann, M. G. (1979). Indicators of stress in policymakers during foreign policy crises. *Political Psychology, 1*, 27–46.

Hermann, M. G. (1980a). Assessing the personalities of Soviet Politburo members. *Personality and Social Psychology Bulletin, 6*, 332–352.

Hermann, M. G. (1980b). Explaining foreign policy behavior using personal characteristics of political leaders. *International Studies Quarterly, 24*, 7–46.

Hermann, M. G. (1983). *Handbook for assessing personal characteristics and foreign policy orientations of political leaders.* Columbus, OH: Mershon Center.

Hermann, M. G. (1984). Personality and foreign policy decision making: A study of 53 heads of government. In D. A. Sylvan & S. Chan (Eds.), *Foreign policy decision-making: Perceptions, cognition, and artificial intelligence* (pp. 53–80). Westport, CT: Praeger.

Hermann, M. G. (1986). Ingredients of leadership. In M. G. Hermann (Ed.), *Political psychology: Contemporary problems and issues* (pp. 167–192). San Francisco: Jossey-Bass.

Hermann, M. G. (1987). Assessing the foreign policy role orientations of sub-Saharan African leaders. In S. Walker (Ed.), *Role theory and foreign policy analysis* (pp. 161–198). Durham, NC: Duke University Press.

Hermann, M. G. (1988). Hafes Al-Assad, President of Syria: A leadership profile. In B. Kellerman & J. Rubins (Eds.), *Leadership in negotiation in the Middle East* (pp. 70–95). Westport, CT: Praeger.

Hermann, M. G. (1995). Advice and advisers in the Clinton presidency: The impact of leadership style. In S. Renshon (Ed.), *The Clinton presidency: Campaigning, governing, and the psychology of leadership* (pp. 149–164). Boulder, CO: Westview Press.

Hermann, M. G. (1999a). *Assessing leadership style: A trait analysis.* Columbus, OH: Social Science Automation.

Hermann, M. G. (1999b). *Leadership profile of Bill Clinton*. Columbus, OH: Social Science Automation.
Hermann, M. G. (2000). An appendum: Making empirical inferences about elite decision making politically relevant. *Political Psychologist, 15*, 24–29.
Hermann, M. G. (2001). How decision units shape foreign policy: A theoretical framework. *International Studies Review, 3*, 47–82.
Hermann, M.G. (2006). *A guide to understanding crisis management through case studies*. Stockholm: CRISMART, Swedish National Defense College and Moynihan Institute of Global Affairs.
Hermann, M. G., & Kegley, C. W., Jr. (1995). Rethinking democracy and international peace: Perspectives from political psychology. *International Studies Quarterly, 39*, 511–533.
Hermann, M. G., & Preston, T. (1994). Presidents, advisers, and foreign policy: The effect of leadership style on executive arrangements. *Political Psychology, 15*, 75–96.
Hermann, M. G., & Preston, T. (1998). Presidents, leadership style, and the advisory process. In E. R. Wittkopf & J. M. McCormick (Eds.), *The domestic sources of American foreign policy: Insights and evidence* (pp. 351–368). Lanham, MD: Rowman & Littlefield.
Hermann, M. G., Preston, T., & Young, M. (1996, April 16–20). *Who leads can matter in foreign policymaking: A framework for leadership analysis*. Paper presented at the annual meeting of the International Studies Association, San Diego.
Hermann, M. G., Preston, T., Korany, B., & Shaw, T. M. (2001). Who leads matters: The effects of powerful individuals. In *Leaders, groups, and coalitions: Understanding the people and processes in foreign policymaking* (pp. 83–131). Boston, MA: Blackwell.
Herr, P. (1986). Consequences of priming: judgment and behavior. *Journal of Personality and Social Psychology, 40*, 843–861.
Herring, E. (1995). *Danger and opportunity: Explaining international crisis outcomes*. Manchester: Manchester University Press.
Herrmann, R. (1985a). *Perceptions and behavior in Soviet foreign policy*. Pittsburgh, PA: University of Pittsburgh Press.
Herrmann, R. (1985b). Analyzing Soviet images of the United States. *Journal of Conflict Resolution, 29*, 665–697.
Herrmann, R. (1988). The empirical challenge of the cognitive revolution: A strategy for drawing inferences about perceptions. *International Studies Quarterly, 32*, 175–203.
Herrmann, R. (1991). The Soviet decision to withdraw from Afghanistan: Changing strategic and regional images. In R. Jervis & J. Snyder (Eds.), *Dominoes and bandwagons* (pp. 220–249). New York: Oxford University Press.
Herrmann, R. K., Voss, J. F., Schooler, T.Y.E., & Ciarrochi, J. (1997). Images in international relations: An experimental test of cognitive schemata. *International Studies Quarterly, 41*, 403–433.
Hess, R., & Torney, J. (1967). *The development of political attitudes in children*. Chicago, IL: Aldine.
Hesterman, J., & Mastors, E. (2011). Internal repression in Syria. *The Counter Terrorist*. Retrieved from http://onlinedigitalpublishing.com/article/INTERNAL_REPRESSION_IN_SYRIA/883798/87543/article.html.

Hewitt, C. (2003). *Understanding terrorism in America: From the Klan to Al Qaeda*. New York: Routledge.

Hewstone, M. (1989). Intergroup attribution: Some implications for the study of ethnic prejudice. In J. P. van Oudenhoven & T. Willemsen (Eds.), *Ethnic minorities: Social psychological* perspectives. Berwyn, PA: Swets North America.

Hewstone, M., & Brown, R. (Eds.). (1986). *Contact and conflict in intergroup encounters*. Oxford: Basil Blackwell.

Hibbing, J. (2019). *Liberals and conservatives: The biology of political differences*. Public presentation at the Foley Institute, Washington State University. Retrieved from www.youtube.com/watch?v=yxvxNVjBDio

Hill, D. (2019). *Two cheers for democracy: How emotions drive leadership style*. Minneapolis: Sensory Logic Books.

Hill, G. W. (1982). Group versus individual performance: Are $N + 1$ heads better than one? *Psychological Bulletin, 91*, 517–539.

Hill, S., Lo, J., Vavreck, L., & Zaller, J. (2013). How quickly we forget: The duration of persuasion effects from mass communication. *Political Communication, 30*, 521–547.

Hirokawa, R. Y. (1980). A comparative analysis of communication patterns within effective and ineffective decision-making groups. *Communication Monographs, 47*, 312–321.

Hirt, E. R., & Markman, K. D. (1995). Multiple explanation: A consider-an-alternative strategy for debiasing judgments. *Personality and Social Psychology Bulletin, 69*, 1069–1086.

Ho, A. K., Sidanius, J., Pratto, F., Levin, S., Thomsen, L., Kteily, N., & Sheehy-Skeffington, J. (2012). Social dominance orientation: Revisiting the structure and function of a variable predicting social and political attitudes. *Personality and Social Psychology Bulletin, 38*, 583–606.

Ho, A. K., Sidanius, J., Kteily, N., Sheehy-Skeffington, J., Pratto, J., Henkel, K. E., Stewart, A. L. (2015). The nature of social dominance orientation: Theorizing and measuring preferences for intergroup inequality using the new SDO7 Scale. *Journal of Personality and Social Psychology, 109*, 1003–1028.

Hobert, R. L., & Tchernev, J. M. (2013). Media influence as persuasion. In J. P. Dillar & L. Shen (Eds.), *The Sage handbook of persuasion: Developments in theory and practice* (2nd ed., pp. 36–52). Thousand Oaks, CA: Sage.

Hoffman, K., & Llagas, C. (2007). *Status and trends in the education of ethnic and racial minorities*. Washington, DC: National Center for Education Statistics.

Hofstede, G., & McCrae, R. R. (2004). Personality and culture revisited: Linking traits and dimensions of culture. *Cross-Cultural Research, 38*, 52–88.

Hogg, M. A. (2000). Self-categorization and subjective uncertainty resolutions: Cognitive and motivational facets of social identity and group membership. In J. P. Forgas, K. D. Williams, & L. Wheeler (Eds.), *The social mind: Cognitive and motivational aspects of interpersonal behavior* (pp. 323–349). New York: Cambridge University Press.

Hogg, M. A. (2004). Social categorization and group behavior. In M. B. Brewer & M. Hewstone (Eds.), *Self and social identity*. Malden, MA: Blackwell.

Hogg, M. A., & Abrams, D. (1988). *Social identifications: A social psychology of intergroup relations and group processes*. New York: Routledge.

Hogg, M. A., & McGarty, C. (1990). Self-categorization and social identity. In M. A. Hogg & D. Abrams (Eds.), *Social identity theory: Constructive and critical advances*. New York: Springer-Verlag.

Hogg, M. A., Turner, J. C., & Davidson, B. (1990). Polarized norms and social frames of reference: A test of the self-categorization theory of group polarization. *Basic and Applied Social Psychology, 11*, 77–100.

Holland, T. (2007). *Persian Fire: The First World Empire and the Battle for the West*. New York: Anchor Books.

Hollander, E. P. (1985). Leadership and power. In G. Lindzey & E. Aronson (Eds.), *Handbook of social psychology* (3rd ed., Vol. 2, pp. 485–537). New York: Random House.

Holsti, O. (1962). The belief system and national images: A case study. *Journal of Conflict Resolution, 6*, 244–252.

Holsti, O. (1967). Cognitive dynamics and images of the enemy. In R. Fagen (Ed.), *Enemies in politics* (pp. 25–96). Chicago, IL: Rand McNally.

Holsti, O. (1969). The belief system and national images: A case study. In J. Rosenau (Ed.), *International politics and foreign policy* (2nd ed., pp. 543–550). New York: Free Press.

Holsti, O. (1970). The "operational code" approach to the study of political leaders: John Foster Dulles' philosophical and instrumental beliefs. *Canadian Journal of Political Science, 3*, 123–157.

Holsti, O. (1977). *The "operational code" as an approach to analysis of belief systems*. Washington, DC: National Science Foundation.

Holtz, R., & Miller, N. (1985). Assumed similarity and opinion certainty. *Journal of Personality and Social Psychology, 48*, 890–898.

Hopkins, D.J., & Sides, J. (2018). *Political polarization in American politics*. New York: Bloomsbury.

Horgan, J. (2014). *The psychology of terrorism*. London: Routledge.

Horowitz, D. (1985). *Ethnic groups in conflict*. Berkeley, CA: University of California Press.

Horowitz, J.M., Brown, A., Cox, K. (2019). Race in America 2019: Public has negative views of the country's racial progress; more than half say Trump has made race relations worse. Pew Research. Retrieved from www.pewresearch.org/politics/2020/06/02/democratic-edge-in-party-identification-narrows-slightly

House, R. J. (1990). Power and personality in complex organizations. In B. M. Staw & L. L. Cummings (Eds.), *Personality and organizational influence* (pp. 181–233). Greenwich, CT: JAI Press.

Howard, J. W., & Rothbart, M. (1980). Social categorization and memory for in-group and out-group behavior. *Journal of Personality and Social Psychology, 38*, 301–310.

Hoyt, P., & Garrison, J. (1997). Political manipulation within the small group: Foreign policy advisers in the Carter administration. In P. 't Hart, E. Stern, & B. Sundelius (Eds.), *Beyond groupthink* (pp. 249–274). Ann Arbor, MI: University of Michigan Press.

Hsu, S. (2006, February 12). Katrina report spreads blame: Homeland security, Chertoff singled out. *Washington Post*.

Huckfeldt, R., Levine, J., Morgan, W., & Sprague, J. (1999). Accessibility and the political utility of partisan and ideological orientation. *American Journal of Political Science, 43*, 888–911.

Human Rights Watch. (1999, March). Leave none to tell the story: Genocide in Rwanda. Retrieved from www.hrw.org/reports/1999/rwanda/Geno1-3-09.htm

Human Rights Watch. (2000). *Human Rights Watch world report 2000.* New York: Author.

Human Rights Watch. (2006). Funding the final war LTTE intimidation and extortion in the Tamil diaspora. Retrieved from http://hrw.org/reports/2006/ltte0306/index.htm

Human Rights Watch. (2007). Darfur 2007: Chaos by design. Retrieved from http://hrw.org/reports/2007/sudan0907/2.htm#_Toc177544425

Human Rights Watch (2021). Yemen: Events of 2020. Retrieved from https://www.hrw.org/world-report/2021/country-chapters/yemen

Hunter, J. D. (1991). *Culture wars: The struggle to define America.* New York: Basic Books.

Hutchison, E. O. (2007). *The Latino challenge to Black America.* Los Angeles: Middle Passage Press.

Huth, P., & Russett, B. (1984). What makes deterrence work? Cases from 1900–1980. *World Politics, 36*, 496–526.

Huth, P., & Russett, B. (1988). Deterrence failure and crisis escalation. *International Studies Quarterly, 32*, 29–45.

Huth, P., & Russett, B. (1990). Testing deterrence theory: Rigor makes a difference. *World Politics, 42*(4), 466–501.

Hymans, J. (2006). *The psychology of nuclear proliferation: Identity, emotions, and foreign policy.* Cambridge: Cambridge University Press.

Ihonvbere, J. O. (1994). *Nigeria: The politics of adjustment and democracy.* New Brunswick, NJ: Transaction Books.

Immelman, A., & Griebie, A.M. (2020). The personality profile and leadership style of U.S. president Donald J. Trump in office. Paper presented at the 43rd Annual Scientific Meeting of the International Society of Political Psychology, Berlin, July 14–16, 2020. Retrieved from http://digitalcommons.csbsju.edu/psychology_pubs/129

Insko, C. A., & Schopler, J. (1987). Categorization, competition, and collectivity. In C. Hendrick (Ed.), *Group processes: Review of personality and social psychology* (Vol. 8, pp. 213–251). Newbury Park, CA: Sage.

Isaak, R. A. (1975). *Individuals and world politics.* North Scituate, MA: Duxbury Press.

Isen, A. (1993). Positive affect and decision making. In M. Lewis & I. Haviland (Eds.), *Handbook of emotions* (pp. 261–277). New York: Guilford Press.

Isenberg, D. J. (1986). Group polarization: A critical review and meta-analysis. *Journal of Personality and Social Psychology, 50*, 1141–1151.

Isikoff, M., & Corn, D. (2006). *Hubris: The inside story of spin, scandal, and the selling of the Iraq war.* New York: Crown.

Iskander, A. (2013). *Egypt in flux: Essays on an unfinished revolution.* New York: American University in Cairo Press.

Iyengar, S. (1990). Shortcuts to political knowledge: The role of selective attention and accessibility. In J. Ferejohn & J. Kuklinski (Eds.), *Information and democratic processes* (pp. 160–185). Urbana, IL: University of Illinois Press.

Iyengar, S. (1991). *Is anyone responsible? How television frames political issues*. Chicago: University of Chicago Press.

Iyengar, S., & Kinder, D. (1987). *News that matters*. Chicago: University of Chicago Press.

Iyengar, S., Peters, M., & Kinder, D. (1982). Experimental demonstrations of the not-so-minimal political consequences of mass media. *American Political Science Review, 76*, 848–858.

Iyengar, S., Peters, M., Kinder, D., & Krosnick, J. (1984). The evening news and presidential elections. *Journal of Personality and Social Psychology, 46*, 778–787.

Izard, C. E. (1977). *Human emotions*. New York: Plenum Press.

Jackman, M. (1978). General and applied tolerance: Does education increase commitment to racial integration? *American Journal of Political Science, 22*, 302–324.

Jackson, A. (2001). Images and police behavior: An analysis of police-community relations. Unpublished doctoral dissertation, Washington State University.

Jackson, D., & Messick, S. (1957). A note on ethnocentrism and acquiescent response sets. *Journal of Abnormal and Social Psychology, 54*, 132–134.

Jacobs, L., & Shapiro, R. (1994). Issues, candidate image and priming: The use of private polls in Kennedy's 1960 presidential campaign. *American Political Science Review, 88*, 527–540.

Jacobson, G. C. (2017). The triumph of polarized partisanship in 2016: Donald Trump's improbable victory. *Political Science Quarterly, 132*, 9–41.

Jacquier, J.D. (2014). An operational code of terrorism: The political psychology of Ayman al-Zawahiri. *Behavioral Sciences of Terrorism and Political Aggression, 6*, 19–40,

James, H. (1989). *A German identity, 1770–1990*. London: Weidenfeld and Nicolson.

James, J. A. (1951). A preliminary study of the size determinant in small group interaction. *American Sociological Review, 16*, 474–477.

Janes, L., & Olson, J. M. (2000). Jeer pressure: The behavioral effects of observing ridicule of others. *Personality and Social Psychology Bulletin, 26*, 474–485.

Janis, I. L. (1972). *Victims of groupthink*. Boston: Houghton Mifflin.

Janis, I. L. (1982). *Groupthink: Psychological studies of policy decisions and fiascos* (2nd ed.). Boston: Houghton Mifflin.

Janis, I. L., & Mann, L. (1977). *Decision making: A psychological analysis of conflict, choice, and commitment*. New York: Free Press.

Jardina, A. (2019). *White identity politics*. Cambridge: Cambridge University Press.

Jennings, M. K. (2004). American political participation as viewed through the political socialization project. In M. G. Hermann (Ed.), *Advances in political psychology*. London: Elsevier.

Jennings, M. K., & Niemi, R. (1974). *Families, schools and political learning*. Princeton, NJ: Princeton University Press.

Jervis, R. (1976). *Perception and misperception in international politics*. Princeton, NJ: Princeton University Press.

Jervis, R. (1995). The drunkard's search. In S. Iyengar & W. McGuire (Eds.), *Explorations in political psychology* (pp. 338–360). Durham, NC: Duke University Press.

Jervis, R., Lebow, R. N., & Stein, J. (1985). *Psychology and deterrence*. Baltimore, MD: Johns Hopkins University Press.

John, L. K., Loewenstein, G., & Prelec, D. (2012). Measuring the prevalence of questionable research practices with incentives for truth telling. *Psychological Science, 23*(5), 524–532.

Johnson, A. L., Crawford, M. T., Sherman, S. J., Rutchick, A. M., Hamilton, D. L., Ferreira, M. B., & Petroceli, J. V. (2005). A functional perspective on group memberships: Differential need fulfilment in a group typology. *Journal of Experimental Social Psychology, 42*, 707–719.

Johnson, D. E., Mueller, K. P., & Taft, W. H. (2002). *Conventional coercion across the spectrum of operations: The utility of U.S. military forces in the emerging environment*. Santa Monica, CA: Rand Corporation.

Johnson, H. H., & Watkins, T. (1971). The effects of message on immediate and delayed attitude change. *Psychonomic Science, 22*, 101–103.

Johnson, M. P., & Ewens, W. (1971). Power relations and affective style as determinants of confidence in impression formation in a game situation. *Journal of Experimental Social Psychology, 7*, 98–110.

Johnson, R. D., & Downing, L. L. (1979). Deindividuation and valence of cues: Effects on prosocial and antisocial behavior. *Journal of Personality and Social Psychology, 37*, 1532–1538.

Johnson, R. T. (1974). *Managing the White House: An intimate study of the presidency*. New York: Harper and Row.

Joint Center for Political and Economic Studies. (2001). Databank. Retrieved from www.jointctr.org/databank/factsht/trendnpov.htm

Jones, B., & Kavanagh, D. (1998). *British politics today* (6th ed.). Washington, DC: CQ Press.

Jones, C. O. (1988). *The trusteeship presidency: Jimmy Carter and the United States Congress*. Baton Rouge, LA: Louisiana State University Press.

Jones, E. E., & Davis, K. E. (1965). From acts to dispositions: The attribution process in person perceptions. In L. Berkowitz (Ed.), *Advances in experimental social psychology* (Vol. 2, pp. 220–266). New York: Academic Press.

Jones, E. E., & Harris, V. A. (1967). The attribution of attitudes. *Journal of Experimental Psychology, 3*, 1–24.

Jowett, G., & O'Donnell, V. (1999). *Propaganda and persuasion* (2nd ed). Thousand Oaks, CA: Sage.

Judah, T. (2000). *Kosovo: War and revenge*. New Haven, CT: Yale University Press.

Judd, C. M., & Krosnick, J. A. (1989). The structural bases of consistency among political attitudes: Effects of political expertise and attitude importance. In A. R. Pratkanis, S. J. Breckler, & A. G. Greenwald (Eds.), *Attitude structure and function*. Hillsdale, NJ: Lawrence Erlbaum.

Judge, T. A., Bono, J. E., Ilies, R., & Gerhard, M. W. (2002). Personality and leadership: A qualitative and quantitative review. *Journal of Applied Psychology, 87*, 765–780.

Juergensmeyer, M. (2000). *Terror in the mind of God: The global rise of religious violence* (3rd ed.). Berkeley, CA: University of California Press.

Kaarbo, J. (1998). Power politics in foreign policy: The influence of bureaucratic minorities. *European Journal of International Relations, 4,* 67–97.

Kaarbo, J., & Beasley, R. (1998). A political perspective on minority influence and strategic group composition. In M. Neale, E. Mannix, & D. Gruenfeld (Eds.), *Research on groups and teams* (Vol. 1, pp. 125–147). Greenwich, CT: JAI Press.

Kaarbo, J., & Gruenfeld, D. (1998). The social psychology of inter- and intragroup conflict in governmental politics. *Mershon International Studies Review, 42,* 226–233.

Kaarbo, J., & Hermann, M. (1998). Leadership styles of prime ministers: How individual differences affect the foreign policy process. *Leadership Quarterly, 9,* 243–263.

Kahn, J. (2000, December 31). Bush filling cabinet with team of power-seasoned executives. *New York Times,* p. A1.

Kahneman, D., & Tversky, A. (1979). A prospect theory: An analysis of decision under risk. *Econometrica, 47,* 263–291.

Kahneman, D., & Tversky, A. (2000). *Choice, values, and frames.* New York: Cambridge University Press.

Kaid, L., & Chanslor, M. (1995). Changing candidate images: The effects of political advertising. In K. Hacker (Ed.), *Candidate images in presidential elections* (pp. 131–134). Westport, CT: Praeger.

Kampf, H. A. (1990). Terrorism, the left-wing, and the intellectuals. *Terrorism, 13,* 23–51.

Kaplan, A. (1981). The psychodynamics of terrorism. In Y. Alexander & J. Gleason (Eds.), *Behavioral and quantitative perspectives on terrorism* (pp. 35–51). New York: Pergamon Press.

Kaplan, J., & Weinberg, L. (1998). *The emergence of a Euro-American radical right.* New Brunswick, NJ: Rutgers University Press.

Karadžić, R. (1996). State of Republic [address]. Retrieved from www.cdsp.neu.edu/info/students/marko/telegraf/telegraf2.html

Karau, S. J., & Williams, K. D. (1993). Social loafing: A meta-analytical review and theoretical integration. *Journal of Personality and Social Psychology, 65,* 681–706.

Katz, D., & Stotland, E. (1959). A preliminary statement of a theory of attitude structure and change. In S. Koch (Ed.), *Psychology: A study of a science* (Vol. 3, pp. 423–275). New York: McGraw-Hill.

Kaufman, S. (2001). *Modern hatreds: The symbolic politics of ethnic war.* Ithaca, NY: Cornell University Press.

Kawakami, J., Dovidio, J. F., Moll, J., Hermson, S., & Russin, A. (2000). Just say no to stereotyping: Effect of training in the negation of stereotypic associations on stereotype activation. *Journal of Personality and Social Psychology, 78,* 871–888.

Kecmanovic, D. (1996). *The mass psychology of ethnonationalism.* New York: Plenum Press.

Keegan, J. (1998). *The First World War.* New York: Vintage Books.

Kellam, M. (2013). Suffrage extensions and voting patterns in Latin America: Is mobilization a source of decay? *Latin American Politics and Society, 44,* 23–46.

Keller, J. W. (2005). Constraint respecters, constraint challengers, and crisis decision making in democracies: A case study analysis of Kennedy versus Reagan. *Political Psychology, 26,* 835–867.

Keller, J. W., & Foster, D. M. (2012). Presidential leadership style and the political use of force. *Political Psychology, 33,* 581–598.

Kellerman, B. (1984). *Leadership: Multidisciplinary perspectives.* Englewood Cliffs, NJ: Prentice-Hall.

Kelley, H. (1967). Attribution theory in social psychology. In D. Levin (Ed.), *Nebraska symposium on motivation* (Vol. 5, pp. 192–240). Lincoln, NE: University of Nebraska Press.

Kelman, H. C. (1958). Compliance, identification, and internalization: Three processes of attitude change. *Journal of Conflict Resolution, 2,* 51–60.

Kelman, H. C. (1961). Processes of opinion change. *Public Opinion Quarterly, 25,* 57–78.

Kelman, H. C. (1965). *International behavior: A social-psychological analysis.* New York: Holt, Rinehart, and Winston.

Kelman, H. C. (1990). Applying a human needs perspective to the practice of conflict resolution; The Israeli–Palestinian case. In J. Burton (Ed.), *Conflict: Human needs theory* (pp. 283–297). New York: St. Martin's Press.

Kelman, H. C., & Hamilton, V. L. (1989). *Crimes of obedience.* New Haven, CT: Yale University Press.

Kelman, H. C., & Hovland, C. I. (1953). "Reinstatement" of the communicator in delayed measurement of attitude change. *Journal of Abnormal and Social Psychology, 48,* 327–335.

Keltner, D., & Robinson, R. J. (1997). Defending the status quo: Power and bias in social conflict. *Personality and Social Psychology Bulletin, 23,* 1066–1077.

Kennedy, C., & Ruiz, N. G. (2020, July 1). Polling methods are changing, but reporting the views of Asian Americans remains a challenge. Pew Research Center. Retrieved from www.pewresearch.org/fact-tank/2020/07/01/polling-methods-are-changing-but-reporting-the-views-of-asian-americans-remains-a-challenge

Kernan, M. C., & Lord, R. G. (1989). The effects of explicit goals and specific feedback on escalation processes. *Journal of Applied Social Psychology, 19,* 1125–1143.

Kernis, M. H. (2003). Toward a conceptualization of optimal self-esteem. *Psychological Inquiry, 14,* 1–26.

Kerr, N. L., & Bruun, S. E. (1981). Ringelmann revisited: Alternative explanations for the social loafing effect. *Personality and Social Psychology Bulletin, 7,* 224–231.

Kerr, N. L., & Bruun, S. E. (1983). Dispensibility of member effort and group motivation losses: Free-rider effects. *Journal of Personality and Social Psychology, 44,* 78–94.

Khong, Y. F. (1992). *Analogies at war: Korea, Munich, Dien Bien Phu, and the Vietnam decisions of 1965.* Princeton, NJ: Princeton University Press.

Kiesler, D. J. (1983). The 1982 interpersonal circle: A taxonomy for complementarity in human transactions. *Psychological Review, 90,* 185–214.

Kille, K. J. (2006). *From manager to visionary: The Secretary-General of the United Nations.* New York: Palgrave.

Kim, K., & McCombs, M. (2007). News story descriptions and the public's opinions of political candidates. *Journalism and Mass Communication Quarterly, 84*, 299–314.

Kimmage, D., & Ridolfo, K. (2007, June). *Iraqi insurgent media: the war of ideas and images.* Radio Free Europe special report.

Kinder, D. (1986). Presidential character revisited. In R. Lau & D. Sears (Eds.), *Political cognition.* Hillsdale, NJ: Lawrence Erlbaum.

Kinder, D. R, & Dale-Riddle, A. (2012). *The end of race? Obama, 2008, and racial politics in America.* New Haven, CT: Yale University Press.

Kinder, D. R., & Nelson, T. E. (2005). Democratic debate and real opinions. In K. Callaghan & F. Schnell (Eds.), *Framing American politics* (pp. 103–122). Pittsburgh, PA: University of Pittsburgh Press.

Kinder, D. R., & Sanders, L. M. (1990). Mimicking political debate with survey questions: The case of white opinion on affirmative action for blacks. *Social Cognition, 8*, 73–103.

Kinder, D., & Sanders, L. (1996). *Divided by color: Racial politics and democratic ideals.* Chicago, IL: University of Chicago Press.

Kinder, D., & Sears, D. (1981). Prejudice and politics: Symbolic racism versus racial threats to the good life. *Journal of Personality and Social Psychology, 40*, 414–431.

King, A. (1998). Why Labour won—at last. In A. King, D. Denver, I. McLean, P. Norris, P. Norton, D. Sanders, & P. Seyd (Eds.), *New Labour triumphs: Britain at the polls.* Chatham, NJ: Chatham House.

King, M., & Taylor, D. M. (2011). The radicalization of homegrown jihadists: A review of the theoretical models and social psychological evidence. *Terrorism and Political Violence, 23*(4), 602–622.

Kipnis, D. (1984). The use of power in organizations and in interpersonal settings. In *Applied Social Psychology Annual* (Vol. 5, pp. 179–210). Newbury Park, CA: Sage.

Kissinger, H. (2014, March 5). How the Ukraine crisis ends. *The Washington Post.* Retrieved from www.washingtonpost.com/opinions/henry-kissinger-to-settle-the-ukraine-crisis-start-at-the-end/2014/03/05/46dad868-a496-11e3-8466-d34c451760b9_story.html

Kitano, H., & Nakaoka, S. (2001). Asian Americans in the twentieth century. In N. Choi (Ed.), *Psychological aspects of the Asian-American experience* (pp. 7–18). New York: Hawthorn Press.

Klandermans, B. (1984). Mobilization and participation: Social-psychological expansions of resource mobilization theory. *American Sociological Review, 49*, 583–600.

Klandermans, B. (1997). *The social psychology of protest.* Oxford: Blackwell.

Klandermans, B., & van Stekelenburg, J. (2013). Social movements and the dynamics of collective action. In L. Huddy, D. O. Sears, & J. S. Levy (Eds.), *The Oxford handbook of political psychology* (2nd ed., pp. 774–811). Oxford: Oxford University Press.

Klandermans, B., Werner, M., & van Doorn, M. (2008). Redeeming apartheid's legacy: Collective guilt, political ideology, and compensation. *Political Psychology, 29*, 331–349.

Klang, C. (1998, February 1). Evil, filthy rotten conspiracy. *Idaho Observer.* Retrieved from http://proliberty.com

Klar, S., Robison, J., & Druckman, J. (2013). Political dynamics of framing. In T. Ridout (Ed.), *New directions in media and politics* (pp. 173–192). New York: Routledge.

Kline, E. (1998). ASF Chechnya Brief. Andrei Sakarov Foundation. Retrieved from www.wdn.com/asf

Knutson, J. (1981). Social and psychodynamic pressures toward a negative identity. In Y. Alexander & J. Gleason (Eds.), *Behavioral and quantitative perspectives on terrorism* (pp. 105–152). New York: Pergamon Press.

Kohut, A. (2012, November 13). Lessons from the 2012 election. Retrieved from www.people-press.org/2012/11/13/lessons

Komorita, S. S., Hamilton, T. P., & Kravitz, D. A. (1984). Effects of alternatives in coalition bargaining. *Journal of Experimental Social Psychology, 20*, 116–136.

Komorita, S. S., & Miller, C. E. (1986). Bargaining strength as a function of coalition alternatives. *Journal of Personality and Social Psychology, 51*, 325–332.

Komorita, S. S., & Nagao, D. (1983). The functions of resources in coalition bargaining. *Journal of Personality and Social Psychology, 44*, 95–106.

Kotter, J. P., & Lawrence, P. R. (1974). *Mayors in action*. Oxford: Wiley.

Kowert, P. A., & Hermann, M. G. (1997). Who takes risks? Daring and caution in foreign policy making. *Journal of Conflict Resolution, 41*, 611–637.

Kravitz, D. A. (1987). Size of smallest coalition as a source of power in coalition bargaining. *European Journal of Social Psychology, 17*, 1–21.

Kressel, N. (1996). *Mass hate: The global rise of genocide and terror*. Oxford: Plenum Press.

Kriesberg, L. (2010). Intractable conflicts. In N. Young (Ed.), *The Oxford international encyclopedia of peace* (pp. 486–490). Oxford: Oxford University Press.

Kriesci, H., Koopmans, R., Duyvendak, J. W., & Guigni, M. G. (1997). New social movements and political opportunities in Western Europe. In D. McAdam & D. A. Snow (Eds.), *Social movements: Readings on their emergence, mobilization, and dynamics* (pp. 52–65). Los Angeles: Roxbury.

Krogstad, J. M. (2020a). Hispanics have accounted for more than half of total U.S. population growth since 2010. Pew Research. Retrieved from www.pewresearch.org/fact-tank/2020/07/10/hispanics-have-accounted-for-more-than-half-of-total-u-s-population-growth-since-2010

Krogstad, J. M (2020b). Most Cuban Americans identify as republican in 2020. Pew Research. Retrieved from www.pewresearch.org/fact-tank/2020/10/02/most-cuban-american-voters-identify-as-republican-in-2020

Krogstad, J. M., Gonzalez-Barrera, G., & Tamir, C. (2020). Latino democratic voters place high importance on 2020 presidential election. Pew Research. Retrieved from www.pewresearch.org/fact-tank/2020/01/17/latino-democratic-voters-place-high-importance-on-2020-presidential-election

Krogstad, J.M., & Lopez, M.H. (2020). Hispanic voters say economy, health care and COVID-19 are top issues in 2020 presidential election. Pew Research. Retrieved from www.pewresearch.org/fact-tank/2020/09/11/hispanic-voters-say-economy-health-care-and-covid-19-are-top-issues-in-2020-presidential-election

Krosnick, J. (1988). Attitude importance in social evaluation: A study of police preferences, presidential candidate evaluations, and voting behavior. *Journal of Personality and Social Psychology, 55*, 196–210.

Krosnick, J. (1989). Attitude importance and attitude accessibility. *Personality and Social Psychology Bulletin, 15*, 297–308.

Krosnick, J., & Kinder, J. (1990). Altering the foundations of support for the president. *American Political Science Review, 84*, 497–512.

Kruglanski, A., & Fishman, S. (2006). The psychology of terrorism: "Syndrome" versus "tool" perspectives. *Terrorism and Political Violence, 18*, 193–215.

Kruglanski, A. W., Chen, X., Dechesne, M., Fishman, S., & Orehek, E. (2009). Fully committed: Suicide bombers' motivation and quest for personal significance. *Political Psychology, 30*, 331–357.

Krupnikov, Y. (2011). When does negativity demobilize? Tracing the conditional effect of negativity on voter turnout. *American Journal of Political Science, 55*, 797–813.

Krupnikov, Y., & Easter, B. C. (2013). Negative campaigns: Are they good for American democracy? In T. Ridout (Ed.), *New directions in media and politics*. New York: Routledge.

Krznaric, R. (2013, May 15). Have we all been duped by the Myers-Briggs test? *Fortune*. Retrieved from http://fortune.com/2013/05/15/have-we-all-been-duped-by-the-myers-briggs-test

Kugler, M. B., Cooper, J., & Nosek, B. A. (2010). Group-based dominance and opposition to equality correspond to different psychological motives. *Social Justice Research, 23*, 117–155.

Kuklinski, J. H., Luskin, R. C., & Bolland, J. (1991). Where is the schema? Going beyond the "s" word in political psychology. *American Political Science Review, 85*, 1341–1355.

Kuklinski, J. H., Riggle, E., Ottati, V., Schwarz, N., & Wyer, R. (1991). The cognitive and affective bases of political tolerance judgments. *American Journal of Political Science, 35*, 1–27.

Kuntner, B., Wilkins, C., & Yarrow, P. R. (1952). Verbal attitudes and overt behavior involving racial prejudice. *Journal of Abnormal and Social Psychology, 47*, 649–652.

LaBaron, A. (1993). The creation of the modern Maya. In C. Young (Ed.), *The rising tide of cultural pluralism: The nation-state at bay?* (pp. 265–284). Madison, WI: University of Wisconsin Press.

La Guardia, J. G., & Ryan, R. M. (2007). Why identities fluctuate: Variability in traits as a function of situational variations in autonomy support. *Journal of Personality, 76*, 1205–1228.

Lake, A. (1994). Confronting backlash states. *Foreign Affairs, 73*, 45–55.

Lambert, A. J., Burroughs, T., & Nguyen, T. (1999). Perceptions of risk and the buffering hypothesis: The role of just world beliefs and right-wing authoritarianism. *Personality and Social Psychology Bulletin, 25*, 643–656.

Lane, R. (1962). *Political ideology: Why the American common man believes what he does*. Oxford: Free Press.

Lane, R., & Sears, D. (1964). *Public opinion*. Oxford: Prentice-Hall.

Langer, E. (1990, July 16). The American neo-Nazi movement today. *Nation, 215*, 82–105.

La Pierre, R. T. (1934). Attitudes versus actions. *Social Forces, 13*, 230–237.

Lasch, C. (1979). *The culture of narcissism*. Oxford: W. W. Norton.

Lasswell, H. (1948a). *Power and personality*. Oxford: Norton.

Lasswell, H. (1948b). The structure and function of communication in society. In L. Bryson (Ed.), *The communication of ideas* (pp. 32–51). New York: Harper.

Lasswell, H. (1960 [1930]). *Psychopathology and politics*. Chicago: University of Chicago Press.

Latane, B., & Darley, J. M. (1970). *The unresponsive bystander. Why doesn't he help?* New York: Appleton-Century-Crofts.

Latane, B., Williams, K. D., & Harkins, S. (1979). Many hands make light the work: The causes and consequences of social loafing. *Journal of Personality and Social Psychology, 37*, 822–832.

Lau, R. (1986). Political schemata, candidate evaluations and voting behavior. *American Journal of Political Science, 29*, 119–138.

Lau, R. (1995). Information search during an election campaign: Introducing a processing-tracing methodology for political scientists. In M. Lodge & K. McGraw (Eds.), *Political judgment: Structure and processes* (pp. 179–205). Oxford: University of Michigan Press.

Lau, R., & Redlawsk, D. (1997). Voting correctly. *American Political Science Review, 91*, 585–598.

Lau, R., & Redlawsk, D. (2006). *How voters decide: Information processing during election campaigns*. Cambridge: Cambridge University Press.

Laughlin, P. R. (1988). Collective induction: Group performance, social combination processes, and mutual majority and minority influence. *Journal of Personality and Social Psychology, 54*, 254–267.

Lav, D. (2007, March 7). The Al-Qaeda organization in the Islamic Maghreb: The evolving terrorist presence in North Africa, MEMRI Inquiry and Analysis. Retrieved from http://memri.org/bin/articles.cgi?Page=archives&Area=ia&ID=IA33207

Lavine, H. (2002). On-line versus memory-based process models. In K. Monroe (Ed.), *Political psychology*. Mahwah, NJ: Lawrence Erlbaum.

Lawler, E. J. (1992). Affective attachments to nested groups: A choice-process theory. *American Sociological Review, 57*, 327–339.

Lawler, E. J., & Thompson, M. E. (1978). Impact of a leader's responsibility for inequity on subordinate revolts. *Social Psychology Quarterly, 41*, 264–268.

Lazarsfeld, P., Berelson, B., & Gaudet, H. (1944). *The people's choice*. Oxford: Duell, Sloan & Pearce.

Lazarus, R. S. (1991). *Emotion and adaptation*. Oxford: Oxford University Press.

Leary, M. R. (1983). *Understanding social anxiety*. London: Sage.

Leary, M. R. (1999). Making sense of self-esteem. *Current Directions in Psychological Science, 8*, 32–35.

Leatherwood, M. L., & Conlon, E. J. (1987). Diffusibility of blame: Effects on persistence in a project. *Academy of Management Review, 30*, 836–847.

LeBon, G. (1960 [1895]). *The crowd: A study of the popular mind*. New York: Viking.

Lebow, R. N. (1981). *Between peace and war: The nature of international crisis*. Baltimore, MD: Johns Hopkins University Press.

Lebow, R. N., & Stein, J. G. (1987). Beyond deterrence. *Journal of Social Issues, 43*, 5–71.
Lebow, R. N., & Stein, J. G. (1989). Rational deterrence theory: I think, therefore I deter. *World Politics, 41*, 208–224.
Lebow, R. N., & Stein, J. G. (1990). Deterrence: The elusive dependent variable. *World Politics, 42*, 336–369.
Lee, M. (1997). *The beast reawakens*. London: Little, Brown.
Lee, R. (1999). *Orientals: Asian Americans in popular culture*. Oxford: Temple University Press.
Leffler, A., Gillespie, D. L., & Conaty, J. C. (1982). The effects of status differentiation on nonverbal behavior. *Social Psychology Quarterly, 45*, 153–161.
Legault, A., & Lindsey, G. (1974). *The dynamics of the nuclear balance*. Ithaca, NY: Cornell University Press.
Legvold, R. (1988). War, weapons, and Soviet foreign policy. In S. Bialer & M. Mandelbaum (Eds.), *Russia and American foreign policy* (pp. 97–132). Boulder, CO: Westview Press.
Leidner, B., Sheikh, H., & Ginges, J. (2012). Affective dimensions of intergroup humiliation. *PLoS ONE 7*, e46375.
Leites, N. (1951). *The operational code of the Politburo*. London: McGraw-Hill.
Leites, N. (1953). *A study of Bolshevism*. New York: Free Press.
Leith, K. P., & Baumeister, R. F. (1996). Why do bad moods increase self-defeating behavior? Emotion, risk taking, and self-regulation. *Journal of Personality and Social Psychology, 71*, 1250–1267.
Leonard, D. J., Mackie, D. M., & Smith, E. R. (2011). Emotional responses to intergroup apology mediate intergroup forgiveness and retribution. *Journal of Experimental Social Psychology, 47*, 1198–1206.
Leonard, D. J., Moons, W. G., Mackie, D. M., & Smith, E. R. (2011). "We're mad as hell and we're not going to take it anymore": Anger self-stereotyping and collective action. *Group Processes & Intergroup Relations, 14*, 99–111.
Lerner, M. J., & Miller, D. T. (1978). Just world research and the attribution process: Looking back and ahead. *Psychological Bulletin, 85*, 1030–1051.
Levin, J., & Levin, W. C. (1982). *The functions of prejudice and discrimination*. New York: Harper and Row.
Levin, S., & Sidanius, J. (1999). Social dominance and social identity in the United States and Israel: Ingroup favoritism or outgroup derogation? *Political Psychology, 20*, 99–126.
Levine, J. M., & Moreland, R. L. (1998). Small groups. In *The handbook of social psychology* (4th ed., pp. 415–469). New York: McGraw-Hill.
Levine, R.A., & Campbell, D.T. (1972). *Ethnocentrism: Theories of conflict, ethnic attitudes and group behavior*. New York: Wiley.
Levy, J. (1991). The role of crisis management in the outbreak of World War I. In A. George (Ed.), *Avoiding war: Problems of crisis management* (pp. 62–102). Boulder, CO: Westview Press.
Levy, J. (1994). Learning and foreign policy: Sweeping a conceptual minefield. *International Organization, 48*, 279–312.
Levy, J. (1997). Prospect theory, rational choice, and international relations. *International Studies Quarterly, 41*, 87–112.

Lewin, K. (1935). *A dynamic theory of personality*. Oxford: McGraw-Hill.

Lewin, K., Lippitt, R., & White, R. (1939). Patterns of aggressive behavior in experimentally created "social climates." *Journal of Social Psychology, 10*, 271–299.

Lewis, T. (2021). The "shared psychosis" of Donald Trump and his loyalists: Forensic psychiatrist Bandy X. Lee explains the outgoing president's pathological appeal and how to wean people from it. *Scientific American*. Retrieved from www.scientificamerican.com/article/the-shared-psychosis-of-donald-trump-and-his-loyalists

Lickel, B., Hamilton, D. L., Wieczorkowski, G., Lewis, A., Sherman, S. J., & Uhles, A. N. (2000). Varieties of groups and the perception of group entiativity. *Journal of Personality and Social Psychology, 78*, 223–246.

Lieb, D.A. (2020). Over 100 state lawmakers accused of misconduct in 3 years. Associated Press. Retrieved from https://apnews.com/article/10aedac91ac64f7e05daacad97408eeb

Lien, P., Conway, M. M., & Wong, J. (2004). *The politics of Asian Americans: Diversity and community*. London: Routledge.

Lifton, R. J. (1986). *The Nazi doctors: Medical killing and the psychology of genocide*. New York: Basic Books.

Light, P. C. (1982). *The president's agenda: Domestic policy choice from Kennedy to Carter*. Baltimore, MD: Johns Hopkins University Press.

Lindner, E. (2006). *Making enemies: Humiliation and international conflict*. Westport, CT: Praeger.

Link, A. (1996). Woodrow Wilson and the constitutional crisis. In K. Thompson (Ed.), *Papers on presidential disability and the 25th Amendment by medical, historical and political authorities* (pp. 53–80). Lanham, MD: Miller Center, University of Virginia and University Press of America.

Link, M., & Glad, B. (1994). Exploring the psychopolitical dynamics of advisory relations: The Carter administration's "crisis of confidence." *Political Psychology, 15*, 461–480.

Linville, P. (1982). Affective consequences as complexity regarding the self and others. In M. Clarke & S. Fiske (Eds.), *Affect and cognition*. Mahwah, NJ: Lawrence Erlbaum.

Linville, P., & Jones, E. (1980). Polarized appraisals of outgroup members. *Journal of Personality and Social Psychology, 38*, 698–703.

Lodge, M. (1995). Toward a procedural model of candidate evaluation. In M. Lodge & K. McGraw (Eds.), *Political judgment: Structure and processes* (pp. 111–139). Ann Arbor, MI: University of Michigan Press.

Lodge, M., & Hamill, R. (1986). A partisan schema for political information processing. *American Journal of Political Science, 80*, 505–519.

Lodge, M., McGraw, K. M., & Stroh, P. (1989). An impression driven model of candidate evaluation. *American Political Science Review, 83*, 399–419.

Lodge, M., Steenbergen, M., & Brau, S. (1995). The responsive voter: Campaign information and the dynamics of candidate evaluation. *American Political Science Review, 89*, 309–326.

Lodge, M., & Stroh, P. (1995). Inside the mental voting booth. In S. Iyengar & W. McGuire (Eds.), *Explorations in political psychology* (pp. 225–263). Durham, NC: Duke University Press.

Loftus, E. (1979). *Eyewitness testimony*. Cambridge, MA: Harvard University Press.

Loftus, E. F. (2001). Imagining the past. *Psychologist, 14*, 584–587.

Lorenz, K. (1966). *On aggression*. New York: Harcourt, Brace, and World.

Lott, A. J., & Lott, B. E. (1965). Group cohesiveness as interpersonal attraction: A review of relationships with antecedent and consequent variables. *Psychological Bulletin, 64*, 259–309.

Lounnas, D. (2019). The Tunisian jihad: Between al-Qaeda and ISIS. *Middle East Policy, 26*, 97–116.

Loyd, A. (1999). *My war gone by, I miss it so*. Harmondsworth: Penguin.

Luce, R. D., & Raiffa, H. (1957). *Games and decisions*. Chichester: Wiley.

Luttig, M.D, & Federico, C.M. (2017). Supporters and opponents of Donald Trump respond differently to racial cues: An experimental analysis. *Research and Politics, 4*(4), 1–8.

Lyons, M. (1997). Presidential character revisited. *Political Psychology, 18*, 791–811.

Maccoby, E., Matthews, R., & Morton, A. (1954). Youth and political change. *Public Opinion Quarterly, 18*, 23–29.

Mackie, D. M. (1986). Social identification effects in group polarization. *Journal of Personality and Social Psychology, 50*, 720–728.

Mackie, D. M., Devos, T., & Smith, E. R. (2000). Intergroup emotions: Explaining offensive action tendencies in an intergroup context. *Journal of Personality and Social Psychology, 79*, 602–616.

Mackie, D. M., & Goethals, G. R. (1987). Individual and group goals. In C. Hendrick (Ed.), *Review of personality and social psychology* (pp. 144–166). Newbury Park, CA: Sage.

Mackie, D. M., & Hamilton, D. (Eds.). (1993). *Affect, cognition and stereotyping: Interactive processes in group perception*. Cambridge, MA: Academic Press.

Mackie, D. M., & Smith, E. R. (2018). Intergroup emotions theory: Production, regulation, and modification of group-based emotions. In *Advances in experimental social psychology* (pp. 1–69). Cambridge, MA: Academic Press.

Mackie, D. M., Smith, E. R., & Ray, D. G. (2008). Intergroup emotions and intergroup relations. *Social and Personality Psychology Compass, 2*, 1866–1880.

MacKuen, M., Marcus, G. E., Neuman, W. R., & Keele, L. (2007). The third way: The theory of affective intelligence and American democracy. In W. R. Neuman, G. E. Marcus, A. N. Crigler, & M. MacKuen (Eds.), *The affect effect: Dynamics of emotion in political thinking and behavior* (pp. 124–151). Chicago: University of Chicago Press.

MacNair, R. (2005). *Perpetration-induced traumatic stress: The psychological consequences of killing*. Oxford: Author's Choice Press.

MacWilliams, M.C. (2020). Trump is an authoritarian. So are millions of Americans. *Politico*. Retrieved from www.politico.com/news/magazine/2020/09/23/trump-america-authoritarianism-420681

Maddi, S. R. (1996). *Personality theories: A comparative analysis* (6th ed.). Washington: Brooks/Cole.

Madigan, T. (2001). *The burning: Massacre, destruction, and the Tulsa race riot of 1921*. New York: St. Martin's Press.

Madsen, K.B. (1961). *Theories of motivation: A comparative study of modern theories of motivation* (2nd ed.). Cleveland, OH: Howard Allen.

Magnavita, J. (2002). *Theories of personality: Contemporary approaches to the science of personality*. Chichester: John Wiley and Sons.

Mahncke, D. (1992). Reunification as an issue in German politics, 1949–1990. In D. Grosser (Ed.), *German unification: The unexpected challenge* (pp. 33–54). Oxford: Berg.

Major, B., Blodorn, A. & Blascovich, G.M. (2018). The threat of increasing diversity: Why many White Americans support Trump in the 2016 presidential election. *Group Processes & Intergroup Relations, 21*, 931–940.

Malici, A., & Malici, J. (2005). The operational codes of Fidel Castro and Kim Il Sung: The last cold warriors? *Political Psychology, 26*, 387–412.

Mani, R. (2000). Contextualizing police reform: Security, the rule of law and post-conflict peacebuilding. In T. T. Holm & E. B. Eide (Eds.), *Peacebuilding and police reform* (pp. 9–26). Portland, OR: Frank Cass.

Manis, M., Nelson, T., & Shedler, J. (1988). Stereotypes and social judgment: extremity, assimilation and contrast. *Journal of Personality and Social Psychology, 51*, 493–504.

Mansour, A. (2021). Sisi's last stand. *Foreign Policy*. https://foreignpolicy.com/2021/01/27/egypt-sisi-human-rights-protests-detention-terrorism-biden-trump

Marcus, G. (2013). *Political psychology: Neuroscience, genetics, and politics*. Oxford: Oxford University Press.

Marcus, G., & MacKuen, M. (1993). Anxiety, enthusiasm, and the vote: The emotional underpinnings of learning and involvement during presidential campaigns. *American Political Science Review, 87*, 672–685.

Marcus, G., Neuman, W. R., & MacKuen, M. (2000). *Affective intelligence and political judgment*. Chicago: University of Chicago Press.

Marfleet, B. G. (2000). The operational code of John F. Kennedy during the Cuban Missile Crisis: A comparison of public and private rhetoric. *Political Psychology, 21*, 545–558.

Marger, M. N. (2003). *Race and ethnic relations: American and global perspectives* (6th ed). Belmont, CA: Thompson Wadsworth.

Marilla Communications Group. (2001). *American attitudes toward Chinese Americans & Asian Americans: A Committee of 100 survey*. New York: Committee of 100.

Marks, M. L., Mirvis, P. H., Hackett, E. J., & Grady, J. F. (1986). Employee participation in a Quality Circle program: Impact on quality of work life, productivity, and absenteeism. *Journal of Applied Psychology, 71*, 61–69.

Markus, G. (1982). Political attitudes during an election year: A report on the 1980 NEW panel study. *American Political Science Review, 76*, 538–560.

Markus, G., & Converse, P. (1979). A dynamic simultaneous equation model of electoral choice. *American Political Science Review, 73*, 1055–1070.

Marques, J., Abrams, D., Paez, D., & Hogg, M. (2001). Social categorization, social identification, and rejection of deviant group members. In M. A. Hogg & S. Tindale (Eds.), *Blackwell handbook of social psychology: Group processes* (pp. 406–424). Malden, MA: Blackwell.

Marques, J., Yeerbyt, V. Y., & Leyens, J. P. (1988). The "black sheep effect": Extremity of judgments towards ingroup members as a function of group identification. *European Journal of Social Psychology, 18*, 1–16.

Marsella, A. J., Dubanoski, J., Hamada, W. C., & Morse, H. (2000). The measurement of personality across cultures: Historical, conceptual, and methodological issues and considerations. *American Behavioral Scientist, 44*, 41–62.

Martherus, J.L., Martinez, A.G., Piff, P.K., Theodoridis, A.G. (2019). Party animals? Extreme partisan polarization and dehumanization. *Political Behavior*, 43, 517–540.

Martin, J. L. (2001). *The authoritarian personality*, 50 years later: What lessons are there for political psychology? *Political Psychology, 22*, 1–26.

Marx, A. (1998). *Making race and nation: A comparison of the United States. South Africa, and Brazil.* Cambridge: Cambridge University Press.

Maslach, C., Stapp, J., & Santee, R. T. (1985). Individuation: Conceptual analysis and assessment. *Journal of Personality and Social Psychology, 49*, 729–738.

Maslow, A. (1954). *Motivation and personality*. New York: Harper and Row.

Mason, L. (2018). *Uncivil agreement: How politics became our identity*. Chicago: University of Chicago Press.

Mastors, E. (2000). Gerry Adams and the Northern Ireland peace process: A research note. *Political Psychology, 21*, 839–846.

Mastors, E. (2008). Can the Ulster Defense Association transition into mainstream politics? *Journal of Policing, Intelligence and Counterterrorism, 3*(1), 7–30.

Mastors, E., & Deffenbaugh, A. (2007). *The lesser jihad: Recruits and the al-Qaida network*. Lanham, MD: Rowman & Littlefield.

Mastors, E., & Norwitz, J. (2008). Influencing and disrupting leaders of armed groups: the case of Ayman al-Zawahiri, in J. Norwitz (Ed.), *Armed groups: studies in national security, counterterrorism and counterinsurgency* (pp. 323–342). New York: McGraw-Hill.

Mastors, E., & Siers, R. (2014). Omar al-Hammami: A case study in radicalization. *Behavioral Sciences and the Law, 32*, 377–388.

Mattoso, K. M. de Queiros. (1986). *To be a slave in Brazil, 1550–1888*. New Brunswick, NJ: Rutgers University Press.

May, E. R. (1973). *Lessons of the past: The use and misuse of history in American foreign policy*. Oxford: Oxford University Press.

Mayer, W. (1996). In defense of negative campaigning. *Political Science Quarterly, 111*, 437–455.

Maznevski, M. L. (1994). Understanding our differences: Performance in decision-making groups with diverse members. *Human Relations, 47*, 531–552.

Mazur, A. (1985). A biosocial model of status in face-to-face groups. *Social Forces, 64*, 377–402.

McAdam, D. (1988). *Freedom summer*. Oxford: Oxford University Press.

McAdam, D. (2016, June). The mind of Donald Trump. *The Atlantic*. Retrieved from www.theatlantic.com/magazine/archive/2016/06/the-mind-of-donald-trump/480771

McCain, B. E. (1986). Commitment under conditions of persistent failure: Escalation and de-escalation. *Journal of Applied Psychology, 71*, 280–284.

McCarthy, J. D., Rafail, P., & Gromis, A. (2013). Recent trends in public protest in the United States: The social movement society thesis revisited. In

J. van Stekelenburg, C. Roggebans, & B. Klandermans (Eds.), *The future of social movement research: Dynamics, mechanisms, and processes* (pp. 369–396). Minneapolis, MN: University of Minnesota Press.

McCarty, N. (2018). What we know and do not know about our polarized politics. In D. Hopkins & J. Sides (Eds.), *Political polarization in American politics* (pp. 1–8). New York: Bloomsbury.

McCauley, C. R. (2002). *The psychology of terrorism*. Washington, DC: Social Science Research Council.

McCauley, C. R. (2004). Psychological issues in understanding terrorism and the response to terrorism. In C. E. Stout (Ed.), *Psychology of terrorism, condensed edition: Coping with the continuing threat* (pp. 33–66). Westport, CT: Praeger.

McCauley, C. & Moskalenko, S. (2008). Mechanisms of political radicalization: Pathways toward terrorism. *Terrorism and Political Violence, 20*, 415–433.

McClain, P., Carter, N., DeFrancesco Soto, V., Lyle, M. Grynaviski, J., Nunnally, S., ... Cotton, K. (2006). Racial distancing in a southern city: Latino immigrants' view of Black Americans. *Journal of Politics, 68*, 578–584.

McClellan, S. (2008). *What happened? Inside the Bush White House and Washington's culture of deception*. Washington, DC: Public Affairs.

McClelland, D. C. (1975). *Power: The inner experience*. North Stratford, NH: Irvington.

McClelland, D. C. (1985). How motives, skills, and values determine what people do. *American Psychologist, 40*, 812–825.

McClelland, D. C., & Boyatzis, R. E. (1982). Leadership, motive pattern and long-term success in management. *Journal of Applied Psychology, 67*, 737–743.

McClosky, H., & Zaller, J. (1984). *The American ethos: Public attitudes toward capitalism and democracy*. Cambridge, MA: Harvard University Press.

McCombs, M., & Shaw, D. (1972). The agenda-setting function of the press. *Public Opinion Quarterly, 36*, 176–187.

McCrae, R. (1993). Moderated analyses of longitudinal personality stability. *Journal of Personality and Social Psychology, 65*, 577–585.

McCrae, R., & Costa, P. T. (1997). Conceptions and correlates of openness to experiences. In R. Hogan, J. Johnson, & S. Briggs (Eds.), *Handbook of personality psychology* (pp. 825–847). San Diego, CA: Academic Press.

McCrae, R., & Costa, P. T. (2006). Reinterpreting the Myers-Briggs type indicator from the perspective of the five-factor model of personality. *Journal of Personality, 57*, 17–40.

McDermott, R. (1998). *Risk-taking in international politics: Prospect theory in American foreign policy*. Ann Arbor, MI: University of Michigan Press.

McDermott, R. (2008). *Presidential leadership, illness, and decision making*. Cambridge: Cambridge University Press.

McDonald, M. M., Navarrete, C. D., & Sidanius, J. (2011). Developing a theory of gendered prejudice: An evolutionary and social dominance perspective. In R. M. Kramer, G. J. Leonardelli, & R. W. Livingston (Eds.), *Social cognition, social identity, and intergroup relations: A festschrift in honor of Marilynn B. Brewer*. Bristol: Psychology Press.

McDonald, M. M., Navarrete, C. D., & van Vugt, M. (2012). Evolution and the psychology of intergroup conflict: The male warrior hypothesis. *Philosophical Transactions of the Royal Society Biological Sciences, 367*, 670–679.

McElwee, S. & McDaniel, J. (2017). Economic anxiety didn't make people vote Trump, racism did. *The Nation*. Retrieved from www.thenation.com/article/archive/economic-anxiety-didnt-make-people-vote-trump-racism-did

McGraw, K. (2000). Contributions of the cognitive approach to political psychology. *Political Psychology, 21*, 805–827.

McGraw, K., Lodge, M., & Stroh, P. (1990). On-line processing in candidate evaluation: The effects of issue order, issue importance, and sophistication. *Political Behavior, 12*, 41–58.

McGraw, K., & Steenbergen, M. (1995). Pictures in the head: Memory representations of political actors. In M. Lodge & K. M. McGraw (Eds.), *Political judgment: Structure and process* (pp. 15–41). Ann Arbor, MI: University of Michigan Press.

McLeod, P. L., & Lobel, S. A. (1992). The effects of ethnic diversity on idea generation in small groups. *Academy of Management Best Paper Proceedings, 22*, 227–231.

McNamara, R. S. (1995). *In retrospect: The tragedy and lessons of Vietnam*. New York: Random House.

McVeigh helped speed militias demise. (2001, June 10). *Idaho Spokesman Review*, p. A10.

Mearsheimer, J. J. (2014). Why the Ukraine crisis is the West's fault. *Foreign Affairs, 93*, 77–89.

Meloen, J. (1994). A critical analysis of forty years of authoritarianism research: Did theory testing suffer from Cold War attitudes? In R. F. Farnen (Ed.), *Nationalism, ethnicity, and identity* (pp. 127–165). New Brunswick, NJ: Transaction Books.

Mendelberg, T. (2001). *The race card: Campaign strategy, implicit messages, and the norm of equality*. Princeton, NJ: Princeton University Press.

Merelman, R. (1969). The development of political ideology: A framework for the analysis of political socialization. *American Political Science Review, 63*, 750–767.

Merelman, R. (1986). Revitalizing political socialization. In M. G. Hermann (Ed.), *Political psychology* (pp. 279–319). San Francisco: Jossey-Bass.

Merkl, P. (1980). *The making of a stormtrooper*. Princeton, NJ: Princeton University Press.

Messe, L. A., Kerr, N. L., & Sattler, D. N. (1992). "But some animals are more equal than others": The supervisor as a privileged status in group contexts. In S. Worchel, W. Wood, & J. A. Simpson (Eds.), *Group process and productivity* (pp. 203–223). Newbury Park, CA: Sage.

Messick, D. M., & Brewer, M. B. (1983). Solving social dilemmas: A review. In L. Wheeler & P. Shaver (Eds.), *Review of personality and social psychology* (Vol. 4, pp. 11–44). Thousand Oaks, CA: Sage.

Michaelsen, L. K., Watson, W. E., & Black, R. H. (1989). A realistic test of individual vs. group consensus decision making. *Journal of Applied Psychology, 74*, 834–839.

Michener, H. A., & Burt, M. R. (1975). Use of social influence under varying conditions of legitimacy. *Journal of Personality and Social Psychology, 32*, 398–407.

Michener, H. A., & Lawler, E. J. (1975). The endorsement of formal leaders: An integrative model. *Journal of Personality and Social Psychology, 31,* 216–223.

Milbank, D. (2001). *Smashmouth: Two years in the gutter with Al Gore and George W. Bush: Notes from the 2000 campaign trail.* New York: Basic Books.

Milburn, M. A. (1991). *Persuasion and politics: The social psychology of public opinion.* Pacific Grove, CA: Brooks-Cole/Wadsworth.

Milburn, M. A., & Conrad, S. D. (1996). *The politics of denial.* Cambridge, MA: MIT Press.

Milburn, M. A., Conrad, S. D., Sala, F., & Carberry, S. (1995). Childhood punishment, denial and political attitudes. *Political Psychology, 16,* 447–478.

Milburn, M. A., & McGrail, A. B. (1992). The dramatic presentation of news and its effects on cognitive complexity. *Political Psychology, 13,* 613–632.

Milgram, S. (1963). Behavioral study of obedience. *Journal of Abnormal and Social Psychology, 67,* 371–378.

Milgram, S. (1974). *Obedience to authority.* New York: Harper and Row.

Miller, A. (1983). *For your own good. Hidden cruelty in child rearing and the roots of violence.* New York: Farrar, Straus & Giroux.

Miller, A., Wattenberg, M. P., & Malanchuk, O. (1986). Schematic assessments of presidential candidates. *American Political Science Review, 80,* 521–540.

Miller, C. E. (1980). Effects of payoffs on coalition formation: A test of three theories. *Social Psychology Quarterly, 43,* 154–164.

Miller, C. E., & Komorita, S. S. (1986). Changes in outcomes in coalition bargaining. *Journal of Personality and Social Psychology, 51,* 720–729.

Miller, J. (2007). Examining the mediators of agenda setting: A new experimental paradigm reveals the role of emotions. *Political Psychology, 28,* 689–717.

Miller, J., & Krosnick, J. (1996). News media impact on the ingredients of presidential evaluations: A program of research on the priming hypothesis. In D. C. Muntz, P. Sniderman, & R. Brody (Eds.), *Political persuasion and attitude change* (pp. 79–100). Ann Arbor, MI: University of Michigan Press.

Miller, W., & Shanks, M. (1996). *The new American voter.* Cambridge, MA: Harvard University Press.

Minard, R. (1952). Race relationships in the Pocahontas coal field. *Journal of Social Issues, 8,* 29–44.

Mindiola, T., Nieman, Y. F., & Rodriguez, N. (2002). *Black–Brown: Relations and stereotypes.* Austin, TX: University of Texas Press.

Minow, M. (1998). *Between vengeance and forgiveness: Facing history after genocide and mass violence.* Boston: Beacon Press.

Mintz, A. (2004). How do leaders make decisions? A poliheuristic perspective. *Journal of Conflict Resolution, 48,* 3–13.

Mintz, A. (2005). Applied decision analysis: Utilizing poliheuristic theory to explain and predict foreign policy and national security decisions. *International Studies Perspectives, 6,* 94–98.

Mintz, A., & Brule, D. (2009). Methodological issues in studying suicide terrorism. *Political Psychology, 30,* 365–380.

Mischel, W. (1968). *Personality and assessment.* Chichester: Wiley.

Mischel, W. (1973). Toward a cognitive social learning reconceptualization of personality. *Psychological Review, 30*, 252–283.
Mitchell, D. (2005). *Making foreign policy: Presidential management of the decision-making process.* Farnham: Ashgate.
Mitchell, D. (2007). Determining Indian foreign policy: An examination of prime ministerial leadership styles. *India Review, 6*, 251–287.
Mitchell, E. (2000). *W: Revenge of the Bush dynasty.* New York: Hyperion.
Moens, A. (2004). *The foreign policy of George W. Bush: Values, strategy, and loyalty.* Farnham: Ashgate.
Moghaddam, F. M. (2005). Staircase to terrorism: A psychological exploration. *American Psychologist, 60*, 161–169.
Moghaddam, F. M. (2007). The staircase to terrorism. In B. Bonger, L. M. Brown, L. E. Beutler, J. Breckenridge, & P. G. Zimbardo (Eds.), *Psychology of terrorism* (pp. 69–80). Oxford: Oxford University Press.
Moghaddam, F.M. (2018). *Mutual radicalization: How groups and nations drive each other to extremes.* Washington, DC: American Psychological Association.
Molm, L. D. (1987). Extending power-dependence theory: Power processes and negative outcomes. In E. J. Lawler & B. Markovsky (Eds.), *Advances in group processes* (pp. 171–198). Greenwich, CT: JAI.
Molm, L. D. (1988). The structure and use of power: A comparison of reward and punishment power. *Social Psychology Quarterly, 51*, 108–122.
Mongar, T. M. (1974). Personality and decision-making: John F. Kennedy in four crisis decisions. In G. J. DiRenzo (Ed.), *Personality and politics* (pp. 334–372). Garden City, NY: Doubleday-Anchor.
Monroe, K. R. (2008). Cracking the code of genocide: The moral psychology of rescuers, bystanders, and Nazis during the Holocaust. *Political Psychology, 29*, 699–737.
Montopoli, B. (2012, December 14). Tea party supporters: Who they are and what they believe. *CBS News.* Retrieved from www.cbsnews.com/news/tea-party-supporters-who-they-are-and-what-they-believe/
Moon, H. (2001). The two faces of conscientiousness: Duty and achievement striving in escalation of commitment dilemmas. *Journal of Applied Psychology, 86*, 535–540.
Mooney, M. J. (2021). Boogaloo boys prepare for civil war. *The Atlantic.* Retrieved from www.theatlantic.com/politics/archive/2021/01/boogaloo-prepare-civil-war/617683
Moore-Berg, S.L., Hameiri, & Bruneau, E. (2020). The prime psychological suspects of toxic political polarization. *Current Opinion in Behavioral Sciences, 34*, 199–204.
Moreland, R. L. (1987). The formation of small groups. In C. Hendrick (Ed.), *Review of personality and social psychology* (Vol. 8, pp. 80–110). Newbury Park, CA: Sage.
Moreland, R. L., & Levine, J. M. (1982). Socialization in small groups: Temporal changes in individual-group relations. In L. Berkowitz (Ed.), *Advances in experimental social psychology* (Vol. 15, pp. 137–192). New York: Academic Press.
Morgenthau, H. J. (1948). *Politics among nations: The struggle for power and peace.* New York: Alfred A. Knopf.

Morris, A. (1999). A retrospective on the civil rights movement: Political and intellectual landmarks. *Annual Review of Sociology, 25*, 517–539.

Morris, W. N., & Miller, R. S. (1975). The effects of consensus-breaking and consensus-preempting partners on reduction in conformity. *Journal of Experimental Social Psychology, 11*, 215–223.

Moscovici, S. (1985). Social influence and conformity. In G. Lindzey & E. Aronson (Eds.), *Handbook of social psychology* (pp. 347–412). New York: Random House.

MSNBC. (2008). No hidden white bias seen in vote. Retrieved from www.msnbc.msn.com/id/2758972

Mullen, B., Brown, R., & Smith, C. (1992). Ingroup bias as a function of salience, relevance, and status: An integration. *European Journal of Social Psychology, 22*, 103–122.

Mullen, B., & Copper, C. (1994). The relation between group cohesiveness and performance: An integration. *Psychological Bulletin, 115*, 210–227.

Mullen, B., Johnson, C., & Salas, E. (1991). Productivity loss in brainstorming groups: A meta-analytic interpretation. *Basic and Applied Social Psychology, 12*, 3–24.

Mumford, M. D. (2006). *Pathways to outstanding leadership: A comparative analysis of charismatic, ideological, and pragmatic leaders*. Mahwah, NJ: Lawrence Erlbaum.

Mumford, M. D., Espejo, J., Hunter, S. T., Bedell-Avers, K. E., Eubanks, D., & Connelly, S. (2007). The sources of leader violence: A comparison of ideological and non-ideological leaders. *Leadership Quarterly, 18*, 217–235.

Mummendey, A., Kessler, T., Klink, A., & Mielke, R. (1999). Strategies to cope with negative social identity: Predictions by social identity theory and relative deprivation theory. *Journal of Personality and Social Psychology, 76*, 229–245.

Mycock, A., & Hayton, R. (2014). The party politics of Englishness. *British Journal of Politics and International Relations, 16*, 251–272.

Myers, D. G. (1978). Polarizing effects of social comparison. *Journal of Experimental Social Psychology, 14*, 554–563.

Myers, D. G., & Lamm, H. (1976). The group polarization phenomenon. *Psychological Bulletin, 83*, 602–627.

Myrdal, G. (1944). *The American dilemma*. New York: McGraw-Hill.

Narvaez, D. (2020). The psychology of Donald Trump. *Psychology Today*. Retrieved from www.psychologytoday.com/us/blog/moral-landscapes/202008/the-psychology-donald-trump

National Society of Hispanic Professionals. (2008). Hispanic stereotypes: How they affect us at work. Retrieved from www.nshp.org/career_and_jobs/hispanic_Stereotypes_how_they_affect_us_at_work

Navarrete, C. D., Olsson, A., Ho, A., Mendes, W., Thomsen, L., & Sidanius, J. (2009). Fear extinction to an out-group face: The role of target gender. *Psychological Science, 20*(2), 155–158.

Nazaryan, A. (2017). Drain the swamp one year later: Is Trump draining or drowning? *Newsweek*. Retrieved from www.newsweek.com/trump-white-house-has-become-swamp-he-promised-drain-686000

Nebehay, S. (2021). UN Syria envoy says constitutional talks in peril. Reuters. Retrieved from www.reuters.com/article/us-syria-un/un-syria-envoy-says-constitutional-talks-in-peril-idUSKBN29Y2G1

Nelson, T., Clawson, R., & Oxley, Z. (1997). Media framing of a civil liberties conflict and its effect on tolerance. *American Political Science Review, 91*, 567–583.

Nelson, T., & Oxley, Z. (1999). Issue framing effects on belief importance and opinion. *Journal of Politics, 61*, 1040–1067.

Nemeth, C. J. (1986). Differential contributions of majority and minority influence. *Psychological Review, 93*, 23–32.

Nemeth, C. J., Connell, J. B., Rogers, J. D., & Brown, K. S. (2001). Improving decision making by means of dissent. *Journal of Applied Social Psychology, 31*, 45–58.

Neuman, W. R. (1986). *The paradox of mass politics*. Cambridge, MA: Harvard University Press.

Neuman, W. R., Marcus, G. E., Crigler, A. N., & MacKuen, M. (2007). Theorizing affect's effects. In W. R. Neuman, G. E. Marcus, A. N. Crigler, & M. MacKuen (Eds.), *The affect effect: Dynamics of emotion in political thinking and behavior* (pp. 1–23). Chicago: University of Chicago Press.

Neustadt, R. E. (1990 [1960]). *Presidential power and the modern presidents: The politics of leadership from Roosevelt to Reagan*. New York: Free Press.

Neustadt, R. E., & May, E. R. (1986). *Thinking in time: The uses of history for decision makers*. New York: Free Press.

Newcomb, T. M. (1943). *Personality and social change*. Hinsdale, IL: Dryden Press.

Newcomb, T. M. (1960). Varieties of interpersonal attraction. In D. Cartwright & A. Zander (Eds.), *Group dynamics: Research and theory* (2nd ed., pp. 104–119). Evanston, IL: Row, Peterson.

Newcomb, T. M. (1979). Reciprocity of interpersonal attraction: A nonconfirmation of a plausible hypothesis. *Social Psychology Quarterly, 42*, 299–306.

Nicholson, N., Soane, E., Fenton-O'Creevey, M., & William, P. (2005). Personality and domain-specific risk taking. *Journal of Risk Research, 8*, 157–176.

Nicol, A., Charbonneau, D., & Boies, K. (2007). Right-wing authoritarianism and social dominance orientation in a Canadian military sample. *Military Psychology, 19*, 239–257.

Nie, N., Verba, S., & Petrocik, J. (1976). *The changing American voter*. Cambridge, MA: Harvard University Press.

Nieburg, H. L. (1969). *Political violence: The behavioral process*. New York: St. Martin's Press.

Niemi, R. (1973). Political socialization. In J. Knutson (Ed.), *Handbook of political psychology* (pp. 117–138). San Francisco: Jossey-Bass.

Niemi, R., & Hepburn, M. (1995). The rebirth of political socialization. *Perspectives on Political Science, 24*, 5–16.

Niemi, R., & Weisberg, H. (Eds.). (1993). *Controversies in voting behavior* (3rd ed.). Washington, DC: Congressional Quarterly.

Nolan, P. (2013). *Northern Ireland peace monitoring report Number 2*. Belfast: Community Relations Council.

Norpoth, H., & Bednarczuk, M. (2013). Primary model gets it right and early. *PS: Political Science and Politics, 46*, 37.

Norris, P. (1997). *Electoral change since 1945*. Oxford: Blackwell.

Norris, P. & Inglehart R. (2019). *Cultural backlash: Trump, Brexit, and authoritarian populism.* Cambridge: Cambridge University Press.

Northcraft, G. B., & Neale, M. A. (1986). Opportunity costs and the framing of resource allocation decisions. *Organizational Behavior and Human Decision Processes, 37,* 348–356.

Northcraft, G. B., & Wolf, G. (1984). Dollars, sense, and sunk costs: A life-cycle model of resource allocation decisions. *Academy of Management Review, 9,* 225–234.

Noueihed, L., & Warren, A. (2013). *The battle for the Arab Spring: Revolution, counter-revolution and the making of a new era.* New Haven, CT: Yale University Press.

NPR (2016). Here's what Clinton and Trump plan on immigration. Retrieved from www.pbs.org/newshour/politics/trump-clinton-immigration-plans

Nunn, C., Crockett, H., & Williams, J. A. (1978). *Tolerance for nonconformity.* San Francisco: Jossey-Bass.

Nydegger, R V. (1975). Information processing complexity and leadership status. *Journal of Experimental Social Psychology, 11,* 317–328.

O'Callaghan, S. (1998). *The informer.* New York: Bantam Books.

O'Dell, J. W. (1968). Group size and emotional interaction. *Journal of Personality and Social Psychology, 8,* 75–78.

O'Hanlon, M. (2000). *Technological change and the future of warfare.* Washington, DC: Brookings Institution Press.

Oliner, S., & Oliner, P. (1988). *The altruistic personality: Rescuers of Jews in Nazi Europe.* New York: Free Press.

Olson, B. D., & Evans, D. L. (1999). The role of the big five personality dimensions in the direction and affective consequences of everyday social comparisons. *Personality and Social Psychology Bulletin, 25,* 1498–1508.

Olson, D.V.A., & Caddell, D. (1994). Generous congregations, generous givers: Congregational contexts that stimulate individual giving. *Review of Religious Research, 36,* 168–180.

Open Science Collaboration (2015). Estimating the reproducibility of psychological science. *Science, 349*(6251), doi:10.1126/science.aac4716.

O'Reilly, K. P. (2012). Leaders' perceptions and nuclear proliferation: A political psychology approach to proliferation. *Political Psychology, 33,* 767–789.

Orr, C. (2019). Why do Trump's biggest fans believe him even when he lies? The answer is in the human brain. *The Independent.* Retrieved from www.independent.co.uk/voices/trump-lies-supporters-fans-believe-fake-news-facts-immigration-border-wall-a8781571.html

Ortony, A., Clore, G., & Collins, A. (1988). *The cognitive structure of emotions.* Cambridge: Cambridge University Press.

Osseiran, H. (2018). How sectarianism can help explain the Syrian war. *The New Humanitarian.* Retrieved from https://deeply.thenewhumanitarian.org/syria/articles/2018/03/06/how-sectarianism-can-help-explain-the-syrian-war

O'Toole, P. (2000, November 21). Hate-figure and hero. *BBC News.* Retrieved from http://news.bbc.co.uk/2/hi/europe/213964.stm

Ottati, V., & Wyer, R. (1990). The cognitive mediators of political choice: Toward a comprehensive model of political information processing. In J. Ferejohn & J. Kuklinski (Eds.), *Information and democratic processes* (pp. 186–215). Urbana, IL: University of Illinois Press.

Ottati, V. C., & Wyer, R. S. (1993). Affect and political judgement. In S. Iyengar & W. McGuire (Eds.), *Explorations in political psychology* (pp. 296–315). Durham, NC: Duke University Press.

Oyovbaire, S. (1984). *Federalism in Nigeria*. New York: St. Martin's Press.

Padilla, A., Hogan, R., & Kaiser, R. B. (2007). The toxic triangle: Destructive leaders, susceptible followers, and conducive environments. *Leadership Quarterly, 18*, 176–194.

Page, B. I., & Jones, C. C. (1979). Reciprocal effects of policy preferences, party loyalties, and the vote. *American Political Science Review, 73*, 1055–1070.

Papic, M., & Noonan, S. (2011). Social media as a tool for protest. *Stratfor Global Intelligence*. Retrieved from www.stratfor.com/weekly/20110202-social-media-tool-protest

Pardos-Prado, S., Lancee, B., & Sagarzazu, I. (2014). Immigration and electoral change in mainstream political space. *Political Behavior, 36*, 847–875.

Park, B. (1993). *Ailing, aging, addicted: Studies of compromised leadership*. Lexington, KT: University Press of Kentucky.

Park, J., & Banaji, M. R. (2000). Mood and heuristics: The influence of happy and sad states on sensitivity and bias in stereotyping. *Journal of Personality and Social Psychology, 78*, 1005–1023.

Parker, C. F., & Stern, E. K. (2005). Bolt from the blue or avoidable failure? Revisiting September 11 and the origins of strategic surprise. *Foreign Policy Analysis, 1*, 301–331.

Parker, C.S. (2016). Race and politics in the age of Obama. *Annual Review of Sociology, 42*, 217–230.

Patterson, M. L., & Schaeffer, R. E. (1977). Effects of size and sex composition on interaction distance, participation, and satisfaction in small groups. *Small Group Behavior, 8*, 433–442.

Patterson, T. (1993). *Out of order*. New York: Alfred A. Knopf.

Paul, A. M. (2004). *The cult of personality testing: How personality tests are leading us to miseducate our children, mismanage our companies, and misunderstand ourselves*. New York: Free Press.

Payin, E. A., & Popov, A. A. (1996). *Chechnya—From past to present*. Santa Monica, CA: Rand Corporation.

Pearce, K. (1977). Police negotiations. *Canadian Psychiatric Association Journal, 22*, 171–174.

Pearlstein, R. M. (1991). *The mind of the political terrorist*. Oxford: Scholarly Resources.

Pearson, C.A.L. (1987). Participative goal setting as a strategy for improving performance and job satisfaction: A longitudinal evaluation with railway track maintenance groups. *Human Relations, 40*, 473–488.

Pearson, C.A.L. (1992). Autonomous work groups: An evaluation at an industrial site. *Human Relations, 45*, 905–936.

Peffley, M., & Hurwitz, J. (1998). Whites' stereotypes of blacks: Sources and political consequences. In J. Hurwitz & M. Peffley (Eds.), *Perception and prejudice: Race and politics in the United States* (pp. 58–99). New Haven, CT: Yale University Press.

Perera, V. (1993). *Unfinished conquest: The Guatemalan tragedy*. Berkeley, CA: University of California Press.

Perina, K. (2002). Suicide terrorism. *Psychology Today, 35*(5), 15.

Perloff, R. M. (1993). *The dynamics of persuasion*. Mahwah, NJ: Lawrence Erlbaum.

Perreault, S., & Bourhis, R. (1999). Ethnocentrism, social identification, and discrimination. *Personality and Social Psychology Bulletin, 25*, 92–103.

Pervin, L. A., & John, O. (1997). *Personality: Theory and research* (7th ed.). Chichester: John Wiley and Sons.

Peterson, S. (2000a, December 11). Heavy civilian toll in Chechnya's "unlimited violence." *Christian Science Monitor*, p. A7.

Peterson, S. (2000b). *Me against my brother: At war in Somalia, Sudan, and Rwanda*. London: Routledge.

Pettigrew, T. (1979). The ultimate attribution error: Extending Allport's cognitive analysis of prejudice. *Personality and Social Psychology Bulletin, 5*, 461–476.

Pettigrew, T. F. (2017). Social psychological perspectives on Trump supporters. *Journal of Social and Political Psychology, 5*, 107–116.

Pettigrew, T., & Martin, J. (1989). Organizational inclusion of minority groups: A social psychological analysis. In J. P. van Oudenhoven & T. Willemsen (Eds.), *Ethnic minorities: Social psychological perspectives* (pp. 169–200). Berwyn, PA: Swets North America.

Pettigrew, T., & Meertens, R. (1995). Subtle and blatant prejudice in Western Europe. *European Journal of Social Psychology, 25*, 57–76.

Petty, R. E., & Cacioppo, J. T. (1986). The elaboration likelihood model of persuasion. In L. Berkowitz (Ed.), *Advances in experimental social psychology* (pp. 123–205). New York: Academic Press.

Petty, R. E., & Wegener, D. T. (1998). Attitude change: Multiple roles for persuasion variables. In D. T. Gilbert, S. T. Fiske, & G. Lindzey (Eds.), *The handbook of social psychology* (pp. 323–390). New York: McGraw-Hill.

Pew Research Center. (2007). Blacks see growing values gap between poor and middle classes. Retrieved from www.pewresearch.org/social-trends/2007/11/13/blacks-see-growing-values-gap-between-poor-and-middle-class

Pew Research Center. (2008a). Fewer voters identify as Republicans. Retrieved from www.pewresearch.org/pubs/773/fewer-voters-identify-as-republicans

Pew Research Center. (2008b). Inside Obama's sweep. Retrieved from www.pewresearch.org/pubs/1023/exit-poll-analysis-2008

Pew Research Center. (2012). Media bias. Retrieved from www.people-press.org/subjects/media-bias

Pew Research Center. (2016a). 2016 campaign: Strong interest, widespread dissatisfaction. Retrieved from www.pewresearch.org/politics/2016/07/07/2016-campaign-strong-interest-widespread-dissatisfaction

Pew Research Center. (2016b). Behind Trump's victory: Divisions by race, gender, education. Retrieved from www.pewresearch.org/fact-tank/2016/11/09/behind-trumps-victory-divisions-by-race-gender-education

Pew Research Center. (2016c). Social and demographic trends. Retrieved from www.pewsocialtrends.org/2013/08/22

Pew Research Center. (2017). Most Americans say Trump's election has led to worse race relations in the U.S. Retrieved from www.pewresearch.org/politics/2018/08/09/for-most-trump-voters-very-warm-feelings-for-him-endured

Pew Research Center. (2019). Partisan antipathy: More intense, more personal. Retrieved from www.pewresearch.org/politics/2019/10/10/how-partisans-view-each-other

Pew Research Center. (2020). In changing U.S. electorate, race and education remain stark dividing lines. Retrieved from www.pewresearch.org/politics/2020/06/02/democratic-edge-in-party-identification-narrows-slightly

Pierce, W. [pseudonym Andrew McDonald] (1978). *The Turner diaries.* Charlottesville, VA: National Vanguard Books.

Pika, J. A. (1988). Management style and the White House. *Administration and Society, 20,* 3–29.

Pittenger, D. J. (1993). Measuring the MBTI ... And coming up short. *Journal of Career Planning & Placement, 51,* 48–52.

Plock, E. (1993). *East German–West German relations and the fall of the GDR.* Boulder, CO: Westview Press.

Plous, S. (1993). *The psychology of judgment and decisionmaking.* New York: McGraw-Hill.

Popkin, S. (1994). *The reasoning voter: Communication and persuasion in presidential campaigns.* Chicago: University of Chicago Press.

Porter, R. B. (1980). *Presidential decision making: The economic policy board.* Cambridge: Cambridge University Press.

Post, J.M. (1984). Notes on a psychodynamic theory of terrorist behavior. *Terrorism: An International Journal, 7,* 241–256.

Post, J.M. (2004). *Leaders and their followers in a dangerous world.* Ithaca, NY: Cornell University Press.

Post, J.M., & Robins, R. (1993). *When illness strikes the leader: The dilemma of the captive king.* New Haven, CT: Yale University Press.

Post, J. M. (1991). Saddam Hussein of Iraq: A political psychology profile. *Political Psychology, 12,* 279–289.

Post, J. M. (1993a). The defining moment of Saddam's life: A political psychology perspective on the leadership and decision making of Saddam Hussein during the Gulf Crisis. In S. A. Renshon (Ed.), *The political psychology of the Gulf War: Leaders, publics, and the process of conflict* (pp. 49–66). Pittsburgh, PA: University of Pittsburgh Press.

Post, J. M. (1993b). Current concepts of the narcissistic personality: Implications for political psychology. *Political Psychology, 14,* 99–122.

Powell, R. (1990). *Nuclear deterrence theory: The search for credibility.* Cambridge: Cambridge University Press.

Power, S. (2002). *"A problem from hell": America and the age of genocide.* New York: Basic Books.

Pratkanis, A. R. (1989). The cognitive representation of attitudes. In A. R. Pratkanis, S. J. Breckler, & A. G. Greenwald (Eds.), *Attitude structure and function* (pp. 71–98). Hillsdale, NJ: Lawrence Erlbaum.

Pratkanis, A. R., & Greenwald, A. G. (1989). A sociocognitive model of attitude structure and function. *Advances in Experimental Social Psychology* (Vol. 22, pp. 245–285). New York: Academic Press.

Pratto, F., Cidam, A., Stewart, A.L., Zeineddine, F.B., Aranda, M., Aiello, A. (2012). Social dominance in context and in individuals: Contextual moderation of robust effects of social dominance orientation in 15 languages and 20 countries. *Social Psychological and Personality Science 4*, 587–599.

Pratto, F., Sidanius, J., Stallworth, L., & Malle, B. (1994). Social dominance orientation: A personality variable predicting social and political attitudes. *Journal of Personality and Social Psychology, 67*, 741–763.

Pratto, F., Stallworth, L.M., Conway-Lan, S. (1998). Social dominance orientation and the ideological legitimization of social policy. *Journal of Applied Social Psychology, 28*, 1853–1875.

Prentice, D. A., Miller, D. T., & Lightdale, J. R. (1994). Asymmetries in attachments to groups and to their members: Distinguishing between common-identity and common-bond groups. *Personality and Social Psychology Bulletin, 20*, 484–493.

Preston, T. (1997). Following the leader: The impact of U.S. presidential style upon advisory group dynamics, structure, and decision. In P. 't Hart, E. Stern, & B. Sundelius (Eds.), *Beyond groupthink: Political group dynamics and foreign policymaking* (pp. 191–248). Ann Arbor, MI: University of Michigan Press.

Preston, T. (2001). *The president and his inner circle: Leadership style and the advisory process in foreign policy making.* New York: Columbia University Press.

Preston, T. (2007/2009). *From lambs to lions: Future security relationships in a world of biological and nuclear weapons.* Lanham, MD: Rowman & Littlefield.

Preston, T. (2008). Weathering the politics of responsibility and blame: The Bush administration and its response to Hurricane Katrina. In. A. Boin, A. McConnell, & P. 't Hart (Eds.), *Governing after crisis: The politics of investigation, accountability, and learning* (pp. 33–61). Cambridge: Cambridge University Press.

Preston, T. (2011). *Pandora's trap: Presidential decision making and blame avoidance in Vietnam and Iraq.* Lanham, MD: Rowman & Littlefield.

Preston, T. (2012). The role of leaders in sequential decision-making: Lyndon Johnson, advisory dynamics, and Vietnam. In C. F. Hermann (Ed.), *When things go wrong: Foreign policy decision making under adverse feedback* (pp. 53–88). New York: Routledge.

Preston, T. (2017). The leadership style of president Donald Trump and its likely impact on US foreign and security policy. Presentation for the Joseph Kruzel Memorial Foreign and Defense Luncheon Series, Washington State University.

Preston, T., & Hermann. M. G. (2004). Presidential leadership style and the foreign policy advisory process. In E. R. Wittkopf & J. M. McCormick (Eds.), *The domestic sources of American foreign policy: Insights and evidence* (4th ed., pp. 363–380). Lanham, MD: Rowman & Littlefield.

Preston, T., & 't Hart, P. (1999). Understanding and evaluating bureaucratic politics: The nexus between political leaders and advisory systems. *Political Psychology, 20*, 49–98.

Pritchard, R. D., Jones, S. D., Roth, P. L., Stuebing, K. K., & Ekeberg, S. E. (1988). Effects of group feedback, goal setting, and incentives on organizational productivity. *Journal of Applied Psychology, 73*, 337–358.

Pronin, E., Puccio, C., & Ross, L. (2002). Understanding misunderstanding: Social psychological perspectives. In T. Gilovich, D. Griffin, & D. Kahneman (Eds.), *Heuristics and biases: The psychology of intuitive judgment* (pp. 636–665). Cambridge: Cambridge University Press.

Pruitt, D. G., & Kimmel, M. J. (1977). Twenty years of experimental gaming: Critique, synthesis, and suggestions for the future. *Annual Review of Psychology, 28*, 363–392.

Pruitt, D. G., & Rubin, J. Z. (1986). *Social conflict: Escalation, stalemate, and settlement.* New York: Random House.

Prunier, G. (2005). *Darfur: The ambiguous genocide.* Ithaca, NY: Cornell University Press.

Rabbie, J. M., & Wilkins, G. (1971). Intergroup competition and its effects on intragroup and intergroup relations. *European Journal of Social Psychology, 1*, 215–234.

Rabie, M. (1994). *Conflict resolution and ethnicity.* Westport, CT: Praeger.

Rabinowitz, J. L. (1999). Go with the flow or fight the power? The interactive effect of social dominance orientation and perceived injustice on support for the status quo. *Political Psychology, 20*, 1–24.

Raden, D. (1999). Is anti-Semitism currently part of an authoritarian attitude syndrome? *Political Psychology, 20*, 323–343.

Raghavan, S. (2008, April 7). Between Iraqi Shiites, a deepening animosity. *Washington Post.* Retrieved from www.military-quotes.com/forum/between-iraqi-shiites-deepening-animosity-t59025.html

Rahn, W., Aldrich, J., Borgida, E., & Sullivan, J. (1990). A social cognitive model of candidate appraisal. In J. Ferejohn & J. Kuklinski (Eds.), *Information and democratic process* (pp. 136–159). Chicago: University of Chicago Press.

Ramakrishnan, K. (2017). The Asian American vote in 2016: Record gains, but also gaps. *AAPI.* Retrieved from http://aapidata.com/blog/voting-gains-gaps

Rane, H., & Ewart, J. (2012). The Framing of Islam and Muslims in the tenth anniversary coverage of 9/11: Implications for reconciliation and moving on. *Journal of Muslim Minority Affairs, 32*, 310–322.

Ratcliffe, R. (2017). Who are the Rohingya and what is happening in Myanmar? *The Guardian.* Retrieved from www.theguardian.com/global-development/2017/sep/06/who-are-the-rohingya-and-what-is-happening-in-myanmar

Raven, B. H. (1965). Social influence and power. In I. D. Steiner & M. Fishbein (Eds.), *Current studies in social psychology* (pp. 371–382). New York: Holt, Rinehart, and Winston.

Redlawsk, D. P., Civettini, A., & Lau, R. R. (2007). Affective intelligence and voting: Information processing and learning in a campaign. In W. R. Neuman, G. E. Marcus, A. N. Crigler, & M. MacKuen (Eds.), *The affect effect: Dynamics of emotion in political thinking and behavior* (pp. 1–23). Chicago: University of Chicago Press.

Remington, R. (1996). The Yugoslav army: Trauma and transition. In C. Danopoulos & D. Zirker (Eds.), *Civil–military relations in the Soviet and Yugoslav successor states* (pp. 153–173). Boulder, CO: Westview Press.

Renshon, S. A. (2012). *Barack Obama and the politics of redemption.* London: Routledge.

Renshon, S. A. (1996). *High hopes: The Clinton presidency and the politics of ambition*. New York: New York University Press.

Reuters Staff. (2020). Lopez Obrador says Trump has "completely changed" attitude toward Mexicans. Retrieved from www.reuters.com/article/us-usa-mexico-president-trump/lopez-obrador-says-trump-has-completely-changed-attitude-toward-mexicans-idUSKBN24B06R

Reyes-Quilodran, C. (2001). The main factors that could determine the behavior of a torturer (Unpublished master's thesis). Washington State University.

Rhodes, E. (1989). *Power and MADness: The logic of nuclear coercion*. New York: Columbia University Press.

Richards, J. M., & Gross, J. J. (1999). Composure at any cost? The cognitive consequences of emotion suppression. *Personality and Social Psychology Bulletin, 25*, 1033–1044.

Richardson, L. (1960). *Arms and insecurity*. Pacific Grove, CA: Boxwood Press.

Ridgeway, J. (1995). *Blood in the face* (2nd ed.). New York: Thunder's Mouth Press.

Ridout, T. N., & Franz, M. M. (2011). *The persuasive power of campaign advertising*. Philadelphia, PA: Temple University Press.

Rigby, A. (2001). *Justice and reconciliation after the violence*. Boulder, CO: Lynne Rienner.

Ringelmann, M. (1913). Research on animate sources of power: The work of man. *Annales de L'Institut National Agronomique* (2nd ed.), *12*, 1–40.

Roberts, B. W., & Donahue, E. M. (1994). One personality, multiple selves: Integrating personality and social roles. *Journal of Personality, 62*, 201–218.

Robinson, R., Keltner, D., Ward, A., & Ross, L. (1995). Actual versus assumed differences in construal: "Naive realism" in intergroup perception and conflict. *Journal of Personality and Social Psychology, 68*, 404–417.

Rodriguez, S. (2020). Why Mexico's president is buddies with Trump despite years of insults. *Politico*. Retrieved from www.politico.com/news/2020/07/07/mexico-president-andres-manuel-lopez-obrador-friends-trump-350974

Rodrik, D. (2018). Populism and the economics of globalization. *Journal of International Business Policy, 1*, 12–33.

Rogers, R., & Prentice-Dunn, S. (1981). Deindividuation and anger-mediated interracial aggression: Unmasking regressive racism. *Journal of Personality and Social Psychology, 41*, 63–73.

Rogow, A. (1963). *James Forrestal: A study in personality, politics, and policy*. New York: Macmillan.

Rokeach, M. (1973). *The nature of human values*. New York: Free Press.

Romano, L. (2001, May 4). An enigma awaits death. *Washington Post*, pp. A1, A3.

Roper Center. (2012). How groups voted in 2012. Retrieved from www.ropercenter.uconn.edu/polls/us-elections

Roper Center. (2016). How groups voted in 2016. Retrieved from https://ropercenter.cornell.edu/how-groups-voted-2016

Rosati, J. A. (1987). *The Carter administration's quest for global community: Beliefs and their impact on behavior*. Columbia, SC: University of South Carolina Press.

Rosati, J. A. (1990). Continuity and change in the foreign policy beliefs of political leaders: Addressing the controversy over the Carter administration. *Political Psychology, 9*, 471–505.

Rosch, E. (1978). Principles of categorization. In E. Rosch & B. Lloyd (Eds.), *Cognition and categorization* (pp. 27–38). Hillsdale, NJ: Lawrence Erlbaum.

Rosenberg, T. (1992). *Children of Cain: Violence and the violent in Latin America*. Harmondsworth: Penguin.

Rosenthal, S. A., & Pittinsky, T. L. (2006). Narcissistic leadership. *Leadership Quarterly, 17*, 617–633.

Ross, J., & Staw, B. M. (1986). Expo 86: An escalation prototype. *Administrative Science Quarterly, 31*, 274–297.

Ross, L. (1977). The intuitive psychologist and his shortcomings: Distortions in the attribution process. In L. Berkowitz (Ed.), *Advances in experimental social psychology* (Vol. 10, pp. 174–221). New York: Academic Press.

Rothbart, M., & Johns, O. (1993). Intergroup relations and stereotype change: A social-cognitive analysis and some longitudinal findings. In P. Sniderman, P. Tetlock, & E. Carmines (Eds.), *Prejudice, politics, and the American dilemma* (pp. 32–59). Stanford, CA: Stanford University Press.

Rothman, J., & Olson, M. L. (2001). From interests to identities: Towards a new emphasis on interactive conflict resolution. *Journal of Peace Research, 38*, 289–305.

Rothschild, J. (1981). *Ethnopolitics: A conceptual framework*. New York: Columbia University Press.

Rothwell, J. & Diego-Rosell, P. (2016). Explaining nationalist political views: The case of Donald Trump. Retrieved from www.semanticscholar.org/paper/Explaining-Nationalist-Political-Views%3A-The-Case-of-Rothwell-Diego-Rosell/b9f844e1dc20689ad32022b8fcb11cd19bcb604a

Rotter, J. B. (1966). Generalized expectancies for internal versus external control of reinforcement. *Psychological Monographs: General and Applied, 80*(1), 1–28.

Roubini, N. (2016). *Globalization's political fault lines*. Retrieved from www.project-syndicate.org/commentary/globalization-political-fault-lines-by-nouriel-roubini-2016-07?barrier=accesspaylog

Rowe, A. J., & Mason, R. O. (1987). *Managing with style: A guide to understanding, assessing, and improving decision making*. San Francisco: Jossey-Bass.

RTI International (2021). Addicted to hate: Understanding the motives of former white supremacists. Retrieved from www.rti.org/impact/addicted-hate-understanding-motives-former-white-supremacists

Rubenstein, C. M., & Shaver, P. (1980). Loneliness in two northeastern cities. In J. Hartog & R. Audy (Eds.), *The anatomy of loneliness*. New York: International Universities Press.

Rubenzer, S. J., & Faschingbauer, T. R. (2004). *Personality, character, and leadership in the White House: Psychologists assess the presidents*. Washington, DC: Bassey's.

Rubin, J. Z., & Brockner, J. (1975). Factors affecting entrapment in waiting situations: The Rosencrantz and Guildenstern effect. *Journal of Personality and Social Psychology, 31*, 1054–1063.

Rucht, D. (2013). Social movement structures in action: Conceptual propositions and empirical illustration. In J. van Stekelenburg, C. Roggebans, & B. Klandermans (Eds.), *The future of social movement research: Dynamics, mechanisms, and processes* (pp. 169–190). Minneapolis, MN: University of Minnesota Press.

Ruder, M. K., & Gill, D. L. (1982). Immediate effects of win–loss on perceptions of cohesion in intramural and intercollegiate volleyball teams. *Journal of Sport Psychology, 4*, 227–234.

Ruiz, N.G., Horowitz, J.M., & Tamir, C. (2020). Black and Asian Americans say they have experienced discrimination amid the COVID-19 outbreak. Pew Research. Retrieved from www.pewresearch.org/social-trends/2020/07/01/many-black-and-asian-americans-say-they-have-experienced-discrimination-amid-the-covid-19-outbreak

Rule, N. O., Freeman, J. B., Moran, J. M., Gabrieli, J.D.E., Adams, R. B., & Ambady, N. (2010). Voting behavior is reflected in amygdala response across cultures. *Social Cognitive and Affective Neuroscience, 5*(2–3), 349–355.

Rumble, A. (2003). Empathy induced cooperation and social dilemmas: An investigation into the influence of attribution type. Unpublished doctoral dissertation, Washington State University.

Rummel, R. J. (1994). *Death by government.* Piscataway, NJ: Transaction Books.

Russell, D., Peplau, L. A., & Cutrona, C. E. (1980). The revised UCLA Loneliness Scale: Concurrent and discriminant validity evidence. *Journal of Personality and Social Psychology, 39*, 472–480.

Ryan, N. (2003). *Into a world of hate.* London: Routledge.

Sabato, L. (1991). *Feeding frenzy: How attack journalism has transformed American politics.* New York: Free Press.

Sabini, J. P., & Silver, M. (1993). Destroying the innocent with a clear conscience: A sociopsychology of the Holocaust. In N. Kressel (Ed.), *Political psychology: Classic and contemporary readings* (pp. 192–217). New York: Paragon House.

Safi, M. (2020, December 17). Life has got worse since Arab spring, say people across Middle East. *The Guardian*. Retrieved from www.theguardian.com/global-development/2020/dec/17/arab-spring-people-middle-east-poll

Sagan, S. D. (1994). The perils of proliferation: Organization theory, deterrence theory, and the spread of nuclear weapons. *International Security, 18*, 66–107.

Sageman, M. (2004). *Understanding terror networks.* Philadelphia, PA: University of Pennsylvania Press.

Sageman, M. (2008). *Leaderless Jihad: Terrorist networks in the 21st century.* Philadelphia, PA: University of Pennsylvania Press.

Sanchez, G. (2006). The role of group consciousness in Latino public opinion. *Political Research Quarterly, 59*, 435–446.

Sanger, D. E. (2002, April 21). War was easy. The rest of the world is a mess. *New York Times.*

Sanger, D. E. (2005, September 22). Bush compares responses to hurricane and terrorism. *New York Times.*

Sary, G. (2015). Syria conflict: Who are the groups fighting Assad. *BBC.* Retrieved from www.bbc.com/news/world-middle-east-34710635

Schafer, M. (1997). Images and policy preferences. *Political Psychology, 18,* 813–827.

Schafer, M., & Crichlow, S. (2000). Bill Clinton's operational code: Assessing source material bias. *Political Psychology, 21,* 559–571.

Schaffner, B. F. (2011). Racial salience and the Obama vote. *Political Psychology, 32,* 963–988.

Schaffner, B.F. (2018). *Follow the racist? The consequences of Trump's expressions of prejudice for mass rhetoric.* Retrieved from www.ashford.zone/images/2018/09

Schaffner, B.F., MacWilliams, M. & Nteta, T. (2018). Understanding White polarization in the 2016 vote for President: The sobering role of racism and sexism. *Political Science Quarterly, 133,* 1: 9–34.

Schafer, M., & Walker, S. (2006). *Beliefs and leadership in world politics: Methods and applications of operational code analysis.* New York: Palgrave Macmillan.

Schatz, E., & Levine, R. (2010). Framing, public diplomacy, and anti-Americanism in Central America. *International Studies Quarterly, 54,* 855–869.

Schelling, T. (1966). *Arms and influence.* Oxford: Yale University Press.

Schelling, T. (1980 [1960]). *The strategy of conflict* (2nd ed.). Cambridge, MA: Harvard University Press.

Schimmack, U., Oishi, S., Diener, E., & Suh, E. (2000). Facets of affective experiences: A framework for investigations of trait affect. *Personality and Social Psychology Bulletin, 26,* 655–668.

Schirmer, J. (1998). *The Guatemalan military project: A violence called democracy.* Philadelphia, PA: University of Pennsylvania Press.

Schlesinger, A. M., Jr. (1965). *A thousand days: John F. Kennedy in the White House.* Boston: Houghton Mifflin.

Schöpflin, G. (1993). The rise and fall of Yugoslavia. In J. McGarry & B. O'Leary (Eds.), *The politics of ethnic conflict* (pp. 172–203). New York: Routledge.

Schopler, J., Gruder, C., Miller, M., & Rousseau, M. (1968). The endurance of persuasion induced by a reward and a coercive power figure. *Human Relations, 20,* 301–308.

Schouten, R., & Silver, J. (2012). *Almost a psychopath: Do I (or does someone I know) have a problem with manipulation and lack of empathy?* Cambridge, MA: Harvard University Press.

Schroder, H., Driver, M., & Streufert, S. (1967). *Human information processing.* New York: Holt, Rinehart, and Winston.

Schultz, D. (1981). *Theories of personality* (2nd ed.). Monterey, CA: Brooks/Cole.

Schultz, T. (2005). *Handbook of psychobiography.* Oxford: Oxford University Press.

Schuman, H., Steeh, C., Bobo, L., & Krysan, M. (1997). *Racial attitudes in America: Trends and interpretations.* Cambridge, MA: Harvard University Press.

Schutz, W. C. (1958). *FIRO: A three-dimensional theory of interpersonal behavior.* New York: Holt, Rinehart, and Winston.

Schwadel, P., & Garneau, C. (2017). The diffusion of tolerance: Birth cohort changes in the effects of education and income on political tolerance. *Sociological Forum, 32,* 748–769.

Schweitzer, Y. (2004, June 18). Suicide bombers. *PBS*. Retrieved from www.pbs.org/wnet/wideangle/shows/suicide/briefing.html

Scott, J. P. (1969). Biological basis of human warfare: An interdisciplinary problem. In M. Sherif & C. W. Sherif (Eds.), *Interdisciplinary relationships in the social sciences* (pp. 121–136). Chicago: Aldine.

Scott, J. P. (1981). Biological and psychological bases of social attachment. In H. Kellerman (Ed.), *Group cohesion*. New York: Grune and Stratton.

Searle-White, J. (2001). *The psychology of nationalism*. New York: Palgrave.

Sears, D. O. (1975). Political socialization. In F. Greenstein & N. W. Polsby (Eds.), *Handbook of political science* (pp. 93–153). Cambridge, MA: Addison-Wesley.

Sears, D.O. (1993). Symbolic politics: A socio-psychological theory. In S. Iyengar & W. McGuire (Eds.), *Explorations in political psychology* (pp. 113–149). Durham, NC: Duke University Press.

Sears, D., Henry, P. J., & Kosterman, R. (2000). Egalitarian values and contemporary racial politics. In D. O. Sears, J. Sidanius, & L. Bobo (Eds.), *Racialized politics: The debate about racism in America* (pp. 75–117). Chicago: University of Chicago Press.

Sears, D., Hetts, J., Sidanius, J., & Bobo, L. (2000). Race in American politics. In D. O. Sears, J. Sidanius, & L. Bobo (Eds.), *Racialized politics: The debate about racism in America* (pp. 1–43). Chicago: University of Chicago Press.

Sears, D., & Kinder, D. (1971). Racial tensions and voting in Los Angeles. In W. Hirsch (Ed.), *Los Angeles: Viability and prospects for metropolitan leadership*. Westport, CT: Praeger.

Sears, D.O. & Savalei, V. (2006). The political color line in America: Many "peoples of color" or Black exceptionalism? *Political Psychology, 27*, 6, 894–924.

Sears, D. O., Sidanius, J., & Bobo, L. (Eds.). (2000). *Racialized politics: The debate about racism in America*. Chicago: University of Chicago Press.

Seashore, S. E. (1954). *Group cohesiveness in the industrial work group*. Ann Arbor, MI: Institute for Social Research.

Sechrist, G. B., & Stangor, C. (2001). Perceived consensus influences intergroup behavior and stereotype accessibility. *Journal of Personality and Social Psychology, 80*, 645–654.

Seelke, C. R., & Finklea, K. (2014). *U.S.–Mexican security cooperation: The Mérida initiative*. Washington, DC: Congressional Research Service.

Serwer, A. (2020). The new reconstruction. *The Atlantic*. Retrieved from www.theatlantic.com/magazine/archive/2020/10/the-next-reconstruction/615475

Settle, J. E., Dawes, C. T., & Fowler, J. H. (2009). The heritability of partisan attachment. *Political Research Quarterly, 62*, 601–613.

Seyd, P. (1998). Tony Blair and New Labour. In A. King, D. Denver, I. McLean, P. Norris, D. Sanders, & P. Seyd (Eds.), *New Labour triumphs: Britain at the polls* (pp. 49–73). Chatham, NJ: Chatham House.

Shakur, S. (1993). *Monster: The autobiography of an L.A. gang member*. New York: Penguin.

Shapley, L. S. (1953). A value for *n*-person games. In H. W. Kuhn & A. W. Tucker (Eds.), *Contributions to the theory of games* (Vol. 2, pp. 53–65). Princeton, NJ: Princeton University Press.

Shaw, J. I., & Condelli, L. (1986). Effects of compliance outcome and basis of power on the powerholder–target relationship. *Personality and Social Psychology Bulletin, 12*, 236–246.

Shaw, M. E. (1981). *Group dynamics: The psychology of small group behavior* (3rd ed.). New York: McGraw-Hill.

Shaw, R. P., & Wong, Y. (1989). *Genetic seeds of warfare: Evolution, nationalism and patriotism*. Boston: Unwin Hyman.

Shehata, D. (2011). The fall of the pharaoh: How Hosni Mubarak's reign came to an end. *Foreign Affairs, 90*, 26–32.

Shenon, P. (2002, July 19). Traces of terror: The terror suspect; 9/11 defendant in guilty plea; judge rejects. *New York Times*. Retrieved from www.nytimes.com/2002/07/19/traces-terror-terror-suspect-9-11-defendeant-guilty-plea-judge-rejects-it-html?pagewanted=all

Sherif, C. W., Sherif, M., & Nebergall, R. E. (1965). *Attitude and attitude change: The social judgment-involvement approach*. Philadelphia, PA: Saunders.

Sherif, M. (1936). *The psychology of social norms*. New York: Harper and Row.

Sherif, M., Harvey, D. J., White, B. J., Hood, W. R., & Sherif, C. W. (1961). *The Robbers' cave experiment*. Norman, OK: Institute of Group Relations.

Shi, T. (1999). Voting behaviour in plebiscitary and limited-choice elections. *The Journal of Politics, 61*(4), 1115–1139.

Shils, E. (1954). Authoritarianism: Right and left. In R. Christie & M. Jahoda (Eds.), *Studies in the scope and method of "the authoritarian personality"* (pp. 24–49). Glencoe, IL: Free Press.

Shimko, K. (1991). *Images and arms control*. Ann Arbor, MI: University of Michigan Press.

Shinkman, P. (2014). Ukrainian president: Russian aggression sparking new Cold War. *US News and World Report*. Retrieved from www.usnews.com/news/article/2014/09/18/uk

Shipler, D. (1997). *A country of strangers: Blacks and whites in America*. New York: Alfred A. Knopf.

Shively, W. P. (1993). *Power and choice*. Boston: McGraw-Hill.

Shuman, H., Steeh, C., Bobo, L., & Krysan, M. (1997). *Racial attitudes in America: Trends and interpretations*. Cambridge, MA: Harvard University Press.

Sidanius, J. (1993). The psychology of group conflict and the dynamics of oppression: A social dominance perspective. In S. Iyengar & W. McGuire (Eds.), *Explorations in political psychology* (pp. 183–219). Durham, NC: Duke University Press.

Sidanius, J., & Kurzba, R. (2013). Toward an evolutionarily informed political psychology. In L. Huddy, D. O. Sears, & J. S. Levy (Eds.), *The Oxford handbook of political psychology* (2nd ed., pp. 205–236). New York: Oxford University Press.

Sidanius, J., & Pratto, F. (1993). The dynamics of social dominance and the inevitability of oppression. In P. Sniderman & P. Tetlock (Eds.), *Prejudice, politics, and race in America today* (pp. 173–211). Stanford, CA: Stanford University Press.

Sidanius, J., & Pratto, F. (1999). *Social dominance: An intergroup theory of social hierarchy and oppression*. New York: Cambridge University Press.

Sidanius, J., Singh, P., Hetts, J., & Federico, C. (2000). It's not affirmative action, it's the Blacks. In D. O. Sears, J. Sidanius, & L. Bobo (Eds.), *Racialized politics: The debate about racism in America*. Chicago: University of Chicago Press.

Siers, R., & Mastors, E. (2017). Lessons from the Abu Nidal organization. In E. Mastors & R. Siers (Eds.), *Theory and practice of terrorism: Alternative paths of inquiry*. New York: Nova Science.

Sigel, R. (1995). New directions for political socialization research: Thoughts and suggestions. *Perspectives on Political Science, 24*, 17–33.

Silber, L., & Little, A. (1996). *Yugoslavia: Death of a nation*. New York: Penguin.

Silber, M. D., & Bhatt, A. (2007). *Radicalization in the west: The homegrown threat*. New York: NYPD.

Silke, A. (2003). Becoming a terrorist. In A. Silke (Ed.). *Terrorists, victims and society: psychological perspectives on terrorism and its consequences* (pp. 29–53). London: John Wiley and Sons.

Silke, A. (2004). Courage in dark places: reflections on terrorist psychology. *Social Research, 71*(*1*), 177–198.

Silke, A. (2011). *The psychology of terrorism*. London: Routledge.

Silver, N. (2016). The mythology of Trump's "working class" support. *FiveThirtyEight*. Retrieved from https://fivethirtyeight.com/features/the-mythology-of-trumps-working-class-support

Simmons, J.P., Nelson, L.D., & Simonsohn, U. (2011). False-positive psychology: Undisclosed flexibility in data collection and analysis allows presenting anything as significant. *Psychological Science, 22*(11), 1359–1366.

Simon, S. (2008). The price of the surge. *Foreign Affairs, 87*, 57–76.

Simon, S., & Takeyh, R. (2006, May 21). Iran's Iraq strategy. *Washington Post*. Retrieved from www.washingtonpost.com/wp-dyn/content/article/2006/05/19/AR2006051901761.html

Simpson, C. (2000, November 14). Quiet soldier who runs Rwanda. *BBC News*.

Sinclair, L., & Kunda, Z. (1999). Reactions to a Black professional: Motivated inhibition and activation of conflicting stereotypes. *Journal of Personality and Social Psychology, 77*, 885–904.

Singer, John D. (1958). Threat perception and the armament-tension dilemma. *Journal of Conflict Resolution, 2*, 90–105.

Siniver, A., & Featherstone, C. (2020). Low conceptual complexity and Trump's foreign policy. *Global Affairs, 6*, 71–85.

Sipress, A. (2001, April 26). Policy divide thwarts Powell in Mideast effort: Defense Department's influence frustrates State Department. *Washington Post*, p. A10.

Skinner, B. L. (1971). *Beyond freedom and dignity*. New York: Alfred A. Knopf.

Skinner, B. L. (1974). *About behaviorism*. New York: Alfred A. Knopf.

Skovertz, J. (1988). Models of participation in status-differentiated groups. *Social Psychology Quarterly, 51*, 43–57.

Sledge, M. (2011, November 10). Reawakening the radical imagination: The origin of Occupy Wall Street. *Huffington Post*. Retrieved from www.huffingtonpost.com/2011/11/10.occupy-wall-street-origins_n_1083977.html

Slothuus, R. (2008). More than weighting cognitive importance: A dual-process mode of issue framing effects. *Political Psychology, 29*, 1–28.
Sluka, J. A. (2000). Introduction: State terror and anthropology. In J. A. Sluka (Ed.), *Death squad: The anthropology of state terror*. Philadelphia, PA: University of Pennsylvania Press.
Smith, A. (1981). *The ethnic revival*. Cambridge: Cambridge University Press.
Smith, C. P., Atkinson, J. W., McClelland, D. C., & Veroff, J. (Eds.). (1992). *Motivation and personality: Handbook of thematic content analysis*. Cambridge: Cambridge University Press.
Smith, E.R. (1989). *The unchanging American voter*. Berkeley, CA: University of California Press.
Smith, E.R. (1993). Social identity and social emotions: Toward new conceptualizations of prejudice. In D. M. Mackie & D. L. Hamilton (Eds.), *Affect, cognition and stereotyping: Interactive processes in group perception* (pp. 297–315). San Diego, CA: Academic Press.
Smith, E. R., & Mackie, D. M. (2015). Dynamics of group-based emotions: Insights from intergroup emotions theory. *Emotion Review, 7*, 349–354.
Smith, H. K. (1988). *The power game: How Washington works*. New York: Ballantine Books.
Smith, R. J. (2000a, November 25). West is tiring of struggle to rebuild Bosnia. *Washington Post*, p. A4.
Smith, R. J. (2000b, November 10). Ethnic hatred permeates Bosnia's bitter peace. *Washington Post*, p. A2.
Smoke, R. (1987). *National security and the nuclear dilemma* (2nd ed.). New York: Random House.
Sniderman, P., Brody, R., & Tetlock, P. (1991). *Reasoning and choice: Explorations in political psychology*. Cambridge: Cambridge University Press.
Sniderman, P., & Carmines, E. (1997). *Reaching beyond race*. Cambridge, MA: Harvard University Press.
Sniderman, P., Crosby, G., & Howell, W. (2000). The politics of race. In D. O. Sears, J. Sidanius, & L. Bobo (Eds.), *Racialized politics: The debate about racism in America* (pp. 236–278). Chicago: University of Chicago Press.
Sniderman, P., Glaser, J., & Griffin, R. (1990). Information and electoral choice. In J. Ferejohn & J. Kuklinski (Eds.), *Information and democratic processes* (pp. 117–135). Urbana, IL: University of Illinois Press.
Sniderman, P., & Hagen, M. (1985). *Race and inequality: A study in American values*. Chatham, NJ: Chatham House.
Sniderman, P., & Piazza, T. (1993). *The scar of race*. Cambridge, MA: Harvard University Press.
Sniderman, P., & Piazza, T. (2002). *Black pride and Black prejudice*. Princeton, NJ: Princeton University Press.
Sniderman, P., Piazza, T., & Harvey, H. (1998). Prejudice and politics: An intellectual biography of a research project. In J. Hurwitz & M. Peffley (Eds.), *Perception and prejudice: Race and politics in the United States*. New Haven, CT: Yale University Press.
Sniderman, P., & Tetlock, P. (1986). Reflections on American racism. *Journal of Social Issues, 42*, 173–187.

Sniderman, P. M., & Theriault, S. M. (2004). The structure of political argument and the logic of issue framing. In W. E. Saris & P. M. Sniderman (Eds.), *Studies in public opinion: Attitudes, non-attitudes, measurement error and change* (pp. 133–165). Princeton, NJ: Princeton University Press.

Snow, D., Rochford, E., Jr., Worden, S., & Benford, R. (1986). Frame alignment processes, micro-mobilization, and movement participation. *American Sociological Review, 51*, 464–481.

Snyder, J. L. (1984). *The ideology of the offensive: Military decision making and the disasters of 1914*. Ithaca, NY: Cornell University Press.

Snyder, M. (1987). *Public appearances/private realities: The psychology of self-monitoring*. New York: W. H. Freeman.

Snyder, T. (2014). Europe and Ukraine: Past and future. *Eurozine*. Retrieved from www.eurozine.com/search.html

Sorensen, T. C. (1965). *Kennedy*. New York: Harper and Row.

Spink, K. S., & Carron, A. V. (1992). Group cohesion and adherence in exercise classes. *Journal of Sport and Exercise Psychology, 14*, 78–86.

SPLC (2019). Hate groups reach record high. Retrieved from www.splcenter.org/news/2019/02/19/hate-groups-reach-record-high

SPLC (2020a). Alt-right. Retrieved from www.splcenter.org/fighting-hate/extremist-files/ideology/alt-right

SPLC (2020b). Proud Boys. Retrieved from www.splcenter.org/fighting-hate/extremist-files/group/proud-boys

SPLC (2020c). White Nationalist. Retrieved from www.splcenter.org/fighting-hate/extremist-files/ideology/white-nationalist

Sprinzak, E. (2000, September/October). Rational fanatics. *Foreign Policy, 113*, 66–73.

Srull, T., & Ottati, V. (1995). Political information processing. In S. Iyengar & W. McGuire (Eds.), *Explorations in political psychology*. Durham, NC: Duke University Press.

Srull, T., & Wyer, R. (1989). Person memory and judgment. *Psychological Review, 96*, 58–83.

Stangor, C., Sechrist, G. B., & Jost, J. T. (2001). Changing racial beliefs by providing consensus information. *Personality and Social Psychology Bulletin, 27*, 486–495.

Stasser, G., Kerr, N. L., & Davis, J. H. (1989). Influence processes and consensus models in decision-making groups. In P. B. Paulus (Ed.), *Psychology of group influence* (2nd ed., pp. 279–326). Hillsdale, NJ: Lawrence Erlbaum.

Stasser, G., & Titus, W. (1987). Effects of information load and percentage of shared information on the dissemination of unshared information during group discussion. *Journal of Personality and Social Psychology, 53*, 81–93.

Staub, E. (1989). *The roots of evil: The origins of genocide and other group violence*. Cambridge: Cambridge University Press.

Staub, E. (1999). The roots of evil: Social conditions, culture, personality and basic human needs. *Personality and Social Psychology Review, 3*, 179–192.

Staub, E. (2000). Genocide and mass killing: Origins, prevention, healing and reconciliation. *Political Psychology, 21*, 367–382.

Staub, E. (2006). Reconciliation after genocide, mass killing, or intractable conflict: Understanding the roots of violence, psychological recovery, and steps toward a general theory. *Political Psychology, 27*, 867–894.

Staw, B. M. (1976). Knee deep in the Big Muddy: A study of escalating commitment to a chosen course of action. *Organizational Behavior and Human Performance, 16*, 27–44.

Staw, B. M., & Fox, F. V. (1977). Escalation: The determinants of commitment to a chosen course of action. *Human Relations, 30*, 431–450.

Staw, B. M., & Ross, J. (1987). Behavior in escalation situations: Antecedents, prototypes, and solutions. *Research in Organizational Behavior, 9*, 39–78.

Staw, B. M., & Ross, J. (1989). Understanding behavior in escalation situations. *Science, 246*, 216–220.

Steel, R. (1969, March 13). Endgame. *New York Review of Books, 12*, 15–22.

Stein, J. G. (1992). Deterrence and compellence in the Gulf, 1990–91: A failed or impossible task? *International Security, 17*, 147–179.

Stein, N., Trabasso, T., & Liwag, M. (1993). The representation and organization of emotional experience: Unfolding the emotion episode. In M. Lewis & J. Haviland (Eds.), *Handbook of emotions* (pp. 279–300). New York: Guilford Press.

Steiner, I. D. (1972). *Group process and productivity*. New York: Academic Press.

Steinert, M. (1977). *Hitler's war and the Germans: Public mood and attitude during the Second World War*. Athens, OH: Ohio University Press.

Stephan, W., & Stephan, C. (1993). Cognition and affect in stereotyping: Parallel interactive networks. In D. Mackie & D. Hamilton (Eds.), *Affect, cognition, and stereotyping: Interactive processes in group perception*. New York: Academic Press.

Stern, E. (1997). Probing the plausibility of newgroup syndrome: Kennedy and the Bay of Pigs. In P. 't Hart, E. Stern, & B Sundelius (Eds.), *Beyond groupthink* (pp. 153–189). Ann Arbor, MI: University of Michigan Press.

Stern, E., & Sundelius, B. (1994). The essence of groupthink. *Mershon International Studies Review, 1*, 101–108.

Stern, E., & Sundelius, B. (1997). Understanding small group decisions in foreign policy: Process diagnosis and research procedure. In P. 't Hart, E. Stern, & B. Sundelius (Eds.), *Beyond groupthink* (pp. 123–150). Ann Arbor, MI: University of Michigan Press.

Stern, J. (2004, June 12). Holy avengers. *Financial Times*. Retrieved from www.ksg.harvard.edu/news/opeds/2004/stern_avengers_ft_061204.htm

Stevenson, R. W. (2005, September 3) In first response to crisis, Bush strikes off-key notes. *New York Times*.

Stewart, C. J., Smith, C. A., & Denton, R. E., Jr. (2012). *Persuasion and social movements* (6th ed.). Long Grove, IL: Waveland Press.

Stewart, P. D., Hermann, M. G., & Hermann, C. F. (1989). Modeling the 1973 Soviet decision to support Egypt. *American Political Science Review, 83*, 35–59.

Stimson, J. A. (1975). Belief systems: Constraint, complexity, and the 1972 election. *American Journal of Political Science, 20*, 393–417.

Stoessinger, J. G. (1985). *Why nations go to war*. New York: St. Martin's Press.

Stogdill, R. M., & Bass, B. M. (1981). *Stogdill's handbook of leadership: A survey of theory and research*. New York: Free Press.

Stoll, D. (1992). Evangelicals, guerrillas, and the army: The Ixtil triangle under Ríos Montt. In R. T. Carmack (Ed.), *Harvest of violence: The Maya Indian and the Guatemalan crisis* (pp. 109–116). Norman, OK: University of Oklahoma Press.

Stone, W., & Schaffner, P. (1988). *The psychology of politics*. New York: Springer-Verlag.

Stoner, J.A.F. (1961). A comparison of individual and group decisions involving risk. Unpublished master's thesis. Massachusetts Institute of Technology.

Stouffer, S. (1955). *Communism, conformity, and civil liberties*. New York: Doubleday.

Strategic Assessment Group. (2003). *The next generation of world leaders*. Washington, DC: Central Intelligence Agency.

Street, P., & DiMaggio, P. (2011). *Crashing the tea party: Mass media and the campaign to remake American politics*. Boulder, CO: Paradigm Press.

Stroebe, W., & Insko, C. (1989). Stereotype, prejudice, and discrimination: Changing conceptions in theory and research. In D. Bar-Tal, C. Graumann, A. Kruglanski, & W. Stroebe (Eds.), *Stereotyping and prejudice: Changing conceptions* (pp. 54–68). New York: Springer-Verlag.

Stroessner, S., & Mackie, D. (1993). Affect and perceived group variability: Implications for stereotyping and prejudice. In D. Mackie & D. Hamilton (Eds.), *Affect, cognition and stereotyping: Interactive processes in group perception* (pp. 63–86). New York: Academic Press.

Stroud, N. J., & Muddiman, A. (2013). The American media system today: Is the public fragmenting? In T. N. Ridout (Ed.), *New directions in media and politics* (pp. 6–23). New York: Routledge.

Stuart, D., & Starr, H. (1981). The "inherent bad faith model" reconsidered: Dulles, Kennedy, and Kissinger. *Political Psychology, 3*, 1–33.

Suedfeld, P., & Leighton, D.C. (2002). Early communications in the war against terrorism: An integrative complexity analysis. *Political Psychology, 23*, 585–599.

Suedfeld, P., & Rank, A. D. (1976). Revolutionary leaders: Long-term success as a function of changes in conceptual complexity. *Journal of Personality and Social Psychology, 34*, 169–178.

Suedfeld, P., & Tetlock, P. (1977). Integrative complexity of communication in international crisis. *Journal of Conflict Resolution, 21*, 169–184.

Sullivan, J., Piereson, J., & Marcus, G. (1979). An alternative conceptualization of political tolerance: Illusory increases, 1950s–1970s. *American Political Science Review, 73*, 781–794.

Sullivan, J., Piereson, H., & Marcus, G. (1982). *Political tolerance and American democracy*. Chicago: University of Chicago Press.

Sumner, W. G. (1906). *Folkways: A study of the sociological importance of usages, manners, customs, mores, and morals*. Boston: Ginn & Co.

Suskind, R. (2004). *The price of loyalty: George W. Bush, the White House, and the education of Paul O'Neill*. New York: Simon and Schuster.

Swain, C., & Nieli, R. (2003). *Contemporary voices of white nationalism in America*. Cambridge: Cambridge University Press.

Swim, J. K., & Miller, D. (1999). White guilt: Its antecedents and consequences for attitudes toward affirmative action. *Personality and Social Psychology Bulletin, 25*, 500–514.

Sylvan, D. A., & Voss, J. F. (eds). (1998). *Problem representation in foreign policy decision-making.* Cambridge: Cambridge University Press.

Tafoya, S. (2004). Report: Shades of belonging. Washington, DC: Pew Hispanic Center.

Tajfel, H. (1970). Experiments in intergroup discrimination. *Scientific American, 223,* 96–102.

Tajfel, H. (1978). Social categorization, social identity, and social comparison. In H. Tajfel (Ed.), *Differentiation between social groups: Studies in the social psychology of intergroup relations* (pp. 61–76). New York: Academic Press.

Tajfel, H. (1982). *Human groups and social categories.* Cambridge: Cambridge University Press.

Tajfel, H., & Billig, M. (1974). Familiarity and categorization in intergroup behavior. *Journal of Experimental Social Psychology, 10,* 159–170.

Tajfel, H., & Turner, J. C. (1979). An integrative theory of intergroup conflict. In W. G. Austin & S. Worchel (Eds.), *The social psychology of intergroup relations* (pp. 38–48). Monterey, CA: Brooks Cole.

Tajfel, H., & Turner, J. C. (1986). The social identity theory of intergroup behavior. In S. Worchel & W. G. Austin (Eds.), *Psychology of intergroup relations* (pp. 1–24). Chicago: Nelson-Hall.

Takaki, R. (2008). *A different mirror: A history of multicultural America.* New York: Back Bay Books.

Talbot, C. (2000, December 23). Rwanda on the offensive in Congo war. *Washington Post.*

Tam, K.-P., Leung, A., & Chiu, C.-Y. (2008). On being a mindful authoritarian: Is need for cognition always associated with less punitiveness? *Political Psychology, 29,* 77–91.

Tambe, E.B. (2016). Who votes in East Asia? *European Journal of East Asian Studies, 15,* 149–173.

Tannenbaum, F. (1947). *Slave and citizen: The Negro in the Americas.* New York: Alfred A. Knopf.

Taylor, D. W., Berry, P. C., & Block, C. H. (1958). Does group participation when using brainstorming facilitate or inhibit creative thinking? *Administrative Science Quarterly, 3,* 23–47.

Taylor, M. (1988). *The terrorist.* London: Bassey's.

Taylor, M. (1991). *The fanatics: A behavioral approach to political violence.* London: Bassey's.

Taylor, M., & Louis, W. R. (2004). Terrorism and the quest for identity. In F. Moghaddam & A. J. Marsella (Eds.), *Understanding terrorism: Psychosocial roots, consequences, and interventions* (pp. 169–185). Washington, DC: APA Press.

Taylor, M., & Quale, E. (1994). *Terrorist lives.* London: Bassey's.

Taylor, P., & Fry, R. (2007). *Hispanics and the 2008 election: A swing vote?* Washington, DC: Pew Hispanic Center.

Taylor, S. E., & Crocker, J. (1981). Schematic bases of social information processing. In T. Higgins, C. P. Herman, & M. P. Zanna (Eds.), *Social cognition: The Ontario symposium.* (Vol. 1, pp. 89–134). Hillsdale, NJ: Lawrence Erlbaum.

Taylor, V. (2013). Social movement participation in the global society: Identity, networks, and emotions. In J. van Stekelenburg, C. Roggebans, & B. Klandermans (Eds.), *The future of social movement research: Dynamics, mechanisms, and processes* (pp. 37–57). Minneapolis: University of Minnesota Press.

Taysi, T., & Preston, T. (2001). The personality and leadership style of President Khatami: Implications for the future of Iranian political reform. In O. Feldman & L. O. Valenty (Eds.), *Profiling political leaders: Cross-cultural studies of personality and behavior* (pp. 57–77). Westport, CT: Praeger.

Teens sharper on Bart than news. (1998, September 6). *Idaho Spokesman Review*, A6.

Teger, A. (1980). *Too much invested to quit.* New York: Pergamon Press.

Tepperman, J. (2002). Truth and consequences. *Foreign Affairs, 81*, 128–145.

Tesler, M. (2016). *Post-racial or most-racial? Race and politics in the Obama era.* Chicago: University of Chicago Press.

Tesler, M., & Sears, S.O. (2010). *Obama's race: The 2008 election and the dream of a post-racial America.* Chicago: University of Chicago Press.

Tetlock, P. (1983). Integrative complexity of American and Soviet foreign policy rhetorics: A time-series analysis. *Journal of Personality and Social Psychology, 49*, 565–585.

Tetlock, P. (1985). Accountability: The neglected social context of judgment and choice. In B. M. Staw & L. Cummings (Eds.), *Research in organizational behavior* (Vol. 7, pp. 297–332). Greenwich, CT: JAI Press.

Tetlock, P., & Belkin, A. (Eds.). (1996). *Counterfactual thought experiments in world politics: Logical, methodological, and psychological perspectives.* Princeton, NJ: Princeton University Press.

Tetlock, P., McGuire, C., & Mitchell, G. (1991). Psychological perspectives on nuclear deterrence. *Annual Review of Psychology, 42*, 239–276.

Tetlock, P., Peterson, R. S., McGuire, C., Chang, S., & Feld, P. (1992). Assessing political group dynamics: A test of the groupthink model. *Journal of Personality and Social Psychology, 63*, 403–425.

Tetlock, P., & Tyler, A. (1996). Churchill's cognitive and rhetorical style: The debates over Nazi intentions and self-government for India. *Political Psychology, 17*, 149–170.

't Hart, P. (1990/1994). *Groupthink in government: A study of small groups dynamics and policy failure.* Baltimore, MD: Johns Hopkins University Press.

't Hart, P. (1997). From analysis to reform of policy-making groups. In P. 't Hart, E.K. Stern, & B. Sundelius (Eds.), *Beyond groupthink: Political group dynamics and foreign policymaking* (pp. 3–33). Ann Arbor, MI: University of Michigan Press.

't Hart, P., Stern, E. K., & Sundelius, B. (1997). *Beyond groupthink: Political group dynamics and foreign policy-making.* Ann Arbor, MI: University of Michigan Press.

Thoemmes, F.J., & Conway, L.C. (2007). Integrative complexity of 41 U.S. presidents. *Political Psychology, 28*, 193–226.

Thomas, D., & Horowitz, J.M. (2020). Support for Black Lives Matter has decreased since June but remains strong among Black Americans. Pew Research. Retrieved from www.pewresearch.org/fact-tank/2020/09/16/support-for-black-lives-matter-has-decreased-since-june-but-remains-strong-among-black-americans

Thomas, E. (2005, September 19). How Bush blew it. *Newsweek.*

Thomas, E., & Wolffe, R. (2005, September 19). Bush in the bubble. *Newsweek.*

Thomas, R. (1996). History, religion, and national identity. In R. Thomas & H. R. Friman (Eds.), *The South Slav conflict: History, religion, ethnicity, and nationalism.* New York: Garland.

Tianjian Shi. (1999). Voting and nonvoting in China: Voting behavior in plebiscitary and limited-choice elections. *Journal of Politics, 61,* 1115–1139.

Time. (2015). Here's Donald Trump's presidential announcement speech. Retrieved from https://time.com/3923128/donald-trump-announcement-speech

Tobias, J. (2008). The role of entrepreneurship in conflict reduction in post- genocide Rwandan coffee industry. Unpublished doctoral dissertation, Washington State University.

Tong, C., Gill, H., Li, J., Valenzuela, S. & Rojas, H. (2020). Fake news is anything they say: Conceptualization and weaponization of fake news among the American public. *Mass Communication and Society, 23,* 755–778.

Tooby, J., & Cosmides, L. (1990). The past explains the present: Adaptations and the structure of ancestral environments. *Ethology and Sociobiology, 11,* 375–424.

Toros, E. (2014). Social indicators and voting: The Turkish case. *Social Indicators Research, 115,* 1011–1029.

Towles-Schwen, T., & Fazio, R. H. (2001). On the origins of racial attitudes: Correlates of childhood experiences. *Personality and Social Psychology Bulletin, 27,* 162–175.

TRCC (Truth and Reconciliation Commission of Canada). (2015). *Final report of the Truth and Reconciliation Commission of Canada: Volume one, summary.* Toronto: James Lorimer & Company.

Trent, S. (2020, December 4). CIA psychological profiler who labeled Trump "dangerous" dies of COVID-19 at 86. *Washington Post.* Retrieved from www.washingtonpost.com/local/jerrold-post-cia-trump-covid-death/2020/12/04/6dd566cc-35b2-11eb-b59c-adb7153d10c2_story.html.

Triplett, N. (1898). The dynamogenic factors in peacemaking and competition. *American Journal of Psychology, 9,* 507–533.

Trost, M. R., Maass, A., & Kendrick, D. T. (1992). Minority influence: Personal relevance biases cognitive processes and reverses private acceptance. *Journal of Experimental Social Psychology, 28,* 234–254.

Tuchman, B. (1962). *The guns of August.* New York: Macmillan.

Tuckman, B. W. (1965). Developmental sequence in small groups. *Psychological Bulletin, 63,* 384–399.

Tuckman, B. W., & Jensen, M.A.C. (1977). Stages of small-group development revisited. *Group and Organization Studies, 2,* 419–427.

Tufekci, Z., & Wilson, C. (2012). Social media and the decision to participate in political protest: Observations from Tahrir Square. *Journal of Communication, 62,* 363–379.

Tumulty, K., Thompson, M., & Allen, M. (2005, September 25). How many more Mike Browns are out there? *Time.*

Turner, J. C. (1982). Toward a cognitive redefinition of the social group. In H. Tajfel (Ed.), *Social identity and intergroup behavior* (pp. 15–40). Cambridge: Cambridge University Press.

Turner, J. C. (1985). Social categorization and the self-concept: A social-cognitive theory of group behavior. In E. J. Lawler (Ed.), *Advances in group processes: Theory and research* (Vol. 2, pp. 77–122). Greenwich, CT: JAI Press.

Turner, J. C. (1986). Social categorization and social discrimination in the minimal group paradigm. In H. Tajfel (Ed.), *Differentiation between social groups: Studies in the social psychology of intergroup relations* (pp. 235–250). New York: Academic Press.

Turner, J. C., Hogg, M. A., Oakes, P. J., Reicher, S. D., & Wetherell, M. S. (1987). *Rediscovering the social group: A self-categorization theory.* New York: Basil Blackwell.

Turner, R. (1978). The role and the person. *American Journal of Sociology, 84,* 1–23.

Tversky, A., & Kahneman, D. (1982). Judgment under uncertainty: Heuristics and biases. In D. Kahneman, P. Slovic, & A. Tversky (Eds.), *Judgment under uncertainty heuristics and biases* (pp. 3–20). Cambridge: Cambridge University Press.

UN Peacekeeper. (n.d.). *Treaty of guarantee.* Retrieved from https://peacemaker.un.org/sites/peacemaker.un.org/files/CY%20GR%20TR_600816_Treaty%20of%20Guarantee.pdf

United Nations Council on Human Rights. (2019a). *Rohingya refugee crisis.* Retrieved from www.unocha.org/rohingya-refugee-crisis

United Nations Council on Human Rights. (2019b). *Detailed findings on the international independent fact-finding mission on Myanmar.* Retrieved from www.ohchr.org/Documents/HRBodies/HRCouncil/FFM-Myanmar/20190916/A_HRC_42_CRP.5.pdf

United States Department of Commerce. (2005). *U.S. Census Bureau news.* Retrieved from www.census.gov/Press-Release

United States Institute of Peace. (2020). *The current situation in Syria: A USIP fact sheet.* Retrieved from www.usip.org/publications/2020/08/current-situation-syria

University Teachers for Human Rights (UTHR). (2003). *Child conscriptions and peace: A tragedy of contractions.* Retrieved from www.uthr.org/SpecialReports/spreport16.htm

Valentino, N. A., & Nardis, Y. (2013). Political communication: Form and consequence of the information environment. In L. Huddy, D. O. Sears, & J. S. Levy (Eds.), *The Oxford handbook of political psychology* (pp. 559–590). Oxford: Oxford University Press.

Valenzuela, S. (2013). Unpacking the use of social media for protest behavior: The roles of information, opinion expression, and activism. *American Behavioral Scientist, 57,* 920–942.

Vallacher, R.R., Coleman, P. T., Nowak, A. & Bui-Wrzosinska, L. (2010). Rethinking intractable conflict: The perspective of dynamical systems. *American Psychologist, 65,* 262–278.

van den Heuvel, H., & Meertens, R. (1989). The culture assimilator: Is it possible to improve interethnic relations by emphasizing ethnic differences? In J. P. van Oudenhoven & T. Willemsen (Eds.), *Ethnic minorities: Social psychological perspectives* (pp. 221–236). Berwyn, PA: Swets North America.

van Doorn, M., Prins, J., & Welschen, S. (2013). "Protest against whom?": The role of collective meaning making in politicization. In J. van Stekelenburg, C. Roggebans, & B. Klandermans (Eds.), *The future of social movement research: Dynamics, mechanisms, and processes* (pp. 59–78). Minneapolis, MN: University of Minnesota Press.

van Egeren, L. F. (1979). Cardiovascular changes during social competition in a mixed-motive game. *Journal of Personality and Social Psychology, 37*, 858–864.

van Evera, S. (1984). The cult of the offensive and the origins of the First World War. *International Security, 9*, 58–107.

van Knippenberg, A., & Ellemers, N. (1990). Social identity and intergroup differentiation processes. In W. Stroebe & M. Hewstone (Eds.), *European Review of Social Psychology* (Vol. 1, pp. 137–169). Chichester: Wiley.

van Oudenhoven, J. P. (1989). Improving interethnic relationships: How effective is cooperation? In J. P. van Oudenhoven & T. Willemsen (Eds.), *Ethnic minorities: Social psychological perspectives* (pp. 201–220). Berwyn, PA: Swets North America.

van Stekelenburg, J. (2013). The political psychology of protest: Sacrificing for a cause. *Political Psychology, 18*, 224–234.

van Zomeren, M. (2013). Discussion: Opening the black box of dynamics in theory and research on the demand side of protest. In J. van Stekelenburg, C. Roggebans, & B. Klandermans (Eds.), *The future of social movement research: Dynamics, mechanisms, and processes* (pp. 79–92). Minneapolis, MN: University of Minnesota Press.

van Zomeren, M., & Iyer, A. (2009). Introduction to the social and psychological dynamics of collective action. *Journal of Social Issues, 65*, 645–660.

van Zomeren, M., Kutlaca, M., & Turner-Zwinkels, F. (2018). Integrating who "we" are with what "we" (will not) stand for: A further extension of the Social Identity Model of Collective Action. *European Review of Social Psychology, 29*, 122–160.

van Zomeren, M., Postmes, T., & Spears, R. (2008). Toward an integrative social identity model of collective action: A quantitative research synthesis of three socio-psychological perspectives. *Psychological Bulletin, 134*, 504–535.

van Zomeren, M., Postmes, T., & Spears, R. (2012). On conviction's collective consequences: Integrating moral conviction with the social identity model of collective action. *British Journal of Social Psychology, 51*, 52–71.

Vertzberger, Y. (1990). *The world in their minds: Information processing, cognition, and perception in foreign policy decisionmaking*. Stanford, CA: Stanford University Press.

Vertzberger, Y. (1997). Collective risk-taking: The decision-making group. In P. 't Hart, E. Stern, & B. Sundelius (Eds.), *Beyond groupthink: Political group dynamics and foreign policymaking* (pp. 275–208). Ann Arbor, MI: University of Michigan Press.

Vertzberger, Y. (1998). *Risk taking and decisionmaking: Foreign military intervention decisions*. Stanford, CA: Stanford University Press.

Victoroff, J. (2005). The "mind of the terrorist": A review and critique of psychological approaches. *Journal of Conflict Resolution, 49*, 2–43.

Victoroff, J., Adelman, J. R., & Matthews, M. (2012). Psychological factors associated with support for suicide bombing in the Muslim diaspora. *Political Psychology, 33,* 791–809.

Volkan, V. (1980). Narcissistic personality organization and reparative leadership. *International Journal of Group Psychotherapy, 30,* 131–152.

Volkan, V. D., Itzkowitz, N., & Dod, A. W. (1999). *Richard Nixon: A psychobiography.* New York: Columbia University Press.

Volpato, C., Maass, A., Mucchi-Faina, A., & Vitti, E. (1990). Minority influence and social categorization. *European Journal of Social Psychology, 20,* 119–132.

Vosoughi, S., Roy, D. & Aral, S. (2018). The spread of true and false news online. *Science, 359,* 1146–1151.

Vidino, L., & Hughes, S. (2015). *Isis in America: From retweets to Raqqa.* Washington, DC: George Washington University. Retrieved from https://extremism.gwu.edu/isis-america

Wade, F. (2019). *Myanmar's enemy within: Buddhist violence and the making of a Muslim "other."* London: Zed Books.

Wagner, R. V. (2006). Terrorism: A peace psychological analysis. *Journal of Social Issues, 62,* 155–171.

Walgrave, S. (2013). Changing mobilization of individual activists? In J. van Stekelenburg, C. Roggeband, & B. Klandermans (Eds.), *The future of social movement research: Dynamics, mechanisms, and processes* (pp. 205–215). Minneapolis, MN: University of Minnesota Press.

Walker, S. G. (1977). The interface between beliefs and behavior: Henry Kissinger's operational code and the Vietnam War. *Journal of Conflict Resolution, 21,* 129–167.

Walker, S. G. (1983). The motivational foundations of political belief systems: A re-analysis of the operational code construct. *International Studies Quarterly, 27,* 179–202.

Walker, S. G. (1995). Psychodynamic processes and framing effects in foreign policy decision-making: Woodrow Wilson's operational code. *Political Psychology, 16,* 697–718.

Walker, S. G., & Falkowski, L. (1984). The operational codes of U.S. Presidents and Secretaries of State: Motivational foundations and behavioral consequences. *Political Psychology, 5,* 237–266.

Walker, S. G., & Schafer, M. (2007). Theodore Roosevelt and Woodrow Wilson: Realist and idealist archetypes? *Political Psychology, 28,* 747–776.

Walker, S., Schafer, M. & Smith, G. (2018). The operational codes of Donald Trump and Hillary Clinton. In Alex Minz & Lesley Terris (Eds.), *The Oxford handbook of behavioral political science* (1–24). Oxford: Oxford University Press.

Walker, S. G., Schafer, M., & Young, M. (1998). Systematic procedures for operational code analysis: Measuring and modeling Jimmy Carter's operational code. *International Studies Quarterly, 42,* 175–190.

Wallace, M. D., & Suedfeld, P. (1988). Leadership performance in crisis: The longevity-complexity link. *International Studies Quarterly, 32,* 439–452.

Wallach, M. D., Kogan, N., & Bem, D. J. (1962). Group influence on individual risk taking. *Journal of Abnormal and Social Psychology, 65,* 75–86.

Waller, J. (2002). *Becoming evil: How ordinary people commit genocide and mass killing.* Oxford: Oxford University Press.

Warren, K. (1993). Interpreting *La Violencia* in Guatemala: Shapes of Mayan silence and resistance. In K. Warren (Ed.), *The violence within: Cultural and political opposition in divided nations* (pp. 1–23). Boulder, CO: Westview Press.

Washington Post. (2021). Trump made 30,573 false or misleading claims as president: Nearly half came during his final year. Retrieved from www.washingtonpost.com/politics/how-fact-checker-tracked-trump-claims/2021/01/23/ad04b69a-5c1d-11eb-a976-bad6431e03e2_story.html

Watson, W. E., Michaelsen, L. K., & Sharp, W. (1991). Member competence, group interaction, and group decision making: A longitudinal study. *Journal of Applied Psychology, 76,* 803–809.

Webb, P. (2013). Who is willing to participate? Dissatisfied democrats, stealth democrats and populists in the UK. *European Journal of Political Research, 52,* 747–772.

Wegener, D. T., & Petty, R. E. (1994). The hedonic contingency hypothesis. *Journal of Personality and Social Psychology, 66*(6), 1034–1048.

Wegener, D. T., Petty, R. E., & Smith, S. M. (1995). Positive mood can increase or decrease message scrutiny: The hedonic messaging view of mood and message processing. *Journal of Personality and Social Psychology, 69,* 5–15.

Weimann, G. (2004, March). *How modern terrorism uses the internet.* Washington, DC: United States Institute of Peace. Retrieved from www.usip.org/publications/wwwterrornet-how-modern-terrorism-uses-the-internet

Weinberger, J., & Westen, D. (2008). RATS, we should have used Clinton: Subliminal priming in political campaigns. *Political Psychology, 29,* 631–651.

Weiner, B. (1986). *An attribution theory of motivation and emotion.* New York: Springer-Verlag.

Weingarten, K. (2004). *Common shock: Witnessing violence every day.* New York: New American Library.

Weise, Z. (2020). The Libyan conflict explained. *Politico.* Retrieved from www.politico.eu/article/the-libyan-conflict-explained

Weinstein, E. (1981). *Woodrow Wilson: A medical and psychological biography.* Princeton, NJ: Princeton University Press.

Weintraub, W. (1981). *Verbal behavior: Adaptation and psychopathology.* New York: Springer.

Weintraub, W. (1986). Personality profiles of American presidents as revealed in their public statements: The presidential news conferences of Jimmy Carter and Ronald Reagan. *Political Psychology, 7,* 285–295.

Weintraub, W. (1989). *Verbal behavior in everyday life.* New York: Springer.

Weir, F. (2000, May 24). Taming Chechnya, Russia too. *Christian Science Monitor,* pp. A1, A5.

Westen, D. (1998). The scientific legacy of Sigmund Freud: Toward a psychodynamically informed psychological science. *Psychological Bulletin, 124,* 333–371.

Westen, D. (2007). *The political brain: The role of emotion in deciding the fate of the nation.* New York: Public Affairs.

White, R. K. (1968). *Nobody wanted war: Misperception in Vietnam and other wars.* Garden City, NY: Doubleday.

White, R. K. (1977). Misperception in the Arab–Israeli conflict. *Journal of Social Issues, 33*, 190–221.

Whitley, B. E., Jr. (1999). Right-wing authoritarianism, social dominance orientation, and prejudice. *Journal of Personality and Social Psychology, 77*, 126–134.

Whitney, K., Sagrestano, L. M., & Maslach, C. (1994). Establishing the impact of individuation. *Journal of Personality and Social Psychology, 66*, 1140–1153.

Whyte, G. (1986). Escalating commitment to a course of action: A reinterpretation. *Academy of Management Review, 11*, 311–321.

Whyte, W. F. (1943). *Street corner society*. Chicago, IL: University of Chicago Press.

Wicklund, R. A., Cooper, J., & Linder, D. (1967). Effects of expected effort on attitude change prior to exposure. *Journal of Experimental Social Psychology, 3*, 41–78.

Widmeyer, W. N., Brawley, L. R., & Carron, A. V. (1990). The effects of group size in sport. *Journal of Sport and Exercise Psychology, 12*, 177–190.

Wiktorowicz, Q. (2005). *Radical Islam rising*. Lanham, MD: Rowman & Littlefield.

Wilder, D. A., & Shapiro, P. N. (1984). Role of outgroup cues in determining social identity. *Journal of Personality and Social Psychology, 47*, 342–348.

Willamson, V. & Gelfand, I. (2019). Trump and racism. What do the data say? *Brookings*. Retrieved from www.brookings.edu/blog/fixgov/2019/08/14/trump-and-racism-what-do-the-data-say

Williamson, V., Skocpol, T., & Coggin, J. (2011). The tea party and the remaking of Republican conservatism. *Perspectives on Politics, 9*, 25–43.

Wilson, E. O. (1978). *On human nature*. Cambridge, MA: Harvard University Press.

Wilson, J. Q. (1973). *Political organizations*. New York: Basic Books.

Wilson, S. (2001a, April 17). Colombian right's "cleaning" campaign. *Washington Post*.

Wilson, S. (2001b, April 21). Colombian massacre large, brutal. *Washington Post*.

Winter, D. G. (1973). *The power motive*. New York: Free Press.

Winter, D. G. (1980). Measuring the motive patterns of Southern African political leaders at a distance. *Political Psychology, 2*, 75–85.

Winter, D. G. (1987). Leader appeal, leader performance, and the motive profiles of leaders and followers: A study of American presidents and elections. *Journal of Personality and Social Psychology, 52*, 196–202.

Winter, D. G. (2003). Assessing leaders' personalities: A historic survey of academic research studies. In J. D. Post (Ed.), *The psychological assessment of political leaders* (pp. 11–38). Ann Arbor, MI: University of Michigan Press.

Winter, D. G. (2011). Scoring motive imagery in documents from four Middle Eastern opposition groups. *Dynamics of Asymmetric Conflict, 4*, 144–154.

Winter, D. G., & Carlson, L. A. (1988). Using motive scores in the psychobiographical study of an individual: The case of Richard Nixon. *Journal of Personality, 56*, 75–103.

Winter, D. G., Hermann, M. G., Weintraub, W., & Walker, S. G. (1991). The personalities of Bush and Gorbachev measured at a distance: Procedures, portraits, and policy. *Political Psychology, 12*, 215–245.

Winter, D. G., & Stewart, A. J. (1977). Content analysis as a technique for assessing political leaders. In M. G. Hermann (Ed.), *A psychological examination of political leaders* (pp. 21–61). New York: Free Press.

Wittenbaum, G., & Stasser, G. (1996). Management of information in small groups. In J. Nye & A. Bower (Eds.), *What's social about social cognition?* (pp. 57–84). Thousand Oaks, CA: Sage.

Wohlstetter, R. (1962). *Pearl Harbor: Warning and decision*. Stanford, CA: Stanford University Press.

Wolfenstein, E. V. (1971). *The revolutionary personality*. Princeton, NJ: Princeton University Press.

Wood, W., Lundgren, S., Ouellette, J. A., Busceme, S., & Blackstone, T. (1994). Minority influence: A meta-analytic review of social influence processes. *Psychological Bulletin, 115*, 323–345.

Woods, J. (2011). Framing terror: An experimental framing effects study of the perceived threat of terrorism. *Critical Studies on Terrorism, 4*, 199–217.

Woodward, B. (1991). *The commanders*. New York: Simon & Schuster.

Woodward, B. (2002). *Bush at war*. New York: Simon & Schuster.

Woodward, B. (2004). *Plan of attack*. New York: Simon & Schuster.

Woodward, B. (2006). *State of denial: Bush at war, part III*. New York: Simon & Schuster.

Woodward, B. (2008). *The war within: A secret White House history 2006–2008*. New York: Simon & Schuster.

Woodward, B. (2018). *Fear: Trump in the White House*. New York: Simon & Schuster.

Woodward, S. (1995). *Balkan tragedy: Chaos and dissolution after the Cold War*. Washington, DC: Brookings Institute.

Worchel, S., & Brehm, J. W. (1971). Direct and implied social restoration of freedom. *Journal of Personality and Social Psychology, 18*, 294–304.

Yam, K. (2020). Asian Americans voted for Biden 63% to 31%, but the reality is more complex. Retrieved from www.nbcnews.com/news/asian-america/asian-americans-voted-biden-63-31-reality-more-complex-n1247171

Young, C. (1976). *The politics of cultural pluralism*. Madison, WI: University of Wisconsin Press.

Young, C. (1983). Comparative claims to political sovereignty: Biafra, Katanga, Eritrea. In D. Rothchild & V. Olorunsola (Eds.), *State versus ethnic claims: African policy dilemmas* (pp. 199–232). Boulder, CO: Westview Press.

Zaccaro, S. J. (1984). Social loafing: The role of attractiveness. *Personality and Social Psychology Bulletin, 10*, 99–106.

Zagare, F. C., & Kilgour, D. M. (1993). Asymmetric deterrence. *International Studies Quarterly, 37*, 1–27.

Zajonc, R. B. (1965). Social facilitation. *Science, 149*, 269–274.

Zajonc, R. B. (1980a). Feeling and thinking: Preferences need no inferences. *American Psychologist, 39*, 139–151.

Zajonc, R. B. (1980b). Compresence. In P. B. Paulus (Ed.), *Psychology of group influence* (pp. 35–60). Hillsdale, NJ: Lawrence Erlbaum.

Zakaria, F. (2002, April 29). Colin Powell's humiliation: Bush should clearly support his secretary of state—otherwise he should get a new one. *Newsweek*, p. 28.

Zaller, J. R. (1992). *The nature and origins of mass opinion*. New York: Cambridge University Press.

Zander, A. (1985). *The purposes of groups and organizations*. San Francisco: Jossey-Bass.

Zartman, W. I. (1989). *Ripe for resolution: Conflict and resolution in Africa*. New York: Oxford University Press.

Zedalis, D. (2004, June). *Female suicide bombers*. Strategic Studies Institute. Retrieved from www.strategicstudiesinstitute.army.mil/pdffiles/PUB 408.pdf

Zenger, T. R., & Lawrence, B. S. (1989). Organizational demography: The differential effects of age and tenure distributions on technical communication. *Academy of Management Journal, 32*, 353–376.

Zhiang, Q. (2015). Perceived intergroup stereotypes, threats, and emotions toward Asian Americans. *Howard Journal of Communications, 26*, 115–131.

Ziller, R. C., Stone, W. F., Jackson, R. M., & Terbovic, N. J. (1977). Self–other orientations and political behavior. In M. G. Hermann (Ed.), *A psychological examination of political leaders* (pp. 337–353). New York: Free Press.

Zimbardo, P. (1971). *The Stanford prison experiment*. Stanford, CA: Stanford University Press.

Zimbardo, P. (2007). *The Lucifer effect*. New York: Random House.

Zorbas, E. (2008). Reconciliation in post-genocide Rwanda. *African Journal of Legal Studies, 1*, 29–52.

Zurcher, L. A., Jr. (1969). Stages of development in poverty program neighborhood action committees. *Journal of Applied Behavioral Science, 15*, 223–258.

Glossary

accountability. To have one's actions be transparent and evaluated by authorities with the power to punish wrongdoing. Political leaders will take greater risks, and be more likely to engage in conflict, the more they lack accountability to a higher power.

adjourning. A group's decision to dissolve. It can be planned or spontaneous.

affect. A generic term for a whole range of preferences, evaluations, moods, and *emotions*.

affect referral heuristic. Describes the mental tool used in voting when the voter feels familiarity with the candidate and also regards the candidate highly.

agenda setting. When the media defines which issues need attention and in what form.

agreeableness. A *Big Five* personality trait. It means a person is trusting, positive, and good-natured.

ally image. A country or group perceived to be equal to the perceiver's country in terms of culture and capability, with good intentions, multiple groups in decision-making roles, and associated with threat or opportunity.

altruists. People who help others and who speak out despite risks to their personal safety.

analogical reasoning. Using analogies to help decide what policies will work in a current situation.

analogy. A decision-making heuristic, or shorthand, in which policymakers see a current event or situation as similar to (or sharing many of the same characteristics as) a previous historical event.

anchoring and adjustment. When individuals make estimates by starting from an initial value that is adjusted to yield the final answer.

assimilation effect. When information similar to other information is perceived as even more similar than it objectively is.

associative networks. *Knowledge structures* embedded in long-term memory, consisting of nodes linked to one another, forming a network of associations.

attitude. An enduring system of positive or negative *beliefs*, affective feelings and *emotions*, and action tendencies regarding an attitude object—that is, the entity being evaluated.

attitude object. The entity about which one has an attitude.

attributions. The explanations generated for the causes of our own and others' behavior.

attribution theory. A psychological theory arguing that people process information as if they are naïve scientists—that is, they search for causes in the behavior of others.

authoritarian personality. A personality type. Originally said to contain the traits of conventionalism (rigid adherence to conventional values), submission to authority figures, authoritarian aggression (i.e., aggressive impulses toward those who are not conventional), anti-intraception (i.e., rejection of tenderness, imagination, subjectivity), superstition and *stereotype* (fatalistic belief in mystical determinants of the future and rigid thinking), high value placed on power and toughness, destructiveness and cynicism, projectivity (i.e., the *projection* outward of unacceptable impulses), and an excessive concern with the sexual activity of others. In Altemeyer's (1996) reconceptualization, the type has three traits: authoritarian submission, authoritarian aggression, and conventionalism.

autokinetic effect. A perceptual illusion that occurs when a single point of light in a darkened room appears to be moving.

availability heuristic. When people predict the likelihood of something based on the ease with which they can think of instances or examples of it.

avoidance of value trade-offs. When people mistakenly believe a policy that contributes to one value also contributes to several other values, even though there is no reason why the world should be constructed in such a neat and helpful manner.

balance. The cognitive harmony that people attempt to achieve and maintain in a situation and their feelings about the situation and its components.

barbarian image. A country or *group* perceived to be superior in capability, inferior in culture, monolithic in decision-making, and associated with extreme threat.

bargaining theory. When coalitions form on the basis of considering expected payoffs.

behavioral genetics. Explains how individual traits and patterns of behavior get passed down from parents to children, as well as how those traits are shared between siblings.

belief system. A clustering of *beliefs*.

beliefs. Associations people create between an object and its attributes.

Big Five. Core personality dimensions or traits: *neuroticism*, *extroversion*, *agreeableness*, *openness to experience*, and *conscientiousness*.

black and white model. A model developed by Converse (1964), describing responses to *attitude* questions, which from some people remain very stable; for others, the responses change in an apparently random pattern.

bolstering. When people limit their exposure to information to find multiple reasons for the correctness of a decision and none (or discounted ones) against it.

Bradley effect. A term referring to White voters' reluctance to say they would not vote for a Black political candidate, causing polls to inaccurately predict the vote for a Black candidate.

bystander phenomenon. When people are part of a *group*, there is a *diffusion of responsibility*, and people feel less compelled to intervene and help.

charisma. A personality characteristic that makes one an attractive leader.

childish games. A bias occurring when people communicate something to another person that is familiar and meaningful to them, but not to the other person.

Christian Identity. An unusual reading of the Bible often adhered to by racist groups in America, which maintains that White people, but not non-Whites, are descended from Adam and Eve. Non-Whites are deemed "mud people."

coalition. A small collection of group members who cooperate in order to achieve a common goal.

coalition of autonomous actors. A decision unit composed of multiple groups that can act independently.

coercive power. The capacity to punish those who do not comply with requests or demands.

cognition. A collective term for the psychological processes involved in the acquisition, organization, and use of knowledge.

cognitive complexity. The ability to differentiate the environment; the degree of differentiation a person shows in describing or discussing other people, places, policies, ideas, or things.

cognitive neuroscience. A field of study that focuses on how the function and structure of the brain and nervous system explain thoughts, feelings, and actions.

cognitive processes. What happens in the mind while a person moves from observation of a stimulus to a response to that stimulus.

cognitive rigidity. An inability to recognize alternatives caused by high-tension situations.

cognitive style. The way a person gathers and processes information from his or her environment.

cohesion. The factors that cause a *group* member to remain in the group.

collective action. "Any action that aims to improve the status, power, or influence of an entire group, rather than that of one or a few individuals" (van Zomeren & Iyer, 2009, p. 646).

collective fences. When individual members of a group avoid behaviors costly to them as individuals, resulting in harm to the group as a whole.

collective trap. Behaviors that reward an individual *group* member can be harmful to the rest of the group, especially if engaged in by enough group members.

collegial management style. Emphasizes teamwork, shared responsibility, and problem-solving within a *group*.

colonial image. A country or *group* perceived as inferior in culture and capability, benign in intentions, monolithic in decision-making, and associated with opportunity.

common-bond groups. These groups, such as social groups, are based mostly on the attachments between group members. In common-bond groups, the attachments to the group are based on such things as member similarity, likeability of fellow group members, and familiarity with group members.

common-identity groups. Groups based primarily on attachments to the group identity.

compensatory strategy. A voting selection strategy that involves the careful assignment of positive or negative values to each issue position. The voter then engages in an assessment of the tradeoffs involved and resolves the conflict with a choice.

competitive frames. People are often exposed to more than one frame, and those frames may provide different competitive pictures of a candidate or issue.

competitive management style. Relatively unstructured information network, with the leader placed in an arbiter position among competing advisers with overlapping areas of authority.

compliance. Doing what one is asked to do by a more powerful member of one's group.

confirmation bias. A bias occurring when people favor information that confirms existing beliefs.

conformity. The tendency to change one's *beliefs* or behaviors so that they are consistent with the standards set by the *group*.

conscientiousness. A *Big Five* personality trait. It means a person is responsible, dependable, and goal-directed.

contact hypothesis. The argument that increasing intergroup contact, exposing people to the complexity of *group* members, breaks down *stereotypes*.

content analysis. A research method wherein written statements are systematically examined in order to infer psychological characteristics of individuals.

contrast effect. A social category serves as an anchor or central reference point for incoming information. When information is compared with that anchor and when it is different from expectations, the contrast effect makes it seem more so.

core community non-nation-states. Countries with a dominant ethnic or sectarian community that believes its members are the primary nation embodied in the country and that identifies with that nation in the strongest terms. In addition, that community tends to have great capability and control of the political system.

coverage bias. A form of media bias referring to how much time or space is devoted to a particular story.

critical bases of power. A typology of group-based power.

culture of terror. An institutionalized system of permanent intimidation of the masses or subordinated communities by the elite, characterized by the use of torture, disappearances, and other forms of extrajudicial *death squad* killings as standard practice. A culture of terror establishes collective fear as a brutal means of social control. In these systems, there is a constant threat of *repression*, torture, and death for anyone who is actively critical of the political status quo.

death squads. "Progovernment *groups* who engage in extrajudicial killings of people they define as enemies of the state" (Sluka, 2000, p. 141).

defense mechanisms. *Unconscious* techniques used to distort reality and prevent people from feeling anxiety. They are also used to defend the *ego*.

degenerate image. A country or *group* perceived as superior or equal in culture and capability, but lacking resolve and will. It is associated with perceptions of opportunity.

dehumanization. A process in which a particular social *group* is regularly described as less than human, and therefore deserving of treatment one would not administer to a human being.

deindividuation. This occurs when people attribute their behavior to the *group*'s behavior and thereby abandon individual responsibility for their own actions. There is a *diffusion of responsibility*.

denial. A *defense mechanism* wherein people may refuse to acknowledge reality (e.g., denying the country is going to war, despite the mobilization of troops) or denying an impulse (e.g., proclaiming that they are not angry when they are).

deterrence. The threat by one political actor to take actions in response to another actor's potential actions, which would make the costs (or losses) incurred far outweigh any possible benefits (or gains) obtained by the aggressor.

dialogue. A conflict resolution and reconciliation process by which individuals engage with each other in an open forum in order to speak about their sides of the story and to also hear the sides of others.

diaspora. Community of one nation that lives outside of that national territory.

diffusion of responsibility. When individuals feel no responsibility for their actions. It occurs when there is more than one person present in the situation to take all or some of the responsibility for the outcomes.

dissonance. An aversive state that results when behavior is inconsistent with *attitudes*.

drunkard's search. An informational shortcut named after the drunkard who loses his keys in the street and looks for them under the lamppost because the light is better there—not because that is where he lost the keys. This is analogous to the use of information in political decisions when people reduce complicated issues and choices among candidates to simple comparisons because that is easier.

dynamics of demand. The dynamics of demand for a social movement include grievances, social comparisons, and emotion.

dynamics of supply or mobilization. Variables at the individual and organizational level that explain why people are mobilized to support a social movement.

ego. The part of the personality that moderates between the *id*, and its desire for pleasure, and the realities of the social world.

egocentric bias. The tendency of individuals to accept more responsibility for joint outcomes than others attribute to them.

Elaboration Likelihood Model (ELM). A model attitude change that focuses on cognition and rests upon the concept of the elaboration likelihood continuum. The continuum delineates how motivated and able people are to assess something by putting in effort to study it and evaluate it. The model proposes two routes to attitude change through persuasion: a central route and a peripheral route.

emotion. A complex assortment of *affects*, beyond merely good or bad feelings, to include delight, serenity, anger, sadness, fear, and more.

empathy. An *emotion* produced when observing another person in need and taking the perspective of that person.

endorsement heuristic. A mental shortcut wherein people select a candidate who has been endorsed by people in whom the voter has confidence.

enemy image. The enemy is perceived as relatively equal in capability and culture. In its most extreme form, the diabolical enemy is seen as irrevocably aggressive in motivation, monolithic in decisional structure, and highly rational in decision-making (to the point of being able to generate and orchestrate multiple complex conspiracies).

entiativity. The extent to which a collection of people is perceived as a coherent entity.

escalation of commitment. This occurs in situations in which some course of action has led to losses, but there is a possibility of achieving better outcomes by investing further time, money, or effort.

ethnocentrism. The view of things in which one's own *group* is the center of everything and looks with contempt on outsiders.

evolutionary psychology. A study of the biological origins of human behavior. Understanding how particular traits and behaviors and abilities evolved over time allows for a richer and more comprehensive understanding of human behavior today.

expected payoffs. Expectations based on *norms* of equity and equality. *Group* members will appeal to whichever norm provides them with the largest payoff.

expert power. Power derived from having expert knowledge or skills. Physicians, for example, are often afforded a great deal of power because of the knowledge and ability they possess. Of course, expert power can only be exerted if the target of power is aware of the power holder's special knowledge or talent.

externals. People who believe the external environment determines strongly what happens to them. They are more susceptible to authority. Contrast with *internals*.

extremist. A person who is excessive and inappropriately enthusiastic and/or inappropriately concerned with significant life purposes, implying a focused and highly personalized interpretation of the world. Politically, it is behavior that is strongly controlled by *ideology*, in which the influence of ideology is such that it excludes or attenuates other social, political, or personal forces that might be expected to control and influence behavior.

extroversion. A *Big Five* personality trait. It means a person is outgoing, talkative, assertive, and likes to socialize.

familiarity heuristic. A short cut that comes into play when people are familiar with one candidate but not the others, and they are at a minimum at least neutral toward that candidate.

forgiveness. The restoration of a positive relationship between perpetrator and victim wherein negative emotions toward the perpetrator are replaced with positive emotions.

formalistic management style. Emphasis upon strictly hierarchical, orderly decision structures.

forming. The first stage of *group* formation. This stage is also referred to as the orientation stage because prospective members are orienting themselves to the group.

framing. The manner in which an issue is presented and the suggestions for how to think about it. People are often exposed to competitive frames about a candidate or issue.

fundamental attribution error. Occurs when people attribute other people's behavior to internal, dispositional causes, rather than to situational causes.

Fundamental Interpersonal Relations Orientation (FIRO). An explanation of how joining a *group* can fulfill psychological needs. According to this perspective, joining a group can satisfy three basic needs: inclusion (the desire to be part of a group); control (the need to organize an aspect of the group); and affection (the desire to establish positive relations with others).

funnel of causality. Distinguishes long-term factors that affect how Americans vote (attachment to a party or *party identification* and *group* interests) from short-term factors (currently important issues and candidates and their qualities).

game of chicken. A hypothetical game in which two drivers race toward one another head on, each assuming that the other will swerve and avoid an accident.

gatekeeping. A form of media bias wherein the editors or program managers decide which stories will be told and which stories are not reported.

genocide. Actions designed to eliminate a *group* of people from the face of the Earth.

Gresham's law of political information. An informational shortcut wherein the use of a small amount of personal information about a candidate dominates a large amount of historical information of that candidate's historical record.

group. A collection of people who are perceived to belong together and who are dependent on one another.

group development. The stages of growth and change that occur in a *group*, from its formation to its dissolution.

group malfunctions. Faulty *group* decision processes.

group polarization. The tendency for individuals' opinions to become more extreme after a *group* discussion than they were before the discussion.

groupthink. Governmental policy *groups*, particularly at high levels, tend to be smaller groups that, in time, develop a pattern of interactions between group members that emphasizes the maintenance of group cohesion, solidarity, and loyalty. This emphasis upon group cohesion can lead to faulty group decision processes, or *group malfunctions*.

Guns of August analogy. An *analogy* based upon the experience of the events leading up to the outbreak of World War I, a war that none of the policy-makers desired or intended to occur.

habit heuristic. The mental shortcut of voting as the same way as the last time.

Hedonic Contingency Model (HCM). Model that posits that mood has an effect on persuasion—for example, when individuals have an expectation of happiness from a message, those in a happy mood pay more careful attention.

heuristic. Mental shortcuts in processing information about others.

Heuristic-Systematic Model (HSM). This model posits the sufficiency principle, which holds that people attempt to maintain a balance between their desire to expend as little cognitive effort as possible and their desire to be accurate in their judgments. If a person uses heuristics to evaluate a message, which are low-effort cognitive devices, but is not confident that they have made a judgment that is as correct or accurate as they would like, the person will engage in systematic information processing, which is essentially the same as the ELM's concept of the central route.

hindsight bias. A bias occurring when people recognize information consistent with pre-existing ideas.

id. The warehouse for all instincts and drives. The id follows the pleasure principle.

identity. A deeply held sense of who a person is, where he or she fits into the political and social world.

ideologue. A person who knows what liberal and conservative values are, what positions on important political issues are liberal and conservative positions, which party represents liberal and which represents conservative principles, and which candidates stand for which issues.

ideology. An elaborate, intertwined, and broad-reaching structure of *attitudes* and *beliefs*.

image. A political psychology concept equivalent to a *stereotype* of a political *group* or country. Images contain information about a country's capabilities, culture, intentions, the kinds of decision-making groups (lots of people involved in decision-making or only a few), and perceptions of threat or opportunity.

image theory. A political psychological concept equivalent to a stereotype of a political group or country. Images contain information about a country's capabilities, culture, intentions, the kinds of decision-making groups (lots of people vs. a small group), and perceptions of threat or opportunity.

imaginability. The tendency to retrieve information that is plausible without any regard for actual probabilities.

imperialist image. A country or *group* perceived to be superior in capability, dominating in culture, exploitive in intentions, and associated with threat.

impression-based model of information processing. The argument that, as information is acquired, it is used to enhance and update the *beliefs* about a candidate or party and the specific details of the information are forgotten.

individuation. The desire to be distinguishable from others in some aspect.

informational social influence. Conformity that results from the use of other people's actions or opinions to define reality.

in-group. *Groups* to which we belong.

inherent bad faith. A belief that another actor is inherently harmful in its intentions toward the perceiver's group or country. This means that actions that appear to be benign are actually caused by external forces, not the actor's intentions.

integrative complexity. A decision-maker's focus on both differentiation—the distinct dimensions of a problem—and integration—the connections made among differentiated characteristics.

internals. People who believe they have considerable control over their fate. They are more likely to resist authority. Contrast with *externals*.

intractable conflicts. Intractable conflicts by definition last a long time, and those involved in them cannot win, and will not agree to a settlement.
irredentism. The desire to join together all parts of a national community within a single territorial state.
issue. A dispute about public policy.
issue frames. Alternative definitions, constructions, or depictions of a policy problem.
knowledge structures. The mental organization of knowledge about political actors and issues.
Leader Trait Assessment (LTA). A content analytic technique for assessing leaders' personality characteristics.
legitimate power. Power to require compliance held by people by virtue of their position. For example, when a military officer orders troops to battle, that officer is exerting legitimate power.
levels of conceptualization. A classification scheme of Americans' political sophistication, ranging from *ideologues*, those who are very sophisticated, to "absence of issue content," those with very little knowledge of politics.
locus of control. View of the world in which an individual does or does not perceive some degree of control over situations in which they are involved and whether government can influence what happens in or to a nation.
Maximalists. Challengers to the *Michigan model*, who argue that people do not necessarily think linearly about politics, that *emotions* play a role as well, and that the average American is more politically sophisticated than the Michigan model maintains.
media bias. A much-debated argument that the media are dominated by political liberals, and their reporting leans in a liberal direction.
Michigan model. A pioneering framework examining the political *attitudes* of Americans. The scholars of the Michigan School developed a model of American attitudes, in which it was assumed that Americans should have an integrated mental map of the political system, connecting candidates, parties, issues, and *groups* to ideological principles, in a consistent manner. Their research revealed that this is fairly rare in the American public.
minimal group paradigm. Competition can occur, even when the stakes are only psychological, and among *groups* that are arbitrarily formed by experimenters with no real interaction or conflict.
minimum-power theory. When coalition members expect payoffs that are directly proportional to their ability to turn a losing coalition into a winning one.
minimum-resource theory. When *group* members form coalitions on the basis of equal input–equal output.
moral disengagement. The suspension of moral principles that enables individuals to commit inhumane acts.
motivation. The reason or reasons why individuals look for alternatives to their present life situations.
motives. Those aspects of personality concerned with goals and goal-directed actions.
Mujahedeen. Holy warriors who fought to get the Soviet Union out of Muslim Afghanistan.

multiethnic or multisectarian state. A country with at least two ethnic *groups*, neither of which is capable of assimilating or absorbing the other nor of seceding and maintaining independence, where primary identity is with the ethnic group.

multinational states. A country in which several *groups* of people, who think of themselves as separate nations and who actually have the capacity to establish viable independent states, live together in a single country.

multiple advocacy. A group decision-making process in which manipulation is avoided by having the deliberation process managed by a neutral person, a custodial manager, while advocates of different positions are allowed to fully develop their proposals and advocate their advantages.

Munich analogy. If you do not stand up to an aggressor, and instead seek to appease them or make concessions to them in the hopes of keeping the peace, the end result will be to only encourage them to be even more aggressive and probably to bring on the very war you sought to avoid.

narcissism. A personality characteristic that causes people to see the world in terms of their own needs and desires rather than objective reality.

nation-state. A state in which the average citizen has a primary identity with the national community, believes that community should be an independent state, and grants that community primary loyalty.

nationalism. The *belief* that a *group* of people, or a community, belong together in an independent country, and a willingness to grant that community primary loyalty.

need for achievement. A personality trait involving concern with excellence and task accomplishment.

need for affiliation-intimacy. A personality trait involving concern for close relations with others.

need for power. A personality trait involving concern for impact and prestige.

negative campaign ads. Ads in which one candidate criticizes another candidate by name.

negativity effect. The tendency to attribute behavior to dispositional rather than situational factors for people we dislike.

neurotic anxiety. A person's fear of being punished for doing something the *id* wants the person to do.

neuroticism. A *Big Five* personality trait. It means that a person is anxious, has maladaptive coping abilities, and is prone to depression.

noncompensatory strategy. A voting selection strategy that essentially avoids conflict among issue positions by not getting complete information.

normal vote. An election in which people voted according to their *party identification* and in which independents are split evenly between the two parties.

normative social influence. Conformity that is a result of the desire to be liked by others.

norming. The third stage of *group development*, a phase in which conflict is replaced by cohesion and feelings of unity.

norms. Expectations about how all group members should behave in a *group*.

openness. A *Big Five* personality characteristic. It means a person is proactive, independent, and tolerant of different viewpoints.

operational codes. Constructs representing the overall *belief* systems of leaders about the world (i.e., how it works, what it is like, what kinds of actions are most likely to be successful).

orientation toward political conflict. Relates to how open a president is to face-to-face disagreements and confrontations among his or her advisers.

out-group. *Groups* to which we do not belong.

paramilitaries. "Organizations that resort to the physical elimination of presumed auxiliaries of rebel groups and of individuals seen as subversive of the moral order ... They mostly operate through *death squads*" (Cubides, 2001, p. 129).

paranoia. A personality characteristic that causes people to believe they are being persecuted. They often respond to those believed to be persecuting them with aggression or narcissism.

party identification. An *attitude* regarding attachment to (identification with) a political party.

performing. The fourth stage of *group development*. Performance usually only occurs when the groups mature and have successfully gone through the previous stages of development. Many groups do not reach the performing stage.

personality. There is no single universally accepted definition of personality. However, it generally refers to relatively stable aspects of an individual's behavior that account for patterns of behavior.

perspective-taking. The practice of empathizing with others, experiencing their perspective and the *emotions* that it generates in them.

persuasion. An effort to convince people to adopt a particular attitude or position on an issue or candidate.

phenomenal absolutism error. When a judgment that the observer makes about the *group* is not perceived as a judgment about the group, but as an attribute of the group itself.

pleasure principle. The motivation to satisfy aggressive and sexual drives.

policy fiascoes. Failures of policy.

politicized collective identity. A social identity that has political meaning for groups of people.

politics-is-complicated model. Also known as the **principled objection model**. The argument that White Americans vary in the degree to which they blame the inequalities between the races on structural factors (such as the historical legacy of slavery and current system-wide discrimination), as opposed to individual factors (individual acts of *prejudice* and discrimination, rather than system-wide factors).

populism. Opposition to the political establishment and elites and belief that the people should govern directly.

positivity effect. The tendency to attribute positive behaviors to dispositional factors and negative behaviors to situational factors with individuals we like.

pragmatism. Having organizational and managerial skills, and the ability to negotiate and to mobilize resources.

predominant leader. A type of group with a powerful leader who can make decisions without consulting other group members.

prejudice. A negative evaluative orientation toward an out-group and consequently an aversion to its members; an attribution of negative characteristics toward a group and its members that is incorrect; and, finally, consistency in the negative orientation toward the group and its members.

priming. When the media points out to the public which elements of which issues are important.

prior policy experience or expertise. Policy-makers' years in a variety of political positions, and their specializations in particular policy domains. There are different advisory group usages among people with little or a lot of experience and expertise.

prisoner's dilemma. When participants cannot communicate with one another, yet the outcome of the game for each person is contingent on what the other person decides.

projection. A defense mechanism attributing one's own objectionable impulses to another person, projecting them onto another.

prophecy. An ability to act as a purveyor of a movement's values and beliefs.

prospect theory. Predicts that individuals will tend to be risk-averse in the domain of gains and risk-seeking in the domain of losses.

protracted crisis approach. The perspective that a crisis should be viewed as a long series of separate and distinct *deterrence* and compellence exchanges running throughout the crisis from the beginning until the end of any episode.

psychoanalytic or psychodynamic theories. Psychoanalytic theories assess the role of the *unconscious* in human behavior and the motives and drives that underlie behavior.

psychobiographies. Involve an examination of the life history of an individual, often a well-known person or political leader.

rationalization. A defense mechanism whereby people reinterpret their own objectionable behavior to make it seem less objectionable.

realistic conflict theory. Proposal that intergroup *stereotyping* and derogation occurs as a result of competition for resources and competitive goals.

reality principle. According to the reality principle, the demands of the *id* will be blocked or channeled in accordance with reality, but also in accordance with the personality.

rebellion. A term referring to a pattern in group behavior whereby people refuse to do what they are told to do because a group member has abused power.

Receive-Accept-Sample (RAS) Model This model argues that individuals have competing opinions on issues. The view that prevails results from what is on one's mind at the time.

reconciliation. Mutual acceptance of groups formerly engaged in conflict.

referent power. The power a person possesses when others identify with that person because the person is similar to them or because they want to be like that person.

relative deprivation theory. A theory that explains political action as resulting from the comparison of one's group with other groups and finding that one's own group has less than it deserves.

representativeness heuristic. A shortcut using probability expectations to make judgments about others.

repression. A defense mechanism in which a person involuntarily eliminates an unpleasant memory.

rescuers. People who help others and who speak out despite risks to their personal safety.

reward power. The ability to control the distribution of positive and negative reinforcers.

right-wing authoritarianism. Submission to perceived authorities, particularly those in the establishment or established system of governance.

risky shift. When *groups* tend to take riskier decisions (and more chances) than do individuals.

rogue image. A country or *group* perceived as inferior in culture and capability, with monolithic decision-making, and associated with threat.

roles. Expectations about how a person ought to behave in a *group*.

satisfice. To make a decision that is adequate rather than optimal and based upon consideration of all relevant information.

scapegoating. Blaming a *group* for society's problems.

schema. A cognitive structure that represents knowledge about a concept or type of stimulus, including its attributes and the relations among those attributes.

scientific method. Four cyclical steps that researchers repeatedly execute as they try to understand and predict behavior: making observations; formulating tentative explanations; making further observations and experimenting; and refining and retesting explanations.

security dilemmas. Conflicts in which the efforts made by one state to defend itself are simultaneously seen as threatening by its opponents, even if those actions were not intended to be threatening.

self-serving bias. A tendency individuals have to take responsibility for successes but not for failures.

sense of efficacy. A presidential stylistic variable involving presidents' confidence and interest in particular policy areas. Presidents give high priority to policy areas in which they have a strong sense of efficacy.

shared sovereignty strategies. An integration strategy in which an ethnic or racial *group* is given some degree of self-rule.

single group. A type of group in which all members collectively make decisions.

social capital. A set of relationships and resources in a community that can be mobilized for the common good.

social causality. During hard times, the *groups* to which people are particularly attracted are those that provide an ideological blueprint for a better world and an enemy who must be destroyed to fulfill the *ideology*.

social comparisons. An inevitable tendency of groups to compare themselves with other relevant groups, hoping that they compare favorably with the others.

social creativity. Changing the basis of comparison between one's group and another group so one's own group can be considered better than the comparison group.

social-decision schemes. The process by which *groups* combine the preferences of all the members of the group to arrive at a single group decision.

social dominance theory. Presents a social dominance orientation measure that differentiates those who prefer social *group* relations to be equal or hierarchical, and the extent to which people want their *in-group* to dominate *out-groups*.

social identity. The part of a person's self-concept that is determined by the *groups* to which the person belongs.

social identity theory. Explores the impact on behavior of *group* identity and desire for positive comparisons with other groups.

Social Identity Model of Collective Action (SIMCA). Explores the motivations of individuals who engage in collective action. The model posits that a perceived sense of injustice about a group's disadvantage will motivate group members to engage in collective action.

social justification. When a *group*'s poor treatment is justified.

social learning theory. The argument that children learn negative *attitudes* and discriminatory behavior from their parents, teachers, family, friends, and others when they are rewarded for such behavior.

social loafing. The tendency of *group* members to work less hard when in a group than when working alone.

social mobility. Leaving one's group to join a more successful group.

social movements. "Social movements are collective challenges by people with common purposes and solidarity in sustained interaction with elites and authorities" (Klandermans, 1997, p. 2).

social movement organizations (SMOs). Institutions designed to further the goals of the social movement.

spiral conflicts. Conflicts in which each side matches and one-ups the actions taken by the other side. This can produce arms races and other types of aggression that result from misunderstanding each other's motives.

statement bias. A form of media bias wherein a member of the media inserts his or her own views into the reporting of a story.

status. How power is distributed among members in a *group*.

stereotypes. *Beliefs* about the attributes of people in particular *groups* or social categories.

storming. The second stage of *group development*, often marked by conflict.

structure. Varies greatly among social movements. Some are hierarchical, others loose and informal.

suicide bomber. A person who is willing to commit suicide in order to ensure maximum effectiveness in a terrorist attack.

superego. The moral arm or conscience of the personality.

symbolic racism. The argument that racism in America still exists, but is disguised as traditional American individualist values.

task–interpersonal emphasis. Relative emphasis in interactions with others on getting the task done versus focusing on feelings and needs of others.

terrorism. "In principle, terrorism is deliberate and systematic violence performed by small numbers of people, whereas communal violence is spontaneous, sporadic, and requires mass participation. The purpose of terrorism is to intimidate a watching popular audience by harming only a few, whereas *genocide* is the elimination of entire communities. Terrorism is meant to hurt, not to destroy. Terrorism is preeminently political and symbolic, whereas guerilla warfare is a military activity. Repressive terror from above is the action of those in power, whereas terrorism is a clandestine resistance to authority." (Crenshaw, 2000, p. 406)

three-stage model of group decision-making. According to Bales and Strodtbeck (1951), *groups* proceed through three stages before eventually arriving at a decision: orientation, discussion, and decision-making.

traits. Personality characteristics that are stable over time and in different situations. Traits produce predispositions to think, feel, and act in a particular way toward people, events, and situations.

transactional leadership. When the leader approaches followers with an eye toward exchanging one valued thing for another.

transformational leadership. When leaders engage their followers in such a way that they raise each other to higher levels of motivation and morality.

truth and reconciliation commission. An investigative commission designed to reveal the truths of political violence and to achieve some measure of reconciliation and forgiveness. It gathers evidence, determines *accountability*, and often recommends policies for the treatment of victims and perpetrators.

ultimate attribution error. The use of *prejudices* and preexisting *beliefs* in evaluation of others.

unconscious. A part of the mind of which people are unaware. Freud introduced the idea that the mind is like an iceberg. Only a small part of the iceberg is visible, floating above water. Around 90% is under water and unobservable. Similarly, people are conscious of only a small part of the mind.

utilitarian integration strategy. A strategy to promote integration by satisfying the population's needs. It requires removing any obstacles to equality of access to important political positions in the country.

values. Deeply held *beliefs* about what should be true, even if it is not currently true.

variable. Something that is thought to influence, or to be influenced by, something else.

viability heuristic. A shortcut involving selecting a candidate based on the likelihood that he or she will win.

Vietnam analogy. This analogy suggests that any U.S. military intervention will likely result in the same outcome as did American intervention in Vietnam during the 1960s and 1970s: an open-ended commitment to a losing cause that will result in tremendous bloodshed for our troops and political unrest at home.

INDEX

Note: Page numbers in *italic* denote figures and in **bold** denote tables.